Women's Crimes, Criminology, and Corrections

Joycelyn M. Pollock
Texas State University

WAVELAND

PRESS, INC.

Long Grove, Illinois

To Gregory and Eric, as always

For information about this book, contact:
Waveland Press, Inc.
4180 IL Route 83, Suite 101
Long Grove, IL 60047-9580
(847) 634-0081
info@waveland.com
www.waveland.com

Contents

Preface   ix

1   Introduction: Framing the Questions   **1**

Criminology and Positivism   1
   Biases and Paradigms   2

Measuring Crime and Crime Correlates   5
   Measuring Crime   5
   Measuring Correlates   7

Feminist Criminology   9
   Domestic Violence: Research, Policy, and
     Unintended Consequences   9
   Phenomenological Research   12
   Other Contributions of Feminist Criminology   12

Sexual Stereotypes and Sex Differences   13
   The Violent Woman   14
   Sex Differences versus Gender Differences   15

Framing the Questions: The Criminology of Women   17

Review Questions   19

2   Women's Crimes   **21**

The Gender Gap   22

Explanations for Convergence   22

Property Crimes   27
   Burglary   28
   Larceny/Theft, Fraud, and Embezzlement   29

Violent Crimes   34
  Robbery   37
  Arson   39
  Assault   39
  Homicide   41
Drug Crimes   46
  Drug-Related Crimes   48
  Roles of Women in the Drug World   48
Other Crimes   50
  Prostitution   50
  Pregnancy as a Crime?   52
Race and Crime   53
Conclusion   55
Review Questions   55

3   Traditional Theories: 1800s–1970s   57

Theoretical Concerns   58
Classical Theory (1700s)   59
Positivism (1800s)   59
The Chicago School (early 1900s)   61
  Cultural Deviance Theory   62
  Differential Association   62
  Social Strain Theory   64
  Differential Opportunity Theory   65
Social Control Theory   68
Labeling and Conflict Theories   71
  Conflict Theories   72
Psychological Theories of Crime   72
  Psychodynamic Theories   73
  Developmental Theories   76
  Learning Theory and Behaviorism   80
  Other Psychological Theories   81
Early Feminist Theories of Crime   82
  Sex-Role Theory   83
  Women's Liberation Theory   84
Conclusion   87
Review Questions   88

4 Current Theories of Crime   **89**

The General Theory of Crime   90
 Tests/Applications of the General Theory   93
 Applications to Girls/Women   94

General Strain Theory   95
 Tests/Applications of the Theory   96
 Applications to Girls/Women   97

Rational Choice Theory   100
 Tests/Applications of Rational Choice Theory   100
 Applications to Girls/Women   101

Social Support Theories   102
 Tests/Applications of Social
   Support/Disorganization Theory   103
 Applications to Girls/Women   103

Sex-Role and Feminist Theories Revisited   103
 Hagan's Power Control Theory and
   Tittle's Control Balance Theory   104
 Economic Marginalization   106

Biological Theories of Crime   107
 Sex Differences and Crime   108
 ADD, Hyperactivity, and Cognitive Functioning   111
 Traits   111
 Critiques of Biological Criminology   114

Conclusion   115

Review Questions   115

5 Life-Course and Pathways Theories   **117**

Life-Course and Integrated Theories   118
 Longitudinal Studies   118
 Findings from Longitudinal Studies   122
 Application of Life-Course Theories to Girls/Women   125

Pathways Research   127
 High Rates of Childhood Sexual Victimization   127
 Criminal Pathways   131

Making Sense of Theoretical Findings   137

Conclusion   139

Review Questions   140

6 Juvenile Offenders   141

Female Delinquency   141
   Race and Ethnicity   145
   Research on Violent Girls   146
   Girl Gangs   149
Delinquency Theories   156
   Applications of Theories to Girls   156
Juvenile Justice System   160
   Programming   162
   Detainment   163
Conclusion   164
Review Questions   164

7 Chivalry, Sentencing, and Jails   167

Disparate Sentencing Laws   168
The Chivalry Hypothesis   168
   Methodological Concerns   169
   Studies of Chivalry   170
   A Selective Chivalry?   173
   Sentencing Guidelines and Other Changes   176
Sentenced to Prison   178
   Race and Ethnicity   179
   Explaining the Increase   181
Sentenced to Death   182
Jails and Jail Inmates   183
   Characteristics of Women in Jail   183
   Issues and Concerns   186
Conclusion   187
Review Questions   188

8 Women's Prisons   189

Women's Prisons   190
The History of Women's Prisons   191
   Early Punishments and Places of Confinement   192
   The Reformatory Era   194
Female Prisoners   200
   Crimes and Criminal History   201
   Race and Ethnicity   202
   Family Background   202
   Childhood Abuse   203
   Intimate Relationships   206
   Drug Use and Abuse   206
   Personality Traits and Characteristics of Female Prisoners   207
   Medical Needs   208

Management Issues in a Women's Prison   212
    Adapting to a Male Standard   212
    Cross-Sex Supervision   213
    Violence, Collective Disturbances,
        and Rule Breaking   213
    Legal Challenges   214
Conclusion   217
Review Questions   217

9   The Prison World   **219**

Entering the Prison   220
    Adjusting to Prison   221
The Prison World   222
    Recreation and Visitation   222
    Rules and Punishments   224
Prisoner Subculture   225
    Deprivation Theory   225
    Importation Theory   226
    The Inmate Code   227
    Argot Roles   227
    The Black Market   228
    Social Organization (Gangs versus Families)   229
    Homosexuality   231
Violence   232
    Sexual Violence   235
Correctional Officers   237
    Sexual Harassment and Assault   241
Conclusion   243
Review Questions   244

10   Classification and Programming   **245**

Classification and Prediction   246
    The Development of the R/N/R Approach   246
    Criticism of the LSI-R   247
    The Use of Prediction Instruments in Prison   250
Programming in Prison   254
Gender-Responsive Programming   256
Drug-Treatment Programming   260
    Drug Treatment Programs   263
Incest Survivor Programming   266

Parenting Programming   267
  Justifications for Parenting Programs   268
  Types of Parenting Programs   272
Conclusion   278
Review Questions   279

11   Release, Recidivism, and   **281**
Recommendations for the Future
Parole   282
  Employment Issues   283
  Housing Issues   284
  Reunification with Children   284
  Obtaining Needed Treatment   286
  Halfway Houses   288
Recidivism   289
Evaluation of Treatment Programs   290
Policy Recommendations   292
  Policy Implications   294
Review Questions   295

Notes   297
Glossary   327
Bibliography   331
Author Index   381
Subject Index   385

Preface

In 2012 (the most current data available as of this writing), there were 108,866 women incarcerated in this nation's federal and state prisons and over a million women on probation and parole, a small fraction of the approximately 4.5 million men under all forms of correctional supervision.[1] Because of these small numbers, women have historically been an afterthought in criminal justice policy making and the criminological enterprise, and this is the basic theme of this book.

More recently, there has been growing attention to the population of female offenders, partly because of their growing numbers, and partly because of the tens of thousands of children who are affected by having their mother in prison or on supervised release. However, the recent attention has not necessarily been a good thing for women, and they are much more likely to be formally prosecuted and incarcerated today than in decades past. This change has come about partly because of policies to "help" women, and partly because of shifts in theorists' beliefs and public perceptions that women and men are similar in their criminal motivations and risk and should, therefore, be treated similarly. This perception is debatable, and this controversy forms a large part of this book.

Structure of the Book

The book is both a criminology text and a corrections text. In Chapter 1, we frame the questions that will be asked in a far-reaching inquiry that covers what criminology has contributed to the study of criminal women and how the field of corrections has responded. In Chapter 2, official statistics are utilized, along with other sources, to describe the prevalence and patterns of crimes committed by women.

Chapters 3 through 5 explore the field of criminology and criminological theories. There are distinct questions that must be addressed. First, why do women commit less crime, especially less violent crime, than men? Second, why does it appear that the rates of crime for men and women are becoming more similar? In some property crime categories women's rates have become equal to men's, at least as recorded by official statistics. Both traditional and current theories are reviewed, including those theories designed primarily to explain male criminality as well as those that focused specifically on women. Some of these theories are revisited in Chapter 6, which explores issues related to female juvenile offenders. There we review crime rates of and criminological theories directed toward juveniles as well as issues related to their detention.

Chapter 7 returns to the discussion of adult offenders and explores the system's response to criminal women. Historically, it was believed that women were more likely to receive leniency by the system, but sentencing practices have undergone dramatic shifts in the last 30 years, and some of these changes have impacted women even more than they have impacted men. We see that the incarceration of women has increased at a higher rate than that of men for the last 30 years or so, and we explore the reasons for this. We also examine the jail sentence and review what we know about female jail inmates. Chapters 8 through 10 discuss prisons. Chapter 8 takes a broad look at the history and current description of women's prisons, Chapter 9 looks inside the women's prison to understand female prisoners and their world, and Chapter 10 takes a closer look at classification and programming. Finally, Chapter 11 addresses issues of release and recidivism and discusses how to reduce crimes by women based on what we know from research.

This book is directed to those in a college course on Women in the Criminal Justice System, but it could also be used as a supplemental text in a criminology course and/or a corrections course. The book not only explores the theories that have been developed to explain female criminality but also discusses what has happened (and what is happening) to female offenders who have entered the criminal justice system. This book combines theory and corrections for a comprehensive look at one group of offenders (girls and women) whose ranks are growing. By understanding the research and recent history of the system's treatment of female offenders, those who read the book can evaluate policy decisions more wisely.

Acknowledgments

Thanks to Neil and Carol Rowe for allowing me the opportunity to create this text. Gayle Zawilla has been an incredible editor, going above and beyond to improve the quality of the book. Ashley Allen helped in organizing sources in the early stages of the five-year process this took to completion. Finally, Eric Lund helped in innumerable ways, including extremely careful proofreading.

ENDNOTE

[1] Carson & Golinelli, 2013, Table 1, p. 2; Maruschak & Parks, 2012, p. 2.

Introduction
Framing the Questions

CHAPTER SUMMARY

- The study of criminology has largely been the study of criminal men because women commit much less crime than men.

- The field of criminology is a social science and, as such, is rife with difficulties of measurement, and biases and assumptions that may threaten the validity of what we think we know.

- Today, women are more likely to be arrested for domestic assaults, even though legislation and policies were put in place to help women.

- It is difficult to separate out real sex differences from sexual stereotypes. Sexual stereotypes of women have included women as more controlled by her biology, more passive, and more emotional. Historically, these images of women have permeated theory and policy.

- Research on violent women continues to show bias stemming from sexual stereotypes in that small numbers of violent women are presented as if they represent all women.

Criminology and Positivism

Although this is a book about women's criminality, it is about men's criminality as well, because one cannot hope to explain women's crimes without also understanding men's crimes. The flip side of this assumption has not been recognized and criminology has, for the most part, been the study of why

1

men commit crime. In the past, studies excluded women entirely from samples because researchers believed it was not cost effective to include them, given they committed so few crimes. Feminist critiques in the 1970s argued that such attempts could not possibly explain human behavior because they excluded one-half of the population. Periodically, efforts were made to explain women's criminality through the use of unique theories of female behavior; but, they too, could be criticized as incomplete since they ignored men. Women and men are different, but if we are ever to understand human behavior—in this case, criminal behavior—it must be through an understanding of both women and men. Thus, this book revisits the standard criminological theories one would find in any criminology textbook. However, we revisit these theories with a focus on how well they explain the sex differences in criminal behavior.

This is also a book about the criminological enterprise. The approach taken is critical of past and recent attempts to develop and test theories of crime. The book's topic—the criminology of female offenders—can be used to illustrate and illuminate larger and more fundamental problems in the attempt to explain criminal behavior.

Positivism is knowledge construction that employs the methods of the natural sciences—specifically, the collection of data, testing of hypotheses, and searching for measurable causal factors. A fundamental premise of this book is that *all* social science research is rife with hidden or not-so-hidden biases, preconceptions, and ethnocentric and/or androcentric values that make it impossible to measure, much less explain, the reality of crime. This premise is obviously not original, nor even very controversial. Many radical and feminist critiques of traditional criminology, as well as more mainstream text treatments, clearly illustrate how early theorists confused stereotypes with facts and carried out research accepting time- and culture-specific views of women, minorities, and economic classes as truth. It should also be acknowledged that the present time period may be operating under its own cultural and time-specific biases that influence research questions and the answers we think we find. It is important to acknowledge the potential weaknesses of social science research and be aware of its limitations in terms of what questions it might be able to answer.

Biases and Paradigms

The belief that criminologists are objective scientists who have no biases or preconceptions regarding crime or human behavior is patently untenable. All of us have preconceptions regarding the nature of humans and the origins of crime. Does human behavior originate from free choice, or is human behavior determined by biological, social, and cultural factors? Whatever answer one chooses, it results in a bias that one possesses before any theory is constructed, and before a test of any theory is undertaken. The premise that humans are fundamentally social and altruistic, or the alternative premise that humans are inherently egocentric and must be controlled, is implicit in all criminal theory. Similarly, the question of whether men and women have fundamental differences beyond reproductive capabilities colors everyone's reading of sex-difference research. This is not to say that researchers cannot approach data with an attempt to keep an open mind, but the presumption that they are not influenced by their biases is to presume that they are not human.

Even the construction of theory itself is based on the *paradigm* that scientific method can explain behavior such as crime through linear causality, and the same scientific approaches from the hard sciences can be used to explain human behavior. From this paradigm comes the logic that a theory should be able to explain all or, at least, most crime and if there are inconsistencies in observed behavior, then the theory should be discarded. Many criminological textbooks approach their critiques of theories as if any particular theory must be able to predict all behavior. For instance, if broken homes "cause" crime, then all criminals should come from broken homes, or all broken homes should produce criminals. But why assume that a theory must have perfect predictive power? Everyone who smokes tobacco does not get cancer, and everyone who has a genetic predisposition to a degenerative disease does not contract that disease. Medical science has come to terms with probabilities. No one seriously doubts the link between smoking tobacco and cancer, despite the fact that some people can smoke tobacco for 50 years and not die from lung cancer; this merely illustrates the awesome variation in human physiology. Why would we assume that social science could be more accurate than medical science in its ability to predict? This paradigm colors the exploration of criminal theory: that a theory must be able to explain all behavior, or at least most of it; otherwise, it is not a valid explanation of any behavior.

Another problem of criminal theory is the necessity of disaggregating and quantifying dynamic life circumstances and experiences. Consider the following quote:

> [Referring to a female offender] She had a record of juvenile delinquency, including membership in a female gang. When discussing her family, she took the blame for her criminality, explaining that she came from a "good" family; that they had clothes to wear and were made to go to school. With further discussion of her upbringing however, she described a mother who was totally under the control of a strict, authoritarian husband. The father controlled the household with fear and intimidation and the girl was punished severely for not living up to his standards in dress, academic performance, or behavior. One incident she recalled was when she was 10 years old and went to a friend's house after school, instead of coming home. When she did return, her father beat her, called her a slut and locked her out of the house, telling her she was no longer his daughter. She was let back into the house, but her childhood became a pattern of engaging in increasingly more delinquent behaviors with consequential beatings and punishments from her father.[1]

How does one explain this woman's criminality? The woman herself understood her criminality in one way; her counselors probably have diagnosed her in another way; the interviewer came away from this interview with yet another understanding of why she eventually engaged in quite serious criminal behaviors. Even if one can figure out how to measure the various factors that make up the sum total of her life, these identified factors may or may not be recognized as correlated individually or through cluster analysis with some measure of crime (e.g., arrest). One might argue that the influence of life factors cannot be broken down to objective, measurable parts—that somehow in that process of abstraction, the meaning and influence of an individual's life circumstances are lost.

In addition to explaining crime at an individual level, as the above paragraph describes, crime is often explained at a societal level (why crime rates go up or down). Societal factors, such as unemployment, the percentage of women employed, urbanization, and so on, are examined to determine their relationship to crime rates. This is a completely different level of causation from the individual level. A problem arises when the two levels of abstraction are confused, or when the problem of ecological fallacy is not fully exposed. An *ecological fallacy* is a misstatement that occurs when one infers something about an individual based upon some factor that is associated with a group in which the individual is a member. For instance, if one assumes that an individual is criminal because he or she lives in a poor area of town or is a member of a minority group, that may be an ecological fallacy (since there are many law-abiding persons in those circumstances as well).

The increase of broken homes can be postulated as a cause of crime. Statistics indicate a positive correlation between the number of single heads of household in a community and crime rates. But why? It may be because broken homes are more likely than two-parent households to contribute to delinquent children who become adult criminals. Perhaps this is because the children receive less supervision and develop less self-control (Gottfredson and Hirschi's general theory of crime), or that single-parent households are more likely to be poor households with children who have nothing and want what their peers have, tempting them to utilize criminal means to get what they want (Merton's original strain theory). However, the association as measured in the aggregate could be that single-parent homes are more likely to be empty (the head of household is likely to be working by necessity), and burglary of an empty house is a more attractive option for would-be criminals. How does one know whether it is an individual causal factor or a factor that affects crime in the aggregate? (In this case, longitudinal research and other studies have confirmed the correlation at an individual level). The point is that certain factors have both societal and individual components; it would be a mistake to apply either without fully understanding the relationship between the factor and criminality.

There are also biases and scientific fads regarding the causes of crime. While early researchers, such as Sheldon and Eleanor Glueck, identified family factors as causal in the development of delinquent children, these theories were largely discarded in the 1970s and 1980s in favor of social (economic disparity) and subcultural factors.[2] Then, in the 1990s, discoveries pointed to the likelihood that parental practices might have something to do with delinquency after all. Today, no one seriously doubts that family factors are important in the genesis of delinquency.

Measuring Crime and Crime Correlates

In order to test any theory of crime, one must be able to measure the dependent variable (crime) and its *correlates*. They are the independent variables (i.e., poverty, drug use, attachment to parents, and so on) presumed to cause or at least be statistically associated with the dependent variable (crime). If one can identify a statistical relationship between the two that meets predetermined levels of significance, one can say that the two are correlated. If the independent variable occurs with the appropriate pattern (consistently before the dependent variable) and one can eliminate all alternative hypotheses (i.e., other factors that may influence one or both factors), then one can cautiously conclude that there is a causal relationship between the two factors. Thus, any factor that has a significant statistical relationship with crime is merely a correlate; a causal factor must meet a much more stringent definition.

The scientific method described above works fairly well (one assumes) in the laboratory with chemical compounds. The laws of chemistry and the laws of physics tend to hold few surprises, although it is also true that even in the so-called hard sciences one may move beyond the simple laws of nature into a realm where prediction is more problematic. At a certain point even physics becomes metaphysics, and there are more questions than answers. Scientific method and theory testing is obviously helpful in understanding human behavior and determining social policies; however, the accuracy of the measurements used to test theories is extremely important.

Measuring Crime

Measures of crime are notoriously problematic. Textbooks in criminology often start with the difficulties of measuring crime. Included in these discussions are descriptions of the weaknesses of the official data sources, such as the Uniform Crime Reports (UCR), as well as problems with self-reports and victimization studies. Even agreeing on a definition of crime is difficult, and radical and critical theorists especially argue that the construction of crime is purely political and power-based. While we all know these problems, tests of criminal theory proceed regardless, perhaps with the blithe assurance that these data sources are "all we have" or "the best available."

The difficulties, however, are fundamental to the enterprise of criminology. How can one explain a social behavior (crime) when there is no agreed-upon definition of what it is? Do criminal theories presume to explain, in addition to street crime such as robbery, the causes behind toxic waste dumping and/or spousal abuse? Income tax evasion? Speeding? Bribery of public officials? Price fixing? Gay bashing? Given a theory of crime, will it explain the crime of drug use? Did it also explain such behavior when drug use was not a crime? And did it explain abortion when it was a crime but now does not explain it, because abortion is no longer a crime (at least in the first trimester)? Does this theory of crime explain prostitution (except in Nevada)? Gambling (except when it is legalized)? Most criminological theories do not explicitly define what crime they seek to explain. Gottfredson and Hirschi's proffered explanation is one of the few theories that do make explicit the range of behavior addressed, and they state that their theory explains *all* crime.[3] Most criminal theories do not even acknowledge the idea that crime is a dynamic relationship between those who perform a behavior and those who define such behavior as criminal.

A careful survey of crime statistics shows that rates of prostitution and other public-order crimes have dropped significantly in the last 30 years. It may be true that there are fewer acts of prostitution; however, it is more likely that the decline is due to jurisdictions that have de-emphasized prostitution as a crime problem or have even decriminalized some forms of prostitution. Another explanation is that prostitution has moved from the streets to computer chat rooms, and, as such, is more difficult to investigate, thus leading to fewer arrests. The point is that arrest numbers may or may not be an accurate representation of incidence. If one then attempts to theorize about the causes for the changing crime rate of prostitution without recognizing these problems of measurement, any such theory is likely to be flawed.

We measure crime through means that capture only a portion of reality. Offenses in the "crimes reported" category leave the vast area of the "dark figure of crime" unexplored. Through victim reports, such as the National Crime Victim Survey (NCVS), we know a little bit more about how much crime is out there and unreported, but this knowledge is subject to the accuracy of victimization studies. When we found that only 29 percent of rapes/sexual assaults were reported to police in 1993 and 26 percent were reported in 2011,[4] we must assume that the victimization survey samples used to generate these findings were representative of the general population, that respondents answered honestly, that they all had a shared understanding of what rape is, and that there were no errors or intentional malfeasance or misfeasance on the part of the survey takers.

Another issue is the categorizing/counting of crime. Reporting practices pigeonhole human behavior into preconceived categories that can be counted, but life is usually not so simple. For example, police officers respond to a domestic call where an ex-husband has come back for his computer equipment that was taken by his ex-wife, because she did not agree that it was his. She is now brandishing a gun and shoots in his general direction while he is breaking her front window with a tire iron and, in the heat of the moment, he swings at and hits the arriving police officer. What *crime(s)* should be counted in this event? Will we count the wife's theft, her assault, his destruction of property, or assault on a police officer? What about another domestic dispute where a mother and daughter's argument escalates into a screaming fight?

When the mother attempts to drag the 16-year-old to her bedroom, the girl pulls away and pushes the mother, who falls to the floor. How many assaults are of the variety described here? Obviously, some crimes are less complex— one burglar committing one burglary is not complicated to count. However, it should never be forgotten that the UCR is comprised of not only simple burglaries, but also the messy, interpersonal conflicts of individuals that sometimes get processed through the system and are called crimes, even though most people would not identify them as such.

How much crime in official reports is more similar to the mother-daughter dispute or the husband-wife dispute than the one-burglar, one-burglary variety? How much crime has been pushed and prodded into crime categories and, in so doing, bears little resemblance to the contextual reality of its occurrence? In a vacuum, we mentally construct a reality of assault, theft, homicide, or rape. When one reads a news report that says assaults are down or thefts have increased, there is a presumption of what assault means and what theft means. These constructions are then used in criminal theory. We should pause to remember, however, that the measures of crime are poor attempts to reconstruct the original reality.

Measuring Correlates

The problems of measuring crime as described above are compounded by problems in measuring the hypothesized correlates of crime being studied. There are problems when attempting to measure any of the variables historically associated with crime. Even factors that are by nature quantitative, such as poverty or socioeconomic status (SES), pose difficulties. What is the poverty line? Are all individuals equally affected by any given income level—that is, do they feel deprivation equally? What if an individual has access to another's money? If one had no income but had access to a parent's, spouse's, or friend's income, would he or she behave differently from someone who had some money but no access to others' wealth? Even unemployment measures are notoriously subject to the whims of political expediency. Should summer college students be counted? Should those who have given up looking for work be counted? Should adjustments be made for seasonal fluctuations in such industries as construction? Intelligence has also been identified by many as a causal factor; yet, there continues to be a vociferous debate on the difficulties of measuring intelligence. All correlates of crime, even those that seem simple, must be measured. The measurement of such factors creates a constructed reality distinct from the factor itself—an IQ score is only a partial reality of intelligence; an unemployment rate is only a partial reality of the level of need in a society.

What makes perfect sense intuitively may be devilishly hard to measure and prove as causal. For instance, Travis Hirschi's early control theory postulated that various bonds to society act to insulate young people from delinquency. One of the bonds identified was attachment, but what is it exactly and how does one measure it? The original research measured attachment by using answers on a paper-and-pencil test given to high school students.[5] Attachment to parents was measured by several questions that asked such things as how often the youths ate dinner with their parents, or how close they felt they were to their parents. Think of how many constructions of reality have been enacted here. First, the researcher develops the idea of attachment, he or she operationalizes it through some questions, the students read the questions and add their own constructions to the ideas and concepts embedded in such questions, the theorist then adds up "scores" that presume to measure the concept of attachment, and finally the statistical relationship between the score and some other measure (i.e., crime or delinquency) is examined.

Earlier works at least provide more detailed explanations of their terms. In some criminological tests of theory today as reported in journal articles, one has to read the footnotes or appendices to discover the elements used to define a major construct, and sometimes a very complicated construct is measured by two or three simple questions on a survey. The fundamental problem of measuring constructs is often ignored in debates pitting two theories against each other, with so little description given of the measurements of constructs that the reader has to trust that the researcher's measures of variables are valid. There are serious issues as to the validity of measurements of such factors as self-control, goals of society, strain, masculinity, social support, or stigma. Methodologists criticize a theory if the terms cannot be operationalized, but one might also criticize the belief that some concepts can be operationalized at all, at least with simple statements and *Likert scales*.

Measurements of crime (despite their difficulties) and measurements of independent variables (despite their difficulties) are then analyzed using increasingly sophisticated statistical tools. Measures of correlation presume integer-level data—that is, to be able to measure correlation there must be quantitatively equal units of measurement in the two variables. This presumption is routinely violated. Using the example of the attachment variable described above, is it possible to measure attachment and assume that one's measurement is composed of equal parts (e.g., that one person is exactly twice as attached as another person, and another person has three times or four times more attachment)? Can human emotions be measured in such a way?

It is true, of course, that there are nonparametric statistical tests to use when working with non-integer data. In fact, it can be argued that there are statistical tests for every conceivable purpose and type of data. However, the basic question here is whether such mathematical manipulations provide us with "truths" regarding the relationship between the stated variables. Of course, we do seek to measure everything, including human emotions, and a Likert scale is as good as any measurement to quantify stress, or liking for parents, or impulsivity, or any other thing. The most problematic element of the criminological enterprise, however, is not that measurements are perhaps only partial realities, or that the statistical tests used may not be appropriate for the type of data; rather, it is the unquestioning acceptance of such research findings as the perceived truth. Truth is then established through multiple citations.[6]

Feminist Criminology

Each of the issues above is relevant to the research on female criminality. Early researchers mixed up *gender* (the sex-role identity that is socialized in us all) and sex differences (biological, not socialized differences), assumed cultural patterns of behavior as the norm, and viewed women through the sexist and classist notions of the time. Even theorists in the 1950s and 1960s assumed that culturally prescribed behaviors of women were "natural," and they believed the "nature of women" to fit predetermined and unexamined patterns evidenced by their socioeconomic position in society.[7]

The most prevalent bias in criminology has been that women are not worthy of study. While we might understand why a 1975 study showed women to be the subject of a miniscule portion of criminology textbooks (an average of only 2.5 percent were devoted to discussing female criminality), it is harder to understand why the percentage had increased to only 4 percent in Wright's 1992 review of textbooks.[8] In a cursory review of current texts, it appears that the subject of criminal women now receives at least a chapter of its own, but the idea of integrating female criminality into all chapters has evidently never occurred to most textbook authors.

Domestic Violence: Research, Policy, and Unintended Consequences

The research on domestic violence illustrates the difficulties of measurement, the influence of values on research, alternative methods of knowing, and the influence academic research does have on policy. Once domestic violence emerged as a social problem in the 1970s, most of the early literature described it as largely a problem of abusive men physically assaulting female partners. Researchers explored why women stayed in such a relationship, they explored why men were violent, and they explored the effects on children. Then, later research emerged that allegedly proved women were just as violent as men. Two facts supported such a conclusion: first, domestic homicide rates were symmetrical—that is, looking just at intimate partner homicides, there were almost as many women killing male partners as there were men killing their female partners. Of course, men killed many more people in addition to their partners, while when a woman killed, the victim was very likely to be her partner. Second, a survey-based violence index was created showing that women self-reported as much—in fact, in some applications of the research, more—violence than did men.[9] Domestic violence was redefined in this research not as a problem of the victimization of women, but rather as violent people swinging at each other. Yet, the emergency-room personnel who observed almost exclusively female victims were not persuaded by this "new evidence"; nor were the shelter personnel, who heard so many similar stories of abuse and emotional terrorism that they could create brochures identifying early markers to predict which men were likely to become abusers.

Rebuttals of such claims came quickly. Other researchers argued that the violence survey (The Conflict Tactics Scale) overestimated and misinterpreted female violence and that men comprised only about 4–5 percent of domestic violence victims.[10] These researchers argued that homicides committed by women were more likely than those committed by men to be in self-defense. The Conflict Tactics Scale did not distinguish motivation (self-defense versus first-strike aggression) or intensity, so a woman who pushed away a spouse who was threatening her was counted as equally violent as a man who pushed his partner down a flight of stairs.[11] More recent data continue to support the conclusion that domestic violence is largely an issue of female victims and male perpetrators. The Bureau of Justice Statistics reports that women are the victims of intimate partner violence in four out of every five cases, a statistic that has not changed since 1994.[12] Further, the so-called sexual symmetry of violence (equal numbers of spousal homicide) is no longer valid. Arguably, after the emergence of battered women's shelters and social services available for these women, they were more likely to leave an abusive relationship than to use lethal self-defense measures. The numbers of women killing their partners declined, but the number of men killing their partners did not decline as much (supporting the notion that the use of lethal force was more likely to be in self-defense for women). Between 1989 and 2001 the rate of female victims declined by 33 percent, but the rate of male victims declined by 45 percent.[13] Today, the disparity is greater: in 2007, for instance, out of 2,340 intimate partner homicides, over twice as many (1,640) were women killed by their male partner compared to men killed by their female partner (700).[14]

The point of this example is not that researchers intentionally mislead, but that our measurements of reality are woefully inadequate to accurately describe crime or any social behavior. The shelter personnel and those in the field who did not accept the statistical reality of symmetrical violence, and who believed that domestic violence was largely a problem of female victims, possess a truth just as valid as the statisticians' numbers. Nancy Wonders, in a discussion of another issue, makes this point:

> Truth . . . is never absolute, uncontested, transhistorical, or transcultural. Instead reality is at best a complex composite of different stories being lived and told by different people.[15]

The danger in social science research, however, is that one truth sometimes has real consequences in policies and societal reactions. In the domestic violence example, research on domestic violence and arrest led to mandatory arrest policies that pressured police officers to make arrests on domestic violence calls. The confusion over types of violence perpetrated by male and female partners, coupled with academic support for the notion that women were as violent as men, led to the tendency of police officers to arrest both partners of domestic violence if there was evidence that the female partner also was violent, regardless of motive or intensity.[16] The myth that the battered woman doesn't fight back was part of the problem. In early studies developing the concept of the cycle of violence, the *learned helplessness theory* was taught to advocates and police officers promoting the idea that true battering involves a helpless victim and a violent aggressor. The reality is that when women are beaten they often fight back, using any implements accessible at the time. It is reported that while 58 percent of women describe their violence as self-defense, only 5 percent of men do.[17]

Before academic and public attention highlighted the problem of domestic violence, police officers often simply separated the parties and told them to not call police again. Their response was described as benign neglect. After the intervention of victim advocates and academic researchers, legislators and law enforcement agencies responded with a shift in arrest policies. Some states passed mandatory arrest laws in cases of domestic violence, and many more police departments changed their formal policies regarding domestic violence. The result has been that now women are more likely to be arrested than in the past, even if their violence was in self-defense.

After the problem of dual arrests was identified, police in some jurisdictions were retrained to identify the so-called primary aggressor (who was usually the man) and arrest only that person. As a result, dual arrests declined but are still believed to be one of the reasons why women's arrests for aggravated assault and assault seem to have converged with men's rates.[18] Studies that look behind these numbers do not support the notion that the violence of men and the violence of women are equivalent. In one qualitative study of female victims of abuse, it was found that three categories of violent behavior by women existed: generalized violent behavior (involving the fewest number of women in the sample), frustration response violence, and defensive behavior. One of the respondents, for instance, became angry at her husband in a bar because he was flirting with another woman, and she pushed him and threw her drink at him. She was arrested and was placed on probation for assault. In this study, the largest number of respondents hit or used a weapon against their partner during a violent incident as a form of self-defense, yet they were subsequently arrested.[19]

> I just can't believe that I'm being arrested! Even though there's a knife wound, but I'm the victim! I called the police five times because there were black eyes, broken shoulders, and here I'm getting hauled off when I was just trying to keep him off of me.[20]

Researchers have found that while women are often highly emotional when police arrive, men are calm and have learned to manipulate the system by calling police first and reporting abuse. Women who have been abused then find themselves in the system as perpetrators, even though they are clearly victims. They are ineligible for victim services and face losing their children if they go to trial, so they often plea bargain even if the evidence clearly points to self-defense. Even the prosecutors and probation officers of these female defendants sometimes refer to them as victims instead of offenders.[21] The result has been that domestic violence intervention, which was originally intended to help female victims of violence, has now most probably led to the increase in assault arrests for women.[22]

Phenomenological Research

The above criticism of criminology does not necessarily lead to a conclusion of futility or resignation that understanding is impossible, but it does promote the need for alternative methods of study. One of the contributions of feminist criminology is the importance given to subjective, qualitative methods of research. The phenomenological world of the individuals studied is every bit as important as quantitative method. Make no mistake, qualitative methods carry just as much reality constructing as do quantitative methods, but usually the researcher is at least a little more aware of the possibility and more humble regarding the results.

While *phenomenological methods* are not unique to the feminist approach; they are associated with it.[23] The use of narratives to understand the world of the offender provides a different type of knowledge from empiricism and asks and answers different questions. The results of such studies have enriched our understanding of the lives of both male and female offenders.[24]

Gilfus,[25] for instance, utilized the phenomenological method in her study of 20 women. The in-depth interviews with the women chronicled their lives as filled with abuse and neglect, racism, economic marginality, early motherhood, economic struggle, rape and other victimization by men, street crimes, prostitution, forgery, and shoplifting. In her descriptions, it becomes clear that crime was a way of taking care of the people in the women's lives. She suggested, in fact, that childhood violence and/or neglect may socialize women to stubbornly cling to caring for anyone who promised love, material success, and acceptance.

Chesney-Lind[26] also used interviews, and her women also described lives filled with sexual and physical victimization, parental drinking and drug use, and *parentalization*. This term refers to the pattern of children in dysfunctional families, especially girls, in taking on parental responsibilities because of drug or alcohol incapacitation of the parent, or long working hours, or the absence of one or both parents. Many of Chesney-Lind's women described having to become the surrogate parent of their younger siblings, and being beaten for staying out late (unlike their brothers). They described running away to escape the responsibilities and controls of home but then becoming pregnant at an early age, which meant going back home for their parents' support.

The narrative approach has its own drawbacks, of course. Numbers are typically quite small, and, therefore, one questions whether interviewees are indeed typical. Carlen's[27] point that women in prison are not representative of all criminal women because of sentencing bias is well taken.

Other Contributions of Feminist Criminology

The contributions of feminist criminologists to the field of study cannot be overstated. They questioned the basic underpinnings of knowledge sets that treated women as "the other" and ignored them in the search for causation. Feminists correctly pointed out that researchers were influenced by their socialization but might also be criticized for wearing their own unique blinders when analyzing others' research. Morris,[28] for instance, criticized early applications of strain/opportunity theory to women and questioned the assumption that girls had different career goals than boys, arguing that there was little support for that assumption. However, she was perhaps applying a late 1980s cultural bias to research that had been conducted in the 1960s. Those early researchers were perhaps accurate in identifying different career goals of girls and boys *at the time.* Furthermore, one might argue that even today, more than 30 years after Morris argued that girls' and boys' career goals were similar, we can still measure differences between the sexes in the importance placed on career versus family.

Feminist criminology has helped to uncover the sexism that influenced all earlier traditional theories of crime. They pointed out that scientific queries should reject the approach of using men as the norm and women as "the other." The problem goes far beyond criminology and touches every aspect of knowledge collection, whether one looks at medicine, law, or other forms of social science. Some feminists also astutely cautioned against considering women as a homogeneous group, ignoring factors such as class, race, and ethnicity.

Daly and Chesney-Lind[29] summarized some of the general points of all (or most) feminist approaches:

- Gender is not a natural fact but rather is a complex social, historical, and cultural product related to, but not simply derived from, biological sex differences and reproductive capacities.
- Gender and gender relations order social life and social institutions in fundamental ways.
- Gender relations and constructs of masculinity and femininity are not symmetrical but are based on an organizing principle of men's superiority and their social and political-economic dominance over women.[30]
- Systems of knowledge reflect men's views of the natural and social world, but the production of knowledge is gendered.
- Women should be at the center of intellectual inquiry, not peripheral, invisible, or appendages to men.

Many feminists disagree with the concept of biological differences between the sexes, arguing that differences other than very obvious physical ones like pregnancy are the product of socialization.[31] *Cultural feminism,* however, recognizes that while most differences between men and women are the product of socialization, sex roles emerged because of biological differences and "natural" sex-role responsibilities such as child care. It is difficult to distinguish real sex differences from sexual stereotypes or socialization differences; however, it is important to address these issues because sex is the strongest correlate of crime.

Sexual Stereotypes and Sex Differences

Clarice Feinman identifies images of women that have existed throughout history and which continue to influence perceptions of women: the "good" image of women as pure, submissive, moral, and passive can be compared to the "bad" image of woman as "worse than men," vicious, and sexually rapacious.[32] These images continue to have power when considering modern media messages regarding female offenders.

Early Greeks, for instance, viewed women as amoral (like children). This belief was still dominant in Cesare Lombroso's work in the late 1800s. A competing view, however, was that women had higher morals than men. Women were viewed in pre-Jacksonian America as the keepers of the hearth and the guardians of societal morality. Morris and Gelsthorpe use an 1891 quote to illustrate this belief:

> The care and nurture of children has been their lot in life for untold centuries; the duties of maternity have perpetually kept alive a certain number of unselfish instincts; these instincts have become part and parcel of women's natural inheritance, and, as a result of possessing them to a larger extent than men, she is less disposed to crime.[33]

Morris and Gelsthorpe use this quotation critically to argue that women have historically been stereotyped as a Madonna figure, a stereotype that constricts them and has no scientific validity. Among feminist criminologists there is strong resistance to the idea that women are "naturally" predisposed to a moral orientation that is relationship-based and results in less criminality among women than men. Interestingly, though, the quote is remarkably close to current findings from biological and psychological research, only some of which will be reviewed in Chapter 5. The fact that the same views were also expressed in 1891 does not necessarily make them wrong.

The Violent Woman

There is a difficulty reconciling the few violent female offenders that have always existed with the idea that women are naturally passive and nonviolent. One reaction, as described above, is to dichotomize women and view violent women as monsters—as even worse than the most violent of male offenders. The second reaction is to believe that women are changing in general and all women are becoming more violent.

The theme of the violent woman as a monster is long standing. Cesare Lombroso, in 1894, and others writing in the early part of the twentieth century, claimed that violent women were more bloodthirsty and more heartless than violent male criminals. They used vignettes drawn from dime-store novels to illustrate the terrible crimes of some female criminals, presuming that these crimes "proved" their assertion that the violent female criminal was much worse than her male counterpart. Interestingly, one continues to see this thread of thought even in modern academic treatments of the subject matter: "Women terrorists have consistently proved themselves more ferocious and more intractable in their acts than their male counterparts."[34]

In modern times this is most clearly depicted, for instance, by the media's treatment of Aileen Wuornos, a female serial murderer. Various other media images of women, such as in women's prison movies from the 1950s and 1960s, and in violent gang-girl images, are examples of the public's fascination with violent women.[35] These depictions are generally one-dimensional and exaggerate women's violence, downplaying factors that might have led to violence.

The so-called discovery of violent female offenders and the corresponding observation that women are becoming more violent seem to be present in every time period and is typically associated with women's increasing liberation and changing sex roles. In every era, either academics and/or popular media seem to believe, contrary to statistical evidence, that women are becoming more violent.[36] Pollock and Davis[37] reviewed how the discovery of the increasingly violent female offender was cyclical and how the latest increases have been in assault crime categories, highly subject to discretion by system actors. These authors noted that the five ways to make women seem more violent were to:

1. Argue against the straw-dog proposition that women aren't violent at all by showing examples of violent women (obviously there has always been a small percentage of violent crime committed by women).

2. Substitute the term aggression for violence and expand the definition to include acts such as gossip, and then switch the discussion back to violence as if they were the same thing.

3. Utilize a small sample of violent women and then bootstrap the characteristics of this unrepresentative sample to make statements for all women.

4. Use percentage increases, which will be large because of small base numbers.

5. Ignore the fact that system responses (decisions to arrest) are a dynamic factor that influences arrest rates.

Chesney-Lind and Eliason[38] describe journalistic accounts of "bad girls" and illustrate that these treatments follow predictable patterns. A news item or profile of a violent female offender is typically presented with percentage increase figures in arrests to prove that violence among women is increasing. This coverage rarely explores more nuanced explanations, any of the factors that are associated with violence (such as childhood abuse), or the idea that changing numbers might be due partially to changes in the system's "counting" rather than real differences in the behavior of girls and women. The debate as to whether women are becoming more violent is rife with preconceptions and biases regarding the nature of sexual stereotypes versus sex differences and the validity of official statistics.

Sex Differences versus Gender Differences

Sex differences are a topic that always creates controversy. Even the term is controversial. Generally, sex differences should be used to denote biological differences between the female and male sexes. For instance, sex differences include women's ability (and men's inability) to give birth and lactate. Average differences in musculature, height, weight, and brain size are also sex differences. Researchers are discovering other physical differences between men and women, such as the hard wiring of the brain and the levels of certain brain chemicals. More controversial are those differences in intellectual predispositions (spatial versus verbal skills) and aggressiveness, since some believe these differences arise due to biological differences, others argue that they are the result of socialization, and still others argue that there is an interaction between biology and environment resulting in the reality of difference. The term gender differences applies to those differences thought to be purely the product of socialization. For many, what is female or male is thought to be largely determined by cultural definitions and proscriptions/prescriptions of behavior inculcated in the individual from birth onward.

One basically chooses between at least two fundamentally different paradigms or perceptions of reality:

- that women and men are essentially the same except for reproductive functions and all observed differences are socially and culturally influenced; or

- that women and men are essentially different in the natural function of reproduction, and *that difference* contributes to an array of behavioral and emotional predispositions that are, in turn, influenced and reinforced by the social and cultural expectations of each sex.

If one presumes the first paradigm, certain anthropological evidence is cited to prove sex differences are almost nonexistent and observed differences between men and women are purely the effect of socialization. Those who give more credence to socialized differences point to converging behavior patterns between men and women as evidence that differences are largely culturally induced. If one presumes the second paradigm, sociobiological sources are utilized to show how physical differences affect behavior and perception. Those who give more credence to biological differences between women and men would point out there is nothing subjective or fictive about pregnancy, childbirth, or lactation, or the effects these phenomena have on the body.

Steffensmeier and Allen's[39] argument that women's moral choices constrain them from behavior that is harmful to others is an illustration of the second paradigm:

> Because women are bound more intimately into a network of interpersonal ties, their moral decisions are more influenced by empathy and compassion, and this ethic of care constructs nonviolence and suggests that serious predatory crime is outside women's moral boundaries.[40]

Messerschmidt, illustrating the first paradigm, argues that these authors "ignore the fact that there exists no scholarship that demonstrates that the greater conformity of women is a function of their special virtues."[41] Yet, to arrive at that conclusion is to completely ignore the work of Carol Gilligan, Nancy Chodorow, and many others.

Messerschmidt then uses examples of female gang members to show that women are not always empathetic and nurturing. For example, he provides a quote from a girl gang member gloating about "fucking up" another girl and exhibiting pride in how bad the victim looked. He argues that a theory proposing that women are more naturally caring and empathetic would have to see this gang member as "simply defective and freakish, not authentically female." However, despite the sensationalistic language, the girl does represent a "freakish" view of violence if one uses the term freakish in a purely statistical sense instead of in the connotation of stigma that Messerschmidt implies. How many women in the United States or any other country would endorse such a view (but how many men)? The girl is also "defective" if one uses the term in a value-neutral way rather than in the condemnatory tone that Messerschmidt places upon it. Such a glorification of violence is not healthy, either emotionally for the individual expressing it or societally. Is the girl "authentically female"? Of course, but she is a female that most probably has grown up in a societal environment that endorses and encourages violent responses, one that provides no hope or support for the future, and a familial environment that devalued her worth and quite possibly subjected her to emotional neglect and physical and/or sexual abuse. Such an environment could obviously overcome any "natural" predispositions toward care and empathy.

Even after finding a behavioral difference between men and women, it is still necessary to identify the mediator—that is, if behavioral changes exist, what is the mechanism by which the difference manifests? For instance, research has fairly consistent findings that girls in school cheat less than boys,[42] but that is a behavioral difference. The reason why, according to one study, is anticipated shame (girls were more likely to anticipate shame and perceived it as being more intense) and this difference, along with others, influenced cheating behavior. The same author also found that anticipated shame was also the reason why men and women differed in intention to commit shoplifting and DWI. Other research has indicated that self-control is more predictive of males' cheating and moral beliefs more predictive of young women's cheating.[43] Thus, it is important to deconstruct sex differences to understand why the observed behavior differences exist.

In Chapter 4 we take up the question of whether differences observed between men and women are the result of biological sex differences interacting with socialization or purely socialization and sexual stereotypes.

Framing the Questions: The Criminology of Women

Otto Pollak's 1950 book was a milestone in the criminology of women. His review of theories in the first half of the 1900s was comprehensive, if flawed, and his observations of female criminality were provocative, if hopelessly biased. He concluded that women and men were equally criminal; women engaged in more deceitful crimes or were instigators of crime, which is why they were not included in official statistics to the same degree as men; and the system was chivalrous toward women, resulting in less likelihood of arrest, conviction, or punishment. These conclusions have not been supported by more current research, as we shall see in later chapters. They do, however, help us begun a new discussion regarding female offenders. The questions below will be addressed in the chapters to follow.

- *Are women and men equally criminal?* Are increased crime rates of women over the last 30 years due more to system changes or actual behavioral changes of women? The *gender gap* (the disproportional ratio of men arrested compared to women) will be explored through crime statistics, with attention to how these numbers may be influenced by definitional differences, official practices, and misinterpretations. Patterns of crime for both adults and juveniles will be reviewed. Chapter 2 addresses this question for adult women, and Chapter 6 reviews the crime patterns of girls.

- *Are women's crimes different?* Do they come to crime through different pathways? Official and other sources will be utilized to describe women's offense patterns and the true nature of such crimes. For instance, if women and men have equal rates of embezzlement, are their actual crimes similar? Chapter 2 looks at crime patterns, and Chapter 5 also addresses this question by examining life course and pathways theories.

- *Which theories of crime help us to understand why some women commit crime?* Some theories seem to be more helpful than others in understanding female criminality, even if they were not originally designed to explore the question. Chapters 3, 4, and 5 address this question.

- *Has the criminal justice system been chivalrous toward women, with decision-makers less likely to arrest, convict, or send women to prison?* If so, has this pattern continued in more recent eras? Sentencing studies will be utilized to discover whether or not women and men receive similar punishments, with the caveat that most studies cannot control for all variables that might influence sentencing decisions. Chapter 7 addresses this question.

- *How are female delinquents different from male delinquents?* Are they treated differently in the system? Chapter 6 describes juvenile delinquency and juvenile justice with a focus on female offenders.

- *What do we do to women who are defined as criminal?* Are their jails and prisons different from those housing men? Are women's experiences on probation and parole dissimilar to those of men's? Chapters 8, 9, and 10 address these questions.

- *How can we reduce female criminality?* Research on recidivism and chronic offending is presented in Chapter 11, and this chapter also addresses policy implications of the accumulated body of information presented in the preceding chapters.

REVIEW QUESTIONS

1. Explain what a paradigm is and provide an example of a paradigm that might affect criminological research.

2. Present an example of an aggregate-level theory of crime and an example of an individual theory of crime.

3. Provide at least four crime correlates and explain how you would measure them.

4. Describe what was called the "sexual symmetry of violence" and explain how it has changed.

5. Explain how domestic violence research has affected public policy.

6. What are some examples of phenomenological methods? How are they different from empirical methods?

7. What are the major points of feminist criminology as summarized by Daly and Chesney-Lind?

8. What are some "images" of women? Find examples of these images in popular media.

9. Describe the five ways proposed by Pollock and Davis to argue that women are becoming more violent.

10. Give some examples of gender differences and some examples of sex differences.

2

Women's Crimes

CHAPTER SUMMARY

- Women account for a small percentage of violent crime relative to men, but the gender gap dissipates as crimes become less "victim-harming" and it disappears in some property crime categories.

- Women's most frequent crimes continue to be the traditional consumer crimes that they have always been more likely to commit, such as larceny, fraud, forgery, and embezzlement.

- Even though women are committing more crime, the motivation for and elements of their crimes are often different from men's.

- Women's and men's crime rates dropped dramatically during the 1990s, but women's lower rate of decline reduced the gender gap in offending.

- Women's less dramatic drop in crime rate has been attributed to changes in formal identification and processing, and to economic marginalization.

The four sources we can utilize to know what crimes are committed and by whom are: crimes reported to police (Uniform Crime Reports), official arrest statistics, self-reports, and victim surveys. Of these sources, only arrest statistics and self-reports tell us much about the criminal because the other two sources require the victim to know something about the offender. If it is a violent, personal crime then the victim is presumed to have seen the offender, but the vast majority of crime is property crime and the victim may not know the age, sex, or race of the offender.

Arrest statistics are measures of official activity as well as offender activity. They measure only those crimes where an arrest is made. *Clearance rates* (when a crime is cleared by an arrest) are fairly high in crimes such as homicide or aggravated assault but low in crimes such as burglary and larceny/theft. Thus, the "dark" figure of crime (crimes not reported to police) and low clearance rates are a problematic issue when using arrest statistics as measures of crime. Also, changes in official arrest statistics may indicate changes of policy, changes of definition, or changes of efficiency, instead of or in addition to changes in offender behavior.

The Gender Gap

In this chapter we look at crimes committed by adult women, broken into general crime categories of property crimes, violent crimes, and drug crimes.

Women's crime rates do indicate that the *gender gap* (referring to the much higher crime rates of men as compared to women) is shrinking. Table 2.1 displays women's arrests for selected crime categories as a percentage of total arrests. This display shows us the ratio of arrests of men to women to determine long-term patterns in the gender gap. Table 2.1 shows that the gender gap has been decreasing for some time in a slow but consistent pattern for many crime categories. In fact, women are now as equally likely to be arrested for embezzlement as men. It is also important to note that in the most serious violent crime categories (murder and non-negligent manslaughter and robbery), women's participation has not substantially changed for decades. Also, the percentage of total arrests for women in 2011 are almost exactly the same as 2010 figures except that the percentage of women dropped to 50 percent for embezzlement and rose slightly to 26 percent of all arrests for all crimes.[1]

It is important to note that both men's and women's crime rates increased in the 1980s and declined substantially, beginning in the mid-1990s. Thus, the decreased gender gap illustrated above has been due in some crime categories to a dramatic decline for men and a smaller decline for women, rather than an increase in overall crime by women. Figure 2.1 (on p. 24) shows the pattern of change in arrest rates of men and women for property crime; Figure 2.2 (on p. 24) shows arrest rates for violent crime categories, and Figure 2.3 (on p. 25) shows arrest rates for drug crimes.

Explanations for Convergence

The most striking fact illustrated in Figures 2.1–2.3 is that the convergence in arrest rates between men and women is largely due to the decreased arrests of men rather than any extreme increase in arrests of women. Women's arrests rates have increased slightly over the long time period, but not dramatically so. Still, several explanations have been offered for why women's and men's rates of crime (especially property crime) are converging:

Table 2.1   Percentage of Women's Total Arrests—Selected Crimes

Crime	1935	1942*	1946*	1950	1955	1960	1965	1970	1975	1980	1985	1990	1995	2000	2005	2010
All violent	7	10	8	9	12	12	11	11	10	10	11	11	15	17	18	19
Murder/manslaughter	10	13	11	14	14	16	16	15	15	13	13	11	10	11	111	11
Robbery	5	5	5	4	4	5	5	6	7	7	8	8	9	10	12	13
Agg Assault	8	11	9	11	16	15	14	13	13	12	13	13	17	20	20	22
Other Assaults[1]	—	—	—	—	—	—	—	—	13	12	14	15	18	21	23	25
Arson	—	—	—	—	—	—	—	—	14	13	15	16	19	18	19	20
All property	5	8	8	7	8	11	15	20	19	22	25	27	28	30	31	37
Burglary	2	2	3	3	2	3	4	5	5	6	7	9	11	14	15	16
Larceny/theft	8	13	13	12	13	17	23	30	31	30	32	33	33	35	37	43
MVT	2	2	2	3	3	4	4	5	7	7	8	9	12	15	18	18
Forgery/ctft	—	—	—	14[2]	15	17	19	24	29	31	33	34	36	38	40	38
Fraud	—	—	—	18[3]	16	16	21	28	31	42	44	45	43	44	46	42
Embezzlemt	—	—	—	—	—	—	—	—	31	29	36	41	44	50	50	51
Drug crimes	—	—	—	16[4]	17	15	13	16	14	13	13	17	17	18	19	19
All crimes	7	12	11	10	11	11	12	15	—	14	16	17	19	20	23	25

*Five-year increments for this time span were unavailable; the closest years have been substituted.

[1]Unavailable.

[2]Previous years unavailable. 1950 unavailable, 1953 is substituted.

[3]Previous years unavailable. Fraud & embezzlement combined until 1975.

[4]1950 unavailable; 1953 substituted.

Source: Simon, R., 1979, p. 36–37; GAO, 1979, p. 70–71; Snyder & Mulako-Wangota, 2013.

Figure 2.1   Arrest Rates of Men and Women, Property Crime

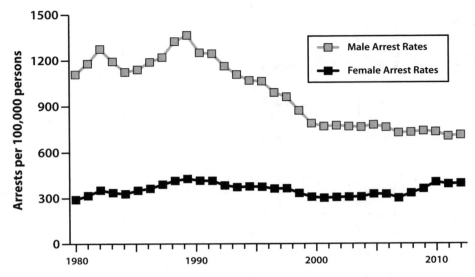

Source: Snyder, H. & Mulako-Wangota, J. *Arrest Data Analysis Tool*. Washington, DC: Bureau of Justice Statistics, August 7, 2013, at www.bjs.gov

Figure 2.2   Arrest Rates of Men and Women, Violent Crime

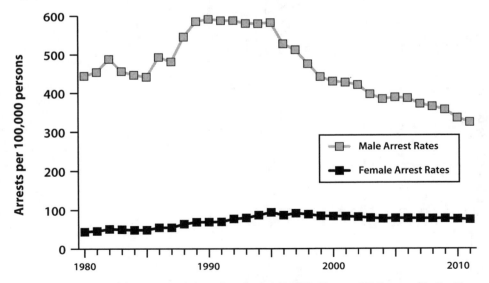

Source: Snyder, H. & Mulako-Wangota, J. *Arrest Data Analysis Tool*. Washington, DC: Bureau of Justice Statistics, August 7, 2013, at www.bjs.gov

Figure 2.3   Arrest Rates of Men and Women, Drug Arrests

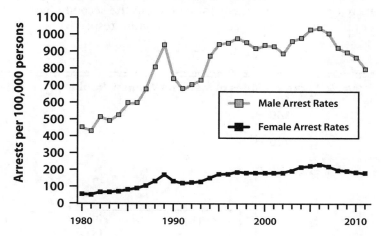

Source: Snyder, H. & Mulako-Wangota, J. *Arrest Data Analysis Tool*. Washington, DC: Bureau of Justice Statistics, August 7, 2013, at www.bjs.gov

- Less chivalrous attitudes toward women and increased pressure to administer law in a neutral way;
- Increased awareness of female criminality leading to greater suspicion and surveillance;
- Police arresting and charging women, despite their having a peripheral role, so they can then coerce them into being informants or testifying against their husbands or boyfriends;
- Improvements in recording practices;
- Changes in sanctioning policies on the part of welfare or retail, leading to more prosecution; and
- White-collar crime (which has always had higher rates of participation by women) becoming the focus of some police divisions and special squads, resulting in more arrests of women.[2]

One of the ways to determine whether there has been a true increase in crime as opposed to arrest rates being influenced by changes in official decision making is to compare official arrest rates as recorded and reported by the FBI with the National Crime Victim Survey (NCVS) rates for the same crimes. If the victimization reports show no difference but arrest rates show an increase over a given time period, one might assume that there are system changes operating to influence the increase in arrests. This is what has been done by Darrell Steffensmeier and his colleagues.[3] In a study covering the time period of 1980 to 2003, these researchers compared homicide and robbery (which are crimes with little discretion available to system actors regarding whether or not to arrest) to assault (where there is a great deal of discretion available to system actors as to whether or not to arrest). As we have noted above, there has been little change in the first category of crime, but an increase in rates of arrests for women in the second. Figures 2.4 and 2.5 present the arrest rates for robbery and assault, respectively.

Figure 2.4   Arrest Rates of Men and Women, Robbery

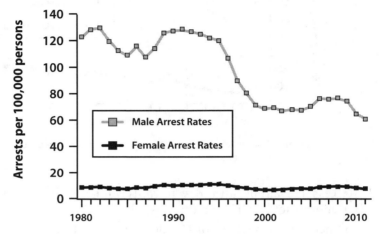

Source: Snyder, H. & Mulako-Wangota, J. *Arrest Data Analysis Tool.* Washington, DC: Bureau of Justice Statistics, August 7, 2013, at www.bjs.gov

Figure 2.5   Arrest Rates of Men and Women, Other Assaults

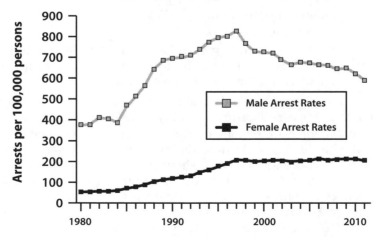

Source: Snyder, H. & Mulako-Wangota, J. *Arrest Data Analysis Tool.* Washington, DC: Bureau of Justice Statistics, August 7, 2013, at www.bjs.gov

Steffensmeier's research revealed that the gender gap in homicide and robbery arrests remained stable over the studied time period; however, the gap narrowed for aggravated and simple assault. Most of the change in arrest rates took place in the 1990s. The NCVS did show an increase in female-perpetrated assaults in the 1980s, but the ratio between male and female perpetrators in victim reports was largely stable (unlike that for arrest rates). Then, starting in the mid-1990s, victim reports showed a substantial decline in female-perpetrated assaults that was not reflected in assault arrests for women over these same years.[4] For the crime of aggravated assault, women's arrest rates doubled between 1980 and 2003, but victim reports reflected in the NCVS declined by more than half.[5]

Steffensmeier and his colleagues also found that the sex ratio in convictions for assault narrowed modestly for convictions and not at all for incarcerations. The researchers' interpretation of this finding was that the increased arrests of women were not for crimes warranting severe punishment, either because of less injury or reduced culpability. They argued that zero tolerance, greater formalization of the system response to family violence, the perception that women are becoming more violent, and a greater willingness of police to utilize a punitive response all contributed to the narrowing of the sex ratio in arrest rates, but that this observed change in arrests may not be a reflection of change in actual behavior patterns (at least for the crime of assault). Other reasons offered by Meda Chesney-Lind and other researchers[6] for increases in girls' arrests are *upcharging* (the practice of defining as assaults behaviors—specifically, mutual aggression in family disputes—that would not have been so defined in years past, thus creating the possibility of detainment)[7], and *bootstrapping* (the idea that girls are originally charged with a status offense and cannot be detained, but if they violate a condition of probation they are charged with contempt and can be detained). It has been reported that twice as many girls as boys are in detention for probation violations in this way,[8] and the criminalization of domestic violence (women being arrested more often as aggressors in ambiguous situations) has also contributed to this trend.[9]

Property Crimes

Most research indicates that the gender gap in arrests has been dramatically reduced in the case of property crimes, which include burglary, larceny/theft, forgery/counterfeiting, fraud, and embezzlement. As Table 2.1 shows, women comprised only 5 percent of total arrests for property crimes in 1935 but accounted for 37 percent of total property crime arrests in 2010.

There is no argument that women are committing more property crimes; however, the debate in this area is how much more and whether women and men commit the same types of property crimes (i.e., whether the motivation, injury or loss, prevalence and career orientation of women are the same as men's). Some argue that women's crimes are still very different from men's and the increase has taken place in what has been called pink-collar crimes, such as shoplifting, passing bad checks, credit card fraud, theft of services, welfare fraud, and small con games that women have always been more likely to commit than other types of crime.[10] Other explanations offered by Steffensmeier for the increase in women's arrests is that greater bureaucratization and more formal methods of policing have inflated women's arrest numbers. For instance, he points out that today "unknown" is used less often on UCR forms asking for the sex of the offender. In the past these were automatically counted as men, and consequently some amount of crime by women was incorrectly attributed to men.[11] While these possibilities may not account for all of the increase, they do illustrate the multitude of factors that affect our crime numbers quite apart from an offender actually committing the crime.

Burglary

Table 2.1 showed that women comprised 2 percent of all arrests for burglary in 1935 and 16 percent in 2010. That might lead one to conclude that women have dramatically increased their participation in burglaries, but Figure 2.6 shows that women's arrest rates for burglary increased only slightly from years past and that their greater percentage of total arrests is due to the dramatic decline of arrests of men for the crime. This illustrates the importance of not just using percentage increase figures or percentage of total figures, but to look at the data in a number of different ways to obtain a complete picture of crime trends.

Research also exists that indicates the profile of female-perpetrated burglary is different from that of men's. A study in the mid-1980s indicated women's

Figure 2.6   Arrest Rates of Men and Women, Burglary

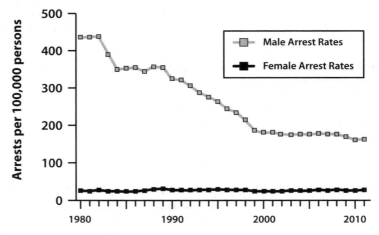

Source: Snyder, H. & Mulako-Wangota, J. *Arrest Data Analysis Tool.* Washington, DC: Bureau of Justice Statistics, August 7, 2013, at www.bjs.gov

burglaries were hastily conceived and yielded smaller profits than burglaries committed by men. It was also reported that women were more likely to work in groups and commit burglaries at a greater distance from their residences.[12]

In another study that compared female and male burglars, Scott Decker and his colleagues found that:

- Men were more likely to commit additional crimes besides burglary.
- Women were more likely to work with accomplices (83 percent versus 39 percent).
- Female burglars were more likely than male burglars to be drug addicted.
- Male burglars started committing burglaries at an earlier age than female burglars.
- Male burglars committed more burglaries than female burglars.
- Female burglars reported less contact with the criminal justice system.
- Both male and female burglars were equally likely to use drugs.[13]

Darrell Steffensmeier points out that women's participation in burglary may have increased because of the reduced risks the crime presents in today's society, in which large percentages of the population leave their houses completely unattended during the day. Women may also take advantage of opportunities to commit burglary that derive from their employment, such as being real estate agents who have access to unattended homes.[14] However, the most important fact to note as evidenced by Figure 2.6 is that the rate of burglary arrests for women has changed very little while the men's rate has decreased dramatically since about 1990.

Larceny/Theft, Fraud, and Embezzlement

Table 2.1 shows that in 1935 women were responsible for 8 percent of all larceny/theft arrests. In 2010, they comprised 43 percent of arrests, and that percentage remained at 43 percent in 2011.[15] Again, the question is whether the convergence is due to an increase in arrests of women, whether those arrests reflect a true change in the incidence of crime, or whether arrest numbers are due to a change in system actors' decisions to arrest. Another question is whether the act of larceny/theft is qualitatively different for women than for men. Figure 2.7 on the following page shows that there has been some increase in the number of arrests, but, again, the major reason for the convergence in arrests is the decrease in arrests of men.

One of the most common types of larceny/theft for both women and men is shoplifting. Three types of shoplifters have been described: the adult occasional shoplifter or pilferer, the amateur shoplifter, and the boosters or professional shoplifters.[16] In one of the few studies of female shoplifters, Mary Cameron reported that more than 90 percent had no prior record and that they were much less likely to recidivate than their male counterparts.[17] Other studies have indicated that women, who are less likely to be organized and professional, steal smaller items and more of them, while men steal fewer, more expensive goods.[18]

Figure 2.7   Arrest Rates of Men and Women, Larceny-Theft

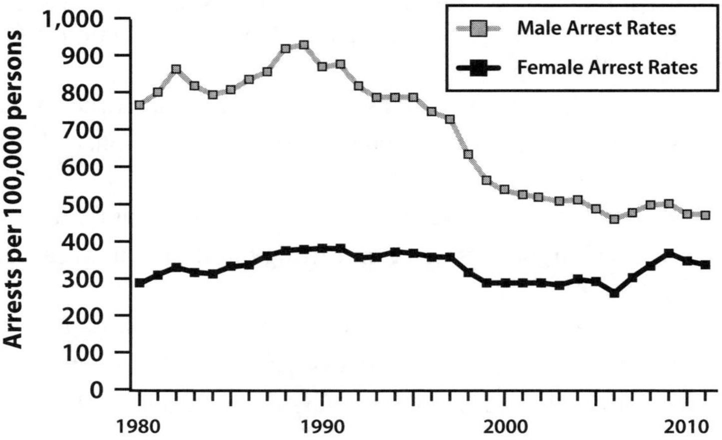

Source: Snyder, H. & Mulako-Wangota, J. *Arrest Data Analysis Tool*. Washington, DC: Bureau of Justice Statistics, August 7, 2013, at www.bjs.gov

In 1950 Otto Pollak speculated that women were responsible for a vast amount of shoplifting and other thefts that were undetected and unreported. He did not allow for the possibility that men also were probably responsible for large amounts of such crime; therefore, he concluded that this "dark" figure represented women's true criminal tendencies. It is important to recognize that statistics of shoplifting and other larceny/thefts are very much affected by official actions; many stores and places of business choose not to prosecute (or have chosen not to prosecute in the past). Policy changes affect arrest rates because if there is an increased willingness to formally prosecute, arrest figures will increase regardless of any changes in actual numbers of shoplifting. Also, stores have become increasingly sophisticated in their methods of detecting and apprehending shoplifters, again leading to higher arrest figures.

Larceny/theft is defined as taking property from another without consent and with no intention to return the property. If other elements are present, the crime becomes a different type of theft: for instance, if one is entrusted with the property but then converts it to one's own use, it is considered as embezzlement. Zietz[19] developed a typology of female embezzlers: the "honest women" who were obsessive protectors and embezzled to meet their perceived responsibilities as wives or mothers; the "romantic dreamers" who embezzled to enhance their relationships with their husbands or lovers; "greedy opportunists" who became dependent on material goods such as expensive cars and houses to enhance their self-worth; "victims" of pressure or persuasion who embezzled because of coercion or undue influence by another; "fraudulent operators" who embezzled from a sense of entitlement, believing that they deserved the money because they had experienced childhood deprivation; and "asocial entrepreneurs" who, unlike the other types, had a career orientation to the crime. Zietz concluded that male embezzlers generally committed their crimes to enhance their status, while female embezzlers were more likely to commit crimes because of relationships, although this conclusion is disputed by some researchers today.[20]

Another type of theft is fraud, defined as obtaining property from another through the use of misrepresentation—for instance, filing fake insurance claims or unemployment claims. Forgery is creating or altering a document that has legal significance—for example, forging a victim's signature on a check or credit card purchase. The rise in the use of credit cards and Internet purchasing has opened the door to many types of fraud, forgery, and identity theft that have no doubt led to increases in the number of women participating in these nonconfrontational, relatively risk-free forms of theft.

Kathleen Daly described the increased crimes by women as petty.[21] Her sample consisted of a group of federal offenders incarcerated for embezzlement, fraud, and forgery. Her findings included the following points:

- Women accounted for very little corporate or organizational crime.
- Women contributed close to 50 percent of bank embezzlement crimes as tellers.
- Women were more likely than men to commit their crimes alone.
- Women obtained less financial gain than men, on average about one-tenth the amount embezzled by men.

Motives in this category were different for men and women, with women more often citing family responsibilities as a pressure to embezzle. Daly found that embezzlement by women typically occurred in low-level sales and clerical jobs where women took money from the cash register or petty cash. Embezzlement by men generally involved greater amounts of money, and the men held positions at higher levels of authority than female embezzlers did. She also found that the female embezzlers were younger, less educated, and earned less than men. Their schemes were less sophisticated and of shorter duration as well.

Very little information is available on women's participation in organized crime. A few women have always been a part of organized crime groups, even though their presence has been ignored or denied by participants. Women have engaged in crime as madams, bookmakers, bankers, and loan sharks.[22] The major finding of all research in this area is, however, that women's crimes involve lesser dollar amounts and, perhaps, occur because of different motivations. For every Leona Helmsley or Martha Stewart, whose crimes were facilitated by their positions of economic power, there are thousands of economically marginalized women working in low-level jobs, such as cashiers, who steal small amounts of money.

In the 1970s, Rita Simon[23] theorized that women would increase their participation in embezzlement and other white-collar crimes as they increased their participation in the workplace and gained access to more opportunities. Figures 2.8a, b, and c show that the gender gap in arrests for fraud and forgery has declined and has disappeared entirely for embezzlement. The figures also show that over the years women's rates for fraud and forgery are remarkably similar in pattern to men's. Rates of arrest for embezzlement do show an increase for women during times of decline for men. Although this supports Simon's theory, the seriousness and type of crime and the motivations for such crimes are largely still under debate.

Figure 2.8a   Arrest Rates of Men and Women, Forgery/Counterfeiting

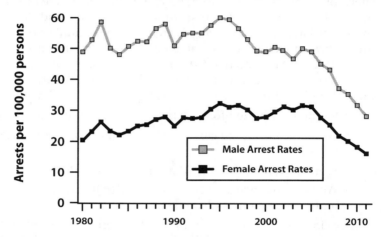

Source: Snyder, H. & Mulako-Wangota, J. *Arrest Data Analysis Tool*. Washington, DC: Bureau of Justice Statistics, August 7, 2013, at www.bjs.gov

Figure 2.8b   Arrest Rates of Men and Women, Fraud

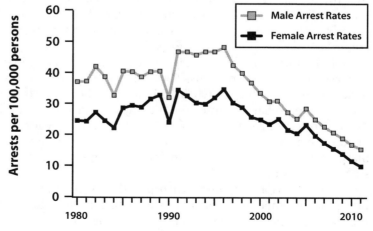

Source: Snyder, H. & Mulako-Wangota, J. *Arrest Data Analysis Tool*. Washington, DC: Bureau of Justice Statistics, August 7, 2013, at www.bjs.gov

Figure 2.8c   Arrest Rates of Men and Women, Embezzlement

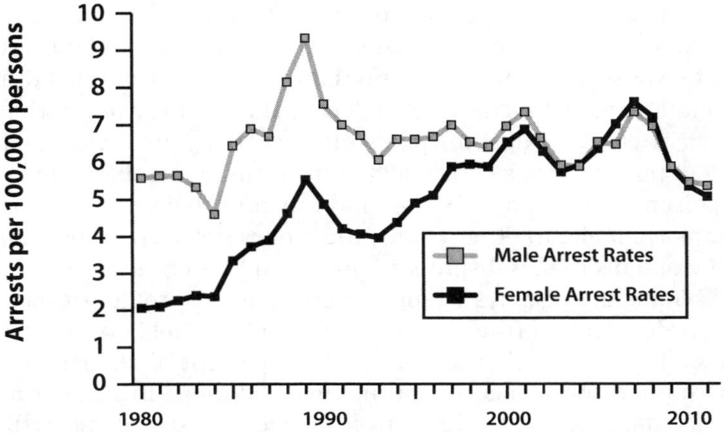

Source: Snyder, H. & Mulako-Wangota, J. *Arrest Data Analysis Tool*. Washington, DC: Bureau of Justice Statistics, August 7, 2013, at www.bjs.gov

Jay Albanese[24] did find a statistical association between the increased number of women in managerial occupations and an increase in women's commission of white-collar crimes such as embezzlement, fraud, and forgery. In 1970, women constituted only 31.7 percent of managerial positions and accounted for roughly 25 percent of white-collar crime. In 1989 women accounted for 44.7 percent of all managerial positions and committed roughly 40 percent of white-collar crimes. While this seems to indicate support for the theory that women would embezzle once they reached the executive suite, Albanese agreed that there was no way to tell whether these women held high-level or low-level managerial positions; and, since crime figures do not indicate seriousness or amount of loss, the increase could represent the petty theft of clerks and officer managers just as easily as it could a new type of crime by female executives.

In conclusion, we see that the big picture, in terms of property crimes and the gender gap, is that women's and men's arrest rates are converging largely because of a decline in men's arrests and a less dramatic decline for women's. Although theorists predicted that women's increased participation in white-collar crimes would follow their entry into professional occupations, there is very little evidence that supports this thesis. The few studies that have looked at female offender populations (as opposed to using macro-level correlations) show that female offenders are qualitatively different than men. On the other hand, at the time of this writing these studies were 20 years old, and the time is ripe to replicate studies such as those conducted by Daly and Zietz.

Violent Crimes

Violent crimes include homicide, aggravated assault, simple assault, robbery, arson, rape, and other sex crimes using force. The most extreme gender gaps are seen when comparing the relative contributions of men and women to total arrests for crimes of violence. There is little doubt that women commit violent crime significantly less often than do men. Otto Pollak's assertion in 1950 that women's choice of victims (family members) and choice of method (poison rather than firearms) hid much of their crime is unsupported by any data available. In other words, there does not seem to be a large "dark" figure of women's crimes disproportionate to men's crimes.

Table 2.1 displays women's percentages of total arrests for violent crimes (murder and non-negligent manslaughter, robbery, rape, and aggravated assault). In 1935 they accounted for 7 percent of all arrests, and in 2010 they accounted for 19 percent of all violent crimes. In murder/manslaughter, the percentage of total arrests has changed hardly at all, while in aggravated assaults the change is quite dramatic (8 percent compared to 22 percent). Figure 2.9 displays aggravated assault arrest rates. The most important thing to note from this figure is that women's rate of increase was less dramatic than men's in the years 1960 through 1990, and their rate of decrease for years

Figure 2.9   Arrests for Men and Women, Aggravated Assault

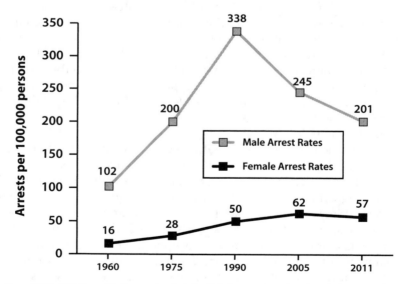

Source: Years 1960–1975 from Steffensmeier, D. & Streifel, C. 1993. Trends in female crime, 1960–1990. In C. Culliver (Ed.), *Female Criminality: The State of the Art*, p. 67. New York: Garland; years 1990–2011 from Snyder, H. & Mulako-Wangota, J. *Arrest Data Analysis Tool*. Washington, DC: Bureau of Justice Statistics, August 7, 2013, at www.bjs.gov

2005–2011 was also less pronounced. The time period 1990–2005, however, showed an increase for women while men's rates had begun to decrease quite dramatically. This is the pattern that is of most interest to researchers.

Several authors have proposed the possibility that this contrary pattern between men and women may be due to official actions rather than offender behavior—specifically, decisions to arrest have changed.[25] Recall from an earlier discussion in this chapter that Darrell Steffensmeier, Jennifer Schwartz, and their colleagues[26] examined this increase by comparing official arrest rates with the NCVS reports and concluded that arrests most probably did not accurately represent a true increase in crime, since a parallel increase was not found in victim reports. Lauritsen, Heimer and Lynch,[27] however, reanalyzed the data. taking into account changes in the administration of the victimization survey (previously known as the National Crime Survey [NCS] and now known as the National Crime Victim Survey [NCVS]). Their statistical corrections were necessary, they argued, because the NCVS undercounted crimes by women. Their results indicated that arrest rates accurately reflected the reality that women's violent crimes (especially assault) did not decline as dramatically as men's, and victim reports also measured a similar pattern. They surmised that the social changes that might have affected the dramatic decline in men's rates (such as male involvement in child rearing, the increased presence of women in public life having a civilizing effect on men, and greater public controls of violence) did not affect women's violence, hence the lack of a similar dramatic decline.

The response of Schwartz, Steffensmeier and colleagues[28] disputed the methodological corrections of Lauritsen and her colleagues, arguing that the new format of the NCVS overestimated female crime by encouraging victims to report ambiguous events and by undercounting black men (who arguably are more likely to be victimized by men) in their sampling. This debate between groups of well-respected researchers indicates how complicated it is to estimate the accuracy of crime statistics in reflecting reality.

What our simple descriptive statistics show is that women's rates of arrest, already low, could not have declined as much as men's. However, there is a troubling period of time in the late 1990s and early 2000s when something was happening to cause increased women's arrests while men's arrests were in decline. Recall that this was also the time period of the dual-arrest problem in domestic violence discussed in Chapter 1. More recently, however, both male and female arrests for violent crimes are decreasing, albeit at different levels.

The majority of the violent crimes committed by women are against intimates and acquaintances. In one study using the FBI's National Incidence Based Reporting System (NIBRS) figures for 1998 from 15 states, 19,945 assaults, 3,656 robberies, and 232 murders were analyzed. Female offenders were likely to victimize intimates (51 percent) and acquaintances (23 percent), and, very rarely, strangers (8 percent).[29]

In studies of violent female offenders, researchers typically use prison samples, which is problematic because a prison sample does not represent all offenders. It is probably the case that violent female offenders in prison represent a subset of all women who commit violent crime. We might assume, for instance, that they are recidivists, that they have engaged in more serious violence, and that they may have had a more primary role in the violence as compared to women who received probation. Thus, extrapolating prison samples to make statements about all violent female offenders is not wise.

In prison samples, researchers have found that female prisoners who have been convicted of violent crimes are more likely than female prisoners not convicted of violent crimes:

- to have been victims of incest and sexual abuse as children,
- to have more extreme drug or alcohol problems,
- to be members of a minority group, and
- to be arrested less frequently than property offenders.[30]

Some studies have enlarged the definition of violent offenders in these prisoner samples to include not only convicted violent offenders, but also those who self-report violent behavior in the year leading up to prison. These studies typically show clear differences between violent and nonviolent women in the above factors, as well as socio-demographic factors (violent women tended to be younger, more likely to be unemployed, and less likely to have children), criminal history (violent women had longer criminal histories that began at a younger age), and gang membership. In these studies, childhood abuse is highly correlated with likelihood of adult violent behavior.[31]

Ira Sommers and Deborah Baskin[32] described an early-onset group and a later entry group of violent female offenders in their prison sample. The group of women who engaged in violent crime early in life also participated in a range of other criminal activities and deviant lifestyle activities. The group of women who committed violent crimes later did so with drugs more likely to be a contributing factor. Sommers and Baskin argued that the same forces that affected male offenders influenced women's commission of violent crimes—specifically, neighborhood effects, drug use, and opportunity structures in city ghettos—and indicated that women's violence was becoming more similar to men's, at least in inner cities.

Kruttschnitt and Carbone-Lopez[33] also used a sample of incarcerated women. Interviews with 66 of them provided information on 106 acts on violence. From this data, these researchers concluded that the field tended to "essentialize" women's victimization as a motivation and factor in their violence, ignoring other motivations, such as disrespect and self-help. They point to Sommers and Baskin's work and Lisa Maher's[34] ethnography of women's criminality as part of the drug world in Bushwick, New Jersey, as illustrating motivations other than victimization for women's violent criminality, including retaliation, response to a collapsing economy, and self-respect. In their analysis of the motivation for the acts of violence described by the 66 women they interviewed, disrespect was the cause of 20 percent of the incidents; jealousy 19 percent; self-defense 18 percent; self-help (debt recovery) 12 percent;

victim precipitation 7 percent; common couple violence 4 percent; and illicit gain 4 percent.[35] These authors observe that rarely is disrespect noted as a reason for women's violence, yet it was pronounced in their sample. They argue that violent responses to disrespect may have less to do with gender and more to do with social location; those who have little cultural or social capital may react to personal affronts more violently. They argue against interpreting women's violence solely by focusing on past victimization and gender relations and state that women's violence is as rational as men's in many instances:

> Women's violence occurs, and expresses itself, in a wide range of circumstances. Its triggers are not limited to victimization and bad domestic relationships but also include the desire for money, respect, and reparation. In this sense, expressions of male and female offending share many similarities and, as we have seen, are often determined by the same sorts of personal and political concerns.[36]

While it is obviously true that not all women's violence occurs in domestic relationships, and that the perception of disrespect as a motivator for violence has been largely ignored for female offenders, it is important to caution that this sample was a prison sample and, as such, not representative of all women. The resort to violence in response to affronts to self-respect is fundamentally a gendered response. The sample of women in this research may have been more similar to violent male criminals, but they were not representative of all female offenders, nor of the general population of women. The fact is that most women do not respond to violence in the situations that these women do. Factors that influence their actions may include social and economic factors, but they also include prior and current victimization and growing up in a culture of violence (as described in the pathways model of women's criminality discussed in Chapter 5). It is important to understand the women who end up in prison, but it is also important not to extrapolate from their behavior that there have been changes in women's violent responses in general. Researchers generally do not find a broad "masculinization" of violent crime by women, even in inner cities.[37] In general, it is not advisable to use prison samples to make statements about changing behaviors of women in the general population.

Robbery

The crime probably least associated with women is robbery. As seen in Table 2.1, only 5 percent of all robbery arrests in 1935 were women and in 2011 they accounted for 12 percent.[38] Figure 2.10 on the following page shows that although robbery arrests for women have inched up slowly, they are down from a high in the 1990s and men's rates are still about 8 times higher than women's. Researchers describe robbery as an almost exclusively male enterprise, one that can be understood as contributing to a male identity, especially for urban black men.[39] When women do engage in this crime, it is often associated with gang membership or with accomplices. Female robbers are less likely to have histories of robbery arrests, and the robberies are often tied directly to prostitution.[40]

Figure 2.10   Arrest Rates of Men and Women, Robbery

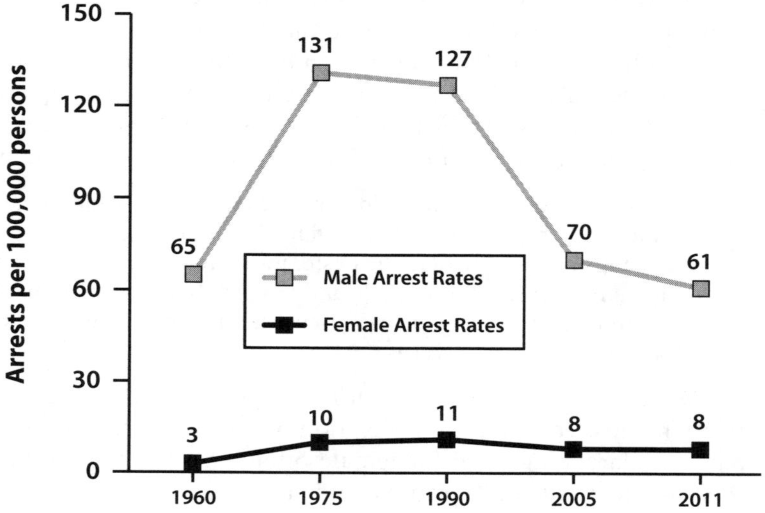

Source: Years 1960–1975 from Steffensmeier, D. & Streifel, C. 1993. Trends in female crime, 1960–1990. In C. Culliver (Ed.), *Female Criminality: The State of the Art*, p. 67. New York: Garland; years 1990–2011 from Snyder, H. & Mulako-Wangota, J. *Arrest Data Analysis Tool*. Washington, DC: Bureau of Justice Statistics, August 7, 2013, at www.bjs.gov

   Some argue that women do not engage in robbery because the risk of victims challenging a woman is greater than when the robber is a man. Violence may be more common when the victim is male, since he may be tempted to offer resistance as this quote indicates: "I put the knife up to his throat and took the money, but as I was coming out of the shop he started to fight me, and three old women coming past the shop went next door and rang the old bill" (called the police).[41]

   Statistics indicate that women do select female and elderly victims more often and, if their target is a man, they are more likely to work with an accomplice. However, in one study of female robbers, the respondent clearly indicated a selection process that was not totally due to concerns about the victim fighting back: "I don't think I'd bop a little ol' lady walking down the block . . . could be my moms, but I might think about takin' one of the other bitches off" (referring to other prostitutes).[42]

   Jody Miller[43] interviewed 14 female and 23 male offenders convicted of robbery, matched roughly for their age and the age of first conviction. Most respondents were black and reported their primary motivation as getting money. These female robbers were less likely to use violence than their male counterparts and always chose female victims except when they committed a robbery with a male accomplice. Gender was important in that female robbers sometimes used sex to lure male targets.

Sommers and Baskin's[44] interviews with 65 female violent offenders included a number of women convicted of robbery. Most of these women committed robberies to obtain money to buy drugs, although some admitted they were motivated by a desire for excitement, vengeance or other reasons. For instance:

> The lady owed me money cause I had gave her money for a bottle of methadone and she never gave me the methadone. She sold me some garbage. So when she got her check, I went there to get my $50 back. She called the cops. It wasn't really robbery.[45]

The women indicated that they chose victims by following people from bars or chose those whom they knew had just received paychecks. They often set up men for robbery using the promise of sex.[46] Although 63 percent of the women in their study committed robbery with accomplices, most accomplices were women (60 percent), which is different from most studies indicating that women are likely to commit robbery with male accomplices.[47] One must be careful of interpreting these results because of the small sample size and the fact that it was a prison sample.

Arson

Data for Table 2.1 were unavailable for arson arrest percentages until 1975, at which point women comprised 14 percent of all arrests. Their contribution to arrests increased to 20 percent by 2010. The Bureau of Justice Statistics (BJS) shows that the rate of arson arrests for women has decreased from 2 per 100,000 in 1980 to 1.3 in 2011 (compared to male rates of 16 in 1980 and 6 in 2011).[48]

Very little information is available on the small number of women who commit arson. In one of the few existing studies, it was found that female arsonists were older than male arsonists and did not gain sexual excitement from the fire, nor did they commit arson for economic reasons (insurance); rather, they set fires to retaliate against individuals they felt had harmed them or with whom they wanted to get even. The women exhibited alcohol and drug abuse problems and, often, mental illness such as personality disorders or schizophrenia. The fires were not premeditated and were simply a way to strike out. The women could have just as easily committed a violent assault to achieve their goal of injury and retaliation.[49]

Assault

Assault is categorized as either aggravated or simple. Aggravated assault is specified in each state's penal code, and the definition usually involves a specific type of victim (either young or old or public servant), the extent of injury, and whether a deadly weapon was used. Simple assault may not necessarily involve injury; it may be as simple as a shove, a pinch, or an unwanted embrace. Simple assault is usually a misdemeanor.

Table 2.1 indicates that women comprised 8 percent of all arrests for aggravated assault in 1935 and 22 percent of arrests in 2010. For simple assault (listed as "other assaults" in Table 2.1), in 1975 (data for earlier years are unavailable) women accounted for 13 percent of all arrests and by 2010 comprised 25 percent of all arrests. Figure 2.5 (p. 26) shows women's arrest rates for simple assault, and Figure 2.9 (p. 34) shows arrest rates for aggravated assault. We see that, for a time in the late 1990s and early 2000s, women's assault rates either increased or remained stable while men's rates declined. For aggravated assault, men's arrest rates declined by 12 percent and male juveniles' rates by 29 percent between 1993 and 2002; but in the same period there was a 25 percent increase for women and an 8 percent increase for female juveniles. For other assaults men's rates declined by 8 percent, but women's increased by 41 percent.[50] Between 2002 and 2011 men's aggravated assault arrests decreased by almost 18 percent, but women's arrests decreased by only about 6 percent.[51]

Generally, women's assault victims are either intimates or acquaintances and are usually other women.[52] Sommers and Baskin's[53] interviews illustrated different patterns, but the sample was not representative of all female arrestees since it was an incarcerated population. In their sample the violence was often related to the drug trade, with women either attempting to retrieve a debt owed or otherwise engaging in drug-trade violence. In some of these vignettes there is a clear element of self-defense:

> . . . he comes back in and he says, bitch, I'll kill you, you know. So he goes in his back pocket, right, and I see he produced a lighter. So I said, you threatening me with a lighter and I have the pen in my hand. I said a few more words to him. All I know, all I can recall, I am sticking him with the pen. . . . Then I turned back and I sees this hole in his heart.

> . . . He said you better get out of my face before I smack you and this and that. I was standing here and he kind of pulled me. He went to put his hand up and I saw it coming. I saw a knife, something just said protect yourself and I grabbed it and I cut him. I stabbed him in his hand, but I was going to go for the arm or anyplace. It just happened.[54]

The vast majority of women's assaults, however, are against family members, intimates, and acquaintances.

Domestic Violence.   A large portion of women's arrests for aggravated and simple assault can be categorized as domestic violence. This category includes child abuse, elderly abuse, and spousal/partner battering. The common belief is that women are more likely to be perpetrators of intimate/domestic abuse compared to acquaintance or stranger assaults, partly because they are disproportionately proximate to the victims of such abuse.

The social problem of domestic violence emerged in the 1970s. Although violence has always been present in the home, battering was considered a private matter until it was brought to the public's attention by victim advocates. In large part, battering and rape victim advocates led the victims' rights movement in the late 1970s and 1980s.

As described in the last chapter, some researchers in the late 1970s and 1980s claimed that in domestic relationships women were just as violent as men.[55] These researchers concluded that women were just as aggressive as men, even if they did not have the physical strength to inflict injuries that were as serious as those inflicted by men. Even though this research was rebutted by others, there seems to be little doubt that arrest patterns have been affected so that women are now being arrested for assault in much greater numbers. In Chapter 1 the research on mandatory arrest policies was reviewed. It is worthwhile to note that the gender gap has decreased in assault categories but not in murder and non-negligent manslaughter, lending some support to the proposition that at least part of the change is due to system practices (since these would affect assault arrest decisions but not homicide arrest decisions).

Many researchers believe that official statistics are misleading in that they mask the self-defense motivations of women and girls involved in domestic violence. Many of these researchers also believe that the public perception that women have become more violent has led to an increased likelihood of arrest in ambiguous circumstances in which women were just as likely to be using violence for self-defense. Of course, no one doubts that there are also violent women who victimize family members for other reasons.

Consistent evidence indicates dynamic relationships between victimization and perpetration of violence. Women who engage in violent crimes against family members or intimate partners are more likely to have been victims of violence as children, and victims of domestic violence are also likely to engage in violence themselves.[56]

Homicide

There has been little change in the statistics on total arrests of women for murder and non-negligent manslaughter. In 1935 women accounted for 10 percent of all arrests, and in 2012 they accounted for 11.3 percent of all arrests.[57] The substantial decline of homicide, from the mid-1990s through the present, is largely accounted for by a decline in homicide committed by black men (who also were responsible for a large percentage of the homicide increase in the 1980s). Women's rates were virtually unchanged through this same time period.[58] Figure 2.11 on the following page shows arrest rates for murder and non-negligent manslaughter. The rate for women was only 0.8 per 100,000 in 2011 compared to men's 6.2. Both of these rates are substantially lower than the highest rates recorded in the mid-1990s.

Interestingly, women also are much less likely than men to commit suicide (rates of suicide range from 14.5 to 27.4/100,000 for men and 4.1 to 7.8/100,000 for women). However, women are more likely to commit suicide than homicide, but men are more likely to commit homicide than suicide.[59]

In historical and even recent popular media, female homicide offenders are portrayed as more evil than their male counterparts.[60] Because the idea of a woman committing a murder seems so foreign to the female sex role and cultural stereotypes, the few women who do kill must be "monsters" and are viewed as extreme in their lack of femininity and lack of humanity.

In Mann's study of 296 female offenders who committed homicide between 1979 and 1983, over three-quarters of the women were black and

Figure 2.11   Arrest Rates of Men and Women, Murder and Non-Negligent Manslaughter

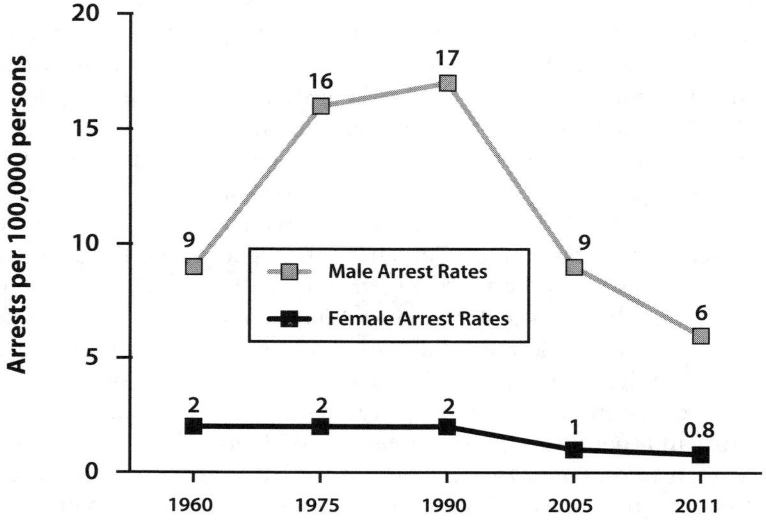

Source: Years 1960–1975 from Steffensmeier, D. & Streifel, C. 1993. Trends in female crime, 1960–1990. In C. Culliver (Ed.), *Female Criminality: The State of the Art*, p. 67. New York: Garland; years 1990–2011 from Snyder, H. & Mulako-Wangota, J. *Arrest Data Analysis Tool*. Washington, DC: Bureau of Justice Statistics, August 7, 2013, at www.bjs.gov

about 9 percent were Latina; most were unemployed, without high school diplomas, and more than half had a criminal record. Most of the homicides were domestic and took place in the home. Alcohol and drugs were involved in the majority of cases. More than half of the male victims had previously been arrested for violent crime. Mann described victim precipitation as present in 84 percent of the domestic homicide cases.[61]

Female homicide offenders are more likely to kill intimates (spouses, girl-friend/boyfriend) and acquaintances than strangers. According to a BJS analysis of homicides between 1980 and 2008, women were most likely to kill an acquaintance, neighbor or someone known to them (about 30 percent of all female arrests for homicide were for killing an acquaintance or known person), then a spouse (24 percent), then any family member other than spouse (17 percent), then a boyfriend/girlfriend (15 percent), with stranger-victims comprising only 12 percent of all arrests. Compare that data with the fact that men's most likely victim was an acquaintance/known associate (56 percent of all victims), then strangers (25 percent), then family members other than spouse (11 percent), and, finally, intimates which includes spouses (7 percent). Only 4 percent of men's victims, but 24 percent of women's victims, were spouses. Both men and women were more likely to kill men.[62]

In a New York study of female homicide offenders, it was found that there were elements of victim precipitation in two-thirds of the cases. The researchers rated more than one-half (57 percent) of the homicides as psychopharmacological drug-related, 12 percent as economic-compulsively drug-related, and 11 percent as systematically drug-related. Only about one-third were not related to drugs in any way. The authors describe female homicide offenders in the following way:

> The lives of the women we studied were complex and filled with patterns of pain, prolonged abuse, and isolation. . . . a host of factors, including abuse, contributed to the wear and tear these women experienced with violence as an integral part of their everyday lives.[63]

Filicide. *Filicide* is the killing of one's child. About half of parents and stepparents who commit murders of children are women. However, official numbers do not tell us what percentage of women are found guilty of child-murder through arrests for "failure to protect" as opposed to committing the murder through direct action. Victims of maternal filicide are about equally likely to be sons as daughters. Mothers are more likely to kill children in infancy, while fathers/stepfathers are more likely to kill children older than eight.[64] In a BJS study of homicides between 1980 and 2008, 63 percent of children under five were killed by parents (33 percent by fathers and 30 percent by mothers).[65]

A study done between 1970 and 1975 examined women who were incarcerated for killing or attempting to kill their children. The researchers developed a typology that included child batterers (36 cases), mentally ill (24 cases), *neonaticides* where women killed immediately after birth (11 cases), retaliating others who killed children to hurt the other parent (9 cases), those who killed unwanted children (8 cases), and mercy killings (one case). There seemed to be quite a bit of overlap in some categories, since 17 of the 36 battering mothers were diagnosed with personality disorders. Eighteen of the sample attempted suicide at the time of the offense or soon afterward. Some of these suicide attempts were linked with the homicide—that is, women would kill their children before attempting to kill themselves.[66]

Another study identified three groups. The first group was murder-suicides—women who tried to kill themselves along with their children. They generally came from very difficult life circumstances, were likely to be clinically depressed, and believed their children would be happier "with God." The second group was neonaticides committed by young women who generally ignored their pregnancy to the point of denial. They gave birth alone and feared the repercussions of the pregnancy. The final group was called fatal assaults. These women had no intent to kill but lashed out in response to misbehavior or crying. They had a host of financial and health problems and were also likely to suffer from clinical depression and exhaustion.[67] It appears that juries and judges tend to be understanding and employ lenient sentencing of neonaticides as compared to infanticide.[68]

More recent research replicates these older findings. Women who kill their children tend to have histories of extreme victimization, and they are likely to be "profoundly" isolated. Researchers describe the women as not even understanding how abusive their childhood was in that they would describe it as good but then describe examples of extreme abuse. They made excuses for their parents, especially their mothers, for why the abuse continued, and they seemed unable to break the cycle of abuse with their own children.[69] It is also important to remember that opportunity and access to child victims are much different for men than for women. Women are overwhelmingly primary caregivers and spend much more time with children.

Serial Murder.   There is very little information available on female serial murderers because, quite simply, there are very few female serial killers. There seem to be differences in the motivations and methods of killing between male serial killers and those few female serial killers who have been prosecuted. For instance, in one study of a small sample of female and male serial murderers, there were differences in the amount of damage inflicted on the victim (men inflicted more damage), the use of torture (men were more likely to torture), and the method of targeting (women "lured" while men "stalked"). Men were more likely to kill with their hands or use an object other than a gun to kill. Men were more likely to have affective motives (emotional or psychological reasons for killing), whereas women in the sample were about equally divided between affective and instrumental motives. Women were more likely to abuse drugs and alcohol. Both women and men were likely to have come from dysfunctional families and to have suffered physical and sexual abuse. The majority of the sample was diagnosed with some form of pathology (antisocial personality or schizophrenia). Women were likely to stay in one location, while men were mobile, moving from city to city, state to state.[70]

Domestic Homicide.   In the 1980s, the *sexual symmetry of violence* referred to the fact that spousal homicide with husbands as victims was about as prevalent as spousal homicide with wives as victims. This fact contributed to the previously described premise that women were as violent as men. Others argued, however, that the motivations for killing were different between male and female spouses, with women's homicides more likely to be related to self-defense. After the advent of battered women's shelters and the increasing prevalence of domestic violence prosecution, the number of wives killing their husbands declined, but the number of husbands killing wives did not.

Between 1976 and 1993, the number of male victims killed by intimates fell by an average of 5 percent per year; however, the number of female victims killed by intimates went down by an average of only 1 percent.[71] In 1977, 54 percent of murder victims killed by intimates were women (roughly the same number as men, showing the symmetry of domestic homicide). By 1992, 70 percent of the intimate-murder victims were women.[72] From 1977 to 1995, the rate for husbands, boyfriends, or other male victims declined by two-thirds (from 1.5 to .5 per 100,000); the decline of female victims was much less, from

1.6 to 1.3 per 100,000.[73] More recent statistics show that the rate of male offenders killing female intimates declined substantially along with all other forms of violent crime by men; however, the disparity between male and female victims of spousal homicide remains. As stated in Chapter 1, out of 2,340 intimate partner homicides in 2007, more than twice as many (1,640) were women killed by their male partners compared to men killed by their female partners (700).[74]

It has also been shown that increased ratios of domestic homicide (more men killing women than women killing men) is associated with higher levels of economic indicators for women (implying they are less likely to kill when they have the means to escape a violent partner).[75] Another study found that male arrestees for domestic violence were more likely to have a generalist arrest history (engaging in other forms of crime and violence), while female arrestees were specialized (more likely to be arrested only for domestic violence). The authors interpreted these results as lending support to the concept that women's domestic violence is more likely to be in self-defense.[76]

Obviously, not all domestic homicides are due to abuse. In an older study of partner homicides, it was found that 30 percent of the women had records of previous arrests for violent crimes, including assault, battery, and weapons charges.[77] However, the domestic homicide is unique from other crimes of violence, since there is a real question as to whether some offenses are actually crimes of violence or acts of self-defense. In several early studies of women incarcerated for homicide, there was clear evidence that they had killed in self-defense after being abused, often in the course of an abuse incident at the time.[78] Ewing, for instance, reports on samples in which between 40 and 78 percent of women who killed their husbands or boyfriends had been abused. Many of these women, historically and currently, serve long prison sentences for their actions. Ewing reports that of the 100 battered women he surveyed, 12 received life sentences and 17 more received sentences in excess of 10 years.[79] Some of the women in prison for killing their husbands would seem to have a legitimate self-defense claim if their descriptions of the homicide are true, as these stories illustrate:

> The night of the killing he was drunk and out of control. When she said she was leaving, he started pushing her. He tried to get a gun, but could not find it. Then he took a knife from his pocket and stabbed her in the thigh. She grabbed a kitchen knife and stabbed him to death.

> One night, after he had been drinking to excess, he heard her talking on the telephone. He thought it was another man and became enraged. He began to strangle her with the telephone cord. She freed herself and ran into the kitchen. He started to strangle her with his hands. She reached into the sink where she found a knife that she then used to stab him to death.[80]

Acceptance of the self-defense argument based on the *battered woman syndrome* has been mixed. Some courts are unwilling to allow jurors to hear expert witness testimony explaining the psychological state of the woman who suffers over a long period of time. Absent that evidence, jurors find it hard to understand why the woman doesn't just leave the abusive husband or seek outside help. In many cases, of course, there is substantial evidence that women have tried to leave, have sought help, and have suffered increased violence and threats because of their attempts. Angela Browne[81] found that battered women who killed their abusers, as compared to battered women who did not kill, more often had husbands who used drugs and alcohol and who were more frequently intoxicated. The men had also used more threats and had exhibited assaultive behavior more often; they had been more likely to threaten not only the woman but also her children or other family members. Many of them had abused the children, and the abuse of their wives was more likely to include sexual abuse.

To summarize, women are very unlikely to commit crimes of violence, and when they do, they are likely to assault or (rarely) kill those they know. Prison studies tend to focus on a group of women who are products of their violent childhood and environment. Little research has been done on the larger group of arrestees (most of whom do not get sent to prison). Some research indicates that increased domestic violence arrests are responsible for some portion of the assault-category arrest increases, and these arrests are due to policy decisions as opposed to actual behavior changes among women. The most important thing to remember, however, is that the gender gap has been reduced largely because of the dramatic decline in men's arrests rather than any substantial increase in women's arrests.

Drug Crimes

Table 2.1 shows that women accounted for about 16 percent of all drug arrests in 1953 and, in 2011, they accounted for about 20 percent of all drug violation arrests and about 30 percent of DUI arrests.[82] Figure 2.12 shows that the rate of arrests for men and women increased exponentially until recently, when it has begun to decline somewhat. In 1960 the rate for men was 50 per 100,000 (and 8 per 100,000 for women); by 2005 the rate had climbed to an amazing 1,028 per 100,000 for men (and 235 for women) but has since declined.

According to Chesney-Lind and others, the War on Drugs was a war on women because of large percentage increases of women arrested for drug crimes.[83] Between 1985 and 1994, women's drug arrests increased 100 percent while men's drug arrests increased only by about 50 percent. More recently, between 2002 and 2011, men's arrests for drug-abuse violations decreased by about 4 percent while women's arrests increased by 8 percent.[84] While some research indicates women are moving into nontraditional drug distribution roles, other evidence disputes this and finds that women continue to participate as mules (drug couriers), low-level dealers, and users.

There are fundamental philosophical and political differences of opinion in the characterization of what is referred to as the drug problem in this country.

Figure 2.12   Arrest Rates of Men and Women, Drug Violations

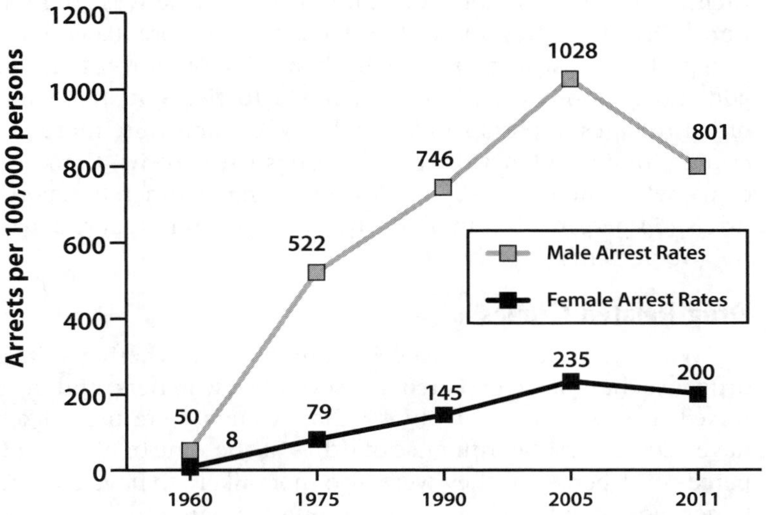

Source: Years 1960–1975 from Steffensmeier, D. & Streifel, C. 1993. Trends in female crime, 1960–1990. In C. Culliver (Ed.), *Female Criminality: The State of the Art*, p. 67. New York: Garland; years 1990–2011 from Snyder, H. & Mulako-Wangota, J. *Arrest Data Analysis Tool*. Washington, DC: Bureau of Justice Statistics, August 7, 2013, at www.bjs.gov

Some argue that it is the scourge of this nation's young and that drugs are responsible for countless crimes and economic losses, not to mention personal tragedies. Others argue that while the rate of use of illicit drugs has gone up and down in the last 100 years, the focus on a so-called drug problem and policies of interdiction and prosecution rather than treatment have been largely responsible for the public's view of drugs as a major social problem. In other words, it is the state reaction to drug use that is the problem, not the drug use itself.

The most comprehensive national statistics are available from the Substance Abuse and Mental Health Services Administration. In their 2012 report, figures from 2011 for those 12 and over indicated the following percentages for the preceding month: 8.7 percent used any illicit drug (compared to 8.3 percent in 2002); 7 percent used marijuana (compared to 6.2 percent in 2002); 2.4 percent used psychotherapeutic drugs (compared to 2.7 percent in 2002), and .5 percent used cocaine (compared to .9% in 2002). This report indicates that there are more male users of illicit drugs (11 percent) than female users (6 percent) in the general population.[85] The report also indicates that about twice as many males 12 years or older as females are dependent on or abusers of illicit drugs. The rate for males was 10.4 percent compared to females' 5.7 percent. In the 12 to 17 age group, however, male and female teenagers' rates of abuse or dependency were equal at about 7 percent.[86]

In older studies, evidence indicated that female offenders in the criminal justice system were more likely than male offenders to be drug abusers (or their addiction was more severe), but the reverse was true for alcohol addiction.[87] Prison studies found that women were more likely than male prisoners to report drug use as a problem in their lives, with over a third admitting drug addiction.[88] More recently, the Bureau of Justice Statistics, using a 2002 survey of jail inmates, reports similar findings. Women were more likely to meet the criteria for dependency or abuse of drugs (61 percent) than of alcohol (39 percent); while men were slightly less likely than women to report dependency on drugs (54 percent) but more likely than women to report dependency on alcohol (50 percent).[89]

Drug-Related Crimes

Whether drug use precedes criminality or whether criminality precedes drug use has been explored by several researchers and results have been mixed. Past studies have shown that women were more likely than men to have been under the influence of drugs at the time of offense (36 percent compared to 31 percent); they were also more likely to have committed an offense to get money to buy drugs (one in four compared to one in six). Women with drug histories were twice as likely to have committed robbery, burglary, larceny and fraud as those who were not on drugs.[90] More recent research also indicates that women were more likely than men to have been under the influence of drugs at the time of their offense (34 percent compared to 25 percent), and less likely than men to have been under the influence of alcohol (22 percent compared to 30 percent).[91]

> I was spending anywhere from $400–$500 a day on drugs. Stealing and resorting to other things like prostitution and burglary . . . taking money from the tricks, stealing from them. [describing prostitution] . . . started off high class, but the deeper I got into my addiction, before I knew it, I was standing on the street corners.[92]

Research has shown that other criminality increases with an increase in drug use among drug-using populations. Crimes by female drug users include prostitution, drug sales, and shoplifting, while crimes by male addicts are more likely to include violent crime, burglary, and drug dealing.[93] Inciardi and his colleagues[94] reported that while heroin and narcotics tended to be associated with prostitution and property crime, crack cocaine was more likely to be linked to violent crime, drug dealing, and sex work. In Baskin and Sommers'[95] research, they found that an early-onset group of women committed criminal acts before drug use, but the late-onset group who committed crime relatively late in life were very likely to begin criminal activities after a period of drug use.

Roles of Women in the Drug World

Several phenomenological studies in the 1980s described the role of women in the subculture of drug use and sales. While a few researchers argued that women were taking their place in higher levels of power in the drug hierarchy, other researchers found that only a few women attained such positions. For most women, the role they played continued to be that of girlfriend, courier (mule), steerer, or low-level dealer.[96]

Maher and Daly[97] described an ethnographic study of female drug users during the years 1989 through 1992 in New York City. They disputed the claim by some researchers that women were advancing and playing increasingly more dominant roles in the drug underworld. Their findings indicated that women continued to play fairly traditional roles in the drug subculture. A few of the women they interviewed acted as *steerers* (or touts) who referred potential customers to dealers. Some women were hired as low-level, temporary street dealers and many women "copped" for others; for instance, a white male would enter the neighborhood, approach the woman, and pay her to buy drugs for him, with or without a sexual exchange as part of the bargain as well. Maher and Daly found that women were not hired as drug sellers because they were perceived as not being "bad" enough. They could not deploy and/or threaten violence to the same extent that men could (making debt collection and protecting the drugs problematic). Although women attempted to run shooting galleries (places where illegal drugs may be obtained, prepared, and taken by injection, often with equipment provided on the premise), they were successful only when they had male partners to keep order and ward off interlopers. The authors suggest that the police department targeted female-owned shooting galleries for harassment and shut them down more often than those run by men. Women also developed special niches, for instance, as "house distributors" (who help male partners run crack houses or "freak houses"), "freak house girls" (who performed sexual services in exchange for drugs), and "smoking partners" (who provide the drugs and company in return for money).[98]

These authors found a strong relationship between sex work and drugs. Many of the addicts described how they were introduced to drugs by boyfriends and how they resorted to sex work because of no opportunities, other than prostitution, to pay for their drug use. They also described how sex work was not paying as well as it used to because women desperate for crack would underbid the street prostitutes. In their descriptions, they commented that there was more violence than in years past by "johns," by strangers who robbed them for their money or even clothing, and by other prostitutes.[99]

The phenomenological studies above describe the drug subculture as one in which women are certainly present but play a different role than men. The advantage of the phenomenological method is the richness of the data; the weakness of the method is that the researcher does not know whether one's informants are representative of others in the same world.[100] By combining the results of a number of phenomenological studies, we might conclude that women are seldom major dealers (although there are some), and they are usually connected to the drug world through a relationship with a man, at least initially. Their roles range from independent dealer to coerced mule—a woman who might have been coerced to carry drugs for little reward. There are also consistent findings that drugs and sex work are intertwined, a concept that we return to in Chapter 5.

Other Crimes

Not all crimes have been discussed in this chapter. Crimes against the family, sex crimes, DUI, vandalism, and other Part II offenses have not been addressed. Recently, women's participation in sex crimes other than rape has been the topic of research. The Uniform Crime Reports indicates that only about 7 percent of arrests for sex crimes other than rape are of women. Women's rate of arrests in 2011 was 3,328 per 100,000 compared to men's rate of 42,872 per 100,000.[101]

Vandiver and Walker found that women made up 2.4 percent of registered sex offenders in 1999. They reviewed 40 cases in one state and described the female sex offender as white, in her thirties, with no criminal history, more likely to be a first-time offender, and more likely to have been the victim of sexual abuse than male sex offenders. These authors suggest that female sex offenders are diverted from the system, which partially accounts for their low numbers.[102] Others also suggest that official numbers underreport female sex offenders given that, in one study, 60 percent of sex offenders in a treatment program report childhood abuse by an adult female.[103] Professionals, at least in the past, have discounted the problem of female sex offenders, although there is growing recognition that they exist. Research indicates that female sex offenders are much less prevalent than male offenders, that they often have been victims of sexual abuse as children, that they target a range of victims (not just teenage boys), and that, generally, victimization by a female offender is just as damaging to the victim as when the offender is a man.[104] It does seem to be the case, however, that today, women who engage in sexual relationships with youth (e.g., teachers and their students) are just as likely to be arrested and prosecuted as male offenders, and the number of female sexual offenders is extremely small.

Up to this point, we have been describing women's participation in crimes that are more commonly associated with men. In the next section we discuss a few crimes that are especially associated with women. Historically, special crimes of women included "scolding," infanticide, and witchcraft. Today, prostitution, injury to a fetus, and other crimes related to pregnancy are associated with female offenders.

Prostitution

Prostitution used to be a crime only when committed by a woman soliciting a man. Today laws have been rewritten to apply to both sexes; however, some argue that law enforcement practices still differentiate.[105] Official numbers are highly suspect in this crime category because prostitution enforcement varies over time and across jurisdictions. Further, official attention, as well as academic attention, has been focused almost exclusively on street prostitution rather than call girls, chat rooms, or other forms of prostitution.[106]

According to the UCR, women accounted for 69 percent of all prostitution arrests in 2011. Prostitution arrests of men have declined 33 percent and arrests for women have declined by only 15 percent between 2002 and 2011[107]; however, whether that is an illustration of male and female offender activity or official response is impossible to say.

As with drug crimes, any discussion of prostitution as a crime must first acknowledge the social, political, and philosophical issues regarding the definition of the activity as a crime. Prostitution, at least when not associated with robbery, "viccing" (taking the money and running), and other forms of prostitution-related victimization, is considered by many to be victimless crime. In fact, in some places prostitution is not a crime at all. Thus, it is hard to view prostitution in the same way as other crimes that are more clearly injurious to innocent victims. Nevertheless, prostitution continues to be associated with the criminal subculture. Prostitutes may victimize their customers or be victimized themselves by customers or pimps. They may also be part of a larger criminal organization that includes gambling and drugs.

Much of the research on prostitution is phenomenological and provides typologies of the different types of prostitutes (e.g., call girls, streetwalkers, bar girls, and so on). Rosenbaum,[108] in a phenomenological study, explored how call girls developed their identity, the power relationships between call girls and their clients, motivations for entering "the life," and other elements of the prostitute's world.

There is continuing debate in the literature over whether entry into prostitution is clearly and solely economic, or whether there is a correlation between entry into prostitution and personal victimization—that is, childhood sexual abuse or deprivation. Many point to the connection between teenage runaways and prostitution. Many teenage girls who run away do so because of dysfunctional families; once on the street they turn to prostitution to survive, or they become emotionally attached to men who encourage and benefit from their prostitution.[109] As mentioned previously, there is a strong association between sex work and drug use.[110] Many prostitutes use drugs; many prostitute to get money for drugs. Interestingly, in interviews, some prostitutes explain that they need drug intoxication in order to engage in sex with a customer (as a type of self-medication); therefore, the relationship in some cases is circular. Women use drugs to help themselves perform as prostitutes, but they also engage in prostitution in order to get drugs. Women engaged in sex work and drug use have reported high levels of injury as well—either by clients or pimps. In one study, 40 percent reported being beaten or raped by clients. In a Miami study using interviews and focus groups with 325 drug-using sex workers, researchers found these workers were likely to encounter violence. More than 40 percent had experienced violence from clients. Almost a quarter (24.9 percent) had been beaten, about 13 percent had been raped, and about 14 percent were threatened with a weapon. The researchers also discovered that nearly half of the sex workers had been physically (44.9 percent) or sexually (50.5 percent) victimized as children.[111]

Most studies indicate that female criminals, regardless of crime, often also have a history of prostitution although it is not clear which came first. Teenage runaways are recruited by street pimps or engage in prostitution independently to survive. Other women are recruited or turn to sex work from compatible occupations that emphasize women's sex role and attractiveness, such as dancing, massage, and bar service. Some women resort to prostitution only after becoming addicted to drugs, although for many others entry into prostitution may predate heavy drug use. Drug dependency always, of course, makes any exit from "the life" more difficult, if not impossible.

James,[112] in an early study, provides a list of reasons why women enter prostitution.

- There is no other occupation available to unskilled or low-skilled women with the potential income of prostitution.
- Sex work offers adventure and independence.
- It is consistent with women's traditional sex role.
- Some women are already labeled deviant because of their sexuality.
- There is a cultural importance placed on wealth and material goods, and sex work offers one avenue to attain these things.

Human sex trafficking has become of interest not just to local law enforcement, but to international law enforcement agencies (such as Interpol) as well. There is a growing body of research regarding the prevalence of trafficking, who is likely to be victimized, the relationship between traffickers and their victims, and interdiction and intervention efforts. It should be noted as well that human trafficking also refers to those who are transported and coerced to work in foreign countries in agriculture or domestic work.[113]

Pregnancy as a Crime?

Obviously, pregnancy is not a crime, but being pregnant has precipitated differential definitions of criminality and court processing for women. For at least some women, being pregnant has become a punishable offense. Historically, women's unique role in procreation led to greater social control. Eugenics movements advocated sterilization of men, but they also employed sterilization or incapacitation of women to control reproduction.[114]

Many authors have written about what has been termed the criminalization of pregnancy, especially those laws used against women who used drugs.[115] In the mid- to late 1980s, the epidemic of so-called crack babies received a great deal of press. According to some accounts, babies exposed to drugs in the womb would be scarred for life and dependent on state monies to house them, as they would not be able to survive outside of institutionalized settings. This media-created perception of an epidemic no doubt spurred lawmakers and prosecutors who either used existing laws or created new laws to punish pregnant women who used drugs.

Some states responded by increasing and/or adapting their use of child-injury laws (either enlarging the definition of "child" to include the fetus or writing new fetal endangerment statutes). Sometimes existing drug laws were utilized with a redefinition of delivery to include the fetus. Civil courts were also used to deprive women of custody at birth. Many states passed informant laws that required hospital or medical personnel to report positive toxicology tests.

By the 1990s, subsequent research contested the "epidemic" literature. While it was true that a certain percentage of babies were exposed to drugs *in utero*, it became apparent that drug use had not created a legion of crack babies who would be institutionalized all their lives. It is difficult to distinguish the effects of drug use from the effects of poor nutrition, smoking, or drinking alcohol—behaviors in which many drug users also engaged. Studies that showed positive toxicology test results were extrapolated to indicate that the infant was born addicted, but a positive toxicology test does not mean that addiction was present or that there would be long-term effects. Also, there was evidence indicating that a far greater problem than drug exposure is the lack of prenatal care, and that this problem was probably responsible for many more long-term problems for more infants than the so-called problem of drug-using mothers.

The criminalization of women may have resulted in exactly the opposite effect desired: Once the word on the street was that medical personnel would report drug use to authorities and women might lose their babies and could face arrest, many drug-using women simply stopped seeking prenatal medical attention, further endangering their developing fetuses.

A more subtle way the system punishes pregnant women is by sentencing women who are before the court for other crimes to prison rather than proba-tion, or giving women longer terms of incarceration *because* of their pregnancy to protect the fetus from further drug use. In several reported cases, judges said on record they were incarcerating a woman rather than giving her proba-tion because of her pregnancy. It is unknown how many other judges do so but don't state it on record.

Race and Crime

Before we conclude the discussion of women's crimes, it is important to note the influence of race and ethnicity on crime rates. The race and ethnicity influence has been mentioned by previous research that goes back decades, and researchers who have looked at prison populations, drug addicts, victim-ization studies, self-reports, and official statistics all note the greater tendency of African American women and, to a lesser extent, Hispanic women to engage in crime. This research indicates that minority women are more likely to engage in crimes of violence than white women (and some studies indicate their rate exceeds that of white men), and that their pattern of criminality shows less of a gender differential than the patterns of white women and white men.[116] Native American women also contribute disproportionate numbers to prison populations. In South Dakota, for instance, where Native Americans are only 7 percent of the population, Native American women represent up to one-third of prison populations, and in Montana, 28 percent of the prison population is Native American.[117] More recent statistics indicate that 20 percent of the men in Montana prisons and 27 percent of the women were Native American, even though they comprise only about 7 percent of the state population. This means that their incarceration rate is three to four times the rate of white residents. Why this might be so is a complicated subject that has been addressed by a number of sources.[118] One potential explanation is differential treatment by the criminal justice system. There is certainly some evidence that indicates minority women do not receive the "chivalrous" treatment that may or may not exist in the system for white women.[119]

Chilton and Datesman[120] presented a number of alternative explanations to address the disproportional contribution of minority women to crime rates and concluded that the best explanation for the criminality of minority women is poverty. African American women are the most likely of all demographic groups to head a household under the poverty line. They are more likely than white women to be unemployed, and, if employed, their average wage is the lowest of any group. They are more likely to be single heads of household and more likely to have teenage pregnancies.

Minority women are more likely than white women to be victimized sexually and physically, both as children and adults. They are more likely to come from broken families and dysfunctional families where alcohol, drugs, and criminality affect their childhood. Minority women are probably more likely to join youth gangs for protection and social support. They may also be more likely to have the opportunity to become part of criminal networks.[121]

There is also evidence of systematic bias. In the 1990s, African American women were twice as likely as white women to be reported to formal authorities for drug use (despite similar use rates), and 10 times more likely than white women to be drug tested in public hospitals.[122] Crenshaw[123] and others discuss the reality that minority women, especially African American women, are overpoliced and underprotected. They are more likely to suffer criminal victimization, but often their experience with the criminal justice system leads to being labeled a criminal rather than a victim. Other social service networks (housing, welfare, education) also are more likely to label African American mothers as offenders deserving of punishment rather than as victims of structural and social disadvantage, which makes it impossible for them to conform to societal definitions of acceptability.[124] Research clearly shows that gender and race affect one's experience with crime and the criminal justice system.

Conclusion

It becomes clear that any discussion of women's contribution to crime must clearly differentiate violent crime from property crime to give the most accurate picture. While violent crime rates continue to show large differences in the relative rates of participation between men and women, property crime rates are converging. For both property crime and violent crime, the gender gap has been reduced largely because of decreases in men's arrests rather than increases in women's arrests.

Changes in arrest decisions may be responsible for some of the change in women's arrest rates in the last 40 years; it is likely, however, that women are indeed committing more crimes. Some evidence indicates that there continue to be qualitative differences between crimes by men and women (i.e., women have different motivations and methods of crime commission). In the next chapter, the so-called chivalry hypothesis is more closely examined. This is the idea that historically women have been less likely than men to be arrested, prosecuted, and/or convicted for crimes they do commit.

REVIEW QUESTIONS

1. What are the major sources of crime data? What do they tell us about the relative crime patterns of men and women?

2. Provide at least three explanations for why women's and men's rates of crime (especially property crime) are converging.

3. Are men's and women's larceny/thefts and embezzlements generally similar or different? Explain your answer.

4. What are the various types of female embezzlers?

5. What are some of the findings of studies that compare violent offenders in prison to other nonviolent offenders? How are they different?

6. Is the reason the gender gap in violent crime categories is decreasing because women's crimes are increasing relative to men's? Explain your answer.

7. What is the meaning of the terms upcharging and bootstrapping?

8. Describe women who commit infanticide and neonaticide.

9. Why have some researchers called the War on Drugs a war on women? What are the findings regarding female and male prisoners and their drug use?

10. Describe some crimes that are almost always or always associated with women.

Traditional Theories
1800s–1970s

CHAPTER SUMMARY

- Criminological theories largely ignored women's criminal behavior or continued with sexist, biological explanations long after theories for men developed into sophisticated psychosocial and/or societal explanations.

- Classical thinkers ignored women, and Lombroso and early positivists viewed women as completely influenced by their biology.

- The early Chicago School theorists virtually ignored women in their development of such theories as cultural deviance, differential association, and strain. Of all traditional theories, social control theory seems to best fit what we know about female criminality.

- Major correlates of crime identified by the traditional theories such as delinquent friends, social bonds, and strain tend to operate similarly for boys/men and girls/women; however, there is always a gender gap left unexplained after controlling for these predictors.

- The liberation theorists predicted that women's crimes would increase in new areas associated with illegitimate opportunities (robbery) or the workplace (work-related embezzlement). Instead, the largest increase in women's crimes has taken place in the so-called pink-collar crimes of shoplifting and check/credit card fraud—areas that have always been traditionally associated with women.

In this chapter, traditional theories of criminality are reviewed. We emphasize those developed by theorists in the United States, and we arbitrarily draw the definition of "traditional theories" as those that developed up until about the 1970s. This is not an exhaustive review; there are dozens of criminology textbooks and more critical treatments of the theories discussed below that the reader is urged to consult. Here, only the main points of the theory are drawn to point out applications to female criminality. It is also important to remember the weaknesses of positivism in understanding human behavior—specifically, that values and paradigms influence research and that substantial difficulties exist in measuring crime and its correlates.

Theoretical Concerns

Why do some people commit crime? Almost everyone you ask on the street, in the classroom, even in a prison, has an answer to that question. Although people's answers will vary somewhat, the elements of the answer usually include family issues (bad parents), individual/personality issues (bad kid), peer issues (bad friends), or societal issues (bad economy). Criminologists have addressed the question for more than 100 years, filling hundreds of books and thousands of articles that argue minutiae as well as fundamental issues in the mysteries of behavior. Not surprisingly, their theories include the same elements enumerated above.

However, if one asked why women commit less crime than men, the person-on-the-street would probably answer with some version of "Because women are taught to be 'nicer' than men" or that women are "naturally nicer" than men. The point made in this chapter is that traditional criminology never satisfactorily answered this question because it was not even addressed.

One of the most ironic facts regarding the field of criminology was that, for the most part, one-half of the population was virtually ignored. If mention was made of women in classic texts, the obvious implication was that the problem of crime was a problem of men. The numbers of women who committed crimes were too small to bother with. Why that fact alone was not enough to intrigue researchers who were supposed to be focused on the causes of crime is interesting. One would think that if a large percentage of a population showed disproportionately low crime rates, it would be imperative to look at factors that distinguished this group from the group that contributed a disproportionate share of crime. The reason women were not the focus of criminologists may have to do with cultural *androcentrism*—that is, the paradigm that what men do is normal; therefore, women's lower rate of criminal activity was abnormal. If the question of why women committed crime was asked, it was asked as a separate question with a different answer.[1]

If a single theory of crime can explain male and female criminal behavior, this would mean that one or a number of causal factors affect men and women differently, or the factors are differentially present among men and women. Thus, we ask the following questions in our review of traditional theories.

- Does the theory explain the sex/gender crime differential (i.e., women's lower rates of arrests in most, but not all crime categories)?

- Does it explain the fact that the sex/gender crime differential decreases with property crime but increases with violent crime?
- Does it explain why the sex/gender crime differential between women and men is decreasing overall, especially in property crimes?

Classical Theory (1700s)

The Classical School is usually described by the contributions of Cesare Beccaria (1738–1794) and Jeremy Bentham (1748–1832). Beccaria was more concerned with remaking the legal system into one that was fair and just, while Bentham could be described as more concerned with fine-tuning the system to improve its efficiency. Both theorists operated under the fundamental assumption that men were rational and operated with free will. Therefore, they assumed that the elimination of crime could be achieved by appealing to men's rationality and, more specifically, that laws promising punishment for offenses would act as a deterrent to crime. The use of a male pronoun in this discussion is not unintentional; philosophers in this time period did not view women in the same manner as men, believing their mental abilities to be more akin to children's.

Bentham[2] proposed that the justice system must employ punishment in such a way that it was slightly more punitive than the perceived profit of the crime contemplated (in order to deter individuals from attempting the crime). Punishment should be adjusted in this way for each offense. It should be no more than necessary to deter. It should be adjusted upward in severity in relation to a decrease in certainty. Thus, the focus of these thinkers was on the legal system; the assumption was that everyone would respond to the legal system in a similar rational manner.

The Classical School included the idea that the threat of punishment could deter rational men from committing crime. Furthermore, punishment that was swift, certain, and proportional to the perceived benefit of the crime was more effective. Since women were not viewed as rational, nor did they commit a great deal of crime (other than prostitution), they were not considered by Classical School philosophers. Women in this time period were under the legal authority of their fathers and husbands, and any crimes committed by them were the responsibility of their male guardians.

The idea that all people will respond equally to a deterrent is not a viable concept, even though it has been resurrected in the rational choice theory (discussed in the next chapter). The Classical School is usually a historical preface to the theories of crime that developed after the rise of Positivism.

Positivism (1800s)

Positivism can be described simply as scientific method, or the search for causes using scientific methods. Cesare Lombroso (1825–1909) is often referred

.to as the Grandfather of Criminology. Lombroso and the Positivist approach can be distinguished from the Classical School approach in that the focus of criminology shifted from the legal system to the offender. Individuals are not presumed to be equally rational or equal in any other way. The cause of crime, in fact, is assumed to lie in the individual. Thus, Lombroso developed his "born criminal" theory, the idea that criminals were born with genetic defects that made them commit criminal acts. It should also be noted that over the course of his career Lombroso developed a more sophisticated typology of criminals.[3]

Since difference was a presumption under Lombroso's theory, it was consistent with the theory to distinguish women from men, and criminal women from noncriminal women. In fact, Lombroso did address the question of women's criminality and, along with his son-in-law, Guglielmo Ferrero, wrote a book on criminal women in 1895.[4] In this work, women were presumed to be biologically and psychologically different from men, which accounted for their lower crime rates. However, some women were evolutionary throwbacks, according to Lombroso, and these so-called primitive women were criminal because, in his theory, all primitive women were more masculine and criminal than "modern" law-abiding women. Interestingly, however, his typology did include other types besides the purely biological criminal, and these types tapped some of the same explanations we use today, such as opportunity, influence, and passion. In his words:

> . . . while the majority of female delinquents are led into crime either by the suggestion of a third person or by irresistible temptation, and are not entirely deficient in the moral sense, there is yet to be found among them a small proportion whose criminal propensities are more intense and more perverse than those of their male prototypes.[5]

According to Lombroso and Ferrero, women were ordinarily held in check by biological traits such as passivity, but when they were criminal, they were worse than male criminals:

> . . . their moral sense is deficient . . . they are revengeful, jealous, inclined to vengeances of a refined cruelty. In ordinary cases these defects are neutralized by piety, maternity, want of passion, sexual coldness, by weakness and an undeveloped intelligence.[6]

Obviously Lombroso and Ferrero's theory of female criminality can be subject to the same criticisms as their theories regarding male criminality, particularly for some gross stereotyping of gender traits. The idea that the behavior of women was solely determined by their biology was a theme that persisted in the theories of crime throughout most of the next century.

One thread of such research was to consider women as the "breeders" of criminality. Nicole Hahn (Rafter)[7] discusses the *cacogenic family studies* of the early 1900s. These studies, funded by wealthy supporters of eugenics, all found that in examples where one man had relations with both a "good" woman and a "bad" woman (the illegitimate lover or prostitute), it was the bad woman's children who were alcoholics, vagrants, and criminals. The studies, of course, ignored the social and economic implications that were involved and identified the mother's "bad seed" as the reason for generations of criminals.

Reviews of older theories point out how such theories identified women's biological traits as suppressing criminality.[8] For instance, one early theorist[9] argued that in the early history of humankind, women did not resort to crime because of their physical incapability (i.e., they were weaker, and all crime was physical). This pattern continued even though certain crimes (e.g., theft or using a firearm to kill) did not require physical strength. These early theories tended to concentrate on why the women who committed crime went against their nature (under the assumption that it was a woman's biological and psychological destiny to be gentle, passive, and noncriminal).

The Chicago School (early 1900s)

If the focus of the Classical School was the legal system and the focus of the Positivists was the individual, then the focus of the early criminologists in the United States was society itself. Early sociology was concerned with urban life, and one of the inescapable elements of urban life in the early 1900s was crime.

Earlier sociologists, such as Adolphe Quetelet (1796–1874) and Émile Durkheim (1858–1917), are credited as establishing the foundations of sociological criminology. Quetelet offered the information that crime occurred in reasonably predictable patterns in society, thus supporting the notion that it was something about society that caused crime rather than crime occurring at random or because of individual causes. Durkheim offered the principle that crime was normal and present in all societies and, if it was not present, it indicated that the society was stagnant and too conformist.

It is the Chicago School, however, that is perceived as the beginning of criminology, when early sociologists at the University of Chicago observed that crime occurred more often in interstitial zones of the city. In these zones, residential, commercial, and industrial activity could be observed; they were also characterized by low home ownership levels, property damage, graffiti, high rates of alcoholism, domestic violence, and mental health problems. Early sociologists discovered that these interstitial zones always had higher crime rates, even though demographic groups moved in and out of them. For instance, in the latter part of the nineteenth century, it was Irish immigrants who lived in the zones, but they eventually moved out—to be replaced by Eastern and Southern Europeans, and then, after World War II, African Americans moving up from the South. Thus, it seemed that there was something about the zone, rather than the people who lived within it, that generated crime. One thing that characterized such zones, of course, was lack of opportunity. Thus, the Chicago School moved into two lines of explanation: the cultural deviance theory (criminal subcultures cause crime), and strain theory (blocked economic opportunities cause crime), with the two merging into the differential opportunity theory of Richard Cloward and Lloyd Ohlin (youths who share similar life circumstances will form groups, and crime is committed by those in the group with blocked opportunities).

Cultural Deviance Theory

In the 1930s, Clifford Shaw and Henry McKay,[10] authors of the "zone theory" described above, also explained that part of what was going on in the zone was the transmission of culture—more specifically, a subculture with deviant values.

> The *boy* who grows up in this area has little access to the cultural heritage of conventional society. For the most part, the organization of *his* behavior takes place through *his* participation in the spontaneous play groups and organized gangs with which *he* had contact outside of the home . . . this area is an especially favorable habitat for the development of *boys'* gangs and organized criminal groups.[11] [emphasis added]

The added emphasis in Shaw's quote reflects the fact that this theory was almost exclusively concerned with the transmission of culture to men, by men. Walter Miller's[12] contribution to this discussion was the idea of focal concerns: trouble, toughness, smartness, excitement, fate, and autonomy. These were developed and perceived as lower-class men's concerns, not women's. Women were largely ignored, even though they obviously lived in the transitional zones alongside the boys and men who were being socialized to criminality.

Differential Association

Edwin Sutherland introduced the theory of differential association in 1939 and later joined with Donald Cressey to reiterate the concepts twenty years later.[13] As was discussed above, cultural deviance theory proposed that different subcultures in a society influence the thoughts and behaviors of those exposed to such subcultures. It is differential association theory that describes the mechanism by which that influence operates. Differential association assumes that delinquency and criminality develop because of an excess of definitions favorable to crime offered by one's close associates. Furthermore, variations of frequency, duration, priority, and intensity of these associations will also affect the likelihood of delinquency. That is, if one's family and friends are criminal, profess criminal values, and teach criminal methods, one will become criminal. This theory assumes that learning takes place predominantly within intimate personal groups, and that learning includes techniques of crime as well as motives, drives, rationalization, and attitudes.[14]

Ron Akers[15] applied social learning principles to differential association. He and Robert Burgess developed the differential association-reinforcement theory, which applied behaviorism and principles of learning to Sutherland's sociological theory.[16] For instance, under their reformulation, the seventh principle of differential association ("differential associations may vary in frequency, duration, priority, and intensity") changes to "the strength of deviant behavior is a direct function of the amount, frequency, and probability of its reinforcement."[17]

Criticisms of differential association and/or Akers' formulation of it include the observation that it is not conceptually distinct from simple learning theory or behaviorism. Others argue that the theory cannot explain irrational crimes, such as crimes of passion. It does not explain so-called "new criminals," those who begin to commit crimes but come from law-abiding families. There is a de-emphasis of personal traits such as aggressiveness, as well as the de-emphasis of choice in a more general sense. One might argue against the theory, for instance, by observing that actors choose associations to support their behavior (e.g., alcoholics who choose to develop new friendships to help them stay sober). The determinism implicit in the differential association-reinforcement theory troubles those who perceive human nature as operating with free will.

Sutherland and Cressey maintained that the theory was general and not specific to male behavior. Yet, in the attempt to explain why women commit less crime, inconsistencies appear unless one assumes that girls and boys receive different messages or have different associations. Indeed, that is what is hypothesized in the application of this theory to female criminality. Burgess and Akers argued, "From infancy, girls are taught that they must be nice, while boys are taught that they must be rough and tough. . . . Girls are schooled in 'anti-criminal behavior patterns.'"[18] However, this presumes that girls receive one model of female normality that is homogenous across social and economic categories, while boys are exposed to varying definitions of masculinity depending on socioeconomic class and geographic location.

If girls are more restricted in their movements and associations and thus have less opportunity to form and/or be exposed to the intimate personal groups that provide criminal definitions (i.e., gangs or delinquent peers), then they receive fewer criminal messages, which would lead to less criminality according to this theory. In the 1930s, women were relegated to hearth and home. Although lower-class women did not have the luxury of being housewives and most likely worked outside the home, they were largely invisible insofar as street culture was concerned. Theorists writing in these early years were accurate in their idea that girls and women did not share the same street culture as boys and men; however, girls' and women's relationships with these men existed in the home and should have, according to the theory, influenced their criminality.

Cultural deviance theories are singularly unable to explain female criminality, much less any changes in female criminality. It evidently was never deemed important to ask whether there were cultural differences in definitions of femininity in the same way cultural differences in the definition of masculinity were identified. Current theories are more careful to note that cultural definitions of femininity may be different, as we discuss in the next chapter.

Early attempts to test differential association for girls posited the idea that girls lacked social support for delinquency; unfortunately, the researchers used different kinds of delinquent acts for boys and girls, hopelessly confusing the results. For boys, surveys identified motor vehicle theft and assaults as delin-

quent acts, but for girls heavy petting or promiscuity were used as the operationalization of delinquency.[19] Many studies have found associations between
delinquent friends and delinquency, although the association has generally
been found to be weaker for girls than for boys.[20]

If we accept that girls and boys learn different things, even in the same
environment and with the same exposures, then differential association theory is a valid explanation for the gender differential in crime. If we can assume
that girls are no longer learning different things and are, in fact, being socialized more similarly to their brothers, then it might also explain the crime-rate
increase for property crime, but it does not explain the relative stability of violent crime by women.

Akers[21] has reformulated his theory to include structural elements. In this
reconceptualization, which he calls the Social Structure and Social Learning
(SSSL) model, an individual's position and placement of structural elements
(age, gender, community, poverty, and other structural variations) mediate
social learning variables (differential reinforcement, peer associations, opportunities, and individual factors). In one test of this newer form of learning theory, researchers found that, other than age, structural factors (gender, social
class, family structure, and community size) had smaller effect sizes than
social learning factors (differential peer association, differential reinforcement, and imitation) on youth's drinking and drug use. For instance, the
direct effect on alcohol and drug use was .06 to .15, but the social learning
variables ranged from .44 to .68. The authors suggested that these findings
supported Akers's SSSL theory that structural factors such as gender are mediated by social learning factors to influence criminal choices.[22]

Social Strain Theory

Thomas Merton's[23] anomie theory of cultural normlessness is the basis for
strain theory, which points to blocked access to cultural goals. According to
this theory, everyone in the United States feels pressure to achieve the same
goal, namely, monetary success. Legitimate means to achieve this goal include
employment, education, family connections, or talent. Those who have no
legitimate means to achieve societal goals feel strain and react with innovation
(i.e., crime). Others may react with other adaptations, specifically conformity
(where one accepts the goals and the means of achieving them) and ritualism
(where one merely goes through the motions expected of them without truly
internalizing the goals of society). Other adaptations are retreatism (where
goals and means are rejected, perhaps through drug abuse or retreating from
society entirely), and rebellion (where one violently rejects societal goals and
means). The capitalist nature of American society leads to high crime because
the societal goal of wealth and acquisition of material goods cannot be
achieved by everyone using legitimate means (education and hard work).
Since everyone in capitalist societies is socialized to believe that they can and
should achieve material success, those who do not have the means feel particular stress. In other cultures, societal structures are more static, vis-à-vis class

(i.e., the poor have no expectations or hope that they will achieve wealth, so there is less pressure or inclination to innovate to get ahead).

Robert Agnew[24] reformulated strain as an individual construct in what has become known as general strain theory. Agnew found that crime was most frequently committed by those who had a high desire for wealth and low expectations of achieving it, but he has also identified a whole range of other factors that may cause strain in an individual. We discuss Agnew's strain theory in more detail in Chapter 4.

Criticisms of strain theory have included the idea that the theory says little about why people respond to strain by making the particular adaptations that they do. For instance, why do some people retreat and others innovate? There is a question as to whether the goals of American society are as homogenous as the theory postulates. Is it true that everyone defines success the same way? Finally, the theory cannot explain crime committed by those who already have great wealth, and it cannot explain why all poor people do not commit crime.[25] The biggest criticism, however, is the inability of the theory to explain the sex differential.

If the strain/opportunity thesis were the ideal explanation of crime, then one would think that women should be more criminal than men because, arguably, they have had fewer opportunities to achieve financial success and therefore should have experienced more strain—at least in past decades. Theorists who attempt to apply the theory to female criminality must argue that women and men have different goals in this society. For instance, one might argue that men have the goal of financial success and women have the goal of financial success through marriage. There is evidence to suggest that women's and men's goals are different in degree (if not in kind), and women may put more value on relational goals (i.e., to get married and to have children). Since these goals are so easily achieved, women are not under the strain that men experience. The application would predict that only those women who are blocked from these goals would turn to crime. Thus, only those women who are blocked from achieving their own version of success (marriage and children) would be expected to innovate through crime or other deviant means.

Differential Opportunity Theory

In 1955, Cohen[26] elaborated upon and expanded Merton's concept of blocked opportunity. In his theory, he proposed that lower-class boys, blocked from legitimate avenues of success, formed delinquent groups to protect their self-respect. School and legitimate employment represented failure to lower-class boys because they could not access these avenues of success; thus, the delinquent boys created an upside-down world of values where short-term hedonism and negative behavior were promoted instead of delayed gratification and conformity. Antisocial activity defined the boys as tough and affirmed their masculinity.

Cohen proposed that when girls resorted to delinquency, their delinquency was associated with their differential goal orientations—specifically, the attention of men. Girls' delinquency, according to Cohen, almost always took the form of sexual promiscuity: "[male delinquency] . . . is versatile, whereas female delinquency is relatively specialized. It consists overwhelmingly of sexual delinquency."[27] Obviously, Cohen confused official reaction with individual deviant adaptation. We don't know that boys' and girls' sexual promiscuity was equal or different, especially in Cohen's time, because the system was more concerned with girls' sexual activities than their other deviant behaviors. Official reports overestimated girls' sexual delinquency, since boys' sexual activities were perceived as neither deviant nor officially sanctioned.

Naffine[28] points out that Cohen's description of the societal values that delinquent boys reject is almost purely a description of stereotypically male traits. Girls fit into Cohen's scheme only peripherally and evidently did not have a need to protect their self-image, even if employment and education opportunities were blocked to them as well. Since Cohen and others believed that girls were only interested in ". . . dating, popularity with boys, pulchritude, 'charm,' clothes and dancing . . ." they believed that it was unnecessary for girls to react to blocked opportunities with an alternative culture.[29]

Cohen's description of female traits ran directly counter to his description of what is normal and admirable: he identified ambition as a virtue and girls as "inactive" and "unambitious." He portrayed altruism as inconsistent with American self-reliance and described girls as nurturing and affiliative. He described rationality as a trait associated with success and described girls as emotional. He identified initiative as a valuable trait in a "get-ahead" society and described girls as timid and harm avoiders. Thus, in Cohen's theory, delinquent boys are actually more "normal" than all girls, if one uses his description of normality that draws heavily from traits associated with masculinity. The delinquent boy may be bad, but at least he is male; and there is even a "glamour and romance" associated with his antics. Although ". . . it may be condemned by others on moral grounds, [delinquency] has at least one virtue: it incontestably confirms, in the eyes of all concerned, his essential masculinity."[30]

Cloward[31] and Cloward and Ohlin[32] restated the basic ideas of strain theory and Cohen's cultural strain theory in their differential opportunity thesis in 1960. The added dimension of the differential opportunity thesis was that some boys were blocked from legitimate *and* illegitimate means to financial success. Some boys have access to avenues associated with organized crime that are just as productive in achieving goals as legitimate means, while others are blocked from even these avenues. Groups then formed based on available avenues of opportunity: the group who had access to legitimate means, the group who had access to illegitimate means, and those who had access to neither. Delinquency occurred primarily in the latter two groups, although the group that had no avenues of opportunity tended to engage in more random and uncontrolled delinquency than the group that had access to illegitimate means.

Criticisms of the differential opportunity thesis include those applied to the anomie-strain theory. Once again, these theorists did not see girls as part of the economic mainstream of society. It was the man, according to Cloward and Ohlin, who "must go into the marketplace to seek employment, make a career for himself, and support a family."[33] Since women were not pressured to achieve economic success, they did not pursue delinquent avenues to reach such goals. Cloward and Ohlin's only mention of girls, in fact, was to blame them for male delinquency, arguing that they were the reason boys felt pressure to have money.[34]

Morris[35] was one early theorist who applied strain theory to female delinquency. She proposed that while boys will turn to delinquency when blocked from achieving goals associated with economic success, girls will turn to delinquency when blocked from affective (relationship) goals, since that is the measure of success for women in society. According to this theory, delinquent girls would be those who came from dysfunctional families and who "rated low in personal appearance and in grooming skills."[36] Her findings supported her theory. In a sample of delinquent boys and girls compared to a control sample of nondelinquents, she found that delinquent girls were more likely to come from broken homes and rate their family life as unhappy. Delinquent girls evidently also displayed slightly poorer grooming habits; however, Morris did not find that personal appearance overall was different between delinquent and control samples of girls.

Other researchers have also followed the line of reasoning that delinquent girls are less able than nondelinquent girls to achieve a female definition of success (which was solely related to marriage and family). Usually this took the form of measuring girls' masculinity or attractiveness or their perception of blocked access to marriage. In an interesting example of tortured reasoning, Sandhu and Allen[37] found that delinquent girls showed less commitment to marriage than a control sample of girls, but they interpreted their findings as showing that the delinquent girls' disinterest was due to their recognition that marriage was unattainable for them. In a similar fashion of ignoring contrary evidence, Datesman and colleagues found there was a stronger association between perceived strain and delinquency for girls than for boys. Then the authors interpreted these findings as if girls interpreted the "success" statements in the survey instrument as relating to marriage and relationship goals, even though the statements specifically related to education and employment.[38]

Smith[39] tested a number of criminological theories, using a large sample of men and women who filled out a self-report of delinquency and criminality. Strain was measured by a number of statements regarding a perception of blocked opportunities/access to such things as education and employment. It was found that strain was an equally valid predictor of delinquency for both men and women, but that after controlling for strain there was still additional male delinquency that was unexplained by strain.

Cernkovich and Giordano[40] also tested the strain theory and found that race complicated the relationship between perceived strain and delinquency. Although strain was a fairly good predictor of delinquency for whites, it did not hold up as well for nonwhites. It operated equally well for men and women for the white sample only.

The problem with using strain theory to explain female criminality is that it assumes many things. First, there is the assumption that women do have different goals from men's. This may be true (or it may have been true in the past), but the assumption that women turn to crime when they are blocked in their specific goal of marriage and family does not logically follow. Note that the goal of financial success is logically related to an innovative strategy of property crime or robbery (in order to achieve money); however, the goal of marriage/children is not logically related to an innovative strategy of crime. Only if one postulates that marriage was solely a financial and economic goal would there be the same logical consistency between strain and crime, and most theorists agree that women emphasize affiliative goals in addition to or instead of economic ones.

The theory assumes that only women who are blocked from marriage resort to crime. Statistics do not clearly support this assumption. Many criminal women are married, and many unmarried women are not criminal. If one argues that marriage is only an avenue to financial success, the argument is supported somewhat better by statistics indicating that poor, single head-of-household women are more likely than other demographic groups to engage in consumer types of crime. If, however, the theory assumes that marriage is the end of the rainbow for women and, once achieved, it is unnecessary to innovate, it denies the fact that marriage itself sometimes leads to criminal behavior—either through the influence of the man, or because the man is unable/unwilling to provide for the women and/or children and the wife engages in crime as a result.

How does the theory account for increasing rates of property crime among women? One would at first assume that because women have more opportunities today, they should be feeling less strain (with reduced crime as a result). On the other hand, if women are less likely to marry, marry later, and/or are less often able to depend on a husband to provide for them, then the theory makes sense because it would support greater rates of property crime. The basic theme of strain theory, as applied to women, is that women have been exempt from feeling the strain of economic independence and responsibility. Arguably, this has been true in the past (at least for middle- and upper-middle class women) and is not so true today; thus, it is not entirely inconsistent with current statistics. It does not explain, however, women's continued lower rates of violent crime.

Social Control Theory

In the 1960s Travis Hirschi[41] developed social control theory (or what has been called control theory, bond theory or social bond theory). Basically, the theory states that the delinquent or criminal is not controlled by bonds to society—specifically, the person experiences no feelings of attachment, commitment, involvement, and belief. Attachment involves relationships; commitment involves the dedication to legitimate work and leisure activities; involvement measures actual time engaged in such activities; and belief refers to acceptance of the basic goals and rules/laws of society. In the research that supported the development of control theory, Hirschi used self-report surveys of large numbers of young people (the Richmond Youth Study) and analyzed self-reported delinquency (validated by comparison to official records) and measures of the bonds to society described above. For instance, attachment was measured by such things as supervision (Does your mother/father know where you are when you are away from home?), communication (Do you share your thoughts and feelings with your mother/father?), and affectional identification (Would you like to be the kind of person your mother/father is?).

This theory postulates that conformity occurs because of ties to society; deviance occurs when those ties are weak or nonexistent. Conformity is associated with good school performance, strong family ties, liking for school, conventional aspirations, and respect for law. Note the difference here between control theory and differential association or cultural deviance theory. While the latter two theories propose that individuals are socialized to criminality, Hirschi's formulation proposes that criminality takes place because of a lack of socialization.

Statistical support for control theory followed, especially the correlation between both attachment and commitment with delinquency, with somewhat less support for involvement and delinquency. Generally, the theory received more support than differential association in studies testing the relative validity of both theories, although some researchers also found that differential association explained delinquency better than social control theory.[42] Criticism of control theory points out that it does not discuss why bonds are weak or strong, nor does it include any possibility of individual action affecting such bonds. The theory also does not seem to explain corporate crime or crimes of passion, although one must take into consideration that social control research tends to focus solely on delinquency as opposed to adult criminality.

In a decision that was heavily criticized by the feminist critiques that emerged in the 1970s, Hirschi chose to drop girls from his sample before analysis began. Naffine[43] pointed out that Hirschi begins his exploration not with the question, "Why do people commit crime?" but rather with "Why don't people commit crime?" Yet he then proceeds to ignore women, the largest group of non-offenders. Naffine notes that Hirschi described law-abiding behavior as "male-like" rather than weak and passive, unlike earlier theorists (such as Cohen and Sutherland) who glamorized the male delinquent as a more masculine than law-abiding youth.[44]

Interestingly, tests of control theory idealize or devalue conformity depending on whether they are testing the theory on women or men. Hagan, Simpson, and Gillis,[45] for instance, note that delinquency is "fun" and that, because girls are more controlled through family associations and other forms of informal control, they do not have as much opportunity for the fun of delinquency. This version of control theory is not at all different from sex-role theory or the earlier applications of differential association to female conformity. Hirschi, on the other hand, conceptualized the delinquent as adrift without meaning or value or friendships; it was the law-abiding teen who was active, dynamic, and having "fun" by engaging in extracurricular and family activities.

Tests of control theory or comparisons of control theory to other theories fill up volumes. Generally, associations are found between measures of the social bonds identified by Hirschi and delinquency. However, support also exists for the view that association with deviant peers mediates the relationship so that weak bonds affect delinquency but also that weak bonds—when coupled with an association with delinquent peers—are more likely to be associated with delinquency.

Greenberg[46] reanalyzed the Richmond Youth Study data and found that most of the relationships proposed by control theory were modest, and also that strain variables were associated with delinquency as well (e.g., educational aspirations). A criticism of most tests of social control theory is that cross-sectional research only measures correlation, not direction. In other words, while there may be a correlation between lack of involvement in school and delinquency, cross-sectional research cannot prove that the lack of involvement came before the delinquency or if the causal ordering of the two factors was reversed (e.g., the delinquency preceded the lack of involvement in school).

Control theory does seem to provide a more adequate explanation for the sex differential in crime rates than some of the other traditional theories discussed above. In studies of delinquency, researchers have found that female adolescents have stronger levels of attachment than male adolescents[47] and that they engage in fewer delinquent acts than male adolescents.[48] Some research links the higher attachment of girls and women to greater feelings of guilt because "they have more to lose."[49] Studies also find, however, that even after controlling for attachment, boys commit more delinquency than girls.[50] As mentioned before, Smith[51] found that girls with low social bonds were still more conforming than boys. Alarid and her colleagues found that parental attachment was significantly stronger as a correlate for delinquency for female as compared to male respondents (in a negative direction). On the other hand, attachment to spouse was correlated positively with criminality.[52] Covington[53] also discovered that social control theory was a better predictor than other theories of women's involvement in crime and attributes this difference to greater parental supervision of female children. A somewhat related finding is that poor environment (arguably with fewer bonds) is more predictive of female delinquency while low self-control is more predictive of male delinquency.[54]

More recent research generally finds that social control factors tend to operate similarly for girls and boys. Although some studies have found social control factors, especially attachment, operate differentially for girls and boys, inconsistent findings exist across several studies.[55] Unfortunately, studies use varying definitions and measures of the relevant variables and samples are often high school or college samples with very little delinquency. Generally, it seems to be the case that those studies that use incarcerated or justice-involved samples find stronger relationships than those studies that use high school samples.

Labeling and Conflict Theories

Labeling theory relies on symbolic interactionism and can be traced to the ideas of Edwin Lemert,[56] George Herbert Mead,[57] and Howard Becker.[58] The theory is unique from those discussed above in that, like radical criminology, it focuses attention on the official labeler as well as the deviant. In fact, deviance (at least *secondary deviance*) is believed to be caused by the actions of the labeler instead of any individual pathology on the part of the offender. The theory raises questions as to why only certain behaviors are labeled deviant, why only certain people are subject to formal sanctions, and how labels of deviance change over time. The main element of labeling theory, however, is that everyone commits primary deviance, but only some get labeled and stigmatized, and the deviant commits secondary deviance in reaction to this labeling and stigmatization after the deviant label is incorporated into one's identity.[59]

While Becker assumed a great deal of volition on the part of the actor in accepting or rejecting labels, later applications of the theory presumed a more passive recipient of the labeling process. More current applications of the theory have operationalized and tested some of the more vague tenets of the theory (such as the process by which the individual absorbs the label). There has also been a focus on practical effects of early labeling—specifically, how labeling during adolescence affects the individuals' opportunities in life to create "cumulative disadvantage."[60]

Criticisms of labeling theory include the observation that no explanation for primary deviance is offered. Also, any accurate testing of whether secondary deviance would not exist except for the labeling is impossible.[61] Labeling does not explain persistent criminality when offenders are not subject to labeling (such as with hidden corporate criminality) and ignores the deterrent effect of official intervention.

There is very little literature by labeling theorists to help us understand female criminality. Although Lemert[62] did discuss prostitution, he presented it as a sexual deviation rather than an economic crime and did not use labeling to explain a woman's decision to commit the crime as secondary deviance. For labeling theory to explain female criminality, one must assume that women are less likely to be labeled as deviant and, therefore, do not internalize deviant labels even if they engage in primary deviance. Other corollaries are that women suffer less stigma if they do come into contact with formal authorities. If true, this would explain their reduced numbers in secondary deviance.

Some support for these premises was offered by early research that found women were less likely to be stigmatized because they were less likely to be formally processed.[63] Others argue that girls are more likely than boys to be processed (at least for status crimes).[64] However, as is discussed in a later chapter, whether women have been or still are treated chivalrously by the system is difficult to determine, given the difficulty of controlling for all aspects of the crime and all aspects of the offender's background. One labeling theorist, Schur,[65] spoke specifically about women. He argued that women were subject to labeling on a greater scale than men, and those who deviated from male-designated norms—especially with regards to sexuality and beauty—were more readily labeled than men. He argued that women who committed deviant acts and/or crime were stigmatized more harshly than men.

Conflict Theories

Radical, critical, or Marxist theories of crime[66] challenge the "science" of criminology and the nature of the exercise, concentrating as it does on the individual "deviant." Critical or radical criminology addressed the process of defining crimes and the nature of law as a method of social control by those in power. Under the Marxist theory of crime, crime exists in the capitalist society as "work." It is an essential element of capitalism. Criminal activity represents false consciousness; the "lumpenproletariat" does not know who their true oppressors are; thus, they steal from and hurt each other. This approach expands the definition of crime—for instance, to the death of workers in unsafe conditions.

Elements of critical criminology include an identification of class-based definitions of crime (street crime is heavily sanctioned, corporate crime is not), a challenge to the ideology of equality (rhetoric does not match reality in governing decisions), and the lack of objectivity in law (the poor are more likely to be the target of legal sanctions).[67] Critics of these theories contend that the view of society is oversimplified and that power coalitions are more complicated and diverse than represented by such theories. Another criticism that can be made is that these types of theories are unable to explain the sex differential.

According to the few theorists who attempt to apply critical criminology to women's crime, sexism keeps women at home and women, therefore, suffer poverty in a way different from men.[68] While men have labor to sell and become disassociated from themselves through the economic exchange of their labor; women, too, are economic commodities under capitalism. However, both their labor and their sexuality are for sale. (Ironically, similarly to Lombroso and Cohen, in Marxist theory prostitution is explained as the most common form of female criminality.)

Psychological Theories of Crime

Criminology has largely ignored psychological theories of deviance and criminology. A quick review of criminology textbooks will reveal that psychology continues to be given little attention, and superficial rebuttals are usually offered to explain the absence of psychological explanations (e.g., the explanation that international crime-rate differences prove that social factors such as poverty and social inequality cause crime, or the fact that crime is so "normal" that psychology cannot help much in explaining criminal decision making.

Psychological theories can be categorized into psychodynamic theories, developmental theories, and learning theories. Of these, both developmental theories and learning theories have their correlates in sociological criminology, so to say that psychology is ignored in criminology textbooks is perhaps a misstatement of facts. Perhaps we could say that psychological theories are merely sociologized.

Psychodynamic Theories

Neither Sigmund Freud nor many of his followers had a great deal to say about crime. The psychodynamic tradition would assume, however, that crime was the result of a weak superego or ego.[69] According to psychodynamic theory, one does not develop in a normal manner when childhood trauma occurs or there is deficient parenting. Crime may occur because of unresolved feelings of guilt and a subconscious wish to be punished, or more likely because of weak superego controls over id impulses—that is, the individual cannot control impulses and pursues immediate gratification.

The difference between psychodynamic theory and sociological theory is that in traditional examples of psychodynamic theory there is usually no mention of gender, race, or class issues as interacting with individual psychodynamic factors in human behavior, as is the case with sociological theory. Sheldon and Eleanor Glueck's[70] early work could be considered an example of the application of psychodynamic theory to explain crime. They identified poor parenting, weak affection, and familial instability as problematic, even though they also pointed to societal factors such as poverty as influential in delinquency prevention.[71]

Historically, psychodynamic theory explained women's behavior as operating from different motivations than men's.[72] Freud had little to say directly about female criminality or deviance, but his theory of psychosexual development is used to explain why women commit crime. Normal development, according to Freudian theory, occurs when the mother is seen as the first and primary sex object (for boys and girls) and the boy attempts to be like his father to gain his mother's love. This acts as the mechanism for role modeling and identification and is healthy and normal. Girls cannot model themselves after the father and feel deficient in that they do not have a penis like their father, thus they attempt to seduce their father to gain his penis. Winning a man's love (because of penis envy) is seen as normal female development. Attempting to be like a man (because of penis envy) is deviant female development, which according to Freudian theory is the case with female criminals. Promiscuous sex is also the result of deviant psychosexual development according to this theory. In Freudian theory, women's criminality is largely sexual because it derives from emotional disturbance. Other crimes by women were explained by narcissism—that is, theft and other crimes of acquisition are committed by women who are totally self-absorbed and consider only their own wants and needs. Narcissism is a more natural trait for women than for men, according to the psychodynamic theory of sex development.

The most obvious contribution of psychological theory to an understanding of criminality is the development of the concept of sociopathy or psychopathy.

The psychopath has been differentiated from the sociopath in the following way: "[the psychopath is] an individual in whom the normal processes of socialization have failed to produce the mechanisms of conscience and habits of law-abidingness that normally constrain antisocial impulses," and sociopaths are defined as "persons whose unsocialized character is due primarily to parental failures rather than to inherent peculiarities of temperament."[73]

The *Diagnostic and Statistical Manual* (DSM) *of Mental Disorders* by the American Psychiatric Association (DSM-V, the most current edition at the time this book was written, was published in 2013) is a sourcebook for diagnosis of mental illness. It has replaced the terms psychopathy and sociopathy with the term antisocial personality disorder. Regardless, these definitions describe an individual who is without a conscience and unable to form sincere, affectionate bonds with others. Of course, this describes many, but not all, of those who engage in criminal behavior. Lykken wrote that criminal behavior develops due to poor parenting and that the increase in crime was due to an increase in the rate of illegitimacy and the number of poor single mothers who did not discipline their children.[74] Interestingly, even as this comment was published, the great American crime decline had begun and continued for about a decade. Since the number of illegitimate births or single parents has not declined by any substantial number, Lykken's proposition is without empirical support. An interesting question to ponder is: if it is bad parenting that causes sociopathy, why are women not equally criminal (since arguably they are equally subject to parental deficiencies)?

Freud's 1933 assumptions about women's reproductive instinct, innate passivity, narcissism, and deceitfulness provided the foundation for the works of others such as Pollak,[75] Konopka,[76] and Vedder and Somerville.[77] One could also add Thomas,[78] the Gluecks,[79] and Cowie, Cowie, and Slater[80] to the list of theorists influenced by Freud. These early psychological theories described female delinquents and criminals as different from men in their needs, desires, and motivations for crime.

In the 1920s, W. I. Thomas postulated a biological/psychological difference between men and women. Women were passive by nature, as opposed to men, who were active. According to Thomas, women had four desires: the desire for new experience, desire for security, desire for response, and desire for recognition. These desires largely accounted for female delinquency and crime. For instance, shoplifting was viewed by Thomas as a desire not only for new experience but also for recognition and response, since girls were likely to steal things that would make them "pretty."[81]

Pollak[82] also used psychological constructs to explain why and how women committed crime, although unlike most of these other theorists he believed that women were just as criminal as men. He discussed the devious nature of girls and women and concluded that deviousness among women, if not biological, was aided by a woman's biology, using as examples the woman's ability to fake sexual response and conceal menstruation. His theory presumed men and women were different in their personality structure, not in their criminality; therefore, differences could be observed only in what crimes were committed and how they were committed.

Most theorists discussed in this section concluded that the personality structure and emotional makeup of men and women were different and that these differences reduced criminality among women. For instance, Konopka[83] was a clinician who observed that female delinquents tended to come from extremely poor home environments. She noted that loneliness, problems with communication, and identification with a delinquent mother characterized the lives of delinquent girls. She concluded that delinquent girls are more dependent than delinquent boys and often come from families that do not give them care and nurturance. Their delinquency stems from their need for support. She argued that official intervention should be to restore, instead of tear down, the girls' self-esteem and proposed a more caring approach to female delinquents than she observed in official reactions. Interestingly, these observations and suggestions have been resurrected in the gender-responsive corrections approach that identifies different needs of female offenders (described in Chapter 5).[84]

Psychodynamic theories are sometimes logically inconsistent and mix up sex-role stereotypes with psychological differences between men and women. For instance, the assertion that women's deviance is largely sexual is unsupported and may have more to do with the formal system's response than with individual behavior. Traditionally, sexual activity was considered normal sexual development for boys but abnormal for girls. Sexual mores continue to be different for boys and girls, but this is a sociological construct, not a psychological difference. The main problem with psychodynamic theories is that they view male and female development as different, yet the theories that attempt to explain female development are obviously ad hoc adaptations of the theories developed for men. Cowie, Cowie, and Slater[85] offered one of the most complete early analyses of the interplay between psychological and other factors in the development of delinquency. They wrote that social and psychological factors, such as poverty or broken and/or poor home environments, seemed to be better explanations for female delinquents than for male delinquents. When delinquent girls were compared with delinquent boys, the girls were found to come from economically poorer homes and were more often from broken homes; experienced more frequent changes of home, more conflict at home, and more disturbed intrafamilial relations; and experienced more mental abnormality in the family, with "worse" moral standards and worse discipline. Cowie and his colleagues argued that girls' motivations for crime "are connected, much more than with boys, with the intimate family, and with the girl's personal relations with her parents."[86] The authors proposed that delinquent girls had "defective" intelligence, deprived childhoods, and often had incestuous fathers. While they identified these environmental factors contributing to delinquency, they believed that biological predisposition had to play a part as well. These are psychological/biological theorists in that they argued that biology ordinarily played a part in restraining women from criminal choices, so that it was only in situations of extreme stress due to environmental factors that women were not controlled by these biological predispositions.[87]

The idea that female delinquents and criminal women were more likely than their male counterparts to come from dysfunctional homes has been tested by numerous researchers. Datesman and Scarpetti,[88] Gora,[89] and Chesney-Lind and Shelden[90] failed to find a consistent relationship that pointed to a higher correlation between family dysfunction and female delinquency. Dembo and colleagues[91] and Rosenbaum[92] did find such a relationship. Widom[93] found that abused or neglected girls were twice as likely as a matched group of non-abused girls to have an adult crime record (16 percent compared to 7.5 percent, respectively); the difference among men was not as dramatic (42 percent versus 33 percent). She also found that male victims of childhood abuse tended to commit violent crimes, while female victims tended to commit property and social-order offenses. Daly[94] also found that the women in her study tended to come from worse backgrounds than the men. This characteristic of female offenders has been fairly well established.

Developmental Theories

This type of theory addresses both cognitive and social development. The general hypothesis is that all individuals progress through similar stages of understanding and maturity regarding the world around them. Those who engage in criminal behavior have, for some reason, become stuck at lower stages of development. They are immature in their response to the world, in their interactions with others around them, and/or in their putting themselves above others.

Piaget[95] and Kohlberg[96] are most commonly identified with the cognitive development field. In Piaget's stage theory of cognitive development, it is assumed that the infant goes through qualitatively different stages of understanding. Only gradually does the child come to understand that others have needs and desires similar to him/herself. Higher levels of maturity are necessary to understand such abstract concepts as altruism and compassion. Kohlberg linked Piaget's work with moral development, arguing that cognitive development was necessary in order to develop a moral conscience, and understandings of right and wrong varied depending on what cognitive level one had reached. For instance, very young children understand that stealing is wrong only because parents have told them so. It is much later that they come to understand more abstract reasons for the wrongness of stealing. Kohlberg developed a stage theory of moral development, positing that everyone goes through certain stages of understanding moral concepts related to their cognitive abilities. These stages are described below.

Pre-conventional Level

Stage 1. Obedience to authority and avoidance of punishment are the elements of moral reasoning. For the young child, what is right is what parents say is right; what is wrong is what is punished. There is little independent thought regarding right and wrong, and an egoistic view of the world prevails.

Stage 2. There is still a strong egoistic element to morality. What is right is what feels good to one's self. There is, however, awareness of relativism—that is, what feels good may be different to different people. There is some commitment to exchange and reciprocity.

Conventional Level

Stage 3. This is Kohlberg's "good boy-good girl" orientation. Role modeling is a major mechanism for shaping values and behavior. Actions are judged by intent as well as consequences.

Stage 4. Morality is associated with doing one's duty and showing respect for authority. Maintaining the social order is seen as the sum result of moral rules.

Post-conventional Level

Stage 5. There is recognition of legalistic agreement in the social order and the realization that the social order may be an arbitrary creation at any particular point in time. "Majority rules" is a rule of morality.

Stage 6. This is the conscience- or principles-based orientation. Social universality and consistency are the themes that are used to determine moral decisions.[97]

Compared to nonoffenders in similar age groups, offenders tend to cluster in stages 1 and 2, whereas most non-offender adults tend to cluster in stages 3 and 4. Few people evidently reach the higher stages. Individuals progress from lower stages when they are raised in environments that include higher-level reasoning, when they are made responsible for their moral choices, and when they are challenged in their moral beliefs. Morality, then, stems purely from reasoning. A more rational, reasonable, intelligent person will be one who is more moral than someone without those qualities.

Kohlberg's theory has not been without its critics. There are arguments that the theory is culturally biased and presents a Western orientation to ethics that probably does not represent other cultures. In fact, it has been shown that individuals from other cultures do not test in the same way as those raised in Western cultures that have a Greek/Roman philosophical tradition. Another criticism is that the stage sequences are sex-biased. This criticism arose primarily from the work of Carol Gilligan, a student and colleague of Kohlberg, who found that women tended to cluster in stage 3 while men clustered in stage 4.[98] Gilligan found that women tend to base their moral decisions on relationship and needs, while men based their moral decisions on principles and laws. Gilligan noted that Piaget's early research documented differences between how boys and girls played, but the differences were not relevant to his study and he ignored them. Observed differences in girls' play included girls' greater tolerance, a greater tendency toward innovation in solving conflict, greater willingness to make exceptions to rules, and lesser concern with legal elaborations (rules).[99]

Gilligan proposed that women do not exhibit a *lower* morality; rather, they represent a *different* morality, one that is inconsistent with the Western philosophical tradition and more consistent with some Eastern religions. In her research she found that only a portion of women exhibited a relationship-based or needs-based moral reasoning, but almost no men did. She found that when resolving moral dilemmas, most people (about two-thirds) focused on either a care concern or a justice concern, but almost every male subject who had a focus exhibited moral reasoning based on justice while women were split (one-third focused on care, one-third focused on justice, one-third had no focus).[100] She concluded that because both women and men are socialized in this country to Western philosophy, it is not surprising that many women adopt such reasoning and display it when asked to resolve a moral dilemma. Another interesting finding of her research was that when sensitized to the approach (to utilize factors of relationships and needs in resolving dilemmas), both women and men could adopt and utilize the reasoning adequately.[101]

Some critics of Gilligan complain that she has merely provided a scientific veneer for the age-old stereotype that women are more nurturing, caring, and "nicer" than men. Smart, for instance, was concerned that Gilligan's work represented a "slide into sociobiology" which "merely puts women back into their place."[102] In a discussion concerning Gilligan's work as well as other research that identified sex differences, Held also worried that such work would lead to continued stereotyping.[103]

Other criticism was directed at Gilligan's methodology. The moral dilemma used to identify the moral stages of subjects was abortion. Arguably this dilemma has special resonance for women, and it is possible that the topic accounted for the differences observed between men and women in the resolution of the dilemma.[104] Later research discovered that people's moral decision making varied by the type of dilemma, and people may make real-life decisions in a different manner than when they analyze hypothetical dilemmas. Studies have found that Kohlberg's dilemmas produce justice-based decision making while personal dilemmas produce more care-based decisions, although females still exhibited more care-based thinking.[105]

Gilligan's findings were consistent with other work in philosophy and psychology. For instance, Chodorow[106] created a model of development that described differences between men and women based on their relationships with their mothers. Female children maintain a connection and identity with their mother, thus developing traits of "responsibility, care, and promotion of peace and love." Boys, however, develop by psychological separation from the mother. This explains women's tendency to connect rather than disengage, to be sensitive to others, and to be nurturing. The ideal of masculinity, however, is autonomy. Chodorow also points out that the very tasks of caring for children and others may promote a caring approach to life. The responsibility of feeding, clothing, and comforting helps to develop a loving relationship. This psychological development would also predict that women would define morality in ways that protected and emphasized human relationships.

Nel Noddings'[107] work in philosophy is also consistent with Gilligan's findings. She proposed a different, "caring" approach that emphasized needs over rights. Since women's lives are centered on relationships, connectedness is valued; while men value rationality, women value care.[108]

One interesting correctional intervention that utilized Kohlberg's stage development theory provides support for Gilligan's assumptions. An early therapeutic intervention based on Kohlberg's theory of moral development was conducted in one prison for men and another prison for women. The prison for men and the prison for women developed into very different entities: women's group meetings took on the characteristics of a family model where individuals provided moral support, while such support was almost nonexistent in the men's program, which was more political. The authors called the women's approach "communitarian" and the men's "political." Another interesting difference was that a closer and more trusting relationship existed between staff and female inmates than between staff and male inmates.[109] These findings are perfectly consistent with what we would expect from men and women given Gilligan's findings.

The relationship between moral development and criminality seems perfectly obvious, yet it has been largely ignored by traditional criminology. The only well-known criminologist who has had much to say about morality and crime is the conservative theorist James Q. Wilson,[110] who proposed that immorality is largely the result of impulsiveness combined with aggressiveness and a lack of empathy. Wilson concluded that there is a biological basis to immorality through the traits of impulsivity and aggression (linked to neurotransmitters, especially dopamine and serotonin).[111]Biological factors in crime causation are discussed in Chapter 4.

Continuing the argument, Wilson proposed that self-control comes from a conscience and that a conscience develops through attachment. He argued that this desire and need for attachment is innate. The relevance of sex/gender differences and Gilligan's work on moral development to Wilson's theory is obvious, and he described Gilligan's findings and others. Wilson argued that the innate aggressiveness of men and the psychological development of women that emphasizes relationship building rather than dominance are responsible for observed behavioral differences:

> Through prolonged involvement in play where sustaining relationships is more important than managing dominance, girls tend to acquire both a moral orientation that emphasizes caring and harmony and a non-hierarchical orientation toward the organization of common undertakings.[112]

Another version of a developmental approach is Rita Warren's I-level theory and classification model.[113] In this developmental model, the individual is viewed as progressing through stages of increasing maturity in interpersonal relationships. Although delinquents are clustered at the lower stages of the model, it is also noted that criminality may occur at any stage, but for different reasons and motivations.

Using her I-level model, Warren observed that the delinquent girls in her study tended to cluster differently from boys, but in this stage-sequence scheme the girls (at least delinquent girls) clustered in higher stages of interpersonal development than delinquent boys. Further, under each sub-type, girls tended to cluster in the stage that emphasized relationships as opposed to group or cultural influences.[114] These intriguing differences are consistent with the idea that women are more tuned to relationships than to principles; and even delinquent girls and criminal women were more similar to other women than to law-breaking men in this regard.

Learning Theory and Behaviorism

Learning theory basically proposes that individuals act and believe the way they do because they have learned to do so. Learning takes place through modeling or reinforcement. Because modeling stems from the desire to be like others, especially those whom one admires, children will act as they see their parents or peers act. The other form of learning is through reinforcement (i.e., one will continue behaviors and beliefs for which one has been rewarded and extinguish those behaviors and beliefs for which one has been punished or unrewarded). Bandura,[115] for instance, argues that individuals are not necessarily inherently aggressive; rather, they learn aggression. He and others also point out that learning is mediated by intelligence and temperament. Personality traits such as impulsivity, activity, and emotionality affect one's ability to absorb learning.

One of the most enduring explanations of why women commit less crime, by both laypeople and criminologists, is the idea that they learn to be law-abiding and that the social sanctions against deviance for women and girls are much stronger than those for boys or men. If this is true, then learning theory is perfectly consistent with the lower crime rates observed for women. Further, it also explains why women tend to cluster in consumer crimes, since women may be more likely to learn how to commit credit-card fraud than armed robbery. Do women learn to control violence, which would explain their lower rates of violent crime? Arguably, girls are taught that violence is not appropriate, while boys are rewarded (or at least not punished as severely) for using violent coping mechanisms.

Learning theory is less able to explain rising rates of female criminality unless one argues that what is being learned is different today than in the past. This could occur in two ways: (1) girls may be learning more criminal techniques and motivations for crime today than they have in the past; or (2) girls are not learning to be law-abiding to the same degree they were in past years when, arguably, there was more social control over their behavior.

Finally, learning theory does not explain the difference in cultural prescriptions for men and women—that is, why women's sex roles exclude the use of aggression and criminal activities more so than men's sex roles.

Although one can avoid the question of whether women and men are *naturally* different in their inclination to violent crime by utilizing learning theory, there remains the question of why societal norms developed to control women's behavior in this way, suppressing their supposedly equally violent tendencies.

Other Psychological Theories

Parsons,[116] although a sociologist, presented a psychological theory proposing sex-role identification as the basis of the different crime patterns of men and women. According to his theory, somewhat similar to Chodorow's described earlier, women's lack of criminality was due to a close and nurturing female figure upon which adolescent girls could model themselves; male children, frustrated by lack of close models, engaged in delinquency as a reaction to the omnipresent female authority figures in their lives. Parsons noted that although women were largely responsible for the socialization of the next generation, including the socialization of ethical behavior, boys see the "goodness" of mothers as weak (since the dominant society disvalues her) and therefore rebel against niceness, creating the tendency for boys to be inclined to antisocial behavior. Girls, on the other hand, have no such sex-identity conflicts and conform to a mother's role model, including the adoption of pro-social values and behaviors.[117]

This theory would lead to the prediction that men would be more likely to be criminal if from a female-headed household, and women would be more inclined to criminality if they came from a dysfunctional household with no good maternal role model. Further, it could be predicted that more "masculine" men would be more criminal and more "feminine" women would be less criminal.

The tests of the theory unfortunately have difficulty operationalizing the constructs, largely because what theorists propose as measures of masculinity and femininity are heavily influenced by sex-role stereotypes. Also, in later studies the tested hypothesis correlated masculinity with delinquency for either sex. Thus, it was hypothesized that criminal women and girls would score higher on masculinity measures than noncriminal women or girls. This is not at all consistent with Parsons' sex-role identity idea that boys rebel against a maternal figure.[118]

Current psychological theorists include Donald Andrews and James Bonta,[119] whose psychological theory of crime includes the characteristics of the immediate environment and individual characteristics to explain crime choices. They point to the attitudes, values, beliefs, and rationalizations held by a person with regard to antisocial behavior, social support for antisocial behavior (perceived support from others), a history of having engaged in antisocial behavior, self-management and problem-solving skills, and other stable personality characteristics conducive to antisocial conduct. Then they relate these to a behavioral explanation of criminality where rewards and costs of crime are mediated by these individual differences. Andrews and Bonta's identification of criminogenic personality traits and thinking patterns are discussed in more detail in Chapter 5.

While we could wish for a more direct analysis of women's criminality in psychological theories, these theories do have the characteristic of accepting individual differences; therefore, differences between men and women, as well as differences between women, are consistent with such theories. Historically, these theories suffered from confusing societally imposed sex-role stereotypes and inherent characteristics of women (and men). Today, psychological theories assume sex-role influences, although they do not necessarily specify why such differences exist or exactly how such influences impact behavior. Psychological theories are much more inclusive of biological sex differences than purely sociological explanations of crime.

Early Feminist Theories of Crime

In the early 1970s, a number of feminist analysts concisely and thoroughly pointed out the bankruptcy of traditional theories of crime that purported to explain criminality yet ignored one-half of the population. They observed that one could not simply apply male-oriented theories to women. Traditional theories used male samples, assumed male behavior was the norm, and operated under assumptions that may have applied to men, but not to women. Klein[120] offered a scathing critical analysis of the major theories of crime that, at the time, largely ignored female criminals. In short order, Rasche,[121] Smart,[122] Crites,[123] Pollock,[124] Leonard,[125] Price and Sokoloff,[126] Heidensohn,[127] Morris,[128] Naffine,[129] Allen,[130] and Howe[131] offered their own critiques of traditional criminology. These critiques stripped traditional criminological theories of their supposed scientific objectivity and pointed out sexist views that colored the researchers' explanations and theories of criminality for women (and men). All critiques pointed out that theories for women seemed to be mired in biological or psychological causes even while theories for men had evolved into identification of sociological factors as causes (e.g., opportunity, subculture deviance, control, and so on).

One of the more interesting viewpoints, offered by Naffine,[132] was that traditional criminology tended to view delinquency and criminality as enjoyable exciting, and glamorous. Therefore, women's conformity was considered weak and abnormal. Only in Hirschi's control theory was conformity considered more "fun" than delinquency.

There is disagreement over exactly what feminist criminology comprises, and feminism itself has been subdivided into more distinct categories (radical, cultural, and so on). However, the central thesis of feminist criminology is that females have largely been invisible or marginal in theories of crime. Unfortunately, feminist criminology has not offered any comprehensive theory to supplant those it has criticized. The attempts have either emphasized women's oppression and their control in and by domestic structures of society,[133] emphasized economic factors and the women's greater poverty,[134] or only offered suggestions toward the construction of a theory.[135] Feminists and nonfeminists alike tend to agree that socialization differences between men and women account for the gender differential in crime.

Sex-Role Theory

During the 1960s and 1970s sex-role theory was more fully developed, in comparison to the passing comments offered by earlier researchers as to why girls and women did not engage in crime as frequently as boys and men. It should be noted that in earlier decades men's and women's sex roles incorporated functions and characteristics that were more exaggerated than today: men were breadwinners and women were homemakers; men were supposed to be strong, assertive, and analytical while women were passive and nurturing. Sex-role theorists saw sex-role socialization as the single best explanatory factor for the crime rate differential.

Hoffman-Bustamante[136] described sex roles as the controlling factor in differential crime rates, arguing that women are rewarded for conformance and men for flouting many conventions. She identified a number of factors that contributed to differential crime rates, including:

- *Different role expectations and socialization patterns.* Girls were expected to be nurturing, and they had more responsibility for home maintenance tasks. They were also less likely to learn skills, such as handling firearms or fighting, that would be important when engaging in delinquent acts.

- *Sex differences in the application of social control.* Girls were more likely than their brothers to have earlier curfews, and they were expected to be at home rather than allowed freedom after school.

- *Differential opportunities to commit particular offenses.* Since girls were more likely to be at home or at someone else's house, there was less opportunity for them to engage in delinquent acts, such as vandalism, fighting, or other forms of delinquency.

- *Sex differences in terms of access to criminal subcultures and careers.* Girls were less likely to belong to gangs or to have other criminal associations.

- *The classification of offenses by the legal structure in a manner that relates to sex-role differences.* By this, Hoffman-Bustamante meant that girls were more likely to be caught up in the system for status offenses rather than delinquent offenses because their sexuality was controlled more so than boys' sexuality.[137]

Smart[138] also presented a sex-role theory to account for the sex differential in crime rates. She argued that girls were more closely supervised while boys were encouraged to be more aggressive, ambitious, and outgoing. Girls did not learn to fight or use weapons and learned to seek protection; consequently, they did not have the skills for crimes of violence, armed robberies, or gang fights. She pointed out, however, that sex-role theory did not explain why the differences in socialized sex roles existed. Smart also observed that sex roles are sometimes used by those who advance a sociobiological basis of behavior, in that what is described as behavior appropriate to one's sex role is easily translated to what is natural or "proof" of the validity of sexual differentiation. She criticized sex-role theory in its inability to explain why certain women rejected their sex role and did engage in crime.[139]

Tests of sex-role theory examined the association between identification with one's sex role and delinquency. The hypothesis was that women with a stronger feminine sex-role identity would be less likely to be criminal. Jensen and Eve[140] proposed that socialized sex roles accounted for most of the gender difference in crime rates. They utilized the Richmond Youth Study (Hirschi's sample of high school students) to test whether delinquency could be predicted by parental attachment and supervision patterns, which they used as proxies for measures of the differences in socialization of boys and girls. Although the associations were in the expected direction, they did not completely account for boys' greater delinquency.

Women's Liberation Theory

The greater attention to female offenders corresponded with an activist era in women's rights; hence the inevitable association was made between the two. Interestingly, this association has been made in almost every era.

In 1923:

> The modern age of girls and young men is intensely immoral and seemingly without the pressure of circumstances . . . [i]s it the result of what we call "the emancipation of woman," with its concomitant freedom from chaperonage, increased intimacy between the sexes in adolescence, and a more tolerant viewpoint towards all things unclear in life?[141]

In 1931:

> In the fight for Emancipation women have won most of their objectives and they have good reason to be jubilant at their success. Yet could they have foreseen the future twenty years ago, they would probably have relinquished the struggle, afraid of the consequences of their coming triumphs. . . . Speaking broadly, it is my belief that many more women have become criminally minded during the past few years than ever before . . . they have shown greater imagination and, in some cases, greater initiative than men.[142]

In 1950:

> Women [sic] with all her success in getting access to new fields and new social roles has not been able to get rid of her more traditional functions. She still is the homemaker, the rearer of children, and the shopper. Man—albeit grudgingly—has accepted her as a competitor, but he has as yet refused to become her substitute in the social sphere. Thus, with her burden of social functions increased, it seems probably [sic] that her opportunities for crime have not just changed but increased correspondingly.[143]

In 1975:

> Like her legitimate-based sister, the female criminal knows too much to
> pretend or return to her former role as a second-rate criminal confined to
> "feminine" crimes such as shoplifting and prostitution. She has had a taste
> of financial victory. In some cases she has had a taste of blood. Her appe-
> tite, however, appears to be only whetted.[144]

In 1990:

> We needn't look to the dramatic example of battle for proof that violence is
> no longer a male domain. Women are now being arrested for violent
> crimes—such as robbery and aggravated assault—at a higher rate than
> ever before recorded in the U.S.[145]

In 1975, Freda Adler proposed that the liberation of women in the 1960s
and 1970s freed women to exhibit more stereotypically masculine traits such
as competitiveness and aggressiveness. She argued that just as women were
entering nontraditional fields such as engineering and construction, they were
also entering nontraditional illegitimate fields such as organized crime, gangs,
and violent crime (robbery).

Critics of Adler's liberation theory argued that percentage increases were a
poor choice to track changes over time in women's arrest rates because this
statistic is subject to the problem of small base numbers. Also, it did not
appear that women increased their criminality in the years that they should
have been affected by women's liberation.[146]

In later work, Freda Adler continued to utilize percentage increases to support the notion that female criminality was increasing at unprecedented rates,
although she did accept that absolute numbers remained small.[147] She also
enlarged the scope of inquiry to other countries. Developing countries, according to Adler, would see their women's crime rate rise in relation to the extent
to which women participated in economic development and attained economic equality with their male counterparts.[148] Her hypothesis included the
notion that "Where the restraining influence of family control continues,
female criminality remains at a low level."[149]

The data collected to test this theory of economic development and women's
criminality included economic indicators and official crime rates. Findings did
not provide overwhelming support for the thesis. While there was a general trend
in the direction predicted, some countries did not seem to fit the model and there
were lower rates of arrests in some developed countries than one might expect.

Rita Simon's[150] version of liberation theory indicated that women's
employment opportunities would create criminal opportunities, and women
would then take advantage of such opportunities to commit those crimes. She
offered the explanation that women would not necessarily become more
aggressive because they would take advantage of employment opportunities to
engage in such nonaggressive crimes as embezzlement and workplace fraud.
Simon believed that women's involvement in violent crime would not increase
because when women killed, it was usually out of frustration and anger and

they usually killed a man. Increased economic and social independence would decrease "their feelings of being victimized and exploited . . . and their motivation to kill will become muted."[151]

In a later edition of her 1975 book, *Women and Crime*, Simon reiterated the thesis that women's liberation enabled women to engage in crime by taking advantage of white-collar positions of responsibility.[152] Simon noted that physical opportunities for women would never be equal, thus such crimes as robbery would probably always be less common for women. It is unclear, however, why this would necessarily pose an obstacle to potential female robbers: a gun would seem to more than equalize any perceived natural advantages, and one could always choose a weaker victim. In fact, as discussed in Chapter 2, in many cases of female-perpetrated robberies the victim is elderly and frail; therefore, it is unclear why women, if they were equal to men in their inclinations, would not be equal in their robbery participation rates.

The critics of Simon's opportunity theory argued that there are four weaknesses in the theory structure as exemplified by these contrary findings:

- Women and men do not act similarly, even given similar circumstances.
- Women's gains in employment do not necessarily consist of positions of power and access to money as Simon predicted.
- Women criminals are not "liberated" and, in fact, espouse more traditional views than women from noncriminal samples.[153]
- Women's increase in larceny/theft crimes are not the types of crimes that Simon predicted would increase.[154]
- The increase in women's crimes occurred to a much greater degree in "consumer" areas (forgery, larceny) than in workplace crimes.
- Many lower-class women had always worked outside the home.[155]

In 2000, Simon again updated her older work, once more utilizing worldwide figures.[156] Women's percentage of total arrests increased in economically developed countries, especially for larceny and fraud. This lends support to Simon's original thesis only if economic opportunities for women were correlated with economic development.

Those researchers who attempted to identify an association between masculine traits and criminality among women have been largely unsuccessful.[157] The correlation between economic opportunity and increased crime has received mixed results. Marshall[158] found that in a sample of Western nations, women's employment figures were positively correlated with increased levels of theft and fraud, although they did not show higher levels of robbery or burglary. The two countries with the highest female crime rates had relatively low ranking on economic participation, while three countries with low female criminality (Denmark, Finland, and Japan) had relatively high levels of economic participation of women.[159]

Steffensmeier, Allen, and Streifel[160] also conducted a cross-national test of the liberation theory using data from 69 countries to examine the relationship between economic development and female criminality. The theories they tested were the gender equality theory (liberation theory), economic marginalization theory (that women were forced into poverty with increasing industrialization and looser social mores), female consumerism (that more consumer goods created more opportunities for theft), and social control (that with increasing economic prosperity came more formal criminal justice decision making, leading to more arrests). Steffensmeier and colleagues concluded that, rather than social liberation, other theories better fit the data. Evidence existed that countries showing higher levels of female criminality could be explained by general opportunity theory (more things to steal). This increase in small consumer goods came at the same time as women's entry into the workforce, and it explained more of the increase than did women's economic liberation. They also found a change in the formal patterns of social control so that countries with higher levels of development utilized more formal processes of arrest and prosecution which, in turn, increased women's arrests.

Other research looked at homicide patterns in the United States and found that gender equality (measured by the male-to-female ratio of median income, employment levels, percentage at management level, and college education) was not related to an increase in homicide. If anything, this study supported a backlash theory in that gender equality seemed to be correlated with an increase of men killing women, but not female-perpetrated homicide.[161]

The tests of Simon's and Adler's theories do not show that crimes by women changed in the manner they predicted, although Simon's theory has generated more support than Adler's.[162] The liberation theorists predicted that women's crimes would increase in new areas associated with illegitimate opportunities (robbery) or the workplace (work-related embezzlement and white-collar crimes). Instead, the largest increase in women's crimes has taken place in consumer crimes or pink-collar crimes (e.g., shoplifting, check and credit-card fraud)—areas that have always been traditionally associated with women.

Criminal women have not changed their criminal activity patterns, nor do they seem to be especially "liberated." Both adult and juvenile female offenders show very little evidence of so-called liberated attitudes or egalitarian views of sex roles.[163]

Conclusion

Most of the theories described in this chapter were developed for men. If women were thought of at all, it was as different; they did not share in the deviant subculture and/or they did not feel strain. Of course, later researchers attempted to adapt the theories and test them with samples of female delinquents and women, but the adaptations seemed forced, the explanations contorted. The implication is clear that women tended to complicate the theory and were better left out. Most tests conducted on these theories found that some amount of sex differential remained even after controlling for theoretical constructs. Thus, the conclusion always ended with some version of sex-role theory (i.e., that women were controlled more, were taught differently, and subsequently acted differently from men).

The liberation theorists proposed that as socialization changed, women would become more like men in their criminality. We live in a completely different social world than the early 1970s when Adler and Simon were developing their liberation theories. Today's women may choose to work in any field they desire. There are greater social freedoms for women and less sex stereotyping. Yet, there are still important differences in socialization patterns. While the gender-gap decrease in property crimes seems to support the liberation theorists, the continuing gender gap in violent crime does not. In the next chapter, we discuss more recent theories of crime.

REVIEW QUESTIONS

1. Compare classical and positivist theories of crime and explain what each has to say about women.

2. Explain how Cloward and Ohlin's theory combined strain and cultural deviance theories. Identify any existing evidentiary support for any or all of these theories.

3. Compare and contrast differential association theory and learning theory.

4. Compare social control and differential association's views on peer networks and their relationship to delinquency. Which theory would be a better fit for what we know of female delinquency and why?

5. Evaluate the evidence to make a case for either social control, labeling, or conflict theory as a better explanation of the crime patterns of women and men.

6. Identify and compare the three categories of psychological theories discussed in the chapter.

7. Explain Gilligan's criticism of Kohlberg's theory of moral development and her findings regarding women's moral development.

8. Explain the elements of sex-role theory (specifically from Hoffman-Bustamante) and compare Parson's and Chodorow's theories of sex-role development and its relationship to crime.

9. Compare and contrast Freda Adler's and Rita Simon's theories of crime.

10. Draw a table that includes all of the theories in the chapter identifying the major theorists, the major premise(s) related to women, the independent variables, how these variables were or could be operationalized, and whether there are consistent or inconsistent findings.

Current Theories of Crime

CHAPTER SUMMARY

- The general theory of crime postulates that low self-control is responsible for crime. Researchers have found that women tend to score higher on self-control than men.

- General strain theory postulates that various environmental strains create an affective state (anger) that leads to crime/delinquency. Research has shown that men and women experience similar levels of strain but react to it differently.

- Rational choice theory has been enlarged to include perceived shame as a risk of crime and, because of this change, researchers have found that differing perceptions of risk of shame distinguish men and women and their different levels of crime.

- Social support/social disorganization theory has received some support in its explanation of why crime occurs in certain communities, but it is a macro-level theory and is not able to explain the sex differential in crime rates.

- Researchers have discovered that a sex/gender effect remains, even after controlling for the independent variables identified by current theories. Thus, sex-role theories and/or biological sex differences are still offered as an explanation for different crime rates.

In this chapter we look at the theories of crime developed since the 1970s. Despite the scathing criticism of traditional theories by feminist researchers in the 1970s, current theories of crime often persist in ignoring sex as a variable in crime causation. While the field of criminology is still largely androcentric, there has been a growing body of work testing both traditional and current theories of crime as to how well they explain female criminality.

The General Theory of Crime

Travis Hirschi's 1969 social control (or bond) theory, discussed in the last chapter, generated a wealth of theoretical and analytical response in criminology in the 1970s. In 1990, along with Michael Gottfredson,[1] Hirschi developed the general theory of crime, which also resulted in a flood of tests and applications in the 1990s through the 2000s. Actually, the two theories are not all that different. While control theory postulates that various bonds to society (attachment, commitment, belief, and involvement) *control* the individual and prevent delinquency, the general theory of crime proposes, simply, that individuals are raised to have either higher or lower levels of self-control and that it is this personal *control* that inhibits some from committing crime. Crime, according to Gottfredson and Hirschi, is composed of "acts of force or fraud undertaken in pursuit of self-interest."[2] In their definition of crime they state that there are no real differences between serious and nonserious crimes: "Murder may be among the least motivated, least deliberate, and least consequential (for the offender) crime."[3] Therefore, one can look for a similar cause for both serious and nonserious crime. In other words, they reject the idea of specialization or the assumption that at least some criminals may be career criminals (adopting a career orientation, committing many crimes of a specialized nature, and developing skills in that area in the same way that any professional would). They also reject the idea that different theories might explain victim-harming versus non-victim-harming crimes. Gottfredson and Hirschi argue that criminals are generalists, citing research that shows most criminals commit a wide range of different types of crimes.

Their conclusion that crime is a unitary construct is contrary to the point made in the first chapter of this book: that crime is composed of a multitude of very different behaviors, and that some behaviors are so different in seriousness, predisposition, and motivation as to prevent a single unitary theory from explaining all criminal behavior. Gottfredson and Hirschi would not agree and proposed that one variable explains all criminal offending: the variable of self-control.[4]

According to the theory, criminal acts provide immediate gratification and are relatively easy, risky, and exciting. These characteristics appeal to low self-control types who lack diligence; are adventuresome, active, and physical; and cannot delay gratification. Crime provides meager long-term benefits, but low self-control types do not think ahead and are not good at planning. Crimes often result in pain or discomfort for the victim, but low self-control types tend to be self-centered, indifferent, or insensitive to the suffering and needs of others. Further, low self-control types also engage in other activities indicative of low self-control, such as smoking, drinking, using drugs, gambling, having illegitimate children, and engaging in illicit sex.[5]

Gottfredson and Hirschi anticipate their critics by arguing that low self-control can explain white-collar crime as easily as it can explain garden-variety opportunistic crime. In describing white-collar criminals they claim that "They too are people with low self-control, people inclined to follow momentary impulse without consideration of the long-term costs of such behavior."[6] According to these theorists, those who embezzle have less self-control than those who do not embezzle (but embezzlers evidently have more self-control than other criminals who did not go to college, graduate, get hired by a business, and maintain a decent reputation long enough to rise to some level of trust that would give them the opportunity to embezzle). White-collar criminality is a problem for this theory, and other researchers[7] have argued that Gottfredson and Hirschi's statement that white-collar crime by professionals is relatively rare flies in the face of evidence that graft, fraud, and other forms of corporate criminality are widespread and, to some extent, standard in the business world.

Gottfredson and Hirschi also anticipate critics who might point to organized crime (Mafia and gangs), since descriptions of such criminal enterprises involve what is apparently a good deal of control in the operation and continuation of such criminal activity., In response to the example of organized crime, these researchers simply disbelieve the existence of organized crime—at least in the traditional sense—and with regard to gangs, they propose that gang members do not trust or like each other and are largely unorganized. They argue that gang membership does not predict delinquency, but rather that low self-control predicts gang membership *and* delinquency.[8]

The major cause of a lack of self-control according to Gottfredson and Hirschi is ineffective parenting. They argue that the conditions necessary to teach self-control include monitoring behavior, recognizing deviant behavior, and punishing such behavior.[9] They argue that the correlates of crime found in the longitudinal research, such as divorced parents, single female heads of households, and percentage of unattached individuals in the community are linked to ineffective parenting.[10] Hirschi,[11] in a later work, argued that the family influenced delinquency in many ways in addition to monitoring the behavior of the youth and teaching them self-control (or not). He argued that the family may also reduce crime by guarding the home, thereby protecting it from potential thieves, vandals, and burglars. He also believed that the family may reduce delinquency by protecting its members—i.e., by deterring potential "fornicators," assaulters, molesters, and rapists (although he does not discuss victimization from relatives inside the home). Finally, according to Hirschi, the family may reduce delinquency by acting as an advocate for the child to the criminal justice system and being willing to guarantee the good conduct of family members.[12]

According to this argument, if a child is from a single-parent family or comes from such a large family that parents are unable to parent effectively, then the advantages above are eliminated. However, after reviewing the evidence Hirschi concludes that the effects of single-parent families on delinquency were small but the number of siblings did have an effect: those with a large number of siblings are reported to score lower on intelligence tests, do worse in school, and complete fewer years of education.[13] Instead of considering intervening or precursor variables, such as income or culture, Hirschi concludes that both large family size and children's delinquency are caused by low self-control on the part of the parents. (His assumption that people with low self-control don't use birth control seems to ignore the many reasons why some couples choose to have large families.)[14]

Gottfredson and Hirschi argued that the age effect (the gradual desistance of crime in individuals who have reached their twenties and early thirties) can be explained by the continued socialization of the individual over the life course. They rejected evidence of other personality differences between delinquents and nondelinquents, describing such research as unimpressive.[15] They also argued against Hirschi's own social control theory (and the social support theory described below), arguing that if a correlation exists—for example, between marriage and lower delinquency levels—it is because low self-control types do not get married, only those with more self-control.[16]

Gottfredson and Hirschi's treatment of sex and gender is, to say the least, brief: "It is beyond the scope of this work (and beyond the reach of any available set of empirical data) to attempt to identify all of the elements responsible for gender differences in crime."[17] One might question, then, why these researchers felt justified in calling it a "general" theory of crime. Interestingly, in an oblique reference to potential explanations of the sex/gender difference, they seem to point to biological differences: "It seems to us to follow that the impact of gender on crime is largely a result of crime differences and differences in self-control that are not produced by direct external control."[18] If we assume that "direct external control" refers to the parenting practices that they described as causal to low self-control, it is unclear what other "differences in self-control" might exist other than biological.

In a later work, Gottfredson and Hirschi[19] restated their general theory of crime and argued that their theory was consistent with findings that established correlations between delinquency and family factors, opportunity theory, and a maturation effect. However, they felt the theory was inconsistent with the career-criminal theory, the existence of organized crime, the idea that adolescent delinquency is different from adult criminality, the belief that white-collar crime is different from street crime, and the idea that crime is learned. They described and responded to some of the criticisms that had been leveled against their theory:

- that it is too general and tautological;
- that it ignores differences in crime across age groups;
- that it ignores important distinctions between the incidence and prevalence of crime;
- that it ignores differences in the level and variety of criminal behavior by gender, class, and race; and
- that it scapegoats mothers as the cause of low self-control.[20]

Another criticism of the theory is that it does not include any concept of the meaning of actions and how personal meaning interacts with and influences self-control. Values, motivations, and meanings interact with individual self-control, explaining why some people show a great deal of self-control in some areas and none in others. Hirschi,[21] in a later work, seems to recognize a broader definition of self-control that includes other elements by viewing self-control as weighing all potential consequences, including what other people think and what might happen in the long term. This broader version seems to overlap with the concept of attachment (from his earlier theory) and other constructs relevant to social control beyond simple parental monitoring and punishment.

Finally, a difference exists between acts that are labeled criminal and those that are merely injurious to one's health because, by the author's own definition, crime includes those acts that "through force or fraud" result in self-benefit by hurting someone else. Many people drink and smoke, but relatively few of us commit acts of force or fraud. It seems that some type of moral sense or judgment is the missing element in this theory. In other words, there are many more "weak" people than there are "harming" people.

Tests/Applications of the General Theory

Studies of the general theory of crime conclude that there is statistical support for a correlation between measures of low self-control and measures of crime/delinquency, although the amount of variance is not especially high (perhaps no more than 20 percent).[22] Findings are mixed regarding the relationship between parenting (monitoring, supervision, closeness) and low self-control.[23] Some studies have failed to find either a direct or indirect relationship between parenting and delinquency/crime.[24] Other studies have found that low self-control is not stable over the lifespan, which is contrary to the theory's assumptions.[25]

Much of the earlier research operationalized low self-control by acts that are also delinquent/criminal,[26] leading critics to claim that the theory was a *tautology*.[27] In other words, it argued that those who committed delinquency/criminality (using it as an independent variable) are more likely to commit delinquency/criminality (using it as a dependent variable). Another issue is the construction of the dependent variable. In order to have enough "crime" to analyze, many studies constructed the dependent variable of delinquency/criminality very broadly, with nonserious acts (running away for juveniles or speeding for adults) included.[28] Although a significant correlation may be found, the approach may not be very helpful in predicting who is likely to commit serious criminality. Other studies[29] use a dependent variable of "willingness to commit delinquent/criminal acts," measured by survey responses. Even though these studies find correlations between low self-control and willingness to commit crime, the application of such findings is speculative at best. Especially in tests of the general theory to women, criminality is often constructed very broadly, including nonserious deviance because women commit so little serious, violent crime.

One of the controversies among researchers is whether self-control is better measured through attitudinal measures or behavioral measures.[30] Behavioral measures run the risk of the tautology mentioned above; therefore, some researchers advocate using attitudinal measures. Grasmick, Tittle, Bursik and Arneklev's scale of self-control is now the standard in the field.[31] It utilizes six scales comprised of *impulsivity* ("I often act on the spur of the moment without stopping to think"); *simple tasks* ("When things get complicated, I tend to quit or withdraw"); *risk seeking* ("Sometimes I will take a risk just for the fun of it"); *physical activities* ("I almost always feel better when I am on the move than when I am sitting and thinking"); *self-centeredness* ("I'm not very sympathetic to other people when they are having problems"); and *temper* ("I lose my temper pretty easily"). Grasmick and his colleagues have tested both types of measures of self-control and found that neither outperformed the other in predicting delinquency/criminality.[32] Others have tested the scale to less success, finding that the physical activity and simple task scales were least predictive.[33]

Some researchers have examined the construct of self-control and found that it is either similar to, or adds no additional value to, the construct of impulsiveness. Using factor analysis, Longshore, Turner, and Stein[34] identified five subscales. Risk seeking and impulsiveness/self-centeredness were as valuable as the overall self-control scale in predicting crimes of fraud, while risk seeking and temper were as valuable as low self-control in predicting crimes of force. The authors proposed that perhaps self-control adds no new explanatory power to the question of criminal choice and that risk taking or impulsiveness may be better related to other sociological theories or neurological theories than self-control.

The two major competing theories to the general theory are differential association/social learning theory (which would predict that delinquent friends would hold more explanatory power than low self-control) and Robert Agnew's general strain theory (discussed in a later section). There are mixed findings regarding the relative value of delinquent friends compared to low self-control. Some studies find that associations are either more powerful or retain explanatory power after controlling for low self-control, supporting a social learning theory over the general theory.[35] The key issue here is causal order. Gottfredson and Hirschi say that low self-control individuals find each other (in other words, low self-control comes first), but learning theory would argue that it is one's peers who influence the likelihood of delinquency. Many researchers now explain the two variables as interactive: delinquent peer associations promote crime most strongly among those with low self-control.[36]

Applications to Girls/Women

The general theory of crime would seem to support the idea that:

(a) girls and women have more self-control than boys and men, at least in restraining their violent impulses (since there is less divergence in non-serious deviance such as minor delinquencies or property crimes), or

(b) although girls and women might have the same levels of self-control as boys and men, opportunity and/or socialization factors are different, creating different levels of crime (especially violent crime) for males and females.

Most research does find that girls/women score higher on measures of self-control.[37] It is also true that, after controlling for self-control, there is still a sex/gender effect, indicating that there is something more than low self-control at work.[38] Zager used Hirschi's own data from the Richmond Youth Study, adding girls back into the analysis (Hirschi had removed them in his analysis), and testing low self-control as an independent variable. She concluded that gender should be seen as an opportunity factor because it did not vary equally across types of crimes (gender had more explanatory power than low self-control for violent crimes).[39]

As mentioned above, many tests or applications of the general theory to girls/women use very minor forms of deviance as the dependent variable—for instance, cheating by students is used as the dependent variable and a proxy for delinquency. Such studies find that boys have less self-control than girls as measured by researchers' instruments (usually a combination of attitudinal and behavioral measures), and girls cheat less than boys. The explanation may lie in girls' greater perceived shame; they seem to be more deterred by feelings of shame than boys.[40] Most studies in this area find that a gender effect remains even after controlling for self-control.[41]

General Strain Theory

Robert Agnew's[42] general strain theory reformulated Robert Merton's strain/anomie theory to the point that it can be considered an entirely separate theory. Recall from the last chapter the premise of the original strain theory: that those who were blocked from legitimate goals would adapt by innovation, an adaptation to blocked goals that might include delinquency/crime. Richard Cloward and Lloyd Ohlin argued that those who are blocked may form delinquent subcultures. Agnew enlarges the concept of strain considerably beyond the original idea that strain derived from being blocked from society's definition of success. (The theory assumed this meant monetary success for most people.)

Agnew's general strain theory (GST) is not unlike Walter Reckless's psychological containment theory, which became popular in the 1960s. Containment theory identified factors that fell into either inner containment (e.g., self-esteem) or outer containment of delinquency (e.g., strong rules and supervision) that counteracted the pushes (discontent, aggressiveness, frustration, boredom) and pulls (delinquent peers) toward delinquency. Like general strain theory, containment theory incorporated a broad range of social control and social learning factors. Reckless also recognized possible biological effects in identifying aggressiveness as a potentially biological push toward delinquency. Thus, both theories describe "pushes" toward delinquency (measures of strain and resulting affective states) and "pulls" away from delinquency (coping skills or resources).

According to general strain theory, strain occurs whenever (a) individuals fail to achieve positively valued goals, (b) there is a removal of something that is positively valued (e.g., through divorce or death), or (c) there are negative/noxious experiences (e.g., criminal victimization, child abuse). These strains create a negative affective state of anger or frustration that leads to the pressure for corrective action. If coping skills or resources are available, the affective state does not result in delinquency/crime, but if they are not available, delinquency/crime results. In later developments of the theory, Agnew has said that strain is more likely to result in delinquency when the events creating the strain are perceived as unjust, and the severity/magnitude, duration, recency, and centrality of the strain is also important. He also has incorporated low self-control (from erratic parental discipline), and high self-control (creating a strain due to parental expectations) into his theory.[43]

The major criticism of the theory is that it seems to include anything as a strain and has the capacity to explain everything by the recognition of so-called conditioning factors (e.g., attitudes, deviant peers, external attributions, self-esteem, and self-efficacy).

These factors are presumed to interact with the affective states that now are described as including anger, depression, guilt, fear, and anxiety. Strains have also been redefined as either objective (things that everyone might strongly react to) or subjective (the individual's perception of the event).[44]

Tests/Applications of the Theory

Similar to all delinquency/criminology theories, many of the tests/applications of the theory use high-school or college students, thus the dependent variable includes fairly nonserious forms of deviance. Further, one might argue that the strains experienced by middle-class college students are probably not equivalent to the strains faced by urban lower-class youth. Other studies use incarcerated populations. The individuals have generally experienced a high level of strain, but since they all have engaged in crime/delinquency, the dependent variable is a matter of degree, not kind. If adolescent offender samples are used, the dependent variable is capturing mostly adolescent misconduct, not necessarily adult crime.

Researchers do find correlations between measures of strain and measures of delinquency/criminality. Some researchers have found that some strains are more associated with delinquency than others—specifically, verbal and physical victimization and work problems are correlated with delinquency, while expected failure to achieve educational or occupational success or unpopularity with peers were not.[45] Individuals also react to strain differently.

Agnew and his colleagues continue to refine and extend GST to include constructs from other theories, such as low self-control. In one study,[46] researchers examined whether those with high negative emotionality and low constraint were more likely than others to react to strain with delinquency. They defined the personality trait of negative emotionality as being more likely to see life events as aversive, having paranoid tendencies, and reacting more quickly with anger to life stressors. Individuals with low constraint were described as impulsive, risk taking, rejecting conventional social norms, and unconcerned with the feelings of others. These researchers saw these personality traits as stemming from both biological and environmental factors, accepting that they were inherited to some degree.

In the study, all types of strain were measured (conflict with parents, school, and neighborhood strains), the personality characteristics of negative emotionality and low constraint were measured, and most were found to be significantly associated with delinquency. Social-control and social-learning variables were significant too, including attachment to parents, parental firmness, school commitment, time spent on homework, school attachment, conscience, and troublesome friends. (Only the variable of educational goals was not significantly related.) Although Agnew and his colleagues found that the personality traits of negative emotionality and low constraint actually "condition" strains so that those who have these traits are more likely than others to engage in delinquency, even those with these particular personality traits are not likely to engage in delinquency when the strain is low.

Some studies do not find that strains as identified by Agnew are related to delinquency once other variables such as age and gender are controlled for, and/or that other variables which are more supportive of social learning (such as delinquent peers) have stronger associations than strain variables.[47] Others found that while the additive effect of strains did predict delinquency, the affective state of anger was a stronger predictor for violent crime than for property crime and depression was not predictive at all. Other conditioning effects described by Agnew showed weak or nonexistent correlations with delinquency.[48]

Others find that strain theory explains delinquency to some extent, especially when considering the conditioning factors. Mazerolle and Maahs,[49] for instance, found in their study that low to high strain levels resulted in different levels of delinquency in the predicted direction (from 43 percent for low levels of strain to 72 percent for high levels of strain). However, exposure to delinquent peers also made a difference. Of those experiencing high levels of strain, delinquency increased from 37 percent (with low levels of peer exposure) to 67 percent (with medium peer exposure), and 93 percent (with high levels of peer exposure). In these more elaborate applications of strain theory, the constructs used overlap with those from social learning and social control.

Applications to Girls/Women

GST would support the notion that:

(a) women experience less strain than men; or

(b) women and men experience similar levels of strain but have a different affective state as a response; or

(c) women and men experience similar levels of strain and/or affective states but have different conditioning factors that lead men to commit more delinquency/crime than women do.

Broidy and Agnew[50] explore these premises and find that women experience as much strain as males—perhaps even more, considering their higher rates of sexual abuse. They found that there is some data to indicate men experience more strain from blocked economic goals, but women experience more strain from relationship stressors. Women report more stress from gender-based discrimination, low prestige in work and family roles, excessive demands from family, and restrictions on behavior. Men report more stress from competitive peers, greater financial strain, conflict, and violent victimization.

Supporting the second premise above, Broidy and Agnew[51] found that males and females differ in their emotional response to strain. While both reacted with anger, females were also likely to react to strain with guilt, depression and anxiety, which in turn was more likely to lead to self-destructive and escapist offenses. Further, there is some evidence to indicate that while men experience anger as moral outrage, women see it as loss of self-control. Broidy and Agnew also indicated that men may be more likely to respond with delinquency when anger and strain are present because they don't have the conditioning elements that moderate the affective state (i.e., self-esteem, social control, coping skills, and emotional/social support). Some data do suggest that women have more coping elements, especially social support. Broidy and Agnew concluded that males and females tend to experience different kinds of strain, with males' strains more conducive to serious violent and property crimes and females' strains more conducive to family violence.

Finally, Broidy and Agnew found that women's need for relationships and their increasing need to financially support families are linked to strain and deviance. These findings have been confirmed by other researchers.[52] In her study using a youth sample, Heimer[53] found that most factors operated similarly for girls and boys. However, when looking at longitudinal data, noxious relations with adults predicted delinquency for girls; for boys, noxious life events in general (e.g., parental unemployment, losing a family member) predicted delinquency. Her findings showed gender differences in how individuals experience strain (anger, blame, or other emotions) and response (negative versus positive response or external versus internal response). Other research replicates the finding that girls experience guilt with anger (e.g., in reaction to family strain), and that the association between strain and delinquency is stronger in boys.[54]

Piquero and Sealock[55] supported Broidy and Agnew's premise that males and females do not experience different levels of the key indicators that are implicated in GST, but that they do experience them differently. Using a juvenile delinquent sample, with self-reported crime as the dependent variable, they found that males and females reported no difference in the amount of strain experienced. Females were more likely to show higher levels of anger and depression, and males were somewhat more likely to report more inter-personal aggression and property offending. Strain was associated with anger for both males and females, but strain and depression were associated for males only, not for females. This study is problematic in that it used a sample of youth who were already involved in the system and thus, one might assume, is not representative of the general population.

Other tests of GST use incarcerated adult populations and find that incarcerated women have experienced higher levels of strain (noxious neighborhood conditions, stressful life experiences, violent victimization) than male offenders. Also, it was found that additive effects of strain are associated with both violent and nonviolent crime. The researchers found that violent victimization was related to violent offending, but not to drug use or nonviolent crimes.[56]

Kaufman's 2009[57] analysis of whether GST is a general theory that can explain both male and female criminality is worth reviewing, not only because of the comprehensive nature of the review of prior studies but also because of the extrapolations made in understanding female deviance. First, Kaufman reviews the evidence that indicates mixed support for the idea that there are gender differences in the affective states resulting from strain. The findings of this study, which used a large national youth sample (National Longitudinal Study of Adolescent Health), supported the hypothesis that the experience of strain is gendered such that (1) males are more likely to be violently victimized while females are more likely to experience other types of victimization; and (2) females are more likely to experience higher levels of strain associated with important relationships (e.g., attempted suicides by family/friends). Kaufman's study also supported a second hypothesis predicting that the emotional response to strain is gendered such that (1) the relationship between strain and non-angry negative emotions (depressive symptoms) is stronger for females than for males, and (2) the relationship between strain and anger is similar for males and females. Other hypotheses were not supported—specifically that females were more likely to respond to strain with suicidal thoughts and nonconfrontational deviance.

Kaufman also suggests a broader definition of the dependent variable to include "nonconfrontational" deviance, because it is a more likely response of females and suggests suicidal thoughts, running away, and eating disorders as some of the additional behaviors to make up the dependent variable of deviance.[58] This is interesting because it is somewhat reflective of the historical approach to female delinquency: girls and boys are described as similarly deviant only when the definition is enlarged to include acts that girls are more likely to engage in. In other words, the theory works better if the dependent variable is redefined as typical delinquency for boys but includes eating disorders and suicidal thoughts for girls. The problem with this is that purging is not a crime, nor are suicidal thoughts. Thus, if the dependent variable is enlarged in this way it is no longer a criminological theory.

Rational Choice Theory

The Classical School has been revived with the advent of rational choice theory. This modern-day theory presumes that criminals rationally choose criminal action because its immediate rewards have a greater influence on decision making than uncertain future punishments do. Cornish and Clarke[59] developed and applied the rational choice theory to residential burglary. Their research indicated that burglars were influenced by such facts as the affluence of the neighborhood; the presence of bushes, nosy neighbors, alarms, and dogs; the placement of the residence on the street; access to major arterials; and other factors. The conclusion is that burglars do not pick houses at random. They identify and target those houses that have the best chance of being burglarized without getting caught. Although the theory makes sense with burglars, it has been applied with less success to other crimes.

Cohen and Felson's[60] routine activities theory is slightly different from rational choice. They argue that predatory crime rates are influenced by routine activities that satisfy basic needs, such as food and shelter. For a crime to occur there must be a motivated offender, suitable targets of criminal victimization, and the absence of guardians of persons or property. Any changes in routine activities lead to changing opportunities for crime. For instance, the increase in the number of working women after WWII meant that more homes were left unattended during the day, creating the opportunity for burglaries to occur. Most sociological theories look at the motivation/decision making of the offender, but these researchers view the existence of motivated offenders as a given. For some, this makes routine activities theory an incomplete theory of crime.

Tests/Applications of Rational Choice Theory

Tests of the theory applying it to women, crimes other than theft, and other countries have obtained less conclusive results than the seminal studies by these researchers.[61] One of the interesting elements in the development of rational choice theory is the enlarged definition of deterrence. The theme of all rational choice theories is that rational people will not commit delinquency when they perceive their chance of being caught is greater than, and the level of punishment is higher than, the likelihood of their benefitting from the delinquent act. Researchers have more recently enlarged the construct of perceived risk to also include perceived potential shame or guilt, finding that those who have higher levels of perceived risk of feeling shame/guilt will be less likely to engage in the delinquency.[62]

It is clear that enlarging the fear of getting caught and resulting punishment to include the concepts of shame, guilt or embarrassment introduces the construct of attachment and belief, because the subjective experience of any of these concepts relies on socialization and connection to others. While this may make the theory more successful in predicting delinquency/criminality, it seems to have muddied the distinctions between rational choice and theories that emphasize constructs inherent in relationships (either attachment in social control/bond theory, the learning that occurs through primary relationships in differential association/learning theory, or the emotional support that comes from others in social support theory).

Piquero and Tibbetts[63] argued that rational choice theory should be combined and tested along with self-control theory to form a more comprehensive approach to the explanation of crime. In other words, a theory that includes both situational factors (opportunity and risk factors) and personal self-control (low or high) will explain more than simply looking at one or the other. They successfully tested their integrated theory with a sample of college students (asking only the likelihood of whether the respondent "might" commit shoplifting or driving while intoxicated). Although they found their predicted correlations between low self-control, measures of rational choice, and deviance, they also found that the total effects for low self-control ranked second to a measure of moral beliefs that was not a variable in either self-control (general theory) or perceived risk (rational choice theory).

Applications to Girls/Women

In order for rational choice theory to explain the gender differential in crime, one must assume that:

(a) women are more rational than men in that they are better able to weigh the consequences of their behavior (ironically opposite to historical beliefs about women and men), and/or

(b) women have more to lose and therefore perceive a greater potential deterrent than men in deciding whether to commit crime.

Those who have adopted the enlarged definition of deterrence to include perceived shame or embarrassment find not only that this informal threat is more powerful than perceived formal threats in predicting delinquency, but also that women report higher levels of perceived threat of shame/embarrassment (providing at least one possible reason for the gender differential in crime).[64]

In a study of anticipated delinquency and deterrence (in which subjects were asked if they "might" commit certain crimes and, if so, what their perceptions of threat were), Blackwell and her colleagues found that both males and females reported similar levels of legal threat (arrest) but that females reported greater perceived threats of shame.[65] These researchers found some variation based on the type of crime and disaggregating the constructs of shame, guilt and embarrassment. In general, however, they found continuing differences over time between men and women and the shame/embarrassment they perceived they would feel if they committed crime.

The finding that women are more likely to be deterred by greater perceived threats of guilt/shame or embarrassment seems to make sense with what we know. However, almost all tests/applications of rational choice theory have used either broad, nonserious deviance or respondents' agreement that they "might" commit the crimes as the dependent variable and "anticipated" threats as one of the independent variables. Further, the inclusion of shame and embarrassment (which depends on relationships) might be argued to have moved rational choice theory away from its original distinctive constructs into a realm more closely aligned with either social control (described in the last chapter) or social support theories (described below).

Social Support Theories

Another type of theory that emerged in the late 1980s and 1990s is the social support or social disorganization theory. Social support theories predict that strong families and other social organizations (family, school, and neighborhood associations) provide support and informal social control to individuals, thus reducing crime/delinquency. Social disorganization theories predict that the lack of informal social controls by these connections would result in higher rates of delinquency/crime. If the rational choice theory has resuscitated the Classical School, then the social support/social disorganization theories of today revive the old Shaw and McKay (Chicago School) ideas of the community as a prime factor in crime causation. These theorists[66] point to the social milieu as affecting victimization rates and/or offending rates.

Sampson,[67] for instance, looked at marital rates. He found that divorce was associated with adult offending and that higher rates of married couples in a community had a negative effect on juvenile offending rates. He also found that higher racial income inequality, poverty, and low occupational status were associated with significantly higher rates of robbery and homicide.

Social support theorists point to the power of informal social control by one's family, church, school and community in controlling both juvenile and adult offending and also propose that public support for the family (e.g., aid for dependent children, strong community associations, health care) are correlated with stronger informal social control.[68]

Social disorganization occurs when the neighborhood cannot help individuals achieve common goals and effective social controls are absent. Social disorganization is measured by such factors as low socioeconomic status, residential mobility, racial heterogeneity, family disruption, weak or nonexistent local social organizations, weak local friendship networks, low organizational participation, and unsupervised teenage groups. Sampson and his colleagues measured the *social efficacy* of neighborhoods (defined as higher levels of variables associated with social support) and found that lower social efficacy was associated with more delinquency.[69]

However, macro-level research, by its nature, cannot identify more specifically how these factors affect crime. For instance, the statistics gathered typically cannot isolate incidence or prevalence patterns—that is, whether a *few* people in the community commit *much* crime or *many* people commit *some* crime—therefore, any statistical associations identified would have to be further researched. The theory also has difficulty explaining the massive drop in crime levels beginning in the mid-1990s, since the levels of social support have certainly not risen in that same time period. Also, the social support/social disorganization theories do not typically address why girls/women in the same social milieu having low social support and high social disorganization commit less crime than their brothers/husbands/fathers.

Tests/Applications of Social Support/Disorganization Theory

Other than research by Sampson and his colleagues (The Project on Human Development in Chicago Neighborhoods), there have been few independent applications or tests of this theory. Those who have tested it have found modest evidence for the hypothesized association between measures of social disorganization and delinquency, although there was less evidence for the idea of social support being negatively correlated with delinquency.[70] Generally, evidence seems to support social disorganization to a greater degree than it does the idea of social support.

Applications to Girls/Women

Like the Chicago School and cultural deviance theories in the 1930s through the 1950s, this theory does not answer the question of why girls/women in neighborhoods with low social efficacy do not commit crime at the same level as their brothers/husbands/fathers. Only with the addition of social learning or sex-role theory is the theory viable as an explanation for why those in socially disorganized communities commit more crime than those who do not, as well as why girls/women in those communities commit less crime than their male relatives and associates.

Sex-Role and Feminist Theories Revisited

More often than not, a sex/gender effect remains after controlling for all the variables in current theories, just as with the traditional theories described in the last chapter. The accepted belief is that, in addition to low self-control, or strain, or lack of social support, there are also sex-role effects that inhibit delinquency or criminality among girls and women.[71] Many theorists, such as Messerschmidt,[72] describe the continued validity of sex roles. They argue that, compared to men, women still hold a subordinate role in social/economic spheres, experiencing greater controls on their sexuality.

Other research finds that young men and women continue to have different socialization experiences, with young women more strictly controlled (although perhaps not as strictly controlled as in past eras). Bottcher[73] compared 40 brother-sister pairs in activities and definitions of delinquency. The sisters committed much less delinquency than their brothers and described very different socialization patterns. Girls tended to have one boyfriend and fewer friends; boys had several girlfriends and a more diffuse association pattern of peers. The comments of the girls and boys indicated their acceptance of sex roles. As one young woman remarked, "I'm married and I got a baby to think of. I can't go around being crazy and wild."[74] Bottcher identified peer pressures that rewarded strength and boldness for boys but not girls, greater family responsibilities for girls, parental controls on girls to prevent early pregnancy, and other controls that inhibited delinquency for girls.

Sex-role theory is an adaptation of social learning theory. Basically, the idea is that socialization is gendered and that boys and girls learn different things. Boys are more likely to learn the values and thought processes of, and perceived support for, delinquent acts, while girls learn that such acts are not as acceptable for them. Variations of sex-role theory can be found in power control and control balance theories, described below.

Hagan's Power Control Theory and Tittle's Control Balance Theory

Hagan,[75] in his power-control theory, posited that family class structure consists of the configurations of power between spouses derived from their work-related status that is important both outside and inside the home. More specifically, Hagan places families on a continuum with patriarchy on one end and egalitarianism on the other; with patriarchy defined as a family structure in which the father has a more important job than the mother, either because of money or status. According to power-control theory, family structure shapes gender relations, and, in turn, delinquency.[76] According to this theory, girls and boys are controlled differently by parents in patriarchal families, which leads to risk preferences (boys prefer more risks than girls because they receive less parental control). Risk preferences then lead to delinquency. Gender also influences delinquency directly, through official designations (i.e., girls are more likely to be targeted for sexual misbehaviors).[77] It is not clear why greater parental controls would create risk-averse girls but not boys. One might argue that it seems just the opposite should occur, in that excessive control should push girls to risky behaviors as rebellion against such control.

The theory argues that as women enter the workforce, the informal controls of the family decrease and the formal controls of state increase. The presumption is that in egalitarian families (where both spouses had equal power) there would be less gender disparity between the delinquency of sons and daughters (because egalitarian families exert less parental controls, leading to lower risk-aversiveness in girls).

In early efforts to test the theory, outside employment was the measure used for egalitarianism in a marriage. As expected, findings showed maternal controls of daughters strongest in patriarchal families and equal to controls for boys in egalitarian and female-headed households.[78] However, findings did not conform to the theory in other ways. Results indicated that controls on sons were highest in female-headed households, which, according to the theory, should mean that boys in such households had the least risk preference and the least delinquency. Yet the findings indicated delinquency was highest for boys in female-headed households and lowest in patriarchal households.

Risk preference was highest for boys in female-headed households, even though control was highest in such households. Although girls' delinquency levels were higher in egalitarian and female-headed households, even in these samples it was still only one-half that of boys.[79]

Morash and Chesney-Lind[80] and others[81] criticize power-control theory for using a simplistic measure of egalitarian households (both partners working would not necessarily mean that there was an equal relationship between the parents), using only measures of direct control for the supervision variable, and ignoring other explanatory factors, such as poverty. The Oklahoma City study was a community survey measuring a large number of social and individual variables as well as self-reported crime and delinquency. Survey results were used in several tests and extensions of power control theory.[82] No difference was found in risk preferences between men and women who were raised in non-patriarchal families (using both father's employment and attitudinal measures to measure patriarchy). Patriarchal families did show differences in risk preference between men and women, but not when using either measure of patriarchy separately. The researchers noted that risk preference need not be tied only to delinquency. Other research showed that women who held nontraditional views indicated less perception of risk (measuring the threat of informal controls such as guilt) than those who held more traditional views.[83]

Differences between studies in measuring patriarchal/egalitarian households and parental supervision make comparisons of studies difficult. The theory does not accommodate single-head-of-household families very well (are these egalitarian or not?). Generally, the idea that egalitarian families are associated with increased delinquency of daughters has received support, but the association between levels of risk preference and delinquency and the idea that boys are less controlled in patriarchal families, less so.[84]

Blackwell[85] provided a thorough review of power control theory and then tested the theory, focusing on the measurement of risk preference as the result of parental controls. She tied power control theory to the latest version of rational choice theory, which includes perceived threat of shame or embarrassment as a deterrent. After reviewing the research that indicates women perceive a higher risk of shame or embarrassment for committing deviance, she tested whether the perception of risk is related to parental control (patriarchal versus egalitarian). She found that those raised in patriarchal families perceived a higher risk of formal sanctions (arrest), but there was no difference between men and women. Another finding was that there was no difference between those raised in patriarchal versus egalitarian families in perceived risk of shame. There was a gender effect in perception of embarrassment in egalitarian households but not in patriarchal families, as the theory would presume.

Along with other colleagues,[86] and using the same data set, Blackwell has compared power-control theory to self-control theory. Her findings show complicated relationships between the measures for household type, self-control, and risk perception. Females in more patriarchal households with more parental controls indicated higher self-control levels, but females in less patriarchal households with more parental controls were associated with lower self-control. Increased parental affection was associated with higher self-control. For males, higher parental controls were associated with higher self-control, irrespective of household type. Females in more patriarchal families with higher parental control were less likely to project future crime. Females with low self-control levels were more likely to project future crime, irrespective of household type. These studies result in complicated findings. Also, because the dependent variable was measured as agreement that the respondent "might" commit specific crimes, it is questionable whether these findings translate to actual delinquency/criminality.

Tittle's[87] control balance theory also utilizes constructs of power to explain delinquent choices. This psychological theory proposes that an individual will react in different ways to control, and it presents complicated scenarios of different alternatives of conformity, submission, and deviance. Tittle also discusses the application of the theory to female offenders. He proposes that higher levels of control lead to acts of rebellion: since girls are under greater controls, they should be exhibiting greater acts of rebellion. Tittle's measures of rebellion included "pouting" and not performing their maternal functions to the degree they should; a redefinition that removes this theory from the arena of criminology.[88]

Both Hagan's power-control theory and Tittle's control-balance theory illustrate the problems of trying to operationalize and test complicated constructs. Neither theory offers substantially more enlightenment concerning female criminality than the old sex-role theory, which proposed that girls are socialized to "be nice" and therefore their delinquency is less likely. Power-control theory suggests a stronger gender differential in patriarchal households. Another premise from these findings is that socialization to the female sex role includes an internalization of greater fear of guilt/embarrassment.

Economic Marginalization

In contrast to Freda Adler's opportunity theory discussed in the last chapter, Chapman[89] proposed that women—especially single women with children—were becoming a growing percentage of the poor in 1980, and she predicted that the numbers of women committing property crimes would increase. This increase would be due, however, not to liberation but to need. Further, she predicted that women's crime would continue to be sex-specific, involving forgery, welfare fraud, and shoplifting. In fact, Chapman's predictions more than 30 years ago have proved to be extremely accurate in that women have increased their participation in pink-collar property crime.

Darrell Steffensmeier[90] and other researchers point to no-fault divorce, increasing numbers of single-head-of-household families, low child-support recovery rates, and depressed wages for the service industry (where female workers predominate) as the reasons why women's financial outlook has actually gotten worse with "liberation."[91] According to economic marginalization theory, women's property crimes (larceny, embezzlement, fraud) have increased because more women are single heads of households and they have few resources other than crime to provide for themselves and their children. This leads them to commit property crimes, but not necessarily violent crimes.

Economic marginalization theory can be tested at the macro or micro level. Macro-level studies measure the levels of economic distress in a community to see if the measures are correlated with levels of crime committed by women. Evidence generally supports this proposition. Macro-level factors such as measures of poverty, income inequality, racial composition, region, population size, age structure, family disruption, residential mobility, population density, and joblessness have been found to affect men's and women's rates of crime.[92] Economic marginalization theory says that women's economic situation relative to men's has changed for the worse since the 1970s, and that has affected crime rates of women specifically.

Others who have tested economic marginalization have reported mixed results. One study found that women's recidivism rates were negatively correlated with the receipt of unemployment checks or employment (i.e., crime decreased as economic support increased),[93] and correlations were found between economic distress and crime for women.[94] However, Karen Heimer[95] and other researchers[96] argue that there is little evidence to support economic marginalization.

An important element of the economic marginalization theory is that it predicts an increase in property crimes, but not in violent crimes. As Chapter 2 indicated, women's property crime rate is reaching parity with men's in some crime categories; but murder and nonnegligent homicide and robbery rates have stayed virtually the same in the past 40 years (although the gender differential has declined in aggravated and simple assault).

Biological Theories of Crime

Biological theories of crime are some of the oldest crime theories as well as the newest. When discussing biological theories, criminology textbooks typically start with Lombroso's theory of the "born criminal" and then briefly describe other early biological theories, such as Sheldon's body type theory (mesomorphs are more likely to be delinquent than ectomorphs or endomorphs), or the XYY theory (those with an extra Y gene are more likely to be criminal). Then the methodological weaknesses of twin studies and adoption studies are reviewed and, finally, authors conclude that there is only weak evidence to indicate criminality might be correlated with inherited traits or, indeed, that there is any biological influence on criminal choices. This is interesting since the three strongest predictors of crime—sex, age, and race—are biological constructs. Of the three, only race shows strongly different patterns cross-culturally. Furthermore, race is mediated by interracial mixing so that most people do not represent pure racial phenotypes.

Part of the reason that biological approaches in criminology have been so completely rejected is that there are serious policy implications for these theories. It is argued that such theories lead to *eugenics* or other methods of control that are repugnant to our democratic ideals. Biological criminology is accused of being racist because it does not automatically reject race-based differences in biological characteristics beyond skin color. Feminists disparage biological theories because they reject the idea that there are biological differences between men and women that might account even partially for the gender differential in crime. Partially because of these concerns, biological research has been given less attention in criminology or has been outright rejected and suppressed. That is beginning to change, however, as our understanding of DNA (which helps us identify genetic inheritance) and neurology (which unlocks the mysteries of the brain, including sex differences) continues to improve.

Biological approaches to crime causation must first be separated from biosocial approaches. *Biosociology* explains patterns of human behavior as adaptive to survival of the species, and different behaviors of men and women are explained in terms of how each contributes to the species' survival. For example, the species' survival depends on women's childbearing and caregiving, which is why, according to biosociologists, they have brain chemistry and neurological hardwiring to be more nurturing than men.[97] Although biosociology is interesting (and controversial), there is no way to test such theories; therefore, they remain purely speculative.

Biological criminology can be categorized into (1) those theories that identify inherited (genetic) traits or characteristics that are associated with criminality, and (2) other theories that identify organic (but not inherited) factors that influence criminal decision making. Genetic factors such as inherited traits may predispose an individual to criminal choices, although this obviously does not predetermine criminality. Organic (nongenetic) factors would include lead poisoning, which damages brain functioning, or a brain tumor that puts pressure on the violence center of the brain. These factors are biological but not inherited. The biological effects of long-term drug use on brain functioning is not inherited; however, the predisposition to drug addiction may be an inherited factor. Twin studies comparing concordance in monozygotic and dizygotic twins (when a trait/behavior appears in both twins) and adoption studies generally support the theory that some traits are inherited, although early studies used small samples.[98]

More recent research continues to use adoption studies and twin studies to determine the role of genetic transmission of criminal predispositions or, more specifically, the biological elements that might increase the likelihood of criminal choice.[99] Differences in neurotransmitters in the brain, specifically dopamine and serotonin, are the most likely mechanism by which behavioral differences emerge.[100] Some researchers conclude that evidence supports the estimation that about 50 percent of criminal choice can be attributed to genetic factors.[101]

Sex Differences and Crime

When describing biological theories, criminology textbooks typically include premenstrual syndrome (which has been argued as a causal factor in women's violent criminality) and XYY syndrome (wherein an extra Y chromosome has been associated with men's violent criminality). Both theories have suffered from weak methodology resulting in ambiguous and/or suspicious findings. A more general criticism is that neither—even if related to criminal choices—explains much crime because these syndromes affect very few people.[102] It is interesting to point out, however, that in both the PMS and XYY explanations, criminality seems to occur because of a surfeit of maleness. Those few women who suffer from clinically diagnosed PMS experience an extreme decrease in female sex hormones (progesterone and estradiol), but testosterone remains high during the time period in question; and XYY men have the extra male chromosome that assumedly does something to their biology.

Walsh[103] views sex as a continuum instead of a dichotomous variable; the continuum is based on neurohormonal criteria from extreme "femaleness" to extreme "maleness." Turner's Syndrome females are excessively "female" since they lack a second sex hormone. They exhibit deficits in right-hemisphere brain functioning and suffer "space-form blindness" due to extremely poor visual/spatial skills. Their mean verbal IQ is significantly greater than their mean performance IQ; in essence their brain has not been "masculinized" at all, not even to the extent of a statistically normal woman. XYY men, on the other hand, are excessively masculine because of the extra Y chromosome. Research indicates that they display hypermasculinity, including aggression and low verbal IQ. All men and women, not just those at the far extremes of the "sex continuum," are affected by their sex hormones, which influence brain chemistry and ultimately behavior.

Testosterone. A fairly impressive body of knowledge has developed regarding the correlation between testosterone and aggression (and/or violent crime), although such research has also been subject to heavy criticism.[104] Although both men and women have testosterone in their bodies, men have about 10 to 15 times more testosterone than women. Basic problems with such research include accurate measurements of testosterone; a valid definition and operationalization of the construct of aggression; and understanding the interactive effect of testosterone production, aggressive behavior, and environmental cues. As with all biological variables, environment and socialization play a large role in how biological factors ultimately influence behavior.[105]

Neural Pathways and Brain Chemicals. The human brain is essentially female and becomes male with an "androgen bath" that occurs between the sixth and eighth week of gestation, at which point male characteristics begin to appear.[106] Walsh and others believe that sex hormones are responsible for emotional and behavioral differences between men and women through their influence on brain chemicals and neural pathways. According to Walsh and others, women's brains are, in essence, pre-wired for altruism and "otherness." They have greater sensitivities to human emotions, and they are less impulsive. They also have greater verbal skills, which reduces frustration that leads to aggression.[107]

Studies of autonomic nervous system factors, brain-wave patterns, cerebral dysfunctions, and cerebral metabolic dysfunctions tend to support the idea that men's and women's brains are different beyond their average size. *Brain lateralization* means that brain functions are more specialized to one hemisphere; in other words, one hemisphere has more neural pathways than the other. There is some evidence to indicate that women's brains are likely to have more neural pathways in the left hemisphere, while men's right hemisphere is more developed. The left hemisphere has been associated with positive emotions, altruism, and emotion.[108] Women's brains also have more neural pathways connecting the two hemispheres.

Low levels of monoamine oxidase (MAO), a chemical found in the brain, is linked to psychopathy, alcoholism, sensation seeking, impulsivity, extraversion, schizophrenia, and criminal behavior.[109] On average, men have about 20 percent less MAO than women, and this difference exists at all ages. Studies have reported findings that MAO levels are linked to delinquency. Boys with low MAO levels were found to be more impulsive and sensation seeking than other boys and were more likely to have drug and alcohol problems.[110] Associations are consistently found between low MAO activity and various correlates of criminal behavior, such as impulsiveness, childhood hyperactivity, learning disabilities, sensation seeking, substance abuse, and extraversion. Age, sex and race all evidently affect MAO activity, and testosterone evidently depresses MAO levels. In fact, testosterone levels are at their highest and MAO levels are at their lowest during the second decade of life (age 10–20, roughly corresponding with the crime-prone age years).[111]

Walsh[112] explains that there is a two- to threefold increase of MAO and a tenfold decrease of testosterone between age 30 and 80. Women have only about seven percent of the testosterone that men have and 15 to 20 percent more MAO. Walsh also states that African American men have 5–10 percent more testosterone and about 10–15 percent less MAO than white men.[113] Determining the exact function of MAO and why or how it might be related to delinquency as well as the other dysfunctional patterns mentioned above is complicated, although it may have something to do with the reaction to stress.[114]

Recently, there has been popular attention to MAO with commentators coining the term "warrior gene."[115] Researchers have found that roughly a third of the general population has the so-called warrior gene that results in low levels of MAO. This, in turn, results in serotonin and other neurotransmitters being less active. The MAOA gene has been linked to aggression cued from environmental stressors. What this means is that those who have the gene do not display generalized aggression, but rather display aggression when environmental cues or stressors are present that provoke violence—hence the name warrior gene. Those without the gene are less likely to display aggression even in high-provocation situations. Beaver and colleagues[116] have found that for girls and women, having the gene does not create the potential for violent behavior as it does for boys and men. The reason may be that the gene's location on the X-chromosome means that females have a second copy of the allele, and perhaps this is the reason why behavioral effects do not occur for girls/women having the gene.

ADD, Hyperactivity, and Cognitive Functioning

Consistent evidence exists that hyperactivity and Attention Deficit Disorder (ADD) are correlated with delinquency.[117] There is also evidence that Attention Deficit Hyperactivity Disorder (ADHD) has a high level of inheritability.[118] Denno[119] reports that delinquency is linked to ADD and hyperactivity as well as overactivity, perceptual-motor impairments, impulsivity, emotional lability, attention deficits, minor disturbances of speech, intellectual defects (learning disabilities), clumsiness, neurodevelopmental lag, psychogenic factors, and minor physical anomalies. These features may be the result of genetic transmission, poor living environment, prenatal or birth trauma, or, most probably a combination of the above.[120] Denno reports that there is higher incidence of prenatal and perinatal mortality and complications, childhood diseases, reading and learning disorders, and mental disabilities in socioeconomically deprived families.[121] Evidence indicates that many children outgrow predisposing factors, but those who do not are more likely to become delinquent.[122]

ADD and hyperactivity tend to be more common in boys than in girls: it has been reported that hyperactivity is four to six times more common for boys.[123] Walsh notes that there are different kinds of ADHD and that the type associated with impulsivity has a higher gender ratio (4:1) than the type that involves inattentiveness (2.7:1).[124] Evidently, men have a higher incidence of prenatal and perinatal mortality and complications, reading and learning disorders, and mental disabilities as well as left-hemisphere deficits.[125] Other evidence indicates that even though many of the biological measures described above are more prevalent for males, biological factors may be more strongly correlated with female criminality than to male criminality.[126] One presumes the reason may be that socialization (e.g., peers) also influences delinquency for boys but not so much for girls; therefore delinquency for girls is more likely to be influenced by individual factors (either familial or individual).

In Moffitt's longitudinal study in New Zealand it was found that delinquents had significantly lower verbal skills, auditory verbal memory, interspatial analysis, and visual-motor integration in elementary school.[127] Such early evidence of cognitive deficits indicates that it is not simply a delinquent lifestyle and/or drug use that causes subsequent lower or different cognitive abilities: there may be problems at birth or genetically transmitted cognitive deficits that affect the child early in school.[128] Denno[129] suggested that the relationship may be one where cognitive deficiencies affect school performance, which, in turn, affects delinquency. She also suggested that lower verbal/language development affects moral development and abstract principles such as altruism and utilitarianism.[130]

Traits

The field of psychology has identified what are known as the Big Five personality traits, each with associated sub-traits. They are:

- *openness* (to experiences), which includes curiosity and creativity;
- *conscientiousness*, which includes self-discipline, dutifulness, and dependability;
- *extraversion*, which includes assertiveness, sociability, stimulation seeking and talkativeness;
- *agreeableness*, which includes compassion and cooperativeness; and
- *neuroticism*, which includes anxiousness, depressiveness, and emotional instability.

Because these traits are on a continuum, a trait may appear in the opposite direction—for instance, the reverse of conscientiousness would be carelessness, unreliability, and irresponsibility. Instead of agreeableness, the other end of the continuum would be suspiciousness, unfriendliness, uncooperativeness and unhelpfulness.

Personality traits such as extraversion,[131] impulsivity, aggressiveness, sensation seeking, and others[132] have long been associated with delinquency/criminality. For instance, a study using samples from New Zealand and the United States found that delinquents scored significantly higher on a personality trait called negative emotionality and another called weak constraint (which is described similarly to low self-control).[133] Recall that Gottfredson and Hirschi's "general theory" isolates the personality trait of low self-control as the causal element in all criminal choices, although they did not characterize it as a biological trait. Researchers[134] who have conducted direct tests to determine whether parenting practices or genetic influence was a better explanation for the association between parents' and children's low self-control found that the statistical evidence for parenting practices was mixed. However, there was clear evidence from neuro-imaging studies that showed a strong genetic influence of prefrontal lobe capacity and development (which is related to executive functioning, including impulse control). Others have also found that incarcerated juveniles, compared to a high school sample, show a lower resting heart rate, demonstrate poorer performance on tasks requiring the prefrontal cortex, and score lower on self-control. Executive functions utilizing the prefrontal cortex are implicated in goal-oriented processes, learning and applying rules, abstract reasoning, problem solving, and sustained attention and concentration.[135]

Eysenck and Gudjonsson[136] argued that three elements of personality—specifically, emotional stability (N), emotional independence (P) and introversion-extraversion (E)—are correlated with the propensity to make criminal choices. The individuals who possess high N scores are anxious, depressed, exhibiting high guilt feelings and low self-esteem; they tend to be tense, irrational, shy, moody, and emotional. Those with high P scores are described as aggressive, cold, egocentric, impersonal, impulsive, antisocial, unempathetic, creative, and tough-minded. Those who have high E scores are sociable, lively, active, assertive, sensation seeking, carefree, dominant, and adventuresome.

The most well-known element of this theory posits that biologically determined low degrees of arousal and arousability in extroverts (and possibly in persons high on the psychoticism scale) lead to behaviors (e.g., risk taking and sensation seeking) that increase the cortical level of arousal to a more acceptable level. Behaviors of this type are not necessarily antisocial. They could be sport-related activities or daredevil stunts that are exciting and produce the level of cortical arousal that extroverts seek. Such activities might be antisocial because behaviors involving aggressive interactions, fast driving, shoplifting, robbery, and so on are risky and result in a thrilling rush of adrenalin that is much more pleasant for sensation seekers than for thrill avoiders. Because extroverts need greater stimuli to respond, they do not learn as well and do not absorb societal lessons that lead to law-abiding behavior.[137]

Another issue, of course, is whether these traits are biological or developmental. Caspi and his colleagues[138] discussed the potential for biological causation in the personality traits linked to delinquency. They proposed that research findings indicating lower serotonin levels in the brains of violent criminals may provide an explanation, since low levels of serotonin might account for both negative emotionality and impulsivity. Raine[139] reviewed studies that showed reduced serotonin and norepinephrine levels in antisocial individuals and argued that this fact can be combined with theories of underactive behavioral inhibition systems in antisocials (meaning that their bodies do not react to stimuli as quickly or as well and, therefore, they do not learn from punishment). Although Raine admits that there are problems with measurement, he concludes that there is evidence to support the idea that antisocials have poor conditionability, and some studies show that criminals from higher socioeconomic-status classes have even lower conditionability than those from lower classes (which would support an interaction effect of social class on delinquency). Also, Raine argued that "a lower resting heart rate has been found to characterize noninstitutionalized, young antisocial groups and probably represented the best replicated biological correlate of antisocial behavior, probably reflecting fearlessness and underarousal."[140]

There is also some evidence to indicate sex differences in personality traits. Men are predisposed to have personality traits of impulsivity and sensation seeking, probably because of brain chemistry differences. As noted above, males seem to have lower conditionability, which generally leads to sensation seeking since it takes more stimulation to satisfy. After reviewing a wide range of studies concerning sex differences in the brain, Eysenck and Gudjonsson[141] concluded that the "masculinization of the brain" and the level of androgens present are related to physique, low arousal, the absence of a "conscience," and a failure to be deterred by pain, among other things.

Behaviors that are evidently androgen influenced and can be influenced by artificially introducing androgens into the system include: assertive erotic sexual behavior, status-related aggressive behavior, spatial reasoning, spacing behavior (including territoriality), pain tolerance, retarded acquisition of aversive conditioning, diminished fearful emotional responses to threats, task control-oriented tenacity, transient bonding tendencies, peripheralization, sensation seeking, and predatory behavior.[142] Walsh notes:

Sensation seeking, impulsivity, aggression, dominance, [and] a propensity toward greater visual/spatial skills relative to verbal skills, are overwhelmingly male traits, they are all androgen-facilitated, and they are all traits linked to behavioral nonconformity of all kinds.[143]

Like all biological criminologists, Walsh[144] recognizes the importance of socialization as well as biological factors in the explanation of criminal behavior. For instance, while he points out differences in brain lateralization between men and women, he also explains that parenting, specifically interaction and communication, may positively affect the development of neural functioning; alternatively, neglect reduces verbal development.[145] Thus, he explains the finding that female delinquents tend to come from more dysfunctional homes than male delinquents because their sex predisposes them to hemispheric integration but their environment sabotages brain development by lack of nurturance. Child-rearing practices ordinarily tend to favor girls who receive more tactile stimulation (from being held more as infants), cuddling, and other forms of contact; thus, behavioral differences between the sexes most probably arise through both biological and child-rearing differences.[146]

Walsh points out that infants are more "plastic" than other mammals in that their brains are more undeveloped at birth with less hardwiring (instinct-driven behavior). Humans benefit because they gain the qualities of rationality and are flexible learners, but the negative effect of plasticity is that humans are vulnerable to environmental effects in the first two years of life while the brain is still developing. Walsh argues that deprived and neglected children are repeatedly exposed to stress, and that such a constant barrage of stress eventually shuts down the body's normal responses to stress (because stress becomes normal and the body stops initiating the fight-or-flight syndrome).[147] Evidence indicates, for instance, that many abused children have been shown to possess autonomic nervous systems that are nonreactive to fear and anxiety. The possible effect of such autonomic nervous system development is that these individuals will become relatively immune to normal stress; they may engage in "fearless" behaviors or antisocial behaviors because their autonomic nervous system does not give them the cues that such behavior is stressful. According to Walsh, some research indicates that those subjected to chronic stress in childhood may react with hypo-reactivity to mild stressors (not responding) but hyper-reactivity to severe stressors (overreacting).[148] One study supported the idea that childhood abuse could affect neuroendocrine processes, finding that violent women (in prison) were more likely to have had violent childhoods (both being victimized and witnessing abuse or death/injury) and lower cortisol levels. It was also found that violent female offenders were more likely to have had minor brain trauma (head injury) than nonviolent offenders.[149]

Critiques of Biological Criminology

Critics of biological theories argue that biology cannot explain criminal choice because crime rates vary across cultures and show patterns related to social factors such as urbanization. The argument is that a constant (inherent nature) cannot explain a variable (crime).[150] Others argue that gender (social-ization) is more powerful than sex (biology) and that all observed sex differ-ences are really the product of socialization.[151] Feminists, especially, scorn biological theories and view them as evidence of patriarchy.[152] Other critics argue that the methodology used to support biological theories is weak.[153] Other problems with biological research concern the practice of assuming prison samples are representative of all criminals and using formal and official reports as accurate measurements of criminal behavior. Also, studies typically do not differentiate between occasional criminals and chronic offenders.

However, it appears that many criminologists are now beginning to accept that criminal choices are at least partially influenced by predisposing biological factors. Those who propose biological theories clearly explain that the factors briefly described here produce only predispositions to criminal choices that inter-act with environmental cues or stressors, and biological factors explain no more than 50 percent of behavioral choices. No one advocates biological determinism in the way some critics mischaracterize biological explanations. Biological theo-ries clearly support the idea that sex differences (in predisposition to aggressive and anti-social behavior) exist and, as such, offer some rationale for why long-standing differences in violent crimes have existed between men and women.

Conclusion

In this chapter, we have described a few current criminological theories. There is more effort today to include women in discussions of crime causation and there have been a few continuing attempts to develop theories specifically to explain women's lower crime rates. The two most dominant theories today are the general theory of crime (self-control) and general strain theory. Neither dealt directly with women in their first iterations, but many researchers have tested these theories to determine their ability to explain women's crime as well as men's. In almost all tests and applications of these theories, once vari-ables are controlled for, there remains a sex difference in crime. Arguably, this remaining difference is due to sex-role theory and/or biological sex differences. In the next chapter, we complete our review of current theories by examining "integrated" or life-course theories (which include biological factors as well as social); and, "pathways" (a life-course theory specific to women).

REVIEW QUESTIONS

1. Compare and contrast Gottfredson and Hirschi's general theory of crime with Hirschi's older theory of social control. How does each theory explain female criminality?

2. What are the two methods of measuring low self-control? What do find-ings show regarding low self-control in women and men?

3. How does GST differ from Merton's strain theory? Review how each would explain women's criminality.

4. Identify the strains and affective states in general strain theory. Then identify the conditioning factors.

5. Compare the Classical School assumptions to the modern theories of rational choice and routine activities. What do each of these theories have to say about women?

6. What is the modern redefinition of risk that moves rational choice to include elements of social bond theory or learning theory? Explain how this change in the operationalization of risk has affected findings regarding the criminality of men and women.

7. Compare the social support/social disorganization theories of today to the Chicago School approach of the 1930s.

8. Compare Hagan's and Tittle's modern versions of sex-role theory to the older theories of the 1970s. Are they different? In what way?

9. Briefly describe the potential influence(s) of the four biological factors discussed in the chapter on the gender gap in criminality.

10. Draw a table that includes all of the theories in the chapter identifying the major theorists, the major premise(s) related to women, the independent variables, how these variables were or could be operationalized, and whether there are consistent or inconsistent findings.

5

Life-Course and Pathways Theories

CHAPTER SUMMARY

- Researchers have discovered that a sex/gender effect still exists, even after controlling for the independent variables specified by all the major theories.

- This sex/gender effect is attributed to sex roles, and some theorists also acknowledge biological sex differences.

- Life-course/integrated theories utilize longitudinal research instead of cross-sectional research and combine biological, psychological, and environmental factors.

- Pathways research is a type of life-course theory developed to understand the specific trajectories of criminal women.

- The pathways approach points to certain sex-specific experiences, including childhood victimization, pregnancy, and negative relationships, as influencing women to follow a different pathway to criminality than what is typical for men.

In the previous chapter most of the major current theories of crime were described, as well as how each theory has been applied to explain the gender/sex differential in criminality. In this chapter we present a different type of theory that utilizes a different type of methodology. Longitudinal research follows cohorts over many years to identify how life events affect the individual. The data derived from longitudinal research have been used to develop life-course or integrated theories. Instead of concentrating on one construct (e.g., low self-control, strain, or peer influence), such theories incorporate these and many other variables to explain criminal choices and changes in the propensity to commit crime across the lifespan. While some longitudinal studies ignored women (yet again), more recent studies have included females in the cohort sample and compared men and women. Pathways research is a type of life-course theory specific to women that is not inconsistent with the main body of life-course research.

Life-Course and Integrated Theories

Longitudinal studies identify a *cohort* (a selected group of individuals) and then follow this group for a long period of time, collecting the same types of information at various points in the lifespan. Typically the follow-up period extends throughout childhood and into adulthood. This is a different approach from cross-sectional research, which utilizes a large sample and collects a great deal of information relevant to the dependent variable (delinquency or crime) and to the independent variables (e.g., age, race, religion, economic status). Then statistical tests are conducted to determine the association between the independent variables and the dependent variable (delinquency). Proponents of longitudinal research argue that cross-sectional research cannot discover how factors work at various times in one's life. Proponents of cross-sectional research argue that one can capture that information by utilizing age as an independent variable, and some argue that factors influence individuals similarly at various times in life; therefore no new information is learned by following cohorts for many years. Unfortunately, because longitudinal research is extremely expensive, researchers have access to a limited number of cohort studies. Longitudinal research has been used to develop life-course or developmental theories.

Longitudinal Studies

Several longitudinal studies have contributed immeasurably to our understanding of how criminal choices change over the lifetime. Some of these studies are listed and discussed below.

Gluecks' Study.   Robert Sampson and John Laub[1] used a data set originally collected by Sheldon and Eleanor Glueck in the 1930s in their groundbreaking life-course research study. Two samples (500 each) of boys born between 1924 and 1935 in Boston, one delinquent and the other nondelinquent, were matched by age, race/ethnicity, general intelligence and neighborhood socioeconomic status. Both groups of boys grew up in high-risk environments. Data was collected when the boys were about 14, 25, and 32. The researchers coded and computerized the longitudinal data for analysis.

Across the life course, Sampson and Laub identified both consistency (antisocial traits during childhood predicted adult criminality) and change (most teenagers who engaged in delinquency did not continue to engage in criminality). They and others identify this finding as a paradox—specifically, that criminal men were usually delinquent boys, but that most delinquent boys do not grow up to be criminal men. One of the findings of this study was that informal social ties affect criminality. Supportive of Travis Hirschi's original social control theory, they found that those men who were strongly attached by a stable job, a strong marriage (the strength of the marriage was predictive, but not the fact of being married itself), and ties to the community were less likely to continue to engage in antisocial behavior despite a history of delinquency. Those who were not bound by marriage and other informal social controls were more likely to engage in adult criminality.[2]

Sampson and Laub argued against Gottfredson and Hirschi's[3] premise that there is consistency in criminal propensities over the life course. They found that marriage, moving, and entry into the armed forces were correlated with a reduction of antisocial behaviors, while unemployment was associated with persistence. These researchers argue that types of social control vary by age. When one is young, social control is provided by the family, school, peer groups, and the juvenile justice system. During young adulthood, one may be controlled through higher education, vocational training, work, marriage, and the adult criminal justice system. Middle adulthood controls include work, marriage, parenthood, investment in the community, and the criminal justice system. They see informal social controls as emerging from the "role reciprocities" and interpersonal bonds linking members of society to one another and to wider social institutions such as work, family, and school.[4]

Cambridge Study in Delinquent Development.   Farrington[5] describes the results of the Cambridge Study in Delinquent Development, which tracked a cohort of British men from age 8 to 32:

> [we] found that the typical offender—a male property offender—tends to be born in a low-income, large-sized family and to have criminal parents. When he is young, his parents supervise him rather poorly, use harsh or erratic child-rearing techniques, and are likely to be in conflict and to separate. At school, he tends to have low intelligence and attainment, is troublesome, hyperactive, and impulsive, and often truants. He tends to associate with friends who are also delinquents.[6]

Farrington goes on to describe the young adulthood of the above offender as characterized by frequent unemployment, versatile deviance, violence, vandalism, drug use, drinking, reckless driving, and sexual promiscuity. Criminality declines in the late twenties when these men get married and have children. Their thirties are described as marked by divorce, periodic unemployment or low-paying jobs, frequent moves, heavy drinking, more violence, and more drug taking.[7]

In this Cambridge study, one-third of the men admitted delinquency but five percent were responsible for 50 percent of all delinquent acts. This illustrates how incidence figures (how many crimes were committed by each individual) tell us something more than merely prevalence figures (how many crimes are committed in a community). There was an absolute decline of antisocial acts among all in the cohort between the ages of 18 and 32, but the worst offenders at 18 were also the worst at 32. Farrington and his colleagues concluded that risk factors associated with a persistence of criminality after age 21 included lack of leisure time with father during childhood, low intelligence, employment instability, and heavy drinking. Desistance was associated with the increasing costs of crime (long prison sentences), the importance of intimate relationships, increasing satisfaction with jobs, and becoming more mature, responsible, and settled with age.[8]

OJJDP Youth Development Study. This multi-wave panel study was conducted in Rochester, Pittsburgh, and Denver. More than 4000 youth were interviewed for nearly a decade. The Rochester study started with an initial sample of 1,000 students in 7th and 8th grades during 1987–1988. Data was obtained at six-month intervals over 4.5 years, and then the respondents were interviewed once a year for next three years. Researchers oversampled at-risk youth and males.[9]

The Pittsburg study was an all-male sample. Researchers identified the causal ordering of factors related to delinquency as: difficult temperament, hyperactivity, overt conduct problems/aggressiveness, withdrawal, poor peer relationships, academic problems, covert or concealed conduct problems, association with deviant peers, delinquency (arrest), and recidivism. Delinquent youth were described as having difficulty mastering tasks and negotiating conflict. Researchers identified three developmental pathways—covert behavior (theft, lying, arson, and injury to animals), overt behavior (bullying, violence), and oppositional behavior (argumentativeness, disobedience, disregard of authority). Delinquency was most likely for those boys who followed multiple pathways.[10]

Philadelphia Cohort Study. One of the first longitudinal studies began with a cohort that was born as early as 1945 and eventually included 9,945 children born in Philadelphia. Wolfgang, Thornberry, and Figlio[11] report findings of this longitudinal study that are very similar to those discussed previously—specifically, that individuals have varying levels of delinquency, and those serious delinquents who commit the most delinquency tend to come from more dysfunctional homes. Five distinct classes from non-offenders to high-rate offenders were identified, but early analyses used only males from this cohort.

In later analyses of this cohort that included females, it was found that while males could be described with five groups of varying incidence of delinquency, females were more aptly described with only three: non-offender, low-rate adolescent limited, and high-rate adolescent limited (which compared in crime frequency to low-rate chronic males). Male chronic offenders made up only 8 percent of the sample but accounted for 42 percent of all crimes. No comparable high crime group (as was identified with the male group) was found within the female group.[12] Another study of the same sample found that the extremely small number of serious and violent female delinquents were more likely than males to go on to adult crimes. Boys outnumbered females in all groups: serious delinquents (3:1), violent delinquents (4:1), chronic delinquents (3:1), serious and chronic delinquents (6:1), and violent and chronic delinquents (7:1).[13]

Philadelphia Collaborative Perinatal Project.   This longitudinal study began with a sample of children born between 1959 and 1962 in the inner city of Philadelphia; 87 percent were African American, and they were born to high-risk mothers who took part in free maternal health care during pregnancy. Data included clinical visits, home visits, medical data, and juvenile data. In 1978, 987 of the original 2,958 were randomly selected, and updated information was obtained.[14]

The data concluded that both social and biological factors were correlated with delinquency. Findings indicated that biological factors, such as brain lateralization, ADD, intelligence, low birth weight, lead poisoning, and head injuries all seemed to have some influence on the likelihood of offending.[15] Other findings were that sex/gender was the most important predictor of crime and that biological factors seemed to be more powerful for women than for men as predictive of criminal choices.[16]

Dunedin Study (New Zealand).   Terrie Moffitt and others[17] report on the Dunedin Multidisciplinary Health and Development study in New Zealand. The sample included 1,037 births between 1972 and 1973 in New Zealand. The cohort was followed through adulthood. Moffitt and her colleagues found that some individuals were life-course persistent offenders, meaning that they engaged in a lot of crime as juveniles and continued to commit high levels of crime throughout adulthood. Adolescent limited delinquents were those individuals who aged out of criminality after adolescence. Life-course persistent offenders could be identified through low self-control (measures included the opposite of traits of caution, rationality, high moral standards, and excitement avoidance) and negative emotionality (individuals with high scores were nervous, vulnerable, prone to worry, unable to cope with stress, suspicious, and likely to seek revenge; expected mistreatment; and thought it fun to frighten others). Researchers found that criminal men and women had the same personality profile.

Other findings from this study included a comparison of partner abuse and general crime. Researchers found that the two were distinct. Low self-control was more likely than partner abuse to be predictive of general crime. Researchers noted that this finding supported the feminist argument that partner abuse was partially due to the power dynamics of traditional marriage.[18]

Other Studies.   Other longitudinal studies include the Seattle Social Development Project, the Montreal Longitudinal Experiment Study, and the Harvard Program on Human Development and Criminal Behavior.[19] Generally, longitudinal studies have similar findings although there are continuing controversies as noted below.

Findings from Longitudinal Studies

Farrington[20] notes that most longitudinal studies use cohorts of urban males in Western cultures. We know quite a bit about this group, but not so much about other demographic groups. From these studies we know that offending peaks in late teenage years between the ages of 15 and 19 and declines rapidly during ages 20–29. There is a marked stability in the ordering of frequency of offending through the life course (high offenders remain high offenders and low offenders remain low offenders). Chronic offenders commit a large fraction of all crimes and also engage in behaviors such as heavy drinking, reckless driving, bullying, and truancy. Most offenses in younger years are committed with other offenders; older criminals are more likely to commit crimes alone. There are different types of offending that are prevalent at different years (e.g., shoplifting occurs more at younger ages). Individual risk factors for delinquency include low intelligence, low school achievement, hyperactivity/impulsiveness, risk taking, antisocial child behavior, family factors (poor parental supervision, harsh discipline and physical child abuse, inconsistent discipline, cold parental attitude, neglect, conflict, broken families, criminal parents), socioeconomic factors, peer factors (delinquent peers, peer rejection), school factors (failure), and neighborhood factors. Life events (e.g., marriage, job, moving to a better area, joining the military) encourage desistance after age 20. Findings regarding women can be summarized as follows (although findings are not consistent across all studies): girls and women participate in crime at lower levels than boys and men at all age levels except for similar participation rates for status offenses during juvenile years. The gender ratio increases up until the mid 20s, but in later years (after 50), men's and women's offending rates become more similar. Late onset criminality appears to be more common with female offenders.[21]

The findings from longitudinal studies have been the basis of so-called integrated theories because a wide range of factors, both biological and environmental, have been incorporated into a life-phase-specific theory of criminal decision making. Latent traits (biological predispositions, such as low cognitive functioning) are recognized, as well as the importance of primary caregivers. Biological traits interact with environment and are more influential in adverse social environments than in supportive environments. In other words, early prevention can be effective in muting the influence of latent traits. During school-age years, the experience in school may either promote pro-social activities or push the child into delinquency through failure, rejection, and labeling and then delinquent peers become important in reinforcing and increasing delinquent behaviors.[22]

Farrington[23] posits a model that includes different stages of developing delinquent/criminal behavior patterns. At first, *energizing factors* (desires for material goods, status among intimates, excitement, boredom, frustration, anger, and alcohol consumption) tempt individuals to commit delinquent acts. Then, in the *directing stages*, socially disapproved methods of satisfying motivations are either habitually chosen or not. The *inhibiting stage* is the process by which antisocial tendencies can be reduced by internalized beliefs and attitudes that are built through the social learning process, a history of rewards and punishments, a strong conscience (which Farrington believes comes from love and close supervision), and empathy (which comes from parental warmth and loving relationships). Those with high impulsivity and low intelligence are less able to build up internal inhibitions against offending. In the *decision-making stage*, the actual choice of criminal action (or not) depends on opportunity costs and benefits and subjective probabilities of different outcomes for each situation.

Sampson and Laub also proposed a developmental theory from their longitudinal research:

- a set of *predisposing factors* (structural and background factors, low family SES, family size, family disruption, residential mobility, parents' deviance, household crowding, being foreign born, mother's employment);

- combined with *individual constructs* (difficult temperament, persistent tantrums, early conduct disorder);

- which interact with *social control processes* (family, lack of supervision, threatening/erratic harsh discipline, parental rejection, school, weak attachment, poor performance, delinquent influence, peer delinquent attachment, sibling delinquent attachment);

- that then lead to *delinquency*, which damages social bonds, weakens labor force attachment, and weakens marital attachment (which in turn creates the likelihood of continued crime).

Sampson and Laub discuss the changes and directions during the life course as turning points and trajectories—in other words, things that happen (divorce, loss of job) can push individuals in one direction, while other types of events (happy marriage, obtaining a degree) can move the individual in a completely different direction. This is the essence of the life-course perspective—that the individual and the environment are both important in whether or not criminality is sustained.[24]

Widom[25] also presented an integrated theory of criminal behavior and psychopathology. Physiological and genetic predispositions (including sex/gender) interact with socialization experiences to produce personality, which then affects situational factors that lead to behavior. Behavior, in turn, leads to society's response that then affects individual attitudes, norms, and expectations about behavior.

Many of these researchers cautiously include biological factors in their developmental schemas as predisposing factors.[26] Denno,[27] for instance, incorporated both biological and sociological factors in an integrated explanation of criminality and delinquency. She identified predisposing factors that were largely genetic or familial (that increase the likelihood of criminality), facilitating variables (that, in combination with predisposing, increase the likelihood of delinquency), and inhibiting variables (that counteract predisposing factors and decrease the probability of delinquency). Different factors affected delinquency over the life course. At birth, individuals are already affected by such factors as culture, gender, prenatal material conditions, pregnancy and delivery complications, socioeconomic status, and family stability. By age seven, other factors such as cerebral dominance, intelligence, and physical and health development have influenced predispositions to delinquency, and during the pre-teen and teen years, school behavior and achievement (affected by intelligence and learning disabilities) affect the likelihood of delinquency and eventually adult crime.[28]

Blumstein and Cohen[29] were instrumental in beginning what became known as career-criminal research, which found that a small number of criminals committed a large portion of all crime. These individuals continued chronic criminality well past the age at which most offenders' criminality declined. Some other life-course and development theorists also identify life-course persistent delinquency as distinct from adolescent-limited delinquency (social delinquency that most youth mature out of). Life-course persistent delinquents are also called early-onset delinquents because they commit crime earlier, commit more crime, and persist in crime later than others. Correlates of early-onset delinquency include low intelligence, high impulsiveness, child abuse, harsh and erratic parental discipline, cold and rejecting parents, poor parental supervision, parental disharmony, separation, and divorce, one-parent female-headed households, convicted parents or siblings, alcoholic or drug-using parents or siblings, non-white race membership, low occupational prestige of parents, low educational level of parents, low family income, large family size, poor housing, low educational attainment of the child, attendance at a high-delinquency school, delinquent friends, and a high-crime area of residence.[30]

Describing the New Zealand cohort, Moffitt[31] identified both an early-onset and an adolescent-onset delinquent group. The delinquent group that began in childhood was more likely to exhibit low verbal ability, hyperactivity, and negative/impulsive personality. The adolescent onset group was more likely to engage in property crime; the childhood onset group was more likely to commit violent crime.[32]

Other researchers have found empirical support for the presence of an early-onset life-course persister group, and there is evidence that the group can be distinguished by biological factors (low birth weight and neurological deficits).[33] More recent research continues to explore the contribution of genetics and finds that genetic influence has a strong and direct correlation with life-course persistent offending that is not mediated by parenting practices.[34]

Gottfredson and Hirschi[35] and Sampson and Laub[36] do not believe these distinct groups exist. They argue that all offenders desist over time and that the only difference is the relative rate of offending, which is consistent over the life span (with high-offending-rate delinquents desisting, but doing so at a level different from the low-offending group). They also argue that while any retrospective analyses may identify persisters, they do not capture those who have died or are incapacitated. In addition, prospective studies do not result in high prediction levels (i.e., many youth who possess the characteristics do not go on to become life-course persisters). Sampson and Laub did, however, identify a small group (about 3%) who were high-rate chronics with a later peak age and later desistance.

To sum up the differences between theorists, Gottfredson and Hirschi believe that low self-control is static throughout life and that the level of self-control predicts high offending or low offending, which remains at a constant level (although all offenders gradually desist). Sampson and Laub believe that life events affect offending and that these life events occur in age-graded patterns (e.g., work and marriage in the second decade of life) that reduce offending in predictable ways. Moffitt and others believe there are individual differences that emerge early and interact with life events. While most offenders' criminality can be predicted using age-graded events as Sampson and Laub propose, one group (early-onset) maintains high levels of crime for a much longer period. This small group (3–5%) is described as having low self-control (which they characterize as a biological construct of impulsivity) as well as other factors (e.g., dysfunctional family and learning disabilities).[37]

Application of Life-Course Theories to Girls/Women

Unfortunately, cohort samples for longitudinal studies have often excluded women. For instance, in the Harvard longitudinal study prenatal cohorts included both boys and girls, but later sampling contained only boys because researchers were concerned with obtaining "a sufficient number of predatory and violent offenders in the study population."[38] In Blumstein, Cohen, Roth, and Visher's[39] longitudinal study no women appeared in the sample, and the sex of the offender was not a study factor in their findings regarding career criminals. Illustrative of the early neglect of women, in a leading text on life-course criminology there are no entries in the index for women, sex, or gender![40] Farrington[41] explains why women were excluded from his longitudinal sample:

> Because of the difficulty of establishing causal effects of factors that vary only between individuals (e.g., gender and ethnicity), and because such factors have no practical implications for prevention (e.g., it is not practicable to change males into females), unchanging variables will not be reviewed. . . . In any case, their effects on offending are usually explained by reference to other, changeable, factors. . . . For example, gender differences in offending have been explained on the basis of different socialization methods used by parents with boys and girls, or different opportunities of males and females for offending.[42]

This is an interesting comment and deserves some attention. At first, he seems to say that because sex is an unchangeable factor, it is not worth studying. This begs the question, however, as to what it is about sex that affects the choice of crime. Then he changes the explanation so that it is not sex that explains the crime differential between men and women, but some other factors such as socialization or opportunities that, arguably, are subject to change. If socialization patterns influenced the inclination to make criminal choices, it seems one would want to study socialization differences. However, if one's sample was composed entirely of boys, it would be impossible to examine how such a factor worked differently on girls and boys to account for their different crime rates.

Farrington[43] goes on to discuss mother-only households, Attention Deficit Disorder (ADD) and hyperactivity (learning disabilities that are much more prevalent among boys), sensation seeking, low physiological arousal, intelligence, poor supervision and erratic discipline, neglectful parenting, broken homes, criminal parents, large families, socioeconomic status, poor housing or public housing, socially disorganized neighborhoods, and peers as causal elements in the development of delinquency. By excluding women from the cohort sample, this study is unable to determine the relative effects of these factors on male and female delinquency and criminality.

The Philadelphia cohort studied by Denno and others did include girls/women. Denno reported that there were 487 male and 500 females in the sample. While 31 percent of the men had at least one police contact prior to age 18, only 14 percent of the women experienced contact with police. These percentages are lower than a general sample of juveniles in Philadelphia at the same time, and the authors speculate that it was possible that the continued attention by researchers to these families protected children from social influences that encourage delinquency (the *Hawthorne effect*). It is possible, then, that biological influences would take on greater importance in this sample because of the reduced power of social influences.

Denno's findings indicated that 17 percent of male offenders and 10 percent of female offenders in the cohort could be defined as chronic, committing two to four offenses. The mean level of seriousness of offenses was nearly 2.5 times greater for the men as compared to the women in the sample.[44] Denno characterized sex as the vehicle of differences in brain lateralization, ADD, MAO levels, and testosterone that were recorded between delinquents and nondelinquents.[45] While the effects of sex can be moderated by the environment, the influence is strong. Further, because socialization and biology both act to insulate women against criminal choices, such factors should be measurably stronger in a female sample in the direction toward delinquency/criminality. In other words, delinquent/criminal women should be expected to have even higher likelihoods of biological factors (e.g., lower IQ), or socialization factors (extreme dysfunctions in family/social environments).[46] Findings generally supported the idea that biological and socialization factors suppressed female criminality. However, even utilizing all the biological and environmental variables identified, Denno was unable to explain a large portion of the variance in behavior.[47] Thus, the relationship between social and biological factors remains largely unexplained.

Moffitt and others find that women are less likely to belong to the life-course persistent group, largely because the biological and psychological characteristics (low birth weight, neuropsychological deficits, birth complications and early conduct disorder) of the group are more commonly found in males. The argument is that the gender differential is less extreme in adolescent years because most adolescent delinquency is social (and both boys and girls engage in social delinquency); but adult crime is more likely to be chronic, and that's when gender differences emerge.[48] The few tests that have been done to determine whether these assumptions are true have had mixed results.[49] In one study to determine if female persisters could be identified, an inmate sample was used. Persistence was measured simply as arrests as both a juvenile and adult (which might be questioned as a good measure of persistence). Researchers found that adult persistence was associated with being a gang member, having a friend arrested as an adult, and having been sexually abused; interestingly, none of the biological factors (head injury, low birth weight, etc.) were significant. On the other hand, the study was fairly small (n = 131) and used an incarcerated population, so the effect sizes of variables would not be the same as in a general population study.[50]

Pathways Research

Traditional sex-role theory explained that females are less likely to engage in delinquency or crime because they are socialized to "be nice" and avoid risk. Pathways research, emerging in the late 1980s and 1990s, identified sex-specific life events that pushed some girls/women into delinquency/crime despite gender-specific socialization against criminal choices. Specifically, this research focuses on the greater likelihood of girls to be subject to childhood victimization that leads to running away, high-risk sexual activity, early pregnancy and single motherhood, drug use, and crime.

High Rates of Childhood Sexual Victimization

One of the most long-standing and consistent findings in studies of correctional populations is that female offenders experience childhood victimization at higher rates than male offenders, and both groups experience higher rates of victimization than the general population.[51] Some studies report up to three-quarters, but usually over half, of female offender populations report childhood victimization (either physical, sexual, neglect, or a combination).[52] Some report that female offenders' lifetime prevalence rate of victimization is two to three times higher than that of the general population.[53] Their rate of victimization is also higher than male offenders': female offenders are seven times more likely to have experienced sexual abuse and four times more likely to have experienced physical abuse, according to one study.[54] Many studies document the finding that female offenders are much more likely than male offenders to report victimization.[55]

More recent studies continue to find high rates of victimization among female offender samples.[56] For instance, the reported lifetime prevalence for the general population is about 15 to 24 percent, but in one sample of incarcerated women, 38 percent reported rape victimization, and 72 percent reported some form of coerced sex. Almost a quarter of these incarcerated women reported that their attacker was someone in authority.[57] In another study, using a random sample of 403 women entering prison, it was found that female prisoners (especially those who had experienced homelessness and/or were single) experienced significantly more traumatic life events (including childhood and adult victimization) than the general population.[58]

One of the interesting findings from some prison researchers using qualitative methodology is that women often don't even realize how dysfunctional and abnormal their childhood was. Far from using childhood victimization as an excuse for their criminality, they more often tend to excuse and rationalize their parents' or other relatives' abuse by saying such things as "I can't blame my parents, I always had a roof over my head," even if under that roof they were emotionally or physically abused.[59] For instance, one female offender was asked, "Did either of your parents abuse you . . . ?" And, the answer was, "No, I just got hit a lot. . . ."[60] Another female inmate told an interviewer that she had a good relationship with her mother and considered her to have been a good mother, but later she explained that her mother was in prison because of drugs and that, as a child, she had to live with other relatives because of her mother's drug use.[61]

The abuse that many female offenders experienced as children was severe, chronic, and devastating in its consequences. Medical science is only just beginning to understand the role of stress on physical health, and traumatic life events are well-known precursors to mental and physical health complications. Many justice-involved women have experienced multiple and/or chronic trauma, including rape, incest, physical beatings, death threats, the murder or serious injury of loved ones, kidnapping, emotional abuse, and other traumatic events. One woman, for instance, described her rape by her father's best friend when she was seven and repeated beatings by her father:

> . . . those people hurt me, man, they hurt me . . . and that's why I guess I got to a point where I said nothing's gonna hurt me no more, nobody's gonna see me shed a tear for nothing that they did to me. I remember when my dad used to put a gun to my head, it took all fear away from me from dying. . . .[62]

It should be noted that the prevalence of victimization is replicated in jail and prison samples, in pre-sentence reports, and in longitudinal studies. In fact, the strikingly different experiential histories of male and female offenders spurred one researcher to write, "Traumatic experiences were so common for women in this sample that trauma could be described as a defining feature of their lives."[63]

Gilfus reinforced others' findings that women experience a constellation of factors from childhood victimization—including living on the street, drug dependence, and high-risk lifestyles—that contribute to their further victimization.[64] Wesely,[65] in a study of homeless women and exotic dancers, many of whom also had criminal justice involvement, found that about half had endured childhood sexual victimization. The majority of the women described horrific childhoods marked by physical, sexual, and emotional abuse. They described how they were told they were worthless and "only good for one thing [sex]." Some were indoctrinated into sex work by their mothers. They left home early, and many entered into relationships with abusive men: "I guess I was trying to get affection from anywhere I could, because I wasn't getting it from my father or my parents. So I guess when the other two guys showed the affection, I just kinda clinged to it."[66]

A sad element of these women's descriptions of their lives is how their own daughters (and sons) experience similar childhoods, being victimized by the women's husbands and boyfriends. Their experiences of violence led them to believe that it was an inevitable part of life: "I thought that's the way life was. Because in the neighborhood I grew up in, it was nothing to see a woman dragged, knocked down, stomped and beat. . . . You were just supposed to take it."[67] The women in Wesely's study had experience with the criminal justice system as victims, and then as offenders. None of their experiences with the criminal justice system were positive and, in fact, some of them reported that police officers were the perpetrators of assault or victimization. About half of the group admitted violence themselves, although typically it was in an effort to stop an assault.

In her qualitative analysis of 24 young girls in custody for assault or robbery, Ryder[68] reports that the girls' lives were characterized by "multiple episodes of loss and violence." Seventy-five percent of the girls were beaten, burned, kicked, hit, bitten, and exposed to other forms of physical abuse, while over a fourth had experienced sexual victimization.

Childhood Victimization and Correlates.   Correlations between childhood victimization and a range of behavioral and emotional effects are also consistent and long-standing. Childhood victimization has been linked to mental health-related complications such as depression, post-traumatic stress disorder, anxiety, low self-esteem, self-hatred, and suicide attempts.[69] Childhood victimization has also been linked to adolescent and adult drug dependency.[70] Arguably, female survivors of rape, incest, and childhood sexual abuse use illegal drugs to self-medicate to alleviate the mental health effects described above.[71] Unfortunately, illegal drug use has become one of the most important factors in the huge increase in the number of women in prison, and studies indicate that there is a constellation of drug use and selling, sex work, and victimization that characterizes the lives of many female offenders.[72]

Researchers have linked childhood sexual victimization to high-risk lifestyles (multiple partners, strangers as partners, no protection against sexually transmitted disease).[73] Others have documented the correlation between childhood sexual victimization and prostitution.[74] Prostitution, as well as a range of property crimes, is often committed to support female offenders' drug addiction.[75] Unfortunately, this life path creates a high risk for recurrent victimization, as one offender describes:

> Street life . . . it's a power game, you know? . . . You have to show you're tough. You have to beat up this broad or you have to shank this person, or . . . it has so much fucking abuse, it has more abuse. . . . I find living on the street I went through more abuse than I did at home.[76]

Recurrent Victimization.   Female offenders are much more likely than male offenders to report adult victimization, including rape and battering. Studies find that women who have been sexually victimized are at a higher risk of subsequent victimization.[77] Browne and Finkelhor[78] reported that 33 to 68 percent of childhood sexual abuse victims were raped later in life compared to 17 percent of a nonvictim group. Also, 49 percent of victims versus 18 percent of non-abused in one study reported being adult victims of domestic abuse. The finding that those who have been sexually victimized are at a higher risk for subsequent victimization is consistent across offender populations and non-offender populations. For instance, one study used a college sample to show the correlation.[79] This is an interesting finding, indicating that structural problems (i.e., poverty or involvement in the drug trade) are not the only factors leading to future victimization, but also suggesting maladaptive behaviors and attitudes as contributing factors. For instance, acceptance of rape myths and sex-role stereotypes, low self-esteem, learned helplessness, substance abuse, and poor partner selection might be some of the factors potentially associated with revictimization.

The high risk of revictimization has also been explained as "traumatic sexualization" (i.e., girls learn to use sex to gain affection and consequently adopt high-risk lifestyles). Another explanation is that the betrayal by trusted adult figures leads to dependency, impaired judgment and vulnerability, and the powerlessness experienced by child-victims leads to learned helplessness. Stigmatization experienced by child-victims who believe they are at fault leads to self-blame and esteem issues, all of which leads to high-risk lifestyles. High correlations between victimization and alcohol use have been found. More psychosocial factors (compulsion to repeat trauma, or disassociation) receive less empirical support.[80]

Childhood Victimization and Crime.   Childhood victimization has been linked to delinquency and adult criminality for both girls/women and boys/men. Researchers, especially Cathy Widom, have identified the link between childhood victimization and crime.[81] In fact, this association seems to be stronger for females than for males.[82] There also seems to be a stronger link between childhood sexual victimization and violent crime than property crime.[83]

In a longitudinal study, a sample of 127 adjudicated female delinquents were reinterviewed as young adults 13 years later. Researchers found that abuse as a teenager (physical or sexual) was the only variable that distinguished higher versus lower criminality among the group as adults. Those with the highest sexual abuse scores as minors were 334 percent more likely than those with the lowest scores to be in the highest offender group. Abuse did not predict levels of adolescent delinquency—only adult crime. It should be remembered that those in the adolescent sample were already institutionalized, so there may not have been enough differences between them for significance between abuse and delinquency to emerge.[84]

In Siegel and Williams'[85] longitudinal study, beginning with a cohort of sexual abuse victims from hospital records and a matched control group, the same correlations between abuse and adult crime was found. Abuse was not correlated with adolescent property delinquency but was associated with running away and violent crimes: 14 percent of those who reported victimization were arrested for violent offenses compared to 6 percent in the control group. For property crime, the respective rates of participation were 9 percent compared to 6 percent.

The relationship between victimization and criminality can be explained by several different crime theories. Under social control (bonds) theory, victimization (which is generally by family members or not prevented by family members) would prevent attachment, which would, in turn, create a greater likelihood of delinquency. Under the general theory, victimization might be considered part of a constellation of factors involved in poor parenting that leads to low self-control. Under general strain, victimization would cause an affective state (anger or depression) that leads to delinquency. Manasse and Ganem reviewed the existing research linking childhood victimization to delinquency/crime and then, using two waves of the National Youth Survey, tested a number of hypotheses related to this link. These researchers found a significant correlation between childhood victimization and delinquency and a correlation between childhood victimization and depression. They discussed the tendency of victimization to result in internalizing behaviors for girls and externalizing behaviors for boys. In other words, girls reacted to victimization with depression, but that depression did not manifest in anger/delinquency as it did for boys. These researchers concluded that their findings supported general strain theory.[86] The findings also are consistent with the pathways approach.

> . . . all of mine [drug use] come from my childhood life 'cos I was raped at the age of 12 . . . by three men. I don't know who they were. I was on my way walking to school . . . and I'm 32 years old and I still think about it. It bothers me a lot. [Then] when I was 15 I been beat up so badly by men [sic] . . . [I stayed with him] because I didn't have nowhere else to go.[87]

There are other ways that past sexual abuse may be linked to criminality. As noted above, one of the consequences of childhood abuse is post-traumatic stress disorder (PTSD). One of the symptoms is hyper (or hypo) arousal and/or flashbacks. It seems likely that some of women's violent crimes may be due to PTSD, as the following quote suggests:

> . . . The officer put his hands on me, and I went right back to the last time I was raped. And I fought like hell. I wasn't ever going to let a man touch me like that again. So I kicked him and tried to grab his gun and if I'd gotten it, I would have shot him. I know I would have. . . . If someone moves towards me too fast, I'll just go off. And then I have nightmares all night long.[88]

Criminal Pathways

Kathleen Daly[89] is credited as being one of the first to organize the findings above to develop the pathways theory of female criminality, although many others have also contributed to the development of the pathways approach.[90] The idea is that female offenders are more likely than male offenders to experience prior victimization, substance addiction, dysfunctional familial relationships, and economic marginalization. This leads to adaptations (running away, drug use, and high-risk sexual behavior, including prostitution) that lead to entrenched criminal lifestyles. Daly offered a typology of female offenders that included:

- Street women—women who flee abusive homes, become addicts, and commit survival crimes (prostitution, drug dealing);
- Drug connected—women who use, manufacture and/or distribute drugs because of an intimate partner or family-based relationship;
- Harmed and harming—women who live in turbulent, chaotic living conditions of abuse and neglect; have a tough, bully-like demeanor; and are as likely to be an aggressor as a victim (and often both in the same relationship);
- Battered women—for whom violence is confined to relationships with violent intimate partners; and
- Other—women who do not fit into any of the types above; crime stems from greed or economic necessity.[91]

Some of the women in Wesely's research,[92] for instance, clearly fit into Daly's "harmed and harming" category. They reacted with disproportional violence to perceived threats or slights. This violence is only slightly understood by the women themselves as a reaction to years of abuse: ". . . but after so many years of taking all my dad's crap, when I got there, I started beating the shit out of her." And: "Men that was violent to me, I didn't do nothing to them. But the one who was sweet to me I'd be violent to." The most violent woman in Wesely's sample was also the most victimized. She was raped by a school janitor in the third grade, her mother tried to kill her, she was molested by her stepfather and gang raped at 14, and her husband beat her. She had served three prison terms for aggravated assault with a firearm, attempted murder, arson, and domestic violence.

DeHart also described women who had experienced extreme, unrelenting victimization as children and grew up to be violent themselves: "She hurt me. I hurt somebody else. . . . The low man on the totem pole got to catch all the weight. . . ."[93] DeHart interviewed 60 women in prison, finding that their earlier victimization led directly or indirectly to criminality. Victimization directly led to criminality when the woman killed or injured her abuser, either in a defensive interaction or as retaliation for past abuse. For instance: "Josie's boyfriend jumped her at her mother's house. Josie stabbed him something like 12 times. She was tired of him flipping on her."[94] Victimization indirectly led to criminality when chronic abuse or early childhood abuse led to drug use; for instance, women who were indoctrinated into drug use and/or prostitution by a parent or older sibling. Another indirect path was when such abuse led to running away and entry into a criminal lifestyle. Abuse as an adult also could set in motion a pathway to crime when, for instance, an abusive ex-husband continually harassed the woman, leading to her eviction from housing and loss of a legitimate job (because of him appearing at her house or job and acting violently). This led, in turn, to her selling drugs to survive.

DeHart, similarly to Robert Sampson in his life-course theory, discussed "turning points" that either led to criminal decisions or the choice of a different, noncriminal way of life. As examples of turning points, she cites the death of a loved one, the loss of a child to child protective services, family disruption (e.g., a parent going to prison), pregnancy and/or childbirth, finding or losing a job, criminal justice involvement, and finding religion. Some of these turning points could be either positive or negative; for instance, pregnancy could spur a woman to get and stay clean or the birth of a new baby could create enough stress to push the woman back into using drugs for coping. Buffers that seemed to avert criminal decision making included a good job and caring adult role models.

Salisbury and Van Voorhis[95] used path analysis with 313 female probationers who had been administered the Women's Needs and Risk Assessment instrument (developed with the support of the National Institute of Corrections). These researchers found that three pathways (identified from the literature) could be identified in their sample of female offenders:

1. a childhood victimization path that included mental illness and substance abuse;

2. a relational pathway that included dysfunctional relationships, domestic violence, adult victimization, low self-esteem, current mental illness, and substance abuse; and

3. a social and human-capital deficit pathway that included very low educational levels and unemployment along with deficits in social/family support.

The most recent research on pathways uses statistical analysis, large samples, and a multitude of variables to determine if types of offenders emerge through factor analysis. Brennan[96] and his colleagues reviewed previous research and concluded that the following female types have emerged in the growing literature using female offender samples:

1. *Normal or situational female offenders.* These women have few risk factors (little abuse, minor school problems, minor family dysfunction), minor histories of property or drug crimes, and few psychological markers indicating distress.

2. *Offenders with an "adolescent limited" pathway.* This title refers to Moffitt's type, characterized by limited delinquency during adolescence and few risk factors.

3. *Offenders with a victimized, socially withdrawn and depressed pathway.* These women have experienced early abuse and childhood trauma (such as witnessing murder). Their childhoods have led them to be mistrustful, hostile, and depressed. They are involved in drug abuse and crime.

4. *Chronic, serious offenders.* Women in this group also experienced early physical and/or sexual abuse, child behavior problems, school and family problems, and delinquency. They are characterized by low self-control, an aggressive, hostile personality, and ongoing criminality. The type is most similar to Daly's "harmed and harming" pathway and Moffitt's life-course persistent offender described earlier.

5. *Socialized offenders and socially marginalized groups:* This pathway identifies poor, marginalized, uneducated women who come from disorganized families, have experienced ineffective parenting, and have been socialized in subcultural and deprived settings.

Brennan and his colleagues[97] then undertake their own statistical analyses to isolate and identify statistical types based on a large number of variables consistent with the pathways approach, including victimization and abuse, mental health markers, intimate relationship conflict or dysfunction, housing safety, family-of-origin variables such as supportive parents, personal and psychological factors such as anxiety and depression, and employment and educational history. Their research led to the identification of eight separate pathways that can be statistically distinguished:

• **Pathway 1:** Drug-abusing young women. Women in this path were usually single and under 30. They had better social resources than those on other paths and came from lower-crime areas. They possessed fewer vocational and educational deficits than others, fewer financial problems, greater residential stability, and more supportive families. Very few had any mental health problems, and there was little evidence of prior victimization of any type. They had minor criminal histories, usually of nonviolent property and drug offenses.

• **Pathway 2:** Drug-abusing older women. The average age in this category was 40. This group had most of the same characteristics of the prior group. The major difference between this group and pathway 1 was age and the fact that this group of women were not actively parenting. Their children were grown.

• **Pathway 3:** Battered women. These women were usually single mothers of children under age 18. Their lives were characterized by lifelong physical and sexual abuse. They exhibited depression and substance abuse and were in adult abusive relationships. The significant others of these women led them to legal trouble. Although they exhibited depression, they did not manifest psychosis or antisocial personality traits. They experienced substantial marginalization (poverty, housing instability, and unemployment). Their criminal history was minor, mostly for drug or property offenses; however, family violence was also a feature. A high percentage of women in this group were in prison for the first time.

• **Pathway 4:** Older battered women. Once again, the major difference between this group and the prior group was age. Drug abuse was chronic. Criminal history was more pronounced as compared to those in previous pathway; however, the women in the previous pathway were more likely than this group to have current family violence charges. Women in Pathway 4 also exhibited higher levels of anxiety related to parenting and more depression than those in Pathway 3.

- **Pathway 5:** Marginalized mothers. This group constituted younger, extremely poor, single mothers in conflicted (but not violent) relationships. They had few social or economic resources and experienced high residential instability. These women experienced high parenting stress, low self-efficacy, and poor social support. There was little evidence of childhood victimization or mental health issues. They possessed an above-average criminal history with prior arrests for drugs, including trafficking, and property crime.

- **Pathway 6:** Older drug-addicted women. These women also experienced extreme marginalization but were not actively parenting children younger than 18. Most were single and older, with an average age of 40 years. These women were less likely than the women in the previous pathway to have significant others who created legal trouble for them.

- **Pathway 7:** Abused and aggressive women. This pathway is similar to Daly's harmed and harming women. They experienced the most extreme childhood victimization, disrupted childhoods (with state placement involvement), and violent adult relationships; and they exhibited significant mental health issues. They were extremely marginalized with little economic or social resources. These women also were likely to have children and experience parental stress. They had above-average criminal histories and multiple prior detentions, violent institutional infractions, but largely nonviolent drug and property offense convictions.

- **Pathway 8:** Abused and addicted single mothers with serious mental health issues. These women exhibited serious mental health issues, including psychosis and suicide ideation. They were also aggressive, violent, and noncompliant. Most had children. They were as extremely marginalized as pathway 7, however psychological factors were even more prominent for this group, with higher than average measures of hostility, antisocial personality, low self-efficacy, aimlessness, and social isolation. Their residential stability was higher than that of women in the previous path and they were more likely to have had a full-time job and be married. They were the most violent group, with the highest rate of prior violent offenses, weapons offenses, disciplinary infractions, and domestic violence incidents.

Brennan and his colleagues discuss the possibility that those studies which do not find links between childhood victimization and criminality may miss the correlation because they analyze female offenders as one group, when in fact there are diverse pathways as described above.[98] For some women (pathways 1, 2, 5, and 6) victimization is not relevant to their criminal decision making, but for other women (pathways 3, 4, 7, and 8) victimization is extremely relevant. Future research no doubt will continue to utilize factor analysis to determine if it is necessary to discuss eight pathways or some smaller number, and how pathways can increase our understanding of criminal decision making and inform treatment options.

Relationship to Life-Course Theories.   It should be noted that pathways research has not, until recently, been as comprehensive as some life-course theories in both in its methodology and its scope of explanation. Life-course theories do take note of traumatic life events in a manner similar to pathways research, but they also measure other differences (e.g., learning deficiencies, brain injuries, school-based experiences, jobs, and so on). In fact, life-course and longitudinal studies that include females in the sample have supported the finding that female offenders are more likely than male offenders to have experienced childhood victimization. The advantage of pathways research over the larger life-course studies is the rich detail of female offenders' lives, clearly showing how criminal choices were sometimes inevitable choices for women who survived horrific childhoods only to re-create such environments for their own children.

It is also important to note that the pathways model, as most theorists refer to it, explains the path to criminality for only some women. Daly found there were many women who committed crime for arguably the same purely acquisitive/economic reasons many men did. More recent research, such as that of Brennan and his colleagues, shows that there are multiple pathways describing very distinct groups of women, not all of whom experienced childhood victimization.

Pathways and Race/Ethnicity.   One's identity as an African American, Hispanic, or white woman in this society influences every aspect of life. Too often, we forget to note that race/ethnicity may be more important, or at least as important, as one's sex in determining one's life choices and experiences.[99] For instance, minority women are differentially impacted by long drug sentences for certain kinds of targeted drugs (crack cocaine) as compared to drugs of choice for middle-class whites (prescription drug abuse), so much so that many call the War on Drugs a de facto war on African Americans, especially African American women.[100]

Researchers[101] have shown, for instance, that social-psychological issues (i.e., family disorganization) seem to be more criminogenic for white women than for African American women, while structural factors (economic marginalization) seem to be more predictive for African American women.

Miller's[102] and Richie's[103] investigations of the crime paths of African American women have helped us understand some of the differences in life paths between racial/ethnic groups. Miller,[104] for instance, concluded that African American women were more likely than white or Latina women to enter crime through domestic networks (i.e., family members), while the other two groups were more likely to do so because of running away or drug use.

Richie[105] identified a number of different pathways for African American women's entry into crime. Being involved with an abusive and criminal partner led to crimes either with him or against him. Faced with few or no economic sources, some black women engage in sex work and other crimes. Richie describes how women of color in the correctional system have experienced physical assaults, emotional degradation, marginalization, and overt racism, all of which create a "web of despair" around them. Despite this, many show resolve and resistance—they are survivors. Arnold[106] also discusses the role of early victimization of African American women in their subsequent dislocation from family and other institutions of society.

Richie urges researchers to approach female criminality, including the correlate of race, as a structural issue. That is, black women's experiences as victims and offenders are often viewed as individual pathology, but economic marginalization, social stigma, lack of social resources, and punitive public policies affect them at every stage of life.[107]

Lujan[108] described Native American women who are also disproportionately represented in the nation's prisons. These women's lives are marked by alcohol and despair. Some statistics indicate that over 70 percent of crimes committed by American Indians are alcohol related.[109] In part because of their small numbers, the experiences of Native American and Hispanic/Latina women in the criminal justice system have not been understood or explored by researchers.

Theories based on power cannot ignore class and race. Simpson and Elis[110] offered one of the few attempts to combine factors of gender and race/ethnicity to understand delinquency and crime. They proposed that "hegemonic" masculinities and femininities are defined within social institutions such as work, family, peer groups, and school, but that gender is modified by race/ethnicity.

Making Sense of Theoretical Findings

While all of the theories and findings in Chapters 3, 4, and 5 may be confusing, it is possible to create an integrated understanding of why female criminality occurs at a lower level than men's (except for certain categories of property crime). First, most theorists now accept that there are some biological sex differences that go beyond reproductive abilities. These brain chemistry differences predispose the female of the species to be more altruistic, nurturing, and relationship oriented and the male of the species to be more aggressive and autonomous. Thus, females are pre-wired for caring. The biological mechanisms of this difference are variances in levels of serotonin, MAO, and neurotransmitters that affect emotions and behavior.

Sex differences affect the development of a conscience that would inhibit victim-harming behavior. Psychological research[111] has found differences between men's and women's analysis of moral judgments (conscience), which tend to be justice or rule-based for both men and women (because we are all socialized similarly) but can be care-based for women (when certain dilemmas are analyzed). Low self-control or impulsivity may explain much delinquency, but the conscience is still an important restraint on behavior.[112] Many biological differences between men and women, such as conditionability and cognitive deficiencies, suggest that learning (which is important for the development of a conscience) is more problematic for boys than for girls. Various studies have indicated that guilt/shame seems to be more potent for girls than for boys. This supports the idea that learning, necessary for development of a conscience, is less subject to deficits in girls than in boys.

Both biological and socialization differences are important.[113] Girls are still raised differently, and sex-role theory is still salient as an explanation for the gender differential in crime. Measurements indicate that girls/women have stronger attachments than boys/men, which strengthens care-based moral thinking and reduces the risk of delinquency and criminality. This may be why female criminality has not expanded into violent crime (the ultimate victim-harming behavior), as predicted by liberation theory, but has increased in property crime areas where empathizing with victims is more difficult.

Of course there are women who do commit crimes, even violent crimes, and there always have been. This can be explained by the simple fact of human variability within groups. There is also evidence to indicate that biological factors (e.g., cognitive deficiencies) or environmental factors (e.g., child abuse) seem to be stronger among female offender samples than in male offender samples. This indicates that these factors must be extreme in order to overcome the predisposition and socialization of women to avoid victim-harming behavior. Concurrently, other evidence indicates that criminal women are much more likely than male offenders to have had extremely dysfunctional and/or abusive childhoods—also indicative that "normal" socialization usually insulates women from criminal life paths.

There is also some evidence to indicate that many crimes by women can be considered affiliative, albeit misdirected. Research indicates that many crimes committed by women have different motives from those committed by men (e.g., to help an intimate partner).[114] The finding that many, if not most, female offenders have been abused as children has been used to speculate that these damaged women are more prone to engage in a lifelong pattern of codependency that often involves committing crimes to hang on to a relationship.

In short, men are predisposed to crime because of biological, psychological, and socialization influences that act as barriers to the development of a care-based conscience and guilt; and women's biological, psychological and socialization influences are congruent with (and indeed strengthen the development of) a care-based conscience. Findings from biological research (brain chemistry differences that predispose women to emphasize affiliation), psychological research (proposing that gender identification leads to "connectedness" and affiliation for women and autonomy for men), or sociological research (arguing that girls are socialized to be more sensitive to others while boys are socialized to be self-centered) support this proposition that there are fundamental differences between men and women that would affect decisions to commit delinquency or crime. It also explains age-graded desistence from crime, since both biological evidence (indicating that brain chemistry changes over the lifespan) and sociological evidence (that attachment bonds increase with marriage and children in the 20s) support the idea that men desist from crime when they become "more like women" (i.e., less testosterone and MAO and more bonds to others). Increasing men's (and some women's) care-based conscience would not necessarily involve the cognitive-based approaches so common in corrections today unless those interventions also addressed such things as egocentricity, responsibility, and empathy.[115]

Conclusion

We have reviewed most of the current criminology theories. The authors of the general theory of crime stated that it was beyond the scope of their work to explain the sex differential. Others who tested the theory's ability to explain the gender differential in crime found that self-control was higher among women, but self-control did not eliminate the gender differential.

General strain theorists have made many attempts to adapt the theory to explain female criminality, with mixed results. Findings indicate that males and females experience similar levels of strain but that the affective response differs (i.e., girls are more likely to experience both anger and guilt), and girls are more likely to engage in nonconfrontational deviance (e.g., running away).

Rational choice theory did not address the sex differential; but later applications enlarged the concept of deterrence to include the threat of feeling guilt or shame and, by doing so, showed the theory worked for both males and females (because girls/women were more likely to anticipate shame).

Social support/social disorganization theories are macro-level theories that help to understand general levels of crime in a neighborhood or society but do not explain individual motivation to commit crime; therefore, they do not address the sex differential.

Sex-role theories, including power-control theory, continue to utilize socialization and supervision differences to explain the crime differential, despite the massive social changes that have occurred in this society over the last 40 years.

The life-course/integration theories explain crime through the use of biological, environmental, and socialization factors. Several life-course theorists have directly addressed the sex differential and showed significant biological, psychological, and environmental differences between boys' and girls' lives that go a long way toward explaining criminal choice differences.

Pathways research is a relatively recent addition that focuses on the dramatic differences in life experiences between male and female offenders, arguing that victimization, early pregnancy, and adaptations to these experiences explain the criminal choices of some female offenders, but not all. Note, however, that pathways research by itself helps us understand why female offenders may commit crime, but it does not explain why most women do not.

REVIEW QUESTIONS

1. How are cohort/longitudinal studies different from cross-sectional studies? What do proponents argue are the benefits of longitudinal research?

2. List some of the findings of longitudinal research summarized by Farrington regarding those likely to engage in delinquency.

3. Describe Sampson and Laub's integrated theory of delinquency.

4. Describe Moffitt's types of delinquents.

5. Describe what longitudinal research studies have discovered regarding girls/women and crime.

6. Describe the major premises of the pathways approach. What are the elements that distinguish women according to pathways researchers?

7. What percent of female offenders have experienced childhood sexual abuse? What are the correlates or effects of such abuse?

8. List and describe Daly's types of women.

9. Do women of other races or ethnicities differ from white women in their pathways to crime? Explain your answer.

10. Describe a gender-specific theory of delinquency/crime using the most persuasive evidence that has been presented in Chapters 3, 4, and 5.

Juvenile Offenders

CHAPTER SUMMARY

- Juvenile crime committed by girls has increased as a percentage of total crime by juveniles.
- The gender disparity between boys and girls in the commission of violent crime has decreased, largely due to dramatic decreases by boys.
- Female offenders have been treated differently from their male counterparts in the past in that they have been more likely to be brought into the system for status offenses.
- Today, girls are still being brought into the system for less serious offenses than boys through the practices of upcharging and bootstrapping.
- Research shows that girls in the juvenile justice system are beginning the "pathway" to criminality described in the last chapter.

In this chapter we pause to look specifically at female delinquency patterns, highlight delinquency theories, and then discuss juvenile court processing of girls.

Female Delinquency

Status offenses are those offenses that would not be crimes if committed by adults (e.g., truancy, incorrigibility, running away, and curfew violations). Delinquent acts, in contrast, are acts that would be crimes if committed by adults. In 1974, the Juvenile Delinquency Prevention Act mandated that states keep status offenders out of institutions housing delinquents. This has resulted, some argue, in an increased likelihood of defining the same behavior that would have been a status offense in past decades as a delinquent act in order to bring the youth into the system.

Many researchers have described dramatic percentage increases in female delinquency. As discussed in a previous chapter, percentage increases are misleading when very small base numbers are involved. Chesney-Lind and Shelden[1] noted that there was a dramatic rise of female arrests between 1965 and 1975, but this increase fell off between 1976 and 1985. Then it rose again in the 1990s and early 2000s.

In Table 6.1, girls' arrests are displayed as a percentage of total juvenile arrests beginning in 1980. There are several points to make concerning the trend over the last 30 years. First, in a few crime categories (homicide, forcible rape) there has been very little change in girls' arrests as a portion of total arrests. However, in almost all other crime categories the percentage of total arrests of girls has increased. The most extreme changes have occurred in aggravated assault, larceny/theft, other assaults, vandalism, and disorderly conduct.

Table 6.1   Percentage of Total Arrests of Females Under 18: Selected Years, Selected Crimes*

Crime	1980	1985	1990	1995	2000	2005	2010
Homicide**	8	9	5	6	11	10	10
Forcible rape	2	2	2	2	1	2	2
Robbery	7	7	9	9	9	9	10
Aggravated Assault	15	15	15	20	23	24	25
Burglary	6	7	8	10	11	11	11
Larceny/theft (Part II Offenses)	26	27	28	32	37	42	44
Other Assaults	21	23	23	27	31	33	35
Forgery/counterfeit	29	31	33	35	32	32	27
Vandalism	8	8	8	11	12	14	15
Weapons	6	7	6	8	11	11	11
Drugs (All)	17	15	11	12	15	17	16
Disorderly conduct	17	19	20	24	28	32	34
Runaway	58	57	56	57	58	58	n/a
All Other	19	20	21	22	25	27	26
Violent crime	10	11	12	15	18	18	18
Property crime	19	20	21	22	25	27	26

*Calculated from total juvenile arrests and female juvenile arrest tables.
**and non-negligent manslaughter

Source: Snyder, H. & Mulako-Wangota, J. *Arrest Data Analysis Tool*. Washington, DC: Bureau of Justice Statistics, July 13, 2013, at www.bjs.gov

There were some dramatic increases in total arrests between 1990 and 1995, particularly in arrests of female juveniles. For instance, in 1990, 9,864 girls were arrested for aggravated assault and in 1995, 16,720 girls were arrested—a 70 percent increase! This compares to only a 30 percent increase in overall arrests. Arrests for other assaults also increased for girls by 73 percent in those five years compared to a 46 percent increase in total arrests. Disorderly conduct has similar numbers: 24,435 girls were arrested in 1990; 41,480 were arrested in 1995 for an 81 percent increase (compared to a 47 percent increase in total arrests). For all drug offenses combined there were 9,076 arrests of girls in 1990 and 24,420 arrests in 1995, for an amazing 169 percent increase. Unlike the assault categories, the increase in arrests was more in line with the increase in total arrests (there was a 141 percent increase in total arrests).[2] Some argue that these dramatic increases in arrest numbers for girls in some crime categories but not other crime categories are evidence that it was decisions to arrest that changed more so than actual behavior of girls.

Since the mid to late 1990s, even though in most crime categories the number of girls arrested has declined or not changed much, property categories of crime experienced a steady increase in girls' *proportion* of arrests. For instance, their percentage of total arrests has almost doubled in the category of larceny/theft.

When using arrest records as a measure of criminal activity, it is important to remember that they are as much a record of official actions as they are of offender behavior. Much of the early literature on female delinquents chronicled the system's predisposition to be almost solely interested in the girls' sexual activity (contrary to the general disinterest in boys' promiscuity).[3] Self-report studies have revealed that girls and boys showed far more similar patterns of activity in nonserious delinquency and status offenses than official arrest statistics indicated, although boys did self-report more delinquent acts and the gender differential was apparent in more serious offenses.[4] It is important to note that self-reports usually include a broad range of behaviors, some of which are not serious criminality (e.g., running away). Thus, researchers who use such data to argue that patterns of offenses are similar between boys and girls need to note that such patterns are not strictly or even mostly *crime* patterns. Almost 30 years ago, Steffensmeier responded to alarm over the increase in female juvenile crime with a careful analysis of self-report data and official arrest statistics.[5] He concluded then that girls showed gains in larceny (shoplifting), liquor law violations, and running away. He concluded that female gang membership had not affected female delinquency, that female delinquency showed no dramatic increase, and that what increase had occurred was consistent with traditional female sex roles.

In both self-reports and official reports, the gender differential is most extreme in violent crime and almost disappears in some other types of delinquency. Girls have been more likely than boys to be arrested for status offenses such as running away from home, incorrigibility, and truancy, and they are more likely to be found in need of care and protection. The most common cause of arrest for boys and girls has been larceny/theft, but the second most common cause for girls has been running away.

Another way to display delinquency is by rates per 100,000, which allows us to compare different years even when there have been population increases or decreases. Figures 6.1 and 6.2 compare male and female juvenile arrest rates. We see that the dramatic decline in male arrests was not matched by dramatic declines in arrests of girls; but on the other hand it would not have been possible to match the magnitude, since girls' arrests started at such low numbers to begin with. The decreased gender differential in crime rates, therefore, has occurred almost entirely due to the dramatic declines in arrests of boys rather than any substantial increase in arrests of girls.

Figure 6.1   Juvenile Arrest Rates—All Property Crimes

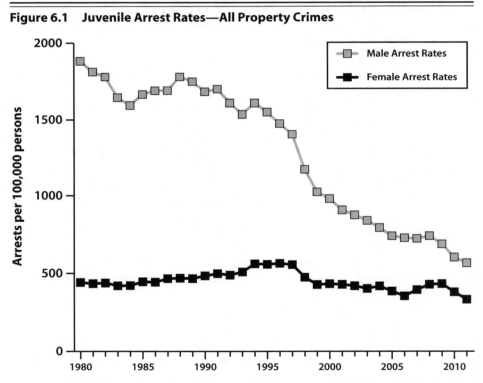

Source: Snyder, H. & Mulako-Wangota, J. *Arrest Data Analysis Tool*. Washington, DC: Bureau of Justice Statistics, July 8, 2013, at www.bjs.gov

Figure 6.2   Juvenile Arrest Rates—All Violent Crimes

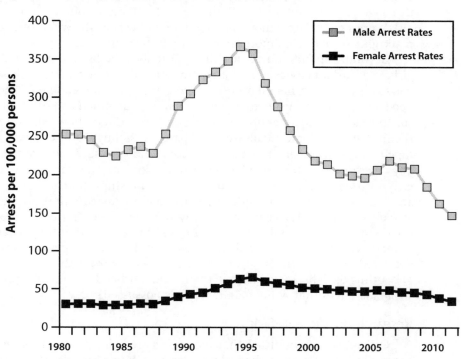

Source: Snyder, H. & Mulako-Wangota, J. *Arrest Data Analysis Tool*. Washington, DC: Bureau of Justice Statistics, July 8, 2013, at www.bjs.gov

Race and Ethnicity

Official statistics and self-report studies seem to indicate that African American and Hispanic female juveniles commit more violent crimes than do Caucasian girls. In 1991, Simpson[6] reported that African American girls have higher rates of homicide and aggravated assault than white girls, and African American girls participate in UCR violent offenses 5.5 times more often than white girls. In a recent study in California, it was found that between 15 and 60 percent of girls arrested in selected counties (Bay Area, Sacramento Valley, and Southern California), between 24 and 74 percent of those detained, and up to 67 percent of those sent to institutions were minorities.[7] Recent research identifies an "intersectionality" between gender and race/ethnicity such that girls are evidently treated differently from boys in the system, but also that minority girls are treated differently than minority boys. Moore and Padavic,[8] using Florida data on juvenile dispositions, found that white girls received what appeared to be more lenient sentencing than black girls until offense seriousness reached a certain threshold. For instance, black girls were 28 percent more likely than whites to receive probation rather than nonjudicial intervention at median offense severity levels, but at the highest levels of offense severity the probability converged. One interesting finding was that for most offense levels, Hispanic girls were sentenced no more harshly than whites, but the worst-offending Hispanic girls were treated more leniently than the worst-offending white girls.

Beyond statistics, however, Miller[9] describes the lives of African American girls in an urban city as a mix of victimized and victimizer. The girls she interviewed grew up in neighborhoods where violence was endemic. They developed self-protective ways to avoid the violence as much as possible but, even so, they lost loved ones to violence and more often than not were victims themselves—of domestic abuse from parents, siblings, and other relatives, of rape by both strangers and acquaintances, and of assault by strangers. While boys were more often the victims of fatal violence and gang-related assault, girls experienced violence in intimate relationships that seemed to be an accepted part of their lot in life. They also had to navigate their social world in school and on the street in such a way that they were not considered "stuck up" (and subject to retaliation for being so), but also so that they would not be sexually victimized. It was a difficult balance. Their life experiences were both gendered (in that they had different experiences from their male relatives) and influenced by race (in that their neighborhoods could not provide the social resources that white neighborhoods possessed).

Research on Violent Girls

Official sources indicate that more girls are being arrested for simple and aggravated assault today than in decades past. Some argue that it is a function of system actors more likely to arrest girls today, while others argue that behavior has actually changed and girls are more likely to commit violent crimes than ever before.

First, it is important to remember that girls' arrests for violent crimes declined during the same period as boys' arrests did, just not as dramatically. Examining the evidence, Chesney-Lind reports that there was an increase of 143 percent of girls arrested for "other assaults" between 1985 and 1994, and arrest rates for violent offenses did show double- and triple-digit increases; however, boys' rates increased as well. Violent crime as a percentage of total arrests showed very little change, and girls' percentage of total arrests for violent crime increased from 11 percent to 14 percent between 1985 and 1994—hardly an earth-shattering increase.[10] Since then, boys' arrests have declined dramatically, but girls' arrests have not. For instance, between 1996 and 2005 girls' arrests for simple assault increased 24 percent, while boys' arrests decreased by 4 percent. In the same time period, girls' arrests for aggravated assault declined by 5 percent while boys' declined by 23 percent.[11] Since 2005, as indicated in Figure 6.2, girls' arrests for violent crimes have declined from 49 per 100,000 to 34 and boys' arrests have declined from 207 in 2005 to 147.

Girls are five times as likely to be arrested for simple rather than aggravated assault, but boys' arrests for simple assault are only 3.5 times higher.

Some argue this finding indicates that girls' nonserious assaultive behavior is being treated more formally than boys' (increasing girls' arrest numbers for simple assault). Another suspicious finding is that assault arrests of girls increased while there was no increase in homicide or robbery. If girls were actually becoming more violent, it should also result in more arrests in these other violent crime categories. Similar to the discussion in previous chapters regarding adult women, some argue that mandatory arrest policies regarding domestic violence have led to these increases. In addition, self-report and the NCVS have not shown the same rate of increase as official arrest numbers.[12]

Steffensmeier and his colleagues[13] have conducted an analysis for juveniles similar to what was previously discussed for adult women, comparing victim reports and self-reports to arrest statistics. Findings indicated that arrest numbers increased while the other two sources did not show similar increases. These authors speculated that arrests are more likely to be made for minor incidents today, there is more formal policing of domestic violence (which comprises a large portion of girls' violence), and there is a less tolerant/less understanding attitude toward girls today. Case studies indicated that girls were arrested for family altercations in incidents of mutual violence or self-defense, or in schools that had zero-tolerance policies (utilizing police officers to arrest in discipline cases that had been dealt with by school officials in past decades).[14] There is some evidence that this is occurring: sources show that 50 percent of juveniles arrested for assault act against a parent, and 50 percent of arrests were made of children under 13 years of age.[15] Buzawa and Hotaling[16] found that 91 percent of girls in domestic violence calls (assaults on parents) were arrested compared to 75 percent of boys. They also reported from other sources that self-reported assaultive behavior of girls did not increase but arrests and convictions did, indicating a system change rather than a behavioral change.

Feld, Chesney-Lind, and others[17] argued that relabeling, upcharging, and bootstrapping (see Chapter 2) have occurred. These researchers note that in the 1970s, three-fourths of all girls were in detention for status offenses rather than delinquency, but the 1974 Juvenile Delinquency Prevention Act barred holding juveniles for status offenses. Then the number declined dramatically. A 1980 amendment to the act allowed judges to confine status offenders if they found the juvenile had violated "valid court orders," which might be orders to go to school or refrain from seeing problematic friends. The contempt of court orders and the subsequent detentions due to contempt orders have increased tremendously, leading to detention rates for females that appear to indicate greater delinquency. In reality, however, the detentions result from behaviors that were typical of girls in the past, such as running away, truancy, and incorrigibility.

Studies have indicated that the media attention to so-called violent girls is misplaced and that many arrests for assaults involve minor assaults on family members, police officers, or case workers in situations of high emotion.[18] Studies that have examined case processing find evidence that white girls' violence is interpreted as needing counseling and treatment while violence by black girls is perceived as requiring punitive responses.[19]

Self-reports have been used by some researchers to understand the motivations and patterns of girls' behaviors beyond arrest numbers. Some researchers conclude that girls' violence is undercounted and underemphasized. For instance, Miller and White[20] interviewed 70 young minority men and women in a depressed area of St. Louis to understand dating violence. They reported that, according to their respondents' reports, boys were more likely to be hit, pushed, shoved, or slapped by girlfriends compared to girlfriends being assaulted in the same ways by boys. Boys were more likely than girls to verbally abuse and cheat on their dating partners. Boys were also more likely to have used a weapon on a girl. Only girls were asked about sexual violence, and 19 percent reported being forced into sex. These researchers described the boys as maintaining emotional detachment, and girls' violence was looked upon with disdain and amusement by boys. Both boys and girls believed boys shouldn't hit girls, and the ideal reaction for boys was to walk away or to stop girls by holding them; but violence by boys was accepted when girls were "out of control" or to "teach them a lesson."

In this study, the perceptions of youth are interesting and shed light on their attitudes toward violence, but using their reports as accurate estimates of frequency might be unwise. There was a discrepancy in the numbers of girls who said they experienced nonreciprocal violence by their boyfriends and boys who admitted they initiated nonreciprocal violence (only two boys in the whole sample admitted such violence). There was also a discrepancy in that they all said boys shouldn't hit girls, but respondents also said they saw it all the time but rationalized it by saying "she deserved it" or "he has a bad temper." Boys reported that they did not intervene when girls were beaten by their boyfriends. The authors of this study discuss the "feminist" inclination to downplay evidence of women's non-self-defensive violence, arguing that their data showed the "reality" of mutual combatants' or girls' self-initiated and nonreciprocal violence. However, their own data indicated that boys' violence toward girls was serious and used in many instances as a power device to control, while girls' violence was perceived even by the victims as nonserious and often amusing.

This is not to say that there is not a problem of violence committed by girls, but it seems to be largely a problem of violence within a sphere of family members and acquaintances. Feld,[21] using official statistics, reports that boys are much more likely than girls to assault and kill victims, but when girls commit assault, their victims are three to four times more likely than boys' victims to be family members. Of homicide victims of boys and girls, girls' victims are five times more likely to be family members. Girls' victims are about equally likely as boys' victims to be acquaintances but much less likely than boys' victims to be strangers.

Batchelor and her colleagues[22] interviewed girls in Scotland about violence and found large percentages of girls who had experienced (41 percent), witnessed (98 percent), or perpetrated (30 percent) violence. The most common experience was verbal threats, taunting, or ridicule (91 percent), and half reported fear of being bullied or threatened. These girls, who came from depressed areas with poverty and social disorganization, did not view sibling or family physical altercations or sexual coercion in relationships as violence. A small percentage (10 percent) was routinely violent. This small group also reported more self-harming behaviors and higher levels of past violent victimization, drug use, and street time. These violent girls had pride in their reputation as bad girls or bullies. For this small group, violence was an acceptable response to perceived threats to one's self or one's reputation. They lived in a constant state of readiness to use physical violence. Common reasons given for their violence were self-defense, or responding to insults, stolen boyfriends, a betrayal of trust, disrespect, or gossip. It should be noted that other researchers have found these same reasons as initiating girls' violence, including violence perpetrated by girls involved in gangs.[23]

In a later work, Batchelor[24] noted an increase in arrests for violence of young women in Scotland but cautioned that high percentage increases didn't mean much when base numbers were so low (violent crimes by girls numbered barely over 100 for the whole country of Scotland). The second study reinforced the earlier findings that a small percentage of girls were violent. Their violence often took place during drug or alcohol use, and their victims were often other young women. Most of the violent girls had been victimized, had attempted suicide and/or had committed self-harming behaviors, a pattern that has been found in other studies as well.[25] Batchelor described these violent girls as utilizing violence in response to the powerlessness they experienced as children in abusive homes. As one girl who committed violence against other girls commented, "I like to see the fear in their eyes. You're in control."[26] Another characteristic that most of them shared was loss of loved ones to death and/or loss of their children to the state. The result was anger, and it involved lashing out in other situations at innocent bystanders. Once again, it was clear that violence was an accepted response to triggers such as disloyalty or disrespect. Disrespect was an important concept for these girls, similar to descriptions of its saliency for boys and men, especially in contexts of gangs. The salience of disrespect as a violence initiator is explained by Batchelor as the fear of girls of being victimized. They react in violence to any threat in order to avoid becoming, as they explained it, "easy prey." The violent girls described a pattern of unstable but intense relationships that involved quick intimacy and then rejection/devaluation (both with men and with friends), thus in some ways replicating their childhoods: "I always [think] the worst of everybody, and I don't like letting people near me because I get hurt. So I'd rather hurt them before they hurt me."[27]

Girl Gangs

The very earliest gang research in the 1950s mentioned girl gangs, but the attention was slight and the analysis superficial.[28] Girl gangs historically had been seen as auxiliary gangs to boys' gangs; girl gang members' contributions were seen as providing sex and as acting in minor ways to assist the violent and criminal activities of the male gang members. Campbell[29] pointed out, however, that it was hard to tell what the role of the female gang member was in earlier decades, since most early researchers were men and that probably affected their interpretation of female activities and membership. In Campbell's historical account of gangs in New York from the early 1800s forward, some girls and women were very active in fighting and other criminal activity. Reviewing other studies of gangs through the 1950s, 1960s and 1970s, Campbell observed that members of some female gangs fought and enjoyed fighting, and some committed crimes.

Walter Miller provided one of the earliest descriptions of a girl gang, the Molls.[30] These girls were white, Catholic, and mostly Irish. They had extensive criminal records, starting at a very young age. Of the 11 members, five had been arrested. The most common charge was truancy, then theft (shoplifting) and drinking. Other female gang studies showed more assaultive crimes than did the study of the Molls. However, compared to male gangs, no female gang was very criminal. The girls in this gang could not be described as liberated. The gang was an auxiliary gang to a male gang, and the girls evidently gloried in the idea that they were the property of the boys.

Academic research directed to gangs was revived in the 1980s and 1990s with an increased interest in female membership, although the whole area of gang research is rife with mixed findings and lack of consistency in definitions. Studies of gang membership are notorious for their wide range of estimates in percentage of juveniles involved, and especially the percentage of female juveniles involved in gang activity. It has been reported that less than 5 percent of all formal arrests or reports of gang members are of girls.[31] Most studies indicate no more than 10 percent of members are female,[32] but some studies have reported female membership as high as 30 percent[33] and 46 percent.[34] A major report of female juvenile offenders showed that between 20 and 48 percent of gang membership was female.[35] It is possible that girls are more active at younger ages and then age out. It is also possible that law enforcement (which provides the lowest estimates) may undercount girls. Of course, gang membership is only part of the issue. The more important issue is whether gang girls commit crime—especially violent crime. Curry and colleagues[36] report that girls account for 13.6 percent of gang-related property crime, 12.7 percent of drug crime, and 3.3 percent of violent crime. Chesney-Lind[37] found that gang girls in Honolulu showed a similar pattern of delinquency when compared with non-gang girls. For both groups, the most common arrest was for larceny/theft. Male gang members, on the other hand, committed more violent crimes than non-gang members.

Esbensen and his colleagues obtained a survey sample of over 5000 middle-school students in several locations. The authors found that 38 percent of the self-identified gang members were girls; however, only 8 percent of all girls reported gang membership while 14 percent of all boys did. Only about a quarter of the self-identified gang members were white. Not surprisingly, gang members, both boys and girls, committed more delinquency than non-gang youngsters. It seems to be the case that gang girls are more engaged in delinquency than non-gang girls and commit more delinquent acts than non-gang boys, but they commit much less delinquency than gang boys.[38] In other reported findings from these authors, the sample cities were described as purposive and chosen specifically because of higher levels of juvenile crime activity, making these findings nonrepresentative of the nation as a whole. Generally, male gang members committed more crimes, especially more violent crimes, than female gang members. For instance, 83 percent of male gang members reported having ever carried a weapon, compared to 65 percent of females. Although 84 percent of male and 81 percent of female gang members admitted they ever "hit someone to hurt," 57 percent of young men compared to 39 percent of females reported "ever attacking" someone, 34 percent of male versus 17 percent of girls reported "ever robbing" someone, and 34 percent of young men versus 21 percent of young women reported "ever shooting at" someone. It was also reported that female gangs were less hierarchical, exhibiting less emphasis on territory, and members were less likely to be arrested for delinquent activities.[39]

Moore and Hagedorn[40] reported that from 1965 to 1994, the number of arrests for violent crime by gang members was 15 boys to 1 girl for nonlethal violence, and 39 to 1 for drug offenses. Only 1.1 percent of gang-related homicide involved girls. However, they also report that in a survey of eighth graders in the mid-1990s, more than 90 percent of both male and female self-described gang members admitted participating in a violent act in the last 12 months (citing Esbensen and his colleagues' findings). In Miller and Decker's[41] interviews with 27 female gang members, 87 percent hit someone; 74 percent used a weapon (but not a gun, usually a knife); most sold marijuana and crack; and a minority reported other serious crime.

Gang research in the 1980s and 1990s split into two camps regarding whether the girl gang member participated in much crime, much less violent crime. Joe and Chesney-Lind[42] indicated that female gang members were no more criminal than non-gang juveniles and engaged largely in social and innocent activities. On the other hand, Taylor[43] and Campbell[44] argued that girl gang members had become increasingly independent from their male gang members, more criminal, and more violent. The differences in these two profiles may be due to methodology and definitional inconsistencies, or gang differences between the different cities studied.

The popular media have presented the latter view (of girls becoming more violent) almost exclusively. The *New York Times*, *Wall Street Journal*, *Time*, and *Newsweek* all ran stories in the early 1990s on female gangs.[45] Television news shows and local news broadcasts also ran stories complete with interviews of girl gang members who described their crimes. Such stories indicated that there was a new type of violent girl criminal. This is described by Chesney-Lind[46] as virtually a repeat of the news splash in the early 1970s over the supposed rise of female crime.

Quicker's[47] 1983 study of Chicana gangs in East Los Angeles discussed 12 different gangs. Intensive interviews were conducted with 13 girls, and less intensive interviews were undertaken with 30 more female gang members. In this study, gangs were described as substitute families for the girls. "Home-girls" provided the social support that families evidently could not provide, because of either poverty and overwork or neglect and abuse. Quicker found no instance of a completely independent girl gang and indicated that both boys and girls showed ambivalence regarding the appropriateness of girls being in a gang.

Quicker and others describe initiation as being "jumped in," which meant the girl was pummeled by other gang members for a short period of time, either standing and taking it quietly or fighting back. Other ways to be initi-ated was a "fair fight" (where only one girl was selected to fight the initiate) or getting "walked in" (which occurred only by agreement when a girl was sponsored by a current gang member). Another method of initiation was get-ting "trained in," which meant having sex with a number of boys in the gang. If the latter initiation occurred, researchers noted that the girl was not respected and was looked down upon by other members.[48]

Leaving the gang was described as a relatively passive occurrence wherein the girl simply stopped hanging around with the gang, or it could be through a "throw"—a fight with several girls.[49] Even in this situation, terminating the relationship was described as much easier for girl gang members than for boys. Status changes such as marriage, pregnancy, or graduation from high school were the most common reasons for leaving. Others note that older girls and women may act as informal advisors or ex-officio members, even though they are excused from playing a more active role after marriage or motherhood.[50]

Leadership tends to be diffuse in girl gangs; the female gang seems more democratic, with more decision making by consensus rather than operating under the strict authoritarian structure more commonly associated with male gangs.[51] Girls described how the gang was their family and their major interest and social outlet, because many of the members hated school and had negative experiences with their families. In fact, gang membership has been described by several authors as a response to social disorganization and cultural break-down in the Hispanic community. A gang identity provides girls with more freedom than traditional culture, even though sex roles and sexual double standards still predominate,[52] as this quote from a male gang member shows:

> To me a Queen (female gang member) is someone waiting for her man, to treat him like a King. If she has a kid, to take care of her kid. A Queen's job isn't to be out banging, it's to stay home and keep the house the way it was taught historically in the Latin race. There's no place for a girl in this. My nation's business is none of her concern.[53]

Campbell's[54] ethnological study of girl gangs in New York utilized an obser-vation and interview method and covered six months with three different gangs. The age ranges of the gang members were between 15 and 30. (One might argue the age range calls into question whether the studied groups were actually youth gangs). Campbell stated that about 10 percent of all gang members were female. She offered the view that girls were not just auxiliaries to male gangs but rather committed the types of crimes associated with gang activity, although she describes girls as holding weapons, acting as lookouts, sometimes setting up a rival male gang member by agreeing to a date with him, and procuring younger girls for gang rapes. Campbell described the female gang member as quite similar to the male gang member in some respects.

> Like the boys in the neighborhood, they enjoy excitement and trouble, which break the monotony of a life in which little attention is given to the future. They like sharp clothes, loud music, alcohol, and soft drugs. They admire toughness and verbal "smarts."[55]

Campbell also offers a follow-up study of Hispanic girl gang members in New York.[56] Her description of their lives is bleak. Almost all will have children while still very young, almost all will raise their children on welfare, and almost all will be socially controlled by men although not economically provided for by them. The gang is important for a short period of time before they settle into motherhood; it provides an escape from reality. The gang is largely a social outlet, providing fun by "hanging out" and/or partying with alcohol and drugs.

Other descriptions of female gangs indicated a more active role in drug sales. In a San Francisco study, the girls were engaged in crack sales and organized shoplifting (boosting); but here, also, gang membership filled an emotional void in the lives of the girls. The authors also described the girls' lives as hopeless, with no opportunities and no expectation that they would be economically provided for by the fathers of their children.[57] Joe and Chesney-Lind's[58] study covered female gangs in Hawaii. They describe the gang in much the same way as these other researchers. The gang provided escape from abuse and violence in the home and offered an antidote to boredom and hopelessness. While fighting was a common pastime for boys, girls were more likely to dance than fight. Joe and Chesney-Lind described the girl gangs as smaller than those of boys, with the favorite activities listed as sports, drinking, and hanging out (for boys it was drinking, fighting, cruising and looking for girls). About three-quarters of the girls had been physically abused (compared to 55 percent of the boys), and 62 percent of the girls reported sexual abuse. Most of the girls and boys had other family members in gangs. Joe and Chesney-Lind also described the gang as taking the place of family in these youngsters' lives. In these studies and others,[59] both boys and girls tended to stay away from home because of abuse, neglect, or general disruption. Gangs provided the love, acceptance, and emotional support that was unavailable through the family.[60]

Taylor[61] described young, African American gang girls in Detroit. Introducing new terminology into the literature, Taylor's interviewees spoke of their gangs as posses or crews. Taylor's description echoed many of the points above—specifically, that the gang filled a void in members' lives and the home life of gang members was dysfunctional and probably abusive. However, his portrayal of gang members' activities described a much more criminal outlook, more criminal activities, and more violent criminal activity on the part of female gang members. Taylor described a typology of different gangs: scavenger gangs, which drift in and out of crime as opportunity presents itself; territorial gangs, which hold power over geographic boundaries; commercial gangs, which have a product and an organization to sell it; and corporate gangs, which have an infrastructure not unlike any business in corporate America. Girls were involved in all types, even the corporate (which meant they ran fairly large-scale drug rings). Scavenger gangs were described as women and children banding together for begging and other hustles. Taylor's work stretches the definitional boundaries of youth gangs, since many of his "posse" girls were in their late twenties, and some of the descriptions indicated that the groupings were transitory and bore little resemblance to the highly structured male gangs in Los Angeles and New York City.

Chesney-Lind[62] criticized Taylor's work as reinforcing the inaccurate premise that women were becoming more violent. She pointed out that it was not clear how many gang members were interviewed, thus calling into question the representativeness of the sampled gang members. However, this criticism could be applied to most of the studies described above. Phenomenological studies provide context and meaning, but they do little to shed light on prevalence or changes in gang activity over time. Another criticism that can be leveled at most of the studies above is the looseness of the definition of gang member; many gangs claim membership by individuals in their late twenties and even thirties. It stretches the definition of such groupings as youth gangs to the breaking point, and it calls into question the whole practice of trying to identify gangs (as opposed to groups of friends, clubs, criminal associations, and so on).

Jody Miller's[63] research on female gang members is extensive and detailed. She and her colleagues have collected both quantitative and qualitative data on female gangs and found, for instance, that females are most actively delinquent in gangs where males are the majority versus those where there is a female majority or membership is gender balanced.[64] Girls in all-girl gangs focused on relationships, friendships, and the social elements of the gang; but girls in almost all male gangs focused on economic benefits from crime.[65]

In the St. Louis studies of girl gang members by Miller and her colleagues, girls reportedly fought over the same things girls outside of gangs fight about: gossip, disrespect, disloyalty, and sleeping with each other's boyfriends. Girls also tended to inhibit male gang members' violent activities: "Sometimes girls usually break it [violence] up. If it wasn't for them, we would have gotten in a whole lot of trouble."[66]

The descriptions of initiation that came from these interviews were similar to those described in earlier studies, except that an additional method of entry was to commit a crime to prove themselves. Girls who were "sexed in" (earlier described as "trained in," which meant participating in serial intercourse with male gang members) received less respect than those who followed other avenues of initiation. There was some disparity in the views of boys and girls, with girls more likely to think they were full gang members and boys more likely to not describe girls as such (except for a very few who were like "honorary men" because of their activities and the way they carried themselves).

Miller proposes that girls join gangs for the same reasons that boys do: exposure to neighborhood gangs, problems with the family, having gang-involved family members; and having unsafe homes. She describes differences in the types of gangs that exist, especially between inner-city gangs on either coast and Midwest gangs.[67]

In other work, she and colleagues[68] describe victimization patterns of girl gang members. As have other researchers, they identify the high likelihood that female gang members come from abusive homes. Girl gang members are also more at risk for violent crime victimization during gang membership—either rape, death, injury from being a bystander in a drive-by shooting, or being involved in physical altercations increased the risk of victimization. For instance, 41 percent of girl gang members interviewed (11 respondents) reported being stabbed.[69] There was a dramatic drop in violent activity of gangs beginning in the mid-1990s, and study authors noted that this might have been because of a shift in gang activity from territorial fighting to drug sales. Whether greater numbers of female members reduced the violence levels of gangs is difficult to prove.

These and other studies contribute to the picture that girl gangs have always been around and that, while some girl gang members may be becoming more active in criminal activities, the majority are still influenced by sex roles and girl gang members are less criminal than male gang members. The activities commonly engaged in by girl members include holding weapons, spying on other gangs, and serving as sex objects and social companions. They can and do leave the gang easily, especially for motherhood or marriage. Membership seems to be a double-edged sword, since girls find support and acceptance in the gang but may be more subject to physical violence, and girls often lose their reputation and become known, especially by prospective male partners, as unworthy partners for anything but sex.[70]

The studies that supported the view that girl gang members were becoming more violent typically were phenomenological.[71] The researchers interviewed small numbers of active gang members who expressed approval for and participation in violence and criminal activity. In fact, some of these young women were shockingly violent. This type of research was very persuasive that female gang members were growing more violent, but those described were not representative of all girls. Any statements that girls as a whole and across the nation are becoming more active in gangs, or that they are becoming more violent, is simply not supported by the evidence.

Delinquency Theories

Delinquency theories are, in essence, the same as the criminological theories reviewed in Chapters 3, 4, and 5. Generally, researchers have found that there is still a sex/gender effect even after controlling for all other variables. They then (typically) attribute the difference to sex roles—the idea that girls are socialized differently than boys and more tightly controlled, although a few researchers, even in the 1970s, admitted the possibility of biological differences.[72]

There are several national representative surveys of schoolchildren that include self-report data that includes a range of nonserious to serious offenses. The National Youth Survey is a large, representative sampling of youth, and sampling occurs in waves, meaning that the same youth are reinterviewed in subsequent years. Questions cover a wide range of topics from crime and misbehavior to parenting practices. Using this survey to understand behavioral differences between boys and girls is obviously better than using arrest data, since arrest data inserts the bias of official decision makers. The downside of using self-reports is that there are generally very small numbers of youth (especially girls) who have committed serious crimes; therefore, studies typically expand the definition to include trivial offenses. Delinquency theorists test the same constructs that we have previously discussed: peer associations, parental practices, strain, and low self-control; but, they do so by using samples of youth and self-reports rather than arrest records.

Applications of Theories to Girls

Social Learning/Peer Associations/Social Control.   Daniel Mears[73] and his colleagues used the National Youth Survey to test whether the sex/gender differential was due to girls' having a stronger moral conscience than boys. The analysis examined self-reports of theft under $5 and found that boys were twice as likely as girls to admit to this form of delinquency. Boys were also twice as likely to report having delinquent friends. The gender differential in self-reported theft dropped by half when the factor of delinquent friends was controlled for. They found that the effect of delinquent peers was stronger for boys than for girls. They found that females were more apt than males to rate criminal behaviors as "very wrong," but sex differences in moral evaluations did not completely explain sex differences in delinquency. Both moral evaluations and peer influence were important. For males, even when personal moral disapproval was strong, delinquent peers still affected behavior (to commit delinquency); for females, strong moral disapproval effectively eliminated the effect of delinquent peers.

The idea that girls are more attached to family members and others and that this attachment partially explains their lower delinquency levels has been supported by a number of studies. Some researchers found that family attachment was only weakly correlated with delinquency for girls;[74] however, most studies do find that stronger attachments exist for girls. One study, for instance, used two samples of youth (a high-school sample and a sample of street kids living in shelters) to explore the effect of friendship on delinquency. Findings indicated that girls had stronger friendships (measured by intimacy and value), and that friendships exerted a negative influence on committing delinquency. This relationship held for both high-school and street girls, and even for high-school boys, but street boys did not exhibit a link between friendships and reduced delinquency.[75]

Rational Choice. Miller[76] discussed how girls joined gangs as a rational choice to pursue economic gain, status, and emotional rewards, and/or to avoid boredom. The girls she interviewed used their femininity in rational ways to avoid detection and achieve their goals; for instance, they knew they came under less suspicion from police officers and were less likely to be stopped and searched. They even utilized their babies or younger brothers and sisters in order to camouflage their criminal activities. Their methods of committing crimes were influenced by their sex as well. If they robbed, they were likely to choose women as victims. Miller concluded that rational choice theory was helpful in understanding individual choices of crime and crime commission, but she did not address the larger issues of structural constraints (e.g., gender inequalities, racial inequalities, class inequalities) that shaped and limited opportunities for the girls.

Sex Roles/Power Control. Heimer[77] tested power control theory along with social learning theory, using several waves of the National Youth Survey (where youth and their families were interviewed annually for several years). She found that favorable attitudes toward deviance affected both girls' and boys' delinquency; but anticipating negative disapproval from friends reduced the chance of later delinquency for girls but not for boys. Accepting gender definitions (of femininity and masculinity) slightly reduced the likelihood of delinquency among girls but not boys (because definitions of masculinity encouraged delinquency), but definitions also occurred in tandem with other factors such as attitudes about deviance. Contrary to other findings, supervision by parents exerted a strong control on boys' delinquency but not on the delinquency of girls. The results supported the notion that peers are just as important, if not more important, as gender identity and families in youths' decisions to commit delinquent acts.

Heimer and DeCoster[78] also used the National Youth Survey to continue the exploration of how gender identity and other factors affect delinquency. Previous studies had shown that lower-socioeconomic (SES) families have less legitimate power over their children; they don't supervise as closely and are more likely to use physical discipline. This upbringing led boys to learn definitions favorable to violence. Lower-SES families are also more likely to be patriarchal and emphasize gender norms of femininity (passiveness, nurturance, emotionality). While boys are more likely than girls to be directly supervised (monitored), girls are also controlled through emotional bonding or attachment as a form of indirect control. The hypothesis of this study was that the definitions of violence will be shaped for girls primarily by indirect control achieved through emotional bonding, and boys' learning will be shaped primarily by more direct, overt parental controls like supervision and coercive discipline.

Findings indicated that learning violent definitions is an important predictor of violent delinquency among both girls and boys. Aggressive peers and coercive discipline had a larger effect on boys' than on girls' learning of violent definitions, while emotional bonds to family influenced girls' but not boys' delinquency. Direct parental supervision of youths' friendships directly reduced violent delinquency for boys, but this type of supervision was unimportant for influencing violent delinquency of girls. Researchers also found that traditional gender definitions significantly reduced violence among girls but did not influence violence among boys. Heimer and DeCoster concluded that boys engaged in more violent delinquency because they learned more violent definitions and have more experience with violent offending, largely because they have weaker emotional bonds.

Other researchers have also measured the link between gender identity and delinquency, especially violent delinquency. In one study,[79] six social practices were identified as inhibiting violent delinquency in girls but not in boys: male dominance, differences in routine daily activities, variations in sexual interests, transitions to adulthood, ideology defining crime as a male activity, and childcare assigned as a female task. In this study, 67 percent of male and 36 percent of female juveniles said they had felt peer pressure to engage in delinquency. In general, sex roles are still dominant in society and affect girls and boys in ways that lead to a reduced likelihood of female delinquency, at least of serious and/or violent delinquency. Males belonged to relatively larger peer groups and gangs, spent time with unsupervised peers, received social support to be delinquent, had access to privacy and to time and space away from home, and enforced gender-defined friendship group boundaries. Girls, on the other hand, were responsible for child care, spent time in sex-segregated friendship groups, and received social messages defining appropriate behavior, which inhibited delinquency.[80]

General Strain Theory.   The National Youth Survey has also been used to examine the role of victimization on delinquency as a test of general strain theory (GST) (since victimization has been described as a type of strain by Agnew and other GST theorists). In one study, researchers found that victimization did lead to depression, but that depression was linked to delinquency only for boys, not girls.[81] Since this study did not control for anger as another emotion, it was unable to isolate the effects of anger from depression. Recall that several studies have now supported the notion that anger accompanies depression for boys, but not for girls.

Pathways.   In the 1970s and 1980s, feminist critiques of criminology were scathing in their criticism of early theories of female delinquency and the presentation of delinquent girls who tended to come from more disturbed family backgrounds as more emotionally "needy."[82] The criticism directed at these researchers implied that the researchers operated under sex-role stereo-types and were wrong in their view that female delinquents had different motivations than delinquent boys related to their entry into delinquency. However, when reading the findings of these early researchers one senses that they might have had a better understanding of the girls they studied than the later critiques acknowledged. Employing phenomenological methods, the early researchers used quotes from girls that illustrated their emphasis on friends and boys, and the deep pain they felt that stemmed from family abuse or neglect. Ironically, the early research on female delinquents has been revived with the pathways approach, which also focuses on how different experiences of women have shaped their entry into crime.[83]

In the last chapter, statistics illustrating the prevalence of adult offenders' childhood sexual victimization was presented. Studies are also available of girls in the juvenile system, some of whom will become the adult offenders in years to come. These studies also report widespread abuse and victimization. For instance, one study reported that between 40 and 73 percent of incarcerated girls reported sexual abuse. This study found that 90 percent of white girls and 70 percent of black girls reported abuse (of any kind), and 62 percent of white girls and 46 percent of black girls reported sexual abuse. White girls were also more likely to report drug and alcohol abuse, a lesser degree of self-esteem, and more suicide/self-injury attempts.[84] One might interpret these findings as supportive for the idea that social/subcultural supports were more influential in black girls' delinquency than in delinquency of white girls (who exhibited more individual motivations).

Across many studies, the picture of female delinquents was one of isolation, pain, and victimization, as these two quotes illustrate:

> I always felt that I was missing something in my life: Drugs and gangs help you replace that.

> My mom lives in the projects. She was always smoking drugs. I was taken away from her because my stepfather raped me. . . . My uncle was the father figure and when he died, everything changed for me. . . . After I got raped, I started getting wild. . . .[85]

Similar to the studies reviewed in the last chapter, studies of juveniles have also found that violent victimization is linked to violent crime, with girls who had experienced violent victimization more than twice as likely to engage in violent acts.[86] Other findings indicate that victimization and other strains that result in anger and depression are more likely to cause externalizing behavior (delinquency) among boys and internalizing behavior among girls.[87] Studies have found that girls and boys are equally likely to experience physical abuse, mental health issues, gang exposure and other strains, but sexual abuse is more common for girls.[88] Other studies have shown that girls are more likely to experience a wide range of negative experiences (strains) throughout childhood, as indicated below in a study of juveniles in a large city juvenile justice system. In this study, predictors of delinquency for girls were

Figure 6.3   Experiences of Female and Male Juveniles

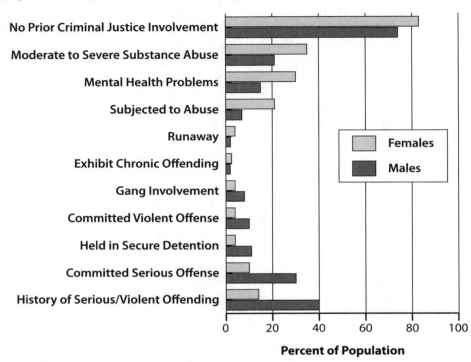

Note: Categories have been arranged with female-predominant problems above, from highest to lowest population percentage, followed by male-predominant problems arranged from lowest to highest overall population percentage.

Source: Adapted from Howell, J. 2003. *Preventing and Reducing Juvenile Delinquency: A Comprehensive Framework*. Thousand Oaks, CA: Sage.

gang involvement, abuse (negative direction), institution or foster care, and substance abuse. For boys, it was gang involvement, mental health problems, institution or foster care, and race. (See Figure 6.3.) The finding that abuse was negatively associated with serious offending was contrary to that of most other studies, but this was a detained population and not representative of the population as a whole.[89]

Juvenile Justice System

Historically, the juvenile justice system treated female delinquents differently than male delinquents in that girls were more likely than boys to be institutionalized for nondelinquent behaviors (such as promiscuity).[90] As described above, studies generally find that girls in the system come from more disordered backgrounds than boys, are more likely to have been victims of sexual abuse, are more likely to be runaways (often running from abuse), and are more likely to have drug or alcohol abuse issues.[91] The explanation for this might be that peer associations and societal messages support male delinquency but not female delinquency; therefore, female delinquents have stronger "pushes" toward delinquency that overcome socialization. In one major study of girls in the juvenile justice system,[92] findings included the following:

- Boys and girls experience similar levels of physical abuse but girls experience more sexual abuse.

- Boys are more subject to ADHD and conduct disorder and girls are more likely to experience depression, anxiety, and PTSD.

- Early puberty combined with family conflict and disadvantaged neighborhoods is associated with girls' delinquency.

Qualitative and quantitative findings are consistent in the finding that girls in the system do tend to have more serious individual issues than boys. Factors associated with female delinquency are lack of parental supervision, inconsistent discipline, parental criminality, unstable home life, maltreatment (both physical and sexual), peers and romantic partners (especially for girls who experience early puberty, associating with older partners affected their use of drugs), socially disorganized neighborhoods, and attachment to school and teachers (negatively associated with delinquency).

Research has shown that juvenile justice staff members generally view most female delinquents as misguided rather than actively dangerous or criminal. In one study, girls were more likely than boys to be described as not criminally dangerous and having emotional or mental health issues and family problems.[93] Other research indicated staff members' belief that girls are more difficult to work with, that girls are more manipulative than boys and are more likely to reoffend, and that girls are more "vicious." These are obviously perceptions that are not borne out by statistical findings.[94] In fact, these research findings strongly parallel much earlier research on staff who worked with adult men and women in prisons. Generally, staff believed women were "worse" than men, probably because they behaved contrary to the feminine stereotype.[95]

Contrary to a general belief that girls are treated more leniently in the system, some studies indicate that girls are just as likely as boys to receive detainment orders and, in fact, may be handled more punitively in that they receive detainment for original status offender charges.[96] (See the discussion on bootstrapping and upcharging in Chapter 2.) Another report indicates that nationally 40 percent of girls in detention are there for probation violations compared to only 25 percent of boys.[97] However, a report from OJJDP indicates that 22 percent of girls incarcerated were there for technical violations compared to 16 percent of boys.[98] *Upcharging*, the practice of defining as assaults behaviors that would not have been so defined in years past, increases the possibility of girls' detainment.[99]

Programming

Once in the system, girls received little gender-specific care (until recently). In one study of 215 programs, only 6 percent could be considered gender-specific.[100] If programs were available, they tended to be "boys' programs with pink covers," meaning that nothing was changed about the program—sometimes not even the male pronoun in program materials.

In 1992, the OJJDP Reauthorization Act mandated that states create gender-specific programming for girls. This has led many states to review their programming for girls and create new gender-specific (or gender-responsive) programs. Such programs, at minimum, create a safe place for girls (single-sex programs rather than co-ed programs allow girls to talk more freely), address past victimization, and emphasize relationships (which have been shown to be more salient for girls' emotional development than for boys'). The difficulty has been that very few evaluations of gender-specific programs exist or, indeed, even evaluations of any programs with gender used as a variable to determine whether the programs worked differently for boys and girls.

One report indicated that of the 392 juvenile programs in the OJJDP database, only 29 reported gender effects in the findings.[101] This same study reported that only nine programs for girls have been evaluated using acceptable evaluation techniques, and only two used random assignment and control samples. For one program, Reaffirming Young Sisters' Excellence (RYSE), findings indicated that although participants were 50 percent more likely to complete probation, there was no difference in recidivism at six months, 12 months or 18 months. Participants were subsequently arrested on less serious charges than nonparticipants, however. Another adequately evaluated program, Working to Insure and Nurture Girls' Success (WINGS), had a lower recidivism rate than the control sample at six months but a higher rate of recidivism at 12 and 18 months. This study also concluded that gender-specific was no more successful than gender-neutral programming.[102] On the other hand, with so few programs having adequate evaluations, it seems much too soon to conclude that gender-specific programs are no better than gender-neutral programs for girls. At least one other recently published program evaluation did find some success with a gender-specific model in reducing subsequent court referrals and fewer post-program detentions.[103]

Hubbard and Matthews[104] provide a discussion of the controversy between the gender-responsive program advocates and those in the "what works" camp who utilize a largely gender-neutral diagnostic device (LSI-R) and advocate cognitive behavioral programming.[105] Generally, there is disagreement in the emphasis on what is important to understand both delinquency and recidivism. Past victimization is emphasized to a greater degree by the gender-responsive theorists, and antisocial attitudes and delinquent peers by the "what works" camp. In at least one study, when matched samples of female and male juveniles were compared, they were found to be similar in criminogenic needs. Although the assessment tool predicted recidivism equally well for both groups, matching treatment services to criminogenic needs was associated with reduced offending only for boys, not girls.[106] Clearly, there is a great need for more research in this area to determine if gender-responsive programs are more effective in improving recidivism rates for female juveniles than the cognitive-based programs promoted by the "what works" approach. This topic is revisited in Chapter 10 in the discussion of correctional programming for adult women.

Detainment

Generally, the description of girls in the juvenile justice system as detailed above also describes girls who end up in detainment. They are very likely to come from disordered, dysfunctional backgrounds with histories of abuse. They are even more likely than girls in the system but not detained to have mental health challenges and suicide attempts. Detained girls are more likely to be girls of color.[107] Other reports also indicate that the predictors of detainment are suicide attempts and more previous offenses than girls in the system but not detained.[108]

Very few female juvenile offenders are transferred to the adult system because of the severity of their crimes. In one study utilizing a small sample of these offenders, researchers noted that they seemed to fit the "harmed and harming" type in Daly's typology in that they had been brutalized by parents and sexually victimized by relatives or family friends. One woman participated in a drive-by shooting that paralyzed her father's friend, who had raped her. Most of them had started "running the streets" from an early age (before 13), either staying out all night or being gone for days at a time. One was kidnapped by a pimp at the age of 13. Interestingly, these girls did not blame their families, even when they were victims of horrific child abuse. Several mentioned that prison saved their lives.[109] These researchers noted that the young women who were sent to prisons for adults did not express much fear of older inmates and, in fact, sometimes received emotional support from them: "A lot of the ladies [adult prisoners] will basically adopt you. And they're like, 'Oh, my baby!' They try to watch over you, they try to mother you. It's mostly nice."[110] Other studies have also described how some girls sent to adult prisons at ages as young as 15 and 16 are literally raised by inmates and correctional staff. They jokingly may even refer to some correctional officers (and more often inmates) as Mom, because these women may be the only mother figures the girls have known.[111]

Unfortunately, some girls who have been detained in state care are further victimized by staff members:

> Specific forms of abuse reportedly experienced by girls from the point of arrest through detention include the consistent use by staff of foul and demeaning language, inappropriate touching, pushing and hitting, isolation, and deprivation of clean clothing. Some strip searches of girls were conducted in the presence of male officers.[112]

Another study by Belknap and colleagues, using focus groups, found that incarcerated girls felt disrespected by staff: "The staff tell us we're 'nothing,' we're not special."[113] These researchers also found that health issues were a significant problem for detained girls. They engaged in self-injury and suicide attempts more often than boys; and they had more medical problems and mental health issues than boys. These challenges were worsened because of the lack of adequate programming. Victimization by staff of girls in juvenile institutions also includes sexual extortion and rape, according to self-reports. In one study, several adult women recounted sexual abuse that took place years earlier when they were incarcerated as juveniles; recalling how powerless they felt as juveniles. Some women had experienced sexual abuse by family members and friends, from pimps and boyfriends on the street, and then also experienced sexual abuse in correctional institutions after detainment.[114]

Conclusion

Official records indicate that juveniles followed the same crime patterns as adults in that there were historically high crime rates in the 1980s, followed by a dramatic decline of both property and violent crime beginning in the mid-1990s and plateauing in the early 2000s. Female juveniles are similar to male juveniles in their rates of minor crimes, but there is a large gender differential in violent and serious crimes. While female juveniles' crimes declined along with those of males, the decline was not as dramatic; therefore, the gender differential was reduced. Some have used this statistic to argue that female juveniles are becoming more criminal. There is more persuasive evidence to indicate that today's system actors are more likely to charge female offenders with crimes for behaviors that might have been dealt with as a status offense in past decades.

Consistent findings indicate that, similar to the descriptions from the early and mid-1900s, female juveniles do come from more disordered, dysfunctional, and abusive backgrounds than male juveniles in the system. They have major challenges in that they are more likely to experience mental health problems, drug or alcohol abuse, and PTSD. Recently, there has been a concerted effort on the national level to encourage gender-specific programming. Evaluations of such programs are only now beginning to emerge in the literature.

REVIEW QUESTIONS

1. Describe the difference between status offenses and delinquent offenses. What has been the pattern of female involvement in delinquency over the last 30 years in percentage of total arrests? In rates per 100,000?

2. Explain how self-reports and official reports do not seem to match regarding female involvement in delinquency. What is the explanation?

3. Explain what researchers mean by intersectionality.

4. Girls seem to be responsible for more arrests for assault and aggravated assault today than in the past. Why do some researchers say this is not necessarily due to changes in behavior?

5. What does the research tell us about girls and gangs? What percentage of girls belong to gangs? What percentage of gangs are girl-only or have female members? What are the differences in the activities of female compared to male gang members?

6. Do females in the juvenile justice system experience chivalry? Explain your answer.

7. Choose the most persuasive theory to explain female delinquency and describe how this theory has more evidentiary support than others.

8. How are females in detention different from male offenders?

9. Explain the pathways theory and how it explains female delinquency.

10. What are the elements of a gender-responsive treatment program for female delinquents?

7

Chivalry, Sentencing, and Jails

CHAPTER SUMMARY

- The so-called chivalry theory proposes that women are arrested, charged, convicted, and punished to a lesser degree than men who commit similar crimes. Mixed evidence indicates that there may have been some chivalry operating for some types of women, but it has declined with the advent of newer sentencing practices such as guidelines.

- Sentencing changes that reduced the discretion of judges (e.g., sentencing guidelines and mandatory minimums) generally increased women's likelihood of receiving a prison sentence and increased the length of their sentences.

- In recent years the rate of imprisonment for black women has declined, while the rate for white and Hispanic women has continued to increase.

- There are 111,387 women incarcerated in prison in this country, and their rate of imprisonment has increased from 7 per 100,000 in 1977 to 67 per 100,000 in 2011.

- Jail inmates are similar to prison inmates in their demographics and needs, but they receive fewer services and programs than prison inmates.

There has been a long-standing assumption that the criminal justice system treats women more leniently than male offenders. The so-called chivalry theory postulates that women are less likely to be arrested, if arrested less likely to be convicted, and if convicted less likely to be sentenced to prison than men in similar circumstances. Is there chivalry in the system and, if so, have there been changes over the years so that women today are treated differently than they might have been 30 years ago? This chapter reviews the chivalry literature before looking at sentencing patterns today.

Disparate Sentencing Laws

Historically, sentencing laws in several states mandated different sentences for female and male offenders. These sentencing laws were premised on the different "nature" of the female offender. She was thought to be more amenable to rehabilitation and able to benefit from an indeterminate sentence with the goal of reform, whereas the male was sentenced primarily for the purpose of punishment.

In the first half of the 1900s, courts justified the different sentencing practices by pointing to sex differences.[1] For instance, in *State v. Heitman* (1919), the Kansas Supreme Court refused to invalidate a statute that imposed fixed sentences on males but gave females indeterminate sentences, rationalizing that the two sexes were different physically and psychologically. Another example of disparate sentencing was the 1913 Muncy Act in Pennsylvania, which took away discretion from the sentencing judge only for female offenders. Because of the Muncy Act, most women were sent to the reformatory for offenses that, if committed by a male, resulted in a county jail term. In *Commonwealth v. Daniel* (1968) the Muncy Act was finally overturned. The court held that there was no rational basis for distinguishing men and women in sentencing.

In later cases throughout the 1960s and 1970s courts found that there were no differences between men and women to justify differential sentencing. A federal district court declared the Connecticut indeterminate sentencing statute to be unconstitutional for much the same reason in *United States ex rel. Robinson v. York* (1968).

Another aspect of differential sentencing appeared in the laws concerning supervision of juveniles, which allowed for longer periods of jurisdiction over females, arguably because they were less mature or independent than males and would benefit from continued contact with the juvenile justice system. New York's Persons in Need of Supervision law was struck down as unconstitutional by the New York Court of Appeals in 1972 because it permitted juvenile court jurisdiction over females, who were considered "persons in need of supervision," for two years longer than males.[2]

Today, disparate sentencing laws no longer exist. However, the discretion still present in sentencing may create disparate effects between men and women. Interestingly, it has been assumed that any disparity benefits girls/women and that they receive shorter, not longer, sentences when compared to boys/men.

The Chivalry Hypothesis

Official records indicate that, except for a very few crimes (e.g., prostitution), women are not arrested as often as men (although, as noted in Chapter

2, the gender differential is decreasing). In 2011, women accounted for 26 percent of arrests.[3] They are even less likely than men to be convicted of a crime. In 2006 (the last year for which data are available), only about 18 percent of all state convictions were of women (13 percent of all violent offenses and 24 percent of all property offenses).[4] Finally, women are even less likely to be sentenced to prison, comprising only about 6.7 percent of the nation's prison population in 2011.[5]

Some, however, dispute the notion that women commit less crime than men and propose, instead, that decision makers treat women differently and are less likely to utilize formal processing. This is called the chivalry hypothesis. Otto Pollak[6] was not the first in 1950 to speculate that women may be just as criminal as men, but he is most associated with the theory that system actors are chivalrous to female offenders.

The chivalry hypothesis has been studied by numerous researchers, and after reviewing the expansive literature the following conclusions can be offered:

- Certain factors that are themselves related to sex can influence sentencing—for example, being a primary caregiver for children, criminal history, and differential culpability in the criminal event (accessory versus primary).

- Later studies were much more sophisticated than early studies by controlling for such factors as prior record, injury, and other sentencing factors that may have affected decision makers instead of, or in addition to, sex. When these factors are controlled for, the apparent preferential treatment for women is reduced but does not disappear.

- The finding by some researchers that women who deviate from normal sex roles are more harshly treated has mixed empirical support.

- Domestic violence law and policy changes that encourage arrest have arguably increased arrests for women and girls in assault and aggravated assault categories, and determinate sentencing and the adoption of sentencing guidelines have impacted women more harshly than men.

Methodological Concerns

To test the chivalry hypothesis, researchers compare sentences given to male and female defendants who commit substantially similar crimes and have substantially similar roles in that crime. Researchers determine whether there are significant differences in the sentences that are unaccounted for by other factors. Many factors may affect sentencing, such as prior record, seriousness of crime, victim injury, offender culpability, motivation, and so forth. Many of these factors appear to be correlated with the sex of the offender. For instance, women are less likely to have criminal records and they (typically) are accessories rather than primary actors when committing a crime with another person (especially with a man). Therefore, any study of differential sentencing must, at the outset, ensure that all these factors are controlled for before assuming that any sentencing differences are due to the sex of the offender. Some studies have been more careful in this regard than others.

More fundamental issues, however, undercut all studies of chivalry undertaken at the sentencing stage. The sentencing decision comes after many previous decision points in processing. A true test of whether the system treats women differentially would have to begin at the point of the arrest decision and carry through to formal booking, the decision to charge (and with what to charge), pre-trial decisions such as bail or release on recognizance (ROR), conviction, and sentencing. Each of the prior decision points are important and may reflect differential processing. The earlier in the system, the more difficult it would be to study decisions—for instance, how could a researcher determine whether police officers were more likely to arrest men than women in similar circumstances? These issues, of course, are the very same issues that are debated relative to the question of whether the system is racist. Even if statistics indicate there is no racial bias at the point of sentencing, it does not tell us much about the other parts of the system. Each step, beginning with the decision to stop and investigate, is part of the larger picture. In the following review of the literature, it is obvious that the weakest aspect of the research is the lack of attention to earlier stages in the formal processing of suspects and defendants.

Daly[7] and Daly and Bordt[8] criticized chivalry studies for not taking into account all factors of sentencing. In other words, purely statistical studies could not capture the context of the crime and thus may mistakenly conclude that unequal treatment was handed out, when in fact the differential sentencing may have been because of the circumstances of the crime. In her New Haven study, Daly looked at 189 cases of female offenders and a random sample of 208 cases of male offenders, drawing from the years 1981 through 1986. She used multiple regression analysis to determine whether there was disparity in sentencing, but she also collected a "deep sample" of 40 male and 40 female cases, matched for factors such as type of crime, to explore more fully. Daly found that men were more likely to be incarcerated than women (the range was between eight and 25 percentage points), and African Americans were more likely to be incarcerated than whites.[9]

Daly's statistical study would have concluded that disparity existed, but she went further with her "deep sample" and utilized narratives of the case histories. She developed what she called a comparative justice metric that evaluated such things as the seriousness of the crime and the level of participation or culpability of the offender. Using the case studies and this comparative tool to control for factors not typically controlled for in statistical studies, she found gender differences were negligible.

Studies of Chivalry

Several studies in the 1970s found that women seemed to be treated more leniently than men in the criminal justice system. They were less likely to be in custody before trial, they were less likely to be convicted, and they were less likely to be sent to prison if convicted. White women received less harsh treatment than African American women, but African American women received less harsh treatment than white men. However, these early studies did not control for seriousness of crime, level of participation or criminal history.

Studies in the 1980s did control for race, offense, and prior record and continued to find that women received shorter sentences; however, these studies typically did not control for level of participation, the types of crimes in prior arrests, or level of injury or loss in the current crime.[10] Wilbanks[11] offered one of the few studies that looked at earlier points in the system, including arrest and charging decisions. Unfortunately, he was not able to control for such factors as seriousness, culpability, or prior record. His findings indicated that women were not treated more favorably at the "front end" of the system, but at the sentencing stage they were, although the effect of sex was inconsistent across offense types. In other words, for some crimes women were treated more harshly than men, and in other crimes they were treated more leniently.

Other studies in the 1980s also concluded that chivalry existed in sentencing;[12] although there were several that concluded that there was no chivalry or that the findings did not clearly support either conclusion.[13] In a very thorough review of the chivalry research that had been conducted up to the early 1980s, Nagel and Hagan[14] concluded that sex appeared to affect decisions differently at different stages in the criminal justice process. At the pretrial stage, sex did affect the decision to release on recognizance (rather than set bail) but did not affect the amount of bail if bail was set. With regard to the decision to prosecute, plea bargain, or convict, they concluded that the available evidence did not clearly support a chivalry hypothesis. Sentencing studies, however, did show differential processing by sex, although the effect was small after controlling for other variables. Other researchers found that the chivalry factor seemed to be dissipating, with changing sentencing patterns in which women received increasingly harsher sentencing.[15]

In the 1990s research continued, with some findings indicating that sentencing decisions were influenced by the sex of the offender.[16] Some researchers, however, showed that the relationship was more complicated than a simple display of chivalry. Steffensmeier, Kramer and Streifel[17] studied sentences from 1985 through 1987 that departed from Pennsylvania's sentencing guidelines. Judges departed from the guidelines in 29 percent of female defendants' cases but only in 15 percent of male defendants' cases. The authors concluded that the reasons for the judges' decisions included a number of social/background factors that were related to the sex of the defendant. Their findings were as follows:

- Sex had a small to moderate effect on the decision to imprison. Men were about 12 percent more likely to be sent to prison.
- Decisions were influenced by women's nonviolent prior records, their minor role in the offense, child-care responsibilities, physical or mental problems, and/or a show of remorse.
- Sex had no effect on the length-of-sentence decision. Women received slightly longer sentences for less serious offenses and slightly shorter sentences for more serious offenses than men.

In 1995, Daly and Bordt[18] conducted an extensive literature review of the chivalry question and also analyzed older data sets of court cases. They found that one-half of the studies showed sex effects favoring women, one-quarter showed mixed effects, and the remaining one-quarter showed no effects. Sex effects were evident in both recent and older data, more likely to emerge in felony offenses, urban courts, and in the decision to incarcerate as opposed to the length of the prison term.

Spohn and Spears[19] looked at case processing from the 1970s of violent offenders in Detroit. They found that 71 percent of males but 65 percent of females were fully prosecuted; and convictions were almost the same (86 percent vs. 85 percent). About 77 percent of men received prison sentences compared to only 48 percent for women. About 50 percent of males received sentences of more than three years compared to 35 percent of females. This appears to strongly support a chivalry hypothesis; however, these researchers noted significant differences between men and women on all independent variables (fewer prior felony convictions, less serious crimes, less likely to be charged with multiple offenses, less likely to have used a gun, less likely to have victimized a stranger, more likely to have a private attorney, and more likely to have been released prior to trial). All of these factors also affect sentencing decisions. Yet another factor was that women were much more likely to be codefendants. The researchers found interaction effects between sex and race: "We found that gender affected the incarceration rate only for blacks and that race affected the incarceration rate only for males."[20] They found that, for any given offense, African American men were most likely to be incarcerated, followed by white men, African American women, and then white women.

Research continues, and recent studies have also found a definite (albeit small) sex/gender effect on sentencing. One study reviewed older research to conclude that, after controlling for other factors, men were between 8 and 26 percent more likely than women to receive a prison sentence and averaged a 12-month longer sentence. Then the researchers examined chivalry in case processing in Christchurch, New Zealand.[21] Using a matched-sample methodology, the researchers tried to match offense, court, plea, number of charges, ethnicity, and age (but it was unclear if they were successful in matching all of these variables). The independent predictor variables included sex, ethnicity, age, employment status, familial situation, criminal history, offense variables (which included number of co-offenders, role, victim injury), presentence report recommendations, and blameworthiness variables (health, negative life experiences). The researchers found that it was impossible to match on some variables; for instance, women were less likely to have paid work, and they had stronger familial ties, less criminal history, were more likely to have poor health and negative life histories; and probation officers were less likely to recommend prison for women. After the variables were controlled for (if possible), the effect of sex dropped close to zero for the decision to incarcerate; but the length of sentence did seem to be affected by sex.[22]

Another more recent study reviewed the literature and concluded that women were 12 to 23 percent less likely to receive prison or jail time, but that there were mixed findings regarding length-of-sentence decisions.[23] These researchers utilized sentencing data from Texas from 1991 and found that females were less likely to be sentenced to prison and, if sentenced, received shorter sentences than men for property and drug crimes. For violent crimes, there was no difference in the decision to imprison, but if women were sent to prison, they received shorter sentences.[24] Like most studies, however, these researchers could not possibly control for all sentencing variables that might also be correlated with sex/gender.

A Selective Chivalry?

Some researchers have suggested that those women who conform to traditional sex roles (such as those who commit so-called women's crimes like shoplifting, or who are wives and mothers, or who appear contrite and demure in court) may be treated differently than women who do not fit the traditional image. Chesney-Lind[25] and Kruttschnitt[26] have argued that the traditional-type women are more subject to the informal social control of family and, therefore, the formal social control of the criminal justice system is less likely to be utilized. Kruttschnitt observed that women are subject to different control devices in this society through economic dependence, marriage, and motherhood. Her hypothesis was that if a woman is seen as controlled by these informal elements, then the courts would tend to treat her with less formal control.

Nagel[27] found that controlling for prior arrests did not seem to reduce the sex effect of sentencing; however, in this study there was no attempt to measure severity of prior crimes. More interestingly, however, marriage seemed to favorably impact women's sentences, but not men's. Farrington and Morris[28] also found that marriage affected women's sentences favorably, but not men's. Eaton[29] also noted that family circumstances seemed to affect judicial decision making. Daly[30] discussed the idea of "familial paternalism" and found that women with dependent children received more lenient sentencing because of their child-care role.

Visher[31] found that race, not marriage or family, affected the gender differential. In her study, she found that young, black, or hostile women received no preferential treatment. Older, white women, especially those whose demeanor was "ladylike," seemed to receive leniency. Other researchers also found that race was a complicating factor in the chivalry discussion.[32]

More recently, Brennan[33] looked only at female defendants in a New York City misdemeanor court. She found that in cases from 1989 and 1991, race/ethnicity did not directly affect sentencing, but black and Hispanic females were more likely to receive jail sentences than whites due to differences in socioeconomic status, community ties, prior record, earlier case processing, and charge severity. She noted that many chivalry studies found black and Hispanic women to be less likely to receive any favorable effect from some type of chivalrous sentencing. Brown[34] also found that native Hawaiian women were more likely than white girls to offend at earlier ages, hold juvenile records, recidivate, and be incarcerated, and that these differences were due to socioeconomic status rather than solely racial/ethnic bias in the system.

Farnsworth and Teske[35] identified and tested three different versions of the chivalry hypothesis:

- The *typicality* hypothesis proposes that women are treated with chivalry only when charges are consistent with female stereotypes.

- The *selective* chivalry hypothesis proposes that only white female offenders receive chivalry in the system.

- The *differential discretion* hypothesis proposes that disparity is most common in the pretrial informal decisions and least common at final sentencing.

Their data were from the 1980s and included larger numbers of cases than many of the other studies, but addressed only two types of charges—theft and assault. They found that African American men, but not African American women, were less likely than other defendants to get charge reductions. They found that women were 14 to 17 percent more likely than men without a record to receive probation and 11 to 16 percent less likely to receive a jail sentence.[36] These authors also found that white women were about twice as likely as minority women to have assault charges at arrest changed to non-assault charges at final sentencing.[37] They concluded that there are sex effects, at least for these two crime categories, that exist apart from any influence of offense seriousness. They found no evidence for the typicality argument, since the sex effects seemed to operate in a similar pattern with both theft and assault, and the authors assumed that assault was a nontypical crime for women. Considering that in the 1980s mandatory arrest policies for domestic violence resulted in more women being arrested for assault, this may have been a false assumption. One might conclude that domestic violence assaults would be treated differently than stranger or acquaintance assaults based on quality of participation, motivation, and presence of self-defense indicators, all of which operate differentially for men and women and no doubt affect sentencing decisions.

A few researchers suggest the possibility that women will be punished and controlled more than men because of their role in reproduction. Early eugenics movements targeted women in broad social policies designed to control population growth of undesirables.[38] More recently, there have been proposals to tie welfare to sterilization, and pregnant women have been incarcerated to "protect" their fetuses. Social control over women has been influenced and continues to be influenced by women's reproductive capabilities. For instance, there has been an increasing tendency to prosecute women for exposing their fetus to alcohol or drugs by using child-endangerment statutes. There have also been some instances where judges have required the use of contraceptives as part of the conditions of probation or parole. Further, some researchers have described state responses toward pregnancy in prison as coercing women either against or toward abortion.[39] Much evidence exists that women are still partially controlled by the state in ways relevant to their procreative functions. This sometimes results in what might be considered leniency (e.g., when a woman is given probation because she is nine months pregnant); or sometimes it might involve more serious punishment solely because of her pregnancy (e.g., anecdotal stories of judges sentencing pregnant drug offenders to prison because of their pregnancy).[40]

Chivalry for Juveniles? As discussed in the last chapter, Chesney-Lind and other researchers[41] found that girls were treated to a double standard and were more subject to control for noncriminal offenses such as promiscuity. Bishop and Frazier[42] found that male delinquents were more likely than female delinquents to be subject to formal intake, to be petitioned to court by prosecutors, to be detained in secure facilities until adjudication, and to receive sentences involving incarceration. Older youths, African Americans, and male delinquents were more likely to be incarcerated. There were, however, significant interaction effects between sex and contempt charges after status offense adjudications. Status offenses are those actions that would not be crimes if committed by an adult (curfew violations, smoking, drinking, running away). While there was no difference in sentencing male and female status offenders to secure facilities, girls were *more* likely to be incarcerated than boys when they were found in contempt after a status-offense finding. These researchers characterized these findings as "striking and dramatic," indicating that this was evidence that the juvenile system continues to treat girls more harshly than boys for status offenses (which include incorrigibility and promiscuity).[43] In further analysis of the same data, the researchers found the "intersectionality" of race/ethnicity and gender in that black girls were *more* likely than white boys to receive detention.[44] A more recent study found that females were less likely than males to receive detention and black females were less likely than white females to be subject to petition (formal processing), although the sample size was very small and the authors did not look at the impact of contempt charges.[45]

Several other authors[46] have also noted the juvenile justice system's pattern of upcharging or bootstrapping (discussed in Chapter 2). In one study, looking solely at sentencing for simple assaults, researchers noted that between 1994 and 2007 girls' convictions for simple assault increased 13 percent, but boys' arrests decreased by 11 percent. The authors speculated that zero-tolerance policies in schools and mandatory arrest policies in domestic violence brings youth into the system, and this occurred more often with girls than boys during this time period. Judges are unable to incarcerate girls for status offenses, but they can for contempt charges that occur after violations of probation, and that seems to happen more frequently to female offenders. The interaction between race/ethnicity and sex, and the complexity of relationships between status offending and delinquency make any general conclusions regarding the system's treatment of female juveniles relative to male juveniles highly speculative.

Sentencing Guidelines and Other Changes

The research discussed above examined whether differential treatment between men and women exists. Another question is: Even if differential treatment existed at one point in time, has it declined because of increased social and economic equality between the sexes? Also, many states changed their sentencing practices in the 1980s by adding mandatory minimum sentences for some crimes, and/or enforcing sentencing guidelines that dramatically curtailed judges' sentencing discretion. Daly and Bordt[47] and Raeder[48] argued that some of the sentencing changes occurring in the 1980s affected women more negatively than men. First, so-called gender neutral approaches such as sentencing guidelines that were adopted by many states offered mitigating factors that could reduce sentence length, but there was no mitigation for family circumstances—arguably a factor more female defendants would ask for. Second, "split the difference" approaches that averaged men's and women's sentences for a presumptive sentence always resulted in longer sentences for women.

Sentencing changes that reduced judicial discretion proved to be a natural experiment in testing the chivalry hypothesis since, arguably, women would be less subject to any favorable treatment by judges when they were forced to apply standard sentences based on type of crime and offender risk score. Several research studies looked at the effect of guidelines in several states that had created them.

Daly and Tonry[49] examined both sex and race as variables in sentencing. They found that after controlling for prior record and offense seriousness, women received shorter sentences before guidelines were enacted. Because the states and federal government used male averages when constructing guidelines, sentenced women received longer sentences than they would have before the guidelines were implemented. Table 7.1 presents information from Daly and Tonry's study along with more recent figures to show that there have not been dramatic changes in either the likelihood of being sentenced to prison or the length of sentence. Women are more likely to be sentenced to prison for some crime categories and less likely for others. Sentence length has decreased for aggravated assault, contrary to most crime categories where sentence length increased.

Other research looked at sentencing in Ohio before and after sentencing guidelines went into effect. The researchers assumed that sentencing would be equalized after guidelines were implemented but then gradually become disparate again because of "substantive rationality," which they described as decision making based on values, mitigating factors, family concerns, and other factors. They found that the percentage of convicted felons receiving prison dropped, and sentence length decreased after sentencing guidelines went into effect in 1996. They found no difference in the likelihood of conviction between men and women, or between pre- and post-guidelines. Women were less likely to be sentenced to prison both before and after guidelines. Black women were less likely to be incarcerated only after guidelines were instituted

Table 7.1 Sentences Imposed on Convicted Defendants, by Gender, 1986, 1990, 2006

Percent receiving an incarceration sentence (prison or jail)

Crime	Men			Women		
	1986	1990	2006	1986	1990	2006
All offenses	70	74	72	50	57	60
Murder	95	96	95	95	88	88
Sexual assault	88	86	82	75	84	69
Robbery	89	91	86	69	79	72
Aggravated assault	74	75	76	44	58	61
Burglary	74	78	75	70	65	72
Larceny	67	70	73	49	49	60
Drug sale	65	79	69	53	69	57
Average prison sentence, by months, by gender						
All offenses	60	54	61	42	36	45
Murder	217	234	256	168	173	212
Sexual assault	129	128	133	124	75	83
Robbery	128	98	105	85	48	71
Aggravated assault	66	52	64	71	42	54
Burglary	57	62	58	54	45	46
Larceny	32	35	39	29	23	34
Drug sale	42	52	58	43	44	46

Source: Daly, K. & Tonry, M. 1997. Gender, race and sentencing. *Crime and Justice 22*, 201–252; 2006 figures from Rosenmerkel, S., Murose, M. & Farole, D. 2009. *Felony Sentences in State Courts—2006,* Statistical Tables, p. 18 (Table 3.3); p. 19 (Table 3.4). Washington, DC: Bureau of Justice Statistics, U.S. Dept. of Justice.

(suggesting judges dealt leniently only with white women). There was no effect of having dependent children on sentencing, and these researchers did not find sex to have an effect on sentence length before or after guidelines.[50]

Other researchers also examined the effect of sentencing changes, such as the elimination of mandatory minimums, and found that there was a gender effect when judges were less constrained by sentencing laws.[51] Even with sentence guidelines in place, a different research study found that female white-collar offenders were 39 percent less likely than male offenders to receive jail over probation and 27 percent less likely to receive a prison sentence. For street crimes (auto theft, unarmed robbery, burglary), women were 42 percent less likely than male offenders to receive prison sentences. Control variables included race, age, crime seriousness (by the guideline score), trial versus plea bargain and whether a male or female judge presided. It is not clear, however, whether participation in crime or prior criminal history were used as controls in this study.[52] Looking at sentencing guidelines and whether they reduced any effect of sex on sentencing, Koons-Witt[53] found that there was no chivalry effect before or after the introduction of sentencing guidelines. Other researchers also found that in Minnesota (which also employed guidelines) no differences between men and women were found when looking at departures from guidelines, indicating no support for a chivalry hypothesis.[54]

In one recent study of federal sentencing cases after federal sentencing guidelines were rendered advisory rather than mandatory, Doerner[55] looked at 194,521 cases (83 percent were male offenders) to determine the effect of judges' increased discretion in federal sentencing. About 85 percent of the male offenders were incarcerated compared to 62 percent of the women. He found that, after controlling for prior record, women were about twice as likely to get downward departures from the guideline sentence; however, there were major differences between male and female offenders. Men were more likely to have multiple offense counts (22 percent to 15 percent), were more likely to go to trial (4.5 percent to 2.5 percent), and were more likely to have a violent offense (6.21 percent to 2.56 percent). After controlling for the variables that could be controlled for, women were about 39 percent less likely to be sentenced to prison. This study indicates that, at least in the federal system, greater discretion of judges may be introducing a new phase of differential sentencing for women. However, important variables may not have been controlled for, just as in earlier studies of chivalry.

To summarize the wide range of studies on chivalry, it appears that there was a small sex effect even after controlling for other independent variables such as prior record. However, it is not at all clear that the shorter sentences for women were unfair in that many factors cannot be controlled for in any statistical test, including remorse, plea bargaining agreements, and participation/culpability in the crime. Sentencing guidelines and other determinate sentencing changes have generally increased the likelihood of and length of prison sentences for women. Finally, chivalry studies tend to be single jurisdiction studies; therefore, it is entirely possible that there is a sex effect in one jurisdiction and not in another. Based on the more recent studies, if there is a sex effect whereby women are less likely to be sentenced to prison or receive a shorter sentence, it is probably a very small effect and may only exist for a subset of women (white women who commit property crimes).

Sentenced to Prison

In 1976 there were 11,000 women in prison; in 1986 there were 26,000.[56] In 1990 there were 44,065 and in 1998, 84,427. In 2009 there were 105,197; and in 2011 there were 111,387.[57] Historically, women comprised about four to five percent of the total prisoner population; today, their percentage has increased to about 6.7 percent. Although the total number of women incarcerated is dwarfed by the number of men in prison, the *percentage increase* of women sentenced to prison over the last three decades has been higher than the rate for men. Between 1990 and 2001, the average annual growth rate was 5.7 percent for men and 7.5 percent for women. Put another way, the number of men in prison increased by 80 percent, whereas the number of women in prison increased by 114 percent.[58] Since 2001, the rate of increase has declined and since 2008, even the actual number of women in prison has declined from 114,612 in 2008 to 111,387 in 2011.[59] National growth trends mask major changes between states, however, and some states (like California) have dramatically reduced their numbers while other states continue to increase the numbers of women sent to prison.

Race and Ethnicity

The intersectionality between race and gender is well known.[60] As Table 7.2 shows, incarceration rates (per 100,000) vary tremendously by race/ethnicity and sex. In 2009, the incarceration rate for women was 67 per 100,000 compared to 949 per 100,000 for men.

Table 7.2   Incarceration Rates by Race/Ethnicity and Sex, 2009/2011

	Males	Females
Total	949/932	67/65
White	487/478	50/51
Black	3,119/3,023	142/129
Hispanic	1,193/1,238	74/71

Source: West, H., Sabol, W. & Greenman, S. 2010. *Prisoners in 2009*, BJS Bulletin. Washington, DC: U.S. Dept. of Justice, p. 28; Carson, E. & Sabol, W. 2012. *Prisoners in 2011*, BJS Bulletin. Washington, DC: U.S. Dept. of Justice, p. 8.

Crenshaw points out that, despite the great differences in rates between men and women, the ratio of black men to white men is roughly the same as that between white women and black women. In Table 7.3 on the following page we see that the ratio between black and white men is about 6 to 1, as is the ratio between black and white women. The relative rate of incarceration for black men to white men is the same as that for black women to white women, and the same ratios between men and women apply to Hispanics as well.

Interestingly, the rate of imprisonment for black women has been declining, even while the rate for white and Hispanic women has been increasing. In 2000, the incarceration rates (per 100,000) looked like this: white women—34, black women—205, Hispanic women—60. In 2009, the rates had changed: white women—67, black women—142, Hispanic women—74.

The incarceration rate for black women is still over double that of white women (see Table 7.4 on the following page), but it is significantly lower than it was 10 years ago when it was about six times the rate of white women.[61] The rate for black women declined by 30 percent between 2000 and 2009 (and declined 10 percent for black men). During that same time period, the rates for whites increased (9 percent for men and 47 percent for women) and the rate for Hispanics also increased (2 percent for men and 23 percent for women).[62]

Table 7.3	Proportional Odds of Incarceration by Race		
	Black–White	**Black–Latino**	**Latino–White**
Male	5.7:1	2:1	2.8:1
Female	6.5:1	2.6:1	2.5:1

Source: Crenshaw, K. 2012. From private violence to mass incarceration: Thinking intersectionally about women, race, and social control. *UCLA Law Review 59*, 1418–1472.

Table 7.4	Trend in Incarceration Rate per 100,000			
Year	**All women**	**White**	**Black**	**Hispanic**
1990	31	19	117	
1992	33	20	136	
1994	45	26	169	
1996	51	30	185	
2009	67	67	142	74*

*Hispanics were grouped with whites in earlier years.

Source: Greenfield, L. & Snell, T. 1999. *Women Offenders* (Bureau of Justice Statistics Special Report, NCJ 175688). Washington, DC: U.S. Department of Justice, p. 10. Rates for 2009 from West, H., Sabol, W. & Greenman, S. 2010. *Prisoners in 2009* (NCJ 231675). Washington, DC: Bureau of Justice Statistics.

It is not clear why the rate of incarceration for black women has decreased. There is a wide disparity in ratios of imprisoned blacks to whites between the states from 15:1 in one state to a low of 2:1[63] (meaning 15 black women are incarcerated for every one white woman in the first state compared to a ratio of two black women to one white woman in the second state); therefore, there may be different explanations relevant to different states. One source suggested that it may be because black women are less likely to be involved in drug and violent crimes today, combined with the fact that methamphetamine arrests are rising (and white and Hispanic women are more likely to be involved in this type of drug crime).[64] It could also be that determinate sentencing changes reduced any race effects that may have operated to increase the likelihood of prison sentences for black women. It could also be that a steady stream of critical press and academic studies that criticized the overuse of prison sentences, especially for drug offenders, has finally begun to affect sentencing decisions and that black women (who were differentially affected by the War on Drugs) are benefitting from this recognition.

At least one study does not support this speculation. Crow and Kunselman[65] examined Florida sentencing data of all female drug offenders for 10 years and found that female drug offenders were more likely to receive prison when judges were allowed more discretion in sentencing (not less, as is speculated above). The increased risk of imprisonment was true for all women, but more so for black women: 27 percent of black women were sentenced to prison when guidelines were mandatory compared to a later point in time when 38 percent of black women were sentenced to prison when guidelines were advisory. Hispanic women were also more likely to receive prison when judges had more discretion (24 percent before the sentencing change received prison compared to 38 percent afterwards). Thus, it is not clear what effect greater discretion might be having on sentencing. On a national level, it appears to be reducing the likelihood of black women receiving prison sentences, but at least one study shows that one state's experience has been the opposite.

Explaining the Increase

The same pattern of increase in the number of female offenders in prison is present in jail and community corrections populations as well. Fifteen years ago women constituted a little under 20 percent of the probation population, about 11 percent of the parole population, and 11 percent of jail inmates.[66] Today, they comprise about 24 percent of the probation population, about 12 percent of the parole population, and about 12 percent of the jail population.[67]

Chesney-Lind[68] points out that between 1985 and 1994 women's crimes increased 36.5 percent, but their rate of incarceration increased by 202 percent. Since then, the rate of increase for women's incarceration has not been as dramatic (22 percent between 2000 and 2009), but it is still higher than men's (16 percent).[69]

Many researchers[70] have argued that part of the rise in women's imprisonment, beginning in the 1980s, has been due to determinate sentencing, "greater formalization" in the system, and a shift in sentencing practices that has been called "equality with a vengeance."[71] Beginning in the 1980s, several researchers found that women were more likely to get prison sentences for any given crime and to be given longer sentences than in years past. In some cases, the chance of being sent to prison doubled.[72] Another factor in the increased numbers of women sent to prison seems to be an increased tendency to revoke parole or probation, usually for failed drug tests.[73] Arguably, the War on Drugs has been the largest single factor in the increased imprisonment of women.

The Drug War and Women's Imprisonment.   The dramatic rise in women's imprisonment has been attributed most often to the criminal justice system's response to drug use and abuse. By all accounts, female offenders who end up in prison are more likely to use drugs than male offenders and to use more drugs than male offenders, are more likely to report drugs as a problem in their lives, and are increasingly more likely to be sentenced to prison for a drug conviction. Danner[74] is one of many who point out how the War on Drugs and this country's punitive sentencing practices have hurt women, not only by placing more of them in prison but also by siphoning public resources away from health and social programs into prison construction and maintenance.

In one study of sentencing trends in New York, California, and Minnesota for the years 1986 through 1996, researchers found that the number of women in prison for drugs increased tenfold. Drug crimes accounted for half of all new imprisonments of women; for men, drug crimes accounted for about one-third of the increase in the same ten years. Drug offenses accounted for 91 percent of the increase in the number of women imprisoned in New York, 55 percent in California, and 26 percent in Minnesota.[75]

During the period 1986 to 1995, total arrests of women increased by 15 percent but drug arrests rose by 61 percent. A further breakdown of drug-related prison commitments showed that of women who were incarcerated, 77 percent of Hispanic women, 59 percent of African American women, and 34 percent of white women were incarcerated for drug crimes.[76]

Women arrested for drugs are not drug kingpins. For the most part, they are low-level users and dealers, and often their foray into the drug world is intertwined with an intimate relationship. Typically, they receive no mitigation in sentencing because they cannot help the prosecution, since they know very little about the drug seller's network.[77]

Nowhere is the impact of drug sentencing felt more strongly than in the federal system. Because of the increasing federalization of drug crimes, the jump in the number of female inmates has been dramatic. Gender-neutral sentencing ignores the fact that women are often involved in drug networks because of an intimate relationship with either a husband, a family member, or a lover. While they may be aware of, benefit from, and perhaps participate in a minor way in the drug enterprise, they typically are not as actively involved as their male codefendants. More importantly, for women to avoid such criminal entanglement would mean terminating the relationship; this is a much different choice than other codefendant relationships, especially if there are children involved.[78]

Supreme Court decisions, including *Booker v. U.S.* (2005), rendered federal sentencing guidelines only advisory, meaning that judges could depart from proscribed guideline sentences. Before *Booker*, sentence length was mandated by federal sentencing guidelines, and sentences for drug crimes were extremely long. Today, after a series of Supreme Court decisions, federal sentencing guidelines are no longer mandatory and federal judges have more discretion to sentence an offender to a shorter sentence than the guidelines specify.

Sentenced to Death

Some women serve their time in prison under a sentence of death. The unique aspects of living under a sentence of death are seldom discussed in relation to female offenders because there are so few of them;[79] however, their numbers are increasing.

Baker[80] found that from 1632 to 1997, only 357 women have been executed in this country. Of these, 39 percent were white, 58.6 percent were African American, 1.5 percent were Native American, and 0.9 percent were Latina (the others' race or ethnic origin was not known). Most were executed for murder, but other crimes included witchcraft (26), arson, and slave revolt. The South Atlantic states were the most frequent site of executions. Baker argues that women were more likely to be executed in times when women were challenging power structures, such as during slave revolts. In 2011, 62 women were under a sentence of death, comprising about 2 percent of the total number of inmates under a death sentence. Of the 62, 42 are white and 16 are black. No woman was executed in 2011. Texas has the most women (nine) under a death sentence. Many states either have no woman under a sentence of death or do not have a death penalty.[81]

Jails and Jail Inmates

Before turning our attention to prisons and prisoners, it is necessary to stop and consider jails and jail prisoners. While there are obviously many similarities between the institutions and the female inmates in prisons and jails, there are enough differences that it is important to identify them. Women in jail experience many of the same fears and deprivations that women in prison do, as well as some unique to the jail experience.

Jail is perhaps more traumatic because it is at the point of the arrest: child care is unsettled, the woman may be experiencing withdrawal from drugs, and the separation from family and children is recent and still extremely painful. Jails are typically in urban locations so there is very little space available; consequently, women may have fewer programs and almost no outdoor opportunities (often jail recreation "yards" are the roof). Because of their small numbers, women typically are housed in a wing or unit of a jail for men, although there are a few women-only jails across the country.[82]

In 1983, women comprised about 7.1 percent of the total jail population; in 1985, 8 percent; in 1989, 9.5 percent; and in 1996 they increased to more than 10 percent.[83] The adult female jail population grew 7 percent annually in the 1990s, compared to an annual 4.5 percent increase for males.[84] In 2012, women's percentage of the total jail population increased to 13 percent.[85]

Characteristics of Women in Jail

Generally, women in jail are similar to women in prison although, as a group, they have committed (or are arrested for) less serious crimes and tend to be younger. Recall that jails also house those who have been accused but not convicted of a crime. Between 50 and 75 percent of jail detainees may be there awaiting trial and/or sentencing rather than serving a sentence. Most personal characteristics of female jail prisoners are similar to those of prison inmates: they are poor and undereducated, minorities are overrepresented, they are likely to be unmarried, a substantial percentage have had family members involved in the criminal justice system, over a third have experienced childhood abuse, and most have also experienced adult abuse. Green and colleagues reported that childhood physical and sexual abuse was linked to drug and alcohol abuse, mental disorders and criminality among a jail sample.[86]

A recent Bureau of Justice Administration report by Lynch and her colleagues[87] surveyed female jail inmates in both urban and rural jails and found that 40 percent had experienced childhood physical abuse, 47 percent experienced childhood sexual abuse, 61 percent witnessed violence, 38 percent had been attacked/robbed, 67 percent experienced partner violence, 45 percent had been the victim of adult sexual assault, 71 percent had a caregiver who had been in jail, and 61 percent had a caregiver with an addiction problem. Those with serious mental health issues were significantly more likely to have experienced these life events.

Domestic violence is extremely common among jail inmates, with estimates at about 60 percent. In one study, a surprising finding was that jail was used as an avenue of escape for women who feared their partners:

> Always in my head my ultimate thing was to leave him and the only way I could do that was to go to jail. And I was safe in jail. I didn't have to worry about getting beat up, you know, and when he would come to visit me, he couldn't beat me up because we were supervised.[88]

It is possible that an even higher number of jail inmates than prison inmates suffer from mental health problems.[89] Veysey found that jailed women are also more likely than jailed men to be diagnosed with mental illnesses (18.5 percent vs. 8.9 percent). The most frequent diagnosis is clinical depression (13.7 percent of women vs. 3.4 percent of men). About a quarter (22.3 percent) of women in jail are diagnosed with post-traumatic stress disorder (PTSD). Further, a dual diagnosis (both mental illness and drug addiction) is very common.[90] More recent studies replicate earlier findings that female jail inmates are more likely than male inmates to suffer from mental health issues.[91] In the recent study by Lynch and her colleagues, 43 percent of the sample of female jail inmates met the criteria for a serious mental illness (lifetime occurrence) and 53 percent met the criteria for PTSD.[92] Not surprisingly, those with serious mental health issues also were more likely to report greater rates of victimization and more extensive offending histories. Serious mental illness was significantly related to early onset of substance abuse, drug dealing, property crimes, fighting/assault charges, and running away.[93]

As with women in prisons, female jail inmates are most likely to have drug problems. Reporting on 1989 figures, a Bureau of Justice Statistics report indicated that more than half of female jail inmates had used drugs in the month prior to their jail incarceration; 40 percent used drugs daily. Cocaine or crack was the most frequently used drug (about 39 percent had used cocaine or crack in month before arrest). About a quarter of the women committed crime to buy drugs. About 20 percent of the women were under the influence of alcohol at time of offense.[94] Teplin and her colleagues[95] reported that about 60 percent of her jail sample had a substance abuse diagnosis, 14 percent suffered from major depression, and 22 percent had current PTSD symptoms.

In a 2002 study, it was found that two-thirds of female jail inmates reported risk factors for drug abuse; one-third were homeless, half had been exposed to infectious diseases, and a quarter were already under mental health care. About 14 percent of the women in this sample were pregnant.[96] In the 2012 study by Lynch and her colleagues, 82 percent of the sample met lifetime criteria for drug or alcohol abuse or dependence.[97]

In a 2005 study of 100 female jail inmates using a convenience sample, the following findings emerged:

- 44 percent had not completed high school,
- the average age was 34 years,
- 87 percent were unmarried,
- 81 were black,
- 11 percent were white,
- 73 percent had children younger than 18,
- 65 percent lived with family/friends/parents,
- 80 percent were awaiting trial,
- 33 percent had charges that were theft related, and
- 21 percent had charges that were drug related.[98]

Interestingly, no substantial differences were found between those awaiting trial and those sentenced, except those awaiting trial had more children and were less likely to have alcohol problems (28 percent versus 50 percent). In this study, it was found that

> 98 percent of respondents had some trauma exposure; the most common was violence by intimate (71 percent). About 62 percent reported childhood trauma; 72 percent reported recent use of illicit substance; and, 74 percent reported an alcohol or substance abuse problem.[99]

Similar to past studies, about half (48 percent) reported childhood sexual molestation, 26 percent reported childhood physical abuse, 58 percent witnessed someone injured or killed, 58 percent reported a family member was killed, 58 percent had been raped, 57 percent had been physically attacked, 71 percent had experienced domestic abuse, and 55 percent had been threatened with a weapon.[100]

The jail inmates in this study had a high level of need for intervention in all areas. Similar to Teplin's study, about two-thirds had a drug dependency problem; about a quarter were diagnosed with a major depressive disorder; and about a third suffered from PTSD. Nearly half of the women had a sexually transmitted disease and participated in high-risk sexual practices. They exhibited low levels of parental functioning with scores indicating high risk for abusive or maladaptive parenting practices, a general lack of understanding of children's developmental capabilities, difficulty in helping children meet their needs, use of corporal punishment in controlling children, and seeing children as objects of adult gratification. A particularly sad finding of this jail study was that 83 percent of the children of the jailed mothers reportedly had witnessed or experienced sexual or physical abuse or other violence.[101]

The perceived program needs of these women (in order) were: job training (93 percent), problem solving (91 percent), stress management (88 percent), relationship counseling (82 percent), health education (82 percent), individual mental health counseling (80 percent), parenting classes (79 percent), anger management (76 percent), and drug education/treatment (75 percent).[102]

Crimes.   When compared with men, a smaller number of women have committed violent crimes, and a greater percentage of women are in jail for drug crimes.[103] In an older Bureau of Justice Statistics report, it was noted that 28 percent of men were in jail for violent offenses, while only 15 percent of women were. Further, 32 percent of women were in for property offenses, 27 percent for drug offenses, 25 percent for public order offenses, and the remainder for "other."[104] More jail inmates than prison inmates are sentenced for prostitution (because these are usually misdemeanor charges where the sentence is to jail, not prison).

Issues and Concerns

As mentioned earlier, because of their small numbers, jailed women probably receive even less programming and fewer opportunities for activity, especially physical activity, than women in prison.[105] Outdoor recreation is especially problematic for women in jails. As with prisons, there is very seldom an attempt to use a gender-specific classification system for women. Consequently, it may be that they are overclassified and housed in higher security settings than they need to be.[106]

Medical and psychological services for women in jail are, in many jurisdictions, inadequate. In one national survey it was reported that less than half of female inmates received a physical exam upon entry.[107] Large percentages of female jail inmates need psychological services, although many do not receive needed help.[108]

It is most probable that a portion of the mental health problems of women in jails is related to prior victimization. As reported above, at least as many, if not more, women in jail report childhood and adult sexual and physical victimization as women in prison. While there is obviously underreporting by men, there is probably a certain amount of underreporting by women as well. It seems clear that, similar to prison inmates, there is a clear difference in the likelihood of prior victimization between male and female jail inmates. Not only do female jail inmates report childhood victimization, a large number also continue to be victimized as adults (often because of their lifestyles). In one study of female jail inmates, 60 percent said they had been physically victimized within the past year and 68 percent reported forced sexual activity. In an open-ended question asking about the "last bad thing" that happened to them, responses included being thrown from a moving car, shot, stabbed, beaten, and gang-raped.[109]

In a 2003 report by Moe and Ferraro,[110] female jail inmates expressed great concerns about the lack of medical care, but they also acknowledged that it was better than what they had access to on the street. The women described a wide range of minor health issues that became serious because of lack of care, such as an infected cut on one woman's foot that burst open with pus and blood because she was unable to get medical assistance. Another woman with Hepatitis C was having complications, and yet another woman described how her undiagnosed stomach pain turned into a burst appendix. As with women in prison, fear of the spread of disease and the lack of medical care is an ever-present reality and one that causes conflict between inmates. Women who give birth must give up their baby immediately and receive no help for postpartum depression or other postnatal health issues.

In this study, women in jail had the same anxiety regarding past victimization, which they typically suppressed: ". . . If I start talking, I'm going to be like Humpty Dumpty. I'm going to fall and you ain't going to find all of those pieces. That's what I'm afraid of, that I'll lose it completely mentally, you know?"[111] However, many women expressed appreciation for drug treatment and saw jail as a "blessing in disguise."

Veysey[112] provides a clear argument that the characteristics of the jail, combined with women's background of victimization, act to re-traumatize the offenders. She notes that about a quarter (22.3 percent) of female jail detainees are diagnosed with PTSD. Symptoms include hypervigilance, startle reflex, phobias, auditory and visual flashbacks to incidents of abuse, and uncontrollable anger or rage. The presence of male officers, strip searches, and an environment characterized by loss of control are elements of the jail that may increase stress and anxiety.

Veysey notes that this not only impacts the woman but also results in associated increased institutional costs, including an increase in health costs, in physical injury, and in greater use of medications. She suggests that there are certain procedural and resource distribution changes that can be made to help reduce women's stress levels. For example, making an effort to give more information to offenders during booking as to what is happening, screening for vulnerable women, crisis and de-escalation intervention counseling, the use of female staff, training of all staff to understand women's issues, a respite from administrative segregation if necessary, architectural changes to improve privacy, reducing contact between female detainees and male detainees in the facility, employment of specialized staff, and community referrals are some of Veysey's suggestions.

Female jail inmates arguably have more problems than their male counterparts and fewer services available to them. They are more likely to have drug and alcohol problems, medical needs, mental health needs, and to experience stress due to the characteristics of incarceration. They are more likely to have major problems related to child care (i.e., finding child placement, experiencing stress due to separation). In some jails women are housed in proximity to male offenders who sexually harass them. There are also numerous reports across the country that male jail staff sexually harass and even assault female jail inmates.[113] Women in jails have similar problems of drug abuse, single parenthood, and mental and physical health challenges but have fewer services available to them than women in state prisons. They may be housed in units designed for male offenders. What seems obvious is that very few jurisdictions make any effort to think about any special needs or differences that characterize female jail populations compared to male populations.

Conclusion

Differential treatment most probably operated in the criminal justice system in past decades, especially in sentencing. However, there is a real question whether treating women differently resulted in less than equal justice or whether such treatment was warranted by differences in the elements of the crime, participation, and motivation (for the crime) of women.

Treatment of women by the formal criminal justice system has changed, arguably, because of a change in the image of women. If public perception has adopted the idea that women are equally criminal as men, then it is predictable that criminal women will be equally sentenced. Yet if one looks closely, their crimes, criminal motivations, and histories are not the same as men's. Women in jails and those sent to prison are more likely to be drug addicted, more likely to have been sexually and physically victimized, more likely to be responsible for small children, and more likely to be imprisoned for a nonviolent crime.

It appears that women are now viewed like men, and this equalization has translated to policy. But arguably this policy is not helpful to female offenders or to society. Women have historically had lower recidivism rates than men, even though they received more so-called lenient treatment. Today women's recidivism rates are increasing. It is possible that the increased tendency to use incarceration instead of other correctional alternatives will lead to more entrenched female criminality.

REVIEW QUESTIONS

1. Describe disparate sentencing laws in the 19th and early 20th centuries.

2. What are the conclusions reached regarding the presence of chivalry in the system?

3. What are the factors that might explain more lenient sentencing of women (instead of or in addition to chivalry) and should be controlled for in any study of sentencing?

4. Some researchers support the notion that a *selective* chivalry exists. Which women may be more likely than others to receive more lenient sentencing?

5. Describe Farnsworth and Teske's three different chivalry theories. Which one received more empirical support?

6. What are the findings regarding recent research regarding gender and race/ethnicity of juveniles?

7. What were some of the sentencing changes that reduced sentencing discretion and led to longer sentences for women?

8. Describe the pattern of growth of women in prison over time using both percentage increase figures and rates per 100,000. Describe how percentages of totals relative to race/ethnicity have changed.

9. Describe the major explanations for the explosive growth in the numbers of women sent to prison.

10. Describe the characteristics of women in jail.

8

Women's Prisons

CHAPTER SUMMARY

- Women's prisons are few in number compared to men's and have a different history and legacy.

- The reformatory era, roughly from 1870 through 1930, refers to the building of reformatories for women that were based on the cottage style of architecture, housed young offenders (some as young as 12), and employed matrons who acted as role models to reform the "dissolute" ways of those sent to the institutions.

- Female prisoners are likely to be slightly older than male prisoners and more likely to have a drug problem. They are typically unmarried, unemployed, or underemployed prior to incarceration, and are likely to be the custodial parent of at least one child. They are also likely to have been a victim of sexual or physical abuse as children and as adults.

- The rate of imprisonment for black women has been declining while an increase in white women's imprisonment rate has occurred, decreasing the ratio of black to white women in prison and decreasing the percentage of black women in prison.

- Management of prisons for women poses different issues, even though the trend has been to "bring them in line" with prisons for men. Women are less likely to commit lethal violence or engage in collective disturbances, but they have greater medical needs and are perceived as harder to supervise.

There are approximately 112,000 women in prison in the United States. This is only 6.7 percent of the total incarcerated population, so women have often been characterized as the "stepchildren" of the system and treated as an afterthought or special problem by central prison administration. While the numbers remain relatively small, the percentage increase of incarcerated women has been higher than men's for most years in the last several decades, although recently the numbers have begun to stabilize and even decline in some states. Chapter 7 described the tremendous increase in women's incarceration rate. In this chapter we look at the number and range of women's prisons across the country; discuss the history of women's prisons; review the research on female prisoners, including differences between male and female inmates; and discuss management issues unique to women's prisons. In the next chapter, we describe the prison world in more detail.

Prisons for men have been the subject of a long tradition of research, starting in the 1940s, with works that have described prisoner subcultures, the relationship between prisoners and guards, victimization, race relations, and other elements of the prison for men.[1] These researchers, with a few exceptions, did not explore the world of female prisoners.[2] Apart from a single history and description published in 1931[3] and a few published studies in the 1960s,[4] most research on women's prisons began in the 1970s and 1980s, focusing on female prison homosexuality[5] and other aspects of the female prisoner subculture.[6] Journalistic accounts of prisons contributed to the literature by adding the voices of prisoners and staff.[7] In the 1990s, several ethnographic studies of women's prisons were presented, including those by Owen,[8] Girshick,[9] and Rierden.[10] Other books covered counseling or other issues of women in prison.[11]

Since the 1990s there have been many more published books, articles, and monographs on women's prisons and female prisoners, and even reality television series. Government studies, such as one commissioned by Eleanor Holmes Norton, examined sentencing issues, the lack of drug treatment, pathways to crime, and sexual abuse by correctional officers.[12] Amnesty International and the Human Rights Watch[13] also published reports condemning the treatment of female prisoners in the United States, describing such treatment as human rights violations and violations of international treaties against torture. The most extreme criticisms were directed at health care, the policy of separating mothers and babies after birth, shackling pregnant women, and the seemingly increasing incidence of sexual assaults by male correctional officers. It was also reported that poor opportunities for treatment existed for women. Even with all the new sources, however, the descriptions of female prisoners and prisons for women remain substantially the same as the descriptions from studies in the 1970s.

Women's Prisons

Women's prisons range from the Bedford Hills turn-of-the-century brick buildings, situated in affluent Westchester County, New York, to brand-new buildings in states that are trying to keep up with growing prisoner populations. In the 1990s some states, faced with exploding female prisoner populations, briefly utilized gymnasiums as dormitories[14] before building their way out of overpopulated institutions. New prisons are often cheaply built, portable buildings surrounded by chain-link fences and razor wire.

Some women's institutions still carry the legacy of their reformatory past. Consequently, institutions for women may very well "feel" different. That is, some older women's prisons may still have "cottage style" architecture, the signs of security are more subtle, and the interactions between staff and inmates appear to be more informal and personal than what occurs in prisons for men. However, the trend has been to build facilities that can and do house men and women interchangeably. Increasingly, staff members, too, are "interchangeable" and are transferred back and forth between facilities for men and women. Staff training, administrative policies, and "unisex" architecture all combine to minimize and de-emphasize any differences between the two population groups.[15] Of course, the model of the "unisex" prison is a male model.

Many states have only one or two institutions for women. This means that, whether housed in smaller building units, a Gothic castle, or a dormitory in a portable-style building, all custody grades and all variety of offenders are housed together in the same state prison. Security is set at medium and maximum security level, even though most women do not need that level of custody. Table 8.1 on the following page shows that only three states have more than 4,000 female prisoners: Florida, California, and Texas.

California has reduced its population of female prisoners dramatically in the last several years. Up until a few years ago, Texas and California had about the same number of women in prison, moving inexorably up every year until both states' populations of women rose to 10,000 and higher. California had 10,989 women incarcerated as recently as 2009. In *Brown v. Plata* (2011), the Supreme Court mandated that the state reduce its total prison population and now the latest figures show only about 6,000 women incarcerated in California's prisons. The "realignment" program has offenders more likely to serve time in the community under a probation sentence or in jail.

The History of Women's Prisons

Until the 1800s, men and women were incarcerated together in *gaols* and women were preyed upon and exploited by male prisoners and guards. Incarceration was considered extremely inappropriate for women (who were under the legal authority of a father or husband). Those few female offenders who were incarcerated because of the seriousness of their crime or because they were older, repeat offenders were considered irredeemable.

Table 8.1	Number of Female Prisoners by State	
Under 250	**250–500**	**500–750**
Vermont (127)	Nebraska (353)	Delaware (566)
Maine (164)	Montana (399)	Alaska (678)
North Dakota (171)	South Dakota (423)	New Mexico (630)
Rhode Island (186)		Utah (639)
Wyoming (238)		Hawaii (688)
		Minnesota (710)
		Kansas (730)
750–1000	**1000–1250**	**1250–1500**
Massachusetts (759)	Idaho (1,008)	South Carolina (1,357)
Iowa (784)	Arkansas (1,060)	Washington (1,395)
West Virginia (805)	New Jersey (1,061)	
Maryland (876)	Connecticut (1,218)	
Nevada (967)	Wisconsin (1,225)	
Idaho (1,008)	Oregon (1,231)	
1500–1750	**1750–2000**	**2000–2250**
Mississippi (1,687)	Michigan (1989)	New York (2247)
Colorado (1,723)		
2250–2500	**2500–2750**	**2750–3000**
Tennessee (2,363)	Indiana (2,566)	Illinois (2,865)
Louisiana (2,389)	Alabama (2,649)	Virginia (2,894)
North Carolina (2,461)	Kentucky (2,685)	
Oklahoma (2,497)	Missouri (2,703)	
	Pennsylvania (2,735)	
3000–3250	**3250–3500**	**2750–3000**
	Arizona (3,631)	Georgia (3,589)
3750–4000	**Over 4000**	
Ohio (3,968)	California (6,098)	
	Florida (6,985)	
	Texas (13,549)	

Source: Carson, E. & Golinelli, D. 2013. *Prisoners in 2012: Advance Counts* (Bureau of Justice Statistics Bulletin, NCJ 242467). Washington, DC: U.S. Dept. of Justice, Table 2, p. 3.

Early Punishments and Places of Confinement

Early English law made it very clear that women and men were different and possessed different rights under the law. Some behavior, for instance, was not considered criminal when committed by men or was punished much less severely, such as adultery. For other crimes, however, women may have been punished less often or less severely than men who committed the identical activity.[16] Women who violated the social order were subject to the ducking stool or *branks*:

> The branks was an iron cage placed over the head, and most examples incorporated a spike or pointed wheel that was inserted into the offender's

mouth in order to "pin the tongue and silence the noisiest brawler." This spiked cage was intended to punish women adjudged quarrelsome or not under the proper control of their husbands.[17]

First fathers and then husbands had almost complete legal control over their daughters and wives. Punishment could be imposed whenever the wife or daughter was considered disobedient or unchaste. Women were sent to monasteries when out of control, and husbands could turn their errant wives over to *bridewells* or poorhouses. Wives had little legal recourse against brutal or improvident husbands. If a woman was married to a drunk who did not give her money to buy food, there was little she could do to provide for herself and her children; consequently, many of the women committed to prisons or bridewells in the 1700s and 1800s were there for theft or begging. Others turned to prostitution, the only other way women could earn money. When sentenced to bridewells, female criminals often received substantially longer sentences than men.[18]

Women in poorhouses and bridewells were expected to do the cooking and cleaning, spinning and sewing required for the institution. Women in bridewells in England found that prostitution was one of the few ways to better their living conditions in the prison.[19] Similarly, female offenders who were transported as indentured servants to Australia were often sexually exploited. In 1812, the Committee on Transportation observed that women were ". . . indiscriminately given to such of the inhabitants as demanded them, and were in general received rather as prostitutes than as servants. . . ."[20]

Feinman[21] described the early treatment of women in the United States as basically egalitarian during the colonial period, and they were considered equal partners to men. With increasing urbanization and industrialization after the American Revolution, women's labor was less essential and the "Cult of True Womanhood" developed in the East. Women were expected to be "pure, submissive, and pious" and expected to confine their activities to the home. Those who did not fit this mold were considered in some ways more deviant than criminal men, since they went against a "natural" order. Freedman explained that the female deviant, whether a prostitute, vagrant, murderess, or thief, "threatened social order doubly, both by sinning and by removing the moral constraints on men."[22]

Descriptions of early places of confinement for women indicate that there was little regard for the safety or health of female prisoners. Before classification of the sexes in Europe and the United States, men and women were housed together in large rooms where the strong preyed upon the weak. Each individual's life was made bearable only by the resources received from his or her family or what could be acquired by begging, bartering, or stealing from other prisoners. After the separation of the sexes, women's lives in prison were only marginally better.[23]

Freedman describes early institutions for women as overcrowded and filthy. In the 1820s, a Philadelphia jail held seven women in a cellar with only two blankets among them; and in Albany, a jail placed fifteen women in one room.[24] In 1825, separate quarters for women were built at a Baltimore prison, and in 1835 officials at Ossining State Penitentiary (Sing Sing) built a separate unit for women.[25] Feinman described Sing Sing Penitentiary in 1843 as a place where women, some with their children, were housed in a room eighteen feet square and where the "hot, crowded, and unsanitary conditions during the summer led to the death of one baby."[26] Floggings and harsh physical punishments led to miscarriages and even death. Women were subject to forced prostitution by male warders.[27] More often than not, women were simply left alone in the wing or building that comprised the women's portion of the institution. Rafter writes that female prisoners held in Auburn Prison in 1825 were housed in an attic and visited only once a day when a steward came to deliver food and remove waste.[28]

The Reformatory Era

In the late nineteenth century, the perception of female criminals changed from being seen as evil and irredeemable to a view that they were misguided and led astray by men. Elizabeth Fry in England and several reformers in this country advocated not only separate housing but also female supervision of women in prison. Fry visited Newgate Prison in 1813 and was "shocked and sickened" by the "blaspheming, fighting, dram-drinking, half naked women" found there. In her words: "All I tell thee is a faint picture of reality; the filth, the closeness of the rooms, the furious manner and expressions of the women towards each other, and the abandoned wickedness, which everything bespoke, are quite indescribable."[29] Her book, *Observations on the Siting, Superintendence and Government of Female Prisoners*, published in 1825, advocated work, training, religion, routine, manners, and supervision of female prisoners by women, not men.[30] Primarily through her efforts, a separate system for female inmates developed in England long before the United States undertook the same reforms.

In this country, reformers such as Dorothea Dix, Mary Wister, Sarah Doremus, and Abby Hopper Gibbons advocated female warders in the 1820s. In 1845, Doremus and Gibbons established a Ladies Association within the New York Prison Association, which became autonomous several years later as the Women's Prison Association of New York. This organization also opened the Isaac Hopper Home for released women.[31] In 1825, a House of Refuge was established in New York City. In 1833 the Magdalene Home for wayward women was created; The House of Shelter was opened in Indiana in 1869; the Home for the Friendless in New York City hired a female manager in 1870; and homes for women opened in Dedham, Springfield, Richmond, and other cities in the 1870s and 1890s. These institutions served homeless women and prostitutes and emphasized religion, education, discipline, reading, and sewing.[32]

Female reformers also advocated female management of women in prison but encountered strong resistance to the notion. Public service was not considered appropriate for women, who were seen as incapable of controlling female prisoners. Gradually the resistance to female administration of prisons for women gave way, and women were hired to run the separate buildings or wings that housed women offenders. In 1822, Maryland became the first state to hire a female jail keeper.[33] In 1827, Connecticut hired a woman to oversee the female department of the state prison. In 1828, a separate building for women was built at Ossining, New York (euphemistically called Mt. Pleasant). In 1830, Maine and Ohio also opened separate buildings for female prisoners.[34]

Elizabeth Farnham, appointed in 1844 as matron of Mt. Pleasant, was very much influenced by Elizabeth Fry. She made many changes in the institutional surroundings, designed to "feminize" the female prisoners there. For instance, she allowed female prisoners to decorate their rooms with curtains and flowers. She brought in a piano and instituted educational classes and readings. Her tenure lasted only two years, however, because of harsh critics who objected to her "atheism" and lack of discipline.[35]

By the late 1800s, female reformers were finally successful in their quest to establish completely separate institutions run by women (instead of wings or separate buildings at prisons for men). At the 1870s Prison Congress, a national meeting of correctional specialists and reformers, one of the principles endorsed by the participants was that women and juveniles should be separated from male offenders. Further, the attendees recognized the value of employing female professionals.[36] Zebulon Brockway, famous for being the first warden of Elmira Reformatory, advocated reformatories for women that could create a "family life, where they [female prisoners] shall receive intellectual, moral, domestic, and industrial training, under the influence, example and sympathy of refined and virtuous women."[37] Brockway had himself dealt with female prisoners and had developed his idea that prisoners should be able to earn limited freedoms through good behavior with female prisoners in a House of Shelter at the Detroit House of Correction during the period from 1865 to 1869.[38]

In the 1870s, separate institutions in Indiana and Massachusetts were built and female staff was hired. In 1881 the New York House of Refuge for female misdemeanants was created, and in 1900 Bedford Hills was built.[39] Houses of Refuge were designed for young women (as young as twelve or fifteen) who had been convicted of minor crimes, such as "petit larceny, habitual drunkenness, or being a common prostitute, of frequenting disorderly houses or houses of prostitution or of any misdemeanor," and who were "not insane or mentally or physically incapable of being substantially benefited" by the discipline found there.[40]

Ironically, the first completely separate institution for women run by women did not follow the reformatory ideal. In 1873, the Female Prison and Reformatory Institution for Girls and Women was opened in Indiana. Here, the reformatory concept was only partially followed. The institution received only felons; it did not originally use indeterminate sentencing; it made no attempt to reform through education; and its architecture did not follow the cottage system (all hallmarks of the reformatory model).[41] In fact, the first prisons for women in Indiana and Massachusetts were described as castle-like—"grim, dark, 'Bastille-like' structure[s]."[42] However, the women in Indiana did have separate rooms and wore gingham dresses instead of prison uniforms.[43]

The early administrators of these institutions were often the same reformers who had struggled so hard to create them. These women believed they had a moral duty to improve the lives of their female charges.[44] In many of these early institutions, however, top administrators were men, because of the belief that only men could solve the management problems and make decisions regarding the management of women. Other men held staff positions to take care of such things as construction and mechanical needs. It was also a struggle to retain female supervisors once they were in place. For instance, Freedman wrote that Clara Barton (the famous Civil War nurse) reluctantly agreed to be superintendent of the women's prison in Framingham, Massachusetts, in 1882 for nine months in order to prevent the governor from appointing a man. Low pay, uncomfortable living conditions, and questionable status made qualified women difficult to find and keep.[45]

Later institutions were more likely to follow the reformatory or House of Refuge model. Institutions like the Hudson House of Refuge, which opened in New York in 1887, were built using the cottage-model architecture, were staffed almost entirely by women, and followed a "domestic" routine. In 1893, Albion Training School for Girls was opened and followed the Hudson model, and in 1901 Bedford Hills was opened. Although primarily for misdemeanants, these facilities also accepted some felony offenders.[46] Those given reformatory terms were young, relatively unhardened, guilty of misdemeanors, or victims of difficult circumstances. Most were under the age of 25, white, and native born. Two-thirds had been married at some time but were widowed, divorced, or separated. Most had no prior convictions and their crimes were minor: more than half had been incarcerated for drunkenness and prostitution.[47]

Lekkerkerker,[48] a Dutch lawyer who toured a number of reformatories for women in the 1930s, viewed them as entirely different from reformatories for men and unique in the world. Part of the reason for their difference was the vague line drawn between crime and sexual immorality. Freedman described the early reformatories as "benevolent matriarchies," which offered a homelike atmosphere free "from the contaminating influences of men."[49] Training consisted of household work, including sewing, knitting, cooking, washing and ironing clothes, gardening, and farming. The institutions offered domestic training and very little else. Academic classes were underfunded, industrial training was opposed by civilian industry, and only a small number of women could get jobs in skilled trades anyway.[50] In Massachusetts, an indenture law was passed in 1879, and 1,500 women went into service in family homes as domestic servants. One-quarter of the prisoners from Albion Reformatory (in New York) were paroled directly to live-in domestic positions. In fact, parole revocation usually occurred because of sexual misconduct or "sauciness" to employers.[51]

At Bedford Hills, women also did outdoor work, such as gardening, slaughtering pigs, and draining a swamp.[52] Other descriptions of reformatories described women who "poured concrete sidewalks, laid floors for new buildings, painted cottages, graded the grounds, filled wash outs, put up fences, planted trees and began a farm."[53]

In Niantic, Connecticut, the women's reformatory, built in 1918, was set in the woods with farmland and a stocked lake. Niantic, called "The Farm," was described in bucolic terms by Lekkerkerker in the 1930s:

> The Farm certainly has charms: the buildings, scattered wide apart, form an attractive whole with the romantic lake, the wood and thicket, the rolling hills and green pasture, which offer the women abundant opportunity for healthy outdoor sports, such as hiking, swimming, fishing, sleighing and skating in winter, picking berries, chopping wood, etc. which, in fact, is often done by them.[54]

The life of a matron was a difficult one. She was expected to live at the institution and, in some institutions, to eat with the prisoners during all meals. She had only one day off each week with vacation days determined by how many years she had worked for the institution. Twelve-hour shifts were not uncommon. Staff members filled both custodial and educational roles; they were sewing instructors and farm supervisors as well as matrons.[55]

Most women incarcerated in the early reformatories were not serious criminals and did not often pose a security risk for the staff. Sympathy and emotion usually were used to appeal to female inmates rather than force; however, harsher punishments included forfeiture of wages, distinctive dress, cutting the hair close to the scalp, and solitary confinement.[56] "Dungeons," rooms with no ventilation or light, were available for those who attacked officers, destroyed property, or threatened safety.[57] Female staff could be as prone to abusive treatment of prisoners as their male counterparts. A scandal at Bedford Hills in 1915 involved the use of physically abusive punishments. Eventually, some of these problems led to riots, such as those at Bedford Hills in the 1920s.[58]

Rafter[59] noted that more women served time in "custodial" prisons than in reformatories. Wings or separate buildings on the grounds of men's prisons continued to be used for older female prisoners or those with criminal histories. Minority women were also more likely to be sent to these custodial institutions. Albion, for instance, was 97 percent white, despite the fact that blacks comprised almost 40 percent of the prison population in 1934.[60] The custodial model was followed most often in new construction after 1930 as the reformatory era was phased out.

In other regions of the country, such as the West and the South, only makeshift arrangements were available for female prisoners long into the 1900s. In the south, prison farms were thought to be extremely inappropriate places for women. Consequently, the female felon was dealt with by alternative methods, unless she was an extremely serious offender or black. If she met either of those criteria, she may have ended up on the prison farm and expected to do less arduous physical work, such as gardening or housework in the home of the warden.[61]

One of the interesting aspects of some early reformatories was the presence of female social scientists who gathered information and conducted experiments on the inmates. At Bedford Hills, the "Bureau of Social Hygiene" became a center of research on female criminality. These female researchers, who were physicians and psychologists, pointed out social factors in crime causation, such as poor family life and temptation, years ahead of their "discovery" by male criminologists. The thrust of this testing and research, however, was *eugenics*. Criminal women were thought to be the breeders of future classes of criminals. Evidently, the goal of the research was to test for defectiveness and then prevent those found to be defective from having children.[62]

Frances Kellor, another early researcher, compared female prisoners to a "normal sample" and found that factors such as nativity and social environment played a part in criminality. Recognizing the interaction between individual and environmental factors, Kellor attributed many of the criminal sample's lower scores in smell, hearing, pain, fatigue, and memory to poor physical health brought on by poor living conditions. Kellor found that workhouse women had even lower scores than penitentiary women on all physical tests and were more likely to come from backgrounds of extreme poverty.[63] Jean Weidensall also studied female prisoners at Bedford Hills in the early 1900s. She reported that reformatory inmates had lower intelligence and mechanical scores than the average of the general population. They were described as easily frustrated, emotionally unstable, suspicious, and unthinking. Weidensall believed that there were several types of female criminals. Some, she wrote, were intelligent but too lazy to work, some were truly criminal, and some were just so unintelligent that they drifted into crime. She believed that this latter type could be guided by moral training.[64]

Spaulding[65] described how the Bureau of Social Hygiene conducted an experiment with "intractable" female inmates who were moved to isolated patient cottages on the grounds of Bedford Hills. These "psychopathic" prisoners were then encouraged to create a type of self-government. Spaulding wrote that the research was not a success; the prisoners wore down the staff by the frequency and seriousness of their outbursts. Soon the self-government attempt was abandoned and institutional discipline reinstated, including "wet packs" and isolation.

Another group of female researchers[66] developed a large number of case studies from female prisoners in the State Prison for Women at Auburn, New York, the New York County Penitentiary, the New York City Workhouse, and the New York Magdalene Home. Two general causal factors were identified: poor economic background, with its resulting impoverished home environment; and inferior mental ability. They found that almost half the women studied had "defective strains" within their families, such as alcoholism, feeblemindedness, neuroticism, or sexual irregularities. Rafter[67] called these studies *cacogenic*, explaining that they identified the woman as a breeder of criminals and elevated her to the status of "social menace." According to Rafter, researchers such as Dugdale[68] believed harlotry (promiscuity and dissolute living) was hereditary and that the bad woman was inevitably the mother of children who would grow up to be criminals and degenerates. This early concern with women's genetic inferiority was part of the reason for the reformatory era's concern with promiscuity and procreation. Women of childbearing years were incarcerated, partially to keep them from becoming pregnant.[69] Even into the mid-1930s, the Gluecks[70] believed that some female offenders should be kept indeterminately or sterilized in order to prevent them from reproducing. These researchers were obviously influenced by Darwinian concepts, but it is interesting that they seemed to believe that the mother's genetic inheritance was more important than the father's—or, perhaps, it was simply that women (and their ability to give birth) were easier to control. The era was also interesting in that these researchers also recognized social factors as they collected their case studies.

Between 1900 and 1935, seventeen states opened women's reformatories; however, after the 1930s the reformatory era was considered to have ended.[71] Reasons given for the demise of the reformatory ideal include the disinterest with prostitution as a national issue and the gradual exit of the zealous reformers described previously. The Depression also hastened the end of interest in reformatories, but women's prisons continued to be built. Between 1930 and 1972, 20 more states built prisons for women.[72] It wasn't until the 1980s, however, that every state had a completely separate prison, and it was also in the 1980s and 1990s that there was a massive building push for both men's and women's prisons. In the 1980s 34 women's prisons were built, so by 1990 there were 71 women's prisons in the country and only five years later there were 105, beginning a building boom that has continued.[73] Only the smallest states (e.g., Rhode Island) do not have a women's prison today, using combined jail/prison institutions or contracting with another state or the Federal Bureau of Prisons to house the few female offenders who are sentenced.

Few published descriptions of women's prisons exist from the time Lekkerkerker did her study in the early 1930s to the mid-1960s, when Giallombardo,[74] Ward and Kassebaum,[75] and Strickland[76] looked again at the women's prison. Strickland described women's institutions in the 1960s as typically small and patterned after the cottage model. Her findings included the following:

- two-thirds had populations of less than 200;
- most of the prisons had less than 150 staff (14 employed fewer than 50);
- many of the prisons were located in the northeast and north central region of the country;
- inmates ranged in age from 16 to 65;
- living units were often cottages (13 institutions); and
- the majority of institutions used simple classification techniques to assign inmates.[77]

Women's institutions have been described as "softer" or "nicer" and as having fewer formal and custodial aspects. According to Strickland, however, a larger number of institutions for women fell closer to the custody end of a continuum than to the treatment end. The variables she used for her determination included the ratio of treatment staff to inmates. This observation was supported by later researchers, such as Burkhardt[78] and Taylor,[79] who also described the women's institution as having many rules and strict policies governing every aspect of the inmate's life. Even current descriptions discuss rules as efforts to infantilize, control, demonize, and diminish the identity of women in prison.[80]

Female Prisoners

Because of their small numbers, women in prison received little attention from correctional policy makers and the research community until the 1970s when a few comprehensive descriptive studies were published, including those of Glick and Neto[81] and the Government Accounting Office.[82] Few articles described female prisoners or explored their issues.[83] In the 1980s, a few more national surveys were conducted. The National Institute of Corrections published a "state of the art" analysis of programs in adult female institutions in 1984.[84] Crawford,[85] under the auspices of the American Correctional Association, surveyed 71 facilities for women and girls, describing female prisoners and the programs in the prisons.

In the 1990s information on women's prisons expanded dramatically. The American Correctional Association[86] and the Bureau of Justice Statistics[87] published statistical summaries on the female offender (and included sections on women in reports on prisons). It should be noted that statistical information on women in prison has changed very little since the first published summaries, except for the fact that there are fewer African American women as a percentage of the prison population today than in the past. The following 1994 report describes female prisoners (compared to male prisoners) as:

- being less likely to have been employed at time of arrest,
- being more likely to be serving time for drug offenses,
- being less likely to have been sentenced for a violent crime,
- being more likely (if having committed a violent crime) to have victimized a relative,
- having shorter criminal records,
- receiving shorter maximum sentences,
- using more drugs,
- being more likely to have committed crime while under the influence of drugs or alcohol, and
- being more likely to have been physically or sexually abused (more than three times as likely to report abuse as a child and six times as likely to report physical abuse as an adult).[88]

Most of these descriptions still apply to female prisoners today. More detailed "needs assessments" of women in prison were done in California,[89] Oklahoma,[90] and Texas.[91] These needs assessments provided more detailed information than the national surveys and fleshed out the picture of prior abuse, economic marginalization, dysfunctional relationships, and the stress of being responsible for children. Finally, there have been a few national studies of prison programs for women that have surveyed existing programs and made recommendations for effective programming.[92]

One must be careful to differentiate between a profile of the female prisoner population and a profile of female offenders who are sentenced to prison. For instance, the percentage of women in prison for violent crime is not a reflection of their representation in arrest or conviction rates because violent offenders serve longer sentences; therefore, the percentage of violent offenders is higher in prison population breakdowns than they are in arrest or conviction breakdowns. Likewise, the state's inclination to send drug offenders to prison will affect the percentage of all other offenders in a prison population breakdown. For example, if we send more drug offenders to prison, the *percentage* of violent offenders will go down, but it will not mean any change has occurred in the *number* of women sent to prison for violent offenses. While there are parallels in demographics and criminal histories when comparing female prison populations to probation or jail populations, there are some differences as well.

Women in prison are disproportionately likely to be members of a minority group (although whites are the majority group in the women's prison), in their 30s, mothers of one child (or more) under 18, drug users, victims of childhood sexual and physical abuse, and undereducated and underemployed or unemployed before incarceration. Compared to men in prison, women in prison tend to be slightly older, slightly more educated, and more likely to be unemployed prior to incarceration (60 percent compared to 40 percent for men in prison).[93] They are more likely than men to have been the primary caregivers of their children. They are also more likely than men to admit to drug problems, although men are more likely to report problems with alcohol. The profile of women in prison is roughly similar whether one utilizes large national samples or smaller state samples.[94]

Crimes and Criminal History

In the 1980s, women admitted to prison were most often sent there for property crimes (51 percent), and only about 10–11 percent of women entering prison were convicted of violent crimes.[95] More recently the Bureau of Justice Statistics reported that in 2009, about 18 percent of newly sentenced females were imprisoned for violent crimes and about 38 percent for property crimes. Drug offenses comprised 34 percent of new court commitments, and about 10 percent of new admittees had been convicted of public-order offenses.[96]

As mentioned before, the percentage of those who committed violent crimes in an existing prisoner population will be higher than the percentage of those convicted of property or drug crimes because violent offenders receive longer sentences. A 1999 "snapshot" of the prisoner population revealed that

28 percent of female prisoners were sentenced for violent crime, 27 percent for property crimes, 34 percent for drug offenses, and 11 percent for public-order offenses.[97] The most recent statistics indicate that 35 percent of female prisoners were sentenced for violent crime, 30 percent for property crimes, 28 percent for drug crimes, and 6 percent for public-order crimes.[98]

In the past, women tended not to have extensive criminal backgrounds, especially compared to those of men.[99] In the 1980s, a little more than half (55 percent) of female prisoners reported having been on probation at least once (compared to 66 percent of the men).[100] By the 1990s almost two-thirds (71 percent) of female prisoners had served a prior sentence of probation or incarceration.[101] Thus it appears that women are more likely to have criminal histories today than in the past, although they still are less likely than men to recidivate.[102]

Race and Ethnicity

In 1982 the population of women's prisons was 50 percent African American, although African Americans comprised only 11 percent of the total population in this country; nine percent Hispanic, when Hispanics were only five percent of the total population; and three percent Native American, although this group comprised only four-tenths of one percent of the total population.[103] In 1999, 48 percent of women in prison were African American; 15 percent were Hispanic, and four percent were "other."[104] As mentioned in the last chapter, the incarceration rate for African American women is declining, although their numbers are still disproportional to their share of the general population. Sabol and Couture[105] noted in 2008 that black women were incarcerated at a rate six times that of white women in 2000, but by 2007 the ratio had declined to 3.7 black women to every white. They also noted that the decreased ratio was due largely to the 51 percent increase in the incarceration rate of white women (not necessarily that black women had seen decreased commitment rates). In 2010, only 25 percent of women in prison were African American, 18 percent were Hispanic, and 46 percent were white.[106] That is quite a dramatic decline and one that most people have not recognized.

Family Background

One of the most consistent findings in research on female prisoners is that they tend to come from dysfunctional families marked by alcoholism or drug addiction, absent parents, mental illness, and abuse. Earlier research showed that women were twice as likely as men in prison to have grown up in single-parent households, and one-third of women (compared to one-fourth of men) reported that their guardians had abused drugs.[107]

Mortality of family members seems to be a theme that comes up consistently in research that utilizes interviews with women's prisoners. Deaths of friends and family members are common and much more frequent than a statistical average.[108] Female offenders lose their relatives to sickness and fatal violence, sometimes explaining that the death spurred their descent into heavy drug use. Another way to lose family members, however, is abandonment. Women in prison often had one or both parents abandon them to other relatives or the state. Many recite sad childhoods of constantly trying to gain the affection of a physically or emotionally absent parent: "Even though my father smoked weed and drank alcohol and shot and stabbed people I still loved him. I thought that he would love me more for being just like him. I was wrong. He didn't care."[109]

Various research studies show that female prisoners are very likely (about 50 percent to 65 percent) to have at least one family member who also had experienced incarceration.[110]

> I have five brothers. Three of them was in the penitentiary. . . . One was on robbery, two was on drugs and my baby brother still going to school. He's 17. And I have a baby sister and she has two husbands that have been killed in the last 2 months since I've been locked up. . . . They took her children, she's an addict also.[111]

Childhood Abuse

The pathways research reviewed in Chapter 5 focused on the prevalence of abuse in female offenders' lives. There is a large body of both qualitative and quantitative research that chronicles this fact.[112] One study of female prisoners found that 45 percent reported physical abuse, 66 percent reported sexual abuse, and 37 percent reported both before age 18.[113] Table 8.2 displays some older statistics that have not appreciably changed over the intervening years.

Table 8.2   Prior Abuse of Prisoners by Sex

| | | Percent Experienced Abuse before Sentence | | | |
| | | Ever | | Before 18 | |
	Total	Male	Female	Male	Female
Ever abused?					
State prison	18.7	16.1	57.2	14.4	36.7
Federal prison	9.5	7.2	39.2	5.0	23.0
Jail	16.4	12.9	47.6	11.9	36.6
Probationers	15.7	9.3	40.4	8.8	28.2
Physically Abused?					
State prison	15.4	13.4	46.5	11.9	25.4
Federal prison	7.9	6.0	32.3	5.0	14.7
Jail	13.3	10.7	37.3	—	—
Probationers	12.8	7.4	33.5	—	—
Sexually Abused?					
State prison	7.9	5.8	39.0	5.0	25.5
Federal prison	3.7	2.2	22.8	1.9	14.5
Jail	8.8	5.6	37.2	—	—
Probationers	8.4	4.1	25.2	—	—

Source: Harlow, C. 1999. *Prior Abuse Reported by Inmates and Probationers* (Bureau of Justice Statistics Bulletin, NCJ 172879). Washington DC: U.S. Dept. of Justice.

About 15 years ago, Harlow[114] reported the following research findings:

- Women in prison were more likely than the general population to have experienced abuse (6–14 percent of male offenders and 23–37 percent of female offenders reported abuse compared to the general population figures of 5–8 percent for males and 12–17 percent for females).
- Male prisoners were more likely to report abuse only as children; women reported abuse as children and adults.
- The abuse of men was by family members; the abuse of women was by family members and intimates.
- Abuse was associated with foster care, parental abuse of drugs or alcohol, and/or criminal history.
- Abused prisoners were more likely to be serving sentences for violent crimes.
- The use of drugs and alcohol was higher among those who had been abused.

McClellan and her colleagues[115] compared male and female Texas inmates on drug use, criminality, and background characteristics. They found that female prisoners were more likely than male inmates to have been sexually abused and were more likely to have come from extremely dysfunctional family backgrounds. About 31 percent of women reported sexual mistreatment or rape compared to one percent of men, although equal percentages reported childhood physical abuse. Women were more likely to be substance dependent, and substance abuse was much more likely to be correlated with depression for women. Women also reported more mental health problems than men.

The greater presence of childhood sexual abuse and mental health issues among female prisoners is not limited to the United States. MacDonald describes how the goal of the DAPHNE III program funded by the Justice Directorate of the European Commission is to increase knowledge and understanding among criminal justice professionals of abuse and of mental health problems of female prisoners in the European Union. Citing statistics from Scotland, she notes that 70–80 percent of the female prison population had mental health problems, 50 percent had a history of sexual abuse, and at least 50 percent were currently in abusive relationships.[116] Past sexual abuse has also been correlated with a greater likelihood of being convicted of violent crimes[117] and with poor prison adjustment.[118] Moore[119] reports that the effects of childhood sexual abuse can include anger and hostility toward others, distrust of authority and adults as juveniles, alienation from others, a negative self-view, substance abuse, emotional volatility (either an overreacting or numb approach to life), inappropriate use of sex and sexuality, and distant or dysfunctional family relationships. Maeve[120] reports that childhood abuse leads to post-traumatic stress disorder, which includes "over-remembering" that may lead to lashing out in inappropriate circumstances, under-remembering (that leads to disassociation), cyclical dysfunctional relationships, and pervasive feelings of self-blame. Note the description of disassociation in this female inmate's description:

> I knew when my father was on the rampage. I just blacked out and I was just not there. . . . I had terrible impending fear of the dark until my 20s. When I am in the presence of raw brutality, I just become not present.[121]

In one recent British study,[122] researchers linked childhood sexual abuse to what they termed "emotional dysregulation," which they characterized as heightened intensity of emotions, poor understanding of emotions, negative reactivity to emotional state, inability to control behaviors when experiencing emotional distress, and maladaptive emotion management. The researchers also identified disassociation as an effect of childhood sexual abuse and pointed out that survivors frequently describe these symptoms, especially when presented with "cues" from past trauma. The researchers hypothesized that these effects (avoidance, disassociation, and numbing) can increase risky sexual behaviors, which may lead to revictimization by (1) diminishing the survivor's sensitivity to potential threat; or (2) increasing the use of alcohol or drugs, leading to risky decisions regarding sexual partners or protective life-style choices. In focus groups with female prisoners, researchers heard a range of maladaptive emotional responses to past sexual victimization, including risky sexual behaviors. The hypotheses were supported that disassociation led to these women not perceiving sexual threats until too late and engaging in lifestyles that exposed them to risk.

Another study identified self-blame as a mediator between childhood sexual abuse and adult sexual victimization.[123] In this study, 64 percent of 224 female prisoners reported childhood sexual abuse (prior to age 14), and the majority experienced multiple events of abuse. The majority of the sample (55 percent) had scores that indicated clinical depression. Half of the sample had attempted suicide at least once, and 75 percent of the sample reported clinically significant levels of dissociation. Researchers found that childhood sexual abuse was significantly correlated with self-blame, and self-blame was associated with symptoms of PTSD and maladaptive coping (e.g., drugs, alcohol, and risky sexual behaviors). Others have also documented the effects of childhood sexual abuse on drug use and dysfunctional and risky sexual behavior.[124] The pathways approach proposes that early childhood abuse leads to anger and negative life paths. Specifically, childhood sexual abuse may lead to running away, high-risk sexual activity, prostitution, and drug abuse.[125]

> When I was eight or nine my mother's boyfriend molested me. I was afraid to say anything. He did it again and I told my mother; they got in a fight and she killed him with a knife. When she went away to prison, nobody talked to me. They acted like it was my fault. It was my fault, I should have stayed silent. I started to drink when I was eleven. A boy raped me on the roof when we were drinking. I was too afraid to tell anyone, even when I became pregnant. Everyone was shocked when I gave birth at thirteen years old.[126]

Intimate Relationships

Research indicates that many women in prison are there because of their involvement with a romantic partner who engaged in criminal activity, typically drug selling. Sometimes they receive long prison sentences because they do not cooperate with prosecutors and refuse to testify against their partners.[127]

As discussed in Chapter 5, women seem to recreate their abusive childhoods in intimate partnerships, becoming involved with abusive partners—sometimes with a succession of abusive partners. Women in prison are even more likely to report experiencing physical and sexual abuse as adults than as children. In fact, childhood victimization is a strong predictor of adult victimization.[128] There are also studies indicating that sexual victimization seems to be correlated with revictimization.[129] As noted above, this may be because childhood sexual abuse leads to high-risk lifestyles (e.g., engaging in sex work and making poor choices in sexual partners). At least one study also identified a greater vulnerability to sexual harassment and coercion from authority figures for those women who had experienced prior sexual victimization.[130]

The irony is that, once in prison, many of these women engage in same-sex partnerships that are also abusive, as described in the next chapter.

Drug Use and Abuse

Bloom and her colleagues report that the percentage of women admitted to prison for drug-related crimes increased from 14.2 percent of total prison admissions in 1982 to 42.2 percent of the total in 1992.[131] About one in three women in American prisons were there for drug crimes in 1991, an increase from the one in 10 in 1979.[132] The percentage has declined to 34 percent of new commitments and 28 percent of the female prisoner population today.[133]

Research has shown that women in prison are often heavier users of drugs than men in prison, and that women's drug-related crimes included property crime and minor roles in violent crime. In one study, substance abusers were more likely to be Caucasian, to come from broken homes, and to have worse employment histories. Substance abuse was also related to age at first arrest (younger), number of prior arrests, and number of prior incarcerations. Problem users were more likely to have family members who were incarcerated, were more likely to have been under the influence at the time of the crime, and were more likely to have committed the crime for money to buy drugs.[134] An older study showed that 40 percent of women (compared to 32 percent of men) had been under the influence of drugs at the time of offense.[135]

In Owen and Bloom's[136] study, almost three-fourths of their sample of incarcerated women reported drinking alcohol before the age of 18; 11 percent reported drinking before age 10; 59 percent reported drug use before 18, and 15 percent began using at 12 or 13. Other needs assessments[137] also show that women in prison are extremely likely to be heavy users of drugs and that their drug use started very early. Another consistent finding was that drugs were often introduced to them by family members.[138]

> I started using marijuana at the age of eight, with my sisters and my cousin. I started drinking about that time too. Then I started cocaine binges. I started running away when I was eleven. It seems like I have always been in trouble. My family was having trouble when I ran away at eleven. I was angry and always fighting.[139]

As discussed in Chapter 2, drug use does not necessarily cause criminality, but heavy drug use is correlated with more frequent and serious criminality.[140] Drug use is related to a constellation of other criminal behaviors for women. The most common crimes connected to drug abuse are crimes related to the drug market with women involved in low-level selling, acting as runners and go-betweens. They also report involvement in other crimes, including prostitution and property crimes.[141] Female drug offenders are less likely than their male counterparts but more likely than non-drug-abusing women to have been involved in violent crime.[142]

Prison samples have shown that those women who reported heavy drug use were more likely to have experienced childhood sexual victimization, have serious thoughts of suicide, and show other signs of mental distress, especially depression. In one prison study, for instance, women were significantly more likely than male prisoners to report mental health problems (66 percent versus 31 percent) and substance-abuse disorders (53 percent versus 27 percent).[143] These factors are more strongly correlated with drug abuse among women than among men.[144] Further studies have reported that drug abusers are more likely than those who do not report heavy drug use to have come from more dysfunctional families with parents or caregivers suffering from addiction and/or mental health issues, to report feeling unloved, to have been abandoned by at least one parent, and to have experienced homelessness or hunger during childhood. The pattern of physical and sexual victimization in childhood carries over into drug-abusing women's adult lives, and significantly more drug abusers than non-drug abusers have experienced adult sexual and physical victimization and homelessness.[145]

Research has supported the notion that the motivation for drug use may be different for male and female offenders. Women tend to use drugs more often to "self-medicate," while men more often use drugs for social or other reasons.[146]

Personality Traits and Characteristics of Female Prisoners

One long-standing belief is that women in prison have very poor self-concepts. Several researchers found that female prisoners reported lower self-esteem than average, although their self-esteem seemed to increase as they neared release.[147] Correctional professionals have also echoed the belief that female prisoners have low self-esteem:

> Women tended not to feel successful with anything. They didn't feel successful as wives. They didn't feel successful as lovers. They didn't feel successful as mothers. They didn't feel successful as daughters. Whereas men felt a lot more success, relatively speaking, I found, than women did. Men

> could say I was a good carpenter or I did this well or I screwed more women than anybody else on the block. . . . Women were always zero in their own eyes.[148]

There are mixed research findings, however, and some studies did not find that female prisoners reported lower levels of self-esteem than male offenders or the general population,[149] or that self-esteem was related to self-identity.[150] Some studies find that higher education was related to lower self-esteem, but others found that it was related to higher self-esteem.[151] Not surprisingly, childhood abuse—even if only emotional—is associated with lower self-esteem.[152]

> I was told I was stupid. I was told I was fat. I was told I was ugly. Just a lot of things. My dad—I think that's his favorite word—we're all stupid. We were never physically abused. I guess the mental and emotional abuse is worse.[153]

Other research has measured female prisoners' "masculinity." This line of research is problematic in that masculinity is measured differently across studies, and some definitions of "masculine values" may be criticized as dependent on sex stereotypes.[154] Findings are mixed, but studies have found that there is little difference between female prisoners and women in the general population, whichever way this concept is measured.[155]

Medical Needs

Typically, female inmates require relatively more medical services than men do. Women in general are more likely than men to seek health care; also, female inmates' lifestyles (drug use, risky sex practices, poor nutrition, lack of preventative care) prior to imprisonment create health problems. There is no question that women in prison suffer from a range of health problems, some very serious.[156] Women show higher rates of AIDS, tuberculosis, depression, and anxiety disorders than do men in prison.[157] Ross and Lawrence,[158] and others, found that the most common medical problems of prisoners included asthma, diabetes, HIV/AIDS, TB, hypertension, unintended/interrupted/lost pregnancy, dysmenorrhea, chlamydia infection, human papilloma virus (HPV) infection, herpes simplex II infection, cystic and myomatic conditions, chronic pelvic inflammatory disease, anxiety, neurosis, and depression. Women in prison are reported to have greater risk than the general population for cervical cancer, substance abuse, suicide, sexually transmitted diseases, HIV, and gynecological problems.[159]

While the reality may be that most women receive better health care in prison than they would have on the outside, there is also evidence that women do not receive adequate care in some prisons. For instance, there have been reports of women who received no care during pregnancy, were misdiagnosed, or did not receive medical care for diagnosed illnesses.[160] Others have had prescribed pills withheld as punishment, but there are also reports that drugs, especially tranquilizers, are used excessively to control the population.[161] Reports describe horrible cases of medical neglect, including women forced to give birth with their legs shackled together, women giving birth in a prison hallway assisted only by an untrained correctional officer, women having a miscarriage because of being forced to clean floors with a heavy buffer while eight months pregnant, women being denied medical care by inmate gate-keepers, and women suffering from a lack of treatment for chronic diseases.[162] In a 1998 National Council on Crime and Delinquency report, findings included that more than half of incarcerated women had one or more health problems, twice as many female as male inmates were diagnosed with AIDS, female inmates were being overmedicated with psychotropics, there was a lack of follow-up medical care, and there was a lack of pre- and postnatal care.[163]

Acoca[164] reported on the increasing trend in prisons to have prisoners pay for health care, arguing that this practice discourages those who need it most. Even though the cost is nominal, women's income in prison is also nominal or nonexistent. Acoca[165] also pointed out that tuberculosis and sexually transmitted diseases (such as hepatitis B and C) may eventually pose even bigger problems than AIDS, with some studies indicating that half of incoming female prisoners tested positive for hepatitis C.

More recent studies continue to document major problems with health services and the greater needs of female inmates as compared to the general population or even as compared to male inmates. There is also the recognition, however, that as bad as prison health care might be, it often is better than what women could access if they were still on the street.[166]

Fear of getting sick in prison is one of the most prevalent concerns expressed by women in prison. Prison etiquette rules (such as excessive concern with cleanliness in shared bathrooms and dormitories) and prison fights that result when an inmate ignores the rules of cleanliness can be understood in the context of the inmates' great fear of being infected by other inmates with hepatitis or other viruses.[167]

A growing problem concerns the medical needs of older women. With growing numbers of prisoners receiving very long sentences, prison systems are seeing increasing percentages of elderly prisoners. A few studies have documented the extensive medical needs of this group of women and the fact that prisons tend not to have the resources and/or inclination to respond to these needs. Researchers point out that elderly women cost three times as much to incarcerate as younger inmates, and their numbers have risen to 12 percent of the prison population.[168] Researchers point to mobility problems, including the lack of wheelchairs or walkers, the lack of grab bars in showers to prevent falls, top bunks that elderly women cannot climb to access, and the requirement of dropping to the ground during security alarms (older women cannot get down as quickly nor rise as easily as younger inmates).[169] It appears that there are more programs for elderly male inmates than for female inmates (probably because of the cost-effectiveness issue). At minimum, prison systems should consider having a hospice program (for terminally ill inmates), a specialized dorm with assistance for the elderly and/or infirm, recreation programs designed for an older age group, and education programs concerning healthy aging.[170]

Research seems to be mixed on whether it is better to have older inmates housed with younger inmates. Many older women express fear of other inmates and report being harassed and victimized: "There are some rough people in here. Sometimes you will be walking to the cafeteria and someone will walk right up to you and shove you and keep going."[171] However, there are also instances of close bonding between older and younger inmates, and instances where younger inmates watch out for and care for older women.

Mental Health.   Many studies report that a greater percentage of female inmates compared to male inmates have diagnosed mental health issues, with some studies indicating that as many as 60 percent of female inmates require mental health services.[172] Another study showed a much lower statistic for those who reported having prior mental health treatment, finding that 24 percent of the female sample (compared to 12 percent of the male sample) had been treated for mental problems.[173] However, other research reports that some mental health disorders are underdiagnosed, especially depression and bipolar disorder.[174]

A large part of treatment has been reported to be the administering of psychotropic drugs.[175] Some observers have noted that there is a greater tendency to characterize women's (as compared to men's) problems as psychiatric. This expectation may influence the estimates of the percentage of women in prison with mental health problems. It is also possible that this expectation or assumption may be somehow projected to women, leading to their self-reported mental health issues. It is important to keep in mind the possibility that estimates of mental illness may be biased by sexual stereotypes. However, considering that a greater percentage of female inmates (than male inmates) have histories of childhood abuse, have drug problems, and come from families with dysfunctions (i.e., alcoholism, abuse, criminality, psychiatric disorders), one could argue that the greater prevalence of mental health problems among female prisoners is probably not merely evidence of stereotyping.

Maeve,[176] for instance, discusses the effects of chronic childhood abuse. She explains that a child who is constantly stressed by being in constant fear of abuse may end up with "hyper-arousal," which means the person is unable to feel calm. Individuals may use drugs or alcohol to mitigate their feelings; other effects include high-risk sexual activity, acting out, eating disorders, risk taking, and self-mutilation. All of these activities release endorphins that suppress the feelings of fear. Physical ailments including hypertension, asthma, and autoimmune disorders are related to chronic stress, which also impairs cognition and logical thinking. Yet another potential effect of abuse is to replay the same script of rescue, injustice, and betrayal over and over again in life relationships. These effects of chronic abuse are gender specific in that women tend to internalize (express through self-blaming and self-injurious behaviors) and men externalize (express through anger and violence).

"Cutting Up" and Suicide.   Women may be more prone than men to expressions of despair that include self-injury. Although many female

inmates attempt suicide or mutilate themselves because of emotional problems that existed prior to imprisonment, there is no doubt that the deprivations of the prison also spur some women to such desperate acts. Women may experience the deprivation of family roles more severely than men do. They may find that the institutionalized lifestyle of the prison provides little comfort or succor. One study in England showed an average of 1.5 incidents of self-injury each week in Holloway Prison. The women involved tended to be younger, with more previous incarcerations or psychiatric institutionalizations, and most had committed self-injury at least once before. They had higher hostility scores, indicating the close relationship between inwardly and outwardly directed aggression. Also, self-injury tended to occur in copycat epidemics at times.[177]

Fox[178] also studied self-mutilation among imprisoned women. His study at Bedford Hills indicated that women were more likely than men to attempt suicide or injure themselves; in other words, women tended to turn their aggression inward, whereas men turned their aggression outward. An officer described this tendency in the following way:

> I have seen it on a number of occasions. She won't harm anybody else but she will start to destruct her own body. I've seen them have cuts from here up to their shoulders. They've had stitches in: brand new stitches were put in and they got back here from the hospital and they would sit here and pull the stitches back out again. If you look at their arms, the men don't do it as much as the women, but if you look at the females' arms, they'll sit and they'll just cut and cut and cut. They don't want to hurt anybody else and the only person that they think of hurting is themselves.[179]

The female inmates also identify different reasons for "cutting up" than male inmates do. Women primarily feel the loss of relationships and support while in prison and release their emotion in a catharsis: 64 percent of the females sampled had this self-release theme in their responses, whereas only 13 percent of the males sampled exhibited this theme.[180] This theme involves the need to express pent-up emotions, with a resulting feeling of relief when the person "explodes."

Another explanation for "cutting up" and suicide has to do with feelings of control and a need to feel something, even if it is pain. Women's life experiences have often been traumatic, and psychological defense mechanisms create a type of disconnection from one's self and emotions (disassociation). "Cutting up" is often experienced by women as a way to reconnect with their emotions, a way to make sure they are still alive.

In studies of both self-mutilation and suicide risk in incarcerated women's populations, it has been clear that risk increases with depression, low self-esteem, and social isolation.[181] One study found that male prisoners are less likely to commit suicide than general population men, but female prisoners are more likely than general population women to commit suicide.[182]

Management Issues in a Women's Prison

Although there are similarities in managing women's and men's prisons, there are differences as well, despite the trend in the last 20 years of bringing women's prisons "into line" with management practices of the prisons for men in state systems.

Adapting to a Male Standard

Administrators of women's prisons have felt pressure in the last several decades to institute changes in the management of the facilities to make them more consistent with the practices in prisons for men. There is some research indicating that those who have worked only in men's prisons and those who have worked only in women's prisons perform their jobs differently and do not understand or agree with the differences displayed by the other group.[183] Differences between men's and women's institutions include security practices (women's prisons are more likely than men's to have extended visitation days), more relaxed rules regarding female inmates' possessions, and less formal interactions between female staff and inmates. Changes brought over from men's institutions have been perceived as overly strict, including more extensive rules and rule enforcement, excessive searches and shakedowns, and reduced concerns for inmate privacy. In the last twenty years, it is likely that most of the correctional staff who had worked only in women's institutions have retired or left, thus leaving only staff who were trained in the era of "prisoner first, woman second."

Observers note that officers who work in facilities for women need to have special training. First, the dislike that officers express toward female offenders ("I'd rather work with 50 men than five women") needs to be addressed, as well as the stigma of being assigned to a women's institution.[184] Second, there needs to be "gender-specific training"—that is, training that informs officers of the issues they need to be aware of when working with women, including women's greater tendency to interact with staff, the likelihood of PTSD related to childhood sexual abuse, and the importance of their social relationships.[185]

Beyond the statistical differences noted above, it is somewhat dangerous to make statements about qualitative differences between male and female prisoners in that we are all prone to be influenced by sexual stereotypes. Several decades ago, descriptions of female inmates were clearly influenced by stereotypes, as illustrated by this quote: "Despite the facade of genuine empathy with the sick girl, an appearance of superficiality was evident. Male relationships appear to be based on firmer fidelities. . . ."[186]

Pollock[187] found that both male and female correctional officers perceived inmates as reflecting sex differences commonly ascribed to males and females in society. For instance, they described female inmates as emotional and manipulative and males as cool and aloof. They also reported that women were more difficult to supervise, primarily because they were less respectful of officers' authority and more argumentative. These perceived differences are still described today; however, it is difficult to know to what degree these perceptions of female inmates are influenced by stereotypes. Consistent descriptions do indicate that female prisoners are less likely to follow the "do your own time" mandate of the male prisoner subculture and are more involved in each other's lives.

> One of the females in the group may be having an emotional problem, may be having a physical problem, a family problem that's got her all upset and all her friends would congregate around her to give her sympathy and console her, to give her direction, to give her moral support, whatever . . .[188]

Correctional officers who have supervised both sexes have stated that they prefer to work with male inmates because they are "more respectful" and don't require the same degree of time and energy as female prisoners.[189] Others do prefer to work in prisons for women, but not always for the right reasons.

Cross-Sex Supervision

The ironic result of equal-protection challenges by women who sought to work in prisons for men[190] is that there are now (in some states) more male officers than female officers working in prisons for women. Male officers in women's prisons have created a number of management challenges, including that of sexual relationships with inmates. Because this topic overlaps with the subject of the next chapter, this discussion is deferred to a section in Chapter 9.

Violence, Collective Disturbances, and Rule Breaking

Although some evidence indicates women may be more likely than men to commit minor rule breaking,[191] research indicates that the higher numbers of infractions coming from women's institutions may be because women are more heavily policed than men. In other words, more minor rules seem to exist in the women's prison, and they are enforced more strictly.[192]

Some research has found that younger, unmarried, urban women with more prior arrests and histories of violence were more likely to commit infractions. Other findings included the fact that long-term inmates may commit more violent infractions than short-time inmates, and inmates are more disruptive near the beginning of their sentences than at the end of their sentences.[193] The woman who is most often disciplined seems to fit the profile of those male prisoners who commit infractions: African American, in their late twenties, incarcerated for manslaughter or narcotics, from urban areas, single, with no children.[194]

One thing is clear: women are much less likely to engage in lethal violence, serious violence, or large-scale riots.[195] Only a few examples of collective disturbances have been documented at women's prisons.[196] Because the idea of violence is so much a part of the prison world, we address inmate-to-inmate violence in the next chapter.

Legal Challenges

The decade of the 1970s brought about many changes in courts' recognition of prisoners' legal rights. After *Holt v. Sarver* (1970), which challenged the conditions of the Tucker and Cummins prison farms in Arkansas and illustrated the sometimes brutal and horrifying conditions of prison, the courts were unable to continue their hands-off approach to prisoner suits. A steady stream of prisoner cases established rights in the areas of religion, censorship, discipline procedures, access to courts, and medical treatment. Basically, courts always balanced the individual inmate's particular interest against the state's interest in security, safety, and order.

Sometimes, when the individual right being litigated was considered paramount and the state could demonstrate no substantial governmental interest in interfering with that right, inmates won. For example, in early cases, courts recognized the inmate's right to practice religion in a way that did not disrupt or endanger the institution. At other times, when the inmate interest might arguably threaten institutional security, the state won.

The view that prisoners did not "check their constitutional rights at the prison door" and that prisoners had many of the rights of free people (except those inconsistent with their status as prisoners) contrasted sharply with the earlier view that prisoners had only those rights given them by prison administrators. More than any single element, this change in perception led to a different burden of proof and a different outcome for many of the cases decided by the Warren Court in the 1960s and 1970s.[197]

Today, courts have retreated to a "deference" position, using a rational relationship test to determine whether the rule or procedure at issue violates the Constitutional rights of the prisoner. In the *rational relationship test*, the state merely has to show a legitimate state interest (such as security) and a rational relationship between that interest and the rule or procedure in question. Using this test, the state almost always wins. The Prison Litigation Reform Act 18 USC Sec. 3626(a)(1)(A) has acted to reduce prisoners' litigation by putting up barriers and limiting the effect of successful lawsuits. This federal act bars injunctions unless they are narrowly drawn and use the "least intrusive" means necessary, requires that the prisoner prove the state has not met requirements, imposes financial penalties on frivolous lawsuits, and reduces attorneys' fees. The effect, of course, has been to drastically curtail prisoner litigation.

Without exception, all the groundbreaking cases in the prisoners' rights arena were brought by male inmates, including *Woff v. McDonnell* (1975), which dealt with the inmates' due process rights in disciplinary hearings; *Estelle v. Gamble* (1976), which established that the deliberate withholding of medical care could constitute unconstitutionally cruel and unusual punishment; and *Procunier v. Martinez* (1974), which established inmates' rights to some due-process protections against censorship. Cases that have challenged the "totality of circumstances" in individual prisons or entire state systems have also involved male inmates. The conditions challenged by male prisoners in these cases are also present in prisons for women, but women have been much less likely to bring suits or seek protection from the courts.

Gabel and her colleagues[198] surveyed several women's prisons to determine why women engage in less litigation than men do. They found that women are less likely to have resources available, they are more likely to focus on child custody issues than on conditions of prison, and they were (at least in the 1980s) less likely to know how to utilize whatever legal resources were available. Others also have found that women are underrepresented in prisoners' rights cases.[199] Some observers noted that in the 1980s, younger and more assertive female inmates may have increased the number of legal challenges brought by women.[200] While legal activity did seem to increase, there is still a disproportional representation between men and women in the number of prisoners' rights cases filed, although in other areas of legal needs (e.g., civil issues such as child custody and divorce), women seem to have the same level of need as men.[201]

Challenges to Programming. "Prison condition" cases for women tend to challenge the quantity or quality of programming, generally arguing that there is an unfair disproportion of inmate opportunities that favors men's prisons. Despite the Equal Protection clause of the Fourteenth Amendment and the Civil Rights Act, the Supreme Court has established a test for sex-based differential treatment (an intermediate standard) whereby the state can justify different treatment on such grounds as that women have different needs, or that the state has a legitimate reason for treating them differently from men. Also, if women are considered not to be "similarly situated" as men, then they do not have to receive the same treatment.

The first several cases in which female prisoners challenged the absence of prison programming and/or wage-earning work were successful.[202] In these earlier cases courts were not persuaded by arguments that the small numbers of women made offering programs cost-prohibitive. The most well-known case concerning the equal protection claim and prison programming was *Glover v. Johnson* (1979), a Michigan case. At the time the suit was filed, male prisoners had access to 22 vocational training programs while women had access to only three. Male prisoners also had more opportunities for education and work. The court ordered more educational courses for the women, an apprenticeship program, a work-release program, and an expanded legal training program. It also ordered the state to stop using the county jail as an overflow facility for female prisoners, since women there deserved the same programs as other state prisoners. More recently, however, cost arguments are received more favorably by the courts as reasons for not offering programs for women, and the sweeping changes ordered by the court in *Glover* probably would not occur today.[203]

Often state constitutions provide broader protections than does the U.S. Constitution. For instance, in *Inmates of Sybil Brand Institution for Women v. County of Los Angeles* (1982), a California court held that the California Constitution required strict scrutiny whenever a fundamental right was violated by a prison regulation. This ruling made it easier to prove unconstitutionality in the procedures and programs for female inmates. In this case, even under strict scrutiny, the court upheld the prison's regulations as advancing the state interest of security.

Challenges to Medical Care.   The Eighth Amendment, which bars cruel and unusual punishment, has also been used to challenge the lack of medical care, especially gynecological care, for women. It is difficult to make an Eighth Amendment case, however, in that the inmate must show that the deficiency is deliberate and malicious.[204] *Todaro v. Ward* (1977) was a case challenging health-care delivery at Bedford Hills in New York. The prisoners' complaints included the charge that no physician was on permanent duty at the institution and that women had to be bused to a local hospital. Their challenge to these conditions was upheld by the court. Cases from other states have also dealt with inadequate medical care for female inmates. Some challenges brought by women have been successful, including some which targeted the lack of prenatal care specifically.[205] There are mixed holdings regarding women's rights to have access to abortions, and they usually target specific practices or regulations of a particular state.[206]

Most states transfer women to local hospitals to give birth, and the lack of immediate care has proved to be a problem, especially when staff members do not call for transportation to take the woman out of the prison facility when she begins labor.[207] Lawsuits have been filed concerning the practice of shackling the woman during labor and vaginal searches after delivery and return to prison. In a 2009 case, the Eighth Circuit considered an appeal from a summary judgment dismissing a female inmate's claim from Arkansas that she was subjected to cruel and unusual punishment when her legs were shackled to opposite sides of the hospital bed during late stages of labor. The inability to move during contractions caused her great pain, and evidence showed that she suffered lifelong hip injuries because of the shackling. The Eighth Circuit held in favor of the prisoner, finding that shackling a woman who posed no security risk and against medical advice was an Eighth Amendment violation.[208]

Today, courts have become increasingly more resistant to finding states liable for deficiencies due to "deliberate indifference."[209] This resistance has carried over to other Eighth Amendment cases and it is harder for inmates to prove that lack of medical care rises to the level of cruel and unusual punishment today. California inmates, however, were successful in convincing the Supreme Court in *Brown v. Plata* (2011) that overcrowding created unconstitutional conditions, including an absence or inadequacy of medical care.

Other Claims and Court Response.   The legality of transferring female prisoners out of the state was first challenged in a Hawaii case in 1972.[210] Hawaii transferred female inmates to the mainland, and the court found that this was more onerous for female prisoners and thus violated the fourteenth and eighth amendments. Generally, however, courts have not barred states from transferring female (or male) inmates out of state.[211]

Collins and Collins, Pollock, and others[212] argue that recent court decisions indicate that federal courts are much more conservative in their analysis of prisoners' rights cases, and they have retreated to a due-deference model (which accords great deference to correctional authorities' expertise) and a rational relationship test (where the challenged practice merely needs to be rationally related to a legitimate state objective). This almost always results in a finding for state correctional authorities.[213] Also, the Prison Litigation Reform Act has constricted the power of federal courts to utilize consent decrees and removes financial incentives for lawyers to take cases.

Conclusion

Early prisons for women treated women like children, had few vocational or educational opportunities, and did not provide much assistance upon release. On the other hand, they had more relaxed security than prisons for men, and women received a bit more privacy and more flexible visitation policies with their children. Today, most of the major differences between men's and women's prisons have been eliminated. Practices and procedures are, for the most part, the same for legal reasons as well as the prevalence of administrators who have worked in prisons for men before transferring to women's prisons.

Studies of female prisoners from the 1980s through the present continue to paint the same basic picture: that female inmates are likely to have come from extremely dysfunctional families with a high prevalence of childhood sexual and physical abuse. Moreover, these women have witnessed or experienced other types of violence, abandonment, and other forms of trauma that have led to early drug use and entry into criminal lifestyles. The pathways model described in Chapter 5 originates largely from prison inmate studies. Women in prison are more likely than male inmates to suffer from serious mental problems, including depression and PTSD. They are also more likely than their male counterparts to be drug abusers and to have begun drug use as a reaction to their life experiences.

Managing women's prisons is different in some ways than managing men's prisons. Greater differences existed in the past than there are today. Although women are much less likely to engage in riots or lethal violence, the more pervasive supervision in women's prisons leads to more rule infractions. Legal challenges tend to be directed at a lack of programming and lack of medical care for women. In the next chapter, we turn to the prison world as experienced by the inmates.

REVIEW QUESTIONS

1. Describe how many women are in prison, the number of women's prisons, and the average size of states' female prisoner populations.

2. Describe early places of confinement for women, mentioning bridewells and houses of refuge and distinguishing confinement in the Northeast from the West and South in this country.

3. Describe the contributions of Elizabeth Fry.

4. When was the first completely separate prison for women built? Describe the pattern of growth in women's prisons from the early 1900s to the 1990s.

5. Distinguish elements of the reformatory institution from the custodial institution.

6. Describe characteristics of the female prisoner, creating a demographic snapshot and including personal characteristics.

7. What percentage of women in prison have suffered from childhood sexual abuse? What are the correlates or effects of childhood sexual abuse?

8. What percentage of women have a drug-abuse problem?

9. Describe the mental health issues of women in prison.

10. Describe the rational relationship test used in prisoners' rights lawsuits. What have been the major issues litigated by women in prison?

9

The Prison World

> **CHAPTER SUMMARY**
>
> - Women's prisons tend to have more strictly enforced minor rules than prisons for men.
> - Prisoner subculture research focused on deprivation theory and importation theory. There is evidence to support both approaches when examining the subculture of a women's prison.
> - There is less of a black market in women's prisons (as compared to men's), less racial tension, and less lethal violence, but less-than-lethal violence may have been underestimated in past studies.
> - National studies report more sexual violence in women's prisons than in men's prisons—both inmate-on-inmate and officer-on-inmate.
> - In some prisons, the majority of correctional officers are men; thus, in effect the women's prison has come full circle back to institutions from the 1800s, before the reformatory era, when women were guarded by men.

Women's prisons are not as violent as men's, and some women say that "if it wasn't for prison, I'd be dead" because of the way they lived on the outside. However, prison is still a terrifying place for those who first enter. According to most female prisoners, the worst part of prison is the ever-present message, often inculcated by correctional officers, that they are "nothing."

Entering the Prison

Entering prison is a frightening experience. Even women who have long criminal histories, including several probation terms and/or stays in jails, report that their first trip to prison gave rise to fears of homosexual rape, guard brutality, and loss of friends and family. Upon entry, a woman is fingerprinted and photographed, stripped, searched, and given prison clothing. Reception may include a medical exam, a psychiatric exam, and educational testing. Because these procedures are often done in groups, women may be forced to stand naked in lines waiting for prison-issue clothing. Prison orientation indoctrinates a woman to the extensive rules and regulations of the prison and what is expected of her. Most women describe this experience as stressful, frightening, and dehumanizing.[1]

> I remember it was scary. We were driving on the way up there. Everybody was talking and laughing, cracking jokes about going to prison. They were all happy because maybe they had been there before, and I am sitting in the back of the bus, 19 years old, wondering, "Why are they so happy that they are going to prison?" . . . They told me about the homosexuals, the lesbians. Since I am young and new, they were going to take what they wanted, which was me. I was like, nah, they don't do that. . . . And (they told me) they fight, and use shanks, which is homemade knives, and three or four different girls can jump you.[2]

In many prisons, newcomers are placed in administrative segregation until they have been classified and/or until beds are available. This means that they are housed in a special wing and have extremely limited movement, with no access to yard privileges, programs, or the central mess hall. The process of entry involves a dehumanizing sequence of shedding one's outer identity and becoming a number, with prison clothes, prison rule books, and prison toiletries (at least until one can gain back some measure of comfort by buying personal items in the commissary). Incoming female inmates may also receive essential items from other inmates. These welcoming procedures have been described as more likely to come from the woman's "tribe"—meaning from other black inmates if she is black, white if she is white, and so on—or from "homegirls" (those from one's own neighborhood). The practice seems to be fairly widespread and not necessarily a grooming procedure for exploitation, as it often is in men's prisons.[3]

Most women's prisons in the country are designated as medium/maximum security prisons. One of the biggest differences between facilities for men and for women is the absence of custody-graded institutions. Typically, only one or two facilities are available for women in the state. Consequently, the single facility must house the whole range of security grades. Men, on the other hand, are sent to prisons that match the risk they present.

Administrative classification systems that utilize risk-factor scores (based largely on prior criminal history, prior institutional history, and present crime) have almost always been developed with and for men, and they may not be useful for a female inmate population in that they overclassify, assigning higher custody scores to women than necessary.[4] In the late 1980s, Crawford[5] found that only 22 percent of female facilities used a classification system designed especially for women; and over ten years later, still only about 25 percent of reporting institutions used a gender-specific classification system.[6]

Adjusting to Prison

New inmates may spend weeks or sometimes months in ad-seg (administrative segregation) or whatever classification unit is used to house newly arrived or due-to-be-transferred inmates, but at some point the woman enters general population. She will live in either a dormitory or a cell shared with one to three other women (in most state systems). Some women continue to be frightened. Learning to live with other inmates is difficult. If the inmate is lucky, she will be helped by other inmates in learning prison etiquette. There are also ways to make prison life more comfortable—for instance, finding one or several other inmates to share food and goods with, and avoiding trouble by staying away from gambling, bartering, and prison relationships.

Adjusting to prison includes deciding how much one wants to participate in "programming"—either work, school, or some combination of the two. Women who feel as if they have "real" jobs appreciate the feelings associated with having work and being of value. Depending on the prison, women may work in the field, with farm animals, in large industrial laundries, on yard crews, performing maintenance tasks or clerical duties, working in jobs set up by private corporations on the prison grounds, or a myriad of other occupations.

One of the hardest things for women to adapt to in prison is being treated like a child.[7] Clark,[8] an inmate herself, discussed the infantilization of prisoners. She noted the hypocrisy of a system that makes women dependent but then tells them they need to be responsible, that calls women girls but expects them to act like adults, that forces women to be become passive and dependent and then expects them to take on all the problems of living immediately upon release. In more recent accounts of prison, women don't describe being treated as a child so much as being treated as worthless, describing how officers call them crack hoes and bitches.[9] This change in the relationship between institutional staff and female inmates is most probably due to the decreasing percentage of female correctional officers and the campaign to make women's prisons more like men's prisons in security procedures and informal policies and procedures.

One of the most difficult elements of adjustment for all women in prison is adjusting to other women: "What bothers me most back here is these stinking-ass women."[10] Older inmates complain about younger inmates, rural white women complain about having to live with blacks (although there is less racial animosity in women's prisons than in men's prisons), and some women complain about other prisoners engaged in same-sex relationships. Women also complain about theft; studies show that almost half of female prisoners have had something stolen.[11] The most typical complaint, however, is that other women are "messy," meaning that prisoners gossip: they gossip to retaliate, to gain power, or just for entertainment; and sometimes gossip leads to violence.[12]

The Prison World

A prisoner's day starts at 6:00 AM, or earlier if she is on kitchen duty, and typically ends at 10:00 PM with "lights out." After breakfast the women are sent to their various assignments: school, training, or work. Relatively few women stay in the living units during the morning or afternoon hours unless they are on "daylock" (in which a woman is locked in her cell all day as punishment) or unless they have a medical excuse for staying in. Inmates come back at 11:30 or 12:00 for count and lunch and then are sent to their afternoon assignments. Dinner is relatively early, sometimes as early as 4:30, in order for kitchen staff to have the meal cooked, served, and cleaned up by a reasonable hour. Evening hours are spent either in recreation (the prison yard or dayroom) or in some type of program (e.g., a college class, group therapy, an art class, a community meeting, an AA meeting, or charity work).

Count is taken periodically during the day, usually before breakfast, before lunch, after dinner, and sometime in the evening. If there is a discrepancy in the figures, women are kept in their cells until the numbers can be reconciled. They may wait for hours if the error cannot be found. The noon count is the most problematic, and an error or a missing inmate may mean that afternoon classes are postponed or canceled, visitors are kept waiting, and women who need to go to the medical unit must wait.

Food in prison is uniformly criticized as bland, starchy, and unappetizing. Some women, if they have the means, ignore the mess-hall meals altogether and use food bought in the commissary. Jean Harris[13] described how she practically lived on cereal, shunning the food and company of the mess hall. In Bedford Hills, women had access to stoves in the living units when Harris was serving time. Groups of women shared supplies and cooked dinners in these small kitchens. Inmates in other prisons may cook in their living units, but if no kitchens exist, they resort to using hotpots or contraband "stingers" (electrical devices that will heat water), or even irons. Prison recipes include ingredients such as Cheez Whiz, corn chips, canned tuna for enchiladas, and other creative fare.

Recreation and Visitation

Recreation is an important component of any institution's offerings; women's institutions offer fewer programs than comparable institutions for men.[14] Women tend to be less enthusiastic about physical team sports such as softball or basketball when they are offered; consequently, authorities justify the lack of such programs by the apparent disinterest on the part of female inmates.

However, women do show interest in participating in any number of charitable activities, including taping books for the blind, sewing teddy bears and dolls for distribution by police officers to traumatized children at crime scenes, knitting blankets for the poor, even beginning the training of seeing-eye dogs. Women who are engaged in these activities do so during evening recreation hours and, although some may be involved because they believe it will speed their release, probably the majority of them do so from a genuine interest in helping others.

Leisure time is also often spent watching television or playing card games and board games. Women look forward to commissary visits when they can buy candy, soda, and luxury items (sometimes not so much luxuries as necessities—for instance, a gentler shampoo than prison issue). Some women spend as much time as they can in their cells, removed from other prisoners by their own choice. Other women are involved in the social organization of the prison and gather around them a group or "family" who provide needed items and social support. Even though many female inmates, like male inmates, insist that you can't trust another inmate, they do develop strong friendships and familial-type relationships with other women in the facility.

Visitation is a necessary and important tool to bolster family ties and smooth reintegration. Unfortunately, many women's prisons are far removed from the urban areas where most prisoners come from and where their families live. Visiting poses problems for the families of female prisoners even more than for the families of male prisoners, because women's prisons are likely to be further away. This problem is especially acute in the federal system, which has only a few institutions for women in the whole country. Despite traveling difficulties, prisons often allow for no flexibility in visiting times; visiting may be restricted to specific hours during the day and may be limited to a couple of days a month. This discourages families who may have to travel hundreds of miles to see an incarcerated woman. Despite these problems, in some studies women have reported more frequent outside communication with family members than did men.[15]

Prison officials remark that visitation rooms in women's prisons are mostly filled with family members (typically mothers and sisters) and children; visitation rooms in men's prisons are usually filled with wives and girlfriends. There is a general tendency for women in prison not to have continued support from the men in their lives; either they are not married, their partner is also serving a prison sentence, or they have been abandoned by husbands and boyfriends.

The increased presence of telephones in prison has changed the visitation situation dramatically. Prior to the 1980s, telephone privileges were rare or reserved for family emergencies. At some point in the 1980s, telephone providers discovered that they could charge extremely high rates for collect calls and reap substantial profits, even after paying states a portion of the profits for allowing telephones into prisons. Now, many prisons have banks of phones in the dayrooms (instead of counselors' offices) and inmates may be able to call as often as several times a week. Observers have complained that the presence of telephones is yet another example of the so-called softening of prison security, but the change in access was largely due to the huge profits that were made at the expense of prisoner families who can usually ill afford the high price of collect calls. In 2014, a ban from the Federal Communications Commission (FCC) went into effect prohibiting excessive charges to prisoners and kickbacks to corrections departments. The ban does not cover video chats (such as Skype), which some suspect will be the next frontier of profit for telecommunications companies that will target prisoner families who are unable to have face-to-face visits with their loved ones.[16] It is likely that inmates maintain more frequent communication today with family members than in the past, and evidence indicates that strong ties with families are linked to success upon release. Many women even prefer telephone visits over face-to-face visits with their children so that caregivers do not have to make the effort to travel to a far-away prison and children do not see their mother in prison uniforms.

Rules and Punishments

The impression one receives on entering a women's institution is that it might be a pleasant, albeit restricted, place to spend some time. Grounds are typically attractive, and rooms may be decorated in homey ways. Upon further examination, however, one discovers that the institutions typically operate by means of dozens of rules (ranging from serious to trivial) governing behavior. Women may not be allowed freedom of movement except in groups and with passes. They may have their letters from or to home read and censored. They may be forced to eat in the cafeteria whether they want to or not; taking food, even an apple, out of the cafeteria can get an inmate written up because it is against the rules. Officers constantly check passes and interrogate women accused of being out of place. Several observers agree that the rules in women's prisons may be stricter and cover more petty details than those in prisons for males.[17] Very early studies of women's prisons described rules that included strictures regarding personal cleanliness, what type of clothing could be worn, and what items were considered contraband (which included "immoral" magazines and dice); and prohibitions against exchanging presents, bartering, offensive language, gambling, and disorderly conduct, including sexual conduct.[18] Similar types of rules still exist today. "Trafficking and trading" (a system of inmate commerce) is prohibited because such activity is a frequent source of violence (when debts are not paid); however, sharing, trading, and selling goods and services are mechanisms that make prison life more bearable. Punishments include daylock, loss of recreation or commissary privileges, loss of visitation or correspondence privileges, solitary confinement, or loss of good time (time off one's sentence for good behavior).

There is a fairly consistent history of findings that document the greater rate of rule breaking by women in prison, with a few studies showing that rule violations by women are 1.5 to 2.0 times the rate of men's.[19] There are other studies that do not show that women are more likely to commit infractions.[20] Also, other researchers like McClellan[21] noted that trivial rules seem to be enforced more stringently in women's prisons, resulting in greater numbers of rule breakers. It is also possible that women are more likely than men to have altercations in front of officers, leading to disciplinary tickets, as this correctional professional describes:

> Women tend to showboat, men don't. Like . . . if a girl was going to fight, quite often she'd wait until she got in the mess hall so that all the girls were around, not just three or four girls on her unit. Where men . . . they'll tend to get you later, on the side of the building and that way nobody gets hurt. I mean not have to go to lock. We've had a couple instances here where a guy has shown up with a black eye and we ask and they give you some bull story about tripping down the stairs and yet after it all comes out eventually you hear that somebody met him out behind the gym or something and cleaned his clock.[22]

Prisoner Subculture

The prisoner subculture is a subterranean culture that exists within but is distinct from the formal culture of the prison and society. It is the *sub rosa* culture of norms, values, and social roles. The formal prison culture, on the other hand, is what is seen; it is the product of all the actors in the prison environment, including prison administrators, staff, and the prisoners themselves. *Prisonization* is the term used to describe the degree to which an individual inmate has adopted the prisoner subculture and its value system.

Early researchers documented the subculture in prisons for men, describing elements of leadership, social roles, race, the role of violence, and the like.[23] A few studied these elements in institutions for women.[24] Unfortunately, researchers merely compared the women's institution to the descriptions of men's institutions rather than approaching the women's world without preconceptions or expectations derived from prior research in men's prisons.

Two competing theories of how prisoner subculture develops are deprivation theory and importation theory. Deprivation theory presumes that inmates experience deprivations of needs and wants (such as privacy, family, sex, and so on) and these deprivations lead to the creation of a subculture to meet those needs. Importation theory presumes that prisoner subculture is merely a variant of street culture and that prisoners bring street culture into the prison. Other theorists believe that both sources are relevant when understanding prisoner subculture. Both theories have been used to explain differences between male and female subcultures.

Deprivation Theory

Gresham Sykes[25] described the pains of imprisonment, including the loss of family and friends, security, privacy, autonomy, and sex. Prisoners must share their living space against their will and must learn to coexist with others with whom they would never associate outside prison. Privacy is nonexistent, since women must shower together and may be observed even when excreting

or taking care of hygiene needs. In these times of overcrowding this deprivation is exacerbated, and rooms that were built to hold two women are often
holding four. Many prisons today use a dormitory style of housing, providing
even less privacy for women.

Some researchers believed that female prisoners suffer the pains of imprisonment more deeply than men do. For instance, Ward and Kassebaum wrote:

> The impact of imprisonment is, we believe, more severe for females than
> for males because it is more unusual. Female inmates generally have not
> come up through the "sandlots of crime," in that they are not as likely as
> men to have had experience in training schools or reformatories.[26]

According to this view, women feel deprivations of family, emotional support, and safety more acutely than men do. Thus, the deprivation of family
ties, for instance, is the reason that women create make-believe families in
prison (described more fully in a later section). The deprivation of emotional
support in prison explains why there is less social distance and isolation
between inmates and officers than one finds in a prison for men.[27] With
increased visitation and telephone calls, this need seems to be increasingly
met through outside contacts, reducing the need to depend on staff. Consequently, the interactions between staff and female prisoners today seems to be
more formalized and distant than in years past.

Other argue, on the other hand, that women do not have as many deprivations as men and therefore have less need of a subculture; for instance,
women's prisons are not believed to be as violent as men's prisons and, thus,
women do not need to create a subculture of gangs for protection.

Still other theorists believe that women have different—not less—deprivation. Harris[28] concluded that women did not experience greater deprivation
than men, although men and women experienced the deprivations of prison
differently. For instance, women in her study identified the lack of relationships as deprivations and men did not.

Importation Theory

The importation theory, developed by John Irwin and Donald Cressey,[29]
presumes that the subculture in a prison is shaped by the prisoners themselves
and what they bring into the prison from the outside. Drug culture in prison,
for instance, nonexistent before the 1960s, was imported when many drug
offenders entered the prison system. In this view, male and female prison subcultures are different because they bring in socialized gender differences from
the outside. For instance, some might argue that women's concerns about
their children tend to diffuse the importance of prison life. Also, women's
criminal backgrounds are typically less extensive than men's, which also
changes the prisoner subculture.

Researchers eventually concluded that both deprivation and importation
play a role in the prisoner subculture for both men and women.[30] Researchers
also found that both importation and deprivation factors tended to explain the

extent and nature of the prisoner subculture for women, but findings were mixed with different studies having different measures, so it is hard to draw many conclusions.[31]

The next several sections discuss the major elements of subculture, including the inmate code and argot roles; the black market (including drugs), social relationships, violence, and relationships with officers.

The Inmate Code

The so-called inmate code was originally described by researchers studying prisons for men in the 1940s and 1950s. The major values endorsed in the code are: "Don't interfere with inmate interests," "Never rat on a con," "Don't be nosy," "Don't have a loose lip," "Keep off a man's back," "Don't put a guy on the spot," "Be loyal to your class," "Be cool," "Do your own time," and "Don't exploit inmates."[32] Female prisoners have never adhered to the code provisions in the same way as men.[33] For instance, although one hears the statement that women should "do their own time," female prisoners seem to be more involved with each other and routinely extend nurturance and sympathy to each other (as well as more negative interactions fueled by jealousy and dislike).[34] Women also do not have strong proscriptions regarding interaction with correctional officers (COs). In a men's prison, inmates tend to avoid officers so as not to be labeled a snitch.

Because of differences in offender criminal background, gender differences, and institutional features (including staff interactions and expectations), it should not be surprising that female prisoners have exhibited different values and a somewhat different inmate code from that found in prisons for men. Unfortunately, researchers have always used the male inmate code as the standard and have typically merely compared the women's prison to this standard. Thus, we have had a somewhat distorted view of the inmate code for women; typically we have been told only what it is not (when it does not conform to men's). We do not have a comprehensive portrait of what it *was*, because early studies merely compared the women's prison to the men's.[35] We also do not have a comprehensive sense of what it *is* today because, except for a few notable exceptions, we have little information of what is currently occurring in women's prisons.

Argot Roles

Argot (social) roles describe the behavior patterns, motivation, and place of the individual in the prison culture. Of course, not all inmates can be categorized into a social role, but some are easily recognizable. Sykes's[36] classic work specified rats, centermen, gorillas, merchants, wolves, ball busters, real men, toughs, and hipsters. Schrag's[37] typology included square johns, right guys, con politicians, and outlaws.

Some social roles were observed in prisons for both men and women (squares, snitches, and homies/homeys/homeboys), and others were similar.[38] Interestingly, sometimes the same social role was explained in different terms.

Giallombardo[39] discussed the "homey" relationship found in the women's prison as making friends with those from one's home neighborhoods to prevent gossipy women from spreading stories from the outside; however, homies exist in prisons for men as well and have not been explained in the same way. Giallombardo's social roles for women included snitchers (common to male prisons), inmate cops (inmates who identify more with the guards than with other inmates), squares (a parallel to square johns), jive bitches (those who lie or spread gossip), rap buddies and homies (common to male prisons), boosters (thieves), pinners (those who facilitate the black market), and the cluster of roles associated with homosexuality.[40]

The role of "real man" applied to old-style cons who possessed characteristics such as generosity, integrity, and stoicism in the face of provocation from guards. Giallombardo wrote that there were no corresponding "real women" because female prisoners did not have the positive qualities associated with the role. Instead, they were described as "spiteful, deceitful and untrustworthy."[41] Heffernan, however, did find a parallel to the real man in a women's prison. This type of inmate was described as responsible, loyal, and willing to stand up for what she believed in. She also identified three types: square, cool (professional criminals), and "the life" (prisonized, recidivistic women), that corresponded almost identically to Irwin and Cressey's square, thief, and con subcultural roles.[42] Other efforts to create typologies exist as well.[43]

Ethnographies of women's prisons published in the 1990s did not describe these social roles, although Owen's[44] description of "the mix" (homosexual activity, drugs, and fighting) seems to be similar to Heffernan's older definition of "the life."

A large part of the inmate code is concerned with the proscription against ratting, or in any way conveying information about inmate activities to prison officials. The common perception is that this concern is present in both men's and women's prisons, but the rule against ratting is much more heavily enforced in men's prisons. In both prisons, social isolation is used against individuals, but in women's prisons, gossip is used and sometimes violence in the form of threats or pushing-and-shoving sessions. Serious violence, however, is extremely rare in women's prisons, although it has occurred. Several reasons can be suggested for these differences, including the fact that the stakes involved are probably not as high in prisons for women. Specifically, women do not engage in the same large-scale drug trafficking that can be found in prisons for men.

The Black Market

All prisoners develop ways of acquiring needed or desired goods. Whereas men tend to operate business-like black market systems, complete with entrepreneurs and corporate mergers, women distribute contraband and goods through family ties, small cliques, and roommate relationships. The other major difference is that female prisoners have less variety and quantity of contraband, including drugs, than men do. It seems likely that women have less ability to obtain drugs from outside prison, and women in prison have fewer resources to purchase drugs from suppliers. Some also speculate that women find it easier to obtain prescribed drugs (anti-anxiety drugs and antidepressants) from prison staff, reducing the need for illicit drugs.

Even for goods other than drugs, the black market does not seem to operate in women's prisons to the extent that it can be found in institutions for men. Although women may engage in petty theft, and contraband goods (e.g., food from the prison kitchen) are distributed in informal circles, the degree of organization observed in prisons for men does not seem to be present in women's institutions. Women more often tend to share legitimate and contraband goods through informal social networks, such as make-believe families, romantic partnerships, friendships, or roommate groups.

Not all of the goods distribution occurs through family or friendship networks; there is some commerce in women's prisons, known in some systems as trafficking and trading, and it is against the prison rules. Those who do not have family or friends who are willing or able to send money must find other ways to get commissary items or other resources. Some sell services (such as doing other inmates' laundry, hair, or creating art projects to sell), some "sell" boxes (that is, a woman receives a box in her name that is actually for another inmate who has exceeded her allowance), and others are described as commissary hustlers who enter into relationships with those who have money in their account in order to share their resources.[45]

Social Organization (Gangs versus Families)

One of the most interesting differences between men's and women's prisons is the relative lack of racial animosity and tension in women's prisons as compared to men's.[46] Although a few reports have described women banding together in racial groupings and discussing racial tensions,[47] women's friendships and make-believe family ties cross racial lines.[48] In most penitentiaries, men self-segregate by race and ethnicity. Women's prisons, even those in California where there is a gang presence, seem to escape the most violent aspects of racial gang groupings:

> . . . racism is not a big issue in here to me . . . you got Crips here, you got Bloods here, you got La Nuestra here, you got all gangs here, you got all colors here, and I have not seen one person disrespect the other. . . .[49]

Women's prisons are not a utopia of racial harmony by any means. Black inmates in some prisons say, "If you're white you're right," and they complain that work assignments are given preferentially to white inmates; in other prisons, whites complain that black staff members favor black inmates. However, violent conflicts over race are almost nonexistent in women's prisons and there is no prevalent fear of racial violence, as in prisons for men.

The social organization of many men's prisons is shaped primarily by gangs. Although some male inmates successfully isolate themselves from gangs, these social groupings are a powerful influence in most men's prisons.

The other major social relationship for men is one between homies (or "road dogs") who are friends (often from one's neighborhood or a prior prison stay).

The social organization of a women's prison is influenced by what are called make-believe or pseudo-family relationships to a greater or lesser degree depending on the institution. Rather than the semipolitical organizations such as gangs, clubs, and associations; women are more likely to group together in familial units, cliques, or dyads. Women take on the roles of mothers (the most frequent), fathers, brothers, sisters, daughters, and sons, along with the attendant characteristics of such relationships (mothers nurture, fathers discipline, and so on).[50]

> The family is when you come to prison, and you get close to someone, if it is a stud-broad, that's your dad or your brother—I got a lot of them here. If it's a femme, then that is your sister. Some who is just a new commitment, you try to school them into doing things right, that is your pup. But if somebody is a three-termer, and doing a lot of time like I have, then that is your dog, road dog—prison dog.[51]

The mother-daughter relationship is the most common, and some mothers may have many daughters in the institution who look to her for comfort and support. She, in turn, listens to their problems and gives advice. In larger, more elaborate family systems, a mother might have a husband who becomes a father to her daughters (but not necessarily). Staff members sometimes even legitimate these relationships by asking "mothers" or "fathers" to control their "children" if the women are having disciplinary issues. This would parallel staff use of gang leaders to control the inmate population in a prison for men.

Commitments to such family systems differ. Often the family relationships are more of a joke or a game than anything more meaningful. What may influence a woman's commitment to the prison family are the other elements that make up her prison life. The pull of the make-believe family is weak when a woman nears release or when she has maintained strong and continuing ties with her natural family, especially her children. When a woman has come from a poor environment on the outside, when she is isolated from other ties, when the prison world is her only world, then often the relationships she develops there become more real than any she had on the outside. In a sense, she may be creating the type of family she wished she had and never did. This inmate described the reasons for families in a similar way:

> I see it like maybe the reason they do that is 'cause they don't know who they [sic] father is, maybe they don't have any sisters or brothers, maybe their mother's passed away, maybe they don't have any kids and want kids, want a mother, want a father, want a brother; want a sister. I don't want none of it. It's not real, for one thing.[52]

The different social organizations found in men's and women's prisons are no doubt partially due to imported gender differences. Hart[53] found that women in prison self-reported higher levels of social support (i.e., close or meaningful friendships with other prisoners and outsiders) than did male prisoners. A statistical relationship between social support and psychological well-being existed for women, but not for male inmates.

The prevalence of these make-believe family structures is decreasing.[54] Permeability (more frequent visitation, telephone privileges, and outside groups coming in to offer programs) decreases dependence on prison life; consequently, the prison family system is less necessary than it was in the past. However, even in fairly recent studies, descriptions of families still emerge:

> Well, we had families in prison. We have these people, you know, a mom and a dad and then we take in the young ones, the girls comin' in who are 18 or 19, we take them under our wing. Prison is a scary place and the young girls are sometimes scared out of their mind and they don't know what to expect so we take them into our family. I had two prison kids, they were small and very sweet and I was their mom. . . .

> [Another inmate:] the only nice thing in prison is that women can be good to one another, they can create a family structure and work together . . . most of us are mothers and miss our kids so the young girls, they substitute for our own kids. . . .[55]

Homosexuality

Early researchers were interested in female prisoners' same-sex prison relationships, almost to the exclusion of any other part of the prison world. Early works described pervasive homosexuality and inmate "marriages," complete with make-believe ceremonies. Except for a small group whose sexual orientation was same-sex before prison, most women are "jailhouse turn-outs"[56] who are "in the life" only during their imprisonment ("gay for the stay") and revert back to a heterosexual lifestyle upon release.[57] Women who are gay have explained that they stay away from *the mix* (homosexual relationships) because of the promiscuity and game playing that goes on.[58]

There are perceived differences in the same-sex relationships found in prisons for women as compared to prisons for men, as this officer describes:

> The homosexuality that is done in the male facilities is usually masked, and there is a percentage of rapes, but I think a lot more of it is permissive; it is sold and so forth. In the female facilities it's not sold, it's not rape, it's just an agreement between two people that they're going to participate and there is a lot of participation.[59]

An inmate echoes this viewpoint:

> I mean, [the men] have sex, but they don't have relationships. But these women, it's more than sex to them. It's a relationship. You can get a woman who comes in off the street that ain't never been gay and is crazy about men, and she'll end up having a relationship. But it's just a substitution, I think, for lack of emotional and, you know, it's one way to try to have your needs met.[60]

One of the first descriptions of female inmate homosexuality was written more than 100 years ago when Otis[61] described "unnatural" relationships between white and black female inmates. Other early works described love notes, nicknames adopted by those participating in same-sex relationships, and prevalence.[62] Estimates of prevalence of homosexuality in women's prisons vary widely. Early studies reported ranges of 19 to 70 percent, depending on whether the source was official reports or staff or inmate estimates.[63] Some research found that prevalence rates were higher in those institutions that were described as more "treatment" oriented.[64] Others did not find much difference in the prevalence levels across various types of institutions.[65]

A woman who displays masculine dress, hair, or behavior patterns may be called a butch, stud broad, drag butch, or hard daddy.[66] Butches and femmes (the term for the other, more feminine partner) sometimes behave in ways that are almost a parody of heterosexual relationships. The "male" acts domineering, is often unfaithful, and demands services, and the other woman often is insecure about keeping the affection of her partner. The cross-gender roles as they appear in men's prisons (punks) and women's prisons (butches) illustrate interesting power relation differences. While butches wield a degree of power in the women's prison, those men forced into cross-gender roles in the men's prison are more often pawns and victims.[67] The choice to take on the "dyke" role is explained by one inmate:

> You either gonna be a femme or you gonna be a dyke, o.k.? If you come in here and nobody is attracted to you as a femme, you gotta belong so you do a complete turnaround, you become the masculine role, you got control, you go after who you want.[68]

Some researchers found that African American women were more likely to be active in homosexual relationships and the inmate subculture, but this is an old finding and has not been replicated.[69] More recent findings have indicated that these relationships are sometimes more complicated than older studies implied; for instance, butches may take on masculine characteristics in order to protect themselves against aggression; femmes may be the violent individual in the relationship; and many long-term romantic relationships bear no obvious outward indices of cross-gender role taking.[70]

Many women in prison choose to isolate themselves and have minimal participation in the social world of the prison, moving between school or work and their cells, seldom venturing outside their created zones of security. Some research indicates that many women report spending the majority of their time in their rooms, partially to avoid trouble that often occurred in recreation or the dayroom.[71]

Violence

Early studies indicated that there was much less violence in the women's prison than in prisons for men.[72] Women are less likely to manufacture or carry weapons, possibly because there are no metal shops or other industries that provide appropriate materials for weapons.[73] Women are probably also less skilled in the manufacture of weapons because of their backgrounds and life experiences. Some women do carry weapons, but they are less sophisticated and less lethal than weapons found in prisons for men. During an altercation, women pick up nearby objects, such as a chair, broom, or iron, to use as a makeshift weapon, or they fight without weapons.

Violence in a women's prison usually is between two people in a romantic relationship or, if not within a relationship, because of perceived thefts or perceived disrespect. Thus the violence is rarely impersonal and very infrequently results in serious injury, although in every prison inmates pass on stories of extreme violence.[74]

Recent studies have given us a much greater understanding of prison violence. While it may be true that serious violence is rare in women's prisons, earlier studies probably underestimated the prevalence of the incidence of intimidation, threats, and assaults that occur. Wolff and her colleagues[75] published several reports of their research comparing violence in men's and women's prisons. Their findings were surprising in that they found that 80 percent of their sample of female inmates reported some type of victimization (broadly defined, including theft) in the prior six months. Slightly more women (15 percent) than men (10 percent) reported being slapped, hit, or kicked.[76] Men were more likely than women to report being victimized with a weapon and almost three times as likely as women to report physical violence by guards (13 percent compared to five percent).[77]

Owen and her colleagues[78] used a qualitative approach to examine gendered violence in women's prisons. In focus groups inmates described a wide range of triggers for violence, but conflict over debts, jealousy or disagreements between romantic partners, and "disrespect" seemed to be the most common. Most women did not feel that the threat of violence permeated the prison, but they did note that an inmate had to be aware of informal rules to avoid conflict with other inmates. Women's advice to avoid violence included keeping to oneself and not getting involved in homosexuality, gambling, and drug use; staying quiet about one's personal life; watching the company one keeps (i.e., avoiding women who gossiped); not having an "attitude"; standing one's ground; being clean; and learning how to say no.[79]

One type of conflict between women that came up frequently in the focus groups of this study (and also mentioned in the last chapter) is when an inmate doesn't follow the informal rules of cleanliness. These rules are different from prison to prison, but they all stem from the same source: a pervasive fear of being infected with a contagious illness in a prison where medical care is considered woefully inadequate. For instance, new inmates learn quickly to clean the sink after they use it, not hang their towels on the bunk or in the dorm space of others, and not to use others' personal hygiene products. Health concerns eclipsed worries about sexual or physical safety. This concern is echoed in other studies as well.[80]

Disrespect was a central theme in conflict between inmates. Butler[81] and others have deconstructed the concept of respect and how it leads to violence in the men's prison. Much of the violence in men's prisons is due to perceived disrespect, and men who are more insecure in their identity are more likely to use physical confrontation to protect their self-respect. It appears that the same motivator that spurs violence among men operates with women—at least possibly those women raised in some socioeconomic environments where one's reputation is often protected by violence. Studies show that women in gang-infested and economically distressed neighborhoods also emphasize their willingness to fight against any perceived disrespect (e.g., "Nobody talks to me like that"). Research documents that some women fight against disrespect on the street,[82] and this type of violence also appears in prisons.[83]

Besides a frontal assault by insult or physical push or dare to fight, women describe being disrespected by those who gossip about them. The gossip could be true or completely made up. It could be intended to get the target in trouble, or just to be malicious by telling secrets that should remain private about one's crime or life outside prison.[84] Trammell provided descriptions of how gossip can lead to conflict and, sometimes, violence in prison.

> I had a girl who told everyone that I was in for child abuse, which is a lie, I sold drugs. I called her out and we yelled at each other. She should not be spreading lies and gossip. She finally started crying and apologized to me, so I won that one. That's how you solve a lot of problems.

> [A different inmate:] Women will fight with words; these words hurt more than the fist. We will lie and make others hate you. . . . we break up friends and girlfriends. Maybe it's boredom or something. . . .[85]

In the focus groups in Owen's study, most women suggested that victims of prison violence "put themselves in that situation" through their own behaviors and actions. When prompted, however, their descriptions of likely victims included those who might be considered to have precipitated their victimization, but also those who had the misfortune to look vulnerable. Vulnerable characteristics included being younger or older than average, being naive about prison, having a slight build, possessing mental or physical disabilities, not speaking English, being either resource-poor or resource-rich, and "acting like a victim." Women also acknowledged that there were some women in prison who were known "predators."[86]

Sadly, much of the physical violence that occurs in women's prisons occurs within intimate partnerships; thus, many women in prison recreate the abusive relationships they had outside. One inmate astutely observes this phenomenon:

> . . . you come in here having been beat by a man or what, when you come in here, you look for the same kind of relationship, whether it is a woman or a man. In your subliminal mind, you are looking for the same thing, and before you know it, you are with an aggressor [in here] that is beating on you. Then you have [those who] become an aggressor. You find and go for a woman that you can control because you like being over her.[87]

This observation also points out the possibility that a woman who has experienced being a victim in either a street or prison relationship sometimes enters into another relationship where she becomes the abuser. Women who were abusers in prison relationships described childhood and adult victimization and expressed very little understanding of how to control their own violence.[88] Because these relationships were so intense, any threat to the relationship could be the catalyst for desperate, and often extreme, reactions.

> Women are clingy and have too many needs. In prison we lose our identities and our dignity. We are our numbers. We feel like pieces of shit. We left our kids outside. So in here, if I find someone to focus on and they look at someone else, I'm gonna beat the shit out of them.[89]

As noted above, both resource-rich and resource-poor women were described as potential victims. Previous findings identified prison relationships that occur because of economic dependency. "Canteen whores" or "commissary whores" have been described as participating in sexual relationships to get access to the resources of the partner.[90] However, in the study by Owen and her colleagues, the direction of these economic and interpersonal relationships was not consistent in terms of who might be considered the victim of economic exploitation. Some women asserted that the woman who had access to a lot of commissary was a likely target for sexual predators (whose primary motive was commissary items rather than a loving relationship); while others felt that someone who was able to purchase friends and sexual partners through her well-funded inmate account was the exploiter. Seemingly, both situations occur.

In Owen's gendered violence study, women laughed over extremely violent incidents and boasted of their ability to seriously injure other women. Although they reacted strongly to officers using physical force against them, many participants expressed the view that officers should leave them alone to fight each other.[91] Batchelor and her colleagues[92] also found that some young incarcerated women did not view certain behaviors or experiences as violent: even such violent incidents as attempted rapes by acquaintances or physical fights with siblings were dismissed. This finding clearly illustrates the extremely abnormal backgrounds of women in prison who have experienced violence as a part of their lives since childhood. One important research finding is that girls and women cannot be neatly categorized into victims and offenders. In fact, Daly's[93] "harmed and harming" women come to mind frequently when listening to the life experiences of violent women in prison.

Sexual Violence

As noted above, early studies indicated that most homosexuality in women's prisons was consensual, and homosexual rape was much more of a threat in men's prisons. More recent studies, however, have found that forms of sexual assault and intimidation short of completed physical rape were much more common in women's prisons than previously believed, and, in fact, more common in women's prisons than in men's prisons. Struckman-Johnson and Struckman-Johnson[94] found that in three prisons for women, prevalence rates ranged from zero to 5 percent for rape and six to 19 percent for sexual assault (the latter including behaviors such as unwanted touching). Most perpetrators were other inmates (ranging from 55 to 80 percent), not correctional officers.

Wolff and her colleagues also reported that sexual violence was much more prevalent in women's prisons than previously thought. One of the problems in this area of study is the lack of consistency in terms, such that sexual assault may or may not mean rape, and acts that do not escalate to completed, unwanted sex acts are called by different names. In the surveys used by Wolff and colleagues, much more specific terms were used. "Nonconsensual sex acts" included forced sex acts, including oral and anal sex; and "abusive sexual contacts" included intentional touching of breasts, buttocks, or the groin area. In Wolff's studies, the rate of inmate-on-inmate sexual victimization in a six-month period was four times higher (212 compared to 43 per 1,000) in women's prisons than in men's, and staff-on-inmate sexual violence was about one and one-half times higher (53 compared to 34 per 1,000).[95]

Congress passed the Prison Rape Elimination Act (PREA) in 2003, which mandated that the Bureau of Justice Statistics determine the prevalence of prison rape. The latest prisoner survey was conducted in 2011,[96] and inmates were randomly selected for participation from 233 prisons, 358 jails and 15 special detainments facilities; 44 of the prisons housed women (7,141 female prisoners participated), and four of the jails housed women. This survey defines "non-consensual sex acts" as oral, anal, or vaginal penetration, masturbation, and other sexual acts. "Abusive sexual contacts" is defined as unwanted contact involving touching of buttocks, thighs, penis, breasts, or vagina in a sexual way. "Sexual victimization" includes both categories.

In the latest results, more women than men in prison reported any type of sexual victimization by other inmates (6.9 percent compared to 1.7 percent). About equal numbers of women and men in prison reported staff sexual misconduct of any type (2.3 percent of women compared to 2.4 percent of men). This survey also was administered in jails. About 3.6 percent of female jail inmates reported any type of sexual victimization by other inmates (compared to 1.4 percent of males), and 1.4 percent of female jail inmates reported sexual misconduct by guards (compared to 1.9 percent of males). Survey results indicated that the most vulnerable inmates were those who reported having mental health issues, were committed for sex offenses, and were homosexual or bisexual (these results are from the combined pool of male and female inmates). Juveniles were not statistically more likely than adults to report victimization. It's important to realize that these national averages mask quite extreme differences between facilities. The report identifies "high-reporting" institutions and "low-reporting" institutions.

Owen and her colleagues, in their qualitative study, found that women did not spontaneously initiate conversations about sexual violence and indicated that it was not a pervasive fear, although they could recite examples of both inmate-on-inmate sexual violence and officer-on-inmate sexual violence when prompted. The types of inmate-on-inmate sexual violence that female inmates described ranged from fairly nonserious sexual comments, joking and touching that women could often ignore or avoid (e.g., remarks about the size of one's breasts when showering) to more persistent forms of those behaviors. Another type of sexual victimization was when a woman was pressured for a relationship which, when extreme, was called a "fatal attraction" (from the movie about a female stalker). Sexual aggressors were those women who were known to engage in serial intimidations. There was also sexual violence within intimate relationships, meaning forced or coerced sex with an unwilling partner. Instances of non-partner rape, sometimes done by a group upon one woman, were mentioned, but rarely. Generally, these incidents occurred in retaliation for some transgression the woman was perceived to have done.[97] Studies indicate that more men than women (21 percent compared to 9 percent) fear being raped in prison.[98]

Correctional Officers

The relationships between officers and inmates in women's prisons seem to have somewhat less social distance and greater informal communication than what is found in prisons for men. There are surprisingly warm relationships between a few inmates (in jails and/or prisons) and the correctional officers who work there, especially between some officers and those women who entered the system when they were very young or those women who have had extremely abusive, dysfunctional relationships with family members and friends. For them, correctional officers may be the first individuals in authority who haven't hurt them:

> For me this is my home away from home 'cuz I don't have nobody on the outside. . . . I know all of the COs here. They're like my uncles and aunts in a way, you know what I'm saying? They're real good people to me. I like them.[99]

However, there is still a pervasive culture of distrust and dislike between officers and inmates, even in the women's prison. Officers stereotype inmates as worthless and dishonest; inmates stereotype officers as lazy and ignorant. The lack of meaningful communication between the two groups makes the job harder for the officer and life more difficult for the inmate. Officers may use their power to withhold necessities or humiliate inmates by forcing them to ask for needed items.

Inmates, especially those in segregation, are dependent on the officers to bring them everything, including food, toilet paper, and tampons. If the officer is busy or irritated, the food cart may sit undistributed until the food is cold. To ask another adult for permission to do such mundane things as go to the bathroom is demeaning and humiliating. Female inmates may adopt an abrasive and hostile attitude as a coping mechanism; thus a request is phrased as a demand, often capped with an obscenity for good measure. This tactic only results in making the situation worse, however, since the officer may then ignore the woman, demand that she rephrase the request, or write her up for insolence.

In descriptions of women's prisons up until about the 1990s, there was a pervasive theme that female inmates were treated like children. Women were called girls or ladies, and the tone was often that used to discipline somewhat dense and naughty children. Older inmates were especially irritated when younger officers treated them this way.

> For a 33 year old woman to have another woman tell her that she is misbehaving, it's funny to me, it's funny! . . . To be 33 and have somebody tell you that you're acting like a little child, and that means that you're going to be punished. It's funny.[100]

Changes that have taken place in women's prisons, including more male officers, officers who have worked in prisons for men, and centralized training, have changed the atmosphere. Women are not treated as children so much anymore, but, instead they are "disrespected." A theme that runs through all research with female inmates is that they feel officers treat them as unworthy of human dignity.

> And I don't care if I'm an inmate or not, I'm still a human being. I'm a woman just like they are. Yeah, I may have committed a crime, but I'm paying for it. I've been paying for it almost a decade of my life. You don't have to talk to me like I'm a dog, 'cause I'm not.[101]

Officers who have worked with both male and female inmates explain that there are differences in working with the two groups; women require more effort on the part of officers.

> The female inmates come over and they always want a little bit more than what's there, you know, if you say you can't have this or this, they'll argue about it. They take up more time because you listen to them, you don't have to. You could say "you can't have it and that's all there is to it" and throw them out the door, but it is very hard to do because you know you prevent a lot of problems if you take the time to talk to them, even if it's just to explain. You know, the rule is changed and they usually then accept it, but they have to argue it all the time.[102]

Interestingly, a very similar comment from a CO was obtained about 17 years later in a different prison:

> The men take answers at face value. When you tell them "no," they go away, but the women want to discuss their particular problem in great detail. When staff are trained at a male institution, they do not know how to deal with it. Women take more time and some staff are [sic] not prepared for that.[103]

Recall that prisons and reformatories for women in the early 1900s were staffed primarily by women because it was believed that female matrons could provide good role models for the female prisoners, as the following quote from the 1930s suggests:

> There is a real place in the reformatory for "matrons" in the good sense of the word, women of great refinement and intelligent social workers, who

know not only to create a fine home atmosphere, but who above all have the confidence of their charges and know how to help them in re-adjusting their personalities. . . . Generally, reformatory officers should be physically and mentally healthy, well-balanced, even-tempered, socially mature women, with steady moral standards and a cheerful disposition. . . .[104]

Most of those hired in early institutions came from social work and teaching backgrounds. They had no experience in custody control and approached their charges as they would a dependent client, child, or student. Consequently, the early histories reported staff and female inmates working together hand in hand to build new buildings or plant in the fields. Many of those attracted to corrections work were educated in women's colleges or possessed an almost religious fervor to change the lives of female offenders for the better.

Although the hiring of female reformers for whom corrections was a calling ceased after the 1930s, new hires continued to be women. Up until the 1980s, correctional officers in women's prisons were almost all women. This was probably part of the reason that men's and women's prisons were so different in terms of atmosphere, policies, and discipline. Legal challenges, brought by female correctional officers who fought to be allowed to work in prisons for men, began in the 1960s, and by the mid-1980s we started to see evaluations of female correctional officers in prisons and jails.[105]

The flip side of equal employment was that male officers also had an equal opportunity to work in women's prisons. By the late 1980s, men comprised about 35 percent of COs in women's prisons, and by 1992 about 46 percent.[106] Today, the percentage varies quite a bit from state to state and has been reported as high as 70 percent in California and 81 percent in Colorado.[107]

This is an amazing change from prior decades when women's facilities were staffed primarily by women. It is not clear why so many more men have ended up in prisons for women, especially while the numbers of women in men's prisons has remained quite small. Probably one reason is that the field of institutional corrections is not an occupation of choice for large numbers of women. Corrections departments fill staff positions in prisons for women with men because, quite simply, primarily men are applying for the jobs.

Male officers in some prisons observe women showering and using the toilet. They may also conduct pat-downs or even strip searches. Zupan[108] found that less than half of the facilities employing male officers made physical changes (i.e., shower curtains) to protect women's privacy. Other states have made policies such as having a same-sex officer on the unit at all times. While some states do not allow male officers to pat down or supervise strip searches, most allow these to occur in "emergencies." Interestingly, the first cases challenging opposite-sex guards were brought by male prisoners who didn't like female officers observing them in states of undress or patting them down. They based their challenges on privacy rights. Courts were generally not sympathetic and held that the female officer's right to work outweighed the privacy rights of inmates, especially if states took the barest effort to protect inmates' dignity (such as rules that prohibited opposite-sex guards from observing strip searches and showers).[109] Later cases that were filed by female prisoners arguing privacy rights against male correctional officers received slightly more sympathy from courts, and judges offered suggestions such as frosted glass in showers, announcing the presence of a male CO in a living unit, and issuing pajamas rather than nightgowns to women.[110]

Female prisoners also (in some cases successfully) used the Eighth Amendment, arguing that female prisoners were likely to be incest and rape survivors and searches and pat-downs by male officers were uniquely cruel and painful for female prisoners.[111] There is some research to indicate that some women physically subdued and/or searched by male officers experience PTSD "flashback" incidents because of past victimization by men.[112] For instance, Heney and Kristiansen[113] noted that about 50 percent of Canadian female prisoners have been subject to prior sexual abuse, and these women are retraumatized in prison by incidences of pat-downs, strip searches, verbal abuse, and other interactions with male officers that emphasize their power-lessness against these men, similar to their experiences on the outside.

Zupan[114] noted in 1992 that in 21 percent of the states she surveyed, male officers conducted pat-downs routinely; in 21 percent of the states, males conducted these searches with restrictions (i.e., with another officer present); and in 29 percent of the states, males could only conduct such searches in emergency situations. In some states, male officers may assist in strip searches as well. Strip searches are usually done by medical personnel but supervised by correctional officers. Courts give great deference to state authorities, especially if "emergency" situations are alleged as the reason for pat-downs or strip searches.

While some argue that some courts are practicing reverse discrimination by protecting women's privacy rights over men's, others point out that the dangers of sexual exploitation, harassment, and assault are much greater when men guard women than when women guard men. Policies allowing men to participate in searching women violate international human rights standards regarding the treatment of female inmates.[115] In 1955, the United Nations adopted "Standard Rules for the Minimum Treatment of Prisoners." These standards mandate that incarcerated women are entitled to bodily integrity when subject to cross-gender supervision. In these standards, as well as others adopted by the United Nations, including "Basic Principles for the Treatment of Prisoners" and "Body of Principles for the Protection of All Persons under Any Form of Detention or Imprisonment," only same-sex guards can be present during personal activities such as showering and use of the bathroom, and during transportation to and from medical visits. In fact, these international standards dictate that only same-sex guards should be permitted in residential housing units.[116] Although these rules are nonbinding, many countries uphold the standards; for instance, Brazil and Venezuela allow only female officers in prisons for women. Other countries allow only same-sex guards to search women. Some argue that binding treaties that the United States has signed, including "The International Covenant of Civil and Political Rights" (ICCPR) and the "Convention Against Torture and Other Cruel, Inhuman, or Degrading Treatment and Punishment" (Torture Convention), also are violated by the practice of allowing male officers to observe women in showers, conduct pat-downs, and sometimes observe strip searches.[117]

Female inmates generally express positive attitudes toward the presence of male officers in the prison, but they do not like men supervising searches or observing them while they shower or use the toilet.[118] Some of the female inmates' positive feelings toward male officers seem to stem from socialized patriarchy—that is, the belief that women prefer to take orders from a man: "Men are dominant and women are used to being told what to do by men and they do it. Women [officers] tell them what to do and inmates buck it."[119]

The larger number of male officers and the increasing practice of transferring officers back and forth between facilities for men and women translates into greater pressure to make prisons for women more "normal"—meaning more like prisons for men. More stringent security measures and more formalized interactions between inmates and COs are two resulting developments.

Sexual Harassment and Assault

Another development resulting from increasing numbers of male officers is the issue of sexual harassment and assault. The most troubling aspect of the increasing numbers of male officers in prisons for women is the continuing and consistent stream of allegations, investigations, indictments, and convictions of sexual assault and sexual harassment of female inmates by male officers. A number of articles and reports have detailed instances of sexual abuses in a number of states.[120] For instance:

> Nearly every inmate we interviewed reported various sexually aggressive acts of guards. A number of women reported that officers routinely "corner" women in their cells or on their work details in the kitchen or laundry room and press their bodies against them, mocking sexual intercourse. Women described incidents where guards exposed their genitals while making sexual suggestive remarks.[121]

Through the years there have been reports of officers making sexually graphic requests of inmates, extorting sex from inmates, groping inmates during searches, taking money from male inmates to allow them into women's cells at night (in a prison that housed both men and women), and raping inmates. One of the worst cases occurred in a federal facility in Dublin, California, where women were being held in the solitary confinement unit of men's prison. These women, who were serving time for nonviolent crimes, were the victims of a prostitution ring whereby prison guards took money from inmates in return for access to the women. Although some women consented to the sexual encounters, one woman who complained after being raped was again savagely raped and beaten in retaliation.[122] Several states have reached out-of-court settlements with female inmates or entered into consent decrees to better train and supervise officers. Other cases have resulted in large monetary judgments against state systems, such as one in Michigan[123] described by Culley.[124] In this case the state of Michigan agreed to pay inmate-plaintiffs $15 million and the total judgment was about $100 million. Another court case involved a woman who had been raped by her father between the ages of two and 10 and then physically abused by her mother and sexually abused by her mother's boyfriends. She ran away and was pregnant by 16, when she was arrested along with three males and one other female for rape. She was so heavily intoxicated during the incident that she didn't remember any of it but received a prison sentence of 20–30 years. In prison she was sexually assaulted by male guards. She did not fight or struggle but experienced depression, anxiety, intrusive thoughts, fear of loud noises, and recurrent nightmares. Her descriptions of the event paralleled classic disassociation and PTSD: "It was kinda like I was really not there anymore . . . I wasn't there."[125] After she was raped a second time by a guard, she overdosed on Haldol.[126]

Struckman-Johnson and Struckman-Johnson[127] found that of inmates reporting sexual assault, 72 percent of male inmates reported inmate assailants and 8 percent named staff members; however, 47 percent of women inmates named inmate assailants and 41 percent reported staff assailants. Wolff and her colleagues also found that women were more likely than men to name staff as assailants.[128] However, national survey results have been surprising, finding much higher-than-expected levels of sexual victimization by officers in prisons for men. As noted above, the latest report from the Bureau of Justice Statistics indicates that about equal numbers of men and women reported staff abuse (about 2.3 percent). This is an average, however, and in some facilities the percentage reporting abuse is much higher.

Owen and her colleagues[129] found that female inmates described a broad range of sexual misconduct between COs and inmates. Some "true love" relationships were described where a couple ended up getting married when the inmate was released. Most often, however, sexual victimization occurred in the form of inappropriate comments and sexually charged conversations with female inmates. Officers sometimes escalated such conversations into open requests for sex or "flashing" (e.g., show me your breasts), with such requests redefined as jokes if the inmate became offended. "Trade" was commonly described as well, with inmates performing sexual acts, letting an officer fondle them, or stripping for the officer in return for a privilege or material item, such as a soda. Abuse of search authority evidently was perpetrated by both male and female officers, and inmates complained just as forcefully about female officers who seemed to take too much pleasure in their duties in this regard and violated the women's sense of dignity. The most extreme sexual victimization was sex coerced through threats (of losing privileges, getting an infraction, or other negative acts taken against the woman by the officer), and forced sex by physical assault (although rare, stories did exist in every prison of such incidences). The most common actions were the sexually charged inappropriate interchanges between officers and inmates.

Other research has also described abuses of search powers, the sexually charged atmosphere that is present in some women's prisons, and so-called trading wherein women received some form of payment for their sexual services. Calhoun and Calhoun quote a female inmate who presents an astute description that could be categorized as supporting both deprivation and importation factors in the development of the culture of trading: "They don't know no other way so when they come in here, in order to get things and stuff, that's how I think a lot of them start playing with the ACOs [correctional officers] to get their needs met.[130]

Most states have laws that make it a felony to have sexual relations with an inmate; generally consent is not a complete defense since inmates are presumed not to be able to give voluntary consent. While some states have considered removing all male officers from living quarters in women's prisons, officers' unions are against such a move. Often, even in those states where criminal laws exist, an officer found to be involved with an inmate is "walked off the tier" and fired or transferred to another prison rather than prosecuted. Inmates report that they are unlikely to report what appear to be consensual interactions, or even assaults, since they feel COs are protected.[131]

As described above, female inmates themselves sometimes initiate the sexual relationship. The inmates in Trammell's study described such numerous cases of trading and active involvement by female inmates that sometimes jealousy over male guards led to inmate fights.

> You know, I saw two women fight over a cop. One was my cellie and she was doing the guy, she got a good work detail for screwing this guy. Well, another chick enters the picture, she's young and cute. Well, my cellie was having none of that, she told this chick to back off. They actually fight over who gets to do this guy.[132]

Obviously women have sexual needs and are attracted to some male officers and, indeed, make their availability clear. However, there can be no real voluntary consent given by a female inmate because of the differential power relationship between an officer and inmate. There is always the implicit or explicit threat to use the officer's authority to make trouble for the female inmate. Women fear retaliation if they report harassment, and if they do report it they have difficulty making authorities believe them instead of the officer. Further, women in prison have often had extremely dysfunctional relationships with men; they may have been sexually abused as children by father figures; thus, men in positions of authority who desire sex from them may be forcing them to relive childhood abuse trauma. In some cases, women have been socialized their whole lives to bargain with their sexuality and have never interacted with men except in sexual relationships. To respond to men in a sexual manner has become a self-defense mechanism for them and a mode of interacting that is reinforced by some male officers who sexualize the prison environment in their references to and treatment of women.

Conclusion

The women's prison today and the subculture found there is obviously not the same as the inmate subculture of even a decade ago. For an approximation of what early prisons and prisoners were like, one must resort to biographical and journalistic information, because no tradition of academic research exists.

Women, like men, must learn to reconcile themselves to prison life. Some inmates do easier time than others because they immerse themselves in the prison culture. For them, prison becomes their life, and they fully participate in pseudo-families and homosexual relationships that provide affection, comfort, and support. Some strong women thrive in a prison environment, as do some men. For these exploiters, the prison allows an opportunity to use their aggressiveness to get what they want with little chance of formal retaliation. Other women remain social isolates, avoiding all but necessary contact with other inmates and leading a solitary existence among the many. For the most part, these women will be left alone unless they verbalize or show their scorn of other inmates, in which case they may be socially or physically sanctioned.

More current studies have indicated that women's prisons may be different from earlier decades. Make-believe families still seem to be present, at least in some prisons, but they may be less relevant now to women who have more access to outside support systems. There seems to be more violence than what earlier studies indicated (even though not usually as serious as what occurs in men's prisons), and more sexual intimidation and forced sexual activity than previously suspected. The increase in the number of male officers has led to a masculinization of the women's prison and a different relationship between inmates and officers. In effect, the women's prison has now come about full circle to those institutions in the late 1800s, before completely separate institutions were built—where female inmates were guarded primarily by men, considered unredeemable, used their sexuality to obtain goods, and/or were sexually victimized by male guards.

REVIEW QUESTIONS

1. What is administrative segregation? What happens there?
2. Do women or men commit more prison infractions? Explain the research findings in this area.
3. Describe the deprivation and importation theories of prison subculture.
4. Describe some deprivations of prison. Are they same for men and women?
5. Describe the elements of the inmate code and any differences that exist between men and women.
6. Describe argot roles in men's and women's prisons and point out any differences.
7. Describe the major forms of social organizations in men's and women's prisons and how they are different.
8. Describe the levels of violence in men's and women's prisons and the reasons for violence. Identify differences between violence as it occurs in men's compared to women's prisons.
9. Describe the levels of sexual violence in women's prisons and who the perpetrator is (inmate or staff person).
10. Summarize the major differences between men's and women's prisons.

Classification and Programming

CHAPTER SUMMARY

- Controversy exists regarding whether the prediction/classification instruments developed and used largely for male offenders work equally well for women.

- Research shows that gender-specific elements added to a gender-neutral instrument improve its predictive ability.

- Treatment advocates for women have championed gender-specific or gender-responsive programming, including drug treatment, incest-survivor and trauma counseling, and parenting programs.

- Parenting programs can be parenting education classes, enriched visitation programs, prison nurseries, halfway houses with accommodations for children, or alternative sentencing programs.

- Evaluations of treatment programs typically do not include women; therefore, less is known about what works for women, but in general, experts and researchers are cautiously optimistic that gender-responsive programs improve outcomes.

This chapter directs our attention to the field of classification, prediction, and programming for female offenders. We focus on prison programs, but the issues of classification, prediction, and programming apply to all stages of the process from jails to parole.

Historically, women's needs have been ignored or misunderstood. During the late 1980s and 1990s, the efforts to improve programming and provide resources to help women help themselves upon release were derailed by the explosive rise in numbers of inmates. Administrators found themselves housing women in gymnasiums and education buildings because prison building could not proceed fast enough; programming was a distinct second priority. Beginning in the 1990s, however, a growing controversy emerged over whether prediction and classification instruments developed with and used for male offenders were equally successful with women. Eventually the call for gender-specific classification instruments was answered, but the controversy has continued as to whether these instruments add any value to existing so-called gender-neutral instruments. The instruments are used primarily to predict recidivism; however, the same or similar instruments have also been used to predict prison misconduct. Further, the LSI-R (Level of Service Inventory-Revised™), the primary prediction tool discussed in this chapter, is based on a theoretical foundation that would discourage corrections dollars from being spent on anything other than so-called "criminogenic needs" and thus would not support gender-specific (or gender-responsive) programming, which has recently become a priority for many state corrections systems.

Classification and Prediction

Classification can be for either security or treatment purposes. Treatment classification would include an educational assessment tool to determine whether an inmate should be placed in adult basic education, a high school completion program, or a vocational training program that requires a high level of reading skill. Treatment classification also would involve physical and mental health assessments.

The other form of classification, however, is for security decisions, and the most important role for classification/prediction instruments in prison is to determine risk of violence to self or others. This assessment then is used to determine the necessary security classification level (maximum, medium, or minimum). Either the same or similar tools are also used to determine recidivism risk, which then influences release decisions or what level of supervision the inmate will require upon parole.

The Development of the R/N/R Approach

The earliest classification instruments were actuarial and used *static factors*, so-called because they were unchanging (e.g., age, criminal history, age at first arrest) to determine the type of person who was most likely to recidivate. This contrasted with the clinical approach, in which a professional interviewed the offender to determine future risk. Neither approach was very accurate in risk prediction.

The so-called third-generation prediction instruments are referred to as risk/need assessments and, in essence, merge the two earlier approaches by combining static factors and dynamic factors (personality tests and clinical interviews). Types of information collected in the risk/needs approach include physical health, vocational/financial situation, education, family and social relationships, residence and neighborhood, alcohol use, drug abuse, mental health, attitude, and past and current criminal behavior.[1] There are several instruments that are considered third generation, including the Wisconsin Risk and Needs Assessment Instrument, the Community Risk-Needs Management Scale, and the Level of Service Inventory-Revised (hereinafter referred to as LSI-R). Most of the discussion that follows concerns the LSI-R.

The LSI-R is a 54-item risk-need assessment instrument that captures both static and dynamic risk factors. The theoretical base of the LSI-R comes from the work of Don Andrews, James Bonta, Paul Gendreau, and others (sometimes referred to as the Canadian School of correctional intervention), and it is largely a social learning approach. Risk factors for criminality in this approach include antisocial attitudes, family functioning, and association with criminal peers.[2] It could also be called the Cincinnati School approach, since the major applications and tests of the LSI-R have come from professors and students from the University of Cincinnati's School of Criminal Justice.

This instrument has enjoyed widespread use that also includes an approach toward treatment programming called Risk/Needs/Responsivity (R/N/R). A large body of work has developed that identifies risks (those *static* factors described above) and criminogenic needs (those *dynamic* factors that have been correlated with recidivism or initial crime), including antisocial values, criminal peers, dysfunctional families, substance abuse, criminal personality, low self-control, education, employment, and financial well-being. Responsivity refers to correctional interventions that respond to these specific risk/need factors (and, according to proponents, no others, since intervention with any other factors would not reduce recidivism). Because these factors may change, the instrument should be reapplied periodically during correctional supervision in order to assess changing risk levels. Two major principles of the R/N/R approach is that only high-risk offenders should be targeted for intervention, and only criminogenic needs should be addressed to reduce recidivism.

The approach assumes that the same factors operate similarly for all offenders. For instance, proponents argue that childhood victimization may cause crime, but it does so through the Big Four (criminal history, criminal thinking, personality attributes, and criminal peers), and it is these risk factors that should be addressed in correctional programming.[3]

Criticism of the LSI-R

While the LSI-R has been used in numerous states and with tens of thousands of offenders, critics note that the assessment instrument ignores other factors that may affect recidivism. The conclusion that only criminogenic needs should be addressed has been criticized as inhumane and unjust. Critics especially target the absence of any recognition of economic need factors (e.g., job skills or unemployment assistance), although these have been added in later revisions of the R/N/R model.[4]

Critics also argue that the LSI-R and R/N/R model ignore special issues of women, primarily because women become "lost" in the much larger numbers of men during statistical analysis and because risk factors may or may not be the same for men and women. In fact, the pathways approach described in Chapter 5 would indicate that they are not and would advocate for instruments that measured such things as past victimization, drug use, mental health indices, abusive adult relationships and other factors.[5] Women's risk factors might also include, for instance, suicide attempts, family structure of childhood home, depression, single parenting, reliance on public assistance, dysfunctional relationships, and adult victimization.[6]

Supporting the idea that a prediction instrument that had been developed by and large with male offenders was not suitable for use with women, earlier studies found that prison classification instruments overclassified female prisoners, meaning they indicated women needed more secure settings than were probably necessary.[7] Earlier studies have found that factors such as child abuse, mental health, substance abuse, and employment were stronger predictors of institutional misconduct for women than were factors that were strong predictors for men, such as age, time to serve, crime of conviction, and prior offenses.[8]

In studies that have examined the predictive ability of the LSI-R for female offenders, some researchers have found that it effectively predicts recidivism for women as well as for men.[9] Other studies have also found that standard risk-prediction instruments apply equally well to women when predicting recidivism and that alternative measures do not appreciably improve prediction.[10]

However, other studies have found that gender-neutral instruments do not predict future criminality/delinquency/misconduct as well for female samples as when gender-specific variables are added.[11] Holtfreter, Reisig and Morash[12] found that the LSI-R was *not* effective in predicting women's recidivism among a community corrections sample of 134 female probationers and parolees because it did not factor in women's economic marginality. They found that women who were given state support were 83 percent less likely to recidivate than those who did not receive economic support. Risk scores did not predict recidivism when poverty status was taken into account.

The same researchers reported in a later article[13] that the LSI-R was highly accurate in predicting recidivism for some women but not others. This research utilized Daly's[14] pathways approach, which identified several different pathways to crime for women. Recall from Chapter 5 that Daly's typology included "street women," "drug-connected women," "harmed and harming women," "battered women," and "other."[15] Using this typology, these researchers were able to classify 87 percent of 400 women in a community supervision sample. Most women fell into the "drug-connected" category (44 percent), followed by the "other" category—women who committed economically motivated crimes (24 percent). Findings indicated that the LSI-R was successful in predicting recidivism for the economically motivated group in the "other" category, but overclassified the "harmed and harming" group of women and underclassified drug-connected women (based on their subsequent recidivism).[16]

Taxman and Cropsey[17] have pointed out that because the *meta-analyses* that have been done on the LSI-R use overwhelmingly male samples, it is not necessarily true that the assessment instrument accurately predicts risk for women. They point to a meta-analysis by Dowden and Andrews[18] as an example of the problems inherent in past research. The study concluded that interventions that addressed high-risk needs were successful in reducing recidivism (presumably for both men and women). However, most women are assessed by the LSI-R as low risk, and the Risk/Needs/Responsivity approach would not have advised intervention for this group; thus, program results applied to the large number of men in the sample but not necessarily to low-risk women.[19] The main two issues regarding the LSI-R and female offenders is: (1) whether it accurately predicts risk, since it ignores gender-specific factors such as prior victimization; and (2) whether it is appropriate to allocate correctional program dollars only to what have been statistically identified as high-risk needs (e.g., antisocial attitudes) when female offenders tend to classify into low-risk categories (which the R/N/R approach indicates should not be allocated services), and yet these women clearly have overwhelming needs not identified by the R/N/R approach.

In an attempt to prove that the LSI-R is equally effective for men and women, Smith and her colleagues[20] conducted a meta-analysis of 25 published studies of the LSI-R's effectiveness. These researchers found no difference in effect sizes between male and female offenders, concluding that the instrument was equally successful in predicting for both groups. The study was later critiqued by Taylor and Blanchette,[21] who referred to an earlier meta-analysis by Holtfreter and Cupp[22] that found the LSI-R didn't predict very well for women. Taylor and Blanchette pointed out that Smith and colleagues did not use all of the studies included in the previous meta-analysis, they used others that were not peer reviewed, and seven of the studies in the Smith meta-analysis had overlapping data.

Morash[23] and others have reviewed the major conflict between the R/N/R approach (which relies on quantitative methodologies) and the pathways approach (which has relied largely on qualitative methodologies) in determining the best approach for corrections for women. The next step in the debate was to compare the LSI-R with gender-specific measures to see if either was more accurate in predicting risk for female offenders. In one study,[24] the LSI-R was compared to gender-specific measures, using a prison sample of 150. Examining prison misconduct at six months and recidivism at 44 months after release, Lowenkamp and colleagues found that the LSI-R was a stronger prediction instrument for recidivism in the community than for prison misconduct, but that it adequately predicted both prison and community outcomes for women. However, the researchers found that the so-called Big Four (criminal history, criminal thinking, personality attributes, and criminal peers) were not the strongest predictors of either prison or community outcomes and that risk for women was linked to financial, educational, living-conditions, and substance-abuse factors.[25] The gender-specific measures did accurately predict prison and community outcomes with the exception that childhood victimization was only predictive of prison misconduct; and adult emotional abuse, harassment, and a summary measure of victimization did not influence prison adjustment but did predict community outcome.

Van Voorhis and her colleagues,[26] with the support of the National Institute of Corrections, developed a gender-specific "trailer" to add to the LSI-R to determine whether it improved the prediction accuracy of the instrument. The trailer included items that have been identified above as relevant to the pathways approach, including past victimization and drug use, and also current symptoms of depression, psychosis, mental health history, family-of-origin support, family-of-origin conflict, relationship support, housing safety, anger/hostility, and educational strengths. Findings indicated that subsets of the gender-responsive scales were significantly better at prediction than the gender-neutral instrument.[27] In this study, Van Voorhis and her colleagues found that in probation samples the strongest predictors of recidivism were criminal history, substance abuse, financial problems, education level, employment, homelessness, current symptoms of mental illness, parental stress, self-esteem, and self-efficacy. Child abuse did not significantly predict recidivism (however, child abuse victimization may influence recidivism differently from initial criminality). For the prison sample (predicting misconduct), findings indicated that predictors were mental health, substance abuse and childhood trauma, relationship dysfunction, family support, and family conflict. In the release sample (measuring success on parole), researchers found that predictors were substance abuse, economic educational and financial variables, current mental health, anger/hostility, family support and current adult domestic violence victimization.[28]

These researchers concluded that gender-neutral models do predict recidivism for women, but the addition of gender-specific factors creates more powerful prediction tools. Some of the items in the LSI-R, such as criminal thinking, were weak predictors for women. For predicting recidivism of women, more important factors were substance abuse, economic and educational factors, and mental health factors. For prison samples (predicting misconduct), it appeared that past histories of trauma, dysfunctional relationships, and mental health concerns were predictive.[29]

The Use of Prediction Instruments in Prison

As noted above, the LSI-R was developed primarily to assess the risk of recidivism, but it has also been used with prison inmate samples to predict prison misconduct. Predicting who will be a danger to other inmates and officers is an important goal, and many researchers have developed and tested prediction instruments. The earliest instruments were quite simple, merely using crimes (violent or not) and past institutional history (escape and/or misconduct). Once again, most of the work in this area has obviously been done using male prisoners, who comprise about 93 percent of all prisoners.

There have been efforts to determine whether gender-neutral instruments are equally successful in predicting prison misconduct of women. One of the problems, however, has been that some research studies do not distinguish between minor and major misconduct, partly because there are so few incidents of serious physical violence in women's prisons. This is an issue because there are obviously differences between minor misconduct (being out of place) and misconduct that involves serious physical injury to others.[30]

As noted above, Van Voorhis and her colleagues have tested whether a gender-specific trailer to the LSI-R that includes items from the pathways research (such as self-esteem, self-efficacy, parenting and relationship problems, and childhood and adult victimization) substantially improved its predictive ability for prison misconduct.[31] The authors have also developed a specific instrument for prison classification of women (the Missouri Women's Risk Assessment) that includes criminal history, family lives, relationships, parenting issues, substance use or abuse, economic issues, mental health issues, friends, anger, educational and employment attainments, adult and childhood victimization, and criminal attitudes.[32]

These researchers have found that substance abuse, mental health, self-concept, and relationship issues better predicted prison misconducts than criminal history alone. In one study of a sample of 272 female prisoners, with six-month and 12-month measures of misconducts, many gender-specific factors were as highly correlated with institutional misconduct as gender-neutral factors, including childhood abuse, depression or anxiety, psychosis, and involvement in unsupportive relationships (with those on the outside).[33] Other factors that were identified through the pathways literature, such as self-esteem, self-efficacy, adult emotional abuse, and adult physical abuse, were not significantly related to institutional misbehavior. The significant gender-neutral risk factors were antisocial attitudes, employment and financial difficulties, family problems, mental illness, and anger. Factors that were not found to be predictive of institutional misconduct were antisocial friends, low education level, and substance abuse. The authors concluded that their risk instruments significantly outperformed the existing prison institutional risk scale and that adding gender-specific factors improved the predictive ability of the gender-neutral instrument.[34]

In another related study by some of the same researchers, it was reported that substance abuse, mental health, child abuse, self-concept, and relationship issues were better predictors of prison misconduct than criminal history. This study found that childhood victimization predicted institutional misconduct but adult victimization (except for emotional abuse) did not. It was also found that women in codependent relationships incurred more prison misconducts than those in relationships that were judged to be low codependent. Other findings were that there was no relationship between parental stress and institutional misconduct and that self-efficacy increased the level of misconduct.[35] In a recent article, the same group of researchers indicate that they are continuing to examine gender-responsive risk and need factors with additional samples. They conclude that women who have experienced past victimization have reported substance abuse and mental health problems, and they have problematic intimate relationships, adapt poorly to the prison environment, and participate in more serious misconduct violations. Their findings are consistent with those of others who find that women with mental health issues, especially co-occurring disorders, and/or those who report prior victimization are more likely to incur prison infractions. The researchers advocate programs addressing each or all of these criminogenic needs and noted that the cognitive-based programs associated with the R/N/R approach could be made more gender-responsive by making them less confrontational and addressing more gender-specific thought processes (such as self-deprecating thoughts of women).[36] The conclusion to be drawn from this research is that gender-specific factors do improve prediction and that the correlates of misconduct are different between men and women in prison.

Other instruments have been developed specifically to predict prison misconduct. For instance, the Risk Assessment Scale for Prison (RASP) was specifically developed to measure the risk of violent incidents in prison.[37] This actuarial instrument uses age, education, prior prison confinement, offender type (property or violent crime), and sentence type (life without parole). It has shown modest success in predicting which inmates commit violent disciplinary infractions. The two strongest predictors of who is likely to engage in violent infractions is age (e.g., younger offenders are more likely to engage in violence) and education (e.g., those with higher than a 9th-grade education level are *less* likely to engage in violence).[38] According to the researchers, the scale was developed using exclusively male offenders, but in a replication study in another state with both male and female prisoners the scale predicted violence better for female prisoners than for male prisoners.[39]

Separately from demographic factors (age, criminal history), women who erupt in violence have also tested higher on scales that measure levels of anger, fear, and distress (discomfort with other inmates, discomfort with correctional officers).[40] The Prison Adjustment Scale (PAQ) has been used to determine the psychological status of prisoners, and measures of distress have been correlated with higher levels of violence. One of the interesting things about research that utilizes scales measuring fear and other elements of discomfort or distress is that female prisoners usually have lower scores of fear and victimization in prison than from the time before prison (indicating how truly dysfunctional their lives were before their imprisonment).[41]

Steiner and Wooldredge[42] also examined factors predicting prison misconduct of female prisoners but looked at institutional as well as individual factors. They used a large data set of prisons and prisoners to examine individual and institutional factors in self-reported assaults and rule infractions. They found that significant predictors for assault were age, race, being married, prior incarceration, having been physically/sexually abused, participation in overnight mental health programs, having been prescribed medication for mental illness, and facility crowding. Significant factors that predicted rule infractions were age, participation in overnight mental health programs, medication for mental illness, and program participation and work assignments. They noted that most variation in both assaults and rule infractions occurred within facilities, but the authors were interested in trying to identify whether institutional factors were influential in the level of misconduct. They point out that most instruments measure only individual factors (not elements of the institution).

The attempt to identify prison factors that may influence the level of misconduct, especially violence, is an important contribution to this field of study. Some previous studies indicate that institutional factors (e.g., crowding) may be as important as individual factors. Interesting research suggests that other institutional factors, like the atmosphere of the prison as measured by a social climate scale,[43] the level of conflict, or the amount of programming, affect the likelihood of inmates reacting with violence. What this means is that inmate and institutional factors interact: some inmates may commit violent infractions anywhere they might be, while others commit violent infractions only because of the influence of certain elements of the prison itself. There is a large body of literature in this area, but most of it is directed to male, not female, prisoners.[44]

In their study of whether importation and deprivation factors differentially predicted misconduct of men and women, Gover and colleagues[45] seem to offer some interesting potential findings as to how the institution impacts male and female prisoners differently. They found that only history of incarceration and length of stay were significantly related to both male and female misconduct. Certain deprivation factors (which are institutional factors) affect men (level of security, holding a prison job) and others affect women (scores on satisfaction with staff, perception of safety). The study probably used too small a sample to be confident about the results, but it does suggest that institutional factors are important for both men and women and that there may be different factors about the prison that affect men and women differently.

The testing of prediction instruments continues, but there are some concerns that should be considered. First, it seems important to not concentrate solely on prediction instruments that look only to individual factors (whether they are static or dynamic), because it seems that institutional factors also influence the level of violent misconduct. It also seems obvious that these factors impact male and female inmates differently; therefore, it is important to continue the work that attempts to isolate and identify both individual and institutional factors for misconduct, especially serious violence, for female prisoners and not assume that findings relative to male prisoners are similar.

Second, relevant to both prison misconduct and recidivism prediction, by acknowledging that some gendered pathways factors may be predictive there is a danger that women's past victimization will operate to further disadvantage them in correctional decision making. If factors such as victimization, relationship dysfunction, or mental health symptoms continue to identify high-risk female offenders, will that then lead to higher classification levels and negative release decisions? Van Voorhis and her colleagues[46] urged a careful rethinking of what is meant by high-risk factors and high-need factors in moving forward.

Programming in Prison

Programming in prison can be categorized into four major areas: (1) maintenance, (2) education, (3) vocational training and industry, and (4) treatment programs. The first category includes those activities necessary for the maintenance of the institution but sometimes touted as training (e.g., clerical work in administration, food service for inmates and staff, and general cleaning and maintenance work around the grounds). Prison maintenance jobs use female inmates to perform needed services and jobs in the prison community. Work assignments are typically menial and often are performed over and over again for the mere purpose of keeping the women busy. For instance, floors may be scrubbed every day or sometimes twice a day. The laundry employs many women and is considered by most to be the worst of assignments because of the heat, the physical toil of the work, and the potential for danger from the chemicals and boiling water available for aggressors. In some states the women's institution houses the laundry for the whole system, and large truckloads of institutional laundry come and go every day filled with prison uniforms, sheets, and towels.

Female inmates are also employed to do clerical tasks in the administration building; at times, if they prove capable, they may be given quite a lot of responsibility. Much of any prison's daily maintenance, in fact, is performed by the inmates who live there. This is true for men's as well as women's prisons. There has been a tendency in women's institutions to employ more outsiders to perform tasks typically sex stereotyped as men's jobs, such as lawn care, electrical and plumbing work, and construction or renovation tasks. More often today, however, female inmates perform these tasks, usually supervised by a civilian foreman.

The second category of programming is education. As is true of men in prison, the majority of female prisoners need remedial education, although some are ready for college programs. There are no current statistics available to describe female prisoners' educational needs. Past reports indicate that about 60 percent were high-school dropouts.[47]

All prisons have some form of education, even if it is only Adult Basic Education and GED courses.[48] Some prisons require women to participate in education programs if they do not have a GED or high school diploma. A few states offer high school diplomas rather than GED certificates.[49] Fewer institutions have college programs, and there are probably less today than there have been in the past—partly because in 1994 PELL grants (federally funded student loans) were made unavailable to prisoners; therefore, college classes had to be funded by some other means, reducing the number of inmates who could take advantage of them. It is reported that less than 5 percent of all prisoners (not just women) participate in postsecondary education.[50]

Most studies indicate that education, especially postsecondary education, is related to lower recidivism rates. Education is also correlated with employment and self-esteem.[51] Additional research shows that prisoners require education in soft skills—that is, personal competencies such as problem solving, interpersonal skills, conflict management, and personal responsibility.[52]

The third category of programming is vocational training and industry. Prison vocational programs in the early 1980s primarily fell into stereotyped areas, such as cosmetology, food service, laundry, nurses' aide training, housekeeping, sewing, garment manufacturing, and clerical work.[53] Most institutions still do not have the resources or interest to offer a broad range of programs for women, although programs today are not quite as limited or sex-stereotyped as in the past. Some prisons offer computer courses and nontraditional programs, such as automotive engineering or heavy equipment driving, although these types of courses are rare. Interestingly, female prisoners tend not to be interested in nontraditional occupations, even though they pay better than traditional "women's work."[54]

One continuing problem seems to be underutilization of some programs, or programs "on paper" that do not translate to real opportunities for women. More research needs to be done to determine why some programs are not being utilized. It may be that the qualifications for program entry are too difficult or have disadvantages attached to them that outweigh the advantages. For instance, many vocational programs, especially in the clerical area, require at least a ninth- or tenth-grade reading level. Many inmates may not meet this entry qualification.

A few prisons have established partnerships with outside companies that bring in the raw materials or tools necessary to do a task and employ women as workers. In these partnerships, women earn free-world wages. Their income is taken away except for a small allowance and used to pay back the state for room and board/child support, and to establish a nest egg for the woman to use upon release. Such partnerships include manufacturing companies (e.g., grinding lenses for eyeglasses) and service industries (central reservation systems, order operators, or data-entry positions). The major trend in all vocational training programs, however, has been a decrease in their number. Lack of funds, the punitive approach that has characterized corrections for the last few decades, and the economic downturn beginning in 2008 have decimated the number of programs in all prisons.

The fourth and final category of programming includes all treatment-oriented programs focused on addressing problems, personal growth, or social skills. Since the 1980s almost all prisons offer some sort of treatment program, even if it is only Alcoholics Anonymous. Most prisons offer some form of drug program and some type of life-skills training. A smaller number offer parenting classes, anger management, or some other form of cognitive program.[55] Programs may be outsourced to private service providers, run by prison staff, or run by the inmates themselves. The most common treatment programs in prison are for drug addiction, covered separately in a later section.

Behavior modification employs the use of rewards to shape behavior. The most common form of behavior modification programs in prison are token economies where prisoners earn greater liberties by exemplary behavior, although aversive conditioning that employs punishment may also be used. Behavior modification may be less effective with female offenders than with male offenders. In one study, female delinquents who were participating in a behavior modification program increased their rate of self-mutilation, vandalism, escape attempts, and assault.[56]

Life-skills or eclectic programs tend to target women's goal setting and anger management behaviors. Generally, these types of programs have reportedly helped women avoid disciplinary infractions and ostensibly provided them with skills to increase their potential for success upon release.[57] One typical program is described as having the following phases:

1. *Assessment*: involves psychological, education, medical testing, and a comprehensive look at life history, criminal history and current needs.

2. *Institute*: a curriculum that includes self-efficacy, problem solving, stress management, anger management, communication, employability skills, negotiation, money and time management, and family and community living.

3. *Individualized reintegration plan*: what a woman is going to do while in prison to prepare for her release, including a periodic update and review of the plan.

4. *Return to community*: involves pairing a released offender with an advocate who meets with her three times each week and provides linkage to support services.[58]

Although both men and women benefit from the range of programs briefly described above, there is a growing recognition that women require programming responsive to their particular needs.

Gender-Responsive Programming

After surveying the "state of the art" in women's programming in the 1980s, Ryan[59] offered suggestions for improvements in women's prisons, most of which could be applied to men's prisons as well. However, he also suggested special training programs for managers and supervisors of female offenders to address women's needs and problem areas and to develop skills, techniques, and tools for addressing these specific needs and problem areas. His suggestion was, for the most part, ignored over the subsequent decade even in the face of tremendous increases in the number of female prisoners. Indeed, correctional equality for women translated to having male standards forced upon them and losing the few anachronistic programs that were designed with their needs in mind. For instance, in the 1980s boot camps for women were more common than parenting programs, even though the dismal results of their evaluations indicated they were not even successful for male offenders.[60]

The call for programming designed for the specific needs of female offenders increased in the mid-1980s through the 1990s.[61] The idea that female

offenders could not necessarily benefit from the same correctional programming as male offenders coalesced into a demand for *gender-responsive* or *gender-
specific programming*. Programs specific to women's needs would address the
characteristics that have previously been identified—specifically (in comparison to male prisoners), women's greater tendency to have been the subject of
sexual victimization as children and adults, their greater vulnerability to drug
addiction (and perhaps a different motivation for drug abuse), greater responsibility for care giving, a greater likelihood of coming from extremely dysfunctional family backgrounds (with alcoholism, drug addiction, and mental
health issues in families of origin), greater mental health needs (due, most
probably, to the previous characteristic), and greater stress due to parenting
responsibilities. As noted elsewhere, female offenders (compared to male
offenders) have less extensive criminal records, are less likely to be convicted
of a violent crime, and have greater health care needs. Observers have noted
that women respond differently to program approaches as well: they respond
better to programs that emphasize empowerment models, skill building, and
connections rather than attack therapy or purely educational approaches.[62]

> [The program] gave me a little bit of hope . . . I didn't have to live in this sick-
> ness anymore and it's not just the alcohol and the drugs. It's the sickness of
> being abused. It was the sickness of . . . the prostitution. It was the sickness
> of the thieving. It was the sickness of the whole thing. . . . What this . . . gave
> me . . . was a little bit of hope that maybe there was another way to live.[63]

Two strands of support for gender-responsive or gender-specific programming exist. The first strand includes the contributions of feminist jurisprudence writers and those who described women-centered corrections. These
authors pointed out that everything about the justice and corrections system
was geared toward the male perspective.[64] Explaining that the female perspective is different, theorists used Nancy Chodorow and Carol Gilligan's work
from psychology[65] and Nell Noddings'[66] work from philosophy to illustrate
how a female perspective might be different.[67] The theme of difference refers
to women's greater emphasis on "connection" through their attachment to
others. This can be a strength, especially when it means that women get more
out of therapy because of strong connections to therapists; but it can also lead
to problems when it influences women to be codependent or make bad choices
based on their romantic relationships. Whether these differences arise from
socialization or are partially biological is irrelevant to the end result, which is
that women view the world differently than men do, and they make decisions
based on their greater attachment to others. Emphasizing women's differences, some have suggested that women would respond especially well to
smaller hostels or houses with good community links and support as places of
correction for women (interestingly very similar to the Houses of Correction
that were popular in the late 1800s).[68]

The other strand of support for gender-responsive programming comes
from the more pragmatic recognition of the different risks/needs of female and

male offenders described earlier in this chapter. Specifically, the pathways approach described in Chapter 5 and the classification/prediction research summarized above directly lead to the call for programming that responds to gender differences, such as the greater likelihood of women to experience childhood victimization and dysfunctional family life.[69]

This push for gender-responsive programming has also occurred in juvenile corrections, with the Office of Juvenile Justice and Delinquency Prevention advocating gender-responsive programming as early as the late 1990s.[70] In an inventory of best practices for female juveniles, needs were identified that were consistent with the pathways approach (i.e., sexual victimization, internalized anger and trust issues, need for safety, suicide prevention, pregnancy prevention), and gender-specific programming was recommended.

Supported by the National Institute of Corrections, Bloom, Owen, and Covington[71] published a summary report that identified the elements essential to gender-responsive programming. These elements include the etiology of addiction, low self-esteem, issues related to race and ethnicity, gender discrimination and harassment, relationships with family and significant others, interpersonal violence, eating disorders, sexuality, parenting, grief related to losing children or other family members, work, appearance and health, isolation from support networks, and life-plan development (including child custody issues).[72] Following are Bloom's[73] suggestions for gender-responsive programming:

- focus on the realities of women's lives;
- address social and cultural factors as well as therapeutic interventions;
- provide a strength-based approach to treatment and skill building;
- incorporate a theory of addiction, trauma, and women's psychological development;
- provide a collaborative, multidisciplinary approach; and
- offer continuity of care.

It is clear that there is a conflict between those who advocate gender-responsive programming and those who advocate the R/N/R approach focusing on cognitive-behavioral interventions to address peer associations and antisocial attitudes. Hubbard and Matthews[74] present a cogent discussion of the conflict as it relates to adolescent girls, but the same issues apply to adult women as well. According to the R/N/R approach, individual factors (personality/temperament, problems with educational/vocational achievement, poor parent/child relations) are correlated with delinquency/criminality equally for male and female offenders. This approach advocates cognitive behavioral programs, including cognitive restructuring (changing belief systems) and cognitive skill training (addressing poor critical thinking). Gender-responsive advocates argue that the focus on individual factors ignores macro-level social factors that affect female criminality, that the approach does not meet females' needs for connectedness and the need to improve self-efficacy. Gender-responsive approaches support trauma-informed, strengths-based approaches.[75]

A multitude of studies (each having a range of methodological concerns) present mixed findings as to whether gender-specific factors are related to recidivism (or even initial criminality). After reviewing all these studies, Hubbard and Matthews advocate a combination of the relational model favored by gender-responsive advocates and cognitive behavioral elements stripped of confrontational methods, replacing them with supportive methods. According to these authors, it is more important, especially for delinquent girls, to address the female's self-blame rather than rationalizations.

The R/N/R approach and others like it focus on changing the individual, with no ability to consider or effect change in environmental factors. A few studies have found that a gender-neutral approach to programming is not as successful with female offenders as it is with male offenders. In one study,[76] for instance, it was found that the R/N/R approach (using gender-neutral assessment) discovered similar criminogenic needs in male and female offenders and was equally successful at predicting recidivism. However, matching correctional services to criminogenic risk factors reduced reoffending only among male offenders, indicating that there were other factors operating to influence criminality/delinquency among female offenders.

Ward and his colleagues[77] have also been critical of the rehabilitation goals of the R/N/R approach—or to be more accurate, these authors have defended their Good Lives Model™ against the criticism of the R/N/R proponents. These two groups of researchers argue about the efficacy of the two approaches and disagree on the overlap between them. Briefly, the Good Lives Model focuses on a strengths-based approach rather than identifying high-risk factors (such as antisocial attitudes), as does the R/N/R model. The basic assumption is that all humans want to live a "good life" with meaning, and all humans seek primary and secondary goods.[78] Crime and delinquency occur either through "barriers" that must be addressed (similar to what the R/N/R model identifies as high-risk needs), or inappropriate seeking of secondary goals (e.g., high-risk sexual activity in search of meaningful relationships). Correctional intervention occurs after a comprehensive assessment of what the offender wants out of life and what barriers must be addressed in order to obtain it. While, arguably, the R/N/R model is based largely on external rewards (change and you won't be arrested again), the Good Lives Model places the goal and mechanism of change within the offender's power, thereby increasing intrinsic motivation. It does appear that the Good Lives Model of rehabilitative programming is more consistent with the pathways approach and gender-responsive programming, although there is a great deal of overlap between the models.

Others have also expressed concern that the actuarial approach (LSI-R and R/N/R) *and* the gender-responsive approach ignore the social factors that continue to victimize female offenders, such as racism, sexual stereotyping, underemployment and poverty, and male oppression that is socially condoned. Pollack[79] questions the gender-responsive approach in that it has emphasized victimization discourse without focusing on societal elements that create the conditions in which women find themselves. She offers the example of female victims of battering who are on parole and must get permission to begin new relationships. This typifies the system's approach of seeing female offenders' problems as individual, rather than as influenced by gender realities in society. According to Pollack, the "psy-ing" of women's social marginalization diverts attention from systemic oppression.[80] Hannah-Moffat[81] has expressed the same concern, especially in regard to domestic violence, where the woman's victimization is translated in correctional policy as a problem of either self-esteem or anger (if she fought back) that requires "fixing" before release.

Gender-responsive programming means different things to different people, but at minimum the concept responds to specific issues of female offenders: drugs (specifically, different motivations for drug use), incest survivor programming, and parenting programming. Each of these is discussed separately below.

Drug-Treatment Programming

One of the most consistent findings regarding female offenders is that drug use seems to be more strongly correlated with their criminality than it does for men. Female offenders report more drug use, and they are more likely than male offenders to be drug abusers or drug dependent. The National Center on Addiction and Substance Abuse (CASA)[82] reports that women are more likely than men to have abuse and/or dependence problems in state prisons (68 percent compared to 65 percent) and jails (67 percent compared to 66 percent) but not in federal prisons, where more males (55 percent) than females (49 percent) reported more drug abuse/dependency.

Female addicts seem to have more medical problems, greater mental health needs, and unique issues related to children. CASA reports that women are significantly more likely than male prisoners to have diagnosed mental health issues (55 percent compared to 31 percent) and co-occurring diagnoses of substance abuse and mental illness (41 percent compared to 23 percent).[83] Drug abusers are at risk for dehydration, weight loss, digestive disorders, skin problems, dental problems, gynecological and venereal infections, tuberculosis, hepatitis B, hypertension, seizures, respiratory arrest and cardiac failure.[84]

It should also be noted, however, that there are concerns that the political and policy reaction to drug use in this country has been reactionary and racist. For instance, some sources indicate that although black pregnant women who use public health services are about as likely to use drugs as white women who give birth in private hospitals, they are ten times more likely to be prosecuted.[85] The crack baby scare in the mid-1980s was largely a media myth in that there is little evidence to show large numbers of damaged children or that drug use was more responsible for poor infant health outcomes than poor nutrition, smoking, or alcohol use. What is more telling, however, is that the media painted the problem largely as one of black mothers injuring their unborn children through unrestrained drug use.[86] Despite these concerns that drug dependency and abuse is a socially created problem and portrayed as largely a problem of inner-city blacks, when a women says that prison saved her life, she typically means that drug addiction almost killed her.

> I woke up in this abandoned house, and shooting gallery, where addicts go and shoot drugs. I hadn't taken a bath in about 3 days. My body hygiene was bad. I had destroyed my face from using cocaine. . . . I had abscesses on my body . . . And I just got tired. . . . I didn't want to live that way anymore.[87]

Before one can help female drug abusers, it is important to understand the sequence of drug use and abuse, and the motivations for it. As might be expected, there is much more literature available on male drug users than on female drug users; however, a few studies exist that provide relevant information.

The National Institute on Drug Addiction has found that men and women are equally likely to become addicted to cocaine, heroin, hallucinogens, tobacco, and inhalants. Women are more likely than men to become addicted to sedatives and anti-anxiety drugs but less likely than men to abuse alcohol and marijuana. Women are also more likely to abuse prescription drugs.[88]

Female addicts evidently are different from male addicts in a number of ways. In one national study, it was found that female drug-abusing offenders:

- started at an early age;
- had greater physical and mental problems;
- were more likely to be unemployed or underemployed;
- had fewer skills or lower education levels;
- had more psychosocial problems (prior victimization);
- were more likely to come from families with a background of addiction, mental illness and/or suicide;
- were more likely to be single parents without supportive family or social networks; and
- were more likely to have family members in the criminal justice system.[89]

Carbone-Lopez and Miller[90] described methamphetamine users as those women who, through life events, adopted adult roles early, largely through exposure to older and/or deviant peers and romantic partners. These older partners provided opportunities for drug use. The females interviewed reported that they left home early, often because of abuse but not always. About a third of this small sample reported early sexual victimization and 74 percent reported family dysfunction, but only a few reported they used drugs as self-medication to forget the abuse. Most women explained they used drugs after being exposed to them through relationships with peers or romantic partners. The results are not consistent with other research indicating women use drugs to deal with past trauma. This may be because of the particular drug studied (methamphetamine); in fact, one theme that came up in the interviews was that these women used the drug because they were young mothers of small children and the drug gave them energy.

Contrary to the previous study, a continuing theme of most research—both survey and phenomenological—is that the motivation for drug use may be different for male and female offenders: women tend to use drugs more often to self-medicate, men more often for experiential rewards (thrills). For instance, Lord observed:

> Drug use becomes a way to numb pain, to take oneself out of a painful and hopeless world. The drug use, in and of itself, is not the problem that needs to be addressed but is only a symptom—of feelings that must be kept in check to ensure survival.[91]

And from a female drug user: "You get high because you're suffering, because you have a lot of problems, because you are in pain, because things aren't going the way you wish they would and you have no way out."[92]

Thus, for women, drugs are used as a solution to life's problems—to blunt the pain of past or current victimization, to bolster feelings of self-worth, to help bond with a male or female partner, or to reduce the stress of single parenthood. Obviously, the solution becomes a bigger problem and leads to choices that ultimately result in prison. The motivators for drug use for women include:

1. violent and coercive relationships (in some relationships the partner encourages drug dependency to have control over the woman);

2. untreated mental illness, particularly depression, anxiety, and PTSD (and since minority and poor women can seldom access legitimate help, they self-medicate); and

3. economic pressures and other life stressors.[93]

Self-medication is not the only motivation for drug use, of course. Rosenbaum and others found that female addicts were attracted to the excitement and risk that is part of the drug subculture, as well as the social nature of the lifestyle (parties and alcohol were ever present).[94] Rosenbaum noted that social norms, even in the drug world, expected more of women than of men: "Men do not suffer the stigma of addiction as severely as women, especially in the area of interpersonal and sexual relationships."[95] Others have echoed this notion.[96] Rosenbaum noted that female addicts are tormented by their failures as mothers, and that addicted women are more harshly judged.[97] Women, therefore, almost always chose other addicts as mates, a choice that made breaking free of the drug virtually impossible.

Other studies have also shown that women tend to play peripheral roles in the drug culture, largely through their relationships with men.[98] Research has also described a phenomenon called crack-house sex—an economic exchange of sex for drugs by desperate female crack addicts. Researchers pointed out that the women who sell themselves for drugs destroyed the economic viability of street prostitution in those neighborhoods where crack was prevalent. Prostitutes then became involved in other types of crime, such as "ripping off johns," to survive.[99] The devastation that crack cocaine had on some communities in the 1980s and early 1990s has dissipated. Researchers in that time period described the life of the crack user as one characterized by poverty, chaos, and disordered family life.

> I've been on dope for most of my life. Dope killed my momma, killed my two brothers, and it's gonna kill my little sister 'cause she out here in a crew that's out cold . . . we all gonna die, just wait and see. . . . Crack is what makes us crazy, but it's the best high I know. This ain't the way I wanted things to work, but that's the way it is. . . .[100]

More recent studies have found no gender differences in educational levels between male and female abusers, but women are less likely to be employed and, if employed, make less money than men. Generally, there are no significant differences in the frequency or severity of drug use between men and women; however, men are more likely than women to have problems with alcohol. Most studies have inconsistent findings regarding differences between men and women on age at first use or patterns of drug use. Consistent findings support the notion that although both men and women give similar reasons for drug use, men are more likely to cite hedonistic or pleasure-seeking motivations and peer acceptance, while women are more likely to identify alleviation of physical or emotional pain, or social reasons (e.g., a spouse who uses). Recent studies continue to find that women are more likely to have been victims of sexual and physical abuse, to have relatives who had a substance abuse problem, and to have a drug-using spouse. More women than men lived with or planned to live with minor children. Women are less likely to have criminal records, although a few studies have found no difference in number of arrests. Findings are inconsistent regarding whether women are more likely to have psychological problems, with more sources finding that female offenders with substance/dependency problems are more likely than male offenders to have co-occurring mental illness.[101]

CASA reports that drug-abusing/drug-dependent female offenders as compared to male counterparts are seven times as likely to have been sexually abused, four times as likely to have been physically abused, and 78 percent more likely to have experienced mental illness in the year before incarceration. In addition, women are 58 percent more likely to have been homeless, 31 percent more likely to have had parents or guardians who abused alcohol or drugs, and were more likely to have lived in foster homes and to have had family members who were incarcerated.[102]

Drug Treatment Programs

Earlier studies indicated that fewer treatment options for women existed in prisons;[103] however, more recent research has found that female offenders are slightly more likely than male offenders to have treatment programs available to them (10 percent compared to 7 percent).[104] Alcoholics Anonymous and/or Narcotics Anonymous (or some hybrid modeled after these 12-step approaches) are the most common programs found in prisons. Many women's treatment programs are simply patterned after programs that were developed for men, leading to complaints that programs are recycled for women after putting a "pink cover" on them. Other than 12-step programs, drug treatment can be psycho-pharmacological, cognitive-behavioral, eclectic, a therapeutic community, or some combination of the above.

Therapeutic communities emphasize inmate participation, open communication, and shared decision making in an isolated tier or living unit. Inmates attend "group" at least once a day and sometimes twice a day. In these groups, discussion centers on such issues as personal responsibility and goal setting. Incidents that occur in the living unit are dealt with and used as part of the learning process. Some programs in women's prisons may be therapeutic communities in name only, practicing none of the elements crucial to the theory behind the therapy.

Therapeutic communities seem to be gender responsive in that they depend on developing and utilizing relationships among the community members for therapeutic success and, usually, employ empowerment rather than attack therapy or confrontational methods. In general, advocates note that programs emphasizing empowerment, support, and skill building work better for women.[105] One woman, referring to trust in therapeutic communities in prison, remarked:

> In a prison system regular doing time there is no such thing [as trust]. You can't afford to let your guard down. You can't afford to let people cross your boundaries. . . . In a therapeutic community that's what they encourage us to do. . . . And another thing that I see different in the therapeutic community . . . is with the officers. . . . If you have a problem you can go to the officer and you can talk to them and they may not understand but they try. . . . Ya know, they don't degrade you, they don't humiliate you.[106]

Some evaluations of therapeutic drug-treatment programs in prison have shown modest success although, typically, the sample size is small.[107] The problem seems to be that the programs do not help to create supportive networks outside prison. Inciardi[108] reported on a successful drug treatment program for female inmates in Delaware using the therapeutic community approach. Results indicated that program participants were much less likely than a comparison group to use drugs after release (35 percent compared to 70 percent) and to be rearrested (18 percent compared to 38 percent).

Reed[109] found that women-centered drug therapy was delivered in a context more consistent with women's socialization and comfort than other types of programs. Women respond less well to attack therapy and better to nurturance; their motivation to change is largely found within their guilt toward their children and others, and their vulnerabilities toward recidivating tend to be found in their low self-worth and inability to cope with stress. These issues must be addressed in any treatment program.

Wellisch, Prendergast, and Aglin[110] conducted a survey of the needs of drug-abusing women offenders, as well as a nationwide survey of community-based treatment programs.[111] They concluded that there were widespread inadequacies in treatment delivery and that women-only programs seemed to offer more gender-responsive services. Most programs offered case management, relapse prevention, HIV/AIDS education, counseling, and 12-step meetings. Few programs made accommodations for children, although women-only programs were more likely to meet women's special needs. They further noted that programs did not generally respond to the multiple needs of female offenders (e.g., dual-diagnosis women having mental illness and drug addiction). They also noted that treatment programs were often too short to be effective and did not provide continuity in service (after release).

Other research supports the notion that many of the elements of successful drug programming are the same for male and female clients (individualized treatment plans, continuity of care, sufficient length, and so on). However, other elements seem to be necessary for the most effective interventions for women. Specifically, the approach should be one of skill building rather than attack therapy, should focus on understanding and coming to terms with women's roles as caregivers (since that is often a source of stress that drives relapses and a source of particular pain for addicts who feel they are failures as mothers), should be delivered in women-only environments (because co-ed groups distract women from recovery), and should deal with motivators for drug use (e.g., incest or other childhood abuse).[112]

The issue of child care and addiction therapy is obviously a gender-responsive concern. Prison programs do not have to make provisions for children, but community-based programs do. Even prison-based programs must contend with the stress of child-care issues in that the female offender may have difficulty concentrating on her own recovery when she is concerned with child care. One source indicated that only 8 percent of all available drug programs addressed child care. Furthermore, it is reported that pregnant addicts may not be able to access treatment because they are denied entrance to programs.[113] This is unfortunate, since it is often their children who provide the motivation to change.

> I had been up for about five to eight days and I was crashing out sleeping, and I seen [sic] her [16 year old daughter] going out the door with her luggage and asked her where she was going, and she said, "Mother, I'm not the cause of what you're doing to yourself, and it's not my problem, but I cannot sit here and watch you destroy yourself anymore." And that's when I really started trying to work on my addiction. . . .[114]

Reed[115] notes that developing gender-responsive drug treatment is difficult because the vast numbers of correctional clients are men, and many programs attempt to serve both men and women—resulting in disproportionate numbers of men and making therapy feel awkward and unsafe for the women in groups. Therapy designed for men tends to not address the shame and secrecy elements of drug use, depression, and prescription drug abuse (because these issues are more relevant to women).

In treatment, women are more likely than men to acknowledge they have a problem and to report extreme levels of depression, anxiety, and low self-esteem. Women also may not recognize drugs as self-destructive behavior and more often blame themselves than others for their drug addiction. Treatment providers make the same observation as correctional staff: men in treatment tend to be isolates, but women in treatment tend to be caught up in a multitude of relationships (e.g., with parents, children, and other family members) that complicate treatment.[116] Core services still needed and lacking in drug programs for women include medical assessment and treatment, child and family services, vocational training, self-esteem and "coping" training, chemical dependency education, legal assistance, and sexuality and intimacy counseling.

Messina and her colleagues[117] have published a number of reports of their studies examining gender-responsive drug programming compared to gender-mixed programs. Generally, results indicate that gender-responsive programs are more successful in reducing arrests and drug use for women. While both groups (gender-responsive participants and mixed-group participants) are shown to benefit from drug treatment by increases in psychological well-being and reduced drug use and arrests, evidence seems to indicate that gender-responsive programs provide greater benefits. Other studies have found that gender-specific programming shows some success with female offenders suffering from PTSD.[118]

Incest Survivor Programming

As stated in Chapter 8, a disproportionate number of female inmates (compared to the general population and also compared to a male inmate sample) have been either sexually or physically victimized as children. Victimization as a child has been found to lead to dysfunctional adult behavior, including increased sexual risk-taking behaviors and drug use.[119] Programs are sometimes available to help female offenders realize that their dysfunctional behavior may be due to unresolved anger and grief issues stemming from childhood abuse. Some women have never acknowledged being an incest victim until they are in an environment where they feel safe enough to confront their past demons.

It is rarely the case that women require only counseling services for past sexual victimization without also needing drug treatment. As chronicled in Chapter 5 and Chapter 8, victims of sexual abuse have a constellation of drug-use and criminality issues that are well established in the literature. Thus, drug treatment programs should address past sexual abuse with those participants for whom it is relevant, and incest-survivor groups must address drug dependency issues.

One study, for instance, pointed out that between 30 and 75 percent of women in drug treatment have been victims of childhood sexual abuse.[120] Root describes the "resistant client" in treatment who is slow to insight, ambivalent or inconsistent about complying with assignments, and prone to sabotaging or handicapping their own progress, and suggests that some of these clients may be women with unrecognized issues related to incest. One important point is that the cessation of alcohol or drug use creates heightened negative affect, because PTSD symptoms are no longer being masked or moderated in any way by chemicals.

Clues that may point to past sexual abuse include vague memories or no memories at all of a period of time; vague memories of having been abused; promiscuous sexual relationships; avoidance of sexual relationships; unexplained or multiple gynecological problems; significant changes in school or conduct over a short time; early use of alcohol or drugs; binge eating in childhood or early adolescence; attempts to be physically unattractive (weight gain or loss, personal grooming); dissociative experiences; abrupt personality changes; recurring nightmares with themes of victimization; inexplicable depression, anxiety, or fear; sudden changes in social, occupational, or academic function; running away; depression, anxiety or irritability.[121] Because women have dealt with feelings related to their victimization by burying them under drug use and lifestyle, any treatment that reduces their coping mechanism may bring about exacerbation of PTSD symptoms. Because this is terrifying for women, especially those who only vaguely remember or understand their victimization, resistance occurs.[122] "I want to get me away from the feeling that something terrible lurks there and is waiting for me: I won't want to find out what it is; I don't think I could cope. Alcohol is my coping . . ."[123]

Studies have found that prison therapy can be successful in reducing PTSD symptoms related to past sexual victimization, including nightmares, avoidance, distancing, and hypervigilance; depression, anxiety, and low self-efficacy also lessened.[124] Several studies have evaluated whether this type of gender-responsive correctional program is more effective than gender-neutral programs. While some studies find that responding to past trauma does not significantly reduce recidivism,[125] others have found that "trauma-informed" gender-responsive treatment is more successful in reducing recidivism with some female offenders.[126]

Parenting Programming

There has been a dramatic increase in the numbers of children affected by a mother's imprisonment; estimates range from two to seven million, depending on how one counts correctional supervision. It should also be noted that it is a race/ethnicity issue as well; black children are nine times more likely than white children to have a parent incarcerated, and Latino children are three times as likely.[127] Another report indicates that 1 in 9 African American children; 1 in 28 Hispanic children; and 1 in 57 white children have a parent in prison.[128]

One of the most important differences between incarcerated men and women is the predominance of children in the lives of female prisoners.[129]

Many researchers have documented the pervasive presence of children in the women's prison. Children are either physically present (in visiting rooms or other programs at the prison), or their presence is felt in the increased social, legal, and psychological problems (e.g., depression) that stem from the female prisoner's caregiver role. Separation from their children is often considered one of the worst aspects of prison for women. While we must be careful to not be reductive in assuming that the parental role is more salient for women than for men, there are many reasons to believe this to be true.

1. The majority of imprisoned women (roughly two-thirds) are mothers of minor children (often more than one) and are more likely than men to have been the primary caregivers of their children before prison.[130] One recent estimate was that 77 percent of women were primary caregivers before prison compared to 26 percent of men.[131]

2. Men are more likely to have their children cared for by the same caregiver who was in place before the prison sentence; but the children of female prisoners are less likely to be cared for by their father(s) (only 10–30 percent) than by other relatives, most typically the maternal grandmother.[132]

3. Only about 10 percent of female prisoners' children are in state care, and most women retain legal custody over at least one of their minor children and expect to resume a primary caregiver role after release.[133]

It should also be noted that a substantial number of female prisoners have lost custody over some (but usually not all) of their children.[134] Women whose children were in foster placements experience fear and frustration due to limited contact and ignorance of what was happening in the children's lives. A federal law regarding adoption mandates that a child may be available for adoption after one year if there has been no contact with the biological parents, and this has created the situation where female prisoners avoid state involvement even when family members are not suitable for placement.[135]

Justifications for Parenting Programs

Parenting programs are an important part of a gender-responsive strategy because of the centrality of parenting to a female offender's life. Parenting programs can be considered correctional programs in that they respond to identified needs of female offenders: fear/anxiety regarding the parental role currently or upon release; problems coping with parenting responsibilities that may affect recidivism; and the reality that 10 percent of women in prison are pregnant. Each of these justifications is discussed, in turn, below.

Parenting programs can also be justified as important social programs apart from the correctional purpose in that the children of imprisoned parents are an especially vulnerable and at-risk population. These children bear a high probability of also being involved in the criminal justice system. Since most prisoners are likely to resume parenting duties, it falls to the correctional system to help the children by helping the parents be better parents.

Addressing Female Offender Needs. One justification for parenting programs in prison is that female prisoners continue to be involved with and focused on their children's lives. Female prisoners may be ecstatic, devastated, or angry because of something that has happened outside of prison that concerns their children; thus, correctional supervisors are dealing with the prisoner as parent, whether or not they do it formally.

Women in prison also do not relinquish all care-giving functions while in prison and so are constantly navigating problems and issues regarding their children. Prison counselors or other staff members are also involved when the prisoners must communicate with child welfare workers, school officials, or caregivers.[136] A female inmate may be faced with losing all parental rights during a prison sentence (if the state chooses to pursue such an action and other conditions are met). This event can lead to violence and/or self-injury.

"Role strain" is said to occur when a female prisoner cannot reconcile her role as prisoner to that of mother. Some women who are comfortable with their children's caregivers may not experience strain, but others do. There are also women who, in prison, for the first time soberly reflect on the deficiencies of their mothering, which causes them stress and anxiety.[137] Enos[138] and others describe the difficulties of women in prison as they try to manage motherhood tasks and identities and negotiate shared rights with outside caregivers. She identifies *identity talk* (defined as conversations in prison that revolve around children to reinforce one's self-perception as a mother) and the "contrastive rhetoric" tendency of women in prison to present comparisons between their actions and those of others (in order to show that they weren't as bad a mother as other women). Both are attempts to reconcile being in prison with being a mother. Parenting programs help female prisoners in this attempt.

Release Considerations. Another justification for parenting programs in prison is that they may alleviate some of the barriers to successful reentry that women face. In order for women to succeed upon release they must learn to handle the responsibilities involved in parenting or make other arrangements (permanent deprivation of parental rights, or formal or informal fostering). Practitioners report that stress related to parenting is one of the causes of relapse for drug-dependent women.

Many women fear that they will have difficulties in reestablishing a relationship, that their children will reject them or not respect them, or they worry about economic problems (e.g., housing and support) related to child care.[139] Addressing these fears should be part of release planning. Other female prisoners have idealistic notions about what it will be like to be a caregiver upon release, yet release often turns out to be a difficult adjustment for many women and their children.[140] Children grow up and develop new friends, new interests, and activities. They are often resentful and angry at their mother for leaving them, and distrustful since they suspect that she may leave again. Further, they may have developed attachments to caregivers. Caregivers may be resentful and distrustful of the released woman's ability to parent.

Some women will have difficulty regaining custody—either formally from the state, or informally from relatives who distrust ex-offenders' abilities to parent. State workers will resist reunification until the mother shows that she has a job and a home to care for the children. Ironically, if she has a job to afford a home, she is not in the best position to show that the children will be cared for adequately. More typically, she struggles to find a job that can support herself, much less her children.

It should be noted that in many cases a female prisoner did not live with all her children as primary caregiver, even though she might have been an important part of the children's lives. Henriques[141] and Enos[142] note that in African American families it is not uncommon for children to be cared for by grandmothers or aunts. In one sense, this is helpful when women go to prison because some children may have already been comfortable with other relatives; however, when these arrangements are viewed through the lens of a white middle-class child welfare or criminal justice professional, it often appears as if the mother was negligent and/or had abandoned her child. Of course, some women, especially those who were drug dependent, had abdicated their responsibility before being incarcerated. Those women, especially, are ill-equipped to take on parenting functions, even though there may be no legal barriers to reunification (if children never entered state care and have been taken care of informally by other relatives).

Pregnancy in Prison.   Another justification for parenting programs in prison is that 4 to 10 percent of this nation's female prison population is pregnant at any given time.[143] Many of these women will give birth during their prison term. As discussed in a previous chapter, prenatal care is often sadly lacking in women's institutions, and women have difficulty meeting the nutritional requirements of pregnancy. The institution's practice of waiting until the woman is in labor before transporting her to the hospital increases the risk of birth complications. The quick return to prison after birth—usually within a day or two—and the separation from the baby in most cases is extremely detrimental to both mother and baby. The experience of having to find alternative placement for a newborn is obviously distressing, but other issues make the experience even worse: there is a pervasive fear of state control and permanent loss of custody; there are often health issues involved (for instance, lactation cessation); there is anxiety over turning the baby over to a family that may have been abusive or neglectful; and there may be the realization that because of a long sentence, the woman may never be truly a "mother" to her child.

One concern is that, unless there has been a prior record of involvement with the child protection service state agency, the state does not step in after birth to evaluate the arranged home placement. While privacy advocates may believe this is appropriate, in those states that do not take on this responsibility, women may place their babies with friends of friends and casual acquaintances in order to avoid state involvement. There is no oversight and no way to know what is happening to these infants—either by the woman or by the state.

Addressing the Needs of the Children.   Perhaps the strongest justification for parenting programs in prison is that, whether we like it or not, most female prisoners will resume (or begin) parenting functions over one or more children upon release. Their children already are at a disadvantage: we know that having a parent who has served a prison term is highly correlated with delinquency and adult criminality, and it is also true that having a mother in prison is more disadvantageous than having a father in prison. It has been reported that the adult children of mothers who have ever been incarcerated are 2.5 times as likely to be incarcerated themselves, compared to the children who had incarcerated fathers, and this increases to three times as likely if the mother had an abuse or dependency problem.[144]

Evidence clearly indicates that children need stability and loving care. It is true that often the children of prisoners lived in a chaotic, unsafe, abusive environment before the prison sentence. Some children may indeed be better off when their parent goes to prison. However, whether or not they are good parents, most prisoners have or will have influence on one or more of their children; thus, it is essential that we understand the effects of incarceration on children and try to help make their lives safer, with opportunities for healthy development.[145]

One of the most troubling findings regarding the placement of children is that they often move, sometimes several times, during the mother's imprisonment. This lack of stability and frequent change of primary caregivers is noted by child development experts as quite detrimental to the child's psychological health and well-being. Reasons for the moves usually involve such issues as illness or old age on the part of the caregiver, or the fact that the caregiver may also become embroiled in the criminal justice system and require other relatives to care for all the children under her care. There may be constant conflict and arguments concerning the child between the caregiver and prisoner. For whatever reason, the lives of these children are very unsettled, and they are often passed around from family member to family member and treated as an economic burden. We know that this negatively affects the child's ability to trust, to feel loved and secure, and to concentrate on such things as learning.[146]

Older studies reported that children, especially infants and children of preschool age, responded to their mother's imprisonment with constant crying, little response to stimulation, little effort to crawl, and incidents of self-punishment. School-age children showed difficulty with social relationships, as well as changes in sleeping patterns and grades. Adolescents exhibited antisocial behavior and school problems.[147] Studies indicate that children may experience sadness, fear, feelings of shame and demoralization.[148] Since these early studies there has been a small but steady stream of evidence that imprisonment is detrimental to the children of incarcerated parents, and that children of imprisoned mothers fare worse than the children of imprisoned fathers.[149]

Although there has been a recent proliferation of national reports on the children of incarcerated parents, with several focusing specifically on the needs of imprisoned mothers and their children,[150] these reports typically review the same small set of academic findings or present descriptions of legislation and/or programs. For instance, the Women's National Law Center published a report that gave states grades for their performance in these areas: shackling during labor or birth, prenatal care, community alternatives, and prison nurseries. This group gave 21 states a D or F grade and only one state (Pennsylvania) received an A.[151]

Well-designed, rigorous research on how maternal imprisonment affects children is lacking. It is difficult to get an objective measure of true effects (for instance, most studies simply ask the imprisoned woman or her caregiver whether they've observed problems with the children).[152] Obviously, a better study would objectively measure learning dips, developmental delays, or other criteria indicative of trauma. Further, few studies are able to separate the effects of the mother's imprisonment from other negative influences in the child's life, such as poverty, dysfunctional family settings, and other environmental factors.[153]

Despite these difficulties, it seems clear that if there was a caregiver-child relationship between mother and child before prison, then a prison sentence negatively impacts the child. Further, many experts believe that a parental separation due to a prison sentence is uniquely different from other types of separation because it also involves shame and stigma. The parenting programs described below are designed to help the mother and the child navigate the prison sentence and maintain (or create) attachment in order to facilitate healthy development.

Types of Parenting Programs

After a national survey of prisons in the late 1990s, Pollock[154] reported that 90 percent of reporting prisons had parenting classes, 73 percent had special visiting areas, 55 percent allowed furloughs for family issues, 35 percent had community facilities (halfway houses) that allowed children, 25 percent reported overnight visitation programs, and only 4 states had nurseries.[155] When asked what problems existed in the implementation of such programs, correctional staff mentioned (in order of frequency):

- transportation difficulties/geographic isolation,
- funding/lack of space,
- time constraints of staff,
- time constraints of inmates,
- negative relationships with caregivers,
- no ability to implement classroom skills (if only parenting classes were in place),
- punitive segregation that takes women out of parenting class,
- no demand,
- poorly paid staff,
- inmates who weren't focused on children, and
- lack of volunteers.

Parenting programs may be as simple as a parenting class offered once a month or as elaborate as a prison nursery and transition to community placement with nurse-practitioners offering support and advice. In the sections below, the major types of programs are discussed.

Parenting Education. Most prisons have some type of parenting education class, either as a stand-alone class or as part of a life-skills program.[156] It may or may not include a special visitation component. Classes vary widely in length and intensity. One common modality is to use the Systematic Training for Effective Parenting (STEP) materials.[157]

Some argue that these courses are not needed and/or not effective in improving parenting skills.[158] Some research indicates that parenting classes in prison are not effective in that they are not culturally sensitive; they don't fit existing behavior patterns for women so they don't get much value from them.[159] On the other hand, this was only one study, and most findings indicate that women generally give very positive ratings to parenting programs in jails and prisons. It does seem to be true that in order to improve parenting, one must have extended contact with one's children. It is also true that many women in prison are not bad mothers and do not need to be taught parenting. Richie,[160] after interviewing women on parole, concluded that parenting classes should be taught by those from same socioeconomic and cultural heritage as the women who attended them.

However, it also seems to be true that many women in prison are grateful for and benefit from educational courses concerning child development and appropriate expectations.[161] Such classes are most appreciated when taught by outside professionals, such as pediatricians and child psychologists. The best format is probably one that combines education and experiential learning (extended contact).

Extended or Enriched Visitation. Most visiting rooms in women's prisons are full of children; however, many women do not want their children to visit with them at all. This may be because they have not told their children that they are in prison (the child is told she is away, or in the hospital, or some other story is used to explain her absence). Another reason is that mothers feel guilty exposing their children to the trauma of the entry process, which includes metal detectors and pat-down searches. Furthermore, the distance between home and prison is often great and the costs involved in visiting are high; mothers refuse to burden caregivers with those costs on top of already caring for their children. Some mothers refuse visitation simply because it is too painful to say goodbye, both for her children and for the woman herself.[162]

During prison visits mothers may have a difficult time adjusting to their role as parent, either trying to be friends with the child or "overparenting."[163] The prison itself is an uncomfortable, intimidating place for children; entry is frightening, the wait may be very long, and there is nothing for children to do while adults talk. Children do not understand security rules regarding running or physical contact with the incarcerated parent.

Attempts to improve visitation include child-friendly areas with toys and smaller chairs, extended or special times (e.g., weekend "camps" that may run for an entire afternoon), free transportation (e.g., buses) from major population centers, and/or "family" visits that include overnight visitation.[164] In one prison, a corner of the visiting room is sectioned off and Sesame Street characters are painted on the wall. Children's furniture and toys further enhance the goal of making children more comfortable. Inmates serve as day-care aides to watch the children when the inmate mother visits with adult family members privately.[165] Another program included actual camping on the prison grounds.[166] Girl Scouts Behind Bars has become a common model to enrich visitation for daughters of female inmates.[167]

Older evaluations found that visitation programs helped to maintain family ties, were helpful in reducing recidivism, and improved order in the institution.[168] Barriers to such programs included distance, inconvenient visitation policies, unwelcoming and discourteous staff, lack of child care, lack of overnight facilities, and surcharges on telephone calls. Programs that help women learn better parenting skills or increase and better utilize the women's visitation time with children are in the greatest demand by female inmates. In one report, women wanted more family programs and services, increased visitation, and increased support in legal and post-release areas.[169]

Prison Nurseries.   Prison nurseries have a long history in women's prisons, and early in the 20th century it was not at all uncommon for women to have their babies with them in prison. Most states closed their nurseries after WWII, however, citing safety or cost concerns, or a belief that prison was "no place for babies."[170] Today, only a few states in the country have prison nurseries: New York (the only prison to have never closed its nursery), Washington, Nebraska, Illinois, Indiana, Ohio, South Dakota, and West Virginia. These programs vary widely in size and policies. For instance, while South Dakota allows women to keep their infants for only three months, Washington State allows infants to stay in the facility for up to three years. The average length of stay is 12–18 months.[171]

There is very little research available on whether babies do better or worse when they are cared for by an imprisoned mother compared to being cared for by someone on the outside. Obviously, randomized assignment will never occur and, therefore, it is difficult to control for all other variables in determining what factors influence children's development. It is also difficult to follow infants after release. There has been at least one longitudinal study of Bedford Hill's nursery program participants. Funded by the National Institute of Health and completed by Mary Byrne and her colleagues in 2008, this study attempted to follow 100 mothers and their infants who had been admitted to the prison nursery program for three years after release. Research staff collected data on mothering skills, attachment, and other developmental milestones of infants at several points over three years. Study results indicated that infants displayed normal developmental progress, and there was a zero percent recidivism rate of mothers the first year after release.[172] This study also showed that the majority of babies in the nursery showed a secure attachment level, even though they were high risk given the mother's background. The mothers showed very low attachment levels to their own caregivers, most probably because of their dysfunctional upbringing; therefore, the level of secure attachment with their own babies was considered a substantial achievement.[173] The babies who spent time in the prison nursery and had the benefit of the program's nurse practitioner and parenting classes for mothers showed higher attachment levels than even low-risk community samples.[174]

Unfortunately, the study had difficulty retaining mother-baby dyads for the subsequent years of the study. Researchers also found that only 24 babies stayed with the mother seamlessly from birth, through the nursery program and out into the community for three years. Most had been separated, at least for a period of time, either during the prison program or after release. The most common reasons for separation were that the mother was ejected from the nursery program, that the baby aged out of the program before the mother's prison term ended, or that the mother re-offended after release and was returned to prison. Of the original 100 mother-baby pairs (or in three cases, twins), 59 children left with their mothers, but the remainder (41) had been separated before the end of the first year in the prison nursery. Of the 59 children who left with their mothers, 49 were still with their mothers at the end of the first year of release. At the end of the third year of release, only 24 children had experienced seamless caregiving by their mothers (meaning there had been no separations). It should also be noted, however, that another 20 children had been only briefly separated from their mothers in this group. Counting these mother-baby dyads, 44 children were still with their mothers at the end of the third year of release from the group who completed the nursery program compared to only 16 who had been separated for some reason during the prison nursery program. Almost three-quarters of the babies from the original 100 were with either the mother or a family-member caregiver at the end of the third year.[175] Researchers noted that mothers faced an array of challenges, including poverty, homelessness, drug relapses, and family issues that interfered with their ability to maintain a parenting relationship with their children; however, it bears repeating that most of the children of prison mothers ended up either with their mothers or related family after release.

In addition to this longitudinal study, one British study utilized experimental design by attempting to use random assignment and a control group to measure the impact of a prison nursery program. Sleed and colleagues[176] had difficulty with their design in that the treatment and control groups were not comparable on race/ethnicity, and high attrition occurred. This was an evaluation of a specific attachment-based program in a prison nursery. Findings indicated that mothers in the control group (who had small babies but did not participate in the nursery program) experienced deterioration in measures of maternal functioning and behavioral interactions with babies over time, contrary to those in the program who did not experience deterioration. Researchers noted that control-group mothers saw their infants as providing emotional support for them. This role reversal (or parentification) of the infant is a risk when the mother has no strong adult emotional support. The nursery program course that was evaluated taught inmate mothers about their babies' internal states, their ways of communicating, and appropriate developmental milestones. The researchers also speculated that the group nature of the program was helpful to reinforce what was learned. In the quote below, a female inmate from a different prison program illustrates the potential learning that can take place in a well-run prison nursery program.

> . . . with all my other kids I was using some sort of substance and I wasn't thinking right. I took care of them the best that I knew, but it is a whole different thing with [her baby born in a prison nursery program]. Like every little thing I notice about him. I notice when his nails are too long. I notice if he gets a new bump. I notice if he's teething. Every little thing on this child I notice whereas before if you asked when my baby got his first tooth I said, "I don't know." . . . I see now that I deprived five of my kids of a lot of love because I didn't know love because my love was the drugs.[177]

Generally, evaluations have shown much lower recidivism rates of nursery participants, ranging from 3 to 13 percent versus a comparison sample of 25 to 38 percent.[178] Of course, since women are selected very carefully for participation, such comparisons may not have controlled for other important variables. In a review of findings, the Women's Prison Association reported mixed results (in terms of infant development outcomes and participants' attachment scores). The conclusion was that nurseries can be healthy environments for infants as long as child development and medical care professionals are involved.[179] This advocacy group for female prisoners also noted that most women in prison nurseries would be appropriate for community release facilities where their children might benefit from access to a greater range of services.

Halfway Houses for Women and Children. Halfway houses for women and their children provide services to women who need help in the transition from prison to the free world. (Alternatively, they can be used as a sentencing option in lieu of a prison sentence.) More states have halfway houses than prison nurseries for mothers and children.[180] Generally, female offenders must meet certain requirements—having no history of violence, child abuse, or neglect; being the primary caregiver of the child before imprisonment; and having a good prison record. The facilities typically require the woman to go to school or work and participate in drug treatment or other counseling during her residence.[181] Some programs offer individual counseling and follow-up services after release.

One difficulty with halfway houses is that women can keep only young children with them. It is difficult to explain to older children that a woman can take only younger siblings to live with her. Another problem that has emerged is that women chafe at the rules regarding their social lives. Specifically, many women are anxious to resume dating and romantic relationships, but correctional staff insist that their focus be on their recovery (if a drug program) and their children.

There are very few evaluations of community-based residential programs for justice-involved mothers and children. One evaluation was of a 15-month jail-diversion intervention for pregnant, nonviolent offenders with a history of substance abuse. Women were provided with extensive "wrap-around" social services during a residential and in-community phase of the program. The evaluation's sample consisted of 20 women and their infants who completed the entire 18-month program. Results indicated that program infants had rates of attachment comparable to rates typically found in low-risk samples (and more favorable than those typically found in high-risk samples). Researchers also found that program mothers scored higher in rates of maternal sensitivity than those in a community sample, and that there was improvement over time in the mothers' depressive symptomology but not in other indices of functioning.[182] Given the fact that there was no control sample and the sample size was extremely small, these results can be considered exploratory only, but they do provide some evidence that parenting programs can improve outcomes in the high-risk group of female offender-mothers.

Alternative Sentencing.   In recognition that many women are not risks to the community, states can develop alternative sentencing for mothers with small children in order to keep them in the community with their children. One example of such an approach is Washington State's Family and Offender Sentencing Alternative Program (FOSA) for both male and female offenders (although there are more female offenders than male offenders in the program). In the FOSA program, judges sentence offenders directly to the program instead of prison. In a related program, the Community Parenting Alternative (CPA) program, offenders who are already in prison are released a year early if they agree to the program's requirements. To be eligible, the offender must be the primary caregiver of young children and meet other stringent requirements.

The community corrections officer is specially selected and trained to monitor the offenders. These correctional professionals work with social workers to ensure that offenders develop parenting skills. Offenders are required to meet all basic requirements of probation/parole but also to participate in parenting development activities, which may be classes or meetings with a social worker/child development expert. The community corrections officer monitors the offenders as to whether they are performing required parenting tasks such as reading to the child(ren) and providing good, nutritious meals. The program has proved to have diverted children from foster care and saved the state money by diverting offenders from prison. Preliminary findings also indicate that recidivism is reduced. Between June of 2010 and January of 2014, only 8 of the 206 women who successfully completed the program have returned to prison on a new felony conviction—a recidivism rate of only .05 percent.[183]

California has a similar law that allows some women who are primary-care providers for children and who have less than two years left of their sentence to be released early. These women must not have been convicted of sex offenses, have no current or prior felony convictions, and have no escape attempt on their record. They would be released to house arrest, residential drug treatment, or a transitional care facility.[184]

Dwyer believes that parenting programs in prison do not put the needs of the child first and even argues that, for minority children, such programs encourage the child to see the prison as "home." Because of this, Dwyer advocates a greater use of parental deprivation proceedings and adoption rather than parenting programs.[185] However, this position can be critiqued as fanciful (since most child development professionals agree that babies are not aware of their surroundings in their first 18 months) and short-sighted, since it fails to consider that women in prison are already mothers and may have additional children after release. Also, depriving them of their parental rights because they are in prison (absent any other finding of neglect or abuse) is not only a violation of due process, it is also a violation of equal protection, since such a stance would impact female parents more than male parents in prison.

While providing parenting programs may be criticized by some as being soft on crime, proponents of such programming argue that it is better to strengthen the skills of the offender-parent, and to pay attention to the healthy development of the children of offenders rather than wait for them to enter the criminal justice system themselves in the years to come.

Conclusion

In this chapter we have described the classification of and treatment programs for female offenders. We should be careful not to define women solely through their roles as mothers; nor should we paint them as hapless victims of childhood abusers and manipulative men. Not all women have been victimized or used drugs as a coping mechanism. However, the realities that have been described in this chapter do represent issues for a great number of women in prison. Further, it seems clear that there are distinct and important differences between women and men that need to be addressed.

The controversy over whether gender-neutral risk instruments outperform gender-specific instruments seems unnecessary if gender-specific instruments now exist. Gender-specific programming has been championed by national organizations like the National Institute of Corrections; however, such programming must be more than a catch phrase used in conferences and monograph reports. Given the lower security risk women pose and their lower rates of recidivism, work-release and community programs for women seem not only advisable, but also an obvious solution to budget pressures brought on by the high cost of incarceration.

REVIEW QUESTIONS

1. Describe the two types of classification. What are some measures (tools) used for each?

2. Explain the difference between static and dynamic factors used in risk prediction. What are third-generation instruments?

3. Explain what responsivity refers to in R/N/R.

4. What has research shown regarding the LSI-R's success in predicting recidivism or prison misconduct? What did Van Voorhis and her colleagues add to the LSI-R?

5. What are the correlates of prison misconduct?

6. Describe the four types of programming in prison.

7. Describe the elements that would make up gender-responsive programming in prison. Describe the conflict between gender-responsive programming advocates and R/N/R advocates.

8. Describe the differences between female and male addicts.

9. Describe the justifications for and different types of parenting programs.

10. What have evaluations of prison parenting programs in women's prisons shown?

II

Release, Recidivism, and Recommendations for the Future

CHAPTER SUMMARY

- Women experience a range of problems upon release including housing issues, inability to secure employment, reunification with children, and difficulty in obtaining needed drug and mental health treatment.

- Halfway houses can provide parolees with a safe and secure setting in order to transition into the community; however, it is difficult for a woman with several children to live with only one of her children in a facility, and many do not allow children at all.

- Recidivism studies have indicated that women are less likely than men to recidivate, but their recidivism rate is higher now than it had been in past decades.

- Factors associated with recidivism include criminal history, housing, employment, and drug dependency. There is continuing controversy over whether prediction instruments that utilize gender-specific factors improve prediction.

- Based on what we know about female offenders, comprehensive family services that address family violence, sexual abuse, and neglect will, long term, affect juvenile delinquency and, eventually adult criminality. For adult offenders, a combination of the cognitive-behavioral treatment programs favored by the "What Works?" literature and gender responsive treatment will most probably be more effective for female offenders than either alone.

This chapter reviews what we know about women on parole (with some attention devoted to probation as well), discusses findings regarding the recidivism of female offenders and evaluations of programs, and offers some final thoughts regarding female offenders and recommendations for correctional policy for the years to come.

Parole

Most women who leave prison do so under some form of parole supervision. The Bureau of Justice Statistics reports that there are 853,900 people on parole in 2011, with women making up 11 percent of the total (93,929). In contrast, there are 4,053,115 people on probation, with women making up about a quarter (1,013,278). While women's percentage of the total probation population has increased slightly since 2000 (from 22 percent to 25 percent), the percentage of the parole population has decreased slightly (from 12 percent to 11 percent). The overall number of individuals on community supervision has declined, but the decline has taken place in the numbers on probation while parole numbers have increased slightly.[1]

Although the issues of women on parole (or probation) are basically the same as men's, there are also differences. Like prison staff, community correctional staff members express the belief that female offenders are harder to supervise.[2] Part of this belief system seems to hold that female offenders need and want more from correctional staff members. They have problems related to regaining child custody, child care, housing, employment, substance abuse, and domestic violence. In one study of probation officers, it was found that male officers were more likely than female officers to believe that female probationers were easier than male probationers to supervise, while female officers were more likely to believe that they were more difficult. About 68 percent of officers said violations were the same for male and female probationers, but the reasons were different (e.g., women were more likely to fail to report because of child-care problems).[3]

Women, like men, suffer from the stigma of a prison sentence. Perhaps more than men, however, they experience guilt and low self-esteem because their actions separated them from their children (especially true with drug-dependent women who often had been neglectful mothers during their addiction). The rejection of others may be especially hurtful to women given their dependence on relationships. This quote from a parolee is fairly typical of what parolees face: "I was going to church 'cause I really found God and everyone was so nice. Then, someone found out I was in prison and everything changed, no one would talk to me anymore. Now I don't go, I just pray at home."[4]

While the majority of this discussion concerns female parolees, many of the same issues apply to female probationers as well. Just as with parolees, female probationers are more likely to be primary caregivers for children, and this role responsibility often interferes with meeting the conditions of probation.[5] It is reported, for instance, that female probationers are more likely than males to get revoked for technical violations as opposed to new crimes. Researchers describe how electronic monitoring programs are difficult for women because it is difficult to explain to their children why they can't go to the park with them or attend a school function. The programs typically require a stringent schedule but, as anyone with young children know, it is impossible to plan the week ahead of time for every hour of every day. Children get sick, they need supplies for school, and/or play dates come up.[6] Typically, men on probation or parole have female caregivers to take care of such things so that they can fulfill the conditions of their supervision.

Employment Issues

Most parolees have difficulty finding jobs, even though Title VII of the Civil Rights Act of 1964 prohibits employers from refusing to hire an individual solely because of a criminal record and there are some tax incentives for businesses to hire ex-offenders.[7] Ex-offenders are subject to a range of collateral consequences that include bans on voting, holding elective office, obtaining professional licenses, and ineligibility for public housing and many forms of public assistance. Offenders may be ineligible for military service, jury duty, and educational grants. They can be denied handgun licenses and jobs in real estate, nursing, and physical therapy and, sometimes, public employment and licenses (e.g., bartending, cosmetology, plumbing).[8]

Female parolees have more difficulty than male parolees finding jobs since they usually have no or little history of employment before prison. There are licensing requirements in about 350 occupations that act as barriers to ex-offenders, some of which are in occupations that are of interest to women, including home health care and working with children.[9]

Female parolees are more likely to be economically supported by others (e.g., boyfriends, husbands, family members), but there is a pervasive feeling of hopelessness among female parolees that they will never find a job given the stigma of a prison sentence.[10] Although many female offenders have been the recipients of public financial support, the Personal Responsibility and Work Opportunity Reconciliation Act of 1996 included a federal ban on welfare benefits to women who have a felony drug conviction. This law prohibited them from receiving food stamps or housing assistance for their lifetime. Note that this ban extended only to drug crimes, not to those convicted of murder or other violent crimes, no matter how heinous. The effect of this law has been extremely detrimental to female offenders because so many of them are drug involved, although about half of all states chose to opt out of the ban.

In addition to low educational achievement and poor or no work history, mental health issues have also been correlated with the lack of employment of ex-offenders. Unfortunately, mental illness diagnoses are pervasive among female parolees. It has been found in many studies that employment is related to successful parole outcomes.[11]

Housing Issues

Recall from previous chapters that a large proportion of imprisoned women have been homeless. Released women also fear they will be homeless, and housing is one of the most important elements in parole success.[12] Many female offenders have lost all contact with family and have nowhere to go to upon release. They may parole to halfway houses, missions, or the homes of friends or relatives with the expectation that they will get their own place quickly, but sometimes this is difficult to do.[13]

> Most people, if they're not in a transitional house for women and children on drug addiction, they live with family members or somebody, a friend, or something where they're always asked to be [gone], after a certain limit of time, "You got to go, you got to go, you got to go." . . . and that pushes you right back out to the wolves.[14]

Those women who went to prison because of their drug abuse and dependency find it difficult to return to the same neighborhood and relationships that they had when they were using drugs because the temptation is so great to relapse, yet it is in these neighborhoods where group housing is often located. It's also true that even these neighborhoods' public housing projects are closed to ex-offenders, because of laws such as the Anti-Drug Abuse Act and policies of housing authorities that bar ex-offenders, or even those who are suspected of crimes, from living in public housing. It is estimated that several million people are barred from public housing and face a dramatically increased risk of homelessness because of these policies. These risks are especially acute for women of color.[15]

Lipsitz[16] describes how women of color are caught in a net of poverty, criminalization, and risk of homelessness. One example of this is the abused spouse who stays in an abusive relationship because she cannot economically provide for her children, but when the abuse becomes life threatening, she ends up in prison for killing her abuser; or a woman in public housing who does not call the police when she is abused because she will be evicted. In fact, one of the most common reasons for homelessness is escape from abuse (from a spouse, intimate partner, or parental figure). He also describes the victimization of Section 8 recipients (federally subsidized housing) who encounter abuse and sexual harassment from landlords. Cases include women who have had landlords fondle them, enter with passkeys and sexually assault them, demand oral sex, and expose themselves to the Section 8 recipients.[17] For ex-offenders, these risks are magnified because they have no one to complain to.

Reunification with Children

Reunification with children is a source of great satisfaction for women but also a cause of stress.[18] In one study, about 47 percent of released women reunited with children directly after release.[19] The majority of women live with their children and other family members immediately upon release, or women live elsewhere but reunite with children through visits and other means.

When children are in state care, the released woman has to make a plan with the state that includes meeting certain requirements (e.g., to have stable employment, safe housing, childcare alternatives, clean drug tests, and so on) before her children are returned to her. It is very distressing to paroled women when their children are in state care and they cannot see them or even know where they are. The Adoption and Safe Families Act of 1997 mandates that a child who is under state care for 15 of the past 22 months must be released for adoption, unless certain specified exceptions apply. This law makes it much more likely that an incarcerated woman will lose her children without any evidence that she was a bad mother before her imprisonment.

In one study,[20] 203 parolee case files and 25 interviews in California were utilized to understand the problems of female parolees. Researchers found that 64 percent of the women lived with their children in the year prior to incarceration, 24 percent had been involved with the state department of human services (child welfare division), but only 17 percent had one or more children taken away (deprivation of parental rights). These authors describe the extreme economic stress female parolees experience. For instance, the state expected women to repay the welfare payments made to the family during her time of incarceration (and this may be in addition to court costs, restitution, daily living costs, and parole costs).[21]

Reunification sometimes involves uprooting children from their existing school/living situation and children may resent it, especially when they have to go to a different school or live in housing that is not as nice as what they have become accustomed to. In addition, incarceration erodes parental authority. Children wonder why they should obey a parent who has been imprisoned. Sometimes caregivers have hostility toward the inmate-mother, perhaps because they were forced to assume the economic burdens of the children or perhaps because they do not want to relinquish care over to the mother (especially if she has shown herself in the past to be neglectful or abusive).[22]

There are other situations where a woman might be economically dependent on abusive partners. In these cases, she is torn between removing her children from an abusive environment and displaying a stable living situation to a parole officer. If she is un- or underemployed, she may feel she does not have the financial resources to leave.[23] Female parolees often see their older children beginning to use drugs, dropping out of school, and being unemployed. Mothers who see their children go down the same path they did have no idea how to stop the process.

While male parolees explain that making appointments and keeping them with parole officers is difficult because of the demands of employment, women describe difficulties related to caring for young children, since it is difficult to bring them on buses to get to the parole office and some offices do not allow children. Richie[24] describes the complexities of the problems of female parolees who attempt to get their children back, avoid drugs, get a job, and avoid past relationships (with friends or romantic partners) that led to drug use or criminality. They have no money to buy decent clothes, they depend on bus transportation that may be irregular with difficult connections. When they are late to appointments it implies they are not committed to success—and sometimes they must navigate all these problems with a parole officer who does not transmit a message that he or she is there to help.[25]

> This is my probation's terms. Three to four times a week, counseling, but you have to pay for it. One girl said she was paying like sixty dollars a week just for three counseling sessions. Every time it was twenty bucks, bang. . . . They expect us to have a full-time job, which is fine, counseling four times a week, on top of community service two hours a day; so that's ten hours a week, so where is the time for your kids? . . . but they don't care. You mess up any step of the law and they're violating you and putting you in prison.[26]

In another study, female probationers and parolees expressed surprisingly positive attitudes toward their correctional supervisors. They indicated that their officers were understanding and concerned and were reliable sources of information: "I'm glad for my parole officer . . . it feels good to be clean and sober and to me she was just an angel to save me. . . ."[27]

Obtaining Needed Treatment

Some women have the added burdens of worrying about drug relapse and/or attempting to seek help for mental health issues. In Richie's[28] interviews with released women, one of the themes that emerged was the difficulties involved in treatment for substance abuse. Women described lack of access and problems with treatment settings, including sexual harassment in mixed-gender programs:

> . . . I couldn't stand how they treated me. Mostly it was the men in the group who always want to get some [have sex]. They offer nicely at first, then they teased me, they just stared at me whenever I talked. . . . Do you know one even offered to get high with me if I'd give him some [sex]? So I stopped going altogether.[29]

Richie's interviews also described serious health problems, including HIV, asthma, diabetes, hypertension, and reproductive health problems. Women also described mental health issues: ". . . I have the kind of emotional problems where I just lose my temper and start banging my head against the wall. Sometimes it gets so bad that I stay in bed for a week, just to not hurt myself or someone else . . ."[30] Many women suffer from symptoms of PTSD, including flashbacks, disorientation and depression. Battered women cannot access victim services because they are also offenders.[31]

It is clear that female parolees need just as much, if not more, help than male parolees to improve their lives and learn how to avoid drugs and criminality.[32] Women, especially, need supportive networks in order to succeed. In California, parolees are required to attend a Parole and Community Team (PACT) meeting that introduces them to many nonprofit agencies which provide resources including housing, employment, educational opportunities, substance abuse, and anger management counseling. About 65 percent of parolees go on to use the services that they have learned about in these meetings.[33] The meetings also include a motivational speech by a former inmate who tells them his or her story and how they succeeded.

Others also reinforce the idea that parolees need an array of accessible services. Richie,[34] for instance, writes that parolees need comprehensive programs, community development and linkages, empowerment and consciousness-raising approaches, and community mentoring. O'Brien,[35] specifically discussing women with drug dependency issues, noted that the women she interviewed had suffered an average of five traumatic life events (e.g., child molestation, abusive relationship, loss of a child, suicide attempt), their first alcohol or drug use was before age 18, and their first pregnancy was around age 16. In short, these women were very much in need of comprehensive services to address life problems that were intertwined with their drug use. An interesting finding in her study was that while most women used drugs immediately upon release from prison, many stopped on their own after six months. National findings indicate that relapse and recidivism rates are highest within the first six months; thus, O'Brien's research indicates that it is possible that at least some offenders may be able to control their drug use if they do not get revoked and sent back to prison.

Up to this point the discussion has largely concerned women paroled from prison; however, those leaving jail have many, if not most, of the same problems described above. If anything, it appears that women exiting jail may be even more likely to suffer from mental health problems. In one sample of 476 women released from New York City jails, researchers found that 83 percent had children but only 25 percent lived with their children at the time of the arrest. Only about a third had completed high school or a GED program, about a third had been homeless, less than a third had worked in the six months prior to arrest, and 26 percent received public benefits. About 63 percent reported past physical or sexual abuse. The median number of arrests was 4, although 29 percent reported 10 or more arrests. About 91 percent reported use of drugs in the six months prior to arrest. Self-identified needs of women recently released from jail were housing (71 percent), substance abuse treatment (69 percent), income (65 percent), and education (40 percent).[36]

The women were reinterviewed after some time in the community, and researchers found that although more women were involved in education, there was no change in employment (less than one third were employed). Fewer women admitted to receiving income from illegal activities (from 38 percent to 19 percent). The most frequent source of income was family and friends. About 39 percent of the women released from jail were rearrested. About a third were homeless. The use of drugs declined significantly (i.e., crack use declined from 65 percent to 20 percent).

The factors associated with rearrest were income from illegal activity, drug- and alcohol-related social problems, homelessness, and a history of previous arrests. Factors associated with non-arrest were income from a legitimate job, and reporting of physical problems related to drug or alcohol use.

Having a child at home and having health insurance reduced the likelihood of dealing drugs. According to these researchers, some of the barriers that kept these women from making it on the outside were food stamp eligibility restrictions, evictions from public housing (because of drug convictions), and the fact that Medicaid coverage was terminated with incarceration (only half reobtained it even though many suffered from chronic health issues).[37]

Halfway Houses

Many states operate facilities, typically called halfway houses, which transition the offender back into the community. There are very few beds for women in most state facilities, and almost none allow women to bring their children with them. Even those that do allow children will only allow young children; thus, the woman still has to find alternative care for her older children.

Ideally, halfway houses should be homes that are small enough to blend in with the neighborhood and not stigmatize the offenders who live within them. Because women are typically not feared, as male criminals are, the problems of community acceptance are generally less severe. Unfortunately, some states' solution to prison overcrowding has been to increase the size of halfway houses so that they are mini-institutions, albeit closer to the community.

Brennan[38] described a halfway house that allowed women to have their small children (under age seven) with them. The Summit House accepted high-risk nonviolent female offenders with felony drug or drug-related offenses, but with no mental diagnoses or personality disorder. There were varying levels of privileges, and residents worked toward goals and objectives, with an average completion time of 18 months. Staff offered cognitive learning theory, life skills, job skills, and parenting skills. One of the women's primary concerns was reconnecting with children who did not live with them and dealing with the resentment these children were feeling because they couldn't live with their mother. The conclusion was that education helped improve the health and nutrition outcomes for both the children and the mothers.

Leverentz[39] also described a halfway house for women. The women interviewed were extremely economically marginalized. Some were in deep debt because of restitution, parole costs, and basic needs. Many were dealing with a variety of mental health issues; many were medicated for depression or anxiety. Leverentz discusses how corrections moved from a mission of rehabilitation to one of monitoring and risk assessment. There is increased use of drug testing and electronic monitoring, but despite large increases in the number of offenders who are drug dependent, there was no corresponding increase in treatment. The women described problems stemming from relationships with men. While romantic relationships and/or marriage are typically associated with pro-social bonding and reduced recidivism for men, just the opposite occurs with women. Those who are involved with men are more likely to recidivate because they are typically involved with men who are drug users and/or still involved in other criminality. The women viewed correctional staff as there only to monitor them, not to help them. They expressed great fear of going back to prison—for example, one woman who had been the victim of a domestic assault did not report it because she was afraid she would be sent back.[40]

Recidivism

In a 2002 study of recidivism, Langan and Levin[41] reported on those who were released from prison in 1994. Women were less likely than men to be rearrested (57 percent compared to 68 percent), less likely to be reconvicted (40 percent compared to 48 percent), less likely to be resentenced to prison (17 percent compared to 26 percent), and less likely to be returned to prison (39 percent compared to 53 percent of those convicted). A recent report indicated that nationally, about 32 percent of all parolees (both men and women) were returned to prison in 2011, which was a lower recidivism figure than in 2000.[42]

In one national study of recidivism where female offenders were compared to the total sample that included both men and women, it was found that 60 percent of the women were rearrested (compared to 70 percent of the total male/female sample); 40 percent had new convictions (compared to 48 percent of the total sample), and 30 percent were returned to prison (compared to 37 percent of the total sample). Drug and property offenders were more likely to recidivate, and the factors most associated with recidivism were number of prior arrests and age at release.[43] Studies have found that chronic (as compared to non-chronic) female offenders are more likely to be younger, a minority, single, a substance abuser, a victim of domestic violence, and more likely to commit crimes alone. They also are more likely to have lower IQ scores and to have experienced family criminality.[44]

Reasons for recidivism typically involve a constellation of economic and personal factors. Morris and Wilkinson[45] interviewed 200 women in England during the early phase of their sentences, at prerelease, and three to five months after release. They found that the following factors seemed to be associated with recidivism: drinking or drug use, unemployment, poor living conditions, and economic marginalization. Consistent with these correlates of failure, O'Brien[46] identified factors of success that included a legal income a home, and a network of supportive relationships. She examined the relationship between needs and recidivism and found that 28 percent of her sample had a housing need and less than half of them had assistance; 38 percent had drug treatment needs, and about half did not receive assistance for it.

Other studies have also associated employment and recidivism (finding that employment reduced recidivism by 83 percent).[47] However, a different study found that employment was not significant for women (but was for men), and the most significant factor for women was completion of a drug program.[48] Yet another study concluded that women who were unmarried and unemployed were more likely to recidivate; but for those who were married, employment had no effect on recidivism. Women who were married and employed had the least risk of recidivating.[49] It appears that employment is differentially important as a predictor depending on marriage.

In a study of a community-based service program, it was found that women who finished the program were more likely to be successful. Number of prior arrests and age were highly correlated with recidivism. Although those with children were also more likely to recidivate, the researchers suggested that this might be a factor of age (with younger women more likely to have children and to be prone to recidivate).[50]

Recall from previous chapters that the LSI-R is used to predict recidivism, and there is a controversy as to whether it can be improved by adding a gender-specific trailer. Studies continue to find the LSI-R's gender-neutral factors are as successful in predicting recidivism of women as they are for men and that gender-specific variables do not substantially improve prediction.[51] However, studies do exist that indicate gender-specific approaches are better. In one study of recidivism, researchers[52] found that poverty status increased the odds of rearrest by a factor of 4.6 and increased the odds of a supervision violation by a factor of 12.7. They found that the LSI-R risk scores failed to predict recidivism once poverty status was taken into account. Women who were provided housing had a recidivism rate that declined by 83 percent from those who were not.

Research by Reisig[53] and his colleagues found that the LS-R worked fairly well for those women whose motivations for crime were similar to men's, but it misclassified women that fell into the "harmed and harming" type as well as the "drug-connected" type. About 46 percent of the women in this sample recidivated.

More recently, a gender-specific trailer was added to the LSI-R, improving its accuracy in prediction. Salisbury and Van Voorhis[54] found that in a study of probationers, family support, employment, and other financial needs are important. Those probationers with lower self-confidence and little family support had greater problems keeping and maintaining a job, which was, in turn, related to recidivism. These researchers, like others discussed above, advocated a holistic treatment approach that addressed housing, education, relationship counseling, family support, substance abuse and mental health treatment, and gender-specific needs—specifically, trauma-informed and relational counseling.

Evaluation of Treatment Programs

Most evaluation studies of treatment programs in prison do not specifically target women. Gendreau[55] cites several principles associated with effective programs (for any inmate):

- services that are intensive and behavioral in nature,
- behavioral programs that address the criminogenic needs of high-risk offenders,
- programs in which contingencies and behavioral strategies are enforced in a firm but fair manner,

- relationships between therapists and offenders that are interpersonally responsive and constructive,
- program structure and activities that promote pro-social behavior,
- relapse prevention strategies provided in the community to the extent possible, and
- advocacy and brokering services between offenders and the community that are attempted whenever community agencies offer appropriate services.

Others have also provided the elements of successful programming after reviewing studies of effectiveness:[56]

- inspired and dedicated leaders,
- a sense of purpose and mission for offenders,
- a unified treatment team,
- participants who are endowed with decision-making power,
- participant development of skills,
- uniqueness of the program,
- adequate community networks, and
- no alienation of formal decision makers.

Unfortunately, because evaluation studies don't include women in the samples (or they are a small portion of the sample and not analyzed separately), most prison evaluation efforts are not very helpful as far as understanding which programs may be most successful with women.

Koons[57] and her colleagues surveyed correctional professionals to discover what was perceived to be the most effective programs or program elements with female offenders. They found that there was some agreement on what administrators felt were elements of successful programming:

- the use of a comprehensive approach,
- a continuum of care,
- individualized and structured programming,
- emphasis on skill development (parenting, life skills, job skills),
- addressing of individual needs,
- caring staff members,
- female staff members who are ex-addicts or ex-offenders,
- separation from the general population,
- partnerships with outside services,
- adequate money and resources, and
- a "homey" environment.

As part of the same research study, Morash and Bynum[58] found that correctional administrators reported the need for more programming in areas of vocational education, work skills, family development, substance abuse, domestic violence, physical and sexual abuse, aftercare, and especially housing. They further concluded that innovative programs share the following elements: well-trained and dedicated staff, women-only programming, program materials focused on skills development and on meeting women's particular needs, willingness to tailor approaches to meet individual needs, treatment with appropriate controls, use of peer support and development of peer networks, formal recognition of participant achievement, and options for women who fail.

In one small study, factors related to reduced recidivism in a therapeutic community program for women included degree of contact with a significant person, having responsibility for children, and identification with their community.[59]

It is clear that treatment programs are essential and that there are not enough programs to accommodate all women who desire to better themselves while in prison. One of the interesting aspects of evaluating treatment programs is that women report highly positive attitudes toward all types of treatment. In fact, their only complaint seems to be that there are not enough available.[60]

> I think I would have been dead. . . . I don't understand why with the overdoses and everything that I went through and the life threatening situations that I would put myself in why I didn't die. . . . In fact, when I went into the _____ program, I didn't go in there looking for a change. I went in there looking to get off the work crew that they have in the prison system. And something was said in there and I met _____, and . . . I saw a care in somebody's eyes who had never been through this before, and it was . . . . I probably would have been back out there and either dead or back in the streets doing what I do best. And I like to use the terms "ripping and running" because it's a nice way to put what I did.[61]

Policy Recommendations

In this last section we briefly recap the findings reviewed in the book and discuss policy recommendations that are suggested from the findings. In the first chapter, we saw that what we think we know about the criminality of women (or men for that matter) is subject to the limitations of research. Further, sometimes researchers argue amongst themselves about how to measure a particular phenomenon (e.g., women's violence) even while policy changes are occurring based on some research findings.

In the second chapter we saw that the so-called gender gap is converging in property crimes but not so much in violent crimes. The convergence has taken place largely because of a decline in men's arrests. Women's arrests have decreased since the mid-1990s but not as dramatically as men's, and they have even shown increases in assault arrests. It should also be noted, however, that assault arrests are influenced by the discretion of system actors.

In Chapters 3, 4, and 5 we reviewed the major criminological theories as they applied to women. We see that most traditional theories excluded women, and most current theories have to adapt the original theory to fit women. Some theories explain women's crime patterns better than others. Hirschi's original social control theory seemed to fit what we knew about women's greater attachment to family, friends, and teachers; thus, most girls/ women are not involved in crime, and those who are do show higher levels of family dysfunction. General strain theory today has been adapted so that it accommodates findings regarding women's greater likelihood of experiencing severe family dysfunction and responding to strain differently than males. Life-course criminology utilizes longitudinal studies and is related to the pathways literature proposing that female offenders come to crime through different "pathways" than male offenders. Specifically, their greater likelihood of child victimization (both sexual and physical), their greater likelihood of serious drug abuse/dependency, their greater mental health needs, and their responsibilities for child care are noted by many researchers. Although many sociological researchers reject biological criminology, there are well-documented differences between the sexes that suggest intriguing possibilities for explaining the gender gap in crime. Longitudinal research has noted some of them. In essence, men are more likely to have low arousal levels and poor conditionability. They are more subject to learning disorders such as ADD and hyperactivity. They are more likely to have poor impulse control and also exhibit greater aggressive tendencies. All of these differences are suggestive of reasons why men are more likely than women to commit crime.

In Chapters 6 and 7, the descriptions of female juvenile offenders and jail inmates make it clear that we are dealing with the same profiles as female prisoners. Generally, the pathways literature findings have been replicated time and time again throughout a multitude of studies. While some researchers are still arguing about whether women receive "chivalry" from the criminal justice system, it is extremely clear that justice-involved girls and women generally are in great need of services to deal with a constellation of negative life experiences and their effects.

In Chapters 8, 9, and 10 prisons for women were described. While the history of women's prisons shows that women were treated differently from men (albeit in a sex-stereotyped and paternalistic fashion), today's approach to corrections has been one of uniformity. Women still form a small portion of the total prison population and, thus, the norm in correctional policy comes from prisons for men. Correctional policies, classification, and programming are all heavily influenced by the male norm in corrections. A more serious problem has been cross-sex supervision and the risk that male correctional officers will abuse their position, exploiting and assaulting female prisoners. Ironically, the field of corrections has come full circle—back to the 1700s and 1800s when female offenders were largely guarded by men before separate institutions for women were established.

Recently, the need for gender-responsive treatment has been recognized (stemming largely from the pathways approach). The controversy continues over whether gender-neutral classification and prediction instruments (like the LSI-R) are equally applicable to women or whether gender-specific instruments and programs are more effective.

Policy Implications

The very same social policy implications emerge from biological research, longitudinal research, the general theory of crime, social support theory, and pathways research. In order to reduce crime, families need to be strengthened. This involves broad societal policies that allow all families to earn a living wage and avoid the stress and disintegration of the family unit that poverty creates. Racism must be addressed since it blocks opportunities, results in different treatment by formal law enforcers, and promotes segregated housing that acts to isolate and polarize communities.

Poverty programs are crime programs in that programs which improve the lives of children will affect crime as these children enter their crime-prone years. This is true for girls and boys: while boys may commit more violent crime, girls who suffer from abuse and dysfunctional families enter criminal pathways that have life-long ramifications. As many policy makers and researchers point out, we will spend money on the same group of children, either earlier (when the children are young) or later (when they are arrested and enter the justice system).

To prevent crime we should increase the affiliation capacity of at-risk youth, meaning the capacity to empathize and care for others. This is more often a deficiency of males but affects females, too, when they are victims of abuse and neglect and have no adult who can provide healthy nurturing. We can ameliorate this situation by improving the economics that hold families together; providing medical and social services that will ensure healthy development; strengthening schools so that teachers can be role models; and, for those children that do enter the system, providing something more than punitive correctional policies.

A healthy conscience may be developed by experiencing loving, caring, attachments that also provide discipline. A variety of sex differences predisposes men to choose crime, especially victim-harming crime. Placed in social settings where violence is tolerated, social networks are weak, and formal social supports are nonexistent, men are more likely than women to make criminal choices. However, women in such environments are more likely than other women to make criminal choices.

From infancy to old age, it is clear that humans are happier, healthier, and more pro-social when they care for and are cared for by others. Because female offenders almost always have children, we have a chance to affect the next generation, yet all too often social policy decisions take the position that the children of offenders are not "correction's problem." However, it is clear that many of these children will become "correction's problem" in the years to come.

For those youth or adults already involved in lawbreaking, official intervention should focus on accountability but should also address pragmatic needs such as employment and housing. Once those needs are met, then programs can concentrate on other elements that lead to criminal decision making. A variety of programs have proved successful in reducing recidivism, and there is no reason not to use the resources available to determine which ones work and which ones are wastes of money. For instance, the Bureau of Justice Administration now has a website that presents evaluation research on a wide range of programs (CrimeSolutions.gov). The existing research seems to indicate that gender-neutral prediction instruments and treatment programs can be improved by adding gender-specific elements. Instead of ignoring the sex differences of crime, we should understand and use this research. Corrections dollars spent on helping female offenders by providing effective programming impacts their children, their children's children, and future generations. Ultimately, such intervention benefits us all.

REVIEW QUESTIONS

1. Review the numbers and percentages of total of women on probation and parole. Are the numbers increasing or decreasing?

2. List and describe the challenges/problems of women after they are released from prison.

3. Provide the findings of the jail inmate study that described female jail inmates and their problems/needs upon release.

4. Describe the issues regarding women in halfway houses.

5. Describe characteristics of female recidivists.

6. Explain the correlates of success (elements that are associated with not being rearrested).

7. Review the controversy regarding the LSI-R and whether or not it can effectively predict recidivism of female offenders.

8. Describe the elements of effective treatment programs.

9. Compare the elements of effective programs with what factors have been identified as important for success with female offenders.

10. Describe the major findings and recommendations for policy regarding female offenders.

Notes

Chapter One

[1] Pollock, 1998, p. 51.
[2] Glueck & Glueck, 1934; see, e.g., Barkan, 1997, p. 62.
[3] Gottfredson & Hirschi, 1990.
[4] Bureau of Justice Statistics. (Number of rape/sexual assaults by reporting to police). Generated using the NCVS Victimization Analysis Tool at www.bjs.gov. 14-Jun-13.
[5] Hirschi, 1969.
[6] Denzin, 1990.
[7] Pollak, 1950, is one example of such research and more will be presented in Chapter 3.
[8] Wilson & Rigby, 1975; Wright, 1992.
[9] See, e.g., Straus et al., 1980; McLeod, 1984; Straus & Gelles, 1986.
[10] Schwartz, 1987 and Dobash et al., 1992.
[11] See Schwartz, 1987; Schwartz & DeKeseredy, 1993. DeKeseredy, Saunders, Schwartz & Alvi, 1997.
[12] Catalano, 2012, p. 2.
[13] Reckdenwald & Parker, 2012, p. 169.
[14] Catalano, Smith, Snyder & Rand, 2009, p. 2.
[15] Wonders, 1996, p. 614.
[16] Dobash & Dobash, 2004; Hirschel & Buzawa, 2002; Finn, Blackwell, Stalans, Studdard, & Dugan, 2004.
[17] Miller, S. 2001, p. 1346.
[18] Hirschi & Buzawa, 2002.
[19] Miller & Meloy, 2006.
[20] Female respondent, from Miller, 2001, p. 1359.
[21] Miller, S., 2001; Miller & Meloy, 2006.
[22] See Chesney-Lind, 2002.
[23] See, e.g., McLeod, 1982; Carlen, 1983, 1985.
[24] See discussions of methods in Daly, 1994a, 1994b; Worral, 1990; Gilfus, 1988; and, Agnew, 2006.
[25] Gilfus, 2006.
[26] Chesney-Lind, 1997, p. 127.
[27] Carlen, 1985, p. 10.
[28] Morris, 1987.
[29] Daly & Chesney-Lind, 1988, p. 504.

[30] See, e.g., Connell, 1987, who defines gender as part of the structured organization of interpersonal relationships; norms of social interaction; division of labor, power transactions, and emotional attachments.

[31] Messerschmidt, 1993; Phillips, 1987.

[32] Feinman, 1983, 1984.

[33] Morris & Gelsthorpe, 1981, p. 52.

[34] Mann, 1984b, p. 29. Also see Pearson, 1997, for a similar application of the "women are worse than men" position.

[35] For discussion, see Chesney-Lind & Eliason, 2006.

[36] For discussion, see Pollock, 1999a, Chesney-Lind & Eliason, 2006; Muncer, Campbell, Jervis & Lewis, 2001. For examples, see Pearson, 1997.

[37] Pollock & Davis, 2005.

[38] Chesney-Lind & Eliason, 2006.

[39] Steffensmeier & Allen, 1988.

[40] Steffensmeier & Allen, 1988, p. 73.

[41] Messerschmidt, 1997, p. 67.

[42] See, e.g., Ward & Beck, 2001; Gibson, Khey & Schreck, 2008.

[43] Tibbetts, 1997; Tibbetts & Herz, 1996; Gibson, Khey & Schreck, 2008.

Chapter Two

[1] Snyder & Mulako-Wangota, 2013.

[2] Steffensmeier & Streifel, 1992, p. 77.

[3] Steffensmeier, Zhong, Ackerman, Schwartz & Agha, 2006; Schwartz, Steffensmeier & Feldmeyer, 2009.

[4] Steffensmeier et al., 2006, p. 82.

[5] Schwartz, Steffensmeier & Feldmeyer, 2009, p. 510; also see Schwartz, Steffensmeier, Zhong & Ackerman, 2009.

[6] For instance, Smith & Jones, 2010; Johnson &Johnson, 2000.

[7] Sherman, 2012, p. 1620.

[8] Dohrn, 2004 (p. 313), reports that twice as many girls as boys are in detention for probation violations in this way.

[9] Steffensmeier et al., 2006; Steffensmeier, Schwartz, Zhong & Ackerman, 2005; Feld, 2009. Chesney-Lind, 2002; Bishop & Frazier, 1992.

[10] Steffensmeier, 1993.

[11] Steffensmeier, 1993, p. 14.

[12] Mann, 1984b, p. 30.

[13] Decker, Wright, Redfern & Smith, 1993.

[14] Steffensmeier, 1993.

[15] Uniform Crime Reports (UCR), 2011, Table 42.

[16] Mann, 1984b, p. 31.

[17] Cameron, 1964.

[18] Chesney-Lind, 1997, p. 106.

[19] Zietz, 1981.

[20] See, e.g., Dodge, 2009.

[21] Daly, 1989c, p. 790.

[22] Block, 1980. Also see Steffensmeier & Allen, 1988.

[23] Simon, 1975, 1976a, 1976b.

[24] Albanese, 1993, p. 126.

[25] See Rennison, 2009.

[26] Steffensmeier et al., 2006.

[27] Lauritsen, Heimer & Lynch, 2009.

[28] Schwartz, Steffensmeier, Zhong & Ackerman. 2009.

[29] Koons-Witt & Schram, 2006.

[30] Harlow, 1999; Silver, Felson & Vanseltine, 2008; Widom & Maxfield, 2001.

[31] Pollock, Mullings & Crouch 2006; also see Kubiak, Kim, & Bybee, 2013.

[32] Baskin & Sommers, 1993, 1998; also see Baskin, Sommers & Fagan, 1993; Sommers & Baskin, 1994, 1993, and 1992 for other articles on the same research project.

[33] Kruttschnitt & Carbone-Lopez, 2006.

[34] Sommers & Baskin, 1993; Maher & Curtis, 1992.

[35] Kruttschnitt & Carbone-Lopez, 2006.

[36] Kruttschnitt & Carbone-Lopez, 2006, p. 345.

[37] Mullins, Wright & Jacobs, 2004; Kruttschnitt, Gartner & Ferraro, 2002; Brownstein, Spunt, Crimmins, Goldstein & Langley, 1994.

[38] Snyder & Mulako-Wangota, 2013.

[39] Katz, 1988, p. 247.

[40] Mann, 1984b; Sommers & Baskin, 1993.

[41] Carlen, 1988, p. 20.

[42] Maher & Curtis, 1992, p. 231.

[43] Miller, 1998.

[44] Sommers & Baskin, 1993.

[45] Sommers & Baskin, 1993, p. 144.

[46] Sommers & Baskin, 1993, p. 146.

[47] Koons-Witt & Schram, 2003.

[48] Snyder & Mulako-Wangota, 2013.

[49] Harmon et al., 1985.

[50] Reported in Pollock & Davis, 2005.

[51] UCR, 2011, Table 33.

[52] Greenfield & Snell, 1999.

[53] Sommers & Baskin, 1993.

[54] Sommers & Baskin, 1993, pp. 151, 152.

[55] Straus, Gelles & Steinmetz, 1980; Straus & Gelles, 1986; Steinmetz, 1978; and McLeod, 1984. See DeKeseredy & Schwartz, 1996, pp. 331–332, for a discussion of the faults of the methodology used in estimating violence by women as compared to men.

[56] Kubiak, Kim & Bybee, 2013; Siegel & Williams; 2003; Magdol, Moffitt, Caspi, & Silva, 1998.

[57] Federal Bureau of Investigation, 2013, Table 42; also see Snyder & Mulako-Wangota, 2013.

[58] Fox & Piquero, 2003.

[59] Batton, 2004.

[60] Blum & Fisher, 1978

[61] Mann, 1996.

[62] Cooper & Smith, 2011, p. 10.

[63] Spunt, Brownstein, Crimmins & Langley 1994, p. viii.

[64] Greenfield & Snell, 1999; Dixon, Krienert, & Walsh, 2013.

[65] Cooper & Smith, 2011, p. 7.

[66] d'Orban 1979, pp. 565–567.

[67] Alder & Baker, 1997.

[68] Oberman, 2002; also see Crimmins, Langley, Brownstein & Spunt, 1997.

[69] Oberman & Meyer, 2008.

[70] Keeney & Heide, 1994, 1995.

[71] BJS, 1998.

[72] BJS, 1994.

[73] Craven, 1996, p. 2.

[74] Catalano, Smith, Snyder & Rand, 2009, p. 2.

[75] Gauthier & Bankston, 1997.

[76] Bouffard, Wright, Muftic, & Bouffard, 2008.

[77] Mann, 1988, p. 45.

[78] Browne, 1987; Ewing, 1987, 2000.

[79] Ewing, 1987, p. 23.

[80] Brownstein, Spunt, Crimmins, Goldstein & Langley, 1994, p. 105.

[81] Browne, 1987.

[82] UCR 2011, Table 42.

[83] Chesney-Lind, 1997.

[84] UCR, 2011, Table 33.

[85] The Substance Abuse and Mental Health Services Administration (SAMHSA), 2012, p. 15.

[86] SAMHSA, 2012, p. 78.

[87] Snell & Morton, 1994; Fletcher, Shaver & Moon, 1993; Pollock, 1998; Deschenes & Anglin, 1992; Hser, Anglin & Chou, 1992.

[88] Bloom, Chesney-Lind & Owen, 1994, p. 5; Pollock, 1998, p. 76.

[89] Karberg & James, 2005, p. 5.

[90] Snell, 1994.

[91] Karberg & James, 2005, p. 5.

[92] From interviews conducted in 1995 by author.

[93] Anglin & Hser, 1987; also see Hser, Anglin & Booth, 1987a, 1987b; Inciardi, 1980; Sanchez & Johnson, 1987; Fletcher et al., 1993.

[94] Inciardi, Lockwood & Pottieger, 1993.

[95] Inciardi et al., 1993, pp. 572–573.

[96] Rosenbaum, 1981, p. 71; Adler, 1993; Huling, 1995; Maher & Daly, 1996; Dunlap, Johnson, & Maher, 1997; Maher & Curtis, 1993; Morgan & Joe, 1997.

[97] Maher & Daly, 1996.

[98] Dunlap, Johnson & Maher, 1997.

[99] Maher & Curtis, 1992.

[100] Maher and Daly, 1996, also point out that one-time interviews are less accurate in obtaining information than ethnographic studies, such as theirs, that cover a longer range of time and consist of multiple interviews over time with the same informants.

[101] UCR, 2011, Tables 33 and 42.

[102] Vandiver & Walker, 2002.

[103] Denov, 2001.

[104] Denov, 2001; also see Gannon & Cortoni, 2010.

[105] See Mann, 1984b; Chesney-Lind, 1997; Rafter (Hahn), 1985.

[106] Weitzer, 2005; Matthews, 2005.

[107] *Uniform Crime Reports* (UCR) 2011, Table 42.

[108] Rosenbaum, 1980.

[109] See Chesney-Lind & Shelden, 2014.

[110] Chesney-Lind, 1997.

[111] Surratt, Inciardi, Kurtz & Kiley, 2004.

[112] James, 1976.

[113] See, for instance, Pollock & Hollier for a review of research, but also note that the entire issue of *Women & Criminal Justice* was devoted to human trafficking. There is a rapidly growing body of research in this area.

[114] Blank, 1993, pp. 57–61; Rafter (Hahn), 1988.

[115] See Boyd, 2004; Merlo, 1993; Sagatun, 1993; Humphries, Dawson, Cronin, Keating, Wisniewski & Eichfeld, 1992; Humphries, 1993; Pollock-Byrne & Merlo, 1991; Feinman, 1992; Maher, 1990, 1992; and Bagley & Merlo, 1995.

[116] See, e.g., Anglin & Hser, 1987; Hser, Anglin & Booth, 1987a&b; Danner, Blount, Silverman & Vega, 1995; French 1978, 1983; Baskin, Sommers & Fagan, 1993; Sommers & Baskin, 1992, 1993; Chilton & Datesman, 1987; Laub & McDermott, 1985; Steffensmeier & Allen, 1988, 1996; and Mann, 1993.

[117] Lujan, 1995, p. 13.

[118] Tonry, 1995; Mann, 1993; Lewis, 1981.

[119] Chilton & Datesman, 1987, p. 166.

[120] Chilton & Datesman, 1987.

[121] See Alarid, Marquart, Burton, Cullen & Duvelier, 1996; Gilfus, 1988.

[122] Maher, 1992, p. 59.

[123] Crenshaw, 2012.

[124] Lipsitz, 2012.

Chapter Three

[1] See, e.g., Lombroso & Ferrero, 1909 or Pollak, 1950.

[2] Bentham, 1843/1970.

[3] Lombroso & Ferrero, 1911/1894.

[4] Lombroso & Ferrero, 1909/1895.

[5] Lombroso & Ferrero, 1909/1895, p. 147.

[6] Lombroso & Ferrero, 1909/1895, p. 151.

[7] Rafter (Hahn), 1979, 1988.

[8] See, e.g., reviews in Gora, 1982; Leonard, 1982; and Pollock, 1978.

[9] Pike, 1876.

[10] Shaw & McKay, 1934/1969.

[11] Shaw, 1951, p. 15; emphasis added.

[12] Miller, W., 1958.

[13] Sutherland, Cressey & Luckenbill, 1992.

[14] Sutherland & Cressey, 1960, pp. 77–79.

[15] Akers, 1985.

[16] Burgess & Akers, 1966.

[17] Akers, 1973, p. 46.

[18] Burgess & Akers, 1966, p. 142.

[19] Morris, 1964.

[20] Hindelang, 1979, 1981; Smith, 1979; Alarid, Burton & Cullen, 2000; McGloin & Dipietro, 2013.

[21] Akers, 1998; 2009.

[22] Lee, Akers & Borg, 2004.

[23] Merton, 1938.

[24] Agnew, 1985, 2001, 2005.

[25] For an expanded discussion, see Leonard, 1982, pp. 56–57.

[26] Cohen, 1955.

[27] Cohen, 1955, p. 141.

[28] Naffine, 1987; also see Naffine, 1996.

[29] Cohen, 1955, p. 147.

[30] Cohen, 1955, p. 140.

[31] Cloward, 1959.

[32] Cloward & Ohlin, 1960.

[33] Cloward & Ohlin, 1960, p. 106.

[34] Cloward & Ohlin, 1960, p. 110.

[35] Morris, 1964.

[36] Morris, 1964, p. 83.

[37] Sandhu & Allen, 1969, p. 110.

[38] Datesman, Scarpetti & Stephenson, 1975, p. 107.

[39] Smith, D., 1979.

[40] Cernkovich & Giordano, 1979.

[41] Hirschi, 1969.

[42] For a review see Costello & Vowell, 1999.

[43] Naffine, 1987

[44] Naffine, 1987, p. 67.

[45] Hagan, Simpson, & Gillis, 1987.

[46] Greenberg, 1999.

[47] Canter, 1982b.

[48] Mears, Ploeger & Warr, 1998; Jensen & Eve, 1976.

[49] Tibbetts & Herz, 1996.

[50] Jensen & Eve, 1976.

[51] Smith, 1979.

[52] Alarid, Burton & Cullen, 2000.

[53] Covington, 1985.

[54] Steketee, Junger & Junger-Tas, 2013.

[55] Booth, Farrell & Varano, 2008; Bjerregaard, & Cochran, 2012.

[56] Lemert, 1951.

[57] Mead, 1934.

[58] Becker, 1963.

[59] Lemert, 1951, p. 76.

[60] Bernburg & Krohn, 2003, p. 1288; Sampson & Laub, 1997.

[61] Akers, 1977.

[62] Lemert, 1951.

[63] Hagan, Simpson & Gillis, 1979.

[64] Chesney-Lind, 1973; 1997.

[65] Schur, 1984.

[66] Although these terms can be distinguished in more careful definitions, for our purposes we will consider the terms as basically referring to the idea that crime is a politically structured concept.

[67] See, e.g., Taylor, Walton & Young, 1998; and Quinney, 1973.

[68] Klein & Kress, 1976.

[69] Andrews & Bonta, 2010; also see Redl & Toch, 1979.

[70] Glueck & Glueck, 1934.

[71] Andrews & Bonta, 2010.

[72] For more complete discussions of early psychological applications of crime theory to women, see Mann, 1984b; Pollock, 1978; Gora, 1982.

[73] Lykken, 1995, pp. 6–7.

[74] Lykken, 1995, p. 18.

[75] Pollak, 1950.

[76] Konopka, 1966.

[77] Vedder & Sommerville, 1970.

[78] Thomas, 1923.

[79] Glueck & Glueck, 1934.

[80] Cowie, Cowie & Slater, 1968.

[81] Thomas, 1923/1969.

[82] Pollak, 1950.

[83] Konopka, 1966, p. 40.

[84] Covington, 1998a; Bloom, Owen & Covington, 2004.

[85] Cowie, Cowie & Slater, 1968.

[86] Cowie, Cowie & Slater, 1968, p. 44.

[87] Cowie, Cowie & Slater, 1968, p. 176.

[88] Datesman & Scarpetti, 1980b.

[89] Gora, 1982.

[90] Chesney-Lind & Shelden, 2014.

[91] Dembo, Williams & Schmeidler, 1995.

[92] Rosenbaum, 1989, p. 1993.

[93] Widom, 1989a, 1989b, 1989c, 1991a, 1991b, 1995, 1996, 2000.

[94] Daly, 1992, 1994a, p. 63.

[95] Piaget, 1965.

[96] Kohlberg, 1981.

[97] Kohlberg, 1976.

[98] Gilligan, 1982.

[99] Gilligan, 1987, p. 22.

[100] Gilligan, 1987, p. 26.

[101] Also see Gilligan, 1990; Gilligan, Rogers & Tolman, 1991.

[102] Smart, 1989, p. 75.

[103] Held, 1987.

[104] Rothbart, Hanley & Albert, 1986.

[105] Wark & Krebs, 1996.

[106] Chodorow, 1978.

[107] Noddings, 1984, 1989.

[108] See Cole & Coultrap-McQuin, 1992, p. 3.

[109] Hickey & Scharf, 1980, p. 93.

[110] Wilson, J., 1993.

[111] Wilson, J., 1993, p. 87.

[112] Wilson, J., 1993, p. 187.

[113] Warren, 1979.

[114] Warren, 1979.

[115] Bandura, 1977.

[116] Parsons, 1954.

[117] Parsons, 1954, p. 306.

[118] Silverman and Dinitz (1974) provide one test of Parsons' hypermasculinity theory, but Cullen, Golden and Cullen (1979) tested both boys and girls for masculinity traits. Widom (1979, 1981) used the Bem Sex-Role Inventory with a sample of 73 women in custody and a control group of 20 women. Offenders were no more masculine than non-offenders, but recidivists were "less feminine."

[119] Andrews & Bonta, 2010.

[120] Klein, 1973.

[121] Rasche, 1974.

[122] Smart, 1976, 1979, 1989, 1995.

[123] Crites, 1976.

[124] Pollock, 1978.

[125] Leonard, 1982.

[126] Price & Sokoloff, 1982.

[127] Heidensohn, 1985, 1986.

[128] Morris, 1987.

[129] Naffine, 1987, 1996.

[130] Allen, 1989.

[131] Howe, 1994.

[132] Naffine, 1987, p. 25.

[133] For instance, Heidensohn, 1985, pp. 161–178.

[134] For instance, Carlen, 1988.

[135] For instance, Naffine, 1987.

[136] Hoffman-Bustamante, 1973, p. 120.

[137] Hoffman-Bustamante, 1973, p. 117.

[138] Smart, 1976, p. 66; also see Smart, 1979.

[139] Smart, 1976, p. 69.

[140] Jensen & Eve, 1976.

[141] Thomas, 1969, pp. 84–85.

[142] Bishop, 1931, pp. 3–4.

[143] Pollak, 1950, p. 75.

[144] Adler, 1975, p. 15.

[145] Crittenden, 1990, p. A14.

[146] Steffensmeier, 1978, 1980b, 1981, 1983; also see Leonard, 1982.

[147] Adler, 1981.

[148] Adler, 1981, p. 10.

[149] Adler, 1981, p. 11.

[150] Simon, 1975; 1976a, 1976b.

[151] Simon, 1975, p. 2.

[152] Simon & Landis, 1991, pp. 3–4.

[153] But see Heimer & DeCoster, 1999, for an opposing view.

[154] Daly & Chesney-Lind, 1988; Leonard, 1982; Steffensmeier, 1980b; Chapman, 1980; Feinman, 1994; Giordano & Cernkovich, 1979; Widom, 1979.

[155] Steffensmeier & Streifel, 1992.

[156] Chernoff & Simon, 2000.

[157] For reviews, see Crites, 1976; Leonard, 1982; Smart, 1976; Steffensmeier, 1978; and Norland & Shover, 1977. But see Heimer & DeCoster, 1999.

[158] Marshall, 1982.

[159] Marshall, 1982, p. 29.

[160] Steffensmeier, Allen, & Streifel, 1989.

[161] Whaley & Messner, 2002.

[162] Steffensmeier, 1978, 1980b, 1981, 1993; Steffensmeier & Streiffel, 1992.

[163] Giordano & Cernkovich, 1979; Campbell, Mackenzie & Robinson, 1987; But also see Cullen et al., 1979; Kruttschnitt & Dornfield, 1993; Heimer, 2000; Owen, 1998; Girshick, 1999; Chesney-Lind & Rodriquez, 1983.

Chapter Four

[1] Gottfredson & Hirschi, 1990.

[2] Gottfredson & Hirschi, 1990, p. 25.

[3] Gottfredson & Hirschi, 1990, p. 43.

[4] Gottfredson & Hirschi, 1990, p. 91.

[5] Gottfredson & Hirschi, 1990, p. 90.

[6] Gottfredson & Hirschi, 1990, p. 191.

[7] Reed & Yeager (1996).

[8] Gottfredson & Hirschi, 1990, p. 208.

[9] Gottfredson & Hirschi, 1990, p. 97.

[10] Gottfredson & Hirschi, 1990, p. 103.

[11] Hirschi, 1994.

[12] Hirschi, 1994, pp. 53–58.

[13] Hirschi, 1994, p. 64.

[14] Hirschi, 1994, p. 66.

[15] Gottfredson & Hirschi, 1990, p. 139.

[16] Gottfredson & Hirschi, 1990, p. 140.

[17] Gottfredson & Hirschi, 1990, p. 149.

[18] Gottfredson & Hirschi, 1990, p. 149.

[19] Hirschi, 1994.

[20] Miller & Burack, p. 1993.

[21] Hirschi, 2004.

[22] Gibbs & Giever, 1995; Evans et al., 1997; Pratt & Cullen, 2000; Vazsonyi, Pickering, Junger, & Hessing, 2001.

[23] Wright & Beaver, 2005.

[24] Latimore, Tittle & Grasmick, 2006.

[25] Hay, 2006.

[26] See Keane, Maxim, & Teevan, 1993; Polakowski, 1994; Caspi, Moffitt, Silva, Stouthamer-Loeber, Krueger, & Schmutte, 1994.

[27] Zager, 1994, for instance defined lack of self-control by alcohol use, marijuana use, obscene phone calls, avoiding payment, strong arming students, and joyriding, and attitudinal measures such as honesty (negative measure), short-sightedness, and concern for victims (negative measure). Also, see Barlow, 1991; Pratt & Cullen, 2000; Tittle, Ward, & Grasmick, 2003.

[28] For instance, see Vazsonyi, Pickering, Junger, & Hessing, 2001. In their cross cultural study of adolescent delinquency, they used a dependent variable that included vandalism, alcohol, drugs, school misconduct, general deviance, theft, and assault. Their finding that self-control was a more powerful predictor of this broad range of deviance than age or sex is not very helpful to our understanding of serious delinquency.

[29] Blackwell & Piquero, 2005.

[30] See Evans et al., 1997; Pratt & Cullen, 2000.

[31] Grasmick, Tittle, Bursik & Arneklev, 2003.

[32] Tittle, Ward & Grasmick, 2003.

[33] Delisi, Hochstetler, & Murphy, 2003.

[34] Longshore, Turner & Stein, 1996.

[35] Evans et al., 1997.

[36] Wright, Caspi, Moffitt & Silva, 2001.

[37] LaGrange & Silverman, 1999; Tibbetts, 1999.

[38] Longshore, Turner, & Stein, 1996; LaGrange & Silverman, 1999

[39] Zager, 1994.

[40] Cochran, Wood, Sellers, Wilkerson & Chamlin, 1998; Cochran, Chamlin, Wood & Sellers, 1999; Tibbetts, 1999; Blackwell, & Eschholz, 2002.

[41] LaGrange & Silverman, 1999.

[42] Agnew, 1985.

[43] Agnew, 2001.

[44] Agnew, 2001.

[45] Agnew, 2001.

[46] Agnew, Brezina, Wright & Cullen, 2002.

[47] Baron, 2004.

[48] Piquero & Sealock, 2000.

[49] Mazerolle & Maahs, 2000.

[50] Broidy & Agnew, 1997.

[51] Broidy & Agnew, 1997; also see Broidy, 2001.

[52] e.g., Mazerolle, 1998.

[53] Heimer, 1995.

[54] Hay, 2003.

[55] Piquero & Sealock, 2004.

[56] Slocum, Simpson & Smith, 2005.

[57] Kaufman, 2009.

[58] Kaufman, 2009, p. 414.

[59] Cornish & Clarke, 1986.

[60] Cohen & Felson, 1979.

[61] Anderson & Bennett, 1996; Elis & Simpson, 1995; Paternoster & Simpson, 1993; Piquero & Tibbetts, 1996; Tibbetts & Herz, 1996; Grasmick, Bursik & Kinsey, 1991.

[62] See Grasmick & Bursik, 1990; Tibbetts, 1999; Tibbetts & Herz, 1996; Piquero & Tibbetts, 1996.

[63] Piquero & Tibbetts, 1996.

[64] Tibbetts & Myers, 1999; Blackwell & Eschholz, 2002.

[65] Tibbetts & Herz, 1996; Blackwell & Eschholz, 2002.

[66] Sampson & Groves, 1989; Byrne & Sampson, 1986; Reiss & Tonry, 1986; Bursik & Grasmick, 1993; Cullen, 1994.

[67] Sampson, 1986a, 1986b; also see Byrne & Sampson, 1986.

[68] Chamlin & Cochran, 1997.

[69] Sampson, Raudenbush & Earls, 1997.

[70] Sun, Triplett, & Gainey, 2004.

[71] See, for instance, Liu & Kaplan, 1999.

[72] Messerschmidt, 1986.

[73] Bottcher, 1993.

[74] Bottcher, 1993, p. 43.

[75] Hagan, 1989.

[76] Hagan, 1989, p. 151.

[77] Hagan, 1989, p. 145.

[78] Hagan, 1989, p. 180.

[79] Hagan, 1989, p. 185.

[80] Morash & Chesney-Lind, 1991.

[81] Chesney-Lind & Shelden, 2014.

[82] See, for instance, Grasmick, Hagan, Blackwell, & Arneklev, 1993.

[83] Grasmick, Blackwell & Bursik, 1999.
[84] McCarthy, Hagan, & Woodward, 1999; Blackwell, 2000.
[85] Blackwell, 2000.
[86] Blackwell & Piquero, 2005.
[87] Tittle, 1995.
[88] Tittle, 1995, p. 232.
[89] Chapman, 1980.
[90] For instance, Steffensmeier, 1983; Steffensmeier & Streifel, 1992; Steffensmeier, Kramer & Streifel, 1993.
[91] Klein & Kress, 1976; Smart, 1976; Chapman, 1980; Datesman & Scarpetti, 1980a, 1980b; Box & Hale, 1983; Chesney-Lind, 1986; Feinman, 1986; Messerschmidt, 1986.
[92] Steffensmeier & Haynie, 2000a, 2000b.
[93] Jurik, 1983.
[94] Box & Hale, 1983.
[95] Heimer, 2000.
[96] Giordano & Cernkovich, 1979.
[97] Walsh, 1995a, p. 175; Walsh, 2011.
[98] Reviewed in Andrews & Bonta, 2010, pp. 162–163; Bohrman, 1996; Mednick, Moffitt & Stack, 1987; Mednick & Christiansen, 1977.
[99] Beaver, 2011; Beaver, 2013.
[100] Barnes, Beaver & Boutwell, 2011.
[101] Miller & Barnes, 2013.
[102] For more on these theories refer to Walsh, 1991, 1995a, 1995b; Mann, 1984b.
[103] Walsh, 1995b.
[104] Olweus, 1987; Eysenck & Gudjonsson, 1989.
[105] Maccoby & Jacklin, 1974; Mednick et al., 1987, p. 250; also Mednick & Christiansen, 1977; Walsh, 1991, 1995a.
[106] Ellis & Coontz, 1990.
[107] Walsh, 1995b, 2011; Mednick et al., 1987.
[108] Walsh, 1995a, p. 89.
[109] Eysenck & Gudjonsson, 1989, p. 135; Walsh, 1991, p. 140.
[110] Walsh, 1991, p. 127.
[111] Walsh, 1995a, pp. 50–54; Ellis, 1991; also see Beaver, Delisi, Vaughn & Barnes, 2010.
[112] Walsh, 1995, p. 54.
[113] Walsh, 1995b, p. 127.
[114] Walsh, 1991a, p. 141.
[115] ScienceDaily.com, 2009.
[116] Beaver, 2011.
[117] Sandhu & Satterfield, 1987.
[118] Walsh, 2011.
[119] Denno, 1990, p. 15.
[120] Denno, 1990.
[121] Denno, 1994.
[122] Denno, 1990; Silberg et al., 1986, p. 78; Farrington et al., 1990.
[123] Eysenck & Gudjonsson, 1989, p. 129; Walsh, 2011.
[124] Walsh, 2011, p. 116.
[125] Denno, 1990, p. 17.
[126] Denno, 1990, p. 56; Denno, 1994.
[127] Moffitt, 1990.
[128] See Moffitt, 1990, p. 112; Eysenck & Gudjonsson, 1989; Andrews & Bonta, 2010; Raine, 1993, p. 233.
[129] Denno, 1990.
[130] See Kohlberg, 1981.
[131] See Eysenck, 1977.
[132] See Caspi et al., 1994.

133 Caspi et al., 1994.
134 Wright & Beaver, 2005.
135 Cauffman, Steinberg & Piquero, 2005.
136 Eysenck & Gudjonsson, 1989, p. 44.
137 Eysenck & Gudjonsson, 1989, p. 55; also see Wood et al., 1997.
138 Caspi et al., 1994.
139 Raine, 1993, p. 93.
140 Raine, 1993, p. 290.
141 Eysenck & Gudjonsson, 1989, p. 140.
142 Eysenck & Gudjonsson, 1989, p. 131.
143 Walsh, 1995b, p. 123.
144 Walsh, 1991, 1995a, 1995b.
145 Walsh, 1991, p. 142.
146 Also see Maccoby, 1985.
147 Walsh, 1991, p. 78.
148 Walsh, 1991, p. 80.
149 Brewer-Smyth, 2004.
150 Gora, 1982, p. 13.
151 Renzetti, Curran & Maier, 2012; Sobel, 1978.
152 See, for instance, Belknap, 2007; Morris, 1987, p. 42; Messerschmidt, 1993, p. 7; and Smart, 1995, p. 18.
153 Gottfredson & Hirschi, 1990.

Chapter Five

1 Laub & Sampson, 2003; Sampson & Laub, 1990.
2 Sampson & Laub, 1993.
3 Gottfredson & Hirschi, 1990, p. 90.
4 Sampson & Laub, 1993, p. 12; Laub & Sampson, 2003.
5 Farrington, 1996.
6 Farrington, 1996, p. 69. Also see Farrington, 1991; Nagin, Farrington & Moffitt, 1993.
7 Farrington, 1996, p. 69. Also see Farrington, Ohlin & Wilson, 1986, p. 2.
8 Farrington, 1996, p. 81.
9 Bernburg & Krohn, 2003.
10 Kelley, Loeber, Keenan & DeLamatre, 1997.
11 Wolfgang, Thornberry & Figlio 1987; also see Wolfgang, Figlio & Sellin, 1972; Tracy, Wolfgang & Figlio, 1990.
12 D'Unger, Land & McCall, 2002.
13 Kempf-Leonard, Tracy & Howell, 2001.
14 Denno, 1990.
15 Denno 1990, pp. 19, 107.
16 Denno, 1994.
17 Moffitt, Caspi, Rutter & Silva. 2001; also see Moffitt, 1993.
18 Moffitt, Krueger, Caspi & Fagan, 2000.
19 Tonry, Ohlin & Farrington, 1991; also see Block, Blokland, van der Werff, van Os & Nieuwbeerta, 2010, for a description of other longitudinal studies.
20 Farrington, 2003.
21 Block et al., 2010.
22 Tonry, Ohlin & Farrington, 1991, p. 23.
23 Farrington, 1996; also see Rowe & Farrington, 1997.
24 Sampson & Laub, 1993.
25 Widom, 1984; also see Widom & Ames, 1988.
26 See, e.g., Moffitt, 1990.

[27] Denno, 1990.

[28] Denno 1990, 1994.

[29] Blumstein & Cohen, 1979; also see Blumstein, Cohen & Farrington, 1988a, 1988b.

[30] Tonry, Ohlin & Farrington, 1991, p. 142; also see Nagin, Farrington & Moffitt, 1995; Nagin & Farrington, 1992a, 1992b.

[31] Moffitt, 1993.

[32] Moffitt, 1993; Bartusch, Lynam, Moffitt & Silva, 1997.

[33] Tibbetts & Piquero, 1999.

[34] Barnes, 2012.

[35] Gottfredson & Hirschi, 1986, 1987, 1988.

[36] Sampson & Laub, 2003.

[37] Wright, Entner, Caspi, Moffitt & Silva, 2001.

[38] Tonry, Ohlin & Farrington, 1991, p. 14.

[39] Blumstein, Cohen, Roth & Visher, 1986.

[40] See Piquero & Mazerolle, 2001.

[41] Farrington, 1996.

[42] Farrington, 1996, p. 104.

[43] Farrington, 1996.

[44] Denno, 1990, p. 43.

[45] Denno, 1990; also see Denno, 1988.

[46] Denno, 1990, p. 27.

[47] Denno, 1990, p. 125.

[48] Moffitt, Caspi, Rutter & Silva, 2001.

[49] Mazerolle, Brame, Paternoster, Piquero & Dean, 2000.

[50] Gunnison & McCartan, 2005.

[51] Sargent, Marcus-Mendoza & Ho Yu, 1993; Pollock, 1998; Greenfield & Snell, 1999; Chesney-Lind & Pasko, 2004; Chesney-Lind & Shelden, 2004; Marcus-Mendoza & Wright, 2003; Mullings, Hartley & Marquart, 2004; Harlow, 1999.

[52] Browne & Finkelhor, 1986.

[53] Siegel & Williams, 2003.

[54] National Center on Addiction and Substance Abuse, 2010, p. 6.

[55] Payne, Gainey & Carey, 2005 (p. 81) found the following reported rates in presentence reports from 1999 to 2002. Note that the prevalence rates here are much lower than in other studies, but the relative ratios between male and female offenders seems to exist: family history of drug abuse (21% male to 33% female), alcohol (23% to 41%), physical abuse (9 to 22%), sexual abuse (3 to 24%), emotional abuse (6 to 18%), neglect (8% to 12%), and family members convicted of felonies (39% to 59%).

[56] See, e.g., Gilfus, 1988, 1992, 2006.

[57] McDaniels-Wilson & Belknap, 2008; Also see Taxman & Cropsey, 2006, p. 9.

[58] Cook, Smith, Tusher & Raiford, 2005.

[59] Pollock, 2002; Gilfus, 1992.

[60] Gilfus, 1992, p. 64.

[61] Hunt, MacKenzie & Joe-Laidler, 2006.

[62] Hunt et al., 2006, p. 61.

[63] Cook et al., 2005, p. 120.

[64] See Gilfus, 2006.

[65] Wesely, 2006; also see Wesely & Wright, 2009.

[66] Wesely & Wright, 2009, p. 226.

[67] Wesely, 2006, p. 310.

[68] Ryder, 2007.

[69] Browne & Finkelhor, 1986; Cauffman, Feldman, Waterman & Steiner, 1998; Eppright, Kashani, Robison & Reid, 1993; Marcus-Mendoza & Wright, 2003; Zlotnick et al., 2008; Cuellar & Curry, 2007; Messina et al., 2008; Messina & Grella, 2006.

[70] Mullings, Hartley & Marquart, 2004; Mullings, Pollock & Crouch, 2002.

[71] Belknap, 2007; Chesney-Lind & Rodriguez, 1983; Pollock, 2002; Sargent et al., 1993; Bush-Baskette, 2000; Dunlap, Johnson & Maher, 1997.

[72] Maher, 1992, 1997; Maher & Curtis, 1992.

[73] Mullings, Marquart & Brewer, 2000; Mullings, Marquart & Hartley, 2003; Cotton-Oldenburg, Jordan, Martin & Kupper, 1999.

[74] Silbert & Pines, 1981; Brown & Finkelhor, 1986; Widom & Kuhns, 1996; Surratt et al., 2004.

[75] Brown, 2006; Bourgois & Dunlap, 1993.

[76] Comack, 2006, p. 41.

[77] McDaniels-Wilson & Belknap, 2008.

[78] Browne & Finkelhor, 1986.

[79] Messman-Moore & Long, 2000.

[80] Breitenbecher, 2001.

[81] Widom, 1989a, 1989b, 1991a, 1991b, 1995, 1996; Widom & Ames, 1988, Widom & Maxfield, 2001, Acoca, 1998, 1999; Siegel & Williams, 2003; Brown, 2006.

[82] English, Widom & Brandford, 2001; Belknap & Holsinger, 2006; Makarios, 2007. Teague, Pazerolle, Legosz & Sanderson, 2008.

[83] Warren, Hurt, Loper, Bale, Friend & Chauham, 2002; Brewer-Smyth, Burgess & Shults, 2004; Makarios, 2007; Pollock, Mullings & Crouch, 2006; Leigey & Reed, 2010.

[84] Cernkovich, Lanctot & Giordano, 2008.

[85] Siegel & Williams, 2003.

[86] Manasse & Ganem, 2009.

[87] From interviews conducted in 1995 by the author.

[88] Richie, 2001, p. 375.

[89] Daly, 1992, 1994.

[90] Bloom, 2000; Bloom, Chesney-Lind & Owen, 1994; Covington, 1998b; Pollock, 1998; Pollock, 2002; DeHart, 2005.

[91] Daly, 1994b.

[92] Wesely, 2006, p. 323.

[93] DeHart, 2005, p. 27.

[94] DeHart, 2005, p. 18.

[95] Salisbury & Van Voorhis, 2009.

[96] Brennan, Breitenbach, Dieterich, Salisbury & Van Voorhis, 2012, pp. 1484–1485.

[97] Brennan et al., 2012.

[98] See Anumba, Dematteo & Heilbrun, 2012, as an example of a study that does not find a correlation.

[99] Henriques, 1995.

[100] Bloom & Chesney-Lind, 2000.

[101] Hill & Crawford, 1990.

[102] Miller, 1986.

[103] Richie, 1996.

[104] Miller, 1986.

[105] Richie, 1996.

[106] Arnold, 1995.

[107] Richie, 2006.

[108] Lujan, 1995.

[109] Lujan, 1995, p. 23.

[110] Simpson & Ellis, 1995.

[111] Gilligan, 1982, 1987, 1990; Brown & Gilligan, 1992; Gilligan, Rogers & Tolman, 1991.

[112] Trasler, 1980, p. 10; Wilson & Hernstein, 1986, p. 35.

[113] Morash, 1983; Pollock, 1999a.

[114] Gilfus, 1992; Arnold, 1995.

[115] See Ross & Fabiano, 1986, Andrews & Bonta, 2010. This discussion continues in Chapter 10.

Chapter Six

[1] Chesney-Lind & Shelden, 2014.

[2] Snyder & Mulako-Wangota, 2013.

[3] See, e.g., Chesney-Lind, 1978.

[4] Weis, 1976; Datesman & Scarpetti, 1980a, 1980b; Figueira-McDonough et al., 1981; Chesney-Lind & Shelden, 2014; Triplett & Myers, 1995.

[5] Steffensmeier, 1978, 1980a.

[6] Simpson, 1991, pp.117–118.

[7] Reported in Sherman, 2012, p. 1618.

[8] Moore & Padavic, 2010, p. 275.

[9] Miller, 2008.

[10] Chesney-Lind, 1997, p. 40.

[11] Zahn et al., 2010, p. 4.

[12] Zahn et al., 2010.

[13] Steffensmeier, Schwartz, Zhong & Ackerman, 2005.

[14] Steffensmeier et al., 2005, p. 366; also see Stevens, Morash & Chesney-Lind, 2010.

[15] Durose, Harlow, Langan, Motivans, Rantala & Smith, 2005.

[16] Buzawa & Hotaling, 2006.

[17] Feld, 2009; Chesney-Lind, 2002; Bishop & Frazier, 1992.

[18] Worrall, 2004.

[19] Alder & Worrall, 2004.

[20] Miller & White, 2003.

[21] Feld, 2009, pp. 254–255.

[22] Batchelor, Burman, & Brown, 2001.

[23] Miller & White, 2004; Sommers & Baskin, 1994.

[24] Batchelor, 2005.

[25] Sommers & Baskin, 1994.

[26] Batchelor, 2005, p. 368.

[27] Batchelor, 2005, p. 369.

[28] See, e.g., Thrasher, 1927; Miller, 1958; Cohen, 1955.

[29] Campbell, 1984; see also Campbell, 1990.

[30] Miller, W., 1980.

[31] Curry, Ball & Fox, 1994, p. 8; Bjerregaard, 2002, p. 80.

[32] Moore & Hagedorn, 1996, 2001.

[33] Moore, 1991.

[34] Esbensen, Deschenes & Winfree, 1999.

[35] Zahn et al., 2010.

[36] Curry et al., 1994, p. 8.

[37] Chesney-Lind, 1997.

[38] Esbensen et al., 1999.

[39] Esbensen et al., 1999.

[40] Moore & Hagedorn, 2001, p. 5.

[41] Miller & Decker, 2001.

[42] Joe & Chesney-Lind, 1995.

[43] Taylor, 1993.

[44] Campbell, 1990.

[45] Chesney-Lind, 1997, p. 39.

[46] Chesney-Lind, 1997.

[47] Quicker, 1983.

[48] Quicker, 1983, p. 14. Also see Portillos & Zatz, 1995; Campbell, 1984; and Miller, 2008.

[49] Quicker, 1983, p. 20.

[50] Sikes, 1997.

[51] Quicker, 1983, p. 22.

[52] Quicker, 1983; Harris, M., 1988.

[53] Sikes, 1997, p. 199.

[54] Campbell, 1984.

[55] Campbell, 1984, p. 7.

[56] Campbell, 1990.

[57] Lauderback, Hansen & Waldorf, 1992.

[58] Joe & Chesney-Lind, 1995.

[59] See, e.g., Sikes, 1997.

[60] For very similar findings, see Lauderback et al., 1992.

[61] Taylor, 1993.

[62] Chesney-Lind, 1997.

[63] Miller, S. 1998.

[64] Miller & White, 2004.

[65] Miller & Brunson, 2000.

[66] Miller & Brunson, 2000, p. 436.

[67] Miller, J., 2001.

[68] Miller & Decker, 2001.

[69] Miller & Decker, 2001, p. 118.

[70] Chesney-Lind & Shelden, 2014; Moore & Hagedorn, 2001.

[71] In addition to those previously cited, see Rosenbaum, 1987.

[72] Jensen & Eve, 1976, p. 445.

[73] Mears, Ploeger & Warr, 1998.

[74] Canter, 1982a; also see Anderson, Holmes, & Ostresh, 1999, for findings that did not support the idea that females were more strongly attached.

[75] McCarthy, Felmlee & Hagan, 2004.

[76] Miller, 2002.

[77] Heimer, 1996.

[78] Heimer & Decoster, 1999.

[79] Bottcher, 2001.

[80] Bottcher, 2001, p. 923.

[81] Manasse & Ganem, 2009.

[82] As examples of this, see Konopka, 1966, and Morris, R., 1964; for examples of criticisms of this early research, see, e.g., Naffine, 1987; Smart, 1976.

[83] See, e.g., Chesney-Lind, 1997.

[84] Holsinger & Holsinger, 2005, p. 216.

[85] Bloom, Owen, Rosenbaum & Deschenes, 2003, p. 126.

[86] Molnar, Browne, Cerda & Buka, 2005.

[87] McGee & Baker, 2003.

[88] Johansson & Kempf-Leonard, 2009; also see Belknap & Holsinger, 2006.

[89] Howell, 2003.

[90] Chesney-Lind, 1982, 1988, 1997; also see Chesney-Lind & Shelden, 2014.

[91] See, e.g., Bloom, Owen, Deschenes & Rosenbaum, 2002; Acoca, 1999; Wolf & Kempf-Leonard, 2009.

[92] Zahn et al., 2010.

[93] Mallicoat, 2007.

[94] Bond-Maupin, Maupin & Leisenring, 2002; Davidson, Pasco & Chesney-Lind, 2011, p. 323.

[95] Pollock, 1984, 1986.

[96] Tracy, Kempf-Leonard & Abramoske-James, 2009, p. 205.

[97] Sherman, 2012, p. 1620.

[98] Hockenberry, 2013, p. 11.

[99] Chesney-Lind, 2002.

[100] Davidson, Pasko, & Chesney-Lind, 2011.

[101] Zahn, Day, Mihalic & Tichavsky, 2009.

[102] Zahn, Day, Mihalic & Tichavsky, 2009.

[103] Davidson, Pasko & Chesney-Lind, 2011.

[104] Hubbard & Matthews, 2008.

[105] There are many sources for the R-N-R approach that are presented in Chapter 11, where this discussion is more fully developed.

[106] Vitopoulos, Peterson-Badali & Skilling, 2012.

[107] Dohrn, 2004.

[108] Zahn, Agnew, Fishbein, Miller, Winn, Dakoff, Kruttschnitt, Giordano, Gottfredson, Payne, Feld & Chesney-Lind, 2010.

[109] Gaarder & Belknap, 2002.

[110] Gaarder & Belknap, 2004, p. 66.

[111] Owen, Wells, Pollock, Muscat & Torres, 2008.

[112] Reported in Acoca, 1999, p. 6.

[113] Belknap, Holsinger & Dunn, 1997, p. 392.

[114] Owen, Wells, Pollock, Muscat & Torres, 2007.

Chapter Seven

[1] Rubick, 1975; Bershad, 1985.

[2] *Patricia A. v. City of New York,* 335 N.Y.S. 2d 33 (1972).

[3] Federal Bureau of Investigation, 2012.

[4] Cohen & Kyckelhahn (BJS), 2010, p. 20 (Appendix Table 3).

[5] Carson & Sabol (BJS), 2012, p. 25 (Appendix Table 5).

[6] Pollak, 1950.

[7] Daly, 1994a, 1994b.

[8] Daly & Bordt, 1995.

[9] Daly & Bordt, 1995.

[10] See, e.g., Moulds, 1980.

[11] Wilbanks, 1986.

[12] See Fenster, 1981; Gruhl et al., 1984.

[13] Curran, 1983; Nagel & Hagan, 1983; Hagan & O'Donnel, 1978; Farrington & Morris, 1983; Feyerhern, 1981a, 1991b; Hindelang, 1981b.

[14] Nagel & Hagan, 1983.

[15] See, e.g., Kempinen, 1983.

[16] See, e.g., Bridges & Beretta, 1994; Nagel & Johnson, 1994.

[17] Steffensmeier, Kramer, & Streifel, 1993, pp. 433–435.

[18] Daly & Bordt, 1995.

[19] Spohn & Spears, 1997.

[20] Spohn & Spears, 1997, p. 37.

[21] Jeffries, Fletcher & Newbold, 2003.

[22] Jeffries, Fletcher & Newbold, 2003, p. 340.

[23] Rodriquez, Curry & Lee, 2006.

[24] Rodriquez, Curry & Lee, 2006.

[25] Chesney-Lind, 1978.

[26] Kruttschnitt, 1982a, 1982b, 1984.

[27] Nagel, 1981, 1983.

[28] Farrington & Morris, 1983, p. 245.

[29] Eaton, 1986.

[30] Daly, 1987a, 1987b, 1989b, 1989c.

[31] Visher, 1983.

[32] Young, 1980; Crew, 1991.

[33] Brennan, 2006.

[34] Brown, 2006.

[35] Farnsworth & Teske, 1995.

[36] Farnsworth & Teske, 1995, p. 38.

[37] Farnsworth & Teske, 1995, p. 41.

[38] Rafter (Hahn), 1989.

[39] Welch, 1997.

[40] Flavin, 2009.

[41] Chesney-Lind, 1973; Smart, 1976; Campbell, 1981; Figueira-McDonough, 1985.

[42] Bishop & Frazier, 1992.

[43] Bishop & Frazier, 1992, p. 1185.

[44] Bishop & Frazier, 1996.

[45] Leiber, Brubaker & Fox, 2009.

[46] Sherman, 2012; Goodkind, 2009; MacDonald & Chesney-Lind, 2001.

[47] Daly & Bordt, 1995, p. 32.

[48] Raeder, 1993a.

[49] Daly & Tonry, 1997.

[50] Griffin & Wooldredge, 2006.

[51] Blackwell, Holleran & Finn, 2008.

[52] VanSlyke & Bales, 2013.

[53] Koons-Witt, 2002.

[54] Stolzenberg & D'Alessio, 1997.

[55] Doerner, 2012.

[56] Bureau of Justice Statistics (BJS), 1989.

[57] West, Sabol & Greenman, 2010, p. 22; Carson & Sabol, 2012, p. 2.

[58] Harrison & Beck 2002, p. 5.

[59] Carson & Sabol, 2012, p. 2.

[60] Mann, 1984a; Bishop & Frazier, 1996; Moore & Padavic, 2010.

[61] West, Sabol & Greenman, 2010, p. 28.

[62] Mauer, 2013, p. 3.

[63] Mauer, 2013, p. 6.

[64] Mauer, 2013.

[65] Crow & Kunselman, 2009.

[66] Beck, 1998.

[67] Glaze & Bonczar, 2009.

[68] Chesney-Lind, 1997, p. 146.

[69] Mauer, 2013, p. 6.

[70] See, e.g., Acoca & Austin 1996; Bloom, Chesney-Lind & Owen, 1994; Bloom, Immarigeon & Owen, 1995; DeCostanzo & Scholes, 1988; Morton, 1998; Owen & Bloom, 1995; Pollock-Byrne, 1992: Pollock, 1998, 1999a; Rafter (Hahn), 1992; Ryan & McCabe, 1997; Steffensmeier, Kramer & Streifel, 1993.

[71] Chesney-Lind & Pollock, 1995; Chesney-Lind, 1991, 1995, 1997, 1998; also see Steffensmeier, Kramer & Streifel, 1993.

[72] Chapman, 1980; Simon & Landis, 1991; Raeder, 1993b.

[73] Chesney-Lind, 1995, p. 112.

[74] Danner, 1998.

[75] Asseo; 1999; Mauer, Potler & Wolf, 2000.

[76] Mauer, Potler & Wolf 2000, p. 22.

[77] Raeder, 1993a, 1993b.

[78] Raeder, 1993b, p. 907.

[79] Although see Coontz, 1983; Morgan, 2000.

[80] Baker, 1999, p. 60.

[81] Snell, 2013, Table 6.

[82] Stohr, Lovrich & Mays, 1997.

[83] Harlow, 1999.

[84] Beck & Mumola, 1999.

[85] Minton, 2013, Table 2.

[86] Green et al., 2005.

[87] Lynch, DeHart, Belknap & Green, 2012, p. 21.

[88] Whaley, Moe, Eddy & Daugherty, 2007, p. 39.

[89] Veysey, 1998; Snell, 1992; Singer et al., 1995; Rice, Smith, & Janzen, 1999; James & Glaze, 2006.

[90] Veysey, 1998, p. 371; also see Veysey, DeCou & Prescott, 1998.

[91] Steadman, et al., 2009.

[92] Lynch, et al., 2012.

[93] Lynch, et al., 2012, p. iii.

[94] Snell, 1992.

[95] Teplin, Abrams & McClelland, 1996.

[96] Alemagno & Dickie, 2002.

[97] Lynch, DeHart, Belknap & Green, 2012.

[98] Green, Miranda, Daroowalla & Siddique, 2005.

[99] Green et al., 2005, p. 140.

[100] Green et al., 2005, p. 142.

[101] Green et al., 2005, p. 143.

[102] Green et al., 2005, p. 144.

[103] Veysey, 1998.

[104] Harlow, 1999.

[105] Koons, Burrow, Morash & Bynum, 1997, p. 513; Connolly, 1983.

[106] Farr, 2000, p. 5.

[107] Harlow, 1999.

[108] Singer, Bussey, Li-Yu & Lunghofer, 1995, p. 103; Rice, Smith & Janzen, 1999; Teplin, Abrams & McClelland, 1996; Veysey, 1998; Steadman & Veysey, 1997; Gray, Mays & Stohr, 1995.

[109] Singer et al., 1995.

[110] Moe & Ferraro, 2003.

[111] Moe & Ferraro, 2003, p. 71.

[112] Veysey, 1998.

[113] See Chapter 9 for a complete discussion of correctional staff sexual misconduct.

Chapter Eight

[1] Sykes, 1958; Clemmer, 1940; Johnson, 2002; Jacobs, 1977; Toch, 1975, 1977; Bowker, 1980; Crouch, 1980; Carroll, 1974; Davidson, 1974.

[2] Bowker, 1979, 1981; Fox, 1975, 1982.

[3] Lekkerkerker, 1931.

[4] Giallombardo, 1966; Ward & Kassebaum, 1965.

[5] Propper, 1976, 1981, 1982.

[6] Heffernan, 1972; Mitchell, 1975.

[7] Watterson, 1996; Burkhardt, 1973; Chandler, 1973; Flynn, 1963.

[8] Owen, 1998.

[9] Girshick, 1999.

[10] Rierden, 1997.

[11] Pollock, 1990, 1998; Harden & Hill, 1998; Faith, 1993; Carlen, 1983, 1985, 1988, 1990.

[12] Santana, 2000.

[13] Amnesty International, 1999; Human Rights Watch, 1996.

[14] Rierden, 1997; Lord, 1995.

[15] See Pollock, 2002a; Carbone-Lopez & Kruttschnitt, 2003.

[16] Dobash, Dobash & Gutteridge, 1986, p. 17.

[17] Dobash et al., 1986, p. 19.

[18] Fox, 1984, p. 16.

[19] Dobash et al., 1986, pp. 24–25; Fox, 1984, p. 16.

[20] Quoted in Dobash et al., 1986, p. 33.

[21] Feinman, 1983.

[22] Freedman, 1974, p. 78. For an example of this type of thinking, see Adams, 1914.

[23] Parisi, 1982.

[24] Freedman, 1974, 1981.

[25] Strickland, 1976, p. 40.

[26] Feinman, 1983, p. 15.

[27] Feinman, 1983; Freedman, 1981.

[28] Rafter (Hahn), 1985, p. 6.

[29] Quoted in Dobash et al., 1986, p. 43.

[30] Freedman, 1974, p. 79.

[31] Freedman, 1974.

[32] Freedman, 1981.

[33] Freedman, 1974, p. 80.

[34] Rafter (Hahn), 1985, p. 17; Freedman, 1974, p. 80.

[35] Freedman, 1981, p. 46; Feinman, 1983, p. 17.

[36] Morton, 1998, p. 5.

[37] Quoted in Rafter (Hahn), 1985, p. 26.

[38] Strickland, 1976.

[39] Freedman, 1974, p. 80.

[40] Lekkerkerker, 1931, p. 102.

[41] Rafter (Hahn), 1985, p. 33.

[42] Freedman, 1981, p. 70.

[43] Lekkerkerker, 1931, p. 99.

[44] Rafter (Hahn), 1985.

[45] Freedman, 1981.

[46] Freedman, 1981; Strickland, 1976.

[47] Freedman, 1981.

[48] Lekkerkerker, 1931.

[49] Freedman, 1974, p. 88.

[50] Freedman, 1981.

[51] Rafter (Hahn), 1985, p. 125; also see Freedman, 1981.

[52] Freedman, 1981.

[53] Strickland, 1976, p. 47.

[54] Lekkerkerker, 1931, p. 121.

[55] Lekkerkerker, 1931; also see Rafter (Hahn), 1985.

[56] Lekkerkerker, 1931.

[57] Freedman, 1981.

[58] Rafter (Hahn), 1985.

[59] Rafter (Hahn), 1985.

[60] Rafter (Hahn), 1985, p. 132.

[61] Rafter (Hahn), 1985.

[62] Freedman, 1981; Rafter (Hahn), 1985.

[63] Kellor, 1900a, 1900b.

[64] Weidensall, 1916.

[65] Spaulding, 1923.

[66] Fernald, Hayes & Dawley, 1920.

[67] Rafter (Hahn), 1979.

[68] Dugdale, 1895.

[69] Zedner, 1991.

[70] Glueck & Glueck, 1934.

[71] Rafter (Hahn), 1985.

[72] Freedman, 1981, p. 144.

[73] Chesney-Lind, 1998, p. 66.

[74] Giallombardo, 1966.

[75] Ward & Kassebaum, 1965.

[76] Strickland, 1976.

[77] Strickland, 1976, pp. 237–240.

[78] Burkhardt, 1973.

[79] Taylor, 1982.

[80] Zaitzow & Thomas, 2003.

[81] Glick & Neto, 1977.

[82] U.S. Government Accountability Office, 1979.

[83] But see Rasche, 1975; Baunach & Murton, 1973, and Chapman, 1980.

[84] Ryan, 1984.

[85] Crawford, 1988a, 1988b.

[86] American Correctional Association, 1990, 1993.

[87] Snell, 1992, 1994; Greenfield & Snell, 1999; Harlow, 1999.

[88] Snell, 1994.

[89] Owen & Bloom, 1995.

[90] Fletcher, Shaver & Moon, 1993.

[91] Pollock, Williams & Schroeder, 1996; also see Pollock, 1998.

[92] Morash & Bynum, 1995; Morash, Haar & Rucker, 1994; Wellisch, Prendergast & Anglin, 1994, 1996; Wellisch, Anglin & Prendergast, 1993.

[93] Greenfield & Snell, 1999.

[94] See, e.g., Chesney-Lind & Rodriquez, 1983; Owen & Bloom, 1995; Pollock, et al, 1996; Fletcher et al., 1993; Richie, 1996; Chesney-Lind, 1997; Bloom, Owen & Covington, 2003.

[95] Crawford, 1988a, 1988b.

[96] Bonczar, 2011.

[97] Greenfield & Snell, 1999.

[98] West, Sabol & Greenman, 2010, Appendix Table 17a.

[99] See, e.g., McDonald & Grossman, 1981.

[100] Goetting & Howsen, 1983, p. 36.

[101] Snell, 1994.

[102] Greenfield & Snell, 1999: also see Jones & Sims, 1997.

[103] Flowers, 1987, p. 150.

[104] Greenfield & Snell, 1999.

[105] Sabol & Couture, 2008, p. 8.

[106] Guerino, Harrison, & Sabol, 2011, Appendix Table 14.

[107] Snell, 1994; also see Velimesis, 1981.

[108] Owen, 1998; Rierden, 1997; Pollock, 1998.

[109] Bedell, 1997, p. 29.

[110] Crawford, 1988a, 1988b; Girshick, 1999; Owen & Bloom, 1995; Fletcher et al., 1993; Pollock et al., 1996.

[111] Pollock et al., 1996.

[112] See, e.g., Owen, 1998; Rosenbaum 1989, 1993; Gilfus, 1988, 1992; Sargent, Marcus-Mendoza & Ho Yu, 1993; Owen & Bloom, 1995; Pollock, 1998; Crawford, 1988a; Harlow, 1999; Fletcher et al., 1993; Blount, Kuhns & Silverman, 1993.

[113] Oregon Department of Corrections, 1992.

[114] Harlow, 1999.

[115] McClellan, Farabee & Crouch, 1997.

[116] MacDonald, 2013.

[117] Widom, 1989a, 1989b, 1996 (note mixed findings); Pollock, Mullings & Crouch, 2006; Snell, 1994; Holsinger & Holsinger, 2005.

[118] Islam-Zwart & Vik, 2004

[119] Messman-Moore & Long, 1994, 2000.

[120] Maeve, 2000.

[121] Owen, Wells, Pollock, Muscat & Torres, 2008, p. 15.

[122] Kuo et al., 2013.

[123] Johnson & Lynch, 2013.

[124] Mullings, Marquart & Brewer, 2000.

[125] See previous chapter, especially Mullings, Marquart & Brewer, 2000; Mullings, Marquart & Hartley, 2003.

[126] Bedell, 1997, p. 28.

[127] Welle & Falkin, 2000; Raeder, 1993a.

[128] Owen et al., 2008; Bloom, Owen & Covington, 2003; Tjaden & Thoennes, 2006; Carlson, 2005; Batchelor, 2005.

[129] Breitenbecher, 2001; Messman-Moore & Long, 2000; Tjaden & Thoennes, 2006, p. 6; Mullings, Marquart & Brewer, 2000; Mullings, Marquart & Hartley, 2003.

[130] Messman-Moore & Long, 2000, p. 498.

[131] Bloom, Chesney-Lind & Owen, 1994, p. 5.

[132] Bloom et al., 1994, p. 5.

[133] Sabol & Couture, 2008.

[134] Blount et al., 1991.

[135] Greenfield & Snell, 1999, p. 8.

[136] Owen & Bloom, 1995.

[137] Sabol & Couture, 2008.

[138] Pollock et al., 1996; Fletcher et al., 1993; Owen & Bloom, 1995; Batchelor, 2005.

[139] Owen, 1998, p. 46.

[140] Anglin & Hser, 1987.

[141] Sommers & Baskin, 1996; Mullings, Pollock & Crouch, 2002.

[142] Covington, 1985; Mullings, Pollock & Crouch, 2002; Pollock, Mullings & Crouch, 2006.

[143] Wolff, Blitz, Shi, Siegel & Bachman, 2007, p. 592.

[144] McClellan, Farrabee & Crouch, 1997; Prendergast, Wellisch & Falkin 1997, p. 320; also see Prendergast, Wellisch & Falkin, 1995; Prendergast, Wellisch & Anglin, 1994.

[145] Mullings, Pollock & Crouch, 2002.

[146] Lord, 1995; Maeve, 2000; Battle et al., 2003.

[147] Tittle, 1973; Hannum, Borgen, & Anderson, 1978.

[148] Reported in Pollock, 1981, p. 76.

[149] Widom, 1979.

[150] Culbertson & Fortune, 1986, pp. 44–48.

[151] Fletcher et al., 1993; Culbertson & Fortune, 1986.

[152] Adelberg & Currie, 1993.

[153] Quote from Pollock, Williams, & Schroeder, 1996.

[154] See Cochrane, 1971.

[155] Widom, 1979.

[156] Ross & Lawrence, 1998; Fogel, 1991; Epp, 1996; Faiver & Rieger, 1998.

[157] Ross & Lawrence, 1998.

[158] Ross & Lawrence, 1998.

[159] Morris & Wilkinson, 1995; Brewer, Marquart, Mullings & Crouch, 1998.

[160] Mann, 1984b; Schupak, 1986.

[161] Mann, 1984b; Amnesty International, 1999; Owen et al., 2008.

[162] Barry, 1989, 1991, 1996.

[163] Acoca, 1998.

[164] Acoca, 1998.

[165] Acoca, 1998.

[166] Proctor, 2009.

[167] Owen et al., 2008.

[168] Williams & Rikard, 2004.

[169] Leigey & Hodge, 2012.

[170] Williams & Rikard, 2004.

[171] Krabill & Aday, 2005, p. 46.

[172] Acoca, 1998; also see Teplin, Abrams & McClelland, 1996; Jordan, Schlenger, Fairbank & Caddell, 1996; Powell, 1999; James & Glaze, 2006; Houser, Belanko & Brennan, 2012.

[173] Panton, 1974, p. 333.

[174] Ross & Lawrence, 1998; Girshick, 1999.

[175] Velimesis, 1981.

[176] Maeve, 2000.

[177] Cookson, 1977.

[178] Fox, 1975, 1982.

[179] Quoted in Pollock, 1981.

[180] Fox, 1975, p. 194.

[181] Scott, Hannum & Gilchrist, 1982.

[182] Dye, M. 2011.

[183] Fleisher et al., 1997; Carbone-Lopez & Kruttschnitt, 2003.

[184] Rasche, 2000.

[185] Cranford & Williams, 1998.

[186] Catalino, 1972, p. 126.

[187] Pollock, 1986.

[188] Reported in Pollock, 1981, but also see more current descriptions in Kerman, 2010.

[189] Pollock, 1986; Owen, 1998.

[190] *Dothard v. Rawlinson,* 433 U.S. 321 (1977).

[191] McClellan, 1994.

[192] Bosworth, 2007.

[193] Casey-Acevedo & Bakken, 2001; also see Gover, Perez & Jennings, 2008.

[194] Faily & Roundtree, 1979; Failey, Roundtree & Miller, 1980; However, Mandraraka-Sheppard, 1986, did not find a race effect.

[195] Crawford, 1988b.

[196] Mann, 1984b, p. 210; Baunach, 1977.

[197] Pollock, 2012.

[198] Gabel, Engel, Josephson & Kates, 1982.

[199] Aylward & Thomas, 1984.

[200] Fox, 1984.

[201] Wheeler et al., 1989; Smith, 1995.

[202] *Barefield v. Leach,* No. 10282 (D. N.M., 1974); *Grosso v. Lally,* No. 4-74-447 (D. Md. 1977)

[203] Collins & Collins, 1996.

[204] *Estelle v. Gamble,* 429 U.S. 97 (1976).

[205] *Morales v. Turman,* 383 F. Supp. 53 (E.D. Tex. 1974)

[206] Pollock, 2002.

[207] Leonard, 1983; Pollock, 2002.

[208] *Nelson v. Correctional Medical Services,* 583 F.3d 522 (8th Cir. 2009).

[209] *Farmer v. Brennan,* 114 S.Ct. 1970 (1994).

[210] *Park versus Thomson,* 356 F. Supp. 783 (D. Hawaii 1976).

[211] Fabian, 1980; *Pitts v. Meese,* 684 F. Supp. 303 (D.D.C. 1987).

[212] Collins & Collins, 1996; Pollock, 2013.

[213] See, e.g., *Women Prisoners of the District of Columbia Dept. of Corrections v. District of Columbia,* 877 F. Supp. 634 (D.D.C., 1994), reversed in part, 93 F.3d 910 (D.C. Cir., 1996).

Chapter Nine

[1] DeGroot, 1998; Owen, 1998; Girshick, 1999.

[2] Owen 1998, p. 67.

[3] Kerman, 2010; Owen, 1998, p. 109.

[4] Burke & Adams, 1991; Farr, 2000; Shaffer, Pettigrew, Bout & Edwards, 1983, discuss the application of the Megargee classification system (using MMPI scores) using a female sample with some success.

[5] Crawford, 1988b, p. 15.

[6] Wellisch, Prendergast & Aglin, 1996; also see Morash & Bynum, 1995; Morash, Bynum & Koons, 1998.

[7] Burkhardt, 1973.

[8] Clark, 1995.

[9] Greer, 2000; Coll, Miller, Field & Matthew, 1997; Owen, Wells, Pollock, Muscat & Torres, 2008; McDonald, 2008.

[10] Owen 1998, p. 116.

[11] Wolff, Shi & Siegel, 2009, p. 183.

[12] Owen et al., 2008.

[13] Harris, 1988.

[14] Mann, 1984b; Pollock, 2002.

[15] Goetting & Howsen, 1983.

[16] *New York Times*, 2014.

[17] Mann, 1984b, p. 209; McClellan, 1994.

[18] Strickland, 1976, p. 114.

[19] Lindquist, 1980, p. 307; Selksky, 1980; McKerracher, Street, & Segal, 1966; Heidensohn, 1985, p. 74; Mandraraka-Sheppard, 1986.

[20] Goetting and Howsen, 1983, p. 37, provide the only contrary finding. In their study, nearly 41 percent of women had been guilty of breaking prison rules during incarceration, but 47.74 percent of men had; men also obtained more serious punishments, such as solitary confinement, loss of good time, or transfer.

[21] McClellan, 1994.

[22] Correctional official, reported in Pollock, 1981.

[23] Schrag, 1944, 1966; Sykes, 1958; Sykes & Messinger, 1960; Hayner, 1961, Irwin & Cressey, 1962; Carroll, 1974; Davidson, 1974.

[24] For example, Giallombardo, 1966; Ward & Kassebaum, 1965; Heffernan, 1972; Hartnagel & Gillan, 1980; Moyer, 1984; Mahan, 1984; Wilson, 1980.

[25] Sykes, 1958.

[26] Ward & Kassebaum, 1965, p. 161.

[27] Ward & Kassebaum, 1965, p. 162

[28] Harris, 1993.

[29] Irwin & Cressey, 1962.

[30] See Pollock, 2012, for discussion.

[31] Hartnagel & Gillan, 1980; Tittle, 1969; Kruttschnitt, 1981.

[32] Sykes, 1958.

[33] Tittle, 1969; Kruttschnitt, 1981; Owen, 1998.

[34] Lord, 1995; Cranford & Williams, 1998.

[35] See, for instance, Ward and Kassebaum, 1965, who compared male and female prisoners' allegiance to the "code" by agreement with hypotheticals developed based on what was known about the male prisoner code.

[36] Sykes, 1958. An even earlier typology was that of Hayner and Ash, 1939, who described *real men, racketeers, smoothies, politicians,* and *dings*.

[37] Schrag, 1966.

[38] Simmons, 1975.

[39] Giallombardo, 1966, p. 279.

[40] Giallombardo, 1966, p. 105–122.

[41] Giallombardo, 1966, p. 130.

[42] Heffernan, 1972.

[43] Mahan, 1984.

[44] Owen, 1998.

[45] Giallombardo, 1966; Owen, 1998.

[46] Carbone-Lopez & Kruttschnitt, 2003; Bosworth, 1999; Owen, 1998.

[47] Mahan, 1984; Rierden, 1997; Kerman, 2010.

[48] Kruttschnitt, 1983.

[49] Carbone-Lopez & Kruttschnitt, 2003, p. 70.

[50] Foster, 1975, Giallombardo, 1966; Culbertson & Fortune, 1986; Toigo, 1962, Rierden, 1997.

[51] Owen, 1998, p. 134.

[52] An inmate quoted by Girshick, 1999, p. 91.

[53] Hart, 1995.

[54] Fox, 1984; Greer, 2000.

[55] Trammell, 2009, p. 274.

[56] Ward & Kassebaum, 1965.

[57] Owen, 1998; Pollock, 1998.

[58] Owen 1998, pp. 146–149.

[59] A CO quoted by Pollock, 1981.

[60] An inmate quoted by Girshick, 1999, p. 86.

[61] Otis, 1913. Also see Selling, 1931.

[62] Kosofsky & Ellis, 1958; Halleck & Herski, 1962.

[63] Ward & Kassebaum, 1965, p. 167.

[64] Mitchell, 1975.

[65] Propper, 1976, 1982.

[66] Giallombardo, 1966; Rierden, 1997; Owen, 1998; Toigo, 1962.

[67] Keys, 2002.

[68] An inmate quoted in Pollock, 1981.

[69] Nelson, 1974.

[70] Owen et al., 2008; Alarid, 2000.

[71] Owen & Bloom, 1995; Girshick, 1999; Owen et al., 2008.

[72] See, for instance, Greer, 2000.

[73] Edgar & Martin, 2003; also see Edgar, O'Donnell & Martin, 2003.

[74] Faith, 1993; Owen, 1998; Rierden, 1997; Girshick, 1999; Owen et al., 2008.

[75] Wolff, Shi & Siegel, 2009; Wolff, Blitz, Shi, Siegel & Bachman, 2007.

[76] Wolff, et al., 2009.

[77] Wolff et al., 2007.

[78] Owen et al., 2008.

[79] Owen et al., 2008.

[80] Moe & Ferraro, 2003.

[81] Butler, 2008.

[82] Jones, 2004.

[83] Trammell, 2009, 2006.

[84] Einat & Chen, 2012; Owen et al., 2008.

[85] Trammell, 2009, pp. 276–277; also see Trammell, 2006.

[86] Owen et al., 2008.

[87] Owen et al., 2008, p. 15.

[88] Owen et al., 2008; also see, Lynch, Fritch & Heath, 2012.

[89] An inmate, quoted in Owen et al., 2008.

[90] Greer, 2000.

[91] Owen et al., 2008.

[92] Batchelor, Burman & Brown, 2001.

[93] Daly, 1994a.

[94] Struckman-Johnson & Struckman-Johnson, 2002, 2006; also see Struckman-Johnson, Struckman-Johnson, Rucker, Bumby & Donaldson, 1996.

[95] Wolff, Blitz, Shi, Bachman & Siegel, 2006, pp. 840–842; also see Wolff, Shi & Bachman, 2008.

[96] Beck, Berzofsky, Caspar & Krebs, 2013, p. 17, Table 7.

[97] Owen et al., 2008.

[98] Fleisher & Kreinert, 2006.

[99] Ferraro & Moe, 2006, p. 84.

[100] Fox, 1984, p. 23.

[101] Girshick, 1999, p. 94.

[102] A CO, quoted in Pollock, 1981.

[103] Owen, 1998, p. 73.

[104] Lekkerkerker, 1931, pp. 265–273.

[105] Peterson, 1982; Zupan, 1986, 1992; Zimmer, 1986; also see Wright & Saylor, 1991; Lawrence & Mahan, 1998.

[106] Crawford, 1988b, p. 13; Nesbitt, 1992.

[107] Owen, 1998, p. 165; Zupan, 1992, p. 200.

[108] Zupan, 1992, p. 306.

[109] *Gunther v. Iowa State Men's Reformatory*, 612 F.2d 1079 (8th Cir. 1980); *Harden v. Dayton Human Rehabilitation Center*, 520 F. Supp. 769 (1981); *Grummet v. Rushen*, 779 F.2d 491 (9th Cir., 1985)

[110] *Forts v. Ward*, 434 F. Supp. 946 (S.D.N.Y.), rev'd and remanded, 566 F.2d 849 (2d Cir. 1977), 471 F. Supp. 1095 (S.D.N.Y. 1979), aff'd in part and rev'd in part, 621 F.2d 1210 (2d Cir. 1980); *Johnson v. Phelan*, 69 F.3d 144 (7th Cir., 1995), cert. denied, *Johnson v. Sheahan* 117 S.Ct. 506 (1996).

[111] *Torres v. Wisconsin* Dept of Corrections, 838 F.2d 944 (7th Cir., 1988), overruled in part 859 F.2d 1523 (1988); *Jordan v. Gardner*, 986 F.2d. 1521 (9th Cir., 1993) (*en banc*) Although for contrary holdings, see *Lee v. Downs*, 641 F.2d 1117 (1981).

[112] Maeve, 2000.

[113] Heney & Kristiansen, 1998.

[114] Zupan, 1992.

[115] Flesher, 2007.

[116] Saliba, 2013.

[117] Saliba, 2013.

[118] Owen, 1998; Zupan, 1992.

[119] An inmate, quoted in Zupan, 1992, p. 304.

[120] Hansen, 1983; Mann, 1984b; Baro, 1997; Cook, 1993; Curriden, 1993; Human Rights Watch, 1996; Amnesty International, 1999; Wojda & Rowe, 1997; Chesney-Lind, 1997; Henriques & Gilbert, 2000; Calhoun & Coleman, 2002.

[121] Reported in Amnesty International, 1999, p. 38.

[122] Henriques & Gilbert, 2000, p. 258.

[123] *Neal v. Michigan Department of Corrections*, 2009 WL 187813 (Mich. App. Jan 27, 2009).

[124] Culley, 2012.

[125] Kubiak, Hanna & Balton, 2005, p. 165.

[126] Kubiak et al., 2005.

[127] Struckman-Johnson & Struckman-Johnson, 2006.

[128] Wolff, Shi & Siegel, 2009.

[129] Owen et al., 2008.

[130] Calhoun & Coleman, 2002, p. 114.

[131] Blackburn, 2006.

[132] Trammell, 2009, p. 279.

Chapter Ten

[1] Van Voorhis, 2004.

[2] Smith, Cullen & Latessa, 2009.

[3] Smith et al., 2009.

[4] Byrne & Taxman, 2005.

[5] Reisig, Holtfreter & Morash, 2006.

[6] Van Voorhis, 2005; Blanchette, 2002.

[7] Farr, 2000; Hardyman & Van Voorhis, 2004.

[8] Van Voorhis & Presser, 2001.

[9] Coulson et al., 1996; Lowenkamp, Holsinger & Latessa, 2001; Bonta, Pang & Wallace-Capretta, 1995.

[10] McShane, Williams & Dolney, 2002.

[11] Blanchette, 2005.

[12] Holtfreter, Reisig & Morash, 2004.

[13] Reisig, Holtfreter & Morash, 2006.

[14] Daly, 1992.

[15] Please refer to Chapter 5 for complete descriptions.

[16] Reisig, Holtfreter & Morash, 2006.

[17] Taxman & Cropsey, 2007.

[18] Dowden & Andrews, 1999.

[19] Taxman & Cropsey, 2007.

[20] Smith, Cullen & Latessa, 2009.

[21] Taylor & Blanchette, 2009.

[22] Holtfreter & Cupp, 2007.

[23] Morash, 2009.

[24] Lowenkamp, Latessa & Holsinger, 2006.

[25] Lowenkamp et al., 2006, p. 570.

[26] See, e.g., Van Voorhis, Wright, Salisbury & Bauman, 2009.

[27] Van Voorhis et al., 2009.

[28] Van Voorhis et al., 2009.

[29] Van Voorhis et al., 2009; also see Salisbury, Van Voorhis & Spiropoulos, 2008.

[30] See Wright, Salisbury & Van Voorhis, 2007.

[31] Van Voorhis et al., 2009.

[32] Wright, Salisbury & Van Voorhis, 2007.

[33] Wright et al., 2007.

[34] Wright et al., 2007.

[35] Salisbury, Van Voorhis & Spiropoulos, 2008.

[36] Wright, Van Voorhis, Salisbury & Bauman, 2012.

[37] Cunningham & Sorensen, 2007.

[38] Cunningham & Sorensen, 2007.

[39] Cunningham & Sorensen, 2007, p. 261.

[40] Wright, 1988; Warren, Hurt, Booker-Loper & Chauhan, 2004.

[41] Warren et al., 2004; also see Bradley & Davino, 2002.

[42] Steiner & Wooldredge, 2009.

[43] See, e.g., Moos, 1968.

[44] See, e.g., Camp & Gaes, 2005; Gaes & Camp, 2009.

[45] Gover, Perez & Jennings, 2008.

[46] Van Voorhis et al., 2009.

[47] Chapman, 1980; Crawford, 1988b, p. 26; Greenfield & Snell, 1999, p. 7.

[48] Chapman, 1980, p. 103; Ryan, 1984.

[49] Ryan, 1984.

[50] Harlow, 2003.

[51] Blitz, 2006; Winterfield, Coggeshall, Burke-Storer, Correa & Tidd, 2009.

[52] Winterfield et al., 2009.

[53] Moyer, 1984.

[54] Pollock, 1998.

[55] Weisheit, 1985.

[56] Ross & Fabiano, 1986, p. 18.

[57] Negy, Woods & Carlson, 1997; Zang, Morash, Paul & Cherry, 1998.

[58] Zang et al., 1998.

[59] Ryan, 1984, p. 29; also see Ryan & Grassano, 1992.

[60] Chesney-Lind & Pollock, 1995; Camp & Sandhu, 1995; Morash & Rucker, 1998; Lutze & Murphy, 1999; Marcus-Mendosa, Klein-Saffon & Lutze, 1998.

[61] DeCostanzo & Valente, 1984; Pollock, 1990, Austin, Bloom & Donahue, 1992; Colley & Camp, 1992; Carp & Schade, 1992; Lord, 1995; Wallace, 1995; Pollock, 1998; Morton, 1998; Zaplin, 1998a, pp. 136–138; also see Zaplin, 1998b; Bloom, 2000.

[62] Zaplin, 1998b; Pollock, 1998; Blanchette & Brown, 2006.

[63] From interviews conducted in 1995 by author.

[64] Harris, 1987; West, 1988; Hannah-Moffat, 1995; Lahey, 1985; Howe, 1990; Daly & Chesney-Lind, 1988, Daly, 1989a.

[65] Gilligan, 1982.

[66] Noddings, 1989.

[67] Daly, 1989a; Heidensohn, 1986; Wheeler, Trammell, Thomas & Findlay, 1989; Carlen, 1989, 1990.

[68] Heidensohn, 1986.

[69] Multiple sources for the pathways approach can be found in Chapter 5 and are not replicated here.

[70] Office of Juvenile Justice and Delinquency Prevention (OJJDP), 1998.

[71] Bloom, Owen & Covington, 2003.

[72] Covington, 1998b.

[73] Bloom, 2000.

[74] Hubbard & Matthews, 2008.

[75] See Covington, 2008.

[76] Vitopoulos, Peterson-Badali & Skilling, 2012.

[77] Ward, Yates & Willis, 2012.

[78] The model follows Aristotle's ethics of virtue in many ways.

[79] Pollack, 2007.

[80] Pollack, 2007.

[81] Hannah-Moffat, 2004.

[82] National Center on Addiction and Substance Abuse at Columbia University (CASA), 2010, p. 30.

[83] Blount, Danner, Vega & Silverman, 1991; Yang, 1990; Biron, Brochu & Desjardins, 1995; Prendergast, Wellisch & Falkin, 1995; Girshick, 1999; CASA, 2010.

[84] Prendergast, Wellisch & Falkin 1997, p. 319.

[85] American Civil Liberties Union (ACLU), n.d., p. 30.

[86] ACLU, n.d., p. 20.

[87] An inmate, quoted in Pollock, 1998, p. 81.

[88] ACLU, n.d.

[89] Wellisch, Prendergast & Aglin, 1996, pp. 29–32. Also see Wellisch, 1994; Wellisch, Anglin & Prendergast, 1993; Prendergast, Wellisch & Anglin, 1994; and Prendergast, Wellisch & Falkin, 1995, 1997.

[90] Carbone-Lopez & Miller, 2012.

[91] Lord, 1995, p. 262.

[92] Hunt, Laidler & Evans, 2002, p. 8.

[93] ACLU, n.d.; Hunt et al., 2002.

[94] Rosenbaum, 1981, pp. 31, 51.

[95] Rosenbaum, 1981, p. 132.

[96] Hunt et al., 2002.

[97] Rosenbaum, 1981; also see Inciardi, 1993, 1996; Hunt et al., 2002; ACLU, n.d.

[98] Adler, 1993.

[99] Inciardi & Pottieger, 1986. This phenomenon was also described by Fullilove, Lown & Fullilove, 1992; Chesney-Lind, 1997; Maher & Curtis, 1992; and Maher & Daly, 1996.

[100] Quote from Taylor, 1993, p. 194.

[101] Pelissier & Jones, 2005; but see CASA, 2010.

[102] CASA, p. 41.

[103] Covington, 1998b.

[104] CASA, p. 47.

[105] Pelissier & Jones, 2005, p. 345.

[106] From interviews in 1995 by author.

[107] Farrell, 2000; Mahan & Prestwood, 1993; Welle, Falking & Jainchill, 1998.

[108] Inciardi, 1996.

[109] Reed, 1987.

[110] Wellisch, Prendergast & Aglin, 1996.

[111] The authors collected information on 165 community-based, 16 jail-based, and 53 prison-based programs. In this report only community-based programs were reported. There were "drug free outpatient" (77), residential (55), and day-treatment (24) programs. The duration was about 30 weeks but ranged from 1 to 105 weeks.

[112] Ryan, 1984.

[113] ACLU, n.d., p. 13.

[114] From interviews conducted in 1995 by author.

[115] Reed, 1987.

[116] Reed, 1987, p. 154.

[117] Messina, Calhoun & Warda, 2012; Messina, Grella, Cartier & Torres, 2010.

[118] Grella, Lovinger & Warda, 2013.

[119] Mullings, Marquart & Brewer, 2000.

[120] Root, 1989, p. 542.

[121] Root, 1989, p. 546.

[122] Root, 1989.

[123] Root, 1989, p. 546.

[124] Valentine & Smith, 2001.

[125] Anumba, Dematteo & Heilbrun, 2012.

[126] Messina et al., 2010; Sacks, McKendrick & Hamilton, 2012.

[127] ACLU, n.d., p. 49.

[128] Krupat, Gaynes, & Lincroft, 2011, p. 14.

[129] Note that this is not a complete list of authors: Catan, 1992; Bloom & Steinhart, 1993; Dressel & Barnhill, 1994; Gabel & Johnston, 1995; Pollock, 1999b; Baunach, 1985; Fogel, 1995; Greenfield & Minor-Harper, 1991; Johnston, 1995b, 1997; Enos, 2001.

[130] Zalba, 1964; Baunach, 1985; Crawford, 1988a; Pollock, 2002.

[131] CASA, 2010, p. 34.

[132] Koban, 1983; Greenfield & Minor-Harper, 1991; Baunach, 1985; Bloom & Steinhart, 1993; Pollock, 1999b, 2002b.

[133] Bloom & Steinhart, 1993; Immarigeon, 1994; Baunach, 1985.

[134] Koban, 1983, p. 174.

[135] Adoption and Safe Families Act of 1997, PL 105-89 (ASFA).

[136] Beckerman, 1989, 1994.

[137] Berry & Eigenberg, 2003; Henriques, 1996.

[138] Enos, 2001.

[139] Baunach, 1985.

[140] McCarthy, 1980.

[141] Henriques, 1982.

[142] Enos, 2001.

[143] Pollock, 2002; although more recent reports indicate only 4 percent are pregnant, Krupat et al., 2011, p. 4.

[144] Dallaire, 2007; as reported in CASA, 2010, p. 34.

[145] Johnston, 1995a, 1995b, 1997a, 1997b.

[146] Muse, 1994; Mustin, 1995; Mumola, 2000.

[147] Baunach, 1985; McGowan & Blumenthal, 1978; Stanton, 1980.

[148] Stanton, 1980; Krupat et al., 2011.

[149] Murray & Farrington, 2008.

[150] See, Nickel, Garland & Kane, 2009; Allard & Greene, n.d.; Women's National Law Center, 2010; Women's Prison Association, 2009.

[151] Women's National Law Center, 2010.

[152] See Fritsch & Burkhead, 1982; Hungerford, 1983; Baunach, 1985; McGowan & Blumenthal, 1978; Sharp & Marcos-Mendoza, 2001.

[153] See Johnston, 1995a, Kempfner, 1995.

[154] Pollock, 1999b, 2002b.

[155] There are more states today that have nurseries, as discussed below.

[156] Pollock, 1999b, 2002b.

[157] Clement, 1993; Boudouris, 1985, 1996.

[158] Johnston, 1997a.

[159] Brown & Bloom, 2009, p. 333.

[160] Richie, 2001.

[161] Showers, 1993.

[162] Owen, 1998; Pollock, 1998; Baunach, 1985; Bloom, 2000.

[163] Kolman, 1983.

[164] Weisheit, 1985; Baunach, 1985; Alley, 1997; Pollock, 1999b.

[165] Haley, 1977.

[166] Weis, 1997.

[167] Driscoll, 1985; Datesman & Cales, 1983; Block & Potthast, 1997, Moses, 1995.

[168] Hairston, 1997; Hairston & Locket, 1985; Hairston, 1991.

[169] Chapman, 1980.

[170] Rierden, 1997; Heffernan, 1992; Blinn, 1997.

[171] Women's Prison Association, 2009.

[172] Byrne, 2009.

[173] Byrne, Goshin & Joestl, 2010; Borelli, Goshin, Joestl, Clark & Byrne, 2010.

[174] Byrne, Goshin & Joestl, 2010.

[175] Byrne, Goshin & Blanchard-Lewis, 2012.

[176] Sleed, Baradon & Fonagy, 2013.

[177] From interviews conducted in 1995 by author.

[178] Women's Prison Association, 2009, p. 18; Goshin & Byrne, 2009.

[179] Women's Prison Association, 2009.

[180] Pollock, 1999b.

[181] Buccio-Notaro, 1998.

[182] Cassidy et al., 2010.

[183] Interview with Susan Leavell, program administrator, August, 2013.

[184] See Thompson, 2013.

[185] Dwyer, 2014.

Chapter Eleven

[1] Maruschak & Parks, 2012.

[2] Seng & Lurigio, 2005.

[3] Seng & Lurigio, 2005.

[4] Dodge & Pogrebin, 2001, p. 50.

[5] Bloom, 2004.

[6] Ansay & Benvenesie, 1999; Maidment, 2002.

[7] Flowers, 2010.

[8] Lipsitz, 2012.

[9] Flowers, 2010.

[10] Richie, 2001.

[11] Flowers, 2010.

[12] Richie, 2001; Schram, Koons-Witt, Williams & McShane, 2006.

[13] Opsal, 2009; O'Brien, 2001. Also see Dodge & Pogrebin, 2001; Richie 2001.

[14] Hall, Golder, Conley & Sawnings, 2012, p. unknown (taken from advance copy).

[15] Lipsitz, 2012; Henriques & Manatu-Rupert, 2001.

[16] Lipsitz, 2012.

[17] Lipsitz, 2012.

[18] Richie, 2001.

[19] Brown & Bloom, 2009, p. 323.

[20] Brown & Bloom, 2009.

[21] Brown & Bloom, 2009, p. 130.

[22] Brown & Bloom, 2009.

[23] Brown & Bloom, 2009.

[24] Richie, 2001.

[25] Richie, 2001.

[26] Ferraro & Moe, 2006, p. 82.

[27] Hall et al., 2012, p. unknown (taken from advance copy).

[28] Richie, 2001.

[29] A female parolee, quoted in Richie, 2001, p. 372.

[30] A female parolee, quoted in Richie, 2001, p. 372.

[31] Richie, 2001.

[32] Opsal, 2009; O'Brien, 2001.

[33] Phua, 2010.

[34] Richie, 2001.

[35] O'Brien, 2006.

[36] Freudenberg, Daniels, Crum, Perkins & Richie, 2005.

[37] Freudenberg et al., 2005.

[38] Brennan, 2007.

[39] Leverentz, 2006.

[40] Leverentz, 2006.

[41] Langan & Levin, 2002.

[42] Maruschak & Parks, 2012, p. 4.

[43] Deschenes, Owen & Crow, 2007.

[44] Danner, Blount, Silverman & Vega, 1995.

[45] Morris & Wilkinson, 1995.

[46] O'Brien, 2001.

[47] Uggen & Kruttschnitt, 1992.

[48] Olson, Lurigio, & Alderden, 2003.

[49] Giordano, Cernkovich, & Rudolph, 2002.

[50] Pearl, 1998.

[51] See Rettinger & Andrews, 2010.

[52] Holtfreter, Reisig & Morash, 2004.

[53] Reisig, Holtfreter & Morash, 2006.

[54] Salisbury & Van Voorhis, 2009.

[55] Gendreau, 1996, pp. 120–125.

[56] Zaitzow, & Thomas, 1993.

[57] Koons, et al., 1997, pp. 523–525.

[58] Morash & Bynum, 1995.

[59] Farrell 2000, p. 40.

[60] Pollock, Williams & Schroeder, 1995; Owen, 1998; Kendall, 1993.

[61] Interviews by author in 1995.

Glossary

Androcentrism—a paradigm that views the world from a masculine point of view (i.e., what men do is "normal" and, if women are different, they are not "normal").

Battered woman syndrome—social science explanation for why battered women stay with their abusers, based on the learned helplessness theory.

Biosociology—study of evolutionary reasons for human behavior.

Bootstrapping—a metaphor referring to advancing or accomplishing something. In the context of describing female juveniles' experience with the justice system, it refers to starting with a status offense and, through a contempt finding, moving the status offense into something that can result in detainment.

Brain lateralization—the tendency to have more neural pathways in one side of the brain than in the other.

Branks—an iron cage placed over the head, often incorporating a spike or pointed wheel that was inserted into the offender's mouth in order to "pin down the tongue and silence the noisiest brawler."

Bridewells—historical institutions that housed minor offenders and vagrants.

Cacogenic studies—family studies based on eugenics; studies assuming degenerative traits in offspring of defective parents.

Clearance rates—the percentage of crimes "cleared" by arrest.

Cohort—a selected group of individuals. Cohort studies follow the same group over a period of time.

Correlates—independent variables (i.e., poverty, drug use, attachment to parents, and so on) presumed to cause or at least be statistically associated with the dependent variable (crime).

Cultural feminism—a type of feminism positing that there are socialized and biological differences between men and women based on different biosocial responsibilities (e.g., child care).

Ecological fallacy—a misstatement that occurs when one infers something about an individual based on some factor that is associated with a group in which the individual is a member.

Eugenics—the science of improving the quality of the human race through genetics (reducing procreation by "defective" individuals).

Filicide—the killing of one's child.

Gaols—an early term for jails.

Gender—one's identity as male or female, developed as part of socialization and socially constructed as opposed to a biological reality.

Gender gap—the disproportional ratio of men arrested compared to that of women.

Gender-responsive/gender-specific programming—programming that addresses the identified needs of female offenders, including past victimization, drug abuse, parenting, and co-dependency inclinations.

Hawthorne effect—a phenomenon that occurs when the subjects of a study act differently because of the attention of the researchers.

Identity talk—conversations in prison that revolve around children for the purpose of reinforcing one's self-perception as a mother.

Learned helplessness theory—a social science theory developed by Lenore Walker. According to this theory, when battered women "learn" that they cannot escape the violence perpetrated upon them by their intimate partners, they stay in the abusive relationships until some of them retaliate violently, often with lethal consequences.

Likert scales—a common measurement tool in survey methodology for measuring attitudes or opinions. Participants are asked to respond to a statement in terms of the extent to which they agree, choosing one of a range of responses from "strongly agree" to "strongly disagree."

meta-analyses—studies that combine the original data sets of a large number of similar studies and reanalyzes results.

Neonaticide—killing of infants that occur very soon after their birth.

Paradigm—a generally accepted model of how ideas relate to one another, forming a conceptual framework within which scientific research is carried out.

Parentalization—the pattern in which children of dysfunctional families, especially girls, take on parental responsibilities because of drug or alcohol incapacitation of a parent, long working hours of a parent, or the absence of one or both parents.

Phenomenological methods—research methods employed in phenomenology (the study of the perceptual reality of the target of study). Phenomenological methods seek to understand the world "through the eyes of the subject" and include in-depth interviews, participant observation and other qualitative methods.

Positivism—knowledge construction that employs the methods of the natural sciences—specifically, the data collection, hypothesis testing, and searching for measurable causal factors.

Prisonization—the term used to describe the degree to which an individual inmate has adopted the prison subculture and value system.

Rational relationship test—a legal test whereby the state merely has to show a rational relationship between a legitimate state interest (e.g., security) and a rule or procedure in question.

Sexual symmetry of violence—In the 1980s spousal homicide with husbands as victims was about as prevalent as homicides where wives were victims; it is no longer true today, and wives are less likely to kill husbands than husbands are to kill wives.

Secondary deviance—in labeling theory, a concept referring to delinquency that results as a consequence of being labeled as delinquent.

Social efficacy—in social disorganization theory, a concept referring to a community's "health" and its power to provide needed social supports to residents.

Static factors—so-called because they were unchanging (e.g., age, criminal history, age at first arrest), these factors were used to determine the type of person who was most likely to recidivate.

Status offenses—acts that would not be criminal if committed by an adult (e.g., truancy, smoking, curfew violations).

Steerers—people who "steer" or direct potential buyers to drug sellers.

Tautology—circular reasoning in which a series of statements purports to support an argument but merely uses different phraseology that states the same thing twice.

Therapeutic communities—residential programs that emphasizes personal responsibility, reduced social distance between staff and inmates, and daily meetings.

Upcharging—the belief that female juveniles are charged with assault or aggravated assault today for actions that in past decades would have resulted in much less serious charges (if any).

Bibliography

Acoca, L. 1998. Defusing the time bomb: Understanding and meeting the growing health care needs of incarcerated women in America. *Crime & Delinquency 44*(1), 49–69.

Acoca, L. 1999. Investing in girls: A 21st-century strategy. *Juvenile Justice 7*(1), 3–13.

Acoca, L. & Austin, J. 1996). *The Hidden Crisis: Women in Prison*. San Francisco: National Council on Crime and Delinquency.

Adams, H. 1914. *Women and Crime*. London: T. Warner Laurie.

Adelberg, E. & Currie, C. 1993. *In Conflict with the Law: Women and the Canadian Justice System*. Vancouver, BC: Press Gang Publishers.

Adler, F. 1975. *Sisters in Crime: The Rise of the New Female Criminal*. New York: McGraw-Hill.

Adler, F. 1981. *The Incidence of Female Criminality in the Contemporary World*. New York: University Press.

Adler, P. 1993. *Wheeling and Dealing: An Ethnography of an Upper-Level Dealing and Smuggling Community* (2nd ed.). New York: Columbia University Press.

Agnew, R. 1985. A revised strain theory of delinquency. *Social Forces 64*, 151–167.

Agnew, R. 2001. Building on the foundation of general strain theory: Specifying the types of strain most likely to lead to crime and delinquency. *Journal of Research in Crime and Delinquency 38*, 319–361.

Agnew, R. 2005. *Pressured into Crime: An Overview of General Strain Theory*. Boston: Oxford University Press.

Agnew, R. 2006. Storylines as a neglected cause of crime. *Journal of Research in Crime and Delinquency 43*(2), 119–147.

Agnew, R., Brezina, T., Wright, J. & Cullen, F. 2002. Strain, personality traits and delinquency: Extending general strain theory. *Criminology 40*, 43–71.

Akers, R. 1973. *Deviant Behavior: A Social Learning Approach*. Belmont, CA: Wadsworth.

Akers, R. 1985. *Deviant Behavior: A Social Learning Approach* (3rd ed.). Belmont, CA: Wadsworth.

Akers, R. 1998. *Social Learning and Social Structure: A General Theory of Crime and Deviance*. Boston: Northeastern University Press.

Akers, R. 2009. *Social Learning and Social Structure: A General Theory of Crime and Deviance*. Piscataway, NJ: Transaction Publishers.

Alarid, L. 2000. Sexual assault and coercion among incarcerated women prisoners: Excerpts from prison letters. *The Prison Journal 80*(4), 391–406.

Alarid, L., Burton, V., Jr. & Cullen, F. 2000. Gender and crime among felony offenders: Assessing the generality of social control and differential association theories. *Journal of Research in Crime and Delinquency 37*(21), 171–199.

Alarid, L., Marquart, J., Burton, V., Cullen, F. & Cuvelier, S. 1996. Women's roles in serious offenses: A study of adult felons. *Justice Quarterly 13*, 431–454.

Albanese, J. 1993. Women and the newest profession: Females as white collar criminals. In C. Culliver (Ed.), *Female Criminality: The State of the Art*, pp. 119–131. New York: Garland.

Alder, C. & Baker, J. 1997. Maternal filicide: More than one story to be told. *Women & Criminal Justice, 9*(2), 15–39.

Alder, C. & Worrall, A. 2004. *Girls' Violence: Myths and Realities*. Albany: University of New York Press.

Allard, P. & Greene, J. n.d. *Children on the Outside: The Pain and Human Costs of Parental Incarceration*. New York: Justice Strategies.

Alemagno, S. & Dickie, J. 2002. Screening for women in jail for health risks and needs. *Women & Criminal Justice 13*(4), 97–108.

Allen, J. 1989. Men, crime and criminology: Recasting the questions. *International Journal of the Sociology of Law 17*, 19–39.

Alley, M. 1997. The Mother Offspring Life Development Program. In *Maternal Ties: A Selection of Programs for Female Offenders*, pp. 151–159. Lanham, MD: American Correctional Association.

American Civil Liberties Union (ACLU). 2005. *Caught in the Net: The Impact of Drug Policies on Women and Families*. Retrieved from https://www.aclu.org/drug-law-reform/caught-net-impact-drug-policies-women-and-families

American Correctional Association. 1990. *The Female Offender: What Does the Future Hold?* Washington, DC: St. Mary's Press.

American Correctional Association. 1993. *Female Offenders: Meeting the Needs of a Neglected Population*. Baltimore, MD: United Book Press.

Amnesty International. 1999, March. *"Not Part of My Sentence": Violations of the Human Rights of Women in Custody*. London, England: Author.

Anderson, T. & Bennett, R. 1996. Development, gender, and crime: The scope of the Routine Activities Approach. *Justice Quarterly 13*, 31–56.

Anderson, B., Holmes, M. & Ostresh, E. 1999. Male and female delinquents' attachments and effects of attachments on severity of self-reported delinquency. *Criminal Justice and Behavior 26*, 435–452.

Andrews, D. & Bonta, J. 2010. *The Psychology of Criminal Conduct* (5th ed.). Cincinnati, OH: Anderson.

Anglin, M. & Hser, Y. 1987. Addicted women and crime. *Criminology 25*, 359–398.

Ansay, S. & Benvenesie, D. 1999. Equal application or unequal treatment: Practical outcomes for women on community control in Florida. *Women & Criminal Justice 10*(3), 121–135.

Anumba, N., Dematteo, D. & Heilbrun, K. 2012. Social functioning, victimization and mental health among female offenders. *Criminal Justice & Behavior 39*, 1204–1218.

Arnold, R. 1995. The processes of victimization and criminalization of black women In R. Price and N. Sokoloff (Eds.), *The Criminal Justice System and Women*, pp. 136–146. New York: McGraw-Hill.

Asseo, L. 1999, November 18. Women, families feeling effects of U.S. drug war. *Austin American Statesman*, p. A20.

Austin, J., Bloom, B. & Donahue, T. 1992. *Female Offenders in the Community: An Analysis of Innovative Strategies and Programs*. San Francisco, CA: National Council on Crime and Delinquency.

Aylward, A., & Thomas, J. 1984. Quiescence in women's prisons litigation: Some exploratory issues. *Justice Quarterly 1*, 253–276.

Bagley, K. & Merlo, A. 1995. Controlling women's bodies. In A. Merlo and J. Pollock (Eds.), *Women, Law and Social Control*, pp. 135–155. Boston, MA: Allyn & Bacon.

Baker, D. 1999. A descriptive profile and socio-historical analysis of female executions in the United States: 1632–1997. *Women & Criminal Justice 10*(3), 57–95.

Bandura, A. 1977. *Social Learning Theory*. Englewood Cliffs, NJ: Prentice-Hall.

Barkan, S. 1997. *Criminology: A Sociological Understanding*. Upper Saddle River, NJ: Prentice-Hall.

Barlow, H. 1991. Explaining crimes and analogous acts, or the unrestrained will grab at pleasure whenever they can. *The Journal of Criminal Law and Criminology 82*, 229–242.

Barnes, J. 2012. Analyzing the origins of life-course-persistent offending: A consideration of environmental and genetic influences. *Criminal Justice & Behavior 40*(5), 519–440.

Barnes, J., Beaver, K. & Boutwell, B. 2011. Examining the genetic underpinnings to Moffitt's developmental taxonomy: A behavioral genetic analysis. *Criminology 49*, 923–954.

Baro, A. 1997. Spheres of consent: An analysis of the sexual abuse and sexual exploitation of women incarcerated in the state of Hawaii. *Women & Criminal Justice 8*(3), 61–84.

Baron, S. 2004. General strain, street youth and crime: A test of Agnew's revised theory. *Criminology 42*, 457–483.

Barry, E. 1989. Pregnant prisoners. *Harvard Women's Law Journal 12*, 189–205.

Barry, E. 1991. Jail litigation concerning women prisoners. *The Prison Journal 24*, 44–50.

Barry, E. 1996. Women prisoners and health care. In K. Moss (Ed.) *Man-made Medicine*, pp. 250–272. Durham, NC: Duke University Press.

Bartusch, D., Lynam, D., Moffitt, T. & Silva, P. 1997. Is age important? Testing a general versus a developmental theory of antisocial behavior. *Criminology 35*, 13–47.

Baskin, D. & Sommers, I. 1993. Females' initiation into violent street crime. *Justice Quarterly 10*, 559–583.

Baskin, D. & Sommers, I. 1998. *Casualties of Community Disorder: Women's Careers in Violent Crime*. Boulder, CO: Westview Press.

Baskin, D., Sommers, I. & Fagan, J. 1993. The political economy of female violent street crime. *Fordham Urban Law Journal 20*(3), 401–417.

Batchelor, S. 2005. 'Prove me the bam!': Victimization and agency in the lives of young women who commit violent offenses. *The Journal of Community and Criminal Justice 52*(4), 358–375.

Batchelor, S., Burman, M. & Brown, J. 2001. Discussing violence: Let's hear it from the girls. *Probation Journal 48*(2), 125–134.

Battle, C., Zlotnick, C., Najavits, L., Guttierrez, M., & Winsor, C. 2003. Post-traumatic stress disorder and substance use disorder among incarcerated women. In P. Ouimette & P. Brown (Eds.), *Trauma and Substance Abuse: Causes, Consequences, and Treatment of Co-morbid Disorders*, pp. 209–225. Washington, DC: American Psychological Association.

Batton, C. 2004. Gender differences in lethal violence: historical trends in the relationship between homicide and suicide rates, 1960–2000. *Justice Quarterly 21*, 423–461.

Baunach, P. 1977. Women offenders: A commentary—Current conceptions on women in crime. *Quarterly Journal of Corrections 1*(4), 14–18.

Baunach, P. 1985. *Mothers in Prison*. New Brunswick, NJ: Transaction Books.

Baunach, P. & Murton, T. 1973. Women in prison, an awakening minority. *Crime and Corrections 1*, 4–12.

Beaver, K. 2011. Genetic influences on being processed through the criminal justice system: Results from a sample of adoptees. *Biological Psychiatry 69*, 282–287.

Beaver, K. 2013. The familial concentration and transmission of crime. *Criminal Justice and Behavior 40*(2), 139–155.

Beaver, K., Delisi, M., Vaughn, M. & Barnes, J. 2010. Monoamine oxidase: A genotype is associated with gang membership and weapon use. *Comprehensive Psychiatry 51*(2), 130–135.

Beck, A. 1998. *Profile of Jail Inmates, 1996*. Washington, DC: Bureau of Justice Statistics.

Beck, A., Berzofsky, M., Caspar, R. & Krebs, C. 2013. *Sexual Victimization in Prisons and Jails Reported by Inmates, 2011–2012* (NCJ 241399). Washington, DC: Bureau of Justice Statistics.

Beck, A. & Mumola, C. 1999. *Prisoners in 1998*. Washington, DC: Bureau of Justice Statistics.

Becker, H. 1963. *Outsiders: Studies in the Sociology of Deviance*. New York: Free Press.

Beckerman, A. 1989. Incarcerated mothers and their children in foster care. *Children and Youth Services Review 11*(2), 175–183.

Beckerman, A. 1994. Mothers in prison: Meeting the prerequisite conditions for permanency planning. *Social Work 39*, 9–14.

Bedell, P. 1997. Resilient women: Risk and protective factors in the lives of female offenders. Unpublished master's thesis, Vermont College of Norwich University, Northfield, VT.

Belknap, J. 2007. *The Invisible Woman: Gender, Crime and Justice* (3rd ed.). Independence, KY: Cengage Brain.

Belknap, J. & Holsinger, K. 2006. The gendered nature of risk factors for delinquency. *Feminist Criminology 1*, 48–71.

Belknap, J., Holsinger, K. & Dunn, M. 1997. Understanding incarcerated girls: The results of a focus group study. *The Prison Journal 77*(4), 381–404.

Bentham, J. 1843/1970. The rationale of punishment. In R. Beck and J. Orr (Eds.), *Ethical Choice: A Case Study Approach*, pp. 326–340. New York: Free Press.

Bernburg, J. & Krohn, M. 2003. Labeling, life chances, and adult crime: the direct and indirect effects of official intervention in adolescence on crime in early adulthood. *Criminology 41*, 1287–1318.

Bershad, L. 1985. Discriminatory treatment of the female offender in the criminal justice system. *Boston College Law Review 26*(2), 389–438.

Berry, P. & Eigenberg, H. 2003. Role strain and incarcerated mothers: Understanding the process of mothering. *Women & Criminal Justice 15*(1), 101–119.

Biron, L., Brochu, S. & Desjardins, L. 1995. The issue of drugs and crime among a sample of incarcerated women. *Deviant Behavior 16*, 25–43.

Bishop, C. 1931. *Women and Crime*. London, England: Chato and Windus Press.

Bishop, D. & Frazier, C. 1992. Gender bias in juvenile justice processing: Implications of the JJDP Act. *Journal of Criminal Law and Criminology 82*(4), 1162–1186.

Bishop, D. M. & Frazier, C. E. 1996. Race effects in juvenile justice decision-making: Findings of a statewide analysis. *Journal of Criminal Law and Criminology 86*, 392–414.

Bjerregaard, B. 2002. Operationalizing gang membership: The impact measurement on gender differences in gang self-identification and delinquent involvement. *Women & Criminal Justice 13*, 79–95.

Bjerregaard, B. & Cochran, J. 2012. The role of school-related bonding factors and gender: Correlates of gang membership among adolescents. *Women & Criminal Justice* *22*, 30–53.

Blackburn, A. 2006. The role perception plays in the official reporting of prison sexual assault: An examination of females incarcerated in the State of Texas. Unpublished doctoral dissertation, San Houston State University, Huntsville, TX.

Blackwell, B. 2000. Perceived sanction threats, gender, and crime: A test and elaboration of power-control theory. *Criminology 38*, 439–488.

Blackwell, B. & Eschholz, S. 2002. Sex differences and rational choice: Traditional tests and new directions. In A. R. Piquero and S. G. Tibbetts (Eds.), *Rational Choice and Criminal Behavior: Recent Research and Future Challenges*, pp. 41–63. New York: Routledge.

Blackwell, B., Holleran, D. & Finn, M. 2008. The impact of the Pennsylvania sentencing guidelines on sex differences in sentencing. *Journal of Contemporary Criminal Justice 24*, 399–418.

Blackwell, B. & Piquero, A. 2005. On the relationships between gender, power control, self-control, and crime. *Journal of Criminal Justice 33*, 1–17.

Blanchette, K. 2002. Classifying female offenders for effective intervention: Application of the case-based principles of risk and need. *Forum on Corrections Research 14*, 31–35.

Blanchette, K. 2005. Field test of a gender-informed security reclassification scale for female offenders. Unpublished doctoral dissertation, Carleton University, Ottawa, Ontario, Canada.

Blanchette, K. & Brown, S. 2006. *The Assessment and Treatment of Women Offenders: An Integrative Perspective*. New York: Wiley.

Blank, R. 1993. *Fertility Control: New Techniques, New Policy Issues*. New York: Greenwood Press.

Blinn, C. 1997. *Maternal Ties: A Selection of Programs for Female Offenders*. Lanham, MD: American Correctional Association.

Blitz, C. 2006. Predictors of stable employment among female inmates in New Jersey: Implications for successful reintegration. *Journal of Offender Rehabilitation 43*(1), 1–22.

Block, A. 1980. Searching for women in organized crime. In S. Datesman and F. Scarpetti (Eds.), *Women, Crime and Justice*, pp. 192–214. New York: Oxford University Press.

Block, C. R., Blokland, A. J., van der Werff, C., van Os, R. & Nieuwbeerta, P. 2010. Long-term patterns of offending in women. *Feminist Criminology 5*, 73–107.

Block, K. & Potthast, M. 1997, March. Living apart and getting together: Inmate mothers and enhanced visitation through Girl Scouts. Paper presented at Academy of Criminal Justice Sciences (NCJ 166449), Retrieved from https://www.ncjrs.gov/App/Publications/abstract.aspx?ID=166449

Bloom, B. 2000, August. Gender-responsive programs and services. Paper presented at the American Correctional Association, San Antonio TX.

Bloom, B. 2004. Women offenders in the community: The gendered impact of current policies. *Community Corrections Report 12*(1), 3–6.

Bloom, B. & Chesney-Lind, M. 2000. Women in prison: Vengeful equity. In R. Muraskin, *It's a Crime: Women and Justice* (2nd ed.), pp. 183–204. Upper Saddle River, NJ: Prentice-Hall.

Bloom, B., Chesney-Lind, M. & Owen, B. 1994. *Women in California Prisons: Hidden Victims of the War on Drugs*. San Francisco: Center on Juvenile and Criminal Justice.

Bloom, B., Immarigeon, R. & Owen, B. (Eds.). 1995. Women in Prisons and Jails. Special Issue. *Prison Journal: An International Forum on Incarceration and Alternative Sanctions 75*(2) (entire issue).

Bloom, B., Owen, B., & Covington, S. 2003. *Gender Responsive Strategies: Research, Practice, and Guiding Principles for Women Offenders*. Washington, DC: National Institute of Corrections.

Bloom, B., Owen, B. & Covington, S. 2004. Women offenders and the gendered effects of public policy. *Review of Policy Research 21*, 31–48.

Bloom, B., Owen, B., Deschenes, E. & Rosenbaum, J. 2002. Improving juvenile justice for females: A statewide assessment in California. *Crime & Delinquency 48*(4), 526–552.

Bloom, B., Owen, B., Rosenbaum, J. & Deschenes, E. 2003. Focusing on girls and young women: A gendered perspective on female delinquency. *Women & Criminal Justice 14*, 117–136.

Bloom, B. & Steinhart, D. 1993. *Why Punish the Children? A Reappraisal of the Children of Incarcerated Mothers in America*. San Francisco: National Council on Crime and Delinquency.

Blount, W., Kuhns, J. & Silverman, I. 1993. Intimate abuse within an incarcerated female population: Rates, levels, criminality, a continuum, and some lessons about self-identification." In C. Culliver (Ed.) *Female Criminality: The State of the Art*, pp. 413–462. New York: Garland.

Blount, W., Danner, T., Vega, M. & Silverman, I. 1991. The influence of substance use among adult female inmates. *The Journal of Drug Issues 21*(2), 449–467.

Blum, A. & Fisher, G. 1978. Women who kill. In I. Kutash, S. Kutash, and L. Schlesinger (Eds.), *Violence: Perspectives on Murder and Aggression*, pp. 187–197. San Francisco, CA: Jossey-Bass.

Blumstein, A. & Cohen, J. 1979. Estimation of individual crime rates from arrest records. *Journal of Criminal Law & Criminology 70*, 561–585.

Blumstein, A., Cohen, J. & Farrington, D. 1988a. Criminal career research: Its value for criminology. *Criminology 26*, 1–35.

Blumstein, A., Cohen, J. & Farrington, D. 1988b. Longitudinal and criminal career research: Further clarifications. *Criminology 26*, 57–74.

Blumstein, A., Cohen, J., Roth, J. & Visher, C. 1986. *Criminal Careers and Career Criminals* (2 Vols.) Washington, DC: National Academy Press.

Bohrman, M. 1996. Predisposition to criminality: Swedish adoption studies in retrospect. In M. Rutter (Ed.), *Genetics of Criminal and Antisocial Behavior*. Chichester, England: John Wiley and Sons.

Bond-Maupin, L., Maupin, J. & Leisenring, J. 2002. Girls' delinquency and the justice implications of intake workers' perspectives. *Women & Criminal Justice 13*, 51–72.

Bonczar, T. 2011. *New court commitments to state prison, 2009: Offense, by sex, race, and Hispanic origin* (Report ncrp0904.csv, Table 4, version 5/5/11). Bureau of Justice Statistics, National Corrections Reporting Program. Retrieved from http://www.bjs.gov/index.cfm?ty=pbdetail&iid=2065

Bonta, J., Pang, B. & Wallace-Capretta, S. 1995. Predictors of recidivism among incarcerated female offenders. *The Prison Journal 75*, 277–294.

Booth, J., Farrell, A. & Varano, S. 2008. Social control, serious delinquency, and risky behavior: A gendered analysis. *Crime & Delinquency 54*(3), 423–456.

Borelli, J., Goshin, L., Joestl, S., Clark, J. & Byrne, M. 2010. Attachment organization in a sample of incarcerated mothers: Distribution of classifications and associations with substance abuse history, depressive symptoms, perceptions of parenting competency and social support. *Attachment and Human Development 12*, 255–374.

Bosworth, M. 1999. *Engendering Resistance: Agency and Power in Women's Prisons*. Dartmouth: Ashgate.

Bosworth, M. 2007. Creating the responsible prisoner: Federal admission and orientation packs. *Punishment & Society 9*, 67–85.

Bottcher, J. 1993. Gender as social control: A qualitative study of incarcerated youths and their siblings in greater Sacramento. *Justice Quarterly 12*, 33–57.

Bottcher, J. 2001. Social practices of gender: How gender relates to delinquency in the everyday lives of high-risk youths. *Criminology 39*, 893–932.

Boudouris, J. 1985. *Prisons and Kids*. Laurel, MD: American Correction Association.

Boudouris, J. 1996. *Parents in Prison: Addressing the Needs of Families*. Lanham, MD: American Correction Association.

Bouffard, L., Wright, K., Muftic, L. & Bouffard, J. 2008. Gender differences in specialization in intimate partner violence: Comparing the gender symmetry and violent resistance perspectives. *Justice Quarterly 25*, 570–594.

Bourgois, P. & Dunlap, E. 1993. Exorcising sex-for-crack: An ethnographic perspective from Harlem. In M. Ratner (Ed.), *The Crack Pipe as Pimp*, pp. 97–132. Lexington, MA: Lexington Books.

Bowker, L. 1979. *Women, Crime and the Criminal Justice System*. Lexington, MA: Lexington Books.

Bowker, L. 1980. *Prison Victimization*. New York: Elsevier Press.

Bowker, L. 1981. The institutional determinants of international female crime. *International Journal of Comparative and Applied Criminal Justice 5*(1), 11–28.

Box, S. & Hale, C. 1993. Liberation/Emancipation, economic marginalization, or less chivalry: The relevance of three theoretical arguments to female crime patterns in England and Wales, 1951–1980. *Criminology 22*, 473–497.

Boyd, S. 2004. *From Witches to Crack Moms: Women, Drug Law, and Policy*. Durham, NC: Carolina Academic Press.

Bradley, R. & Davino, K. 2002. Women's perceptions of the prison environment: When prison is "the safest place I've ever been." *Psychology of Women Quarterly 26*(4), 351–359.

Breitenbecher, K. 2001. Sexual revictimization among women: A review of the literature focusing on empirical investigations. *Aggression and Violent Behavior 6*, 415–432.

Brennan, P. 2006. Sentencing female misdemeanants: An examination of the direct and indirect effects of race/ethnicity. *Justice Quarterly 23*, 60–95.

Brennan, P. 2007. An intermediate sanction that fosters the mother-child bond: A process evaluation of Summit House. *Women & Criminal Justice 18*(3), 47–80.

Brennan, T., Breitenbach, M., Dieterich, M., Salisbury, E. & Van Voorhis, P. 2012. Women's pathway to serious and habitual crime. A person-centered analysis incorporating gender-responsive factors. *Criminal Justice & Behavior 39*, 1481–1508.

Brewer, V., Marquart, J., Mullings, J. & Crouch, B. 1998. AIDS-related risk behavior among female prisoners with histories of mental impairment. *Prison Journal 78*, 101–119.

Brewer-Smyth, K. 2004. Women behind bars: Could neurobiological correlates of past physical and sexual abuse contribute to criminal behavior? *Health Care for Women International 25*, 835–852.

Brewer-Smyth, K., Burgess, A. & Shults, J. 2004. Physical and sexual abuse, salivary cortisol, and neurologic correlates of violent criminal behavior of female prison inmates. *Biological Psychiatry 55*(1), 21–31.

Bridges, G. & Beretta, G. 1994. Gender, race and social control: Toward an understanding of sex disparities in imprisonment. In G. Bridges & M. Myers (Eds.), *Inequality, Crime, and Social Control*, pp. 158–175. Boulder, CO: Westview Press.

Broidy, L. 2001. A test of general strain theory. *Criminology 39*, 9–35.

Broidy, L. & Agnew, R. 1997. Gender and crime: A general strain theory perspective. *Journal of Research in Crime and Delinquency 34*, 275–306.

Brown, L. & Gilligan, C. 1992. *Meeting at the Crossroads: Women's Psychology and Girls' Development*. Cambridge, MA: Harvard University Press.

Brown, M. 2006. Gender, ethnicity, and offending over the life course: Women's pathways to offending in the Aloha state. *Critical Criminology 14*, 137–158.

Brown, M., & Bloom, B. 2009. Reentry and renegotiating motherhood. *Crime & Delinquency 55*(3), 313–336.

Browne, A. 1987. *When Battered Women Kill*. New York: Free Press.

Browne, A., & Finkelhor, D. 1986. Impact of child sexual abuse: A review of the research. *Psychological Bulletin 99*, 66–77.

Brownstein, H., Spunt, B., Crimmins, S., Goldstein, P. & Langley, S. 1994. Changing patterns of lethal violence by women: A research note. *Women & Criminal Justice 5*(2), 99–118.

Buccio-Notaro, P. 1998. An innovative solution: The Neil J. Houston House. In J. Morton (Ed.), *Complex Challenges, Collaborative Solutions: Programming for Adult and Juvenile Female Offenders*, pp. 141–151. Lanham, MD: American Correctional Association.

Bureau of Justice Statistics. 1989. *Prisoners in 1988*. Washington, DC: Author.

Bureau of Justice Statistics. 1994. *Domestic Violence: Violence between Intimates* (Bureau of Justice Statistics Selected Findings, NCJ 149259). Washington, DC: Author.

Bureau of Justice Statistics. 1998. *Violence by Intimates: Analysis of Data on Crimes by Current or Former Spouses, Boyfriends, and Girlfriends* (Bureau of Justice Statistics Factbook, NCJ 167237). Washington, DC: Author.

Bureau of Justice Statistics. 2013, June 14. Number of rape/sexual assaults by reporting to police. Data generated using the NCVS Victimization Analysis Tool at www.bjs.gov.

Burgess, R. & Akers, R. 1966. A differential association-reinforcement theory of criminal behavior. *Social Problems 14* (Fall), 128–147.

Burke, P. & Adams, L. 1991. *Classification of Women Offenders in State Correctional Facilities: A Handbook for Practitioners*. Washington, DC: National Institute of Corrections.

Burkhardt, K. 1973. *Women in Prison*. Garden City, NJ: Doubleday.

Bursik, R. & Grasmick, H. 1993. *Neighborhoods and Crime: The Dimensions of Effective Community Control*. New York: Lexington Books.

Bush-Baskette, S. 2000. The war on drugs and the incarceration of mothers. *Journal of Drug Issues 30*, 919–928.

Butler, M. 2008. "What are you looking at?" Prisoner confrontation and the search for respect. *British Journal of Criminology 48*, 856–873.

Buzawa, E. & Hotaling, G. 2006. The impact of relationship status, gender, and minor status in the police response to domestic assaults. *Victims & Offenders 1*, 373–393.

Byrne, J. & Sampson, R. (Eds.). 1986. *The Social Ecology of Crime*. New York: Springer-Verlag.

Byrne, J., & Taxman, F. 2005. Crime (control) is a choice: Divergent perspectives on the role of treatment in the adult corrections system. *Criminology and Public Policy 4*(2), 291–310.

Byrne, M. 2009. *Prison Nursery Research*. New York: Maternal and Child Outcomes of a Prison Nursery Program, Columbia University Institute for Family and Child Policy. Retrieved from http://www.nursing.columbia.edu/byrne/prison_nursery.html

Byrne, M. W., Goshin, L. & Blanchard-Lewis, B. 2012. Maternal separation during the reentry years for 100 infants raised in a prison nursery. *Family Court Review 50*, 77–90.

Byrne, M., Goshin, L. & Joestl, S. 2010. Intergenerational transmission of attachment for infants raised in prison nursery. *Attachment and Human Development 12*, 375–393.

Calhoun, A., & Coleman, H. 2002. Female inmates' perspectives on sexual abuse by correctional personnel: An exploratory study. *Women & Criminal Justice 13*(2/3), 101–124.

Cameron, M. 1964. *The Booster and the Snitch*. New York: Free Press.

Camp, D. & Sandhu, H. 1995, August. Evaluation of Female Offender Regimented Treatment program (FORT) (Final Report). *Journal of the Oklahoma Criminal Justice Research Consortium,* Vol. 2, 50–57.

Camp, S. & Gaes, G. 2005. Criminogenic effects of the prison environment on inmate behavior: Some experimental evidence. *Crime & Delinquency 51,* 425–442.

Campbell, A. 1981. *Girl Delinquents*. Oxford: Basil Blackwell.

Campbell, A. 1984. *The Girls in the Gang*. Oxford: Basil Blackwell.

Campbell, A. 1990. Female participation in gangs. In C. R. Huff (Ed.), *Gangs in America,* pp. 163–192. Newbury Park, CA: Sage.

Campbell, C., Mackenzie, D. & Robinson, J. 1987. Female offenders: Criminal behavior and gender-role identity." *Psychological Reports 60,* 867–873.

Canter, R. 1982a. Sex differences in self-reported delinquency. *Criminology 20,* 373–393.

Canter, R. 1982b. Family correlates of male and female delinquency. *Criminology 20,* 149–167.

Carbone-Lopez, K. & Kruttschnitt, C. 2003. Assessing the racial climate in women's institutions in the context of penal reform. *Women & Criminal Justice 15*(1), 55–79.

Carbone-Lopez, K. & Miller, J. 2012. Precocious role entry as a mediating factor in women's methamphetamine use: Implications for life-course and pathways research. *Criminology 50,* 187–220.

Carlen, P. 1983. *Women's Imprisonment: A Study in Social Control*. London: Routledge & Kegan Paul.

Carlen, P. (Ed.). 1985. *Criminal Women: Autobiographical Accounts*. Cambridge, England: Polity Press.

Carlen, P. 1988. *Women, Crime and Poverty*. Philadelphia, PA: Open University Press.

Carlen, P. 1989. Feminist jurisprudence—or women-wise penology? *Probation Journal 36*(3), 110–114.

Carlen, P. 1990. *Alternatives to Incarceration*. Philadelphia, PA: Open University Press.

Carlson, B. 2005. The most important things learned about violence and trauma in the past 20 years. *Journal of Interpersonal Violence 20*(1), 119–126.

Carp, S. & Schade, L. 1992. Tailoring facility programming to suit female offender needs. *Corrections Today 54*(6), 152–159.

Carroll, L. 1974. *Hacks, Blacks and Cons*. Lexington, MA: Lexington Press.

Carson, E. & Golinelli, D. 2013. *Prisoners in 2012—Advance Counts* (Bureau of Justice Statistics Bulletin, NCJ 242467). Washington, DC: U.S. Department of Justice.

Carson, E. & Sabol, W. 2012. *Prisoners in 2011*. Washington, DC: Bureau of Justice Statistics.

Casey-Acevedo, K. & Bakken, T. 2001. The effect of time on the disciplinary adjustment of women in prison. *International Journal of Offender Therapy and Comparative Criminology 45*(4), 489–497.

Caspi, A., Moffitt, T., Silva, P., Stouthamer-Loeber, M., Krueger, R. & Schmutte, P. 1994. Are some people crime-prone? Replications of the personality-crime relationship across countries, genders, races, and methods. *Criminology 32,* 163–195.

Cassidy, J., Ziv, Y., Stupica, B., Sherman, L., Butler, H., Karfgin, A., Cooper, G., Hoffman, K. & Powell, B. 2010. Enhancing attachment security in the infants of women in a jail-diversion program. *Attachment and Human Behavior 12,* 333–353.

Catalano, S. 2012. *Intimate Partner Violence 1993–2010* (NCJ 239203). Washington, DC: Bureau of Justice Statistics.

Catalano, S., Smith, E., Snyder, H. & Rand, M. 2009. *Female Victims of Violence*. Washington, DC: Bureau of Justice Statistics.

Catalino, A. 1972. Boys and girls in a co-educational training school are different, aren't they? *Canadian Journal of Criminology and Corrections 14*, 120–131.

Catan, L. 1992. Infants with mothers in prison. In R. Shaw (Ed.), *Prisoners' Children: What Are the Issues?*, pp. 26–42. New York: Routledge.

Cauffman, E., Feldman, S., Waterman, J. & Steiner, H. 1998. Posttraumatic stress disorder among female juvenile offenders. *Journal of the American Academy of Child & Adolescent Psychiatry 37*, 1209–1216.

Cauffman, E., Steinberg, L. & Piquero, A. 2005. Psychological, neuropsychological and physiological correlates of serious antisocial behavior in adolescence: The role of self-control. *Criminology 43*, 133–176.

Cernkovich, S. & Giordano, P. 1979. A comparative analysis of male and female delinquency. *Sociological Quarterly 20*, 131–145.

Cernkovich, S., Lanctot, N. & Giordano, P. 2008. Predicting adolescent and adult antisocial behavior among adjudicated delinquent females. *Crime & Delinquency 54*(1), 3–33.

Chamlin, M. & Cochran, J. 1997. Social altruism and crime. *Criminology 35*, 203–228.

Chandler, E. 1973. *Women in Prison*. New York: Bobbs-Merrill.

Chapman, J. 1980. *Economic Realities and Female Crime*. Lexington, MA: Lexington Books.

Chernoff, N. & Simon, R. 2000. Women and crime the world over. *Gender Issues 18*(3), 5–20.

Chesney-Lind, M. 1973. Judicial enforcement of the female sex role. *Issues in Criminology 8*(2), 51–69.

Chesney-Lind, M. 1978. Chivalry reexamined: Women and the criminal justice system. In L. Bowker, *Women, Crime and the Criminal Justice System*, pp. 197–225. Lexington, MA: Lexington Books.

Chesney-Lind, M. 1982. Guilty by reason of sex: Young women and the juvenile justice system. In B. Price & N. Sokoloff (Eds.), *The Criminal Justice System and Women*, pp. 77–105. New York: Clark Boardman.

Chesney-Lind, M. 1986. Women and crime: The female offender. *Signs: Journal of Women in Culture and Society 12*(1), 78–96.

Chesney-Lind, M. 1988. Girls in jail. *Crime & Delinquency 34*(2), 150–168.

Chesney-Lind, M. 1991. Patriarchy, prisons and jails: A critical look at trends in women's incarceration. *The Prison Journal 71*(1), 51–67.

Chesney-Lind, M. 1995. Rethinking women's imprisonment: A critical examination of trends in female incarceration. In B. Price & N. Sokoloff (Eds.), *The Criminal Justice System and Women, Offenders, Victims, and Workers* (2nd ed.), pp. 105–117. New York: McGraw-Hill.

Chesney-Lind, M. 1997. *The Female Offender: Girls, Women and Crime*. Thousand Oaks, CA: Sage.

Chesney-Lind, M. 1998. Women in prison: From partial justice to vengeful equity. *Corrections Today* (December), 66–73.

Chesney-Lind, M. 2002. Criminalizing victimization: The unintended consequences of pro-arrest policies for girls and women. *Criminology & Public Policy 2*(1), 81–90.

Chesney-Lind, M. & Eliason, M. 2006. From invisible to incorrigible: The demonization of marginalized women and girls. *Crime, Media, Culture 2*(1), 29–47.

Chesney-Lind, M. & Pasko, L. 2004. *The Female Offender: Girls, Women, and Crime* (2nd ed.). Thousand Oaks, CA: Sage.

Chesney-Lind, M. & Pollock, J. 1995. Women's prisons: Equality with a vengeance. In A. Merlo and J. Pollock, (Eds.), *Women, Law and Social Control*, pp. 155–175. Boston: Allyn & Bacon.

Chesney-Lind, M. & Rodriquez, N. 1983. Women under lock and key: A view from the inside, *The Prison Journal 63*(2), 47–65.

Chesney-Lind, M. & Shelden, R. 2014. *Girls, Delinquency, and Juvenile Justice* (4th ed.). Hoboken, NJ: Wiley.

Chilton, R. & Datesman, S. 1987. Gender, race, and crime: An analysis of urban arrest trends, 1960–1980. *Gender and Society 1,* 152–171.

Chodorow, N. 1978. *The Reproduction of Mothering.* Berkeley: University of California Press.

Clark, J. 1995. The impact of the prison environment on mothers. *Prison Journal 75*(3), 306–329.

Clemmer, D. 1940. *The Prison Community.* New York: Holt, Rinehart & Winston.

Clement, M. 1993. Parenting in prisons: A national survey of programs for incarcerated women. *Journal of Offender Rehabilitation 19,* 89–100.

Cloward, R. 1959. Illegitimate means, anomie, and deviant behavior. *American Sociological Review 24,* 164–176.

Cloward, R. & Ohlin, L. 1960. *Delinquency and Opportunity.* New York: Free Press.

Cochran, J., Chamlin, M., Wood, P. & Sellers, C. 1999. Shame, embarrassment, and formal sanction threats: Extending the Deterrence/Rational Choice Model to academic dishonesty. *Sociological Inquiry 69*(1), 91–105.

Cochran, J., Wood, P., Sellers, C., Wilkerson, W. & Chamlin, M. 1998. Academic dishonesty and low self-control: An empirical test of a general theory of crime. *Deviant Behavior 19,* 227–255.

Cochrane, R. 1971. The structure of value systems in male and female prisoners. *British Journal of Criminology 11,* 73–79.

Cohen, A. 1955. *Delinquency in Boys: The Culture of the Gang.* New York: Free Press.

Cohen, L. & Felson, M. 1979. Social change and crime trends: A routine activity approach. *American Sociological Review 44,* 588–608.

Cohen, T. & Kyckelhahn, T. 2010. *Felony Defendants in Large Urban Counties, 2006* (NCJ 228944). Washington, DC: Bureau of Justice Statistics.

Cole, E. & Coultrap-McQuin, S. 1992. *Explorations in Feminist Ethics.* Bloomington, IL: Indiana University Press.

Coll, C., Miller, J., Fields, J. & Matthews, B. 1997. The experiences of women in prison: Implications for services and prevention. *Women & Therapy 20*(4), 11–28.

Colley, E. & Camp, A. 1992. Creating programs for women inmates. *Corrections Today* (April), 208–209.

Collins, W. & Collins, A. 1996. *Women in Jail: Legal Issues.* Washington, DC: National Institute of Corrections.

Comack, E. 2006. Coping, resisting, and surviving: Connecting women's law violations to their histories of abuse. In L. Alarid & P. Cromwell (Eds.), *In Her Own Words: Women Offenders' Views on Crime and Victimization,* pp. 33–45. Los Angeles, CA: Roxbury.

Connell, R. 1987. *Gender and power: Society, the person and sexual politics.* Stanford, CA: Stanford University Press.

Connolly, J. 1983. Women in county jails: An invisible gender in an ill defined institution. *Prison Journal 63,* 99–115.

Cook, R. 1993, June 24. Prison guard acquitted on all counts. *Atlanta Journal,* p. C1.

Cook, S., Smith, S., Tusher, C. & Raiford, C. 2005. Self-reports of traumatic events in a random sample of incarcerated women. *Women & Criminal Justice 16*(1/2), 107–126.

Cookson, H. M. 1977. Survey of self-injury in a closed prison for women. *British Journal of Criminology 17*(4), 332–347.

Coontz, P. 1983. Women under sentence of death: The social organization of waiting to die. *The Prison Journal 63*(2), 88–98.

Cooper, A. & Smith, E. 2011. *Homicide Trends in the United States, 1980–2008: Annual Rates for 2009 and 2010.* (Patterns & Trends, NCJ 236018). Washington, DC: Bureau of Justice Statistics.

Cornish, D. & Clarke, R. 1986. *The Reasoning Criminal: Rational Choice Perspectives on Offending*. New York: Springer-Verlag.

Costello, B. & Vowell, P. 1999. Testing control theory and differential association: A reanalysis of the Richmond Youth Project data. *Criminology 37*, 815–842.

Cotton-Oldenburg, N., Jordan, B., Martin, S. & Kupper, L. 1999. Women inmates' risky sex behaviors: Are they related? *The Journal of Drug and Alcohol Abuse 25*, 129–150.

Coulson, G., Ilacqua, G., Nutbrown, V., Giulekas, D. & Cudjoe, F. 1996. Predictive utility of the LSI for incarcerated female offenders. *Criminal Justice and Behavior 23*, 427–439.

Covington, J. 1985. Gender differences in criminality among heroin users. *Journal of Research in Crime and Delinquency 22*, 329–354.

Covington, S. 1998a. The relational theory of women's psychological development: Implications for the criminal justice system. In R. Zaplin (Ed.), *Female Crime and Delinquency: Critical Perspectives and Effective Interventions*. Gaithersburg, MD: Aspen.

Covington, S. 1998b. Women in prison: Approaches in the treatment of our most invisible population. In J. Harden and M. Hill (Eds.), *Breaking the Rules: Prison & Feminist Therapy*, pp. 141–155. New York: Harrington Park Press.

Covington, S. 2000. Helping women to recover: Creating gender-specific treatment for substance-abusing women and girls in community corrections. In M. McMahon (Ed.), *Assessment to Assistance: Programs for Women in Community Corrections*, pp. 171–233. Lanham, MD: American Correctional Association.

Covington, S. 2008. Women and addiction: A trauma informed approach. *Journal of Psychoactive Drugs 5*, 377–385.

Cowie, J., Cowie, B. & Slater, E. 1968. *Delinquency in Girls*. London: Heinemann.

Cranford, S. & Williams, R. 1998. Critical issues in managing female offenders. *Corrections Today 60*, 130–134.

Craven, D. 1996. *Female Victims of Violent Crime* (Bureau of Justice Statistics Special Report, NCJ 162602). Washington, DC: U.S. Department of Justice.

Crawford, J. 1988a. *Tabulation of a Nationwide Survey of Female Offenders*. College Park, MD: American Correctional Association.

Crawford, J. 1988b. *Tabulation of a Nationwide Survey of State Correctional Facilities for Adult and Juvenile Female Offenders*. College Park, MD: American Correctional Association.

Crenshaw, K. 2012. From private violence to mass incarceration: Thinking intersectionally about women, race, and social control. *UCLA Law Review 59*, 1418–1472.

Crew, B. 1991. Sex differences in criminal sentencing: Chivalry or patriarchy? *Justice Quarterly 8*, 60–78.

Crimmins, S., Langley, S., Brownstein, H. & Spunt, B. 1997. Convicted women who have killed children: A self-psychology perspective. *Journal of Interpersonal Violence 12*, 49–70.

Crites, L. 1976. *The Female Offender*. Lexington, MA: Lexington Books.

Crittenden, D. 1990, January 25. You've come a long way, moll. *Wall Street Journal*, p. A14.

Crouch, B. 1980. *The Keepers: Prison Guards and Contemporary Corrections*. Springfield, IL: Charles C. Thomas.

Crow, M. & Kunselman, J. 2009. Sentencing female drug offenders: Reexamining racial and ethnic disparities. *Women & Criminal Justice 19*, 191–216.

Cuellar, J. & Curry, T. 2007. The prevalence and comorbidity between delinquency, drug abuse, suicide attempts, physical and sexual abuse, and self-mutilation among delinquent Hispanic females. *Hispanic Journal of Behavioral Sciences 29*, 68–82.

Culbertson, R. & Fortune, E. 1986. Incarcerated women: Self-concept and argot roles. *Journal of Offender Counseling, Services and Rehabilitation 10*(3), 25–49.

Cullen, F. 1994. Social support as an organizing concept for criminology: Presidential address to the Academy of Criminal Justice Sciences. *Justice Quarterly 11*, 528–559.

Cullen, F., Golden, K. & Cullen, J. 1979. Sex and delinquency: A partial test of the masculinity hypothesis. *Criminology 17*, 301–327.

Culley, R. 2012. The judge didn't sentence me to be raped. *Women & Criminal Justice 22*, 206–225.

Cunningham, M., & Sorenson, J. 2006. Actuarial models for assessing prison violence risk: Revisions and extensions of the Risk Assessment Scale for Prison (RASP). *Assessment 13*(3), 253–265.

Curran, D. 1983. Judicial discretion and defendant's sex. *Criminology 21*, 41–58.

Curriden, M. 1993, September 20. Prison scandal in Georgia: Guards traded favors for sex. *National Law Journal*, p. 8.

Curry, G., Ball, R. & Fox, R. 1994. *Gang, Crime and Law Enforcement Record Keeping* (NCJ 148345). Washington, DC: National Institute of Justice.

Dallaire, H. 2007. Incarcerated mothers and fathers: A comparison of risks for children and families. *Family Relations 56*, 440–453.

Daly, K. 1987a. Discrimination in the criminal courts: Family, gender, and the problem of equal treatment. *Social Forces 66*(1), 152–175.

Daly, K. 1987b. Structure and practice of familial-based justice in a criminal court. *Law and Society Review 21*(2), 267–290.

Daly, K. 1989a. Criminal justice ideologies and practices in different voices: Some feminist questions about justice. *International Journal of the Sociology of Law 17*, 1–18.

Daly, K. 1989b. Neither conflict nor labeling nor paternalism will suffice: Intersections of race, ethnicity, gender, and family in criminal court decisions, *Crime & Delinquency 35*(1), 136–159.

Daly, K. 1989c. Gender and varieties of white-collar crime. *Criminology 27*, 769–791.

Daly, K. 1992. Women's pathways to felony court: Feminist theories of lawbreaking and problems of representation. *Southern California Review of Law and Women's Studies 2*, 11–52.

Daly, K. 1994a. *Gender, Crime and Punishment*. New Haven, CT: Yale University Press.

Daly, K. 1994b. Gender and punishment disparity. In G. S. Bridges & G. Beretta (Eds.). *Inequality, Crime, and Social Control*, pp. 117–133. Boulder, CO: Westview Press.

Daly, K. & Bordt, R. 1995. Sex effects and sentencing: An analysis of the statistical literature. *Justice Quarterly 12*, 141–168.

Daly, K. & Chesney-Lind, M. 1988. Feminism and criminology. *Justice Quarterly 5*, 497–535.

Daly, K. & Tonry, M. 1997. Gender, race, and sentencing. *Crime and Justice 22*, 201–252.

Danner, M. 1998. Three strikes and it's women who are out: The hidden consequences for women of criminal justice policy reforms. In S. Miller (Ed.), *Crime Control and Women*, pp. 1–11. Thousand Oaks, CA: Sage.

Danner, T., Blount, W., Silverman, I. & Vega, M. 1995. The female chronic offender: Exploring life contingency and offense history dimensions for incarcerated female offenders. *Women & Criminal Justice 6*(2), 45–64.

Datesman, S. & Cales, G. 1983. "I'm still the same mommy": Maintaining the mother/child relationship in prison. *The Prison Journal 63*, 142–154.

Datesman, S. & Scarpetti, F. (Eds.) 1980a. *Women, Crime and Justice*. New York: Oxford University Press.

Datesman, S. & Scarpetti, F. 1980b. Female delinquency and broken homes. In S. Datesman and F. Scarpetti (Eds.), *Women, Crime and Justice*, pp. 129–150. New York: Oxford University Press.

Datesman, S., Scarpetti, F. & Stephenson, R. 1975. Female delinquency: An application of self and opportunity theories. *Journal of Research in Crime and Delinquency 12*, 107–132.

Davidson, J., Pasko, L. & Chesney-Lind, M. 2011. "She's way too good to lose": An evaluation of Honolulu's girls' court. *Women & Criminal Justice 21*, 308–327.

Davidson, T. 1974. *Chicano Prisoners: The Key to San Quentin*. New York: Holt, Rinehart & Winston.

Decker, S., Wright, R., Redfern, A. & Smith, D. 1993. A woman's place is in the home: Females and residential burglary. *Justice Quarterly 10*, 143–162.

DeCostanzo, E. & Scholes, H. 1988. Women behind bars: Their numbers increase. *Corrections Today 50*(3), 104–108.

DeCostanzo, E. & Valente, J. 1984. Designing a corrections continuum for female offenders: One state's experience. *The Prison Journal 64*(1), 120–128.

DeGroot, G. 1998. A day in the life: Four women share their stories of life behind bars. *Corrections Today* (December), 82–86.

DeHart, D. 2005. *Pathways to Prison: Impact of Victimization in the Lives of Incarcerated Women* (Doc. No. 208383). Washington, DC: National Institute of Justice.

DeKeseredy, W. & Schwartz, M. 1996. *Contemporary Criminology*. Belmont, CA: Wadsworth.

DeKeseredy, W., Saunders, D., Schwartz, M. & Alvi, S. 1997. The meaning and motives for women's use of violence in Canadian college dating relationships: Results from a national survey. *Sociological Spectrum 17*(2), 199–222.

Delisi, M., Hochstetler, A. & Murphy, D. 2003. Self-control behind bars: A validation study of the Grasmick et al. scale. *Justice Quarterly 20*, 241–263.

Dembo, R., Williams, L. & Schmeidler, J. 1993. Gender differences in mental health service needs among youth entering a juvenile detention center. *Journal of Prison and Jail Health 12*, 73–101.

Denno, D. 1988. Human biology and criminal responsibility: Free will or free ride? *University of Pennsylvania Law Review 137*, 615–667.

Denno, D. 1990. *Biology and Violence: From Birth to Adulthood*. New York: Cambridge University Press.

Denno, D. 1994. Gender, crime, and the criminal law defenses. *Journal of Criminal Law and Criminology 85*(1), 80–180.

Denov, M. 2001. A culture of denial: Exploring professional perspectives on female sex offending. *Canadian Journal of Criminology 43*(3), 303–329.

Denzin, N. 1990. Presidential address on the sociological imagination revisited. *Sociological Quarterly 31*, 1–22.

Deschenes, E. & Anglin, D. 1992. Effects of legal supervision on narcotic addict behavior: Ethnic and gender influences. In T. Mieczkowski (Ed.), *Drugs, Crime and Social Policy*, pp. 167–196. Needham, MA: Allyn & Bacon.

Deschenes, E., Owen, B. & Crow, J. 2007. *Recidivism among female offenders: Secondary analysis of the 1994 BJS Recidivism data set* (Doc. No. 216950). Washington, DC: Bureau of Justice Statistics.

Dixon, S., Krienert, J. & Walsh, J. 2013. Filicide: A gendered profile of offender, victim, and event characteristics in a national sample of reported incidents, 1995–2009. *Journal of Crime & Justice*. Advance online publication. doi: 10.1080/0735648X.2013.803440

Dobash, R. & Dobash, R. 2004. Women's violence to men in intimate relationships. *The British Journal of Criminology 44*(3), 324–349.

Dobash, R., Dobash, R. & Gutteridge, S. 1986. *The Imprisonment of Women*. New York: Basil Blackwell.

Dobash, R., Dobash, R., Wilson, M. & Daly, M. 1992. The myth of sexual symmetry in marital violence. *Social Problems 39*(1), 71–91.

Dodge, M. 2009. *Women and White-Collar Crime*. Upper Saddle River, NJ: Pearson.

Dodge, M. & Pogrebin, M. 2001. Collateral costs of imprisonment for women: Complications of reintegration. *The Prison Journal 81*, 42–54.

Doerner, J. 2012. Gender disparities in sentencing departures: An examination of U.S. federal courts. *Women & Criminal Justice 22*, 176–205.

Dohrn, B. 2004. All Ellas: Girls locked up. *Feminist Studies 30*(2), 302–324.

Dowden, C. & Andrews, D. 1999. What works for female offenders: A meta-analytic review. *Crime & Delinquency 45*(4), 438–452.

d'Orban, P. 1979. Women who kill their children. *British Journal of Psychiatry 134*, 560–571.

Dressel, P. & Barnhill, S. 1994. Reframing gerontological thought and practice: The case of grandmothers with daughters in prison. *The Gerontologist 34*, 685–691.

Driscoll, D. 1985. Mother's day once a month. *Corrections Today* (August), 18–24.

Durose, M., Harlow, C., Langan, P., Motivans, M., Rantala, R. & Smith, E. 2005. *Family Violence Statistics: Including Statistics on Strangers and Acquaintances* (NCJ 207846). Washington, DC: Bureau of Justice Statistics.

Dugdale, R. 1895. *The Jukes: A Study in Crime, Pauperism, Disease and Heredity.* New York: Putnam.

Dunlap, E., Johnson, B. & Maher, L. 1997. Female crack sellers in New York City: Who they are and what they do. *Women & Criminal Justice 8*(4), 25–55.

D'Unger, A., Land, K. & McCall, P. 2002. Sex differences in age patterns of delinquent/criminal careers: Results from Poisson Latent Class Analyses of the Philadelphia cohort study. *Journal of Quantitative Criminology 18*(4), 349–275.

Dwyer, J. 2014. Jailing black babies. *Utah Law Review*, forthcoming, 2014. William & Mary Law School Research Paper No. 09-239. Retrieved from http://papers.ssrn.com/sol3/papers.cfm?abstract_id=2231562

Dye, M. 2011. The gender paradox in prison suicide rates. *Women & Criminal Justice 21*, 290–307.

Eaton, M. 1986. *Justice for Women: Family, Court and Social Control.* Philadelphia, PA: Open University Press.

Edgar, K. & Martin, C. 2003, February. Conflicts and violence in prison, 1998–2000 [computer file]. Colchester, Essex: UK Data Archive [distributor]. SN: 4596.

Edgar, K., O'Donnell, I. & Martin, C. 2003. Tracking the pathways to violence in prison. In M. Lee & E. Stanko (Eds.), *Researching Violence: Essays on Methodology and Measurement*, pp. 69–87. London: Routledge.

Einat, T. & Chen, G. 2012. Gossip in a maximum security female prison: An exploratory study. *Women & Criminal Justice 22*, 108–134.

Ellis, L. 1991. Monoamine oxidase and criminality: Identifying an apparent biological marker for antisocial behavior. *Journal of Research in Crime and Delinquency 28*, 227–251.

Ellis, L. & Coontz, P. 1990. Androgens, brain functioning and criminality: The neurohormonal foundations of antisociality. In L. Ellis and H. Hoffman (Eds.), *Crime in Biological, Social and Moral Contexts*, pp. 162–193. New York: Praeger.

Ellis, L. & Simpson, S. 1995. Informal sanction threats and corporate crime: Additive versus multiplicative models. *Journal of Research in Crime and Delinquency 32*(4), 399–424.

English, K., Widom, C. & Brandford, C. 2001. *Childhood Victimization and Delinquency, Adult Criminality, and Violent Criminal Behavior: A Replication and Extension.* Washington, DC: National Institute of Justice.

Enos, S. 2001. *Mothering from the Inside: Parenting in a Women's Prison.* Albany: State University of New York Press.

Epp, J. 1996. Exploring health care needs of adult female offenders. *Corrections Today 13*, 96–97, 105, 121.

Eppright, T., Kashani, J., Robison, B. & Reid, J. 1993. Comorbidity of conduct disorder and personality disorder in an incarcerated juvenile population. *American Journal of Psychiatry 150*, 1233–1236.

Esbensen, F., Deschenes, E. & Winfree, L. 1999. Differences between gang girls and gang boys: Results from a multistate survey. *Youth and Society 31*, 27–35.

Evans, T., Cullen, F., Burton, V., Dunaway, R. & Benson, M. 1997. The social consequences of self-control: Testing the General Theory of crime. *Criminology 35*, 475–503.

Ewing, C. 1987. *Battered Women Who Kill*. Lexington, MA: Lexington Books.

Ewing, C. 2000. *Fatal Families: The Dynamics of Intrafamilial Homicide*. Thousand Oaks, CA: Sage.

Eysenck, H. 1977. *Crime and Personality*. London: Routledge.

Eysenck, J. & Gudjonsson, G. 1989. *The Causes and Cures of Criminality*. New York: Plenum.

Faily, A. & Roundtree, G. 1979. Study of aggressions and rule violations in a female prison population. *Journal of Offender Counseling, Services and Rehabilitation 4*(1), 81–87.

Faily, A., Roundtree, G. & Miller, R. 1980. Study of the maintenance of discipline with regard to rule infractions at the Louisiana Correctional Institute for Women. *Corrective and Social Psychiatry and Journal of Behavior Technology Methods and Therapy 26*(4), 151–155.

Faith, K. 1993. *Unruly Women: The Politics of Confinement and Resistance*. Vancouver, Canada: Press Gang Publishers.

Faiver, K. & Rieger, D. 1998. Women's health issues. In K. Faiver (Ed.), *Health Care Management in Correction*, pp. 133–141. Lanham, MD: American Correctional Association.

Farnsworth, M. & Teske, R. 1995. Gender differences in felony court processing: Three hypotheses of disparity. *Women & Criminal Justice 6*(2), 23–44.

Farr, K. 2000. Classification for female inmates: Moving forward. *Crime & Delinquency 46*(1), 3–17.

Farrell, A. 2000. Women, crime and drugs: Testing the effect of therapeutic communities. *Women & Criminal Justice 11*(1), 21–49.

Farrington, D. 1991. Childhood aggression and adult violence: Early precursors and later life outcomes. In D. Pepler & K. Rubin (Eds.), *The Development and Treatment of Childhood Aggression*, pp. 5–29. Hillsdale, NJ: Lawrence Erlbaum.

Farrington, D. 1996. The explanation and prevention of youthful offending. In J. Hawkins (Ed.), *Delinquency and Crime: Current Theories*. New York: Cambridge University Press.

Farrington, D. 2003. Developmental and life-course criminology: Key theoretical and empirical issues—The 2002 Sutherland Award address. *Criminology 41*(2), 221–255.

Farrington, D., Loeber, R. & Van Kammen, W. 1990. Long-term criminal outcomes of hyperactivity-impulsivity-attention deficit and conduct problems in childhood. In L. Robins & M. Rutter (Eds.), *Straight and Devious Pathways from Childhood to Adulthood*, pp. 62–82. New York: Cambridge University Press.

Farrington, D. & Morris, A. 1983. Sex, sentencing and reconvictions. *British Journal of Criminology 23*, 229–276.

Farrington, D., Ohlin, L. & Wilson, J. 1986. *Understanding and Controlling Crime: Toward a New Research Strategy*. New York: Springer-Verlag.

Farrington, D. & West, D. 1993. Criminal, penal and life histories of chronic offenders: Risk and protective factors and early identification. *Criminal Behavior and Mental Health 3*, 492–523.

Federal Bureau of Investigation. 2013. Arrests by sex, 2012. *Crime in the United States, 2012*, Table 42. Washington, DC: Bureau of Justice Statistics. Retrieved from http://

www.fbi.gov/about-us/cjis/ucr/crime-in-the-u.s/2012/crime-in-the-u.s.-2012/tables/42tabledatadecoverviewpdf

Feinman, C. 1976. Imprisoned women: A history of the treatment of women incarcerated in New York City, 1932–1975. Unpublished doctoral dissertation, New York University.

Feinman, C. 1983. An historical overview of the treatment of incarcerated women: Myths and realities of rehabilitation. *The Prison Journal 63*(2), 12–26.

Feinman, C. 1992. *The Criminalization of a Woman's Body.* New York: Haworth Press.

Feinman, C. 1994. *Women in the Criminal Justice System* (3rd ed.). New York: Praeger.

Feld, B. 2009. Violent girls or relabeled status offenders? *Crime & Delinquency 55*(3), 241–265.

Fenster, C. 1981. Societal reaction to male-female co-defendants: Sex as an independent variable. *California Sociologist 4*, 219–232.

Fernald, M., Hayes, M. & Dawley, A. 1920. *A Study of Women Delinquents in New York State.* New York: Century.

Ferraro, K. & Moe, A. 2006. The impact of mothering on criminal offending. In Alarid, L. & Cromwell, P. (Eds.), *In Her Own Words: Women Offenders' Views on Crime and Victimization*, pp. 79–92. Los Angeles, CA: Roxbury.

Feyerhern, W. 1981a. Gender differences in delinquency quantity and quality. In L. Bowker (Ed.), *Women and Crime in America*, pp. 82–93. New York: Macmillan.

Feyerhern, W. 1981b. Measuring gender differences in delinquency self-reports v. police contacts. In M. Warren (Ed.), *Comparing Female and Male Offenders*, pp. 46–54. Beverly Hills, CA: Sage.

Figueira-McDonough, J. 1985. Gender differences in informal processing: A look at charge bargaining and sentence reduction in Washington, DC. *Journal of Research in Crime and Delinquency 22*, 101–133.

Figueira-McDonough, J., Barton, W. & Sarri, R. 1981. Normal deviance: Gender similarities in adolescent subcultures. In M. Warren (Ed.), *Comparing Female and Male Offenders*, pp. 17–45. Beverly Hills, CA: Sage.

Finn, M., Blackwell, B., Stalans, L., Studdard, S. & Dugan, L. 2004. Dual arrest decisions in domestic violence cases: The influence of departmental polices. *Crime & Delinquency 50*(4), 565–589.

Flavin, J. 2009. *Our Bodies, Our Crimes: The Policing of Women's Reproduction in America.* New York: New York University Press.

Fleisher, M. & Krienert, J. 2006. *The Culture of Prison Violence.* Washington, DC: National Institute of Justice.

Fleisher, M., Rison, R. & Helman, D. 1997. Female inmates: A growing constituency in the Federal Bureau of Prisons. *Corrections Management Quarterly 1*(4), 28–35.

Flesher, F. 2007. Cross gender supervision in prisons and the constitutional right of prisoners to remain free from rape. *William and Mary Journal of Women and the Law* (Spring), 841–867.

Fletcher, B., Shaver, L. & Moon, D. 1993. *Women Prisoners: A Forgotten Population.* Westport, CT: Praeger.

Flowers, R. 1987. *Women and Criminality: The Woman as Victim, Offender and Practitioner.* Westport, CT: Greenwood Press.

Flowers, S. 2010. *Gender-Responsive Strategies for Women Offenders.* Boulder, CO: National Institute of Corrections.

Flynn, E. 1963. *The Alderson Story: My Life as a Political Prisoner.* New York: International Publishers.

Fogel, C. 1991. Health problems and needs of incarcerated women. *Journal of Prison and Jail Health 10*(1), 43–57.

Fogel, C. 1995. Pregnant prisoners: Impact of incarceration on health and health care. *Journal of Correctional Health Care 2*, 169–190.

Foster, T. 1975. Make-believe families: A response of women and girls to the deprivations of imprisonment. *International Journal of Criminology and Penology 3*, 71–78.

Fox, J. 1975. Women in crisis. In H. Toch (Ed.), *Men in Crisis*, pp. 181–205. Chicago: Aldine Atherton.

Fox, J. 1982. Women in prison: A case study in the social reality of stress. In R. Johnson and H. Toch (Eds.), *The Pains of Imprisonment*, pp. 205–220. Long Grove, IL: Waveland Press.

Fox, J. 1984. Women's prison policy, prisoner activism, and the impact of the contemporary feminist movement: A case study. *The Prison Journal 64*(1), 15–36.

Fox, J. & Piquero, A. 2003. Deadly demographics: Population characteristics and forecasting homicide trends. *Crime & Delinquency 49*(3), 339–359.

Freedman, E. 1974. Their sister's keepers: A historical perspective of female correctional institutions in the U.S. *Feminist Studies 2*, 77–95.

Freedman, E. 1981. *Their Sister's Keepers: Women's Prison Reforms in America, 1830–1930.* Ann Arbor: University of Michigan Press.

French, L. 1978. The incarcerated black female: The case of social double jeopardy. *Journal of Black Studies 8*, 321–335.

French, L. 1983. A profile of the incarcerated black female offender. *The Prison Journal 63*(2), 80–87.

Fritsch, T. & Burkhead, J. 1982. Behavioral reactions of children to parental absence due to imprisonment. *Family Relations 30*(1), 83–88.

Freudenberg, N., Daniels, J., Crum, M., Perkins, T. & Richie, B. 2005. Coming home from jail: The social and health consequences of community reentry for women, male adolescents and their families and communities. *American Journal of Public Health 95*(10), 1725–1736.

Fullilove, M., Lown, M. & Fullilove, R. 1992. Crack 'hos and skeezers: Traumatic experiences of women crack users. *The Journal of Sex Research 29*(2), 275–287.

Gaarder, E. & Belknap, J. 2002. Tenuous borders: Girls transferred to adult court. *Criminology 40*, 481–518.

Gaarder, E. & Belknap, J. 2004. Little women: Girls in adult prisons. *Women & Criminal Justice 15*, 51–80.

Gabel, K., Engel, K., Josephson, B. & Kates, E. 1982. *Legal Issues of Female Inmates.* Northampton, MA: Smith College School for Social Work.

Gabel, K. & Johnston, D. 1995. *Children of Incarcerated Parents.* New York: Lexington Books.

Gaes, G. & Camp, S. 2009. Unintended consequences: Experimental evidence for the criminogenic effect of prison security level placement on post release recidivism. *Journal of Experimental Criminology 5*, 139–162.

Gannon, T. & Cortoni, F. 2010. *Female Sex Offenders: Theory, Assessment, and Treatment.* New York: Wiley.

Gauthier, D. & Bankston, W. 1997. Gender equality and the sex ratio of intimate killing. *Criminology 35*(4), 577–600.

Gendreau, P. 1996. The principles of effective intervention with offenders. In A. T. Harland (Ed.), *Choosing Correctional Options That Work.* Thousand Oaks, CA: Sage.

Giallombardo, R. 1966. *Society of Women: A Study of a Women's Prison.* New York: Wiley.

Gibbs, J. & Giever, D. 1995. Self-control and its manifestation among university students: An empirical test of Gottfredson and Hirschi's General Theory. *Justice Quarterly 12*(2), 231–256.

Gibson, C., Khey, D. & Schreck, C. 2008. Gender, internal controls, and academic dishonesty: Investigating mediating and differential effects. *Journal of Criminal Justice Education 19*(1), 1–18.

Gilfus, M. 1988. Seasoned by violence/tempered by law: A qualitative study of women and crime. Unpublished doctoral dissertation, Brandeis University, Waltham, MA.

Gilfus, M. 1992. From victims to survivors to offenders: Women's routes of entry and immersion into street crime. *Women &Criminal Justice 4*(1), 63–88.

Gilfus, M. 2006. From victims to survivors to offenders: Women's routes of entry and immersion into street crime. In L. F. Alarid & P. Cromwell (Eds.), *In Her Own Words: Women Offenders' Views on Crime and Victimization.* Los Angeles: Roxbury.

Gilligan, C. 1982. *In a Different Voice: Psychological Theory and Women's Development.* Cambridge, MA: Harvard University Press.

Gilligan, C. 1987. Moral orientation and moral development. In E. Kittay and D. Meyers (Eds.), *Women and Moral Theory,* pp. 19–23. Savage, MD: Rowman and Littlefield.

Gilligan, C. 1990. Joining the resistance: Psychology, politics, girls and women. *Michigan Quarterly Review 29*(4), 501–536.

Gilligan, C., Rogers, A. & Tolman, D. 1991. *Women, Girls and Psychotherapy: Reframing Resistance.* New York: The Haworth Press.

Giordano, P. & Cernkovich, S. 1979. On complicating the relationship between liberation and delinquency. *Social Problems 26*, 467–481.

Giordano, P., Cernkovich, S. & Rudolph, J. 2002. Gender, crime, and desistence: Toward a theory of cognitive transformation. *American Journal of Sociology 107*, 990–1064.

Girshick, L. 1999. *No Safe Haven: Stories of Women in Prison.* Boston, MA: Northeastern University Press.

Glaze, L. & Bonczar, A. 2009. *Probation and Parole in the United States, 2008* (NCJ 228230). Washington, DC: Bureau of Justice Statistics.

Glick, R. & Neto, V. 1977. *National Study of Women's Correctional Programs.* Washington, DC: National Institute of Law Enforcement and Criminal Justice.

Glueck, S. & Glueck, E. 1934. *Five Hundred Delinquent Women.* New York: Knopf.

Goetting, A. & Howsen, R. 1983. Women in prison: A profile. *The Prison Journal 63*(2), 27–46.

Goodkind, S. 2009. Are girls really becoming more delinquent? Testing the gender convergence hypothesis by race and ethnicity, 1976–2005. *Child & Youth Services Review 31*, 885–945.

Gora, J. 1982. *The New Female Criminal: Empirical Reality or Social Myth?* New York: Praeger.

Goshin, L. S. & Byrne, M. W. 2009. Converging streams of opportunity for prison nursery programs in the United States, *Journal of Offender Rehabilitation 48*, 271–295.

Gottfredson, M. & Hirschi, T. 1986. The true value of Lambda would appear to be zero: An essay on career criminals, criminal careers, selective incapacitation, cohort studies and related topics. *Criminology 24*, 213–234.

Gottfredson, M. & Hirschi, T. 1987. The methodological adequacy of longitudinal research on crime. *Criminology 24*, 581–614.

Gottfredson, M. & Hirschi, T. 1988. Science, public policy, and the career paradigm. *Criminology 26*, 37–56.

Gottfredson, M. & Hirschi, T. 1990. *A General Theory of Crime.* Stanford, CA: Stanford University Press.

Gover, A., Perez, D. & Jennings, W. 2008. Gender differences in factors contributing to institutional misconduct. *The Prison Journal 88*(3), 378–403.

Grasmick, H., Blackwell, B. & Bursik, R. 1993. Changes in the sex patterning of perceived threats of sanctions. *Law and Society Review 27*, 679–705.

Grasmick, H. & Bursik, R. 1990. Conscience, significant others, and rational choice: Extending the deterrence model. *Law and Society Review 24*, 837–862.

Grasmick, H., Bursik, R., Jr. & Kinsey, K. 1991. Shame and embarrassment as deterrents to non-compliance with the law: The case of an antilittering campaign. *Environment and Behavior 23*(2), 233–251.

Grasmick, H., Hagan, J., Blackwell, B. & Arneklev, B. 1996. Risk preferences and patriarchy: Extending power-control theory. *Social Forces 75*(1), 177–199.

Grasmick, H., Tittle, C., Bursik, R. & Arneklev, B. 1993. Testing the core empirical implications of Gottfredson and Hirschi's general theory of crime. *Journal of Research in Crime and Delinquency 30*, 5–29.

Gray, T., Mays, L. & Stohr, M. 1995. Inmate needs and programming in exclusively women's jails." *Prison Journal 75*, 186–203.

Green, B., Miranda, J., Daroowala, A. & Siddique, J. 2005. Trauma exposure, mental health functioning, and program needs of women in jail. *Crime & Delinquency 51*(1), 133–151.

Greenberg, D. 1999. The weak strength of social control theory. *Crime & Delinquency 45*(1), 66–81.

Greenfield, L. & Minor-Harper, S. 1991. *Women in Prison* (Bureau of Justice Statistics Special Report, NCJ 134732). Washington, DC: U.S. Department of Justice.

Greenfield, L. & Snell, T. 1999. *Women Offenders* (Bureau of Justice Statistics Special Report, NCJ 175688). Washington, DC: U.S. Department of Justice.

Greer, K. 2000. The changing nature of interpersonal relationships in a women's prison. *The Prison Journal 80*(4), 442–468.

Grella, C., Lovinger, K. & Warda, U. 2013. Relationships among trauma exposure, familial characteristics and PTSD: A case control study of women in prison and in the general population. *Women and Criminal Justice 23*, 63–79.

Griffin, T. & Wooldredge, J. 2006. Sex-based disparities in felony dispositions before versus after sentencing reform in Ohio. *Criminology 44*, 893–923.

Gruhl, J., Welch, S. & Spohn, C. 1984. Women as criminal defendants: A test for paternalism. *Western Political Quarterly 37*, 456–467.

Guerino, P., Harrison, P. & Sabol, W. 2011. *Prisoners in 2010* (NCJ 236096). Washington, DC: Bureau of Justice Statistics.

Gunnison, E. & McCartan, L. 2005. The role of different developmental experiences: A theoretical examination of female persistence. *Women & Criminal Justice 16*(3), 43–65.

Hagan, J. 1989. *Structural Criminology.* New Brunswick, NJ: Rutgers University Press.

Hagan, J. & O'Donnel, N. 1978. Sexual stereotyping and judicial sentencing: A legal test of the sociological wisdom. *Canadian Journal of Sociology 3*, 309–319.

Hagan, J., Simpson, J. & Gillis, A. 1979. The sexual stratification of social control. *British Journal of Sociology 30*, 25–38.

Hagan, J., Simpson, J. & Gillis, A. 1987. Class in the household: A power-control theory of gender and delinquency. *American Journal of Sociology 92*, 788–816.

Hahn, N. 1979. Too dumb to know better: Cacogenic family studies and the criminology of women. Paper presented at the American Society of Criminology Meeting, Philadelphia, PA.

Hairston, C. 1991. Family ties during imprisonment: Important to whom and for what? *Journal of Sociology and Welfare 18*(1), 87–104.

Hairston, C. 1997. Family programs in state prisons. In C. McNeece & A. Roberts (Eds.), *Policy and Practice in the Justice System*, pp. 143–159. Chicago: Nelson-Hall.

Hairston, H. & Lockett, D. 1985. Parents in prison: A child abuse and neglect prevention strategy. *Child Abuse and Neglect 9*, 471–477.

Haley, K. 1977. Mothers behind bars: A look at the parental rights of incarcerated women. *New England Journal of Prison Law 4*(1), 141–155.

Hall, M., Golder, S., Conley, C. & Sawnings, S. 2012. Designing programming and interventions for women in the criminal justice system. *American Journal of Criminal Justice 38*, 27–50.

Halleck, S. & Herski, M. 1962. Homosexual behavior in a correctional institution for adolescent girls. *American Journal of Orthopsychiatry 32*, 911–917.

Hannah-Moffat, K. 1995. Feminine fortresses: Woman-centered prisons? *The Prison Journal 75*(2), 135–164.

Hannah-Moffat, K. 2004. Losing ground: Gendered knowledges, parole risk, and responsibility. *Social Politics 11*(3), 363–385.

Hannum, T., Borgen, F. & Anderson, R. 1978. Self-concept changes associated with incarceration in female prisoners. *Criminal Justice and Behavior 5*(3), 271–279.

Hanson, L. 1983. Women prisoners: Freedom from sexual harassment—A constitutional analysis. *Golden Gate University Law Review 13*, 667–696.

Harden, J. & Hill, M. (Eds.). 1998. *Breaking the Rules: Women in Prison and Feminist Therapy*. New York: Haworth Press.

Hardyman, P. & Van Voorhis, P. 2004. *Developing Gender-Specific Classification Systems for Women Offenders*. Washington, DC: National Institute of Corrections.

Harlow, C. 1997. *Profile of Jail Inmates 1996* (Bureau of Justice Statistics Special Report, NCJ 164260). Washington, DC: U.S. Department of Justice.

Harlow, C. 1999. *Selected Findings: Prior Abuse Reported by Inmates and Probationers* (NCJ 172879). Washington DC: Bureau of Justice Statistics.

Harlow, C. 2003. *Education and Correctional Populations* (Bureau of Justice Statistics Special Report, NCJ 195670). Washington, DC: U.S. Department of Justice.

Harmon, R., Rosner, R. & Wiederlight, M. 1985. Women and arson: A demographic study. *Journal of Forensic Sciences 30*(2), 467–477.

Harris, J. 1988. *They Always Call Us Ladies*. New York: Charles Scribner & Sons.

Harris, J. 1993. Comparison of stressors among female v. male inmates. *Journal of Offender Rehabilitation 19*(1/2), 43–56.

Harris, M. 1987. Moving into the new millennium: Toward a feminist vision of justice. *The Prison Journal 67*, 27–38.

Harris, M. 1988. *Cholas: Latino Girls and Gangs*. New York: AMS Press.

Harrison, P. & Beck, A. 2002. *Prisoners in 2001* (NCJ 195189). Washington, DC: Bureau of Justice Statistics.

Hart, C. 1995. Gender differences in social support among inmates. *Women & Criminal Justice 6*(2), 67–88.

Hartnagel, T. & Gillan, M. 1980. Female prisoners and the inmate code. *Pacific Sociological Review 23*, 85–104.

Hay, C. 2003. Family strain, gender, and delinquency. *Sociological Perspectives 46*(1), 107–135.

Hay, C. 2006. The development of self-control: Examining self-control theory's stability thesis. *Criminology 44*, 739–774.

Hayner, N. 1961. Characteristics of five offender types. *American Sociological Review 26*, 97–98.

Hayner, N. & Ash, E. 1939. The prisoner community as a social group. *American Sociological Review 4*,(3), 362–369.

Heffernan, R. 1972. *Making It in Prison: The Square, the Cool and the Life*. New York: Wiley.

Heidensohn, F. 1985. *Women and Crime: The Life of the Female Offender*. New York: New York University Press.

Heidensohn, F. 1986. Models of justice: Portia or Persephone? Some thoughts on equality, fairness and gender in the field of criminal justice. *International Journal of the Sociology of Law 14*, 287–298.

Heimer, K. 1996. Gender, interaction, and delinquency: Testing a theory of differential social control. *Social Psychology Quarterly 59*, 39–61.

Heimer, K. 2000. Changes in the gender gap in crime and women's economic marginalization. In Office of Justice Programs (Ed.), *The Nature of Crime: Continuity and Change*, pp. 427–483. Washington, DC: National Institute of Justice.

Heimer, K. & DeCoster, S. 1999. The gendering of violent delinquency. *Criminology 37*, 277–317.

Held, V. 1987. Feminism and moral theory. In E. F. Kittay and D. T. Meyers (Eds.), *Women and Moral Theory*, pp. 111–128. Savage, MD: Rowman and Littlefield.

Heney, J. & Kristiansen, C. 1998. An analysis of the impact of prison on women survivors of childhood sexual abuse. In J. Harden and M. Hill (Eds.), *Breaking the Rules: Women in Prison and Feminist Therapy*, pp. 29–44. New York: Haworth Press.

Henriques, Z. 1982. *Imprisoned Mothers and Their Children: A Descriptive and Analytical Study.* Washington, DC: University Press of America.

Henriques, Z. 1995. African American women: The oppressive intersection of gender, race and class. *Women & Criminal Justice 7*(1), 67–80.

Henriques, Z. 1996. Imprisoned mothers and their children: Separation-reunion syndrome. *Women & Criminal Justice 8*(1), 77–95.

Henriques, Z. & Gilbert, E. 2000. Sexual abuse and sexual assault of women in prison. In R. Muraskin (Ed.), *It's a Crime: Women and Justice* (2nd ed.), pp. 253–268. Upper Saddle River, NJ: Prentice-Hall.

Henriques, Z. & Manatu-Rupert, N. 2001. Living on the outside: African American women before, during, and after imprisonment. *The Prison Journal 81*(1), 6–19.

Hickey, J. & Scharf, P. 1980. *Toward a Just Correctional System.* San Francisco, CA: Jossey-Bass.

Hill, G. & Crawford, E. (1990). Women, race and crime. *Criminology 28*, 601–623.

Hindelang, M. 1979. Sex differences in criminal activity. *Social Problems 27*, 143–156.

Hindelang, M. 1981a. Variations in sex-race-age-specific incidence rates of offending. *American Sociological Review 46*, 461–474.

Hindelang, M. 1981b. *Measuring Delinquency.* Beverly Hills, CA: Sage.

Hirschel, D. & Buzawa, E. 2002. Understanding the context of dual arrest with directions for future research. *Violence against Women 8*(12), 1449–1474.

Hirschi, T. 1969. *Causes of Delinquency.* Berkeley: University of California Press.

Hirschi, T. 1994. Family. In T. Hirschi & M. Gottfredson (Eds.), *The Generality of Deviance*, pp. 47–69. New Brunswick, NJ: Transaction Publishers.

Hirschi, T. 2004. Self-control and crime. In R. F. Baumeister & K. D. Vohs (Eds.), *Handbook of Self-Regulation: Research, Theory and Applications*. New York: Guilford Press.

Hockenberry, S. 2013. *Juveniles in Residential Placement, 2010* (National Report Series Bulletin, NCJ 241060). Washington, DC: Office of Juvenile Justice and Delinquency Prevention.

Hoffman-Bustamante, D. 1973. The nature of female criminality. *Issues in Criminology 8*, 117–123.

Holsinger, K. & Holsinger, A. 2005. Differential pathways to violence and self-injurious behavior: African American and white girls in the juvenile justice system. *Journal of Research in Crime and Delinquency 42*, 211–242.

Holtfreter, K. & Cupp, R. 2007. Gender and risk assessment: The empirical status of the LSI-R for women. *Journal of Contemporary Criminal Justice 23*(4), 363–382.

Holtfreter, K. & Morash, M. 2003. The needs of women offenders: Implications for correctional programming. *Women & Criminal Justice 14*, 137–160.

Holtfreter, K., Reisig, M. & Morash, M. 2004. Poverty, state capital, and recidivism among women offenders. *Crime and Public Policy 3*(2), 185–208.

Houser, K. A., Belenko, S. & Brennan, P. K. 2012. The effects of mental health and substance abuse disorders on institutional misconduct among female inmates. *Justice Quarterly 29*, 799–828.

Howe, A. 1990. Prologue to a history of women's imprisonment: In search of a feminist perspective. *Social Justice 17*(2), 5–33.

Howe, A. 1994. *Punish and Critique: Toward a Feminist Analysis of Penality.* London: Routledge.

Howell, J. 2003. *Preventing and Reducing Juvenile Delinquency: A Comprehensive Framework.* Thousand Oaks, CA: Sage.

Hser, Y., Anglin, D. & Booth, M. 1987a. Sex differences in addict careers: Addiction. *American Journal of Drug and Alcohol Abuse 13*, 155–157.

Hser, Y., Anglin, D. & Booth, M. 1987b. Sex differences in addict careers: Initiation of use. *American Journal of Drug and Alcohol Abuse 13*, 231–251.

Hser, Y., Anglin, D. & Chou, C. 1992. Narcotics use and crime among addicted women: Longitudinal patterns and effects of social intervention. In T. Mieczkowski (Ed.), *Drugs, Crime and Social Policy,* pp. 197–221. Needham, MA: Allyn & Bacon.

Hubbard, D. & Matthews, B. 2008. Reconciling the difference between the gender responsive and what works literatures to improve services for girls. *Crime & Delinquency 54*(2), 225–258.

Huling, T. 1995. Women drug couriers. *Criminal Justice 9*(4), 14–20.

Human Rights Watch. 1996. *All Too Familiar: Sexual Abuse of Women in U.S. State Prisons.* New York: Author.

Humphries, D. 1993. Mothers and children, drugs and crack: Reactions to maternal drug dependency. In R. Muraskin & T. Alleman (Eds.), *It's a Crime: Women and Justice,* pp. 130–146. Englewood Cliffs, NJ: Prentice-Hall.

Humphries, D., Dawson, J., Cronin, V., Keating, P., Wisniewski, C. & Eichfeld, J. 1992. Mothers and children, drugs and crack: Reactions to maternal drug dependency. *Women & Criminal Justice 3*, 81–99.

Hungerford, G. 1993. The children of incarcerated mothers: An exploratory study of children, caretakers and inmate mothers in Ohio. Unpublished doctoral dissertation, The Ohio State University, Columbus.

Hunt, G., Laidler, K. & Evans, K. 2002. The meaning and gendered culture of getting high: Gang girls and drug use issues. *Contemporary Drug Problems 29*(2), 375–295.

Hunt, G., MacKenzie, K. & Joe-Laidler, K. 2006. "I'm calling my mom": The meaning of family and kinship among Latina homegirls. In L. Alarid & P. Cromwell (Eds.), *In Her Own Words: Women Offenders' Views on Crime and Victimization,* pp. 57–68. Los Angeles: Roxbury.

Immarigeon, R. 1994. When parents are sent to prison. *National Prison Project Journal 9*(4/5), 14–16.

Inciardi, J. 1980. Women, heroin and property crime. In S. Datesman and F. Scarpetti (Eds.), *Women, Crime and Justice,* pp. 214–223. New York: Oxford University Press.

Inciardi, J. (Ed.) 1993. Drug use and crime among two cohorts of women narcotics users: An empirical assessment. *Journal of Drug Issues 16*, 1–105.

Inciardi, J. 1996, June. *A Corrections-Based Continuum of Effective Drug Abuse Treatment* (NIJ Research Preview). Washington, DC: National Institute of Justice.

Inciardi, J., Lockwood, D. & Pottieger, A. 1993. *Women and Crack Cocaine.* New York: Macmillan.

Inciardi, J., & Pottieger, A. 1986. Drug use and crime among two cohorts of women narcotics users: An empirical assessment. *Journal of Drug Issues 16*, 91–106.

Irwin, J. 1970. *The Felon.* Englewood Cliffs: Prentice-Hall.

Irwin, J. & Cressey, D. 1962. Thieves, convicts and inmate culture. *Social Problems 10*, 142–155.

Islam-Zwart, K. & Vik, P. 2004. Female adjustment to incarceration as influenced by sexual assault history. *Criminal Justice and Behavior 31*(5), 521–541.

Jacobs, J. 1977. *Statesville: The Penitentiary in Mass Society.* Chicago: University of Chicago Press.

James, D. J. & Glaze, L. E. 2006. *Mental Health Problems of Prison and Jail Inmates* (Bureau of Justice Statistics Special Report). Washington, DC: U.S. Department of Justice.

James, J. 1976. Motivations for entrance into prostitution. In L. Crites (Ed.), *The Female Offender*, pp. 177–206. Lexington, MA: Lexington Books.

Jeffries, S., Fletcher, G. & Newbold, G. 2003. Pathways to sex-based differentiation in criminal court sentencing. *Criminology 41*, 329–353.

Jensen, G. & Eve, R. 1976. Sex differences in delinquency: An examination of popular sociological explanations. *Criminology 13*, 427–448.

Joe, K. & Chesney-Lind, M. 1995. Just every mother's angel: An analysis of gender and the ethnic variations in youth gang membership. *Gender & Society 9*, 408–430.

Johansson, P. & Kempf-Leonard, K. 2009. A gender-specific pathway to serious, violent, and chronic offending? *Crime & Delinquency 55*(3), 216–240.

Johnson, K. & Lynch, J. 2013. Predictors of maladaptive coping in incarcerated women who are survivors of childhood sexual abuse. *Journal of Family Violence 28*, 43–52.

Johnson, R. 2002. *Hard Time* (3rd ed.). Belmont, CA: Wadsworth, Cengage Learning.

Johnston, D. 1995a. Parent-child visitation in the jail or prison. In K. Gabel and D. Johnston (Eds.), *Children of Incarcerated Parents*, pp. 135–143. New York: Lexington Books.

Johnston, D. 1995b. Effects of parental incarceration. In K. Gabel and D. Johnston (Eds.), *Children of Incarcerated Parents*, pp. 259–263. New York: Lexington.

Johnston, D. 1997a. Developing services for incarcerated mothers. In C. Blinn (Ed.), *Maternal Ties: A Selection of Programs for Female Offenders*, pp. 1–9. Lanham, MD: American Correctional Association.

Johnston, D. 1997b. The Center for Children of Incarcerated Parents, In C. Blinn (Ed.), *Maternal Ties: A Selection of Programs for Female Offenders*, pp. 15–25. Lanham, MD: American Correctional Association.

Jones, M. & Sims, B. 1997. Recidivism of offenders released from prison in North Carolina: A gender comparison. *Prison Journal 77*(3), 335–348.

Jones, N. 2004. "It's not where you live, it's how you lie": How young women negotiate conflict and violence in the inner city. *Annals of Applied Social Science 595*, 49–62.

Jordan, B., Schlenger, W., Fairbank, J. & Caddell, J. 1996. Prevalence of psychiatric disorders among incarcerated women: Convicted felons entering prison. *Archives of General Psychiatry 53*(6), 513–519.

Jurik, N. 1983. The economics of female recidivism. *Criminology 21*, 3–12.

Karberg, J. & James, D. 2005. *Substance Dependence, Abuse, and Treatment of Jail Inmates, 2002* (Bureau of Justice Statistics Special Report, NCJ 209588). Washington, DC: U.S. Department of Justice

Katz, J. 1988. *Seductions of Crime: Moral and Sensual Attractions of Doing Evil.* New York: Basic Books.

Kaufman, J. 2009. Gendered responses to serious strain: The argument for a general strain theory of deviance. *Justice Quarterly 26*, 410–444.

Keane, C., Maxim, P. & Teevan, J. 1993. Drinking and driving, self-control, and gender: testing a general theory of crime. *Journal of Research in Crime and Delinquency 30*, 30–46.

Keeney, B. & Heide, K. 1994. Gender differences in serial murderers: A preliminary analysis. *Journal of Interpersonal Violence 9*(3), 383–398.

Keeney, B. & Heide, K. 1995. The latest on serial murderers. *Violence Update 4*(3), 1–4.

Kelley, B., Huizinga, D., Thornberry, T. & Loeber, R. 1997. *Epidemiology of Serious Violence.* Juvenile Justice Bulletin. Washington, DC: Office of Juvenile Justice and Delinquency Programs.

Kelley, B., Loeber, R., Keenan, K. & DeLamatre, M. 1997. Developmental pathways in boys' disruptive and delinquent behavior. *Juvenile Justice* (December). Washington, DC: Office of Juvenile Justice and Delinquency Prevention.

Kellor, F. 1900a. Psychological and environmental study of women criminals. *The American Journal of Sociology 5*, 527–543.

Kellor, F. 1900b. Criminal sociology: Criminality among women. *Arena 23*, 516–524.

Kempf-Leonard, K., Tracy, P. & Howell, J. 2001. Serious, violent, and chronic juvenile offenders: The relationship of delinquency career types to adult criminality. *Justice Quarterly 18*, 449–478.

Kempfner, C. 1995. Post-traumatic stress reactions in children of imprisoned mothers. In K. Gabel & D. Johnston (Eds.), *Children of Incarcerated Parents*, pp. 89–100. New York: Lexington.

Kempinen, C. 1983. Changes in the sentencing patterns of male and female defendants. *Prison Journal 63*, 2–11.

Kendall, K. 1993. *Program Evaluation of Therapeutic Services at the Prison for Women.* Ottawa: Correctional Service of Canada.

Kerman, P. 2010. *Orange Is the New Black: My Year in a Women's Prison.* New York: Random House.

Keys, D. 2002. Instrumental sexual scripting: An examination of gender-role fluidity in the correctional institution. *Journal of Contemporary Criminal Justice 18*(3), 258–278.

Klein, D. 1973. The etiology of female crime: A review of the literature. *Issues in Criminology 8*, 3–29.

Klein, D. & Kress, J. 1976. Any woman's blues: A critical overview of women, crime and criminal justice. *Crime and Social Justice 5*, 34–45.

Koban, L. A. 1983. Parents in prison: A comparative analysis of the effects of incarceration on the families of men and women. *Research in Law, Deviance and Social Control 5*, 171–183.

Kohlberg, L. 1976. Moral stages and moralization: The cognitive development approach. In T. Lickona (Ed.), *Moral Development and Behavior: Theory, Research and Social Issues*, pp. 31–53. New York: Holt, Rinehart and Winston.

Kohlberg, L. 1981. *The Philosophy of Moral Development.* San Francisco: Harper and Row.

Kolman, A. 1983. Support and control patterns of inmate mothers. *The Prison Journal 63*(2), 155–116.

Konopka, G. 1966. *The Adolescent Girl in Conflict.* Englewood Cliffs, NJ: Prentice-Hall.

Koons, B., Burrow, J., Morash, M. & Bynum, T. 1997. Expert and offender perceptions of program elements linked to successful outcomes for incarcerated women. *Crime & Delinquency 43*(4), 512–532.

Koons-Witt, B. 2002. The effect of gender on the decision to incarcerate before and after the introduction of sentencing guidelines. *Criminology 40*, 297–328.

Koons-Witt, B. & Schram, P. 2006. Does race matter? Examining the relationship between co-offending and victim characteristics for violent incidents involving female offenders. *Feminist Criminology 3*(2), 125–146.

Kosofsky, S. & Ellis, A. 1958. Illegal communications among institutionalized female delinquents. *Journal of Social Psychiatry 48*, 155–160.

Krabill, J. & Aday, R. 2005. Exploring the social world of aging female prisoners. *Women & Criminal Justice 17*(1), 27–53.

Krupat, T., Gaynes, E. & Lincroft, Y. 2011. *A Call to Action: Safeguarding New York's Children of Incarcerated Parents*. New York: Osborne Association.

Kruttschnitt, C. 1981. Prison codes, inmate solidarity and women: A re-examination. In M. Warren (Ed.), *Comparing Male and Female Offenders*, pp. 123–141. Beverly Hills, CA: Sage.

Kruttschnitt, C. 1982a. Respectable women and the law. *Sociological Quarterly 23*, 221–234.

Kruttschnitt, C. 1982b. Women, crime and dependency. *Criminology 19*, 495–513.

Kruttschnitt, C. 1983. Race relations and the female inmate. *Crime & Delinquency 29*(4), 577–592.

Kruttschnitt, C. 1984. Sex and criminal court dispositions: The unresolved controversy. *Journal of Research in Crime and Delinquency 21*(3), 213–232.

Kruttschnitt, C. & Carbone-Lopez, K. 2006. Moving beyond stereotypes: Women's subjective accounts of their violent crime. *Criminology 44*, 321–351.

Kruttschnitt, C. & Dornfield, M. 1993. Exposure to family violence: A partial explanation for initial and subsequent levels of delinquency? *Criminal Behavior and Mental Health 3*, 61–75.

Kruttschnitt, C., Gartner, R. & Ferraro, K. 2002. Women's involvement in serious interpersonal violence. *Aggression and Violent Behavior 7*, 529–565.

Kubiak, S., Hanna, J. & Balton, M. 2005. "I came to prison to do my time—Not to get raped": Coping within the institutional setting. *Stress, Trauma, and Crisis 8*, 157–177.

Kubiak, S., Kim, W. & Bybee, D. 2013. Differences among incarcerated women with assaultive offenses: Isolated versus patterned use of violence. *Journal of Interpersonal Violence 28*(12), 2462–2490.

Kuo, C., Johnson, J., Rosen, R., Wechsberg, W., Gobin, R., Reddy, M., Peabody, M. & Zlotnick, C. 2013. Emotional dysregulation and risky sex among incarcerated women with a history of interpersonal violence. Advance online publication (forthcoming in *Women & Health*). doi: 10.1080/03630242.2013.850143.

LaGrange, T. & Silverman, R. 1999. Low self-control and opportunity. *Criminology 37*, 41–72.

Lahey, K. 1985. "Until women themselves have told all that they have to tell." *Osgood Hall Law Journal 23*(3), 519–541.

Langan, P. & Levin, D. 2002. *Recidivism of Inmates Released in 1994* (Bureau of Justice Statistics Special Report, NCJ 193427). Washington, DC: U.S. Department of Justice.

Latimore, T., Tittle, C. & Grasmick, H. 2006. Childrearing, self-control, and crime: Additional evidence. *Sociological Inquiry 76*(3), 343–371.

Laub, J. & McDermott, J. 1985. An analysis of serious crime by young black women. *Criminology 23*, 81–98.

Laub, J. & Sampson, R. 2003. *Shared Beginnings, Divergent Lives: Delinquent Boys to Age 70*. Cambridge, MA: Harvard University Press.

Lauderback, D., Hansen, J. & Waldorf, D. 1992. Sisters are doin' it for themselves: A black female gang in San Francisco. *The Gang Journal 1*, 57–72.

Lauritsen, J., Heimer, K. & Lynch, J. 2009. Trends in the gender gap in violent offending: New evidence from the National Crime Victimization Survey. *Criminology 47*, 361–400.

Lawrence, R. & Mahan, S. 1998. Women corrections officers in men's prisons: Acceptance and perceived job performance. *Women & Criminal Justice 9*(3), 63–87.

Lee, G., Akers, R. & Borg, M. 2004. Social learning and structural factors in adolescent substance use. *Western Criminology Review 5*(1), 17–34.

Leigey, M. & Hodge, J. 2012. Gray matters: Gender differences in the physical and mental health of older inmates. *Women & Criminal Justice 22*, 289–303.

Leigey, M. & Reed, K. 2010. A woman's life before serving life: Examining the negative pre-incarceration life events of female life-sentenced inmates. *Women & Criminal Justice 20*, 302–323.

Lekkerkerker, E. 1931. *Reformatories for Women in the U.S.* Gronigen, Netherlands: J. B. Wolters.

Lemert, E. 1951. *Social Pathology: A Systematic Approach to the Theory of Sociopathic Behavior.* New York: McGraw-Hill.

Leonard, E. 1982. *Women, Crime and Society: A Critique of Theoretical Criminology.* White Plains, NY: Longman.

Leonard, E. 1983. Judicial decisions and prison reform: The impact of litigation on women prisoners. *Social Problems 31*(1), 45–58.

Leverentz, A. 2006. The love of a good man? Romantic relationships as a source of support or hindrance for female ex-offenders. *Journal of Research in Crime and Delinquency 43*, 459–488.

Lewis, D. 1981. Black women offenders and criminal justice: Some theoretical considerations. In M. Warren (Ed.), *Comparing Female and Male Offenders*, pp. 89–105. Beverly Hills, CA: Sage.

Leiber, M., Brubaker, S. & Fox, K. 2009. A closer look at the individual and joint effects of gender and race in juvenile justice decision-making. *Feminist Criminology 4*, 333–358.

Lindquist, C. 1980. Prison discipline and the female offender. *Journal of Offender Counseling, Services and Rehabilitation 4*, 305–319.

Lipsitz, G. 2012. "In an avalanche, every snowflake pleads not guilty": The collateral consequences of mass incarceration and impediments to women's fair housing rights. *UCLA Law Review 59*, 1746–1809.

Liu, X. & Kaplan, H. 1999. Explaining the gender difference in adolescent delinquent behavior: A longitudinal test of mediating mechanisms. *Criminology 37*, 195–216.

Lombroso, C. & Ferrero, G. 1911. *Criminal Man: According to the Classification of Cesare Lombroso.* New York: Putnam. (Original work published 1894).

Lombroso, C. & Ferrero, W. 1909. *The Female Offender.* New York: Appleton. (Original work published 1895).

Longshore, D., Turner, S. & Stein, J. 1996. Self-control in a criminal sample: An examination of construct validity. *Criminology 34*, 209–227.

Lord, E. 1995. A prison superintendent's perspective on women in prison. *Prison Journal 75*(2), 257–269.

Lowenkamp, C., Holsinger, K. & Latessa, E. 2001. Risk/need assessment, offender classification, and the role of childhood abuse. *Criminal Justice and Behavior 28*(5), 543–563.

Lowenkamp, C., Latessa, E. & Holsinger, K. 2006. The risk principle in action: What have we learned from 13,676 offenders and 97 correctional programs? *Crime & Delinquency 52*, 77–93.

Lujan, C. 1995. Women warriors: American Indian women, crime, and alcohol. *Women & Criminal Justice 7*(1), 9–33.

Lutze, F. & Murphy, D. 1999. Ultramasculine prison environments and inmates' adjustment: It's time to move beyond the "boys will be boys" paradigm. *Justice Quarterly 16*, 709–733.

Lykken, D. 1995. *The Antisocial Personality.* Hillsdale, NJ: Lawrence Erlbaum.

Lynch, S., DeHart, D., Belknap, J. & Green, B. 2012. *Women's Pathways to Jail: the Roles and Intersections of Serious Mental Illness & Trauma.* Washington, DC: Bureau of Justice Assistance. Retrieved from https://www.bja.gov/Publications/Women_Pathways_to_Jail.pdf

Lynch, S., Fritch, A. & Heath, N. 2012. Looking beneath the surface: The nature of incarcerated women's experiences of interpersonal violence, treatment needs, and mental health. *Feminist Criminology 7*, 381–400.

Maccoby, E. 1985. Social groupings in childhood: Their relationship to prosocial and antisocial behavior in boys and girls. In D. Olweus, J. Block, & M. Radke-Yarrow (Eds.), *Development of Antisocial and Prosocial Behavior: Theories, Research and Issues*, pp. 263–285. Orlando, FL: Academic Press.

Maccoby, E. & Jacklin, C. 1974. *The Psychology of Sex Differences*. Stanford, CA: Stanford University Press.

MacDonald, J. & Chesney-Lind, M. 2001. Gender bias and juvenile justice revisited: A multiyear analysis. *Crime & Delinquency 47*, 173–195.

MacDonald, M. 2013. Women prisoners, mental health, violence and abuse. *International Journal of Law and Psychiatry 36*, 293–303.

Magdol, L., Moffitt, T., Caspi, A. & Silva, P. 1998. Developmental antecedents of partner abuse: A prospective-longitudinal study. *Journal of Abnormal Psychology 107*(3), 375–389.

Maeve, M. 2000. Speaking unavoidable truths: Understanding early childhood sexual and physical violence among women in prison. *Issues in Mental Health Nursing 21*, 473–498.

Mahan, S. 1984. Imposition of despair: An ethnography of women in prison. *Justice Quarterly 1*, 357–385.

Mahan, S. & Prestwood, D. 1993. A radical analysis of a treatment program for cocaine-abusing mothers. In C. Culliver (Ed.), *Female Criminality: The State of the Art*, pp. 503–515. New York: Garland.

Maher, L. 1990. Criminalizing pregnancy—The downside of a kinder, gentler nation? *Social Justice 17*(3), 111–135.

Maher, L. 1992. Punishment and welfare: Crack cocaine and the regulation of mothering. *Women & Criminal Justice 3*, 35–70.

Maher, L. 1997. *Sexed Work: Gender, Race, and Resistance in a Brooklyn Drug Market*. New York: Oxford University Press.

Maher, L. & Curtis, R. 1992. Women on the edge of crime: Crack cocaine and the changing contexts of street-level sex work in New York City. *Crime, Law and Social Change 18*(3), 221–258.

Maher, L. & Daly, K. 1996. Women in the street-level drug economy: Continuity or change? *Criminology 34*, 465–491.

Maidment, M. 2002. Toward a "woman-centered" approach to community-based corrections: A gendered analysis of electronic monitoring (EM) in eastern Canada. *Women & Criminal Justice 13*(4), 47–68.

Makarios, M. 2007. Race, abuse, and female criminal violence. *Feminist Criminology 2*(2), 100–116.

Mallicoat, S. 2007. Gendered justice: Attributional differences between males and females in the juvenile courts. *Feminist Criminology 2*(1), 4–30.

Manasse, M. & Ganem, N. 2009. Victimization as a cause of delinquency: The role of depression and gender. *Journal of Criminal Justice 37*, 371–378.

Mandraraka-Sheppard, A. 1986. The dynamics of aggression in women's prisons in England. *The Howard Journal of Criminal Justice 25*(4), 317–319.

Mann, C. 1984a. Race and sentencing of female felons: A field study. *International Journal of Women's Studies 7*, 160–172.

Mann, C. 1984b. *Female Crime and Delinquency*. Birmingham: University of Alabama Press.

Mann, C. 1988. Getting even? Women who kill in domestic encounters. *Justice Quarterly 5*(1), 33–53.

Mann, C. 1993. *Unequal Justice: A Question of Color*. Bloomington: Indiana University Press.

Mann, C. 1996. *When Women Kill*. Albany: State University of New York Press.

Marcus-Mendosa, S., Klein-Safffon, J. & Lutze, F. 1998. A feminist examination of boot camps: Prison programs for women. In J. Harden & J. Hill (Eds.), *Breaking the Rules: Women in Prison and Feminist Therapy*, pp. 173–185. New York: Haworth Press.

Marcus-Mendoza, S. & Wright, E. 2003. Treating the woman prisoner: The impact of a history of violence. In S. Sharp (Ed.), *The Incarcerated Woman: Rehabilitative Programming in Women's Prisons*, pp. 107–118. Upper Saddle River, NJ: Prentice-Hall.

Marshall, I. 1982. Women, work, and crime: An international test of the emancipation hypothesis. *International Journal of Comparative and Applied Criminal Justice 6*(1), 25–37.

Maruschak, L. & Bonczar, T. 2013. *Probation and Parole in the United States, 2012*. (NCJ 243826). Washington, DC: Bureau of Justice Statistics.

Maruschak, L. & Parks, E. 2012. *Probation and Parole in the United States, 2011*. (NCJ 239686) Washington, DC: Bureau of Justice Statistics.

Matthews, R. 2005. Policing prostitution. *British Journal of Criminology 45*, 877–895.

Mauer, M. 2013. *The Changing Racial Dynamics of Women's Incarceration*. Washington, DC: The Sentencing Project.

Mauer, M., Potler, C. & Wolf, R. 2000. The impact of the drug war on women: A comparative analysis in three states. *Women, Girls and Criminal Justice 1*(2), 21–22, 30–31.

Mazerolle, P. 1998. Gender, general strain, and delinquency: An empirical examination. *Justice Quarterly 15*, 67–91.

Mazerolle, P., Brame, R., Paternoster, R., Piquero, A. & Dean, C. 2000. Onset age, persistence, and offending versatility: Comparisons across gender. *Criminology 38*, 1143–1172.

Mazerolle, P. & Maahs, J. 2000. General strain and delinquency: An alternative examination of conditioning influences. *Justice Quarterly 17*, 753–778.

McCarthy, B. 1980. Inmate mothers: The process of separation and reintegration. *Journal of Offender Counseling, Services and Rehabilitation 13*, 5–13.

McCarthy, B., Felmlee, D. & Hagan, J. 2004. Girl friends are better: Gender, friends, and crime among school and street youth. *Criminology 42*, 805–835.

McCarthy, B., Hagan, J. & Woodward, T. 1999. In the company of women: Structure and agency in a revised power-control theory of gender and delinquency. *Criminology 37*, 761–814.

McClellan, D. 1994. Disparity in the discipline of male and female inmates in Texas prisons. *Women & Criminal Justice 5*(2), 71–97.

McClellan, D., Farabee, D. & Crouch, B. 1997. Early victimization, drug use, and criminality: A comparison of male and female prisoners. *Criminal Justice and Behavior 24*(4), 455–476.

McDaniels-Wilson, C. & Belknap, J. 2008. The extensive sexual violation and sexual abuse histories of incarcerated women. *Violence against Women 14*(10), 1090–1127.

McDonald, D. 2008. Gender-responsive treatment and the need to examine female inmates' lives in prison and prior to prison. *Corrections Compendium 33*(6), 7–14.

McDonald, D. & Grossman, J. 1981. *Analysis of Low Return Among Female Offenders*. Albany, NY: Department of Correctional Services.

McGee, Z. & Baker, S. 2002. Impact of violence on problem behavior among adolescents. *Journal of Contemporary Criminal Justice 18*(1), 74–93.

McGloin, J. M. & Diepietro, S. 2013. Girls, friends, and delinquency. In Cullen, F. T. & Wilcox, P. (Eds.), *The Oxford Handbook of Criminological Theory*, Chapter 15. New York: Oxford University Press.

McGowan, B. & Blumenthal, K. 1978. *Why Punish the Children? A Study of Children of Women Prisoners*. Hackensack, NJ: National Council on Crime and Delinquency.

McKerracher, D., Street, D. & Segal, S. 1966. A comparison of the behavior problems presented by male and female subnormal offenders. *British Journal of Psychiatry 112*, 891–899.

McLeod, E. 1982. *Women Working: Prostitution Now.* London, England: Croom-Helm.

McLeod, M. 1984. Women against men: An examination of domestic violence based on an analysis of official data and national victimization data. *Justice Quarterly 1*, 171–194.

McShane, M., Williams, F. & Dolny, H. 2002. Do standard risk prediction instruments apply to female parolees? *Women & Criminal Justice 13*(2/3), 163–182.

Mead, G. 1934. *Mind, Self and Society.* Chicago: University of Chicago Press.

Mears, D., Ploeger, M. & Warr, M. 1998. Explaining the gender gap in delinquency: Peer influence and moral evaluations of behavior. *Journal of Research in Crime and Delinquency 35*, 25–41.

Mednick, S. & Christiansen, K. 1977. *Biosocial Bases for Criminal Behavior.* New York: Gardner.

Mednick, S., Moffitt, T. & Stack, S. (Eds.). 1987. *The Causes of Crime.* New York: Cambridge University Press.

Merlo, A. 1993. Pregnant substance abusers: The new female offender. In R. Muraskin and T. Alleman (Eds.), *It's a Crime: Women and Justice*, pp. 146–159. Englewood Cliffs, NJ: Prentice-Hall.

Merton, R. 1938. Social structure and anomie. *American Sociological Review 3*(6), 672–682.

Messerschmidt, J. 1986. *Capitalism, Patriarchy, and Crime: Toward a Socialist Feminist Criminology.* Totawa, NJ: Rowman and Littlefield.

Messerschmidt, J. 1993. *Masculinities and Crime: Critique and Reconceptualization of Theory.* Lanham, MD: Rowman and Littlefield.

Messerschmidt, J. 1997. *Crime as Structured Action: Gender, Race, Class and Crime in the Making.* Thousand Oaks, CA: Sage.

Messina, N., Calhoun, S. & Warda, U. 2012. Gender responsive drug court treatment: A randomized control trial. *Criminal Justice and Behavior 39*, 1539–1558.

Messina, N. & Grella, C. 2006. Childhood trauma and women's health outcomes in a California prison population. *American Journal of Public Health 96*, 1842–1848.

Messina, N., Grella, C., Cartier, J. & Torres, S. 2010. A randomized experimental study of gender-responsive substance abuse treatment for women in prison. *Journal of Substance Abuse Treatment 38*, 97–107.

Messina, N., Marinelli-Casey, P., Hillhouse, M., Ang, A., Hunter, J. & Rawson, R. 2008. Childhood adverse events and health outcomes among methamphetamine-dependent men and women. *International Journal of Mental Health and Addiction 6*, 522–536.

Messman-Moore, T. & Long, P. 1994. Child sexual abuse and its relationship to revictimization in adult women: A review. *Clinical Psychology Review 16*, 397–420.

Messman-Moore, T. & Long, P. 2000. Child sexual abuse and revictimization in the form of adult sexual abuse, adult physical abuse and adult psychological maltreatment. *Journal of Interpersonal Violence 15*, 489–502.

Miller, E. 1986. *Street Woman.* Philadelphia, PA: Temple University Press.

Miller, H. & Barnes, J. 2013. Genetic transmission effects and intergenerational contact with the criminal justice system: A consideration of three dopamine polymorphisms. *Criminal Justice and Behavior, 40*(6), 671–689.

Miller, J. 1998. Up it up: Gender and the accomplishment of street robbery. *Criminology 36*, 37–66.

Miller, J. 2001. *One of the Guys.* New York: Oxford University Press.

Miller, J. 2002. Reconciling feminism and rational choice theory: Women's agency in street crime. In A. Piquero & S. Tibbetts (Eds.), *Rational Choice and Criminal Behavior*, pp. 219–239. New York: Routledge.

Miller, J. 2008. *Getting Played: African American Girls, Urban Inequality, and Gendered Violence*. New York: New York University Press.

Miller, J. & Brunson, R. 2000. Gender dynamics in youth gangs: A comparison of males' and females' accounts. *Justice Quarterly 17*, 420–448.

Miller, J. & Decker, S. 2001. Young women and gang violence: Gender, street offending, and violent victimization. *Justice Quarterly 18*, 115–140.

Miller, J. & White, N. 2003. Gender and adolescent relationship violence: A contextual examination. *Criminology 41*, 1207–1248.

Miller, J. & White, N. 2004. Situational effects of gender inequality on girls' participation in violence. In C. Alder & A. Worrall (Eds.), *Girls' Violence: Myths and Realities*, pp. 130–182. Albany: State University of New York Press.

Miller, S. (Ed.). 1998. *Crime Control and Women*. Newbury Park, CA: Sage.

Miller, S. 2001. The paradox of women arrested for domestic violence. *Violence against Women 7*(12), 1339–1376.

Miller, S. & Burack, C. 1993. A critique of Gottfredson and Hirschi's general theory of crime: Selective (in)attention to gender and power positions. *Women & Criminal Justice 4*(2), 115–134.

Miller, S. & Meloy, M. 2006. Women's use of force: Voices of women arrested for domestic violence. *Violence against Women 12*(1), 89–115.

Miller, W. 1958. Lower class culture as a generating milieu of gang delinquency. *Journal of Social Issues 14*, 5–19.

Miller, W. 1980. Molls. In S. Datesman and F. Scarpetti (Eds.), *Women, Crime and Justice*, pp. 238–254. New York: Oxford University Press.

Minton, T. 2013. *Jail Inmates at Midyear, 2012—Statistical Tables* (NCJ 241264). Washington, DC: Bureau of Justice Statistics.

Mitchell, A. 1975. *Informal Inmate Social Structure in Prisons for Women: A Comparative Study*. San Francisco: R & E Research Associates.

Moe, A. & Ferraro, K. 2003. Malign neglect or benign respect: Women's health care in a carceral setting. *Women & Criminal Justice 14*(4), 53–80.

Moffitt, T. 1990. The neuropsychology of juvenile delinquency: A critical review. In M. Tonry & N. Morris (Eds.), *Crime and Justice: A Review of Research*, Vol. 12, pp. 99–171. Chicago: University of Chicago Press.

Moffitt, T. 1993. Adolescence-limited and life-course persistent antisocial behavior: A developmental taxonomy. *Psychological Review 100*, 674–701.

Moffitt, T., Caspi, A., Rutter, M. & Silva, P. 2001. *Sex Differences in Antisocial Behavior: Conduct Disorder, Delinquency, and Violence in the Dunedin Longitudinal Study*. Cambridge, UK: Cambridge University Press.

Moffitt, T., Krueger, R., Caspi, A. & Fagan, J. 2000. Partner abuse and general crime: How are they the same? How are they different? *Criminology 38*, 199–232.

Molnar, B., Browne, A., Cerda, M. & Buka, S. 2005. Violent behavior by girls reporting violent victimization. *Archives of Pediatric Medicine 159*, 731–739.

Moore, J. 1991. *Going Down to the Barrio: Homeboys and Homegirls in Change*. Philadelphia, PA: Temple University Press.

Moore, J. & Hagedorn, J. 1996. What happens to the girls in the gang? In R. Huff (Ed.), *Gangs in America* (2nd ed.), pp. 205–218. Thousand Oaks, CA: Sage.

Moore, J. & Hagedorn, J. 2001. Female gangs: A focus on research. *Juvenile Justice Bulletin* (March). Washington, DC: Office of Juvenile Justice and Delinquency Prevention.

Moore, L. D. & Padavic, I. 2010. Racial and ethnic disparities in girls' sentencing in the juvenile justice system. *Feminist Criminology 5*, 263–285.

Moos, R. 1968. The assessment of the social climates of correctional institutions. *Journal of Research in Crime and Delinquency 5*(2), 174–188.

Morash, M. 1983. An explanation of juvenile delinquency: The integration of moral reasoning theory and sociological knowledge. In W. Laufer & J. Day (Eds.), *Personality Theory, Moral Development, and Criminal Behavior*, pp. 385–414. Lexington, MA: Lexington Books.

Morash, M. 2009. A great debate over using the Level of Service Inventory-Revised (LSI-R) with women offenders. *Criminology & Public Policy 8*(1), 173–181.

Morash, M. & Bynum, T. 1995. *Findings from the National Study of Innovative and Promising Programs for Women Offenders*. Washington, DC: National Institute of Justice.

Morash, M., Bynum, T. & Koons, B. 1998. *Women Offenders: Programming Needs and Promising Approaches* (NIJ Research in Brief). Washington, DC: National Institute of Justice.

Morash, M. & Chesney-Lind, M. 1991. A reformulation and partial test of the power control theory of delinquency. *Justice Quarterly 8*, 347–377.

Morash, M., Haarr, R. & Rucker, L. 1994. A comparison of programming for women and men in U.S. Prisons in the 1980s. *Crime & Delinquency 40*(2), 197–221.

Morash, M. & Rucker, L. 1995. A critical look at the idea of boot camps as a correctional reform. In S. Miller (Ed.), *Crime Control and Women*, pp. 32–46. Thousand Oaks, CA: Sage.

Morgan, E. 2000. Women on death row. In R. Muraskin (Ed.), *It's a Crime: Women and Justice*, pp. 269–283. Upper Saddle River, NJ: Prentice-Hall.

Morgan, P. & Joe, K. 1997. Uncharted terrain: Contexts of experience among women in the illicit drug economy. *Women & Criminal Justice 8*(3), 85–109.

Morris, A. 1987. *Women, Crime and Criminal Justice*. London: Basil Blackwell.

Morris, A. & Gelsthorpe, L. 1981. False clues and female crime. In A. Morris and L. Gelsthorpe (Eds.), *Women and Crime*, pp. 49–70. New York: Cambridge University Press.

Morris, A. & Wilkinson, C. 1995. Responding to female prisoners' needs. *Prison Journal 75*, 295–306.

Morris, R. 1964. Female delinquency and relational problems. *Social Forces 43*, 82–88.

Morton, J. 1998. *Complex Challenges, Collaborative Solutions: Programming for Adult and Juvenile Female Offenders*. Lanham, MD: American Correctional Association.

Moses, M. 1995. *Keeping Incarcerated Mothers and Their Daughters Together: Girl Scouts Beyond Bars* (NIJ Program Focus). Washington, DC: National Institute of Justice.

Moulds, E. 1980. Chivalry and paternalism: Disparities of treatment in the criminal justice system. In S. Datesman & F. Scarpetti (Eds.), *Women, Crime and Justice*, pp. 277–299. New York: Oxford University Press.

Moyer, I. 1984. Deceptions and realities of life in women's prisons. *The Prison Journal 64*(1), 45–56.

Mullings, J., Hartley, D. & Marquart, J. 2004. Exploring the relationship between alcohol use, childhood maltreatment, and treatment needs among female prisoners. *Addiction & Treatment 39*, 277–305.

Mullings, J., Marquart, J. & Brewer, V. 2000. Assessing the relationship between child sexual abuse and marginal living conditions on HIV/AIDS-related risk behavior among women prisoners. *Child Abuse and Neglect 24*(5): 677–688.

Mullings, J., Marquart, J. & Hartley, D. 2003. Exploring the effects of childhood sexual abuse and its impact on HIV/AIDS risk-taking behavior among women prisoners. *The Prison Journal 83*(4), 442–463.

Mullings, J., Pollock, J. & Crouch, B. 2002. Drugs and criminality: Results from the Texas women inmates study. *Women & Criminal Justice 13*(4), 69–97.

Mullins, C., Wright, R. & Jacobs, B. 2004. Gender, streetlife, and criminal retaliation. *Criminology 42*, 911–940.

Mumola, C. 2000. *Incarcerated Parents and Their Children*. Washington, DC: Bureau of Justice Statistics.

Muncer, S., Campbell, A., Jervis, V. & Lewis, R. 2001. "Ladettes," social representations, and aggression. *Sex Roles 44*(1), 33–44.

Murray, J. & Farrington, D. 2008. The effects of parental imprisonment on children. *Crime and Justice 37*, 133–206.

Muse, D. 1994. Parenting from prison. *Mothering 72*, 99–105.

Mustin, J. 1995. Parenting programs for prisoners. *Family and Corrections Network Report 5*, 1–2.

Naffine, N. 1987. *Female Crime: The Construction of Women in Criminology*. Sydney, Australia: Allen & Unwin.

Naffine, N. 1996. *Feminism and Criminology*. Philadelphia, PA: Temple University Press.

Nagel, I. 1981. Sex differences in the processing of criminal defendants. In A. Morris & L. Gelsthorpe (Eds.), *Women and Crime*, pp. 104–124. New York: Cambridge University Press.

Nagel, I. 1983. The legal/extralegal controversy: Judicial decisions in pre-trial release. *Law and Society Review 17*, 481–575.

Nagel, I. & Hagan, J. 1983. Gender and crime: Offense patterns and criminal court sanctions. In M. Tonry & N. Morris (Eds.), *Crime and Justice: An Annual Review of Research*, Vol. 14, pp. 91–144. Chicago: University of Chicago Press.

Nagel, I. & Johnson, B. 1994. The role of gender in a structured sentencing system: Equal treatment, policy choices, and the sentencing of female offenders under the United States sentencing guidelines. *The Journal of Criminal Law & Criminology 85*, 181–221.

Nagin, D. & Farrington, D. 1992a. The stability of criminal potential from childhood to adulthood. *Criminology 30*, 235–260.

Nagin, D. & Farrington, D. 1992b. The onset and persistence of offending. *Criminology 30*, 501–523.

Nagin, D., Farrington, D. & Moffitt, T. 1995. Life-course trajectories of different types of offenders. *Criminology 33*, 111–139.

National Center on Addiction and Substance Abuse at Columbia University (CASA). 2010. *Behind Bars II: Substance Abuse and America's Prison Population*. Retrieved from http://www.casacolumbia.org/templates/Publications_Reports.aspx?keywords=prison.

Negy, C., Woods, D. & Carlson, R. 1997. The relationship between female inmates' coping and adjustment in a minimum security prison. *Criminal Justice and Behavior 24*(2), 224–233.

Nelson, C. 1974. A study of homosexuality among women inmates at two state prisons. Unpublished doctoral dissertation, Temple University, Philadelphia, PA.

Nesbitt, C. 1992. The female offender: Overview of facility planning and design issues and considerations. *Corrections Compendium 17*(8), 4–20.

New York Times Editorial Board. 2014, January 6. Unfair phone charges for inmates. *New York Times*, A22. Retrieved from http://www.nytimes.com/2014/01/07/opinion/unfair-phone-charges-for-inmates.html?_r=0

Nickel, J., Garland, C. & Kane, L. 2009. *Children of Incarcerated Parents: An Action Plan for Federal Government*. New York: Council of State Governments, Justice Center.

Noddings, N. 1984. *Caring: A Feminine Approach to Ethics and Moral Education*. Berkeley: University of California Press.

Noddings, N. 1989. *Women and Evil*. Berkeley: University of California Press.

Norland, S. & Shover, N. 1977. Gender roles and female criminality. *Criminology 15*, 87–104.

Oberman, M. 2002. Understanding infanticide in context: Mothers who kill, 1870–1930 and today. *Journal of Criminal Law and Criminology 92*, 707–738.

Oberman, M. & Meyer, C. 2008. *When Mothers Kill: Interviews from Prison*. New York: New York University Press.

O'Brien, P. 2001. *Making It in the Free World: Women in Transition from Prison*. Albany: State University of New York Press.

O'Brien, P. 2006. Maximizing success for drug-affected women after release from prison: Examining access to and use of social services during reentry. *Women & Criminal Justice 17*(2), 95–113.

Office of Juvenile Justice and Delinquency Prevention. 1998. *Guiding Principles for Promising Female Programming: An Inventory of Best Practices*. Washington, DC: Author.

Olson, D., Lurigio, A. & Alderden, M. 2003. Men are from Mars, women are from Venus, but what role does gender play in probation recidivism? *Justice Research and Policy 5*(2), 33–54.

Olweus, D. 1987. Testosterone and adrenaline: Aggressive antisocial behavior in normal adolescent males. In S. Mednick, T. Moffitt, &S. Stack (Eds.), *The Causes of Crime*, pp. 263–283. New York: Cambridge University Press.

Opsal, T. 2009. Women on parole: Understanding the impact of surveillance. *Women & Criminal Justice 19*, 306–326.

Oregon Dept. of Corrections. 1993. *Childhood Abuse and the Female Inmate: A Study of Teenage History of Women in Oregon Prisons*. Salem: Oregon Dept. of Corrections, Information Services Division.

Otis, M. 1913. A perversion not commonly noted. *Journal of Abnormal Psychology 8*, 113–116.

Owen, B. 1998. *"In the Mix": Struggle and Survival in a Women's Prison*. Albany: State University of New York Press.

Owen, B. & Bloom, B. 1995. Profiling women prisoners: Findings from national surveys and a California sample. *The Prison Journal 75*(2), 165–185.

Owen, B., Wells, J., Pollock, J., Muscat, B. & Torres, S. 2008. *Gendered Violence and Safety: A Contextual Approach to Improving Security in Women's Facilities*. Washington, DC: National Institute of Justice.

Panton, J. 1974. Personality differences between male and female prison inmates measured by the MMPI. *Criminal Justice and Behavior 1*(4), 332–339.

Parisi, N. 1982. Exploring female crime patterns: Problems and prospects. In N. Rafter & E. Stanko (Eds.), *Judges, Lawyer, Victim, Thief*, pp. 111–129. Boston, MA: Northeastern University Press.

Parsons, T. 1954. *Essays in Sociological Theory* (rev. ed.). Glencoe, IL: Free Press.

Paternoster, R. & Simpson, S. 1993. A rational choice theory of corporate crime. In R. Clarke & M. Felson (Eds.), *Routine Activity and Rational Choice: Advances in Criminological Theory*, pp. 37–58. New Brunswick, NJ: Transaction Publishers.

Payne, B., Gainey, R. & Carey, C. 2005. All in the family: Gender, family crimes, and later criminality. *Women & Criminal Justice, 16*(4), 73–89.

Pearl, N. 1998. Use of community based social services to reduce recidivism in female parolees. *Women & Criminal Justice 10*(1), 27–52.

Pearson, P. 1997. *When She Was Bad*. New York: Viking.

Pelissier, B. & Jones, N. 2005. A review of gender differences among substance abusers. *Crime & Delinquency 51*(3), 343–372.

Peterson, C. 1982. Doing time with the boys: An analysis of women correctional officers in all-male facilities. In B. Price & N. Sokoloff (Eds.), *The Criminal Justice System and Women*, pp. 437–460. New York: Clark Boardman.

Phillips, A. 1987. *Feminism and Equality.* Oxford, UK: Basil Blackwell.

Phua, C. 2010. Parolees get help in putting lives back together. *Sacramento Bee*, June 23. Retrieved from http://cdcr-star.blogspot.com/2010_06_23_archive.html

Piaget, J. 1965. *The Moral Judgement of the Child.* New York: Free Press.

Pike, L. 1876. *A History of Crime in England.* London: Smith, Edler & Co.

Piquero, A. & Mazerolle, P. 2001. *Life-Course Criminology: Contemporary and Classic Readings.* Belmont, CA: Wadsworth.

Piquero, N. & Sealock, M. 2000. Generalizing general strain theory: An examination of an offending population. *Justice Quarterly 17*, 449–484.

Piquero, N. & Sealock, M. 2004. Gender and general strain theory: A preliminary test of Broidy and Agnew's gender/GST hypothees. *Justice Quarterly 21*, 125–159.

Piquero, A. & Tibbetts, S. 1996. Specifying the direct and indirect effects of low self-control and situational factors in offenders' decision making: Toward a more complete model of rational offending. *Justice Quarterly 13*, 481–510.

Polakowski, M. 1994. Linking self and social control with deviance: Illuminating the structure underlying a general theory of crime and its relation to deviant activity. *Journal of Quantitative Criminology, 10*(1), 41–78.

Pollack, S. 2007. "I'm just not good in relationships": Victimization discourses and the gendered regulation of criminalized women. *Feminist Criminology 2*(2), 158–174.

Pollak, O. 1950. *The Criminality of Women.* Philadelphia: University of Pennsylvania Press.

Pollock, J. 1978. Early theories of female criminality. In L. Bowker, *Women, Crime and the Criminal Justice System*, pp. 25–50. Lexington, MA: Lexington Books.

Pollock, J. 1981. Interviews conducted with correctional officers.

Pollock, J. 1984. "Women will be women": Correctional officers' perceptions of the emotionality of women inmates. *The Prison Journal 64*(1), 84–91.

Pollock, J. 1986. *Sex and Supervision: Guarding Male and Female Inmates.* New York: Greenwood Press.

Pollock, J. 1995. Women in corrections: Custody and the "caring ethic." In A. Merlo & J. Pollock (Eds.), *Women, Law and Social Control*, pp. 97–116. Boston: Allyn & Bacon.

Pollock, J. 1998. *Counseling Women in Prison.* San Francisco: Sage.

Pollock, J. 1999a. *Criminal Women.* Cincinnati, OH: Anderson.

Pollock, J. 1999b. A national survey of parenting programs in women's prisons. Unpublished monograph available from the author.

Pollock, J. 2002a. *Women, Prison and Crime* (2nd ed.). Belmont, CA: Wadsworth.

Pollock, J. 2002b. Parenting programs in women's prisons. *Women & Criminal Justice 14*(1), 131–154.

Pollock, J. 2012. *Prisons and Prison Life: Costs and Consequences* (2nd ed.). New York: Oxford University Press.

Pollock, J. & Davis, S. 2005. The continuing myth of the violent female offender. *Criminal Justice Review 30*(1), 5–29.

Pollock, J. & Hollier, V. 2010. T Visas: Prosecution tool or humanitarian response. *Women & Criminal Justice 20*(1), 127–146.

Pollock, J., Mullings, J. & Crouch, B. 2006. Violent women: Findings from the Texas Women Inmates' Study. *Journal of Interpersonal Violence 21*(4), 485–502.

Pollock, J., Williams, S. & Schroeder, S. 1996. The needs of Texas women prisoners—Final report. Unpublished report.

Pollock-Byrne, J. 1992. Women in prison: Why are their numbers increasing? In P. Benekos & A. Merlo (Eds.), *Corrections: Dilemmas and Directions*, pp. 79–95. Cincinnati, OH: Anderson.

Pollock-Byrne, J. & Merlo, A. 1991. Against compulsory treatment: No quick fix for pregnant substance abusers. *Criminal Justice Policy Review 5*, 79–99.

Portillos, E. & Zatz, M. 1995. Not to die for: Positive and negative aspects of Chicano youth gangs. Cited in M. Chesney-Lind (1997), *The Female Offender: Women, Girls and Crime*. Thousand Oaks, CA: Sage.

Powell, T. 1999. Women inmates in Vermont. Paper presented at the American Psychological Association, Boston, MA. Cited in Bradley, R. & Davino, K. (2002). Women's perceptions of the prison environment: When prison is "the safest place I've ever been." *Psychology of Women Quarterly 26*(4), 351–359.

Pratt, T. & Cullen, F. 2000. The empirical status of Gottfredson and Hirschi's general theory of crime: A meta-analysis. *Criminology 38*, 931–964.

Prendergast, M., Wellisch, J. & Anglin, M. 1994. *Drug-Abusing Women Offenders: Results of a National Survey* (NIJ Research in Brief). Washington, DC: Bureau of Justice Statistics.

Prendergast, M., Wellisch, J. & Falkin, J. 1995. Assessment of and services for substance-abusing women offenders in community and correctional settings. *Prison Journal 75*(2), 240–56.

Prendergast, M., Wellisch, J. & Falkin, G. 1997. Assessment of and services for substance-abusing women offenders in community and correctional settings. In J. Marquart & J. Sorensen (Eds.), *Correctional Contexts: Contemporary and Classical Readings*, pp. 318–327. Los Angeles, CA: Roxbury.

Price, B. & Sokoloff, N. 1982. *The Criminal Justice System and Women*. New York: Clark Boardman.

Proctor, J. 2009. The impact imprisonment has on women's health and health care from the perspective of female inmates in Kansas. *Women & Criminal Justice 19*, 1–36.

Propper, A. 1976. Importation and deprivation perspectives on homosexuality in correctional institutions: An empirical test of their relative efficacy. Unpublished doctoral dissertation, University of Michigan, Ann Arbor.

Propper, A. 1981. *Prison Homosexuality: Myth and Reality*. Lexington, MA: D. C. Heath.

Propper, A. 1982. Make-believe families and homosexuality among imprisoned girls. *Criminology 20*, 127–139.

Quicker, J. 1983. *Homegirls: Characterizing Chicana Gangs*. San Pedro, CA: International Universities Press.

Quinney, R. 1973. *Critique of Legal Order: Crime Control in a Capitalist Society*. Boston: Little, Brown.

Raeder, M. 1993a. Gender issues in the federal sentencing guidelines. *Journal of Criminal Justice 8*(3), 20–25.

Raeder, M. 1993b. Gender and sentencing: Single moms, battered women and other sex-based anomalies in the gender free world of federal sentencing guidelines. *Pepperdine Law Review 20*(3), 905–990.

Rafter, N. 1985. *Partial Justice: State Prisons and Their Inmates, 1800–1935*. Boston: Northeastern Press.

Rafter, N. 1988. *White Trash: The Eugenics Family Studies, 1877–1919*. Boston: Northeastern University Press.

Rafter, N. 1989. Gender and justice: The equal protection issue. In Goodstein, L. & MacKenzie, D. (Eds.), *The American Prison: Issues in Research and Policy*, pp. 89–109. New York: Plenum Press.

Rafter, N. 1990. *Partial Justice: Women, Prisons, and Social Control*. New Brunswick, NJ: Transaction Books.

Rafter, N. 1992. Equality or indifference. *Federal Prisons Journal 3*, 16–18.

Raine, A. 1993. *The Psychopathology of Crime: Criminal Behavior as a Clinical Disorder.* San Diego, CA: Academic Press.

Rasche, C. 1974. The female offender as an object of criminological research. *Criminal Justice and Behavior 1,* 301–320.

Rasche, C. 1975. The female offender as an object of criminological research. In A. Brodsky, (Ed.), *The Female Offender,* pp. 9–28. Newbury Park, CA: Sage.

Rasche, C. 2000. The dislike of female offenders among correctional officers: Need for specialized training. In R. Muraskin (Ed.), *It's a Crime: Women and Justice* (2nd ed.), pp. 237–252. Upper Saddle River, NJ: Prentice-Hall.

Rave, J. 2009, February 26. Percent of American Indians in jail is high. *The Bismarck Tribune.* Retrieved from http://bismarcktribune.com/news/state-and-regional/percent-of-american-indians-in-jail-is-high/article_3de882e7-003a-5785-81aa-4eaed3da4be6.html

Reckdenwald, A. & Parker, K. 2012. Understanding the change in male and female intimate partner homicide over time: A policy- and theory-relevant investigation. *Feminist Criminology 73*(3), 167–195.

Redl, F. & Toch, H. 1979. The psychoanalytic perspective. In H. Toch (Ed.), *Psychology of Crime and Criminal Justice,* pp. 183–197. New York: Holt, Rinehart & Winston.

Reed, B. 1987. Developing women-sensitive drug dependence treatment services: Why so difficult? *Journal of Psychoactive Drugs 19*(2), 151–164.

Reed, G. & Yeager, P. 1996. Organizational offending and neoclassical criminology: Challenging the reach of a general theory of crime. *Criminology 34,* 357–382.

Reisig, M., Holtfreter, K. & Morash, M. 2006. Assessing recidivism risk across female pathways to crime. *Justice Quarterly 23,* 384–403.

Reiss, A. & Tonry, M. 1986. *Communities and Crime.* Chicago: University of Chicago Press.

Rennison, C. 2009. A new look at the gender gap in offending. *Women & Criminal Justice 19,* 171–190.

Rennison, C. & Welchans, S. 2000. *Intimate Partner Violence* (Bureau of Justice Statistics Special Report, NCJ 178247). Washington, DC: U.S. Department of Justice.

Renzetti, C., Curran, D. & Maier, S. 2012. *Women, Men, and Society* (6th ed.). Upper Saddle River, NJ: Pearson.

Rettinger, J. & Andrews, D. (2010). General risk and need, gender specificity and the recidivism of female offenders. *Criminal Justice and Behavior 37*(1), 29–46.

Rice, A., Smith, L. & Janzen, F. 1999. Women inmates, drug abuse, and the Salt Lake County Jail. *American Jails 13* (July/Aug), 43–47.

Richie, B. 1996. *Compelled to Crime: The Gender Entrapment of Battered Black Women.* New York: Routledge.

Richie, B. 2001. Challenges incarcerated women face as they return to their communities: Findings from life history interviews. *Crime & Delinquency 47,* 368–389.

Richie, B. 2006. Women and drug use: The case for a justice analysis. *Women & Criminal Justice 12,* 137–143.

Rierden, A. 1997. *The Farm: Life Inside a Women's Prison.* Amherst: University of Massachusetts Press.

Rodriquez, S., Curry, T. & Lee, G. 2006. Gender differences in criminal sentencing: Do effects vary across violent property, and drug offenses? *Social Science Quarterly 87*(2), 318–328.

Root, M. 1989. Treatment failures: The role of sexual victimization in women's addictive behavior. *American Journal of Orthopsychiatry 59*(4), 542–548.

Rosenbaum, M. 1981. *Women on Heroin.* New Brunswick, NJ: Rutgers University Press.

Rosenbaum, J. 1987. Social control, gender, and delinquency: An analysis of drug, property, and violent offenders. *Justice Quarterly 4*, 117–132.

Rosenbaum, J. 1989. Family dysfunction and female delinquency. *Crime & Delinquency 35*(1), 31–44.

Rosenbaum, J. 1993. The female delinquent: Another look at the family's influence on female offending. In R. Muraskin & T. Alleman (Eds.), *It's a Crime: Women and Justice*, pp. 399–416. New York: Prentice-Hall.

Rosenbaum, K. 1980. Female deviance and the female sex role: A preliminary investigation. In S. Datesman & F. Scarpetti (Eds.), *Women, Crime and Justice*, pp. 106–127. New York: Oxford University Press.

Ross, R. & Fabiano, A. 1986. *Female Offenders: Correctional Afterthoughts*. Jefferson, NC: McFarland.

Ross, P. & Lawrence, J. 1998. Health care for women offenders. *Corrections Today 60*(7), 122–129.

Rothbart, M., Hanley, D. & Albert, M. 1986. Gender differences in moral reasoning. *Sex Roles 15*, 640–655.

Rowe, D. & Farrington, D. 1997. The familial transmission of criminal convictions. *Criminology 35*, 177–196.

Rubick, R. 1975. The sexually integrated prison: A legal and policy evaluation. *American Journal of Criminal Law 3*(3), 301–330.

Ryan, T. 1984. *Adult Female Offenders and Institutional Programs: A State of the Art Analysis*. Washington, DC: National Institute of Corrections.

Ryan, T. & Grassano, J. 1992. Taking a progressive approach to treating female offenders. *Corrections Today* (August), 184–186.

Ryan, T. & McCabe, K. 1997. A comparative analysis of adult female offenders. *Corrections Today 59*(4), 28–30.

Ryder, J. 2007. "I wasn't really bonded with my family": Attachment, loss and violence among adolescent female offenders. *Critical Criminology 15*, 19–40.

Sabol, W. & Couture, H. 2008. *Prison Inmates at Midyear 2007* (Bureau of Justice Statistics Bulletin, NCJ 221944). Washington DC: U.S. Department of Justice.

Sacks, J., McKendrick, K. & Hamilton, Z. 2012. A randomized clinical trial of therapeutic community treatment for female inmates: Outcomes at 6 and 12 months after prison release. *Journal of Addictive Diseases 21*, 258–269.

Sagatun, I. 1993. Babies born with drug addiction: Background and legal responses. In R. Muraskin & T. Alleman (Eds.), *It's a Crime: Women and Justice*, pp. 118–130. Englewood Cliffs, NJ: Prentice-Hall.

Saliba, S. 2013. Rape by the system: The existence and effects of sexual abuse of women in United States prisons. *Hastings Race and Poverty Law Journal 10*, 293–320.

Salisbury, E. & Van Voorhis, P. 2009. Gendered pathways: A quantitative investigation of women probationers' paths to incarceration. *Criminal Justice & Behavior 36*(6), 541–566.

Salisbury, E., Van Voorhis, P. & Spiropoulos, G. 2008. The predictive validity of a gender responsive needs assessment: An exploratory study. *Crime & Delinquency 54*(4), 225–258.

Sampson, R. 1986a. Crime in cities: The effects of formal and informal social control. In A. Reiss & M. Tonry (Eds.), *Understanding and Preventing Violence*, pp. 271–311. Washington, DC: National Academy Press.

Sampson, R. 1986b. Neighborhood, family structure and the risk of personal victimization. In J. Byrne & R. Sampson (Eds.), *The Social Ecology of Crime*, pp. 25–36. New York: Springer-Verlag.

Sampson, R. & Groves, W. 1989. Community structure and crime: Testing social-disorganization theory. *American Journal of Sociology 94*, 774–802.

Sampson, R. & Laub, J. 1990. Crime and deviance over the life course: The salience of adult social bonds. *American Sociological Review 55*, 609–627.

Sampson, R. & Laub, J. 1993. *Crime in the Making: Pathways and Turning Points Through Life*. Cambridge, MA: Harvard University Press.

Sampson, R. & Laub, J. 1997. A life-course theory of cumulative disadvantage and the stability of delinquency. In T. Thornberry (Ed.), *Developmental Theories of Crime and Delinquency*, pp. 133–161. New Brunswick, NJ: Transaction Books.

Sampson, R. & Laub, J. 2003. Life-course desisters? Trajectories of crime among delinquent boys followed to age 70. *Criminology 41*, 301–340.

Sampson, R., Raudenbush, W. & Earls, F. 1997. Neighborhoods and violent crime: A multilevel study of collective efficacy. *Science 277*, 918–924.

Sanchez, J. & Johnson, B. 1987. Women and the drugs-crime connection: Crime rates among drug-abusing women at Rikers Island. *Journal of Psychoactive Drugs 19*(2), 200–216.

Sandhu, H. & Allen, D. 1969. Female delinquency: Goal obstruction and anomie. *Canadian Review of Sociology and Anthropology 6*, 107–110.

Sandhu, H. & Satterfield, H. 1987. Childhood diagnostic and neurophysiological predictors of teenage arrest rates: An eight year prospective study. In S. Mednick, T. Moffitt & S. Stack (Eds.), *The Causes of Crime*, pp. 146–168. New York: Cambridge University Press.

Santana, A. 2000, February 1. Female prison ranks double: Citing study, Norton plans bills to improve conditions. Washington Post.com. Retrieved from http://washingtonpost.com/wp-srv/Wplate/2000–02/01/1131–020100–idx.html

Sargent, E., Marcus-Mendoza, S. & Ho Yu, C. 1993. Abuse and the woman prisoner. In B. Fletcher, L. Shaver & D. Moon (Eds.), *Women Prisoners: A Forgotten Population*, pp. 55–73. Westport, CT: Praeger.

Schrag, C. 1944. Social types in a prison community. Unpublished master's thesis, Department of Sociology, University of Washington, Seattle.

Schrag, C. 1966. A preliminary criminal typology. *Pacific Sociological Review 4*, 11–39.

Schram, P., Koons-Witt, B., Williams, F. & McShane, M. 2006. Supervision strategies and approaches for female parolees: Examining the link between unmet needs and parolee outcome. *Crime & Delinquency 52*, 450–471.

Schupak, J. 1986. Women and children first: An examination of the unique needs of women in prison. *Golden Gate University Law Review 16*, 455–474.

Schur, E. 1984. *Labeling Women Deviant: Gender, Stigma and Social Control*. New York: Random House.

Schwartz, J., Steffensmeier, D. & Feldmeyer, B. 2009. Assessing trends in women's violence via data triangulation: Arrests, convictions, incarcerations, and victim reports. *Social Problems 56*(3), 494–525.

Schwartz, J., Steffensmeier, D., Zhong, H. & Ackerman, J. 2009. Trends in the gender gap in violence: Reevaluating NCVS and other evidence. *Criminology 47*, 401–426.

Schwartz, M. 1987. Gender and injury in spousal assault. *Sociological Focus 20*(1), 61–75.

Schwartz, M. & DeKeseredy, W. 1993. The return of the "Battered Husband Syndrome" through the typification of women as violent. *Crime, Law and Social Change 20*, 249–265.

ScienceDaily.com. 2009, June 9. "Warrior gene" linked to gang membership, weapon use. Retrieved from http://www.sciencedaily.com/releases/2009/06/090605123237.htm

Scott, N., Hannum, T. & Gilchrist, S. 1982. Assessment of depression among incarcerated females. *Journal of Personality Assessment 46*, 372–379.

Selksky, D. 1980. *Assaults on Correctional Employees*. Albany, NY: Department of Correctional Services.

Selling, L. 1931. The pseudo-family. *American Journal of Sociology 37*, 247–253.

Seng, M. & Lurigio, A. 2005. Probation officers' views on supervising women probationers. *Women & Criminal Justice 16*(1/2), 65–85.

Shaffer, E., Pettigrew, C., Bout, D. & Edwards, D. 1983. Multivariate classification of female offenders MMPI profiles. *Journal of Crime and Justice 6*, 57–65.

Sharp, S. & Marcus-Mendoza, S. 2001. It's a family affair: Incarcerated women and their families. *Women & Criminal Justice 12*(4), 21–49.

Shaw, C. 1951. *The Natural History of a Delinquent Career*. Philadelphia, PA: Albert Saifer.

Shaw, C. & McKay, H. 1969. *Juvenile Delinquency and Urban Areas*. Chicago: University of Chicago Press. (Original work published 1934).

Sherman, F. 2012. Justice for girls: Are we making progress? *UCLA Law Review 59*, 1617–1660.

Showers, J. 1993. Assessing and remedying parenting knowledge among women inmates. *Journal of Offender Rehabilitation 20*, 35–45.

Siegel, J. & Williams, L. 2003. The relationship between child sexual abuse and female delinquency and crime: A prospective study. *Journal of Research in Crime and Delinquency 40*(1), 71–94.

Sikes, G. 1997. *8 Ball Chicks: A Year in the Violent World of Girl Gangsters*. New York: Anchor Books.

Silbert, M. & Pines, A. 1981. Sexual child abuse as an antecedent to prostitution. *Child Abuse & Neglect 5*, 407–411.

Silberg, J., Meyer, J., Pickles, A., Simonoff, E., Eaves, L., Hewitt, J., Maes, H. & Rutter, M. 1996. Heterogeneity among juvenile antisocial behaviors: Findings from the Virginia twin study of adolescent behavioral development. In M. Rutter (Ed.), *Genetics of Criminal and Antisocial Behavior*, pp. 76–87. New York: John Wiley and Sons.

Silver, F., Felson, R. & Vaneseltine, M. 2008. The relationship between mental health problems and violence among criminal offenders. *Criminal Justice and Behavior 35*(4), 405–426.

Silverman, I. & Dinitz, S. 1974. Compulsive masculinity and delinquency: an empirical investigation. *Criminology 11*, 498–515.

Simmons [Moyer], I. 1975. Interaction and leadership among female prisoners. Unpublished doctoral dissertation, University of Missouri, Columbia.

Simon, R. 1975. *Women and Crime*. Lexington, MA: Lexington Books.

Simon, R. 1976a. Women and crime revisited. *Social Science Quarterly 56*, 658–663.

Simon, R. 1976b. American women and crime. *The Annals of the American Academy of Political and Social Science 1976*, 423–452.

Simon, R. & Landis, J. 1991. *The Crimes Women Commit and the Punishment They Receive*. Lexington, MA: Lexington Press.

Simpson, S. 1991. Caste, class, and violent crime: Explaining difference in female offending. *Criminology 29*, 115–135.

Simpson, S. & Elis, L. 1995. Doing gender: Sorting out the caste and crime conundrum. *Criminology 33*, 47–79.

Singer, M., Bussey, J., Li-Yu, S. & Lunghofer, L. 1995. The psychosocial issues of women serving time in jail. *Social Work 40*(1), 103–113.

Sleed, M., Baradon, T. & Fonagy, P. 2013. New beginnings for mothers and babies in prison: A cluster randomized controlled trial. *Attachment and Human Behavior 15*, 349–367.

Slocum, L., Simpson, S. & Smith, D. 2005. Strained lives and crime: Examining intra-individual variation in strain and offending in a sample of incarcerated women. *Criminology 43*, 1067–1110.

Smart, C. 1976. *Women, Crime and Criminology: A Feminist Critique*. London: Routledge & Kegan Paul.

Smart, C. 1979. The new female criminal: Reality or myth? *British Journal of Criminology 19*, 50–57.

Smart, C. 1989. *Feminism and the Power of Law*. London: Routledge.

Smart, C. 1995. *Law, Crime and Sexuality*. London: Sage Ltd.

Smith, B. 1995. *A Vision Beyond Survival: A Resource Guide for Incarcerated Women*. Washington DC: National Women's Law Center.

Smith, D. 1979. Sex and deviance: An assessment of the major sociological variables. *Sociological Quarterly 20*, 183–195.

Smith, P., Cullen, F. & Latessa, E. 2009. Can 14,737 be wrong? A meta-analysis of the LSI-R and recidivism for female offenders. *Criminology & Public Policy 8*(1), 183–208.

Snell, T. 1992. *Women in Jail, 1989* (Bureau of Justice Statistics Special Report, NCJ 134732). Washington, DC: U.S. Department of Justice.

Snell, T. 1994. *Women in Prison: Survey of State Prison Inmates, 1991* (Bureau of Justice Statistics Special Report, NCJ 136949). Washington DC: U.S. Department of Justice.

Snell, T. 2013. *Capital Punishment, 2011—Statistical Tables* (NCJ 242185). Washington, DC: Bureau of Justice Statistics.

Snell, T. & Morton, D. 1994. *Women in Prison* (Bureau of Justice Statistics Special Report, NCJ 145321). Washington, DC: U.S. Department of Justice.

Snyder, H. & Mulako-Wangota, J. 2013. *Arrest Data Analysis Tool*, Bureau of Justice Statistics. Data compiled on August 7, 2013, from http://www.bjs.gov/index.cfm?ty=datool&surl=/arrests/index.cfm

Sobel, E. 1978. The aggressive female. In E. Sobel (Ed.), *Violence: Perspectives on Murder and Aggression*, pp. 267–285. San Francisco: Jossey-Bass.

Sommers, I. & Baskin, D. 1992. Sex, race, age and violent offending. *Violence and Victims 7*(3), 191–201.

Sommers, I. & Baskin, D. 1993. The situational context of violent female offending. *Journal of Research in Crime and Delinquency 30*(2), 136–162.

Sommers, I. & Baskin, D. 1994. Factors related to female adolescent initiation into violent street crime. *Youth & Society 25*(4), 468–489.

Sommers, I. & Baskin, D. 1996. The structural relationship between drug use, drug dealing, and other income support activities among women drug sellers. *Journal of Drug Issues 26*(4), 344–378.

Spaulding, E. 1923. *An Experimental Study of Psychopathic Delinquent Women*. New York: Rand McNally.

Spohn, C. & Spears, J. 1997. Gender and case processing decisions: A comparison of case outcomes for male and female defendants charged with violent felonies. *Women & Criminal Justice 8*(3), 29–50.

Stanton, A. 1980. *When Mothers Go to Jail*. Lexington, MA: Lexington Books.

Steadman, H., Osher, F., Robbins, P., Case, B. & Samuels, S. 2009. Prevalence of serious mental illness among jail inmates. *Psychiatric Services 60*(6), 761–765.

Steadman, H. & Veysey, B. 1997. *Providing Services for Jail Inmates with Mental Disorders* (NIJ Research in Brief). Washington, DC: National Institute of Justice.

Steffensmeier, D. 1978. Crime and the contemporary woman: An analysis of changing levels of female property crime, 1960–1975. *Social Forces 57*, 566–584.

Steffensmeier, D. 1980a. Assessing the impact of the women's movement on sex-based differences in the handling of adult criminal defendants. *Crime & Delinquency 26*, 344–357.

Steffensmeier, D. 1980b. Sex differences in patterns of adult crime, 1965–1977: A review and assessment. *Social Forces 58*, 1080–1108.

Steffensmeier, D. 1981. Patterns of female property crime, 1960–1975: A postscript. In L. Bowker (Ed.), *Women and Crime in America*, pp. 59–65. New York: Macmillan.

Steffensmeier, D. 1983. Organization properties and sex-segregation in the underworld: Building a sociological theory of sex differences in crime. *Social Forces 61*, 1010–1043.

Steffensmeier, D. 1993. National trends in female arrests: 1960–1990: Assessments and recommendations for research. *Journal of Quantitative Criminology 9*, 411–441.

Steffensmeier, D., & Allen, E. 1988. Sex disparities in arrest by residence, race, and age: An assessment of the gender convergence/crime hypothesis. *Justice Quarterly 5*, 53–80.

Steffensmeier, D. & Allan, E. 1996. Gender and crime: Toward a gendered theory of female offending. *Annual Review of Sociology 22*, 459–487.

Steffensmeier, D., Allan, E. & Streifel, C. 1989. Development and female crime: A cross-national test of alternative explanations. *Social Forces 68*, 262–283.

Steffensmeier, D. & Haynie, D. 2000a. Gender, structural disadvantage, and urban crime: Do macrosocial variables also explain female offending rates? *Criminology 38*, 403–438.

Steffensmeier, D. & Haynie, D. 2000b. The structural sources of urban female violence in the United States: A macrosocial gender-disaggregated analysis of adult and juvenile homicide offending rates. *Homicide Studies 4*, 107–134.

Steffensmeier, D., Kramer, J. & Streifel, C. 1993. Gender and imprisonment decisions. *Criminology 31*, 411–445.

Steffensmeier, D., Schwartz, J., Zhong, H. & Ackerman, J. 2005. An assessment of recent trends of girls' violence using diverse longitudinal sources: Is the gender gap closing? *Criminology 43*, 355–405.

Steffensmeier, D. & Streifel, C. 1992. Time-series analysis of the female percentage of arrests for property crimes, 1960–1985: A test of alternative explanations. *Justice Quarterly 9*, 77–103.

Steffensmeier, D. & Streifel, C. 1993. Trends in female crime, 1960–1990. In C. Culliver (Ed.), *Female Criminality: The State of the Art*, pp. 63–101. New York: Garland.

Steffensmeier, D., Zhong, H., Ackerman, J., Schwartz, J. & Agha, S. 2006. Gender gap trends for violent crimes, 1980 to 2003: A UCR-NCVS Comparison. *Feminist Criminology, 1*(1), 72–98.

Steiner, B. & Wooldredge, J. 2009. Individual and environmental effects on assaults and nonviolent rule breaking by women in prison. *Journal of Research in Crime and Delinquency 46*, 437–467.

Steinmetz, S. 1978. The battered husband syndrome. *Victimology 2*, 499–509.

Steketee, M., Junger, M. & Junger-Tas, J. 2013. Sex differences in the predictors of juvenile delinquency: Females are more susceptible to poor environments; males are influenced more by low self-control. *Journal of Contemporary Criminal Justice 29*, 88–105.

Stevens, T., Morash, M. & Chesney-Lind, M. 2010. Are girls getting tougher, or are we tougher on girls? Probability of arrest and juvenile court oversight in 1980 and 2000. *Justice Quarterly 28*, 710–744.

Stohr, M., Lovrich, N. & Mays, G. 1997. Service v. security focus in training assessments: Testing gender differences among women's jail correctional officers. *Woman and Criminal Justice 9*(1), 65–85.

Straus, M. & Gelles, R. 1986. Societal change and change in family violence from 1975–1985 as revealed by two national surveys. *Journal of Marriage and the Family 48*, 465–480.

Straus, M., Gelles, R. & Steinmetz, S. 1980. *Behind Closed Doors*. Garden City, NY: Anchor Books.

Stolzenberg, L. & D'Alessio, S. 1997. The impact of prison crowding on male and female imprisonment rates in Minnesota: A research note. *Justice Quarterly 14*, 793–809.

Strickland, K. 1976. *Correctional Institutions for Women in the U.S.* Lexington, MA: Lexington Books.

Struckman-Johnson, C. & Struckman-Johnson, D. 2002. Sexual coercion reported by women in three mid-western prisons. *Journal of Sex Research 39*(3), 217–227.

Struckman-Johnson, C. & Struckman-Johnson, D. 2006. A comparison of sexual coercion experiences reported by men and women in prison. *Journal of Interpersonal Violence 21*(12), 1591–1615.

Struckman-Johnson, C., Struckman-Johnson, D., Rucker, L., Bumby, K. & Donaldson, S. 1996. Sexual coercion reported by men and women in prison. *Journal of Sex Research 33*(1), 67–76.

The Substance Abuse and Mental Health Services Administration (SAMHSA). 2012. *Results from the 2011 National Survey on Drug Use and Health: Summary of National Findings*, NSDUH Series H-44, HHS Publication No. (SMA) 12-4713. Rockville, MD: Substance Abuse and Mental Health Services Administration. Retrieved from http://www.samhsa.gov/data/NSDUH/2k11Results/NSDUHresults2011.pdf

Sun, R., Triplett, R. & Gainey, R. 2004. Neighborhood characteristics and crime. *Western Criminological Review 5*(1), 1–16.

Surratt, H., Inciardi, J., Kurtz, S. & Kiley, M. 2004. Sex work and drug use in a subculture of violence. *Crime & Delinquency 50*(1), 43–59.

Sutherland, E. H., Cressey, D. R. & Luckenbill, D. F. 1992. *Principles of Criminology* (11th ed.). Holden, MO: General Hall.

Sykes, G. 1958. *The Society of Captives*. Princeton, NJ: Princeton University Press.

Sykes, G. & Messinger, S. 1960. The inmate social system. In R. Cloward (Ed.), *Theoretical Studies in the Social Organization of the Prison*, pp. 5–19. New York: Social Science Research Council.

Taxman, F. & Cropsey, K. 2007. Women and the criminal justice system: Improving outcomes through criminal justice and non-criminal justice responses. *Women & Criminal Justice, 17*(2), 5–26.

Taylor, B. 1982. *Sexual Inequities Behind Bars*. Ph.D. dissertation, Claremont Graduate School, Claremont, CA.

Taylor, C. 1993. *Girls, Gangs and Drugs*. East Lansing: Michigan State University Press.

Taylor, I., Walton, P. & Young, J. 1998. *The New Criminology* (2nd rev. ed.). New York: Harper and Row.

Taylor, K. & Blanchette, K. 2009. The women are not wrong: It is the approach that is debatable. *Criminology & Public Policy 8*(1), 221–229.

Teague, R., Pazerolle, P., Legosz, M. & Sanderson, J. 2008. Linking childhood exposure to physical abuse and adult offending: Examining mediating factors and gendered relationships. *Justice Quarterly 25*, 313–348.

Teplin, L., Abrams, K. & McClelland, G. 1996. Prevalence of psychiatric disorders among incarcerated women. *Archives of General Psychiatry 53*(2), 505–512.

Thomas, W. I. 1969. *The Unadjusted Girl*. Boston: Little, Brown. (Original work published 1923).

Thompson, D. 2013, September 13. California mothers could win early release. *Huffington Post*. Retrieved from http://www.huffingtonpost.com/2011/09/13/ca-inmate-mothers-could-w_n_960923.html

Thrasher, F. 1927. *The Gang*. Chicago: University of Chicago Press.

Tibbetts, S. 1997. Gender differences in students' rational decisions to cheat. *Deviant Behavior: An Interdisciplinary Journal 18*, 393–414.

Tibbetts, S. 1999. Differences between women and men regarding decisions to commit test cheating. *Research in Higher Education 40*(3), 323–342.

Tibbetts, S. & Herz, D. 1996. Gender differences in factors of social control and rational choice. *Deviant Behavior 17*, 183–208.

Tibbetts, S. & Myers, D. 1999. Low self-control, rational choice, and student test cheating. *American Journal of Criminal Justice 23*(2), 179–200.

Tibbetts, S. & Piquero, A. 1999. The influence of gender, low birth weight, and disadvantaged environment in predicting early onset of offending: A test of Moffitt's interactional hypothesis. *Criminology 37*, 843–877.

Tittle, C. 1969. Inmate organization: Sex differentiation and influence of criminal subcultures. *American Sociological Review 34*, 492–505.

Tittle, C. 1973. Institutional living and self-esteem. *Social Problems 20*(4), 65–77.

Tittle, C. 1995. *Control Balance: Toward a General Theory of Deviance*. Boulder, CO: Westview Press.

Tittle, C., Ward, D. & Grasmick, H. 2003. Self-control and crime/deviance: Cognitive vs. behavioral measures. *Journal of Quantitative Criminology 19*(4), 333–365.

Tjaden, P. & Thoennes, N. 2006. *Extent, Nature, and Consequences of Rape Victimization: Findings from the National Violence against Women Survey*. Washington DC: National Institute of Justice.

Toch, H. 1975. *Men in Crisis*. Chicago: Aldine-Atherton.

Toch, H. 1977. *Living in Prison*. New York: Free Press.

Toigo, R. 1962. Illegitimate and legitimate cultures in a training school for girls. *Rip Van Winkle Clinic Proceedings 13*, 3–29.

Tonry, M. 1995. *Malign Neglect: Race, Crime, and Punishment in America*. New York: Oxford University Press.

Tonry, M., Ohlin, L. & Farrington, D. 1991. *Human Development and Criminal Behavior: New Ways of Advancing Knowledge*. New York: Springer-Verlag.

Tracy, P., Kempf-Leonard, K. & Abramoske-James, S. 2009. Gender differences in delinquency and juvenile justice processing: Evidence from national data. *Crime & Delinquency 55*(3), 171–215.

Tracy, P., Wolfgang, M. & Figlio, R. 1990. *Delinquency Careers in Two Birth Cohorts*. New York: Plenum.

Trammell, R. 2006. Accounts of violence and social control: Organized violence and negotiated order in California prisons. Unpublished doctoral dissertation, University of California, Irvine.

Trammell, R. 2009. Relational violence in women's prison: How women describe interpersonal violence and gender. *Women & Criminal Justice 18*, 267–286.

Trasler, G. 1987. Some cautions for the biological approach to crime causation. In S. Mednick, T. Moffitt, & S. Stack (Eds.), *The Causes of Crime*, pp. 7–25. New York: Cambridge University Press.

Triplett, R. & Myers, L. 1995. Evaluating contextual patterns of delinquency: Gender-based differences. *Justice Quarterly 12*, 59–84.

Uggen, C. & Kruttschnitt, C. 1998. Crime in the breaking: Gender differences in desistance. *Law and Society Review 32*(2), 339–366.

Uniform Crime Reports. 2011. *Crime in the United States 2011*. Washington, DC: Federal Bureau of Investigation. Retrieved from http://www.fbi.gov/about-us/cjis/ucr/crime-in-the-u.s/2011/crime-in-the-u.s.-2011

U.S. Government Accountability Office. 1979. *Female Offenders: Who Are They and What Are the Problems Confronting Them?* (Report #GGD-7973). Retrieved from www.gao.gov/products/GGD-79-73

Valentine, P. & Smith, T. 2001. Evaluating traumatic incident reduction therapy with female inmates: A randomized controlled clinical trial. *Research on Social Work Practice 11*, 40–51.

VanSlyke, S. & Bales, W. 2013. Gender dynamics in the sentencing of white collar offenders. *Criminal Justice Studies 26*(2), 168–196.

Van Voorhis, P. 2004. An overview of offender classification systems. In P. Van Voorhis, M. Braswell & D. Lester (Eds.), *Correctional Counseling and Rehabilitation* (5th ed.), pp. 133–160. Cincinnati, OH: Anderson.

Van Voorhis, P. 2005. Classification of women offenders: Gender-responsive approaches to risk/needs assessment. *Community Corrections Report 12*(2), 19–20.

Van Voorhis, P. & Presser, L. 2001. *Classification of Women Offenders: A National Assessment of Current Practices*. Washington, DC: National Institute of Corrections.

Van Voorhis, P., Wright, E., Salisbury, E. & Bauman, A. 2009. Women's risk factors and their contributions to existing risk/needs assessment: The current status of a gender-responsive supplement. *Criminal Justice and Behavior 37*(3), 261–288.

Vandiver, D. & Walker, J. 2002. Female sex offenders: An overview and analysis of 40 cases. *Criminal Justice Review 27*(2), 284–300.

Vazsonyi, A., Pickering, L., Junger, M. & Hessing, D. 2001. An empirical test of a general theory of crime: A four nation comparative study of self-control and the prediction of deviance. *Journal of Research in Crime and Delinquency 38*(2), 91–131.

Vedder, C. & Somerville, D. 1970. *The Delinquent Girl*. Springfield, IL: Charles C Thomas.

Velimesis, M. L. 1981. Sex roles and mental health of women in prison. *Professional Psychology 12*(1), 128–135.

Veysey, B. 1998. Specific needs of women diagnosed with mental illnesses in U.S. jails. In B. Levin, A. Blanch & A. Jennings (Eds.), *Women's Mental Health Sources: A Public Health Perspective*, pp. 368–389. Thousand Oaks, CA: Sage.

Veysey, B., DeCou, K. & Prescott, L. 1998. Effective management of female jail detainees with histories of physical and sexual abuse. *American Jails 12* (May/June), 50–54.

Visher, C. 1983. Gender, police arrest decision, and notions of chivalry. *Criminology 21*, 5–28.

Vitopoulos, N., Peterson-Badali, M. & Skilling, T. 2012. The relationship between matching service to criminogenic need and recidivism in male and female youth: Examining the RNR principles in action. *Criminal Justice & Behavior 39*, 1025–1041.

Wallace, B. 1995. Women and minorities in treatment. In A. Washton (Ed.), *Psychotherapy and Substance Abuse*, pp. 470–491. New York: Guilford.

Walsh, A. 1991. *Intellectual Imbalance, Love Deprivation and Violent Delinquency: A Biosocial Perspective*. Springfield, IL: Charles C. Thomas.

Walsh, A. 1995a. *Biosociology: An Emerging Paradigm*. Westport, CT: Praeger.

Walsh, A. 1995b. Genetic and cytogenetic intersex anomalies: Can they help us to understand gender differences in deviant behavior? *International Journal of Offender Therapy and Comparative Criminology 39*, 151–166.

Walsh, A. 2011. *Feminist Criminology Through a Biosocial Lens*. Durham, NC: Carolina Academic Press.

Walters, G. 1990. *The Criminal Lifestyle: Patterns of Serious Criminal Conduct*. Newbury Park, CA: Sage.

Ward, T., Yates, P. & Willis, G. 2012. The Good Lives Model and the Risk Needs Responsivity Model: A critical response to Andrews, Bonta, and Wornith. *Criminal Justice and Behavior 39*(1), 94–110.

Ward, D. & Beck, W. 2001. Gender and dishonesty. *The Journal of Social Psychology 130*, 333–339.

Ward, D. & Kassebaum, G. 1965. *Women's Prison: Sex and Social Structure*. Chicago: Aldine-Atherton.

Wark, G. & Krebs, D. 1996. Gender and dilemma differences in real-life moral judgment. *Developmental Psychology 32*, 220–230.

Warren, J., Hurt, S., Booker-Loper, A. & Chauhan, P. 2004. Exploring prison adjustment among female inmates. *Criminal Justice and Behavior 31*(5), 624–645.

Warren, J., Hurt, S., Loper, A., Bale, W., Friend, R. & Chauhan, P. 2002. Psychiatric symptoms, history of victimization, and violent behavior among incarcerated female felons: An American perspective. *International Journal of Law and Psychiatry 25*, 129–149.

Warren, M. 1979. The female offender. In H. Toch (Ed.), *Psychology and Criminal Justice*, pp. 444–469. Long Grove, IL: Waveland Press.

Watterson, K. 1996. *Women in Prison: Inside the Concrete Womb*. (Rev. ed.). Boston: Northeastern University Press.

Weidensall, J. 1916. *The Mentality of the Criminal Woman*. Baltimore: Warwick and York.

Weis, J. 1976. Liberation and crime: The invention of the new female criminal. *Crime and Social Justice 6*, 17–36.

Weis, R. 1997. Camp Dismas. In C. Blinn (Ed.), *Maternal Ties: A Selection of Programs for Female Offenders*, pp. 141–151. Lanham, MD: American Correctional Association.

Weisheit, R. 1985. Trends in programs for female offenders: The use of private agencies as service providers. *International Journal of Offender Therapy and Comparative Criminology 29*(1), 35–42.

Weitzer, R. 2005. New directions in research on prostitution. *Crime, Law & Social Change 43*, 211–235.

Welch, M. 1997. Regulating the reproduction and morality of women: The social control of body and soul. *Women & Criminal Justice 9*(1), 17–38.

Welle, D. & Falkin, G. 2000. The everyday policing of women with romantic codefendants: An ethnographic perspective. *Women & Criminal Justice 11*(2), 45–65.

Welle, D., Falkin, G. & Jainchill, N. 1998. Current approaches to drug treatment for women offenders: Project WORTH. *Journal of Substance Abuse Treatment 15*(2), 151–163.

Wellisch, J., Anglin, D. & Prendergast, M. 1993. Treatment strategies for drug abusing women offenders. In J. Inciardi (Ed.), *Drug Treatment and Criminal Justice*, pp. 5–29. Newbury Park, CA: Sage.

Wellisch, J., Prendergast, M. & Anglin, J. 1994. *Bureau of Justice Statistics Report: Drug Abusing Women Offenders. Results of a National Survey*. Washington DC: U.S. Department of Justice.

Wellisch, J., Prendergast, M. & Anglin, D. 1996. Needs assessment and services for drug-abusing women offenders: Results from a national survey of community-based treatment programs. *Women & Criminal Justice 8*(1), 27–60.

Wesely, J. 2006. Considering the context of women's violence: Gender, lived experiences, and cumulative victimization. *Feminist Criminology 1*(4), 303–328.

Wesely, J. & Wright, J. 2009. From the inside out: Efforts by homeless women to disrupt cycles of crime and violence. *Women & Criminal Justice 19*, 217–234.

West, H., Sabol, W. & Greenman, S. 2010. *Prisoners in 2009*. Washington, DC: Bureau of Justice Statistics.

West, R. 1988. Jurisprudence and gender. *The University of Chicago Law Review 55*(1), 1–72.

Whaley, R. & Messner, S. 2002. Gender equality and gendered homicides. *Homicide Studies 6*(3), 188–210.

Whaley, R., Moe, A., Eddy, J. & Daugherty, J. 2007. The domestic violence experiences of women in community corrections. *Women & Criminal Justice 18*(3), 25–45.

Wheeler, P., Trammell, R. Thomas & Findlay, J. 1989. Persephone chained: Parity or equality in women's prisons?" *The Prison Journal 69*(1), 88–102.

Widom, C. 1979. Female offenders: Three assumptions about self-esteem, sex-role identity and feminism. *Criminal Justice and Behavior 6*(4), 365–382.

Widom, C. 1981. Perspectives of female criminality: A critical examination of assumptions. In A. Morris & L. Gelthorpe (Eds.), *Women and Crime*, pp. 33–48. Cambridge, England: University of Cambridge Institute of Criminology.

Widom, C. 1984. *Sex Roles and Psychopathology.* New York: Plenum Press.

Widom, C. 1989a. Child abuse, neglect, and violent criminal behavior. *Criminology 27*, 251–366.

Widom, C. 1989b. Does violence beget violence? A critical examination of the literature. *Psychological Bulletin*, 1063–1028.

Widom, C. 1989c. The cycle of violence. *Science 244*, 160–166.

Widom, C. 1991a. Childhood victimization: Risk factor for delinquency. In M. E. Colten, & E. Gore (Eds.), *Adolescent Stress: Causes and Consequences*, pp. 201–221. New York: Aldine De Gruyter.

Widom, C. 1991b. Avoidance of criminality in abused and neglected children. *Psychiatry 54*, 162–174.

Widom, C. 1995. *Victims of Childhood Sexual Abuse—Later Criminal Consequences.* Washington, DC: National Institute of Justice.

Widom, C. 1996. Childhood sexual abuse and criminal consequences. *Society 33*(4), 47–53.

Widom, C. 2000. Childhood victimization and the derailment of the girls and women to the criminal justice system. In B. E. Richie, K. Tsenin, & C. S. Widom (Eds.), *Research on Women and Girls in the Criminal Justice System*, Vol. 3, pp. 27–35. Washington, DC: National Institute of Justice.

Widom, C. & Ames, A. 1988. Biology and female crime. In T. Moffitt & S. Mednick (Eds.), *Biological Contributions to Crime Causation*, pp. 308–331. Boston, MA: Martinus Nijhoff.

Widom, C. & Kuhns, J. 1996. Childhood victimization and subsequent risk for promiscuity, prostitution and teenage pregnancy: A prospective study. *American Journal of Public Health 86*, 1607–1612.

Widom, C. & Maxfield, M. 2001. *An Update on the "Cycle of Violence"* (NIJ Research in Brief, NCJ 184894). Washington, DC: National Institute of Justice.

Wilbanks, W. 1986. Are female felons treated more leniently by the criminal justice system? *Justice Quarterly 3*, 517–529.

Williams, M. & Rikard, R. 2004. Marginality or neglect: An exploratory study of policies and programs for aging female inmates. *Women & Criminal Justice 15*(3/4), 121–141.

Wilson, J. 1993. *The Moral Sense.* New York: Free Press.

Wilson, J. & Hernstein, R. 1986. *Crime and Human Nature.* New York: Simon & Schuster.

Wilson, N. 1980. Styles of doing time in a coed prison. In J. Smykla (Ed.), *Co-Corrections*, pp. 160–165. New York: Human Services Press.

Wilson, N. & Rigsby, C. 1975. Is crime a man's world? Issues in the exploration of criminality. *Journal of Criminal Justice 3*(2), 131–139.

Winterfield, L., Coggeshall, M., Burke-Storer, M., Correa, V. & Tidd, S. 2009. *The Effects of Post-Secondary Correctional Education: Final Report.* Washington, DC: Urban Institute.

Wojda, R. & Rowe, J. 1997. *Women Behind Bars.* Lanham, MD: American Correctional Association.

Wolf, A. & Kempf-Leonard, K. 2009. Gender issues in juvenile and criminal justice. *Crime & Delinquency 55*(3), 167–170.

Wolff, N., Blitz, D., Shi, J., Bachman, R. & Siegel, J. 2006. Sexual violence inside prisons: Rates of victimization. *Journal of Urban Health: Bulletin of the New York Academy of Medicine 83*(5), 835–848.

Wolff, N., Blitz, D., Shi, J., Siegel, J. & Bachman, R. 2007. Physical violence inside prisons: Rates of victimization. *Criminal Justice and Behavior 34*, 588–604.

Wolff, N., Shi, J. & Bachman, R. 2008. Measuring victimization inside prisons: Questioning the questions. *Journal of Interpersonal Violence 23*, 1343–1362.

Wolff, N., Shi, J. & Siegel, J. 2009. Understanding physical victimization inside prisons: Factors that predict risk. *Justice Quarterly 26*, 445–475.

Wolfgang, M., Thornberry, T. & Figlio, R. (Eds.). 1987. *From Boy to Man, From Delinquency to Crime*. Chicago: University of Chicago Press.

Wolfgang, M., Figlio, R. & Sellin, T. 1972. *Delinquency in a Birth Cohort*. Chicago: University of Chicago Press.

Women's National Law Center. 2010. *Mothers Behind Bars*. Washington, DC: The Rebecca Project for Human Rights, Women's National Law Center.

Women's Prison Association (WPA). 2009. *Mothers, Infants and Imprisonment*. New York: Women's Prison Association.

Wonders, N. 1996. Determinate sentencing: A feminist and postmodern story. *Justice Quarterly 13*, 611–648.

Wood, P., Gove, W., Wilson, J. & Cochran, J. 1997. Nonsocial reinforcement and habitual criminal conduct: An extension of learning theory. *Criminology 35*, 335–366.

Worrall, A. 1990. *Offending Women*. London: Routledge.

Worrall, A. 2004. Twisted sisters, ladettes, and the new penology: The social construction of violent girls. In C. Alder & A. Worrall (Eds.), *Girls' Violence: Myths and Realities*, pp. 41–60. Albany: State University of New York Press.

Wright, B., Caspi, A., Moffitt, T. & Silva, P. 2001. The effects of social ties on crime vary by criminal propensity: A life-course model of interdependence. *Criminology 39*, 321–351.

Wright, B., Entner, R., Caspi, A., Moffitt, T. & Silva, P. 2001. The effects of social ties on crime vary by criminal propensity: A life-course model of interdependence. *Criminology 39*, 321–351.

Wright, E., Salisbury, E. & Van Voorhis, P. 2007. Predicting the prison misconducts of women offenders: The importance of gender-responsive needs. *Journal of Contemporary Criminal Justice 23*, 310–340.

Wright, E. M., Van Voorhis, P., Salisbury, E. J. & Bauman, A. 2012. Gender-responsive lessons learned and policy implications for women in prison review. *Criminal Justice and Behavior 39*, 1612–1632.

Wright, J. & Beaver, K. 2005. Do parents matter in creating self-control in their children? A genetically informed test of Gottfredson and Hirschi's theory of low self-control. *Criminology 43*, 1169–1202.

Wright, K. 1988. The relationship of risk, needs, and personality classification systems and prison adjustment. *Criminal Justice and Behavior 15*, 454–471.

Wright, K. & Saylor, W. 1991. Male and female employees' perceptions of prison work: Is there a difference? *Justice Quarterly 8*, 505–524.

Wright, R. 1992. From vamps to tramps to teases and flirts: Stereotypes of women in criminology textbooks, 1956 to 1965 and 1981 to 1990. *Journal of Criminal Justice Education 3*(2), 224–242.

Yang, S. 1990. The unique treatment needs of female substance abusers in correctional institutions: The obligation of the criminal justice system to provide parity. *Medicine and Law 9*, 1018–1027.

Young, V. 1980. Women, race and crime. *Criminology 18*, 36–44.

Zager, M. 1994. Gender and crime. In T. Hirschi & M. Gottfredson (Eds.), *The Generality of Deviance*, pp. 71–79. New Brunswick, NJ: Transaction Publishers.

Zahn, M., Agnew, R., Fishbein, D., Miller, S., Winn, D-M., Dakoff, G., Kruttschnitt, C., Giordano, P., Gottfredson, D., Payne, A., Feld, B. & Chesney-Lind, M. 2010. *Girls Study Group: Causes and Correlates of Girls' Delinquency* (NCJ 226358). Washington, DC: Office of Juvenile Justice and Delinquency Prevention.

Zahn, M., Day, J., Mihalic, S. & Tichavsky, L. 2009. Determining what works for girls in the juvenile justice system. *Crime & Delinquency 55*(3), 266–293.

Zaitzow, B. & Thomas, J. (Eds.). 2003. *Women in Prison: Gender and Social Control*. Boulder, CO: Lynne Reinner.

Zalba, A. 1964. *Women Prisoners and Their Families*. Los Angeles: Delmar Press.

Zang, N., Morash, M., Paul, G. & Cherry, R. 1998. Life skills programming for women offenders, Michigan Dept. of Corrections. In J. Morton (Ed.), *Complex Challenges, Collaborative Solutions: Programming for Adult and Juvenile Female Offenders*, pp. 173–187. Lanham, MD: American Correctional Association.

Zaplin, R. 1998a. A systems approach to the design and implementation of a day program for women offenders. In J. Morton (Ed.), *Complex Challenges, Collaborative Solutions: Programming for Adult and Juvenile Female Offenders*, pp. 129–141. Lanham, MD: American Correctional Association.

Zaplin, R. 1998b. *Female offenders: Critical Perspectives and Effective Interventions*. Gaithersburg, MD: Aspen.

Zedner, L. 1991. *Women, Crime and Custody in Victorian England*. Oxford: Clarendon Press.

Zietz, D. 1981. *Women Who Embezzle or Defraud: A Study of Convicted Felons*. New York: Praeger.

Zimmer, L. 1986. *Women Guarding Men*. Chicago: University of Chicago Press.

Zlotnick, C., Clarke, J., Friedmann, P., Roberts, M., Sacks, S. & Melnick, G. 2008. Gender differences in comorbid disorders among offenders in prison substance abuse treatment programs. *Behavioral Sciences and the Law 26*, 403–412.

Zupan, L. 1986. Gender-related differences in correctional officers' perceptions and attitudes. *Journal of Criminal Justice 14*, 349–361.

Zupan, L. 1992. Men guarding women: An analysis of the employment of male correctional officers in prisons for women. *Journal of Criminal Justice 20*, 297–309.

Table of Cases

Barefield v. Leach, No. 10282 (D. N.M., 1974).

Booker v. U.S., 543 U.S. 224 (2005).

Brown v. Plata, 131 S.Ct. 1910 (2011).

Commonwealth v. Daniel, 430 Pa. 642, 243 A.2d 400 (1968).

Dothard v. Rawlinson, 433 U.S. 321 (1977).

Estelle v. Gamble, 429 U.S. 97 (1976).

Farmer v. Brennan, 114 S.Ct. 1970 (1994).

Forts v. Ward, 434 F. Supp. 946 (S.D.N.Y.), rev'd and remanded, 566 F.2d 849 (2d Cir. 1977), 471 F. Supp. 1095 (S.D.N.Y. 1979), aff'd in part and rev'd in part, 621 F.2d 1210 (2d Cir. 1980).

Glover v. Johnson, 478 F. Supp. 1075 (E.D. Mich.) 1979).

Grosso v. Lally, No. 474447 (D. Md. 1977).

Grummet v. Rushen, 779 F.2d 491 (9th Cir., 1985).

Gunther v. Iowa State Men's Reformatory, 612 F.2d 1079 (8th Cir.), cert. denied, 446 U.S. 966 (1980).

Harden v. Dayton Human Rehabilitation Center, 520 F. Supp. 769 (1981).

Holt versus Sarver, 309 F. Supp. 362 (E.D. Ark. 1970).

Inmates of Sybil Brand Institution for Women v. County of Los Angeles, 130 Cal. App. 3d 89, 181 Cal. Rptr. 599 (1982).

Johnson v. Phelan, 69 F.3d 144 (7th Cir., 1995), cert. denied.

Johnson v. Sheahan, 117 S.Ct. 506 (1996).

Jordan v. Gardner, 986 F.2d 1544-1545 (9th Cir. 1993).

Lee v. Downs, 641 F.2d 1117 (1981).

Morales v. Turman, 383 F. Supp. 53 (E.D. Tex. 1974).

Neal v. Michigan Department of Corrections, 2009 WL 187813 (Mich. App. Jan 27, 2009).

Nelson v. Correctional Medical Services, 583 F.3d 522 (8th Cir. 2009).

Park v. Thomson, 356 F. Supp. 783 (D. Hawaii 1976).

Patricia A. v. City of New York, 335 N.Y.S. 2d 33 (1972).

Pitts v. Meese, 684 F. Supp. 303 (D.C.Cir. 1987).

Procunier v. Martinez, 416 U.S. 396 (1974).

State v. Heitman, 105 Kan. 139, 181 P. 630 (1919).

Timm v. Gunter, 917 F.2d 1093 (9th Cir. 1990).

Todaro v. Ward, 431 F. Supp. 1129 (S.D.N.Y. 1977), aff'd, 565 F.2d 48 (2d Cir. 1977).

Torres v. Wisconsin Dept of Corrections, 838 F.2d 944 (7th Cir., 1988), overruled in part 859 F.2d 1523 (1988).

United States ex rel. Robinson v. York, 281 F. Supp. 8 (D. Conn. 1968).

Woff v. McDonnell, 418 U.S. 359 (1975).

Women Prisoners of the District of Columbia Dept. of Corrections et al., v. District of Columbia et al., 877 F. Supp. 634 (1994).

Author Index

Acoca, L., 209
Adler, F., 85, 87
Agnew, R., 65, 95, 96, 97, 98
Akers, R., 62, 63, 64
Alarid, L., 70
Albanese, J., 33
Allen, D., 67
Allen, E., 16, 86
Andrews, D., 81, 247, 249
Anglin, J., 264
Arneklev, B., 94
Arnold, R., 137

Baker, D., 182
Bandura, A., 80
Barton, C., 196
Baskin, D., 36, 39, 40, 48
Batchelor, S., 148, 149, 235
Beaver, K., 110
Beccaria, C., 59
Becker, H., 71
Belknap, J., 164
Bentham, J., 59
Bishop, D., 175
Blackwell, B., 105
Blanchette, K., 249
Bloom, B., 206, 258
Blumstein, A., 124, 125
Bonta, J., 81, 247
Bordt, R., 170, 172
Bottcher, J., 103, 104
Brennan, P., 173, 288
Brennan, T., 133, 134, 135

Brockway, Z., 195
Broidy, L., 98
Brown, M., 174
Browne, A., 46, 130
Burgess, R., 62
Burkhardt, K., 200
Bursik, R., 94
Butler, M., 233
Buzawa, E., 147
Bynum, T., 291
Byrne, M., 274

Calhoun, A., 242
Calhoun, H., 242
Cameron, M., 29
Campbell, A., 150, 151, 152, 153
Carbone-Lopez, K., 36, 261
Carlen, P., 12
Caspi, A., 113
Cernkovich, S., 67
Chapman, J., 106
Chesney-Lind, M., 12, 13, 15, 46, 76, 105, 142, 146, 147, 150, 151, 153, 154, 173, 181
Chilton, R., 54
Chodorow, N., 78, 257
Clark, J., 221
Cloward, R., 66, 95
Cohen, A., 65, 66
Cohen, J., 124, 125
Cohen, L., 100

Collins, A., 217
Collins, W., 217
Couture, H., 202
Covington, S., 258
Cowie, B., 75
Cowie, J., 75
Crawford, J., 200
Crenshaw, K., 54, 179
Cressey, D., 62, 63, 226, 228
Crites, L., 82
Cropsey, K., 248
Crow, M., 180
Culley, R., 241
Cupp, R., 249
Curry, G., 150

Daly, K., 13, 31, 49, 76, 131, 136, 170, 172, 173, 176, 177, 235, 248
Datesman, S., 54, 67, 76
Davis, S., 15
Decker, S., 29, 151
DeCoster, S., 157, 158
DeHart, D., 132
Dembo, D., 76
Denno, D., 111, 123, 126
Dix, D., 194
Doerner, J., 178
Doreumus, S., 194
Dowden, C., 249
Dugdale, R., 198
Durkheim, É., 61
Dwyer, J., 278

Eaton, M., 173
Eliason, M., 15
Elis, L., 137
Enos, S., 269, 270
Esbensen, F., 150
Eve, R., 84
Eysenck, J., 112, 113

Farnhan, E., 195
Farnsworth, M., 174
Farrington, D., 119, 120, 122, 125, 126, 173
Feinman, C., 13, 193, 194
Feld, B., 147, 148
Felson, M., 100
Ferraro, K., 186
Ferrero, G., 60
Figlio, R., 120
Finkelhor, D., 130
Fox, J., 211
Frazier, C., 175
Freedman, E., 193, 196
Fry, E., 194

Gabel, K., 215
Ganem, N., 131
Gelsthorpe, L., 14
Gendreau, P., 247, 290
Giallombardo, R., 228
Gibbons, A. H., 194
Gilfus, M., 12, 128
Gilligan, C., 77, 78, 257
Gillis, A., 69
Giordano, P., 67
Girshick, L., 190
Glick, R., 200
Glueck, E., 4, 73, 199
Glueck, S., 4, 73, 199
Gora, J., 76
Gottfredson, M., 90, 91, 92, 119, 124, 125
Gover, A., 253
Grasmick, H., 94
Green, B., 183
Greenberg, D., 70
Greenman, S., 179
Gudjonsson, G., 112, 113

Hagan, J., 69, 104, 171
Hagedorn, J., 151

Hahn, N., 60, 198
Hannah-Moffat, K., 260
Harlow, C., 204
Harris, J., 222, 226
Heffernan, R., 228
Heidensohn, F., 82
Heimer, K., 35, 98, 107, 157, 158
Held, V., 78
Henriques, Z., 270
Hirschi, T., 7, 68, 69, 90, 91, 92, 93, 95, 119, 124, 125
Hoffman-Bustamante, D., 83
Holtfreter, K., 248, 249
Hotaling, G., 147
Howe, A., 82
Howell, J., 160
Hubbard, D., 162, 258, 259

Inciardi, J., 48
Irwin, J., 226, 228

James, J., 52
Jensen, G., 84
Joe, K., 151, 153

Kassebaum, G., 226
Kaufman, J., 99
Kellor, F., 198
Klein, D., 82
Kohlberg, L., 76, 77
Konopka, G., 75
Koons, B., 291
Koons-Witt, B., 177
Kramer, J., 171
Kruttschnitt, C., 36, 173
Kunselman, J., 180

Langan, P., 289
Laub, J., 119, 123, 124, 125
Lauritsen, J., 35
Lawrence, J., 208
Lekkerkerker, E., 196, 197
Lemert, L., 71
Leonard, E., 82
Leverentz, A., 288
Levin, D., 289
Lipsitz, G., 284
Lombroso, C., 14, 59, 60
Longshore, D., 94

Lord, E., 262
Lowenkamp, C., 249
Lujan, C., 137
Lykken, D., 74
Lynch, J., 35, 184
Lynch, S., 183

Maahs, J., 97
MacDonald, M., 204
Maeve, M., 204, 210
Maher, L., 36, 49
Manasse, M., 131
Mann, C., 41, 42
Marshall, I., 86
Matthews, B., 162, 258, 259
Mazerolle, P., 97
McClellan, D., 204, 224
McKay, H., 62
Mead, G. H., 71
Mears, D., 156
Merton, T., 64
Messerschmidt, J., 16, 17
Messina, N., 266
Miller, E., 136
Miller, J., 38, 146, 148, 151, 154, 155, 157, 261
Miller, W., 62, 150
Moe, A., 186
Moffitt, T., 111, 121, 124, 125
Moore, J., 151, 204
Moore, L. D., 145
Morash, M., 105, 248, 249, 291
Morris, A., 12, 14, 67, 82, 173, 289

Naffine, N., 66, 69, 82
Nagel, I., 171, 173
Neto, V., 200
Noddings, N., 79, 257
Norton, E. H., 190

O'Brien, P., 287, 289
Ohlin, L., 66, 67, 95
Otis, M., 231
Owen, B., 190, 206, 228, 233, 234, 235, 236, 242, 258

Padavic, I., 145
Parsons, T., 81

Piaget, J., 76, 77
Piquero, A., 101
Piquero, N. L., 98
Pollack, S., 259, 260
Pollak, O., 17, 30, 34, 74, 169
Pollock, J., 15, 82, 212, 217, 272
Prendergast, M., 264
Price, B., 82

Quetelet, A., 61
Quicker, J., 152

Rafter, N., 194, 197, 198
Raine, A., 113
Rasche, C., 82
Reckless, W., 95
Reed, B., 264, 265
Reisig, M., 248, 290
Richie, B., 136, 137, 285, 286, 287
Rierden, A., 190
Root, M., 266
Rosenbaum, J., 76
Rosenbaum, K., 51
Rosenbaum, M., 262
Ross, P., 208
Roth, J., 125
Ryan, T., 256

Sabol, W., 179, 202
Salisbury, E., 133, 290
Sampson, R., 102, 119, 123, 124, 125, 133
Sandhu, H., 67
Scarpetti, F., 76
Schrag, C., 227
Schur, E., 72

Schwartz, J., 35
Sealock, M., 98
Shaw, C., 62
Shelden, R., 76, 142
Siegel, J., 130
Simon, M., 86, 87
Simon, R., 31, 85
Simpson, J., 69
Simpson, S., 137, 145
Slater, E., 75
Smart, C., 78, 82, 83
Smith, D., 67, 70
Smith, P., 249
Sokoloff, N., 82
Sommers, I., 36, 39, 40, 48
Spaulding, E., 198
Spears, J., 172
Spohn, C., 172
Steffensmeier, D., 16, 25, 27, 28, 29, 35, 86, 87, 106, 143, 147, 171
Stein, J., 94
Steiner, B., 252
Streifel, C., 86, 171
Strickland, K., 199
Struckman-Johnson, C., 235, 242
Struckman-Johnson, D., 235, 242
Sutherland, E., 62, 63
Sykes, G., 225, 227

Taxman, F., 248
Taylor, B., 200
Taylor, C., 151, 153
Taylor, K., 249
Teplin, L., 184
Teske, R., 174

Thomas, W. I., 74
Thornberry, T., 120
Tibbetts, S., 101
Tittle, C., 94, 106
Tonry, M., 176, 177
Trammell, R., 234, 243
Turner, S., 94

Van Voorhis, P., 133, 250, 251, 253, 290
Vandiver, D., 50
Veysey, B., 184, 187
Visher, C., 125, 173

Walker, J., 50
Walsh, A., 109, 110, 111, 113, 114
Ward, D., 226
Ward, T., 259
Warren, R., 79
Weidensall, J., 198
Wellisch, J., 264
Wesely, J., 128, 132
West, H., 179
White, N., 148
Widom, C., 76, 123, 130
Wilbanks, W., 171
Wilkinson, C., 289
Williams, L., 130
Wilson, J. Q., 79
Wistyer, M., 194
Wolff, N., 233, 236
Wolfgang, M., 120
Woolredge, J., 252

Zager, M., 95
Zietz, D., 30, 31
Zupan, L., 239, 240

Subject Index

Abuse. *See* Adult victimization; Childhood abuse; Domestic violence; Physical abuse; Sexual abuse
Administrative segregation (ad-seg), 221
Adoption and Safe Families Act of 1997, 285
Adult victimization
    childhood victimization as strong predictor of, 206
    crime correlated with, 132
    of female jail inmates, 186
    prevalence in female prisoners, 128, 130, 184, 186
    relational pathway of, 133
    self-blame associated with, 205
    as women's risk factor, 248
    by women who were abusers in prison relationships, 235
African American girl gangs, 153
African American women
    chivalry studies and, 170, 172
    drug arrests for, 182
    incarceration rates for, 179–180, 202
    likelihood of victimization, 54

    pathways theories and, 136–137
    percent of prison population, 200
    in prison, 202
    tendency to engage in crime, 53–54
African Americans
    gender disparity in charge reductions among, 174
    juvenile, as victims and victimizers, 146
Age effect/maturation effect, 92
Androcentrism, 58
Argot (social) roles, 227–228
Arrest rates
    aggravated assault, 34
    burglary, 28–29
    counterfeiting/forgery, 32
    drug crimes, 25, 47
    embezzlement, 29, 31–33
    explanations for convergence between men and women, 22–27
    of female vs. male delinquents, 143–144
    forgery/counterfeiting, 32
    fraud, 29–33
    juvenile property crimes, 144
    juvenile violent crimes, 145–146

    larceny-theft, 30
    murder and non-negligent manslaughter, 42
    narrowing of sex ratio in, 27
    other assault, 26
    percentage of women's total arrests, 23
    property crimes, male vs. female, 24
    robbery, 26, 38
    violent crimes, 24
Arson, 39
Assault
    aggravated vs. domestic, 34, 39–40
    by correctional officers in women's prisons, 241–242
    domestic violence, 40–41
    other, arrest rates of men and women, 26
    sexual harassment and assault by COs, 236, 241–243
Attention Deficit Disorder (ADD), 111
Attention Deficit Hyperactivity Disorder (ADHD), 111

Battered women, 45, 132, 134–135
Bedford Hills, 190, 195–198, 211, 216, 222

Behavior modification programs, 255–256
Behaviorism and learning theory, 80–81
Biological criminology, 108–110, 114, 293
Biological theories of crime, 107–115
    critiques of, 114–115
    sex differences and, 108
Biosociology, 108
Black market, 228–229
Body type theory, 107
Booker v. U.S. (2005), 182
Bootstrapping, 27, 175
Brain chemicals and neural pathways, 109–111
Brain lateralization, 110, 114, 121, 126
Branks, 192
Bridewells, 193
Brown v. Plata (2011), 191, 216
Bureau of Social Hygiene, 198

Cacogenic family studies, 60, 198
Cambridge Study in Delinquent Development, 119–120
Canadian School of Correctional Intervention, 247
Career-criminal research, 124
CASA. *See* National Center on Addiction and Substance Abuse
Chicago School
    cultural deviance theory, 62
    differential association theory, 62, 64
    differential opportunity theory, 65–68
    social strain theory, 64–65
Chicana girl gangs, 152
Child care
    addiction therapy and, 265
    alternative sentencing and, 277–278
    in halfway houses, 276–277

as "natural" sex-role responsibility, 13
post-release concerns, 269–270
prison nurseries, 274–276
problems for female jail inmates, 187
See also Parent programming
Childhood abuse/victimization
    behavioral/emotional effects correlated with, 129
    chronic, potential effects of, 210
    dysfunctional families and, 128
    early-onset delinquency correlated with, 124
    female crime/delinquency linked to, 127, 130
    higher rates for women than for men, 127–128
    hyper-arousal correlated with, 210
    and incest survivor programming, 266
    likelihood of violent adult behavior correlated with, 36
    link to mental illness, drug dependency, and high-risk lifestyle, 129
    neuroendocrine processes affected by, 114
    physical. *See* physical abuse
    as predictor of prison misconduct, 248, 251
    as predictor of recidivism, 250
    prevalence among prisoners, 203–205
    of prisoners by sex, 203
    relational pathway of, 133
    as risk factor for delinquency, 122
    sexual. *See* Childhood sexual abuse

as strong predictor of adult victimization, 206
women's arrests for, 40
women's criminality correlated with, 128, 135, 138, 293
Childhood sexual abuse
    drug use/abuse correlated with, 207, 263
    dysfunctional adult behavior correlated with, 266
    of girls in juvenile institutions, 164
    link to female crime/delinquency, 130–131
    link to high-risk lifestyles, 129
    mental health problems correlated with, 186
    more common in girls than in boys, 159
    prevalence in female inmates, 127–129, 183, 185–186, 201, 203–205, 207
    recurrent victimization correlated with, 130
    self-blame associated with, 205
    women in drug treatment correlated with, 266–267
Children
    of inmates, addressing the needs of, 271–272
    parenting programs addressing the needs of, 271–272
    reunification issues after release, 284–286, 288
Chivalry hypothesis, 168–178
    differential treatment in sentencing guidelines, 173–178
    double standard for juvenile girls, 175
    methodological concerns regarding, 169–170
    studies pertaining to, 170–173

Cincinnati School of Criminal Justice, 247

Classical School, 59, 61–68, 100

Classification/prediction instruments, 246–253, 258

Clearance rates, 21

Cognitive behavioral programs/interventions, 258

Cognitive functioning, correlation with delinquency, 111

Cohort studies. *See* Longitudinal research

Commonwealth v. Daniel (1968), 168

Community as a prime factor in crime causation, 102

Community Parenting Alternative (CPA), 277

Community-based treatment programs. *See* Therapeutic communities

Conflict theories, 72

Containment theory, general strain theory vs., 95

Control theory, 7–8, 90–91. *See also* Social control theory

Correctional officers

change in relationship with female inmates, 221

disrespect of female inmates, 238

early history of, 239

gender-specific training for, 212

male officers in women's prisons, 239–241

men's vs. women's interactions with, 227

potential of male COs to exploit female prisoners, 293

preference to work with male inmates, 212–213, 238

relationships between inmates and, 237–239

sexual harassment and assault by, 236, 241–243

stereotyping of female inmates by, 237

Correlates of crime (independent variables), measuring, 5, 7–8

Crack-house sex, 262

Crime

categorizing/counting of, 6–7

correlation with childhood victimization, 130–131

"dark figure" of, 6

difficulties in defining, 6

drug-related, 48

explaining at individual level vs. societal level, 4

measurement, problems in, 5–8

policy implications for reducing, 294–295

statistical sources on, 21–22

theories of. *See* Theories

violent, 34–36

Criminal pathways, 131–137

race and ethnicity's influence on career pathways, 136–137

Criminality

early, causal factors of, 198

heavy drug use correlated with, 207

informal social ties affecting, 119

sex-role effects inhibiting, 103–104

Criminogenic (dynamic) needs, 247, 259

Criminology biases and paradigms, 2–5

Critical criminology, 72

Cult of True Womanhood, 193

Cultural deviance theory, 62–63

Cultural feminism, 13

Current theories of crime

biological, 107–115

economic marginalization, 106–107

general theory of crime, 90–95

rational choice theory, 100

sex-role and feminist theories revisited, 103, 106

social support/disorganization theories, 102–103

"Dark" figure of crime, 22

Death penalty for female offenders, 182–183

Delinquency

ADD and hyperactivity linked to, 111

adolescent-limited, 124

childhood victimization correlated with, 130

differential opportunity theory and, 65–68

early-onset, 124–125

effects of single-parent families on, 91–92

egalitarian vs. patriarchal families and, 105

female. *See* Female delinquency

general strain theory and, 96–97

life-course persistent delinquency, 121, 124, 126–127

low self-control and. *See* Low self-control

personality traits linked to, 111–113

risk preference and, 105

sex-role effects inhibiting, 103–104

social efficacy of neighborhoods and, 102

social/biological factors correlated with, 121

strain theory explanation of, 97

See also Juvenile offenders

Delinquency theories, application to girls, 156–160
Deprivation theory, 225–226
Detainment of delinquent girls, 163–164
Developmental theories, 76–80, 123
Diagnostic and Statistical Manual of Mental Disorders (DSM-V), 74
Differential association theory, 62–64, 94
Differential discretion hypothesis, 174
Differential opportunity theory, 65–68
Disparate sentencing laws, 168
Disrespect, 37, 149, 233–234, 348
Domestic homicide, 44–46
Domestic violence, 40–41
  domestic homicide, 44–46
  feminist research on, 9–11
  prevalence in female jail inmates, 183–184
  recidivism and, 289
  research, policy, and unintended consequences of, 9–11
Drug crimes, 25, 46–50
Drug subculture, role of women in, 48, 50
Drug treatment programs, 260–266
Drug use/abuse
  characteristics of drug-abusing women, 206, 261, 263
  childhood sexual victimization correlated with, 129, 207
  different motivations for male and female offenders, 207, 262
  dysfunctional family life correlated with, 263
  education level and, 263

employment correlated with, 263
  among female jail inmates, 184
  female methamphetamine users, 261
  female vs. male reasons behind, 263
  impact on imprisonment of women, 202
  mental illness correlated with, 263
  pathways research on, 134–135
  prevalence in female prisoners, 184, 206–207
  problems of female addicts, 260–261
  sequence of/motivations for, 261–262
  strong correlation with women's criminality, 260
  U.S., reactionary/racist political policy and reaction to, 260
Drug violations, arrest rates of men and women, 47
Dunedin Study (New Zealand), 121
Dysfunctional families
  childhood victimization and, 128
  delinquency correlated with, 120, 163
  drug use/abuse correlated with, 207, 263
  early-onset delinquency, 125
  friendships with COs and women from, 237
  gang membership and, 154
  recidivism correlated with, 247, 250
  women's criminality correlated with, 132, 138, 202–203, 294
Dysfunctional relationships
  abusive intimate relationships, 206, 243

with family/friends, 201, 204
  as predictor of prison misconduct, 250
  relational pathway including, 133
  as women's risk factor, 248

Early-onset delinquency, 124–125
Ecological fallacy, 4
Economic marginalization as cause of women's criminality, 132, 201
Economic marginalization theory, 85, 87, 106
Economic opportunity/participation theory, 86
Educational programs, 254–255
Egalitarian families, 105
Embezzlement, 29, 31–33
Emotional dysregulation, correlation with childhood sexual abuse, 205
Employment, difficulty securing after release, 283
Estelle v. Gamble (1976), 214
Ethnicity. *See* Race/ethnicity
Eugenics, 60, 108, 174, 198

Familial paternalism and sentencing leniency, 173
Families
  as critical factor in reducing women's crime and recidivism, 294
  dysfunctional. *See* Dysfunctional families
  patriarchal vs. egalitarian, studies of, 105
  pseudo-family relationships in women's prisons, 229–231
Family and Offender Sentencing Alternative Program (FOSA), 277
Female consumerism theory, 87

Female delinquency, 141–155
  application of theories to
    girls, 156–160
  arrest rates for females
    under age 18, 142–143
  detainment of juvenile
    girls, 163–164
  girl gangs, 149–155
  race and ethnicity's
    impact on, 145–146
  research on violent girls,
    146–149
Female offenders
  adult victimization of, 130
  Brennan's typology of,
    133
  Daly's typology of, 132
  elements of successful
    programming for, 291
  embezzlers, typology of,
    30–31
  high rates of childhood vic-
    timization in, 127–129
  increase in incarceration
    rate for, 181–182
  recurrent adult victimiza-
    tion in, 130
  statistically distinguished
    pathways for, 134–135
  See also Female delin-
    quency; Female prison-
    ers; Girls; Women
Female prisoners
  abusive intimate relation-
    ships prior to/during
    incarceration, 206
  adjusting to prison life,
    221–222
  characteristics of, 200–201
  childhood sexual victim-
    ization prevalent
    among, 128–129
  daily maintenance per-
    formed by, 254
  economic marginaliza-
    tion, 106–107
  elderly, health concerns
    regarding, 209
  entry experience for new
    inmates, 219–221

family background of,
    202–203
  fewer services available in
    women's vs. men's
    prisons, 187
  human rights violations
    against, 240–241
  infantilization of, 221, 238
  inmate-on-inmate sexual
    violence, 237
  in jails, 183–187
  legal challenges regarding
    rights of, 214–217
  low self-esteem among,
    207–208
  measuring the percentage
    vs. the number of
    offenders, 201
  medical needs of, 208–211
  numbers by state, 192
  pat-downs/strip searches
    by male COs, 239–240
  personality traits/charac-
    teristics of, 207–208
  prevalence of childhood
    abuse among, 203–205
  prevalence of drug use/
    abuse among, 206–207
  prison population vs.
    offenders who are sen-
    tenced to prison, 201
  programming for specific
    needs of, 256–260
  race/ethnicity of, 202
  relationships with correc-
    tional officers, 237–239
  sexual abuse/assault by
    correctional officers,
    236, 241–243
  sexual relationships with
    correctional officers,
    243
  types of crimes and crimi-
    nal backgrounds of,
    201–202
  use of prediction instru-
    ments with, 250–253
  view of problems as indi-
    vidual rather than soci-
    etal, 260

See also Incarceration;
    Women's prisons
Feminist criminology, 9–13
  criticism of biological
    criminology, 108, 115
  domestic violence
    research, 9–11
  other contributions of,
    12–13
  phenomenological
    research methods, 12
Feminist theories of crime
  early theories, 82–88
  economic marginaliza-
    tion, 106–107
  sex-role theory, 83–84
  women's liberation theory,
    84–87
Filicide, 43–44
Forgery/counterfeiting,
    31–32
Fraud, 29–33
Freudian theory, 73–74

Gangs, 149–155
  Chicana girls, 152–153
  female, in Hawaii, 153
  low self-control and mem-
    bership in, 91
  racial gang groupings in
    prison, 229–230
  research on girl gangs,
    154–155
  typology of, 154
Gaols, 191
Gender
  differences in juvenile
    arrest rates, 142–144
  disparities in sentencing,
    174–178
  feminist perspective on
    gender relations, 13
  selective chivalry and,
    173–175
Gender differences vs. sex
    differences, 15–17
Gender equality theory. See
    Liberation theory
Gender gap in crime, 18, 22,
    24–25, 292

Gender-responsive/gender-specific programming
classification/prediction research supporting, 258
criticisms and concerns regarding, 259–260
drug treatment programs, 265–266
elements essential to, 258
incest survivor programming, 266–267
for juvenile girls, 162–163
need for, 256–258
R/N/R approach vs., 258–260
Gender-responsive risk and need factors, 251
Gender-specific training for corrections officers, 212
Gender-specific vs. gender-neutral measures of prediction, 248–250, 290, 293, 295
General strain theory, 95–99
application to delinquent girls, 158–160
applications to girls/women, 97–99
criticism of, 96
strain as an individual construct, 65
tests/applications of, 96–97
victimization, 131
General theory of crime, 90–95
applications to girls/women, 94–95
criticisms of, 92–93
differential association/social learning theory vs., 94
major competing theories, 94
tests/applications of, 93–94
victimization and, 131
Genetic transmission of criminal predispositions, 107–108

Girl gangs, research on, 149–155
Girl Scouts Behind Bars, 274
Girls
chivalry hypothesis applied to, 175
delinquency theories applied to, 156–160
detainment of delinquent girls, 163–164
gender-specific programming for, 162–163
general strain theory applied to, 97–99, 158–160
general theory of crime applied to, 94–95
girl gang research, 91, 149–155
life-course theory applied to, 125–127
pathways theory applied to, 158–160
power control theory applied to, 157–158
rational choice theory applied to, 101–102, 157
sex-role theory applied to, 158
social control/social learning theory applied to, 156–157
violent, research on 146–149
See also Juvenile offenders
Glover v. Johnson (1979), 215
Good Lives Model, 259
Hagan's power-control theory, 106
Halfway houses, 276–277, 288–289
Hawthorne effect, 126
High-risk behaviors, correlation with childhood abuse, 129, 205, 210
Hispanic girl gangs, 152–153
Hispanic women
drug arrests for, 182
percent of prison population, 202

sentenced to death, 182
tendency to engage in crime, 53
Hispanics
Chicana girl gangs, 152–153
incarceration rate for, 179
percentage of prison population, 202
Holt v. Sarver (1970), 214
Homelessness, 128, 184, 207, 250, 263, 275, 284, 287
Homicide crimes
committed by women, 41–43
domestic homicide, 44–46
filicide, 43–44
serial murder, 44
Homosexuality, 190, 231–232, 235
Houses of refuge, 194–196
Housing, difficulty securing after release, 284
Hyperactivity and cognitive functioning, 111
Hyper-arousal, correlation with chronic childhood abuse, 210

Identity talk, 269
I-level theory and classification model, 79–80
Importation theory, 226–227
Impulsivity, 79–80, 94, 110–114, 123, 125, 138
Incarceration
increase in women's imprisonment due to War on Drugs, 181–182
intersectionality between race and gender, 179–181
jails and jail inmates, 183–187
percent of women's crime resulting in, 185
trend in rates by race/ethnicity, 179–180
See also Female prisoners

Incest survivor programs, 266–267
Independent variables, 5, 8
Industrial training programs, 255
Inmate code, 227
Inmates. *See* Female prisoners; Jail inmates
Inmates of Sybil Brand Institution for Women v. County of Los Angeles (1982), 215
Integrated theory, 122–124
Intimate relationships, prison-based, sexual violence in, 237

Jail inmates
 characteristics of female prisoners, 183–186
 drug dependency problem among, 184–185
 issues and concerns regarding, 186–187
 with mental health problems, 184
Jails, prisons vs., 183
Juvenile corrections, push for gender-responsive programming in, 258
Juvenile Delinquency Prevention Act of 1974, 141
Juvenile girls. *See* Girls
Juvenile justice system
 detainment of female offenders in, 163–164
 gender-specific programming for girls, 162–163
 male vs. female treatment/ experiences within, 160–164
Juvenile offenders, 141–164
 chivalry hypothesis applied to, 175
 female delinquency, 141–155. *See also* Delinquency
 girl gangs, 91, 149–155
 sexual victimization by staff, 164

Labeling theory, 71–72
Larceny/theft, arrest rates for, 29–33
Latinas. *See* Hispanic women; Hispanics
Learned helplessness theory, 10, 130
Learning theory and behaviorism, 80–81
Legal challenges regarding prisoners' rights, 214–217
Level of Service Inventory-Revised (LSI-R), 247–250
Liberation theory, 84–87
Life-course persistent delinquency, 121, 124, 126–127
Life-course theories
 application to girls/ women, 125–127
 longitudinal studies, 118
 relationship to pathways research, 136
Life-skills/eclectic programs, 256
Likert scales, 8
Longitudinal studies
 in biological criminology, 293
 Cambridge Study in Delinquent Development, 119–120
 Dunedin Study (New Zealand), 121
 findings from, 122–125
 Gluecks' study/Sampson and Laub's research, 118–119
 OJJDP Youth Development Study, 120
 Philadelphia Cohort Study, 120–121
 Philadelphia Collaborative Perinatal Project, 121
Low constraint, 96–97
Low self-control
 characteristics of individuals with, 90

chronic, serious offenders characterized by, 134
 crime/delinquency correlated with, 70, 90–91, 93, 112, 138
 delinquent friends and, 94
 differences between theorists regarding, 125
 erratic parental discipline and, 91–93, 96, 112, 131
 general theory of crime and, 92–93
 higher in than in girls than in boys, 95
 impulsiveness and, 94
 in life-course persistent offenders, 121
 parenting practices and, 92, 96, 112, 131
 predictive of future crime in girls, 106
 predictive of gang membership, 70, 91, 138
 white-collar crime associated with low level of, 91
 See also Self-control
Low self-esteem, 112, 129–130, 133, 207–208, 211, 258, 266, 282
LSI-R (Level of Service Inventory-Revised), 249–250, 290

Madonna figure, sexual stereotype of, 14
Maintenance programs, 254
Marital rates, impact on adult and juvenile offending, 102
Marxist theory of crime, 72
Maternal imprisonment, impact on children, 271–272
Maturation effect/age effect, 92
Measurement
 of correlates, 7–8
 of crime, 5–7
 validity of, 8

Medical care
concerns in women's prisons, 186
legal challenges, 216
Mental health problems/issues
childhood and adult sexual/physical victimization correlated with, 129, 183, 186
drug use/abuse correlated with, 263
in female jail inmates, 184–185, 187
likelihood of prison infractions correlated with, 252
as predictor of prison misconduct, 248, 251
as predictor of recidivism, 250
Merton's strain/anomie theory, 95
Meta-analyses, 248
Monoamine oxidase (MAO), 110–111
Moral development, stage theory of, 76–79
Muncy Act of 1913, 168
Murder and non-negligent manslaughter, arrest rates of men and women, 42
Murder, serial, 44

National Center on Addiction and Substance Abuse (CASA), 260, 263
National Crime Victimization Survey (NCVS), 6, 25, 27, 35
National Institute on Drug Addiction, 261
National Youth Survey, 156–158
Native Americans
disproportionate representation of women in prison, 137
percentage of prison population, 202

percentage of women in prison population, 54
sentenced to death, 182
Negative emotionality, 96–97
Neonaticide, 43
Neural pathways and brain chemicals, 109–111
Nurseries in women's prisons, 274–276

Observations on the Siting, Superintendence and Government of Female Prisoners (Fry), 194
OJJDP Reauthorization Act of 1992, 162
OJJDP Youth Development Study, 120
Opportunity theory, 86
Opportunity Theory (Simon), 85–86
Organized crime, 31
Ossining (Sing Sing) State Penitentiary, 194

Pains of imprisonment, 225–226
Parentalization, 12
Parenting, ineffective, lack of self control due to, 91–93, 96, 125
Parenting programs
addressing female offender needs, 269
addressing the needs of children in, 271–272
alleviating barriers to successful reentry through, 269–270
alternative sentencing programs, 277–278
community-based residential programs, 277
extended/enriched visitation in, 273–274
halfway houses for women and children, 276–277
justifications for, 268–272

parenting education classes/life-skills programs, 273
pregnant inmates' need for, 270
prison nurseries, 274–276
reconciling imprisonment with motherhood through, 269
release considerations, 269–270
types of, 272–278
visitation in prison, 223, 273–274
See also Child care
Parole/probation
employment issues for women, 283
halfway houses for women, 284–289
problems concerning women's reunification with children, 284, 286, 288
women's vs. men's issues regarding, 282–283
Pathways research/approach
application to delinquent girls, 158–160
criminal pathways, 131–137
high rates of childhood sexual victimization in, 127–131
relationship to life-course theories, 136
support for gender-responsive programming, 258
See also Prediction/classification instruments
Patriarchal families, 104–106, 157, 173
Peer associations, impact on female delinquents, 156–157
Personal Responsibility and Work Opportunity Reconciliation Act of 1996, 283

Personality traits
   correlation with crime, 81,
      207–208
   sex differences in,
      111–114
Phenomenological research
   methods, 12
Philadelphia Cohort Study,
   120–121
Philadelphia Collaborative
   Perinatal Project, 121
Physical abuse
   adult, prevalence in
      female offenders, 200
   drug use/abuse correlated
      with, 263
   juvenile delinquency cor-
      related with, 161
   mental health problems
      correlated with, 186
   as pathway to women's
      criminality, 293
   prevalence among jail
      inmates, 127, 183, 185,
      201, 203–205
Pink-collar crimes, 28, 87,
   106
Policy changes, arrest rates
   affected by, 30
Policy recommendations, 292
Positivism, 2, 59, 61
Post-traumatic stress disorder
   (PTSD), 131, 184,
   204–205, 240, 242, 267
Poverty
   economic marginalization
      and, 106–107
   impact on criminality/
      rates of crime, 102,
      107, 198
Poverty programs, improving
   children's lives to avoid
   criminal pathways as
   adults, 294
Power, explaining delinquent
   choices through con-
   structs of, 105–106
Power control theory
   application to delinquent
      girls, 157–158

household-type power
   control and risk per-
   ception, 105–106
measuring risk preference
   as result of parental
   controls, 105
self-control theory vs.,
   105–106
Prediction/classification
   instruments, 246–253
   Level of Service Inventory-
      Revised (LSI-R),
      247–250
   R/N/R approach, 246–247
   use in women's prisons,
      250
Pregnancy
   institutional shortcom-
      ings for pregnant
      women, 270
   in prison, state responses
      toward, 174–175
   as punishable offense,
      52–53
Premenstrual syndrome,
   108–109
Primary deviance, 71
Prison
   incarceration rates by
      race/ethnicity, 179,
      181
   misconduct, predictors of,
      248–253
   percentage increase of
      women sentenced to,
      178
   sentencing disparities
      between men and
      women, 173
   sex discrepancies in sen-
      tencing, 172
   See also Women's prisons
Prison Adjustment Scale
   (PAQ), 252
Prison Litigation Reform Act,
   18 USC Sec.
   3626(a)(1)(A), 214
Prison Rape Elimination Act
   of 2003 (PREA), 236
Prison reformers, 194–195

Prison subculture
   argot (social) roles,
      227–228
   black market, 228–229
   deprivation theory/pains
      of imprisonment,
      225–226
   importation theory,
      226–227
   inmate code, 227
   same-sex prison relation-
      ships, 190, 231–232, 235
   social organization (gangs
      vs. families), 229–231
Prisonization, 225
Prisons. See Women's prisons
Privacy issues in women's
   prisons, 225–226
Privacy rights, 239–240
Probation, strongest predictors of recidivism in, 250
Procunier v. Martinez (1974), 214
Programs/programming
   drug-treatment, 260–266
   gender-responsive,
      256–260. See also Gen-
      der-responsive pro-
      gramming
   gender-specific, 162–163,
      257
   incest survivor, 266–267
   legal challenges, 215–216
   life-skills/eclectic, 256
   parenting, 267–278
   partnerships with outside
      companies, 255
   rehabilitative, Good Lives
      Model of, 259
   successful, elements of,
      290–291
   treatment, evaluation of,
      290–292
   types of, 254–256
   in women's prisons, legal
      challenges to, 215–216
Project on Human Develop-
   ment in Chicago Neigh-
   borhoods, 103
Property crimes, 27–33
   burglary, 28–29

convergence of gender gap
in, 292
juvenile arrest rates, 144
larceny/theft, fraud, and
embezzlement, 29–33
pattern of change in male
vs. female arrest rates
for, 24
Prostitution, 50–52, 129, 262
Psychodynamic theories, 72–76
Freudian, 73–74
learning theory/behavior-
ism, 81
Psychological theories
containment theory vs.
general strain theory, 95
developmental, 76–80
learning theory/behavior-
ism, 80
psychodynamic, 72–76
psychopathy, 73–74
PTSD. *See* Post-traumatic
stress disorder.
Punishment
Bentham on, 59
in early English law, 193
in women's prisons,
224–225

Qualitative research, importance in feminist crimi-
nology, 12

Race/ethnicity
differential treatment of
juveniles for noncrimi-
nal delinquent
offenses, 175
of female prisoners, 202
impact on female delin-
quency, 145–146
incarceration rates by,
179–180
influence on career path-
ways, 136–137
influence on crime rates,
53–54
life-choices and experi-
ences impacted by,
136–137

Rape
childhood, 131–132, 163,
185, 204–205
"harmed and harming"
women and, 132
homosexual, in prison, 231
pathways research on,
127–128
percentage of arrest for
females under 18, 142
prevalence in women's
prisons, 236–237
by prison guards, 164,
241–242
recurrent victimization,
130
See also Sexual abuse/vic-
timization,
Rational choice theory
application to delinquent
girls, 157
applications to girls/
women, 101–102, 157
self-control theory com-
bined with, 101
tests/applications of,
100–101
Rational relationship test,
214
Reaffirming Young Sisters'
Excellence (RYSE), 162
Recidivism
gender-neutral vs. gender-
specific prediction of,
246–250, 253
gender-specific vs. gender-
neutral studies on, 290
Reform era
advent of separate institutions run by women,
195
early reformatories for
women, 196–198
early research on factors
affecting women's
criminality, 198
Elizabeth Farnham's
"feminization" of
women's institutions,
195

Elizabeth Fry's work in
England, 194
female management of
women's prisons, 194
House of Refuge model,
196
houses of refuge, 194–196
reasons for demise of, 199
Relationship issues
as predictor of prison misconduct, 251
Research
career-criminal, 124
early, on causal factors of
crime, 198
feminist, 9–13
longitudinal. *See* Longitudinal studies
phenomenological meth-
ods of, 12
on violent girls, 146–149
Richmond Youth Study, 70,
84, 95
Risk Assessment Scale for
Prison (RASP), 252
Risk factors associated with a
persistence of criminal-
ity, 120
Risk/need assessment instruments, 247. *See also* Pre-
diction/classification
Risk preference and parental
controls, 105–106
R/N/R approach, 249,
258–259
Robbery, 26, 37–39
Robinson v. York (1968), 168
Role strain, 269
Routine activities theory, 100
Rule breaking, 213, 224, 252.
See also Prison miscon-
duct

Scavenger gangs, 154
Scientific method, explanation of crime through, 3,
5
Secondary deviance, 71
Selective chivalry hypothesis,
174

Self-concept, poor
    as predictor of prison mis-
        conduct, 251
    prevalence in female pris-
        oners, 207
Self-control
    attitudinal vs. behavioral
        measures of, 94
    Grasmick et al. scale of, 94
    low. *See* Low self-control
    rational choice theory and,
        101
    values, motivations, and
        meanings interacting
        with, 93
Self-control theory, 105–106
Self-defense, domestic homi-
    cide in, 45
Self-esteem
    in general strain theory,
        95–96
    lower levels correlated with
        childhood abuse, 208
Self-mutilation, 210–211, 256
Sentencing
    decisions, correlation with
        sex of offender,
        171–173
    disparate sentencing laws,
        168
    gender disparities in,
        174–178
    guidelines, impact on sen-
        tences imposed,
        176–177
    sex and race as variables
        in, 176–178
    sex-gender effect on,
        172–173
Serial murder, 44
Sex, prior abuse of prisoners
    by, 203
Sex crimes, women's partici-
    pation in, 50
Sex differences
    and crime, 108–111
    gender differences vs.,
        15–17
    personality traits and,
        111–114

Sex-role identification the-
    ory, 81
Sex-role stereotyping
    description of female
        inmates colored by, 213
    early theories of female
        delinquency colored by,
        159
    female prisoners being
        "worse" than men, 161
    in prison vocational pro-
        grams, 255
    in psychodynamic theo-
        ries, 75
    research on female prison-
        ers' "masculinity," 208
    revictimization associated
        with, 130
    typicality hypothesis and,
        174
Sex-role theory, 83–84
    application to delinquent
        girls, 158
    control balance theory,
        106
    current, 103–106
    as explanation for gender
        differential in crime,
        138
    power control theory,
        104–106
    tests of, 84
Sexual abuse/victimization
    adult, prevalence in
        female prisoners, 184,
        206
    assault by correctional
        officers, 164, 241–243
    childhood. *See* Childhood
        sexual victimization
    delinquency correlated
        with, 161
    drug use/abuse correlated
        with, 207, 263, 266
    of girls in juvenile institu-
        tions, 164
    juvenile, more common in
        girls than in boys, 159
    mental health problems
        correlated with, 186

    as pathway to women's
        criminality, 293
    prevalence in female
        offenders, 127, 200,
        203–205
    re-victimization corre-
        lated with, 206
    in women's prisons,
        235–237
Sexual stereotypes
    early Greek, 14
    violent woman, 13, 15
Sexual symmetry of violence,
    10, 44
Sheldon's body type theory,
    107
Shoplifting, 29–30
Sing Sing Penitentiary, 194
Single-parent households
    effect on delinquency,
        91–92, 94
    women in prison from, 202
Social and human-capital
    deficit pathway, 133
Social control theory, 68–70,
    87, 90
    application to delinquent
        girls, 156–157
    criticism of, 92
    victimization, 131
Social efficacy, 102
Social learning theory/
    differential association
    theory
    applications to delinquent
        girls, 156–157
    general theory of crime
        vs., 94
Social organization of
    women's vs. men's pris-
    ons, 229–231
Social strain theory, 64–65
Social Structure and Social
    Learning (SSSL) model,
    64
Social support/disorganiza-
    tion theories, 102–103
Socialization, explanation of
    criminal behavior
    through, 114

Sociological theory vs. psychodynamic theory, 73
Sociopathy, 73–74
Stage theory of cognitive/moral development, 76–79
Standard Rules for the Minimum Treatment of Prisoners, 240
State v. Heitman (1919), 168
Static factors, use in predication/classification instruments, 246
Statistical tests, measuring crime with, 8
Status offenses, 141, 143, 147, 175
Steerers/touts, 49
Strain, gendered emotional response to, 98–99
Strain theory, 65–68. *See also* Differential opportunity theory; General strain theory
Substance abuse
  childhood abuse correlated with, 183
  as criminogenic need, 247
  depression correlated with, 204
  drug abuse. *See* Drug use/abuse
  female parolees' problems with, 282
  female vs. male reasons behind, 263
  greater risk for women in prison, 208
  jail-diversion intervention for pregnant, nonviolent offenders with history of, 277
  low MAO activity correlated with, 110
  mental illness correlated with, 184, 186
  need for more programming in, 292
  pathways theory and, 133–134

  as predictor of delinquency, 160
  as predictor of prison misconduct, 248, 251
  recidivism correlated with, 250, 289
  relational pathway of, 133
  revictimization correlated with, 130
  treatment, problems for female parolees, 286–288
Substantive rationality, 176
Suicide, 210–211
Systematic Training for Effective Parenting (STEP), 273

Tautology, 93
Telephones in prison, 223–224
Testosterone, 109–110
Theory(ies)
  Chicago School, 61–62
  Classical School, 59, 61–68
  conflict theories, 72
  cultural deviance, 63
  current, 89–115
  of delinquency, 156–160
  developmental, 76–80
  differential opportunity theory, 65–68
  early feminist, 82–88
  economic development theory, 85
  general strain theory, 65
  integrated theory, 122–124
  labeling theory, 71–72
  learning theory and behaviorism, 80–81
  life-course/integrated, 118, 125–127
  making sense of theoretical findings, 137
  opportunity theory, 85–86
  positivism (1800s), 59, 61
  psychodynamic, 73–76
  psychological, 72
  questions and concerns regarding, 58–59

  sex-role theory, 83–84
  social control theory, 68–70, 87
  social strain theory, 64–65
  traditional, 57–58
  women's liberation theory, 84–87
Therapeutic communities, 264–265, 290, 292
Todaro v. Ward (1977), 216
Touts/steerers, 49
Trafficking and trading, 224
Traits, personality, 5, 81, 111–114
Traumatic sexualization, 130
Treatment programs
  definition of, 255
  difficulty in obtaining after release, 286–288
  evaluation of, 290–292
  R/N/R approach, 247
Typicality hypothesis, 174

Upcharging, 27, 161, 175

Validity of measurements, 8
Victimization
  filicide linked to, 44
  of girl gang members, 155
  inmate-on-inmate vs. staff-on-inmate, 236–237
  of minority women, 54
  patterns for girl gang members, 155
  prison violence, 234–235
  prostitution-related, 51
  recurrent, 130
  relationship between criminality and, 131
  sexual, in women's prisons, 236–237
  of urban African American female delinquent offenders, 146
  See also Adult victimization; Childhood abuse/victimization; Sexual abuse/victimization

Violence
   disrespect as motivation
      for, 37, 149, 234
   domestic, 40–41
   profile of female prisoners
      prone to, 213
   sexual. *See* Sexual abuse/
      victimization
   in women's prisons,
      232–237
Violent crimes, 34–46
   arrest rates for men and
      women, 24
   arson, 39
   assault, 39–41
   juvenile arrest rates, 145
   prevalence among female
      drug offenders, 207
   robbery, 37–39
Violent girls, research on,
   146–149
Violent woman, theme of,
   14–15
Visitation in prison parenting
   programs, 223, 273–274
Vocational training programs,
   255

War on Drugs, 46, 180–182
Warrior gene, 110
White-collar crimes, 25, 31,
   33
Woff v. McDonnell (1975), 214
Women
   application of life-course
      theories to, 125–127
   belief in genetic inferiority
      of, 198
   as "breeders" of criminal-
      ity, 60–61
   death penalty imposed on,
      182–183
   economic marginalization
      theory and, 106–107
   general strain theory
      applied to, 97–99
   general theory of crime
      applied to, 94–95

imprisoned. *See* Female
   prisoners; Women's
   prisons
jailed, characteristics of,
   183–186
life-course theories
   applied to, 125–127
rational choice theory
   applied to, 101–102
role in drug subculture,
   48, 50
social support theories
   applied to, 103
Women and Crime (Simon), 86
Women's liberation theory,
   84–87
Women's National Law Cen-
   ter, 272
Women's Needs and Risk
   Assessment instrument,
   133
Women's prisons
   adapting to a male stan-
      dard, 212–213
   administration of,
      194–195, 197
   classification/prediction
      instruments used in,
      220–221, 246–253
   cross-sex supervision in,
      213
   current status of, 190–191
   drug treatment programs
      in, 263–266
   drug use and abuse in,
      206–207
   early punishments/places
      of confinement, 192,
      194
   health-related etiquette
      rules in, 209
   history of, 191–200
   human rights violations
      in, 190
   inmates. *See* Female pris-
      oners
   lack of research on, 190,
      199

male correctional offic.
   in, 239–241
management issues in,
   212–217
many rules/strict policies
   governing, 200
mental health issues in,
   210
nurseries in, 274–276
orientation experience, 220
parenting programs in,
   267–278. *See also* Parenting programs
predictors of prison mis-
   conduct, 24–251
pregnancy in, 174–175,
   270
prisoners. *See* Female prisoners
privacy issues in, 225–226
programming in, 254–278.
   See also Programs/pro-
   gramming
race relations in, 229
racial/ethnic makeup of
   population, 202
recreation/visitation in,
   222–224
reformatory era, 194–200
rules and punishments in,
   224–225
self-injury and suicide in,
   210–211
state responses toward
   pregnancy in, 174–175
subculture of, 225–232. *See
   also* Prison subculture
typical daily routine in,
   222
violence in, 213, 232–237
See also Incarceration
Working to Insure and Nurture Girls' Success
   (WINGS), 162

XYY theory/syndrome, 197,
   109